Getting Wired with Lotus®

JOIN US ON THE INTERNET VIA WWW, GOPHER, FTP OR EMAIL:

WWW: http://www.itcpmedia.com
GOPHER: gopher.thomson.com
FTP: ftp.thomson.com
EMAIL: findit@kiosk.thomson.com

WebExtra^{sm}

WebExtra gives added value by providing updated and additional information about topics discussed in this book. Included in the WebExtra for *Getting Wired With Lotus* is:

• Headline news items that keep you up to date on the latest announcements about Lotus and its Internet products as well as developments about the Internet and business.

The WebExtra feature outlined above is available free of charge (except for the charges associated with accessing the Internet and the World Wide Web). Just go to the Web Site for International Thomson Computer Press. The URL is:

http://www.itcpmedia.com

A service of I ⓣ P™

Getting Wired with Lotus®

Paul Lavin

INTERNATIONAL THOMSON COMPUTER PRESS

I(T)P An International Thomson Publishing Company

London • Bonn • Boston • Johannesburg • Madrid • Melbourne • Mexico City • New York • Paris
Singapore • Tokyo • Toronto • Albany, NY • Belmont, CA • Cincinnati, OH • Detroit, MI

Getting Wired with Lotus

Copyright © 1997 International Thomson Computer Press

I ⒯ P A division of International Thomson Publishing Inc.
The ITP logo is a trademark under licence.

For more information, contact:

International Thomson Computer Press
Berkshire House
168-173 High Holborn
London WC1V 7AA
UK

International Thomson Computer Press
20 Park Plaza
Suite 1405
Boston, MA 02116
USA

Imprints of International Thomson Publishing

International Thomson Publishing GmbH
Königswinterer Straße 418
53227 Bonn
Germany

International Thomson Publishing Asia
60 Albert Street #15-01
Albert Complex
Singapore 189969

Thomas Nelson Australia
102 Dodds Street
South Melbourne, 3205
Victoria
Australia

International Thomson Publishing Japan
Hirakawacho Kyowa Building, 3F
2-2-1 Hirakawacho
Chiyoda-ku, 102 Tokyo
Japan

Nelson Canada
1120 Birchmount Road
Scarborough, Ontario
Canada M1K 5G4

International Thomson Editores
Seneca, 53
Colonia Polanco
11560 Mexico D. F. Mexico

International Thomson Publishing South Africa
240 Old Pretoria Road
PO Box 2459
Halfway House
1685 South Africa

International Thomson Publishing France
Tours Maine-Montparnasse
33 Avenue du Maine
75755 Paris Cedex 15
France

WebExtra is a Service Mark of Thomson Holdings Inc.

Lotus and Lotus Notes are registered trademarks of Lotus Development Corporation. All references to Lotus and Lotus Notes in this work are solely representative of the views of the author.

Products and services that are referred to in this book and its accompanying CD-ROM may be either trademarks and/or registered trademarks of their respective owners. The Publisher/s and Author/s make no claim to these trademarks.

The Publisher states that it is using trademarked names only for editorial purposes and to the benefit of the trademark owner with no intention of infringing upon that trademark.

Whilst the Publisher has taken all reasonable care in the preparation of this book and its accompanying CD-ROM the Publisher makes no representation, express or implied, with regard to the accuracy of the information contained in this book and cannot accept any legal responsibility or liability for any errors or omissions from the book or the consequences thereof.

The programs in this book and on its accompanying CD-ROM have been included for their instructional value. While every precaution has been taken in the preparation of this book, the Publisher and the Author assume no responsibility for errors or omissions, or for damages resulting from the use of information herein. In no event shall the Publisher and the author be liable for any loss of profit or any other commercial damage, including but not limited to special, incidental, consequential or other damages.

British Library Cataloguing-in-Publication Data
A catalogue record for this book is available from the British Library

Library of Congress Cataloging-in-Publication Data
A catalog record for this book is available from the Library of Congress

First Printed 1997

ISBN 1-85032-268-6

Typeset by Lorraine Hodghton
Cover Designed by Button Eventures
Printed in the UK by Clays Ltd, St Ives plc.

Contents

Foreword

By the time you read this foreword, you will already have made the wise decision to explore what Paul Lavin has to say about how you should think about acquiring new technologies and/or integrating new technologies to enhance your productivity or that of others with whom you work. The acquisition of new technology should not be about acquiring the latest technology toy; it should, rather, be a much more sensible and considered process, with an extreme degree of relevance to your personal goals and business objectives. It should not, for example, be merely about whether you can get connected to the World Wide Web, but must also address what you will accomplish once connected. No one understands this better than Paul Lavin who has written a tremendous resource for those looking to leverage today's emerging communications and network capabilities, particularly the Internet.

For the past 14 years, Lotus has been working to make the experience of computing as simple as possible for individuals and as productive as possible for organizations and businesses of all sizes. This has been Lotus' constant mission in the constantly evolving context of what those of us in the business of building information technology refer to as "the industry." For many, running a 1-2-3 spreadsheet on an IBM PC was a maiden voyage. Nearly 15 years later, much has changed. The industry has seen a number of major transitions: minicomputer to workstation; character-based user interface to graphical user interface; portable to laptop. But none of these developments has had as dramatic an impact upon the entire notion of personal computing as the expansion of that experience beyond the contained experience of one's world brought about by the emergence and ubiquity of networks and, more recently, the Internet. The definitive emergence of the network – and the Internet is the best example – as the focal point of the computing experience, the place where information resides, where security clearance and access to information is brokered, where meaningful transactions take place, where people meet in the virtual sense to collaborate, communicate and coordinate their actions and ideas – has dramatically altered the potential for individuals who in other times might have thought and written and calculated in isolation to expand their worlds.

New technologies in combination with the Internet and the World Wide Web are making it possible in richer ways every day for individuals to seek information from others, share information with others and build both material and intellectual value with others, or even simply witness the thoughts and ideas of other people who are geographically distant. Lotus is on the edge of this technological transformation which is making our planet a very different place to be than it was only ten years ago, and Paul Lavin's *Getting Wired* will prove an excellent resource for you to explore how Lotus technologies should best be applied to your particular challenges.

During the past decade, we have invested hundreds of millions of research and development dollars in ensuring that all of our products address the need of customers to expand their worlds beyond their own desktops. Customers began to realize the benefits of this investment in 1989 when Lotus introduced Lotus Notes Version 1.0. Lotus Notes quickly defined a new category of software referred to as "Groupware." Since 1989, Lotus Notes has made the notion of participation in a global business world less daunting for many entrepreneurs and large businesses, and simplified the process of sharing, managing and distributing business information inside organizations large and small as well as across organizational boundaries. And Notes has helped customers automate strategic businesses processes that improve their bottom lines. Because it offers a robust and elegant messaging infrastructure coupled with a sophisticated application development environment, Notes has proven an ideal tool for a wide range of communications challenges across the widest spectrum of workgroups and organizations.

Today, more than 8000 companies and 4.5 million individuals have incorporated Lotus Notes solutions into their strategic business operations. Building on our technology, they've created thousands of business applications that improve their operations through enhanced communication, collaboration and coordination.

We have applied this same vision of expanding the dimensions of computing to our entire product line, including cc:Mail, now the world's most popular electronic mail product, and SmartSuite, Lotus' integrated suite of business applications.

Today, the Internet is an integral part of every development project at Lotus, and whether you are a freelance writer or accountant working out of your home, office manager at a small business or CIO of a Fortune 1000 company, you can derive tremendous value from Lotus products by using them to access information that resides far away or by establishing a presence for your product or service on the World Wide Web. You may want to build your home page in Ami Pro or navigate the World Wide Web from within Lotus Notes. Whatever your need, getting "up and running" needn't be complicated, and that's where Paul Lavin comes in.

Paul has done an excellent job of identifying the questions that you need to contemplate once you've made the decision to take advantage of the Internet and the tremendous benefits it has to offer. You will find Paul's understanding of the importance of integrating new technology with minimal disruption and maximum leverage of previous technology investment particularly useful. I also believe you will find throughout this book that Paul has an excellent understanding of who you are as well as the technologies you are already using today.

So quick! – Don't waste another minute. Turn the page and get wired – with Lotus.

Jeff Pappas
President
Lotus Development Corp

Preface

This book is for executives, managers and business owners who are continually faced with myriad business challenges – only one of which is embracing new technology like the Internet. Rather than create yet another book about the Internet and all its wondrous capabilities, this book instead is about meeting your business objectives using the software that you already run on your PCs and servers by harnessing the business power of the Internet.

This Book's Readers

This book is not for techno-weenies or even wannabe techno-weenies. The bookshelves are full of Internet titles that will thrill the technically inclined with the deep and mystical elements of TCP/IP, the nitty gritty of HTML, and the manifold commands available in a well-implemented FTP program. This book is also not a travel guide for cyber-surfers in suits.

This book, rather, is for the people who make tactical and strategic business decisions, e.g. the managers, coordinators, executives and leaders. *The OnLine Office: Getting Wired with Lotus* is intended to help those people understand the advantages that the Internet can provide in resolving a laundry list of business challenges.

Got a problem turning ideas around and getting consensus on a complicated project? Email can provide slack for a tight schedule and get input from coworkers and customers wherever they are. Millions of businesses worldwide have discovered how much value there is in intra-company email. Internet email can be a time machine and you may already have the Lotus software you need to use it.

Need to test your ideas in the marketplace or reach a global audience? A World Wide Web server may be the perfect tool for you to put a toe in the water. Lotus Notes can make it easy to publish, update and collect valuable marketing material.

This book can also be for software shoppers. If you don't already have Lotus Notes, cc:Mail or the Internet-enabled Smart Suite, this book will show you what's there and how they can be made to work in your business.

However, the Internet is not a universal panacea for all business ills; it can even exacerbate pre-existing problems. This book preaches the appropriate application of Internet capabilities to business situations. It aims to provide a complete understanding of the various elements of today's Internet and how they can be applied to increase operational efficiency and profitability without radically changing the software tools in which you have already invested.

If you have some responsibility for running a business in the late 90s, you have already made your acquaintance with office technology. It's all around you – there's a PC on your desk for sure, and you might even take work home or on the road with a notebook computer. Your company probably has a local area network (LAN) server hiding in some corner of the room, sharing files, printers and communications resources within a workgroup.

Bigger organizations will undoubtedly also have some sort of UNIX box around the place running mission-critical applications like accounting and order control, and, if you are part of a large enterprise, there is probably some truly heavy-duty computing equipment sitting in a glasshouse tended by its own priesthood.

One thing is universally true for all computerized businesses: the money invested in hardware and software at any end of the scale is dwarfed by the investment in the training and business policies and practices that have been built on your technical computing platform. Adding Internet capabilities to the business tools you already have is the most effective way of moving your business ahead today. You get maximum gain for minimum pain.

No matter what the scale of your organization, or the amount or kind of computing technology you employ, your business is about to be touched by the Internet, and there is no doubt about it. The Net (to its friends), by virtue of its tremendous growth, is becoming a potent business tool. As this book is written, there are estimated to be over 60 million Internet users of one sort or another. At current growth rates, that may have climbed to over 70 million by the time this book is in your hands. The Internet has been doubling in size every year for the past four years. Next year? A 100 million?

Robert Metcalfe, doctorate engineer, co-inventor of Ethernet and now business sage, illuminated a fundamental principle of networking in what is now known as Metcalfe's Law: The value of a network to its users increases with the square of the number of network users. And the Internet is already bigger than any other terrestrial network: there are even orbital Internet terminals now! When you apply Metcalfe's Law, the Internet is, and will be for some time to come, the most useful network on the planet by any metric. Successful businesses will seize the leverage that the Internet has to offer.

Making the capabilities of the Internet useful for your particular set of business problems requires a three-pronged approach. To apply the Internet to your business you must have a thorough understanding of the business issues that are presenting themselves to you at this point in your business' evolution. You also need to anticipate the challenges ahead as you move toward future business goals. There's not a lot that this book can do for either of these two analytical elements – you need to turn to specialist sources of business information that were created by or for other businesses in the same sector as yourself, whether you are a retailer, a professional or a service provider.

However, once you have an inkling of the first two elements, where you are and what you want to do with your business, this book will help you plug into the Internet using the technology infrastructure that you already have. In the vast majority of cases that means PCs. And since the first IBM PC rolled out 15 years ago, PCs have meant Lotus software. In fact Lotus 123 is the software application that is credited with kickstarting the PC revolution.

You don't have to clear your desk to use the Internet. Whether you have a standalone PC or notebook, connected to a LAN or UNIX box, you can quickly and easily get wired to the Internet. The Internet, however, is a multi-headed beastie that you must use correctly. And that requires analysis of your business objectives/challenges and careful matching of Internet capabilities to them in a cost-efficient way. Recall the worm Oroboros.

You will need to acquire the services of one caliber or another of Internet Access Provider (IAP) but you may also, optionally, want to buy more or better hardware or some additional software. But you can undoubtedly get on the Internet using most of what you already have and, together with this book and access to modest technical resources, begin solving business problems and increasing your organizational efficiency with a comparatively small outlay.

The Scope Of This Book

No single book can talk to all businesspeople. *The OnLine Office: Getting Wired with Lotus* shoots for the middle ground of the

Lotus-using business population that is equipped with Microsoft Windows, Windows for Workgroups, Windows 95, Windows NT or OS/2. Small businesses and departments within larger organizations are well within the ambit of this book but the independent worker has not been left out by any means.

There are several places in this book where it will descend into a hands-on approach to the minutiae of getting Lotus software to work with the Internet. These examples are meant to be illustrative and are, of necessity, aimed at the smaller business or corporate road warrior with standalone or portable PCs or small LANs. There is no intention to provide omnibus technical guidance for getting corporate networks established on the Internet or sorting out cc:Mail, email gateways or developing Internet-empowered Notes applications – I refer you and your technical staff to books that are dedicated to taking a technical problem solving approach. And, while almost everything that you do on a LAN can be scaled upward, the internetworking of enterprise systems is well outside the scope of this book.

The Pitch

Just as PCs were the business phenomenon throughout the 80s, the Internet will be the business buzz of the 90s. The current media hype is not so much hype as perhaps embarrassed over-reaction for not recognizing the possibilities inherent in the Internet a long time ago. It has been said that the only mistakes made in forecasting the growth and impact of the Internet thus far have been underestimates of what has come to pass.

The Internet is now a powerful force for business. It will be even more so in the very near future. The late 90s business survival question may become: "Can I take better advantage of the Internet than my competitors?"

Typographical Conventions

The following typographical conventions are used in this book:

- Italics are used for the names of files, directories, commands and programs.
- Typewriter font is used for examples, URLs, and text that should be entered literally.
- Bold is used for new terms as they are defined.
- Square brackets are used to indicate that an item is optional.

The Sidebars

The OnLine Office: Getting Wired with Lotus is arranged to deliver the printed and bound equivalent of a multi-tasking, windowed computer environment like Microsoft Windows or OS/2. The margins of each page will contain material that supplements the main text. In addition to captioning the illustrations found on the main part of the page, the marginal spaces will be graced with a number of icons to signal the type of information being provided.

This icon means additional definition for a technical topic in the main text.

This icon signals case study material from one of a number of Internet business users.

This icon is used for brief checklists.

This icon is used for hints and tips.

This icon is used to provide Internet Web addresses (URLs) where additional information can be found on the discussion at hand.

check the
WebExtra

This icon is used to remind you to check out the Web Extra book extension which will have the latest developments and Internet business happenings that arrived too late for this printed edition.

Acknowledgments

This book owes a lot to the Internet Society and the Internet Engineering Task Force, that body of self-selected individuals whose back-room efforts have made the Internet the incredibly adaptive business tool that it is today. Many ideas incorporated in this book came from the never-ending stream-of-management-consciousness emanating from Usenet newsgroups which reflect the sheer diversity of thought which courses through the Internet.

I would especially like to thank all those who contributed ideas, answered my many queries and provided guidance in the preparation of this book: William Poel, my partner in the InfoHighway newsletter, Chris Vezey (Lotus), Graham J. H. Smith (Bird and Bird, solicitors), the team at UUNET PIPEX plc. For allowing the use of copyright material including illustrations I'd like to thank Neil Ellul (former Editor, *Internet* magazine), Silicon Graphics Inc., Lotus, Bird and Bird, and Roger McGuinn for the soundtrack.

Server applications used in the research of this book were run on a 90 MHz Pentium ICL TeamServer, with Asante and Intel networking products, Adaptec and Western Digital mass storage products, and the usual combination of baling wire, bubble gum and elbow grease. High bandwidth Internet connectivity was provided by UUNET PIPEX plc and aided by a Telebit Netblazer router with an ISDN terminal adapter from Controlware Ltd. The hard working OKI laser I used worked flawlessly.

Client-side applications were run on a mixture of home-brew and Apricot Pentium PCs. The Apricots, in particular, were fast, configurable and as reliable as bricks.

I would especially like to thank Liz Israel Oppedijk, chief kvetch for International Thomson Publishing, for her help in developing the concept of this book and her later efforts as editor (a fitting reward?) and, of course, my wife, Catherine, who continually seeks to make sure I put my best foot forward rather than in my mouth.

Introduction

The Internet has been covered in newspapers, magazines, TV specials and video tapes. Amidst all the pop phenomenon hyperbole, there has been little discussion of its real-world applicability to today's business problems. As a consequence, many business users have tuned out the Internet message, dismissing it as another fad.

If you had your mind on your business and missed Internet 101, here is a brief Internet primer to provide a good foundation for the material in the rest of this book. This chapter goes on to describe some exciting future developments that will make the Internet even more appealing for business users – make sure to check out the latest news available with our Web Extra (see Appendix.)

With all the media coverage given to the Internet, you could be forgiven for thinking that it is some mythical combination of supercomputers kept running by legions of dedicated computer nerds. The Internet is actually just a big computer network, not too different from the ones that run in most businesses today.

What is different about the Internet is its scope: the Internet spans the globe, not just your office or your company. But for all its size, it is nothing more than a network of networks. Each of the constituent networks can be made from one, several or thousands of computers: there are approximately five million host computers on the Internet at the time of writing. Each of those computers can have one or several users. As each new network joins the Internet, it brings all of its users along – each a potential producer and consumer.

In 1996 the Internet doubled in size, as it has every year since 1988. The Internet has come a long, long way from its governmental origins over 20 years ago. Some of the features that were originally built in way back before the dawn of personal computing, and the global networks, still serve us well today, despite having been created long before today's business computing infrastructure was even a twinkle in Bill Gates' eye.

However, there are a number of "features" that have not been quite so adaptive to new modes of use and rapid growth, notably the Internet addressing scheme and some of the original hard-core denizens of the Internet. Regardless, the Internet and the society of individuals and businesses that use and extend it have become a model of accommodation that has supported the fantastic growth rates that the Internet has exhibited over the past five years.

The Internet was originally set up as a US Department of Defense project to interconnect several networks in a fault tolerant fashion. Resilience was of prime importance to the military because of the need to withstand a bomb or two being dropped on various locations on the network. Obviously, a network that required that a message pass directly from A to B in order to reach C would not work. If the enemy wiped out B, then A and C could not talk.

The Internet is designed so that a message component, known as a packet (which could be part of an email, part of a Gopher request or part of a Web graphic image – they are all treated the same), would not follow a pre-ordained routing from its origin to its destination. It could happen that two successive packets could travel opposite ways around the world, depending on traffic congestion … or open warfare.

" *TCP/IP (Transmission Control Protocol/ Internet Protocol) is the lingua franca of the Internet. It is a networking protocol that can be used to allow virtually any computer to talk to any other.* **"**

What was proof against an anticipated rain of missiles that thankfully never came was also sufficient to insulate the Internet from random power failures, equipment glitches and misdirected utility workers that dug up the wrong cable. After a time, academic researchers were granted access to the ARPAnet (as the precursor of the Internet was called) and quickly they became keen users. Research is best carried out if all interested parties can share ideas, exchange data and critique results. The Internet provided a means to do all of this better than it could have been done on the telephone, by letter or in published journals.

It soon became clear that worldwide internetworking was going to be required in the years ahead. At about the same time the academic community was getting wired in a big way, work began on an open standard for networking by the International Standards Organization (ISO). Their careful deliberations produced a seven-layer protocol for networking that would allow products from any vendor to interoperate with products from any other.

However, while the ISO was grinding out their standard, Internet users chugged ahead with their own protocol called TCP/IP. The contrived elegance of the ISO protocols was commercially under-appreciated in relation to the "get it done today" attitude that suffused the thousands of users that had to interconnect different type of computers. Practicality won.

For a long time TCP/IP was considered to be just an appetizer for the OSI main course but it didn't work out that way. The expected OSI products that could all sing and dance together never materialized while TCP/IP software that could proliferated. You can get TCP/IP implementations for almost any computer imaginable, from mighty IBM mainframes right down to pocket PCs.

Once you have a computer that can talk TCP/IP down a network connection or to a modem, you have another potential jumping-off point for the Internet. In the world of personal computers there is a small but lively group of software developers who are striving to make TCP/IP easy to install and as feature-filled as a business user could endure. Microsoft and IBM arrived somewhat late to the TCP/IP party but made up for it with free basic TCP/IP bundles for Windows for Workgroups and OS/2. TCP/IP is now a standard networking protocol shipped with Windows 95, Windows NT and OS/2.

Internet Features And Functions

Subject to permission, any computer on the Internet can "talk" to any other computer. It can request files (the basis of FTP and the

World Wide Web), execute commands or run programs (Telnet or Gopher) or send messages (electronic mail). The incredible utility of the Internet for business comes from its global reach and the ability for any two computers to transfer bits and bytes by speaking the same language. Apples can talk to IBM mainframes and PCs can talk to Sun workstations.

Electronic mail is today's most frequently used Internet facility. Chapter 2 will go through the business and technical issues that must be confronted to harness rapid, low cost, electronic communication.

The force that is driving the growth of the Internet today, however, is the World Wide Web. This multimedia, hypertext-linked, page-centric phenomenon has piqued the interest of students, housewives, and businesspersons of all stripes. Read more about this exciting development in Chapter 6.

Other facilities that are available on the Internet are discussed throughout the book. How about fast and free technical support for your computers, peripherals and software? Can you use access to research facilities on subjects as diverse as the gas fields of Turkmenistan, property development in Hawaii or hotels in Key Largo?

The Internet has brought a bulging portfolio of applications and capabilities for businesses. Many Internet technologies are not only useful for reaching a customer on the other side of the world but are also apropos to disseminating information to the department down the hall. The so-called "intranet" is a boom area for medium to large sized businesses that are leveraging globe-spanning Internet communications capabilities inside their own organizations.

However, historically there have been a couple of show-stoppers for conservative businesspeople. One, the Net's lack of obvious financial foundation; two, its lack of obvious management structure; and, three, an antipathy on the part of the original settlers in cyberspace for commercial interests.

Can You Believe The Net Is Free?

The marginal cost of an Internet email message is zero. Rather than being greeted with open arms, this promise of a "free lunch" has caused many businesses to distrust the Internet as one of those deals that are too good to be true. One problem that plagued the Internet, in the eyes of the business community at least, was its lack of obvious means of support. The contrast between cost and value was especially stark given the astronomical charges levied by private network operators which are now scrabbling to compete with the Internet.

Internet users pay a monthly fee (or are entitled to free use via a university or their employer) and get unlimited access to the networked world. Business managers had difficulty reconciling their telephone bills which charged by distance and by time units with Internet billings which seemed to take neither into account. What businessperson wouldn't be suspicious when confronted with a "something for nothing" proposition?

Not to fear, the Internet is entirely paid for. There is no mystical hocus-pocus. No lead is being transmuted into gold. The mechanism for funding the Internet is just much less obvious than the telephone bill that turns up in the post.

Your subscription to an Internet service provider, combined with the tithes from thousands of others, pays for some of it. Also, the calls you make to your provider (or the leased line you have) are certainly not free – as your financial controller will certainly explain, with your telecoms bills in hand. The government also makes a contribution (although this is now much less than in the past). You know where the government's money comes from, right? The Internet isn't free – the payment mechanism is just well disguised.

One aspect of the Internet that is actually free is the helpfulness of many of your fellow Internet users. Sometimes, the advice that you get from the Usenet newsgroups is worth exactly what you pay for it: zero. However, the Internet can be a treasure-trove of technical and not-so-technical knowledge that it's yours for the asking.

Another "free" aspect of the Internet that takes some getting used to is the availability of free software. There is a lot of technical talent in the world and not all of it works for the companies that line the shelves of PC stores with gaily colored boxes. There are evidently a lot of people who create useful (and some not-so-useful) programs for their own use or just to show off their coding prowess. There are others that create good software but lack the business nous to hit the big time. Many of these people use the Internet to distribute their software as "freeware" or "shareware." You can use FTP (see Chapter 5) to get this software and you can use it according to the license limitations placed on it by the authors.

Lotus, Microsoft, Oracle and other big software companies are all posting software on the Net that's free for the taking right alongside the little guys who lack the marketing clout to be heard above the noise level of the computer industry. However, there is often limited technical backup and the quality can be uneven. The possibility of viral contamination, too, means that business users should cautiously evaluate the "cost" of ostensibly free software.

Who Is In Charge Here Anyway?

Another bugbear that business has held against the Internet is its lack of formal management structure. Ed Krol, author of the *Whole Internet User's Guide and Catalog*, likened the Internet to a church. It's also a lot like a voluntary organization or social club. You can belong or not, participate or not and have an opinion or not on every element of the organization's structure or operation. There isn't a CEO and there is no five-year plan. But even without a formal management structure, highly paid executives and a comprehensive business plan, the affairs of the Internet are nevertheless attended to.

The Internet is "run" to the extent that it is run by the Internet Society (ISOC). This is a purely voluntary organization and anyone interested in promoting global information exchange is eligible to join. The membership is a rather heterogeneous mixture of big computer company representatives, academics, businesspersons, students, government officials and private individuals. ISOC appoints the Internet Architecture Board (IAB) from a pool of volunteers. It is the IAB that does much of the hands-on guiding work to keep the Internet running and growing.

Another layer of management is embodied in the Internet Engineering Task Force (IETF). This band of volunteers meets regularly to decide near-term technical issues and chew over operational challenges. The IETF works by setting up working groups which consider the merits or otherwise of separate topics of interest. There is an Internet Research Task Force which looks ahead at future technological developments that will have impact on the Internet.

Progress is made through a process where Requests for Comments (RFC) are made to the Internet community. Replies are considered carefully before any policy or technology is made into an Internet standard. This process is cumbersome and reaching a consensus takes some time but the RFC method provides the stability that millions of Internet users can count on. There is also a remarkable lack of commercial bias – a factor that is mostly a plus but does sometimes exact a price.

It may seem a bit laissez faire but the Internet's management structure works. It is independent of any outside commercial influence and its Board and Task Force members are selected after lengthy peer review. It is an excellent demonstration of a functioning technocracy. The Internet Society, through its constituent parts, has muscle as well as brains. Lately the IETF has issued pronouncements that will cause sweeping changes in the Internet's addressing standards. We will all follow suit if we want to use the Internet in the future.

No company owns any part of the Internet's technology and the RFCs are freely available for examination by anyone. This lack of proprietary ownership has not kept the computer industry from competing aggressively to market the best implementations and fullest-feature sets of Internet networking protocols and applications.

Business Hostile?

Given the prolonged phase of its evolution that was within the sway of the academic community, there was a deep-seated suspicion about the advent of commerce on the Internet. The NSFnet, a major building block of the Internet in the US, has strict appropriate-use policies that all but exclude commercial traffic from their section of the North American Net. They jealously defend their right to remain a conduit for knowledge without the taint of money. But the Internet is big enough for all of us.

Now that the US Internet is largely out of government hands (at least from a primary financial support perspective) and parallel capacity has been built alongside NSFnet, this is no longer of any significance to commercial users. However, there are still some hangovers from the old academic heyday (especially in the minds of the old hands) that today's business users will still need to allow for in the next few years.

While commercialism has run riot on the World Wide Web and businesses routinely use email without a second thought, the Usenet newsgroups on the Internet still harbor a community of users that can object, sometimes quite colorfully and forcefully, to commercial messages. Their reactions (and over-reactions) are based on the premise that the Internet and Usenet (especially) belong to the private public and the usurpation of it to carry commercial messages consumes part of the individual's or group's bandwidth without first seeking permission.

We are in a transition period where the old hands are giving way to new blood, and lots of it, too. Until the diehards can be convinced that commercial messages can have information content and that their sometimes reflexive dislike of proprietary products is a form of censorship, businesses on the Internet will have to tread a fine line and observe proper netiquette.

Because all of the computers on the Internet are peers, each organization that runs a host computer has to look after its own security: unauthorized users must be kept out, authorized users must be allowed access to only those capabilities that are appropriate (both inside and outside the organization) and viral infections from outside must be prevented. Because this is clearly a well-held preoccupation of any business considering hitching their wagon to the Internet, Chapter 2 looks at the manifold security implications.

The New Age Internet: The World Wide Web

In mid-1993, the Internet was transformed from a rather dry, technical environment to a multimedia extravaganza. The World Wide Web was created in Geneva, Switzerland at CERN, to allow research physicists at that world-famous institution to share their experimental notes and graphs. With the creation of a Microsoft Windows edition of a Web "browser" called Mosaic, any of the 100 million or so PC users could access rich text documents, images, video clips, sounds and other documents, anywhere in the world, with the click of a mouse button. Mosaic and the Web made the power of the global Internet accessible to completely non-technical users.

The Web is built on hypertext links. As you read a Web document you will notice some words or images that have been highlighted. If you click on a highlighted area, your computer will immediately load the document, image or sound file selected. Since you are on the Internet, it doesn't make any difference if that next file is on the same hard disk or half a world away. The Web became woven together in an increasingly dense cloud of interconnected documents. Cybersurfing was born.

While the Web is built on hyperlinks, hyperlinked pages are created with HTML, the Hyper Text Markup Language which is related to a familiar publishing tool, Standard Generalized Markup Language (SGML). It's amazingly easy to create your own home page and to hang out your company's shingle for business on the Internet. However, stunning commercial results take talent as well as technical ability. The advertising agency of the 21st century will have to demonstrate mastery of Web skills.

While the Internet doubled itself last year, the World Wide Web grew by a factor of almost 20. Explosion is perhaps the most accurate way to describe the creation of over 30 million

check the
WebExtra

multimedia Web pages in the past year. Among those pages are corporate flagships and virtual shop fronts – glimpses of a whole new way of doing business for the future.

The Web is big: it's a faster growing phenomenon than any other communications medium ever. It's bursting into full bloom faster than the telephone, television, fax, portable telephones or the personal computer did in the past. Six months is a long time in the Web world – business should start now.

The Web is a great economic leveller. The wherewithal to drive your stake in commercial cyberspace is modest. That means your Web presence will not suffer from poor location, inadequate capital or require expensive advertising to reach a diffuse marketplace. With initiative and creative thought, your Web pages can put even those of Lotus into the shade. Chapters 6 and 7 will cover all of these issues in depth.

We are beginning to see the usual jostling for position among the big technology companies in the new Internet marketplace created by the World Wide Web. The World Wide Web Consortium (W3C) has been set up as a talking shop to spot the opportunities for standards-making before any innovating trail-blazers can create proprietary gotchas that would lead to sundering the global unity of the Web. Already some divergence has occurred. Whether W3C can stay in front and hold its own against commercial juggernauts bent on domination remains to be seen.

The biggest problem facing a business user of the Internet and the World Wide Web is finding what you need and making sure that potential customers and suppliers can find you. It's daunting to have a world connected to your screen and keyboard! Thankfully, there are some facilities available to make the Internet much less haphazard than you might think. Chapter 5 will cover this in detail.

The Internet is pretty new, which means that many of the business issues you take for granted in your normal work day may not be quite so settled in cyberspace. Chapter 8 will take a long look at the potential pitfalls of doing business on the Internet.

While the Web and many future attractions will become reality soon enough and there are bound to be more tantalizing technologies just over the horizon, you don't have to wait to get your business wired into the Internet. There's plenty of value out there today and it's easy to access with Lotus software.

1 Planning for the Internet

There is no time like the present for getting your company on the Internet. However, you need to approach the task with at least as much forethought as opening a new office or starting a new distribution channel. You must carefully consider all of the positive and negative impacts that it will have on your present organization

The Business Issue

The Internet is big now and going to get a lot bigger very quickly. Rosy forecasts predict that the Internet will account for 1.3 percent of the US economy, or $45.8 billion, by the year 2000. Worldwide Internet business estimates vary from twice to four times that figure. Even if those predictions are off by a factor of 100 percent, an Internet presence is almost a corporate necessity this year. Remember, however, the most consistent mistake made about the Internet in the past was underestimating its growth and impact.

In a very short time, the expansion and ever-present press coverage of the Internet and the World Wide Web have gone a long way toward convincing businesses that the Internet is the place to be, even if they have not convinced them of the viability of actually doing business on the Internet yet. But you can't just snap your fingers and plug into the Net and hope to gain much positive impact from the experience.

Companies must now make the far-reaching decision about whether they will be part of the mainstream businesses to reap benefits from the Internet or whether they will be at the margin. The core of the Internet business community of the near future will consist of companies that can offer products and services by wire, transaction-oriented businesses like banks and, at the bottom of the totem pole, Internet access providers.

Besides the hard-core Internet-enabled businesses, any business that sells into the Internet's demographics sweet spot, the one-quarter to one-third of the population that enjoys a relatively high income, should have a presence, too. Even smaller companies may find that Internet and Web technology can ease the burden of customer and prospect handling, cutting costs even if it doesn't generate revenue.

Depending on your goals and your sense of urgency, you can spend between $100,000 and $10 million to create an Internet presence. With such a substantial investment required, some careful planning is indicated.

First Steps

You've bought the book and read a bit. By now, you have probably got an inkling about why and how you might put the Internet to work in your office. However, there is a considerable gap between knowing how and why, and making it all happen in a way that has a positive effect on your profitability. Like all long journeys, it begins with a few easy steps. There are ten simple, not necessarily expensive, steps you can take to help you get there.

- Don't try to run before you can walk.
- Get your team together.
- Know your starting point: take an inventory.
- Read up – get Internet wise.
- Build your Internet Wish List.
- Select an Internet access provider and software.
- Nail down your name.
- Don't forget the intranet.
- Build your case.
- Allocate management resources.

"*It's more than important to set goals when you contemplate getting on the Net. We have probably wasted quite a bit of money just 'getting wired' because we didn't have any idea of what we really wanted out of the experience. Yet being too rigid in your ideas without any experience on the Net is probably a bad thing, too.*"

Don't Try To Run Before You Can Walk

And watch out where you are stepping! If you haven't already done so, you will probably need to start your Internet adventure with a single-user dial-up account. While you and your fellow managers and in-house technical resource people are still debating the means by which the Internet is harnessed for your business strategy, get on your bike (with training wheels and all) and tool around the Internet and see what's there. This has the dual benefit of acquainting you with the lie of the land and test-driving the support and connectivity services of an Internet access provider. Better yet, sign up for service from more than one IAP!

While it may not be fast, a dial-up account is cheap and secure. You won't be imperilling your business-critical LAN or database. The gut feeling you get for an IAP can save you big money when you are ready to move up to a dedicated Internet connection. In fact, if you let the access provider know that you are just looking for a taster before the big commitment, they may grant a period of free access so that they can show their wares. More about selecting an Internet access provider can be found in Appendix A: Getting Connected.

There is nothing like experience for a teacher. While this book and many others can set out lists of pointers and give technical advice, actually being on the Net will help immeasurably when it comes time to start prioritizing your Internet task list. There are a large number of things connected to the Internet that are "nice to have." Business needs to focus on the "got to haves" first.

Get Your Team Together

Locate the Internet enthusiasts in your organization. Proselytize at meetings. The more helpers and fellow advocates you can assemble, the easier the transition to cyberbusiness will be. Get early input from your network and system administrators – their eagerness and cooperation is irreplaceable.

As any organizational theory book will tell you, it's a lot easier to make a change in a business environment if all concerned understand that they have something to gain by enduring the pain of transformation. You may need to sell the Internet at several levels inside your business and the ability to call on a number of allies is not to be underestimated.

Know Your Starting Point: Take An Inventory

Just what do you have in the way of an information infrastructure and what changes will be needed to get the company on the Internet? If you already have a LAN, what protocol is it running? Get a handle on what else you will need in terms of servers, gateways, software, training and maintenance. Will your stretched technical management be able to cope?

If you are already running a TCP/IP LAN (this traditionally went hand in hand with having UNIX servers around), you may be in for an easy ride. Usually, TCP/IP network "stacks" must be loaded on all computers that will be communicating with the Internet.

While TCP/IP used to be an extra-cost package, most new releases of operating systems come bundled with TCP/IP support. Microsoft Windows NT and Windows 95 users get it free (and Windows 3.11 users can get a free upgrade). Apple Macs got it in Mac OS 7.5. IBM includes it with OS/2 Warp Connect. You may be faced with the purchase of third-party TCP/IP software or upgrading to the newest level of operating system. This is not a bad thing to consider anyway because third-party TCP/IP, like Netmanage Chameleon, frequently comes with extra utilities and polish not found in the bundled packages.

If you are running a Netware LAN, in some cases it may be possible to avoid a switch to TCP/IP. Products are available that encapsulate TCP/IP in other network protocols. Sun's Netra Internet server has an IPX gateway. Firefox Communications sells Novix which runs as an NLM (NetWare Loadable Module) on NetWare servers and encapsulates TCP/IP into NetWare's IPX protocol. This approach can deliver a security bonus, too. Novell's own product line can also help in this regard.

But the switch to an Internet-enabled office isn't a just a matter of buying and configuring software and hardware. Management "bandwidth" is required as well. For instance, TCP/IP brings with it the need to assign and manage IP addresses. Every computer running TCP/IP on a network must be assigned a unique number as its IP address. A company connecting to the Internet is assigned banks of IP addresses through a central registrar (InterNIC). While your Internet access provider can take care of the paperwork for getting IP addresses, these addresses must then be passed out and managed by nobody but you.

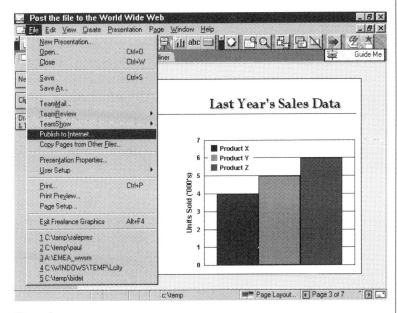

Figure 1

This is no small task. Some companies may already be using unregistered IP addresses of their own, figuring that they will never need to connect to the outside world. Chaos will ensue if these computers are connected to the Net. If you thought maintaining your company telephone list was a big job, you will have some idea about the IP management nightmare.

There is some help available, though, from clever software. You may want to talk to your network managers about installing automated TCP/IP management services, such as DHCP (Dynamic Host Configuration Protocol) which is available on SunSoft Solaris or Windows NT. There is no substitute for putting someone in charge, however.

Figure 1

Freelance is the presentation graphics package of choice, allowing you to publish on the World Wide Web or post your material directly to an intranet Web site for internal discussion. While overhead projectors aren't ready for the scrap heap yet, you need to have Web publishing as part of your presentational arsenal.

"There was a real tug of war between the marketing department that was go-go-go, the MIS staff that was frankly worried about security and additional workload and the bean counters that wanted to be sure that the costs could be justified."

Read Up – Get Internet Wise

The first step above is an important one (that's why it's first) however, there's a lot more to learn about the Internet than you can easily get by just surfing. In addition to buying books from the reference library, get subscriptions to Internet magazines. Subscribe to appropriate listservs and newsgroups. Get a feeling for who's who and what's what.

You will find that the Internet has many of the same aspects as an exotic foreign culture. You need to see the sites, eat the food and drink in the same bars as the natives to have any hope of understanding the possibilities that reside on the Internet. No matter how clever your plans are for cutting costs and creating revenue, if you have formulated them without any full-contact Internet exposure, you are undoubtedly missing something.

Hit the exhibition trail. Not only are the usual PC and Mac conventions sprouting Internet-related exhibits but there are a number of specialist shows that showcase the Internet or online markets. You can always find some kindred spirits as well as keen vendors of Internet products and services. You are not alone! Check out the action at your Lotus users' group if there is one that holds meetings nearby.

Build An Internet Wish List

Once you get your feet wet on the Net, brainstorm with your employees and fellow managers about aspects of your business where the Internet can save time and money. Look at the savings relevant to job categories, functional units, and even on a per task basis. What do those faxes to Australia cost in a month? How much money are you paying to courier documents about town on motorbikes or via a long-distance courier service? How much of your telephone bill is to information or service providers that are already accessible on the Net?

Select An Internet Access Provider And Software

Do the rounds of Internet access and software providers. You will want someone that knows connecting businesses (and not just cybersurfers) to the Internet. Ideally, they will need to know about cc:Mail and Lotus Notes configuration issues.

For businesses, the cost of getting wired isn't concentrated in the actual Internet access fee or the phone line. You should be able to establish a connection to the Internet from your network for under $3,000, with all hardware and software included. Be aware that some providers take an à la carte view of Internet service and be sure that all the parts are included. Take a hard look at all up-front costs and make sure they are comparable and competitive.

While some Internet access providers bill a flat rate for a month's subscription (the norm when ISDN or a leased line is involved), you may choose a provider that charges by units of time. However, if you have a band of far-ranging operatives you may choose to go with both methods of connection and payment.

If your users establish accounts with one of the large commercial online providers that are branching out into the Internet, such as America Online (AOL), CompuServe or Prodigy, each user is charged for his or her time online. When multiple users are all connecting to the Internet with their own accounts, costs multiply fast. An ideal solution is one that allows users to share a single account and be charged to a single account.

POP Goes The Phone Bill

A major cost of Internet access is the money you pay to the telephone company. This can be greatly minimized if you choose an Internet access provider that has a "Point-of-presence" (POP) near you or several in areas where your employees live or travel. POP refers to phone numbers that your access provider makes available for establishing your connection to the Internet. Many large access providers set up a series of POPs so you can dial in to the one that is closest to your company's location and save a bundle on the phone bill. Other Internet access providers provide 0800 numbers so that you can call at local rates from anywhere in the country. It's not free though; this facility is undoubtedly concealed in their rate structure. It may still work out cheaper for your company depending on your pattern of use.

Software Selection

There's lots to choose from on the software front. Having Lotus software on your site simplifies the seemingly endless task of choosing the right applications for your Internet debut. The training and capital costs that you have already invested can be leveraged into your Internet adventure. If there is some feature that you can't get, you probably won't have to wait long because of the pace at which Lotus is sharpening its Internet-equipped applications.

Changing horses in mid-stream would be pure folly. However, you may choose to supplement your stable Lotus

"You can find out if a domain name has been claimed by running a utility program called whois. For a US domain name (ending in .com, for instance), you would type whois internic.net ibm to find out if the name "ibm" was registered. For other countries' domain hierarchies, you have to use their route hub instead of internic.net."

applications with tools or utilities from other vendors. The number and variety of these are increasing daily. It's a full-time job in itself just to keep up. That's where WebExtra comes in.

Nail Down Your Name

To make sure that your customers and suppliers have a good chance of finding you on the Internet, you need to get your name enshrined on the list of domain names at InterNIC. Getting a domain name (`yourcompany.com` or `ourcompany.co.uk`, for example) is easy once you have selected your Internet access provider – they will do all the work. However, the best names may be already taken and TLAs (Three Letter Acronyms) are frowned on. There is now a charge for registering your name so if you have a laundry list of great names, it will cost you to stake a claim for all of them.

You domain name is vital. There are a surprising number of Fortune 500 companies that have found that their domain name is the property of someone else because they didn't wake up and smell the Internet coffee. A law-suit resulted when MTV found that `mtv.com` was registered to the Metaverse organization (oddly, Metaverse was started by disaffected MTV staffers). Registering your domain name even while you are still agonizing over the extent or means of your Internet commitment is a move that can save expense later.

Don't Forget The Intranet

Look for internal applications for Internet technologies and products. Are there documents and databases that Web-based access would be helpful for in-house? Scheduling or event calendars? Time planning? How about in the human resources department? What about your service policies and procedure manuals? There is nothing better than letting the left hand know what the right hand is up to!

Intranets, as their name suggests, are closely related to the Internet. Both share the same software and networking standards and protocols. The only difference is that the global Internet is open to all while intranets exist only to serve users within organizations. They run on private networks within firms and between their branch offices, walled off from the public Internet by "firewalls" which are like one-way mirrors that allow employees to look out, but keep others from seeing in.

The Internet has been getting all of the press attention but intranets are growing just as fast or even faster. Forrester Research determined that 22 percent of the United States' 1000 biggest companies had already deployed Internet technology in an intranet. Netscape Communications, the Web browser market leader, says that nearly three-quarters of its sales are to internal corporate networks. Zona Research, a Californian market-research firm, says that by 1997, the sales of all intranet software will reach $4 billion.

Instead of photocopying a vacation schedule report and stapling on a route slip for internal distribution, a company can put a single copy on an intranet server for all employees to read. No excuses need to be entertained about how the memo got lost in the company mail. An entire company, including its geo-graphically distributed offices, can share a single client or product database, ensuring that everyone uses the most up-to-date information. This is where Lotus Notes users have a leg up on anyone else in the move toward the Internet or intranet.

Figure 2

Build Your Case

Before you can get your company wired, you have to sell your plans to senior management (unless, of course, you ARE senior management!). Brush up on your presentational skills. Assemble a suite of demonstration software complete with lists of relevant Internet resources. Prepare careful budgets for expenditure. Provide truthful estimates of the amount of money that can be saved if you take advantage of Internet services. Use the Net and the information resources to argue your side.

Figure 2
Smart Centre puts all of the resources of the Internet (and your own company intranet) at your finger tips when you use Lotus SmartSuite.

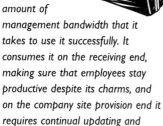

" *The surprising thing we learned about the World Wide Web is the amount of management bandwidth that it takes to use it successfully. It consumes it on the receiving end, making sure that employees stay productive despite its charms, and on the company site provision end it requires continual updating and fresh thought to keep it attractive to callers.* **"**

Allocate Management Resources

If you have successfully made your case to "wire" your company, you have to be sure that you have sufficient resources available to make a good job of it. This means more than a budget to draw on: the project management time required to assemble all the bits of a commercial-grade Internet presence is considerable. Technical management is also required in large measures.

Internet services like Web sites and FTP (File Transfer Protocol) servers on the Internet are very management intensive. Fortunately, you don't have to do everything. Many Internet services can be farmed out to a dependable Internet access provider. However, some facilities take so much "hands on" updating that it would be folly to try to push the job out the door.

Web space is cheap and is even free (up to a point) with some Internet access providers. If you lack conviction that the Internet is the place to be, a small amount invested in a managed Web site on somebody else's server is the perfect way to test the water. If you are truly committed, you might still want to undertake a facilities management contract. For instance, if you were trying to sell photographs across the Net, you would want a very high bandwidth connection to give your customers fast response. That connection's bandwidth might have to be bigger than you could afford. Renting space on a well-connected server could be a viable alternative.

Another service that you may or may not want to have in-house is DNS. For access to the Internet, DNS (Domain Name Service) is required. The Internet and the World Wide Web would be a fraction of its size today if everyone had to enter the numeric address of a site to use it. It would be a lot harder to find Lotus on the Web if you couldn't use `www.lotus.com`! A DNS host allows you to access sites using their names which are a lot easier, even intuitive, to use. Do you need your own DNS? Probably not – you usually get this service from your Internet access provider. But don't forget that DNS requests take up precious bandwidth, and bandwidth in-house is cheaper than out on the Net.

On the other hand, if you intend to make heavy use of Usenet newgroups, you may want to take a select news-feed in-house rather than use a public one (that has far more troublesome and distracting material in and amongst the good). You would then need to set up and run an NNTP (Network News Transfer Protocol) server. For Internet email, a very basic Internet service, you will need an SMTP (Simple Mail Transfer Protocol) host. You will probably want to administer your own email after you have found your feet, but it may be easier to farm it out in the beginning.

To guide your company through the Internet minefield, an experienced consultant can be a time and money saver. However, not all cowboys wear spurs that jingle jangle jingle. Make sure you take up references and commit to a written plan of action to avoid paying too much or not getting all of what you bargained for.

Depending on who you are, where you are and what you decide you want to do with the Internet, there may be other points for you to address. The rest of this book explores some of the other areas that need resolution.

check the
WebExtra

2 Securing Your Business on the Internet

The Internet and security considerations are seemingly at odds with each other. The Internet, born of the open systems movement and nurtured for decades in academia, was originally designed for easy accessibility by many users. Commercial users need to tip that balance to create a safe business environment.

The Business Issue

Poor system security costs money whether the Internet is involved or not. In the period from 1988 to 1994, the number of security violations reported to the Computer Emergency Response Team (CERT) leapt from 100 to 2400. When anything increases by 240 times in just six years, there is cause for concern. Unfortunately, the increase in reported security violations is growing faster than the Internet.

These figures may be conservative: fewer than half of all security breaches were reported according to a DataPro study in 1992. There are probably a further number of attacks carried out by professionals that went undetected or system crashes that were the result of amateurs covering their tracks.

Many security issues can be prevented by the application of low cost hardware or software. But the biggest increase in security comes from management attention: understanding the risks, formulating effective policy and ensuring that the policy is executed.

Security Requires A State Of Mind

The Internet today is largely based on UNIX systems and they are inherently networked – built from the ground up for connectability. However, now that open systems have matured and taken their place in the commercial computing pantheon and the Internet's business role is coming to the fore, tight but efficient systems security is a necessity.

A study by RDI (a US market research company) showed that people are very concerned with security on the Internet, with 93 percent feeling that Internet security is a moderate or high concern to them. Only seven percent responded with a low level of concern. No one had "no opinion"!

If you want a completely secure computer, don't connect it to the Internet. In fact, don't even turn it on. About the only place you will find a perfectly secure computer is inside a cement overcoat at the bottom of the sea! However, that degree of security perfection makes it utterly useless to your business. Utility and security must be balanced.

"Computer security" is a very broad umbrella. It can legitimately include systems availability and data management as well as access control and other topics. In connection with the Internet, you will hear the term "firewall" chanted like some techno-mantra. None of these areas are new or unique to open systems and computer networks in any way – the problems in these areas were well understood by previous generations of IT managers and comprehensively dealt with by the providers of data center hardware and software.

In the open, distributed, internetworked systems world, alas, there are new "challenges" galore created by the network multiplication factor. With networks, the risks of compromise are increased with every access point. Until recently, Internet systems security concerns may not have aroused much user interest because few organizations had committed core business applications to their networks. With money to be gained or lost, the focus has changed.

Risk assessment in a business context requires quantification of
• The likelihood of the risk
• The consequences of the risk
• The cost of prevention.

Despite the ever-present Internet marketing drive, most firms are proceeding cautiously. Mission-critical data (that's what big companies call their account and order control systems) are still largely preserved on host systems rather than distributed on servers likely to be directly connected to the Internet, although "downsizing" to open systems is inevitable, as are connections of some sort to the Internet.

Security concerns are one major reason for the slow migration of conservative systems managers to the Internet. Pushing the system evolution equilibrium in the other direction are users. Users want the Internet to get better access to the world of data that's "out there" in order to do their jobs more efficiently. Marketing-types see the Internet as a vital new channel for getting electronic brochures into the hands of prospective customers and gathering information about market dynamics.

To get the benefits (and as few of the burdens as possible) from the Internet, some old-time mainframe savvy must be used to secure the system. But before implementing draconian network security, it is vital to set your priorities and understand strategic goals, balancing data confidentiality, system integrity and availability.

The right mix of these elements is crucial – a church social club needs one degree of system security, an Army base quite another. When implementing security measures, the level of security must be commensurate with anticipated risks and threats. Security costs money either in hardware, software, training or lost efficiency and can also adversely affect system performance and, indeed, the functioning of the organization.

It may not be entirely possible to reconcile Internet accessibility with the need for internal security. This can result in a standalone machine used in the business for outgoing Internet access. This gets the Net on the inside without connecting it to the business-critical systems. Although access is constricted, it is available nonetheless.

The same method can be used to create a secure (from the business' perspective) Web server. Connected to the Internet and not the internal network, it can perform its Web duties with no chance of inappropriate infiltration. Updates to the Web pages would have to be done via "sneakernet" (i.e. walking a floppy or tape across to the server) but a high degree of internal network security can be maintained albeit with diminished functionality. However, with a bit of work you can get the Internet and your internal network to coexist quite happily.

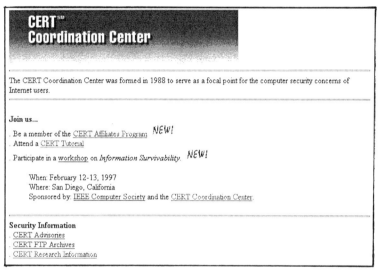

Figure 3

Managers may be pleased to discover that network security in the age of the Internet is amenable to the same budgetary control as any other facet of business enterprise. Security measures are in the correct balance when the cost of protection and the cost of exposure hit the same point. Discovering the exact costs, in some cases, may be a bigger problem than implementing changes.

Another of the basic concepts of information security, in open or proprietary systems, is separation of duties. Separating responsibilities imposes checks and balances. For example, the person who manages computer operations should be different from the person managing data – the programmer who develops a payroll system should not enter data into that system.

The tools available to manage Internet systems security provide a rich reservoir from which to select the proper mix for a given application. They include:

Figure 3
CERT isn't going to win any prizes for a snazzy Web site – but their site contains vital information needed to keep your network secure.

- Physical access control: Simply, don't leave the barn door open on either your servers, workstations or your network wiring.

- Identification or authentication: Password control is the most common implementation of this. A step higher up the technology ladder are smart ID cards and a bit further along the trail to Intelligence community-grade-paranoia come hand prints, voice prints and retinal pattern scanning. Because user authentication comes early in the process of system access, many analysts hold it to be the most vital. It is often the cheapest security measure to implement.

- Access control: Who can do what, basically. All UNIX-based systems contain rudimentary control over who can read, write or execute a file. Advanced systems use access control lists, which define who can run an application and who can create, read or write a file. Access control systems protect networks from inadvertent loss of information, malicious destruction or compromise of data and disruption from virus attack.

  Access control, properly implemented, lets the system assign a user the privileges necessary to accomplish the task at hand, and no more. For instance, this type of security is vital in the health care field where information must be shared between concerned profes-sionals but the patient's confidentiality must be safeguarded simultaneously.

- Accountability and auditing: The system must be able to link changes made by any user to the effect as well as provide a system history for investigation of breaches of security. This security function is also relatively inexpensive to implement.

- Accuracy: The system should protect against unautho-rized or undesired modification of data. This includes modifications to the system. For example, viruses should not be allowed to lodge themselves within systems by hiding inside legitimate system or end-user programs.

- Availability of service: The system needs to protect itself against intentional or accidental monopolization by any user. No user should be able to commandeer 100 percent of the CPU or disk space, or interfere with time-

http://www.securid.com/

critical operations. Plans to deal with power interruption and hardware faults come under this heading.

- Secure data exchange: The system must promote the secure transmission of data over communications channels. Encryption is often used to achieve this security goal. Recently, commercial open systems security products have begun to proliferate as the level of open systems business users has exploded.

Choice, a basic tenet of open systems philosophy on which the Internet is based, is widely available for system security products. These products perform a variety of functions for system administrators. The consensus of security analysts is that users now need automated tools to maintain a secure environment.

The acute problem is one of staffing and expertise. Where once many people were managing a single system, now only a few people are managing hundreds, maybe thousands, of systems in multi-vendor, geographically distributed systems. As networks grow, the threat of a security compromise increases. Every new workstation, router or cable run elevates the vulnerability level.

It cannot be said enough: managing system security issues is a matter of matching the right tool to the job. There is a lot of technology out there that can be used – finding a good fit is the trick. If security interferes with getting the job done, users will find ways around it or the company will lose out through decreased efficiency. One such product that provides a tight seal without onerous user burden is Security Dynamics' Secure ID Card. This technology provides a convenient way to overcome the "crackability" shortcomings in static password systems.

However, it is nothing more than a way to implement a security management policy. That policy is the first line of defense. Without a management policy, you are missing an essential and fundamental element to providing security for business data. A lack of policy reduces security to a list of tactical attempts that over time will utterly fail to do the job. Even the best security in the world is useless if a user walks away from his or her workstation and doesn't log out!

In addition to user authentication and access control, audit techniques are an invaluable asset in managing network security. The auditing functions make an indelible record of the security-relevant events that occur on a system. This can include users' logins and logouts, data file access, printer jobs, password control, and more as appropriate. Auditing is probably the single most important feature for commercial use of an Internet system. It tells you who is interested in your site, keeps honest people honest and helps catch dishonest ones.

But auditing doesn't stop with marketing data collation or implementation of software controls. Like most management issues, auditing of policy and implementation must be a continuing process. Great ideas, leading edge technologies and thorough implementation all fall foul of the erosion of time.

Security is not a goal to be arrived at and then forgotten. It is a process that needs careful monitoring so that oversights can be corrected and a closer fit to a company's needs can be crafted. In the final analysis, system security issues are a combination of technology and personnel challenges. While the perfectly secure computer may never be created, a carefully thought out and deliberately implemented set of security procedures will go a long way to providing commercial open systems users with all of the safeguards they need to regulate access to the data held on their open systems.

Internet Risk Assessment

What is it about the Internet that gets otherwise sober systems administrators quaking in their boots? Is it the menace of viruses? Is it hacker damage to their carefully tended systems? Is it the loss of confidential material into unauthorized hands? It is probably the fear of the unknown. You can't appreciate the holes in your carefully woven security blanket unless you have budgeted time and talent to continually prospecting for flaws.

Given the size of the Internet, the chances of some computer delinquent picking your server out of the hundreds of thousands on the Net are pretty low. There are indications that most computer hacks are conducted from inside or by disgruntled employees recently shown the door. That does not mean, however, that your system won't be the needle in the haystack that gets found.

Without the proper security protection, an Internet connection gives unscrupulous individuals the chance to intercept, corrupt, or even alter your vital business information as well as interfere with the orderly conduct of your business. The threats to your business can be lumped into five categories:

- Eavesdropping. Electronic spies can obtain information
  covertly by intercepting email intended for someone
  else, or even by analyzing the traffic flowing between

"While you may be distracted by the hacker menace, don't forget the peril from within. Disgruntled employees or ex-employees with technical skills may create the worst hazard for your system security. Compartmentalization is the accepted cure: never let developers directly access the operational system."

organizations, allowing them to learn about impending deals or confidential business relationships. Eavesdropping can cost organizations a lot if it affects trading margins, legal liabilities, or your relationship with customers or suppliers.

- Fraudulent transactions. By impersonating an authorized user, thieves can conduct unauthorized business transactions. The financial services sector would be a prime target for this type of mischief but it can happen to small businesses processing orders for office stationery, too.

- Data corruption. Intruders that penetrate a company database can corrupt data – inadvertently or as part of some attempt to alter the target company's competitive stance. If done well, this can be almost impossible to detect.

- Theft of data, services and processing power. If it isn't nailed down, somebody will try to steal it. In the information economy, information is worth money, as is the computing horsepower required to run complex software. This kind of break-in can cause loss of revenue to the company that is hacked. If hackers get into your system, they can use it for a free ride on the Internet or worse yet, steal your expensive processor power for their own pet projects.

- Denial of services. Attacks on a company's computer system can prevent a company from performing its business mission. This can have obvious commercial ramifications. Fortunately, this is the threat that is easiest to detect.

How Hackers Find The Weak Links

Getting hacked is usually a case of bad luck unless you have aroused the animus of a particular individual or group by your business field or practices. While unauthorized access to computer systems is against the law there are few prosecutions. But the hackers that are caught make big news in the media. This in itself may be a strong disincentive for companies to move against hackers. Who wants to admit their failings and suffer adverse publicity or lose clients' trust?

Aside from the criminal who has a pecuniary motivation for getting inside your network, most hackers approach their art for reasons akin to Sir Edmund Hillary's mountain climbing motivations: because they are there. It's your duty to make sure that those mountains they want to climb are as hostile and forbidding as the Himalayas.

Hackers are computer and communications experts. They don't have to work with 'em, they love 'em. As a result they may be better appraised about your security issues than you are. Several former hackers are now making a very comfortable living (once they got out of jail) as security consultants.

Several "open doors" that are inviting to the wrong sort of person usually exist in a company:

- "Social engineering" attacks. If anyone ever calls you and says that they are from MIS or the telephone company or a computer subcontractor and asks for your password to "check out" your system, you are under attack. This simple ruse is extremely effective against security-lax employees, harried executives or even inattentive MIS technicians. Any hacker can sound authoritative on the phone and lying convincingly to non-technical business users is an easily acquired talent.
- Trashing or dumpster diving. It's surprising what can be found in the company's waste bins! Many hackers get vital clues for gaining entry through the simple expedient of rooting around in your dumpsters! If you don't have a shredder, get one. If you have one, use it!
- Application attacks. Some applications, especially older ones that were built before the online explosion, have inherently weak security. Some applications even send passwords over the Internet as clear text. It won't take another Einstein to get access to an application of this sort – or perhaps the whole system! Common Internet applications such as Telnet, email, FTP and HTTP servers all have flaws. Until recently, you could crack some Web servers merely by sending too much data to them. The overflow lets hackers get at the system prompt, the first step on the road to unrestricted access to your computer.
- Computer assisted hacks. Once a hacker gets in, it can be frighteningly easy to access your files and services. Too many users select easy-to-guess passwords for their logins. A password cracker can use the power of your own computer to automatically try a long list of commonly used passwords against all of the user accounts on that computer. With a little luck and persistence, the attacker will get in! It only takes a few hours' time to try every word in the dictionary. Once

http://www.cert.org/

the door is opened a crack, it is much easier to pry the lid off full access privileges.

- Spoofing. Sometimes poorly guarded computers or applications will trust each other based on their network address. However, it is relatively easy to configure any address you want on any computer connected to the Net. Relying on this kind of security alone is extremely hacker-friendly. It helps if you can hide some of your computer resources behind gateway machines.

- Wire tapping. It's not just telephone calls that can be tapped. If a hacker can get physical access to your network for even a brief time, he or she will have the ability to collect your network traffic until an easy way in is uncovered.

The antidote for most of these methods of attack is an effective security policy that is adhered to by all. That policy should include regular password changes, hard to crack passwords and reporting any attempts by "social engineers" or questionable servicemen. Applications developed by users that aren't up to speed with security implications can also be a danger if deployed on an internal network connected to the Internet.

The Internet-connected business has a few potential gateways to ne'er-do-wells and nuisance mongers. On the bright side, with so many individuals and businesses joining the Internet you become a much smaller target statistically and the number of minds working on security issues (from both a user and a vendor viewpoint) also increase.

Some guys in white hats are watching over us. The CERT (Computer Emergency Response Team) routinely sends out security bulletins that expose security-related software bugs in various commercial applications and operating systems. The products from Sun, IBM, HP and Microsoft all have had anywhere from a couple to a couple of dozen security-related bugs flagged by CERT. These loopholes, if exploited, can be a means of gaining access to any site that is using these software environments.

The risks to your system that come courtesy of the Internet are the following.

Email Risks

Internet email servers have had a checkered career as a welcome mat for hackers. In addition to gaining access via poorly selected passwords, binary files attached to email messages can contain software that can open a loophole or damage your system. However, email connectivity itself can be used as a weapon.

Businesses can also run the risk of mail-bombing if they are engaged in a controversial business. A mail bomb is an overload of your mail server by a large quantity of sizeable mail items. When Canter and Siegel perpetrated their unprincipled Usenet sales campaign, they were mail-bombed and effectively excluded from the Internet for a period of time.

Binary files are the danger here but even application files like spreadsheets and word processed documents can contain macro instructions that, if executed, can cause data loss or inconvenience. Still, the value of passing live spreadsheets and carefully formatted proposals or presentations around is very high. The best defense against this Internet pitfall is a competent virus checker that is not only used regularly but also updated for the latest in virus tricks.

If this is a serious consideration for your business, you can either switch from cc:Mail to an email package that has automatic virus checking for binary attachments or ban attachments altogether and use FTP file transfer which can be manually checked for viruses before loading into a live application.

"You can never be too careful: even software from recognized companies can put you at risk. Our company caught the Concept Word macro virus from a CD direct from Microsoft. So much for the security of CDs and known software sources!"

FTP Risks

Whenever you put new software on your network or desktop machine, you are taking a chance, no matter where you got it from. Sharing software with coworkers and like-minded acquaintances on the Net can save time and money but there is a downside from software that behaves badly, either accidentally or intentionally.

Buying your software from recognized commercial sources minimizes the risk but it is still not foolproof. Heard the one about the user with the brand new PC that was contaminated with a virus by his dozy dealer? Magazine cover disks can be tainted – get the CD-ROM versions if you are concerned. But even the best virus scanning isn't guaranteed foolproof!

On the Internet, when you download software you are on your own! If you see a piece of software that you want, take care before you push the download button. Try to use official sources. If you are after a bug fix for Windows, get it from ftp.microsoft.com. It's as close to being safe coming from Microsoft's own FTP server as any Microsoft product will be!

Use a virus checker to test the integrity of any software you get, from the Net or anywhere else.

If you are technically minded, get uncompiled source code if possible. Then read it before you install it to be sure that it isn't up to no good. Before installing software of questionable provenance on a business-critical system (and maybe this should go for all software), check it out on a safe computer. A backup is the single best thing you can do to any important computer. Be methodical and do complete and incremental backups according to a well-considered plan.

One particularly worrisome attack on your computer system can be carried out by a program called a keystroke logger. This program can be downloaded accidentally and lacks the signature that would give it away to a virus detector. It could arrive as a so-called trojan horse program – inside another program that provides some legitimate benefit.

Once the keystroke logger is installed it can sit quietly and monitor your keystrokes whenever your computer is on – looking for passwords or credit card numbers or anything that it can be programmed to filter out of your keyboard activity. When it gets what it is looking for, it is a simple matter to surreptitiously email the contraband data to an email box obtained with false identification information or one established on a third party's system during an earlier break-in.

Depending on your predisposition to take this sort of risk attendant to downloading software from the Internet, a policy forbidding the downloading of software by anyone outside MIS could save you money.

World Wide Web Risks

Incoming Web risks are the same as for FTPed software. If you click on a link that brings an executable file to your disk, be on guard. Don't worry about text and images, though, unless they contravene a local decency statute. Don't forget that images can persist in a computer cache for a considerable length of time. What's legal today may be illegal tomorrow!

Outgoing Web services aren't free from trouble either, unfortunately. Recently there has been a spate of World Wide Web site vandalism. A movie company found that some hackers had gained access to their advertisements for a new film and drawn beards on the faces of the star actors. This "harmless" fun could presage vulnerability to real commercial damage.

For instance, what if the site had advertised flights between the UK and the United States and the miscreants had decreased the prices? The air carrier would be flooded with requests from potential passengers that could not be met. The Virgin Atlantic airline has been fined for incorrect pricing on their Web site already. Who needs this trouble?

Dealing With Internet Security Risks

The Good News

Any business can make their computer systems resources as secure as necessary with currently available security software, hardware and appropriate management procedures. Properly implemented, these security mechanisms can protect the company from intruders who attempt to enter the internal network while still allowing authorized users with access to Internet services such as the Web, FTP, email, Telnet, Usenet news and Gopher.

The Tools Of The Trade

Effective Internet security solutions are based on several tools and technologies that can be combined to protect information and computers from unauthorized access or loss of information. They include passwords, encryption, firewalls, and appropriate security policies and procedures. Since policy is a management issue, we'll start there.

http://www.bbn.com/

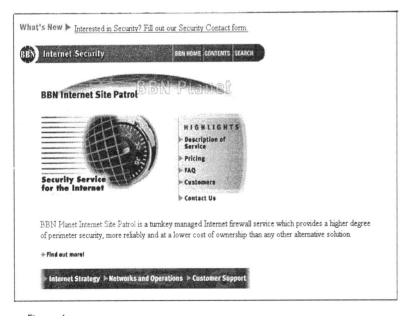

Figure 4

Figure 4
BBN Planet offers a broad range of Internet services to the business community. Their consultants can match your security fears and expectations against available products and techniques.

A good password should be:
- *at least six characters long*
- *a mixture of upper case, lower case, numbers or punctuation*
- *not a word in the dictionary*
- *not an easily guessed combination of letters: adjacent keyboard keys, your name, your company's name, a well-known landmark, etc.*

Security Policies And Procedures

The platform on which to build a sound Internet security solution is a comprehensive security policy that precisely identifies who, and under what circumstances, should have access to a company's internal network and what resources on the Internet are available to employees. It's easy to overlook the basics in the rush to get online and often this initial fault can make a mockery of the money budgeted for technology-implemented facets of security.

BBN Planet, an Internet consultancy that sells security products and services, sees network security policies as a continuum that ranges from promiscuous at one end to paranoid at the other extreme. A promiscuous security policy allows everyone unimpeded passage between the Internet and the organization's internal network. A paranoid policy doesn't give anyone access between these two networks, at all. In between are two more workable alternatives, the permissive and prudent policies.

The permissive policy allows all traffic except that which is explicitly disallowed. This requires the configuration and maintenance of a router or firewall that filters the packets between the LAN and the Internet, stopping those that are pre-determined to be forbidden. This requires an exhaustive filter mechanism that needs continual updating and can prevent certain desirable and necessary communication. On the other hand, it is cheap from an equipment standpoint, requiring only configuration of the gateway router that you will have to have in any event. While packet filtering is useful in fending off intruders, it should not be relied upon as a total Internet security solution.

A prudent policy, on the other hand, works in the opposite fashion. It disallows all traffic from flowing between the two networks except that which is explicitly allowed. Prudent policies are implemented by application proxies, a major constituent of a well-built Internet firewall.

Only after a security policy has been defined should you move on to implementation with software and hardware devices.

Passwords – A Link In The Chain

Passwords give you a good and cheap layer of defense. However, few business users appreciate the impact that poorly chosen passwords can have. Most people choose passwords that are easy to remember. Unfortunately, what is easy for you to remember is oftentimes easy for a hacker to discover. CERT estimates that 80 percent of computer break-ins are caused by poor password choice.

Remember, when it comes to passwords, it's computers that do all the work. A PC can take as long as it wants trying out passwords without even taking a break for lunch. Remember the film *War Games*? You can usually make it very hard for some persistent but dumb computer to guess your password. Most password crackers pick common words from the dictionary and simple names.

However, it is difficult for many people to conceive of a password that will meet all the suggested criteria and still be easy to remember! Passwords that can't be remembered create an administrative workload and lead to users adopting the sort of passwords that are easily cracked.

There are lots of ways to construct practical password mnemonics – give your people a handful of suggestions. A helpful trick is to pick the first letters of a favorite phrase like MpIeTr! (My password Is easy To remember!) or the first letter on each line of a certain page of a desktop reference book you always have to hand. Try your kid's name backwards combined with the month of his or her birth or your dog's name with suitable punctuation. Anything (almost) is better than the most common (and easily guessed) password in computer history: the word "password."

When you install a PC or server, make sure that you assign passwords to the default accounts that come with the system software, if any. Leaving the default passwords in place for root, system, maint or guest logins is inviting trouble. Everyone that has the same computer or version of the operating system will have the same passwords as you!

Another means of increasing the potency of your password protection is to change it regularly. Some operating systems have a password diary system as part of their standard password mechanism. This decreases the impact of any hacker discovering your password – if it is only good for a week and no further holes are exploited, any hacker will be off the system in an average of 3.5 days! Don't use the same password for more than one system. And never, never, never, never write your password down.

Management must be careful to remove user accounts from the system when an employee leaves. It might even be smart to disable the accounts of workers that will be absent for weeks at a time. To reduce the risk of "inside" compromise, a company

http://www.rsa.com/

may consider performing background checks on security system personnel, and separate security management and auditing systems to prevent an administrator from altering the audit of management actions.

Encryption

Encryption encodes information so that it can only be decoded by an authorized individual with the right "key." At a stroke, encryption can prove who a message is from, that it has not been tampered with and has been held in confidence in transit.

When information is encrypted, it is first translated into a numerical form, and then encrypted using a mathematical algorithm. The algorithm requires a key or keys in order to encode or decode the information. The algorithm cannot decode the encrypted information without a decoding key.

The two types of encryption algorithms available in the market today are public key and, less frequently, symmetric key. Public key encryption relies on a pair of keys to encrypt and decrypt data. One key is called the public key and is published publicly by trusted servers. The other is a private key known only to the key's owner. Messages encrypted with the public key can only be decrypted with the private key and vice versa. Most public key systems available in the market today are based on the RSA algorithm patented by Public Key Partners.

Public key encryption is so hard to crack that many governments are concerned that it is too strong, giving protection to criminals and foreign spies. The US government has classified it as a munition and restricts its export. France does not allow any encryption to be used by private individuals. Nonetheless, strong public key encryption is available worldwide, thanks to the Internet. One implementation, PGP (Pretty Good Privacy), is well known and respected. It is said that if a message is encrypted with strong public key encryption, there is not enough time before the sun burns out to decrypt the message using brute-force calculation techniques and the fastest computer available today!

Symmetric key encryption relies on a single key known by both parties. Messages encrypted with a key must be decrypted with the same key. Because keys must be shared between communicating parties, the tasks of sharing the keys and managing the keys can provide loopholes. There are several symmetric key management systems that can help, however.

The best known symmetric key encryption is the Kerberos authentication system developed at MIT for the Athena project.

Kerberos makes use of the Data Encryption Standard (DES) algorithm. The security of Kerberos encryption and the DES algorithm have been compromised but can still provide a useful level of security: they can still be used to keep honest people honest.

Building A Firewall

A firewall is the element of an overall security solution that makes many Internet risks manageable. Installing an efficient firewall between your internal network and the Internet effectively eliminates the Internet as a direct source of security threats. The most important job of a firewall is to shield the potentially security-bug-ridden computers on your internal network from direct contact with the Internet. Passwords and configurational issues cannot be forgotten but they become another layer in a compound solution.

"You are never done with security. You have to test and retest and then make sure that the tests are themselves valid. Security is a process not a goal. This is one aspect of maintaining an Internet-connected system where you dare not rest on your laurels."

You can't go to the computer store and buy an Internet firewall off the shelf, plug it in and relax. A firewall is composed of many separate pieces; some are provided in the operating system, others are included with your Internet service software such as the Web server. Some firewall elements come in the form of add-on software packages, others can be provided by your Internet access provider and still others are the product of the management decisions and policy implementations discussed above. None of it works at all without some understanding of the way in which Internet host machines work and where the weak points are. If you think of security as a process instead of a goal you will wind up with a secure system. The day after you think the job is done, cruel fate may inform you otherwise.

Internet application proxy firewalls are, in BBN's terminology, a prudent perimeter security solution. Sitting between the Internet and your internal network, they act as a traffic cop. A firewall provides application proxies for most of the popular Internet applications and often can be made to work like a one-way mirror.

Rather than directly passing packets between the internal network and the Internet, the firewall requires client applications to establish an application service connection to the firewall. The firewall then maintains the connection with the outside server. The firewall only passes data for the applications that it is configured to support.

Even if there are grievous security lapses on the internal network, they are not visible to the Internet and therefore cannot be exploited by the hacking fraternity. Commonly your own

Internet application servers sit just outside the firewall, eliminating the need for outside traffic to try to reach the Web, FTP and Telnet services through the firewall.

Firewalls aren't forever. Today's ten foot high wall may be down around your knees by next year. Maintaining the integrity of a firewall calls for continuous monitoring and upgrades. You will have an on-going relationship with your firewall vendor or outside security consultancy. Choose well!

Testing Your Security Process

It does you no good to sit back and think that you have the Internet security nut cracked when in fact you do not. Because a smug attitude is an invitation to catastrophe, a couple of programmers created a package to wipe that smile off the faces of inattentive Internet users. SATAN is a fiendishly clever software tool for testing Internet hosts or entire networks for security lapses. SATAN tests host systems to determine which Internet services are present and whether or not those services are badly configured or contain weak spots that an unprincipled intruder could exploit.

But SATAN doesn't leave you in security Hell. It goes so far as to offer ways to correct some of the vulnerabilities that it finds as well providing a brief tutorial on Internet host security. Despite a certain amount of press hysteria, SATAN is merely an analysis and reporting tool and does not actually break into systems. No doubt some guys in black hats are using SATAN, too, but wouldn't you rather know about your system's weak spots than be surprised one Monday morning?

SATAN was placed in the public domain by its authors and is available without cost over the Internet from a variety of FTP sites all over the world. SATAN runs on specially configured UNIX systems and can be configured so that only users with system-level privileges or root privileges may execute the software. SATAN runs on UNIX systems from Sun Microsystems, Silicon Graphics and others, and the list of operating systems that it supports is being increased by popular demand.

The National Institute for Software Testing recommends that sites should develop policies for using SATAN responsibly and efficiently and promptly correct all vulnerabilities before vulnerable systems could be attacked. In addition, sites should be on the lookout for illicit scans of their networks by SATAN or similar tools.

Legal Protection

Not everything on your Internet server can be protected by newfangled technology. As your company publishes Web pages that include your logo, product names, copyright material and other so-called intellectual property, the importance of understanding the legal protections available (and not available) assumes an important role in dealing with one sort of Internet security risk. These elements are covered in Chapter 8. Talk to your insurers to find out which risks are covered and which aren't.

Unless you uncover an international espionage ring or big-time commercial fraudsters operating out of your computing system, you may have trouble interesting local, let alone national, law enforcement in your travails. They probably just don't have the manpower or the skills necessary to get deeply involved in detecting or prosecuting data security breaches. The likelihood of a successful prosecution, the pay-off for the boys in blue suits, is much less than for a run-of-the-mill breaking and entering, due to jurisdictional headaches, high costs and so forth. Even if you do succeed in getting the police interested, this may well put legal and financial responsibilities on your company that you could well do without.

If you do need to institute a lawsuit or initiate a criminal action that could have commercial consequences, you must be aware of all the nuances of collecting and preserving evidence. Your own corporate counsel needs to be consulted very early in the process otherwise vital evidence may become unusable. A good source of information on collecting and preserving computer evidence is Peter Sommer, a forensic computer scientist at the London School of Economics Computer Security Research Centre. He is author of the Hacker Handbook Series.

Lotus And Internet Security

If you use Lotus Notes, many Internet security concerns regarding access to sensitive data are non-issues. You still have to manage access to your network with a firewall but the data inside Lotus Notes can be made very safe indeed. Notes handles its own security across all of its supported operating systems and networking environments. The encryption used by Notes utilizes technology licensed from RSA, the owner of public key encryption patents and a leading commercial encryption vendor.

"Notes security is very tight indeed and it benefits from continual tweaking from Lotus based on user feedback. But it isn't the end of the story for your organization's security. A hacker at the operating system level can cause problems even if Lotus Notes is proof against illicit data access."

Notes provides four classes of security to cover all of the usual loopholes thorough which information (and hackers) can slip:

- Authentication. Notes uses RSA public key certification and X.500 hierarchical naming syntax to identify users, servers, and encryption key certifiers. The Notes authentication process is symmetrical and bi-directional, e.g. servers authenticate the identity of users, and users authenticate the identity of servers to provide near crack-proof security. Notes authentication is used whenever any user communicates with a server or whenever two servers communicate with each other.
- Digital signatures. It is vital to know that the purported author of a message is actually the real author – otherwise disgruntled hackers within would find it amusing to give everyone the boss's birthday off. Digital signatures also provide guarantees that a message has not changed since the user signed it.
- Encryption. As mentioned above, Notes encryption can scramble messages so that they cannot be understood if accessed by the wrong person. Encryption is available at three levels of the system to provide a tight seal on confidentiality. Individual messages can be encrypted for one or more intended recipients; network-level encryption prevents tapping into traffic over the LAN, dial-up links or the Internet. In Notes database fields, encryption can be designed in so that only authorized users can access the information in them.
- Access control. Notes closely controls access to shared databases, documents, views, forms, and fields. Server access can be controlled for individual users by either allowing or denying access to specific Notes servers within the organization. Every Notes database has an access control list which is controlled by the manager of that database.

Notes has particularly fine-grained control over the access attributes for each database. The levels of access range from managers who can change access and privileges to users who are permitted only to read the database policy statement. Provisions are made for database designers, document editors, document authors, readers and document depositors. These classifications may overlap, which can enhance usability but in certain circumstances leads to inappropriate access. It is up to the database designer and manager to grant or deny appropriate access.

cc:Mail depends on the host operating system for much of its security. The amount of security actually delivered can therefore vary according to the platform, version and the degree of attention given by the system administrator. Of course, if you use Note Mail then you have the added bonus of Notes security outlined above.

With Notes, Lotus has done a good job in wrapping a thick security cocoon around the core program. However, there may be latent errors in Notes (especially after new versions are released), and there may be lapses in implementation or operational faults that your company's programmers create. If security is viewed as a process, Notes databases can actually become more secure over time.

What To Do If You Have An Internet Security Incident

The head in the sand routine will ill serve you if you have a breach of security. The key to improving levels of security is to learn from mistakes – if you deny that you have security problems, you will never remedy them.

The first intimation of a breach is when something happens that you can't explain. Don't put it down to a bad case of Monday morning blues. While most burglaries happen at night, computer break-ins can happen any time of day, on any day. Don't forget that broad daylight where you are is midnight somewhere on the Internet. You are only a Telnet away.

If your hacker is careful, you may never know that your defenses have been penetrated unless you are extremely vigilant. UNIX systems will tell you the time of last login and this can provide a strong clue that someone else has been using your computer or your network account. Most server systems maintain a system of event logs. Generally they are never examined unless there is a problem. Part of the ongoing security process is to make use of those logs as a routine matter, spot-checking and identifying any out-of the-ordinary patterns. Alarms can often be set to alert administrators to trigger events.

If an important file is deleted or changed and you don't remember doing it or even if your machine starts running uncharacteristically slow, this could be a pointer toward an intrusion. Unfortunately, many users miss the early signs of unauthorized and unwelcomed access. Alert the system administrator. He or she will look at the user logs, the password files

check the
WebExtra

and the list of running tasks to see if anything is awry. Don't back-up, erase files or change anything until you get expert help.

Tracking down a hacker requires a methodical approach that surpasses the application and intuition of TV's Columbo. While the temptation is to exclude the miscreant from your system at once, a more deliberative approach could pay off in the long run and provide law enforcement officials with a good case for prosecution.

If you find an intruder and seal up the entrance he or she was using, you aren't done yet! If the intruder is capable and has been on your system for a while, he or she has doubtless arranged some insurance against the day when the jig is up.

The Business Bottom Line

Internet security is a major concern for businesses. Statistically, the chances of a break-in are remote but the consequences can be expensive. Providing adequate security requires balancing risks and benefits that are unique for each company's plans for getting value from an Internet connection. There are many things that can be done to enhance computer security that have a near zero cost basis. Satisfactory security levels can be maintained by a combination of hardware, software and management involvement, all of which should be budgeted for on a continuing basis.

3 | Moving Money! Electronic Payment over the Internet

After security issues, how to pay and get paid are the second most important questions that businesspeople have about doing business on the Internet. Not everyone is looking for the Net to be a marketing turbocharger – they want to know, bluntly, how the Net can make them money.

Credit cards and new forms of electronic money are going to be vital for any Net business. However, there are pluses and minuses for traditional and hot new payment technologies. Getting the right exchange medium from the growing list of alternatives will be important for building electronic commerce. The changes in this area are starting to mount, so stay tuned to the Web Extra.

The Business Issue

Nowhere does the Internet security issue come to a finer point than electronic commerce. Keeping future business plans, confidential data and private conversations secure is one thing; keeping tabs on your money, credit cards, and bank balances are perceived to be problems of more urgent dimensions. Financial institutions are concerned because of the huge losses they might sustain if Net payment systems are compromised. Vendors keen to get on the Internet are concerned, too, that lack of security in transactions could deliver hidden and unanticipated overheads or be a turn-off for shoppers. Customers, obviously, want to make sure that their money is spent only when they say so and in the sums they authorize and that there is recourse if transactions don't conclude to their satisfaction.

Credit History

The rapid growth of the Net has created demand for a cheap and secure means of making and taking payments. Consumers want to buy and sellers want to sell – and the Net can be the place to do both. The alternatives for payment that are now available and the additional ones that are being created reflect the popular push for the Net to become a channel for commerce.

The commercial possibilities for the Internet could be virtually limitless, if only if there were a safe, wired way to pay for whatever it is has you (or your customers) metaphorically reaching for your wallet. Never fear, though, because a lot of bright people are working to close the loop so that the Internet can become the info mall of the future. Whether this is a development that will be universally welcomed remains to be seen, however.

It's a time of choice. The decisions that are made today will influence not only our economic lives but also that part of our existence that we may wish to hold private. For instance, do you want some market-research company to know which daily paper or magazines you read and target you with special offers tailored for that readership? In some parts of the world, the paper you read is tantamount to a declaration of political party affiliation. While some of us are vocal about our political preference, not everyone would want to have that information available publicly.

Keen marketers would love to have access to information that would allow them to zero in on the prospects that will be most likely to succumb to their offerings. Some marketing plans would also like to avoid making the offer to the "wrong kind" of prospect. Is there any wonder that electronic money is a topic hotly debated by civil libertarians as well as businesspeople? There are electronic forms of cash being created to protect Net buyers from intrusion on their purchases while other forms of Internet payment would allow the collection of marketing data.

The conundrums of Net commerce aren't theoretical or in the future: there is already commerce on the Net. And there has been for some time. It has followed a gradual evolution, guided by the immediacy desired by both customers and vendors and by their level of comfort with new concepts and perceived risks.

The first payments for goods or services bought on the Internet weren't even done over the Internet. It was done with the simple expedient of a cheque through the mail or a fax with a credit card number and a signature. This was, and is, slow for both parties and expensive for the vendor. It can take days for a cheque to clear and, if the item being purchased can be distributed over the Net (some software or information that could be delivered instantly), then this means of settlement leaves a great deal to be desired from the buyer's perspective. The drawbacks of this kind of payment system are further exacerbated by the global aspect of the Internet. Try buying a piece of US software with a Japanese cheque! It could take months!

A number of pioneering sales operations are already at work on the Internet regardless. A good example is the Future Fantasy Bookshop. You use the World Wide Web to browse the considerable catalogs of old, new, and not yet released book titles (http://www.futfan.com) and, when you find what you want, it's as easy as filling in a browser form to send off an email order. But you haven't bought anything yet because, in common with other 21st century mail merchants, the Future Fantasy Bookshop doesn't want to take your credit card details over the Internet due to the potential problem of eavesdroppers taking your number and misusing it.

Hesitation on the part of buyers and sellers means that some additional form of communication by fax, telephone call or letter is necessary before consummating a transaction. And from the merchant's side, this all drives up the cost of doing business and provides an obstacle that deters impulse buyers.

While none of this order processing is too onerous for a couple of books from the Future Fantasy Bookshop, that reduction in the spontaneity of a sale hurts. Students of retail psychology

http://www.netchex.com/

know that when punters want to buy, you take their money as nicely and quickly as possible before they change their minds.

Today's Internet hasn't found the one payment method that is cheap, easy, universal and secure … but rest assured that many clever people are working on it. A variety of solutions exist and it is a crucial choice for anyone trying to sell over the net. Below we look at the role played by the conventional credit card companies in old and trusted types of transactions as well as in new and unusual implementations like NetChex, CyberCash and First Virtual Holdings payment products, and also at new payment enablement mechanisms like stored value smart cards and even a reinvention of money in an electronic form with DigiCash.

NetChex

Net shoppers with a US check account can take advantage of the facilities of NetChex, a fusion of Internet technology and the familiarity of conventional checks. Nothing out of the ordinary is required – there is no need to set up a special account or apply at a new bank. NetChex can be used with existing credit and debit card accounts, too. It uses proprietary security software so that an authorized user is the only person who can write a check against a NetChex account. No one can defraud or misuse an account either intentionally or accidentally.

Figure 5
Netchex leverages conventional money handling mechanisms so that Net commerce can get off the ground with the minimum of unfamiliarity.

Figure 5

The dynamic signature key used by NetChex is generated before each and every transaction so that a determined hijacker of account information will have little to gain by persistence. Sensitive information like bank account numbers are never sent in clear ASCII text over the Internet.

If you're a merchant, NetChex assures you that payment has been made, making "the check's in the mail" a promise you won't have to hear again. Once NetChex receives an authorized electronic check from an enrolled buyer, the actual check made payable to you is generated and sent to your bank for deposit within 24 hours. As an added value to its service, NetChex automatically notifies you as soon as the electronic check has been received. NetChex does not actually hold on to any money due to the merchant. Therefore there are no chargebacks, reserves or volume requirements. For all its good points, NetChex is very much a US initiative in its early days with only a few merchants signed up. The rest of the world is still waiting.

Another aspect of the Internet exposes an additional shortcoming of putting a cheque in the post or using a device such as NetChex: what if the information you want to buy isn't worth dollars but just cents? So-called micro-transactions are thought to add up to big business on the Net of the future. They will only ever emerge if the right kind of payment mechanism can be developed.

But delay is the biggest enemy to Net commerce today. To cut out a large piece of the delay, Net shoppers turned to their flexible friends, credit, charge and debit cards. If you want to use a commercial service or buy a piece of information, you simply send your credit card details to the service provider involved. Their credit card acquirer handles this payment like any other mail or telephone order.

While dealing with the desire for immediacy, there are some risks to this practice. When credit card details are transmitted over the Internet, the sender doesn't know exactly how these details will reach the receiver. The email or Web form can pass through multiple systems on its way to the vendor and there is a chance that someone, somewhere along the way, could be using an illicit network sniffer to intercept strings of digits just like the ones used for credit cards.

That risk could be easily dealt with by encryption. Using encrypted credit card details requires standards. Both the buyer and the seller would have to use a standard package. Unfortunately, that standard is not yet set. And the cost of the

http://www.visa.com/
http://www.mastercard.com/

transaction would still be prohibitive if the subject of the exchange was a database entry worth a few cents.

Our Flexible Friends (Mastercard And VISA)

Even with safely encrypted credit card numbers, other problems linger. When the buyer and seller aren't physically present for the transaction, it is often useful to use a commercial intermediary like a credit card company to ensure payment or performance. You would think that the Net and credit cards could be made for each other – except for the increased opportunity for fraud on the part of both parties.

While unencrypted credit card details sent onto the Internet are susceptible to "eavesdropping" and subsequent misuse (it is difficult to judge the actual level of this type of activity at the present time), the main risk of buying something over the Net lies in the unsatisfactory legal relationship between buyer and seller if you use a credit card when you are not physically present for the transaction.

Any time you give the details of your credit or charge card you are in the lap of the gods, whether it is over the phone or over the Internet! Because neither Mastercard nor VISA, the two biggest credit card companies, discriminates between Internet-borne sales transactions and more conventional phone orders or mail orders, it is vital to know what their position is.

The precise details are liable to vary according to the legal jurisdiction (or jurisdictions) in which the transaction falls, or which credit card acquirer is used, but certain generalizations are possible. The laws of each jurisdiction may provide certain protections for credit card users. Any time you give your card number and details to a merchant and you are not physically present, you are liable for whatever charges the merchant puts through on your account. It doesn't matter where the source of error arises. You have to pay the bill. Fortunately most merchants can be trusted and hardly any transactions become a source of difficulty.

Spokespersons for both Mastercard and VISA expressed a belief that the vast majority of the problems reported are simple, honest mistakes and most of the remaining balance are merely misunderstandings on one part or another. The honest mistakes and misunderstandings are usually solvable with a single telephone call or letter. Only a very tiny minority of disputes, the card companies assure us, are caused by fraudulent use of the card by the cardholder or the vendor.

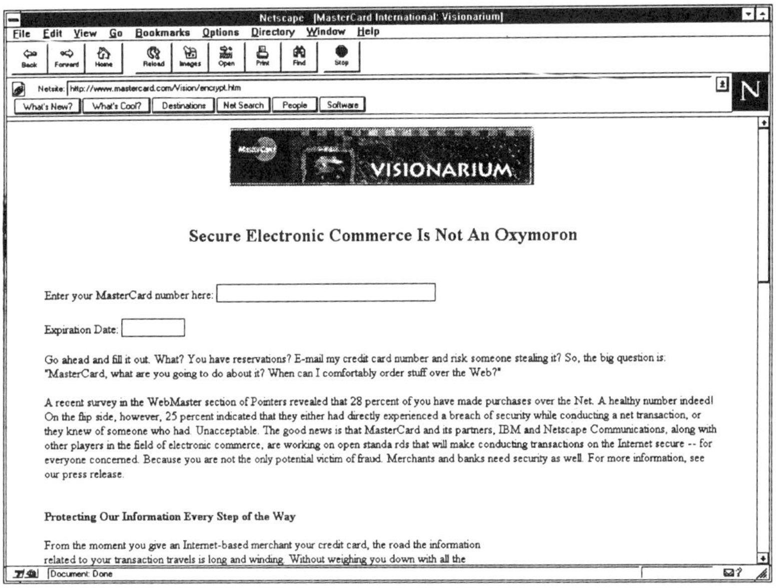

Figure 6

It is convenient to quote your card in email but convenience can have an unexpectedly dear price. Unless some other local law applies (The Sale of Goods Act) or some bonding organization (like ATOL or ABTA for holiday bookings in the UK), you are left with some rather informal procedures on the part of the card companies or recourse to court to get your money back.

If you have a beef, the card companies say that they will take the matter up on your behalf. This is not the same as unquestioningly crediting your account with the amount in controversy. They will expect a letter from you outlining the problem which they will then forward to the merchant involved. They can recommend solutions and encourage settlement but in the end it's up to the merchant to initiate any refund or credit.

The phrase "take the matter up on your behalf" is less than completely reassuring. While the card companies can sanction repeat offenders by removing their ability to take charges, that "remedy" won't do you, or any other bilked buyers, any good for past transgressions. The reassurances from premium card companies like Diners Club are somewhat more mollifying but in the end, it may come down to a matter of proof and persistence.

Since many credit card transactions now conducted over the Net are not protected by any sort of public key encryption, a printout of an email is pretty poor proof of the substance of a transaction or the identity of the correspondents. Anyone could

Figure 6
Mastercard dares you to type your credit card number into the Internet! This is a powerful demonstration of the way unfamiliarity can feed distrust. We don't hesitate to hand over our cards at restaurants do we?

http://www.mastercard.com/set/
set.htm

fabricate or edit an email message to prove almost any point, so it is impossible to say if the copy tendered as documentation for the intended transaction is a true and exact copy of the original.

Recourse to the courts is to be avoided if at all possible. It certainly won't be cheap and there will be many complex legal issues to be determined. If an Internet transaction goes badly wrong, litigation could easily span several jurisdictions. An ounce of prevention is worth a pound of cure.

While small claims courts are accessible (no lawyer required, low filing fees, and simplified procedures) to almost anyone with a claim below a modest jurisdictional amount, it can be a time-consuming process and you will be confronted by the problems of proof even in the much more relaxed evidentiary regime of the small claims courts. Also, once you have won a judgment, you still have to collect the money from the merchant. This can take even more time and trouble, especially if the merchant is located in another state or country. It could be impossible if the merchant has absconded or gone into liquidation.

If you are buying something from abroad, an unsatisfactory transaction may be even more difficult to remedy. The major cards all have international divisions that will chase problems around the globe but their help is voluntary and the sanctions that they can bring against offending merchants are limited from your perspective.

To avoid problems you should insist on a confirming fax or, better still, letter so that the details of the transaction are established concretely before you turn the merchant loose with your card details. Also a bit of circumspection as to the type of merchant you deal with will help. Few would have a problem giving their card numbers to Harrods or American Airlines or Hertz. But how much can you trust a vendor you found in the back of some PC magazine in Timbuktu? (I'm sure that there are lots of honest PC suppliers in Mali.) If in doubt, the best way to protect yourself from credit card fraud is to pay by cheque.

The above recitation is hardly a sweeping endorsement of doing business on the Internet with today's credit cards but until the law is fashioned to provide a clearer relationship between the shopper and the vendor in this type of transaction, buyers will beware and businesses will have a hard time dragging sales out of the Net. Both Mastercard and VISA state that until a safe way to use credit cards on the Net is devised, cardholders should refrain from using their plastic on the Net.

On the side of the seller, caution is appropriate, also.

Becoming involved in a fraudulent transaction as an innocent vendor is no way to make money. If you plan to take credit cards over the Net as payment, you may want to exceed the minimum identification requirements specified by your card acquirer. A telephone confirmation or email could save wasting time or losing your merchandise.

*http://home.netscape.com/info/
security-doc.html*

Netscape To The Rescue

One important measure of comfort supplied in the past year or so is Netscape's browser secure communications facility. Netscape's business model is to give away its Navigator Web browser but it hopes to sell expensive secure software for the other end of Net transactions – consequently there are lots of Netscape browsers out there giving shoppers the thumbs up for Net Commerce. Netscape's Netsite server line includes the Netsite Communications Server and the Netsite Commerce Server. The two products incorporate Netscape's Secure Sockets Layer (SSL), based on public key encryption technology from RSA Data Security.

Netscape's was the first secure server software available for Internet use and they have published the specification, in true open systems style, so that other software client developers can use their method on the client side for mercantile transactions. They have submitted it to the IETF to enshrine it as a Net standard.

Using the Netscape Navigator SSL-enfolded forms submission, your credit card numbers are safe. However, you must still be willing to trust the server operator with your credit card number before you enter into a financial transaction because they will be able to do whatever they want once they have access to your credit card number and your recourse is limited, just as it is on the phone. If someone breaks in and physically steals their server, they'll have your number, too.

Since Netscape's browser has dominated the market, all other competing browsers have to support the SSL security protocol until the market changes. However, the specification for the underlying security protocol has been placed in the public domain and anyone can look at the specification and write their own applications.

As new forms of Net money are accepted, the problems related to today's credit card sales will abate. Hopefully, they will not be replaced with new ones.

Microsoft, Mastercard, VISA And Secure Electronic Transaction Technology

No global transaction software need could go unaddressed by everyone's favorite software and credit card companies, Microsoft, Mastercard and VISA (MMV). Soon any Windows user will be able to make secure credit card purchases over the Internet using security software developed jointly by the three.

Because of the anonymous nature of the Internet, MMV struggled to develop procedures to substitute existing methods used in face-to-face or mail order and telephone order transactions. They addressed the issues of authentication of the cardholder by the merchant as well as the need for the cardholder to authenticate that the merchant can accept Secure Electronic Technology (SET) transactions and is authorized to accept bank card payments. Both parties must be happy.

SET uses public key and secret key cryptography to provide confidentiality of information, ensure payment integrity and authenticate both merchant and cardholder. The specifications were crafted to enable greater bank card acceptance, with a level of security that will encourage buyers and businesses to make wide use of cards on the Internet because the card companies only make money when someone uses the cards.

The parties realized that the SET specifications had to respect and preserve the relationship between merchants and acquirers, and between cardholders and issuers, and had to address all electronic bank card payments sent over private or public networks otherwise there would be delays and the startup costs would swamp the immediate benefits. The task was further complicated by the need to make the specifications work on a variety of hardware and software platforms. And, needless to say, it had to be easy to use and cheap as well for both buyers and sellers!

The task was a daunting one and was further bedevilled by the difficulty of two competitors working closely with a very headstrong software leader. Obviously some things fell outside the perimeter of SET. MMV's SET specification does not cover message protocols for offers, shopping baskets, or order status inquiries. The three decided not to touch the operational issues such as the criteria set by individual financial institutions for the issuance of cardholder and merchant credentials.

Because SET is a standard that hopefully many software companies will base their own creative products on, the standard didn't include screen formats or content, presentation, or layout of order entry forms. To make it as general as possible, transaction transport mechanisms such as HTTP, electronic mail, file transfer, or point-to-point connections weren't specified.

SET will make big changes to card clearing and settlement, lowering the cost of doing business and perhaps lowering the charges levied for using the system in the future. The process where a merchant receives payment for a transaction using a bank card is often a two-step process: the merchant authorizes the transaction and later requests payment. The process of requesting payment is known as clearing and the process of moving the funds from the cardholder's financial institution to the merchant's financial institution is known as settlement.

As you might imagine, clearing and settlement are critical components of the present bank card payment systems. Both SET specifically and electronic commerce in general will have an impact on this process. The relationship between the merchant and the acquirer as well as the rules of the bank card association define the clearing and settlement processes and policies. To avoid disturbing the relationship between the merchant and acquirer and to encourage the widest acceptance of these specifications, no new clearing and settlement process was included in the first version of SET specifications. SET transactions will be cleared through existing processes, giving a fast start to Net commerce. As SET usage broadens and electronic commerce volume grows, the marketplace will determine the need for specifications supporting network-based clearing processes.

SET changes the way that participants in the payment system interact. In a face-to-face retail transaction or a mail order transaction, the electronic processing of the transaction begins with the merchant or the acquirer. However, in an SET transaction, the electronic processing of the transaction begins with the cardholder sitting at a PC or terminal.

Dual Signature

SET introduces a new application of digital signatures, namely the concept of dual signatures. To understand how this works to the benefit of both the buyer and the seller, consider the following transaction: Al wants to send Barbara an offer to purchase a piece of office equipment and an authorization to his bank to transfer the money if Barbara accepts the offer, but Al doesn't want the bank to see the terms of the offer nor does he want Barbara to see his account information. Further, Al wants to link the offer to the transfer so that the money is only transferred if Barbara accepts his offer. He accomplishes all of this by digitally signing both messages with a single signature operation that creates a dual signature.

If Barbara accepts Al's offer, she can send a message to the bank indicating her acceptance and including the message digest of the offer. The bank can verify the authenticity of Al's transfer authorization by checking its digest from the dual signature and ensure that the acceptance is for the same offer by comparing the message digest presented by Barbara to the one in the dual signature. The bank can also check the authenticity of the offer against the dual signature, but the bank cannot see the terms of the offer.

Within SET, dual signatures are used to link an order message sent to the merchant with the payment instructions containing account information sent to the acquirer. When the merchant sends an authorization request to the acquirer, it includes the payment instructions sent to it by the cardholder and the transaction identifier from the order message. The acquirer compares the transaction identifier from the merchant with the one in the payment instructions to link them to the order message to confirm the linkage of the order and payment instructions.

It sounds complex but most of the hard work will be done by software inside the computers of the buyer, seller and credit card acquirer. The hard part will be selling the concept to businesses and Internet buyers – convincing everyone that it is really safe and easy!

Registered Net Shoppers And Merchants

According to VISA, before the first purchase can be made, cardholders must register their VISA card directly online with their bank. This easy step is similar to the current process of calling your bank to activate a new VISA card when you get it in the mail. It takes only minutes. Cardholders have to fill out a registration form on the PC screen with basic information – name, account number, expiration date, billing address, and whatever else the bank requires for purposes of identification.

Once transmitted, this information is encrypted and securely sent to the computers of the VISA card issuer. In doing so the bank checks to make sure the account is authentic. Then it issues an electronic certificate by putting its digital signature on the cardholder's public key. This certificate proves the card is valid. The cardholder stores the certificate on his or her PC for future use.

SET PROCESSING FLOW

CARDHOLDER REGISTRATION
Credential Authority Sends Credential
Cardholder Receives CA Credential
Cardholder Requests Credentials
Credential Authority Creates Cardholder
Credentials
Cardholder Receives Credentials

MERCHANT REGISTRATION
Credential Authority Sends Credential
Merchant Receives CA Credential
Merchant Sends Credential Request
Credential Authority Creates Merchant
Credentials
Merchant Receives Credentials

CARDHOLDER ORDER
Merchant Sends Credentials
Cardholder Receives Credentials and Shops
Cardholder Sends Order
Merchant Processes Order Message
Cardholder Receives Order Acknowledgment
↓
PAYMENT AUTHORIZATION
Merchant Requests Authorization
Payment Server Processes Authorization
Request
Merchant Receives Authorization Response

Merchants will have to register, too. To participate in secure Net shopping vendors will fill out basic information on their PC screen, including their merchant IDs. The card acquirer then gives a certificate to the merchant.

A Walk Through

Only after you have registered and received your VISA certificate online can you begin shopping. Before deciding to purchase anything from a particular cybershop, the merchant

While there is a lot happening behind the scenes, SET has been designed to be simple to use by the customer and safe for all parties.

needs to provide the customer with its VISA certificate. The merchant can do this in variety of ways, such as sending a copy to the cardholder by electronic mail, for instance, or by publishing a copy on the Web so that anyone can easily see that they are an authorized trader.

If the merchant has VISA's approval, the cardholder can send an order electronically to the merchant and the merchant requests authorization for the amount of the purchase from the acquirer. Once the approval is completed, the order is processed and confirmed with the cardholder. Your software (or whatever) can be on its way!

As the source of the world's most popular client software, Microsoft is in a good position to drive this financial development. With over half a billion cardholders on the planet, Mastercard and VISA are in a pretty good spot, too, for laying down a transaction standard. Nonetheless, it will take time for a large portion of the Net to get comfortable with the concepts and technology.

SET will interface with VISA's VisaNet payment system to authenticate buyers and sellers and to ensure transaction security in the same fashion as an OLE application, allowing it to work in conjunction with other OLE-compliant applications like spreadsheets, personal finance packages or email. Mastercard have their own plans for implementation.

Microsoft, Mastercard and VISA are doing their best to remove transactional hurdles. If everyone does their job right, users will be able to make secure payments from within desktop computer applications by doing nothing more complicated than clicking an appropriate icon and then typing in their credit card number.

Some transaction hurdles cannot be crossed by widespread use of standard technologies alone. The Internet presents shoppers and resellers with new opportunities and new problems. Selling information or software on the Net could be big business for information providers but regular credit card charges are too dear for a deluge of anticipated micro-transactions.

Imagine if you wanted access to a collection of consumer magazine dishwasher evaluations. That information could be worth perhaps 20 cents per article. If thousands of shoppers "bought" there could be a good return for the author or publisher but even if a credit card transaction costs pennies, that might make micro-information too dear for widespread sales.

A Chink In The Plastic Armor

However carefully your credit card details are encrypted and however sure you are that the merchant you are dealing with is authorized and trustworthy, there is a potential problem with ever typing your credit card number in at your PC keyboard: the keyboard logger trojan horse.

It isn't just a bug in a single program, and it is therefore not something that can be patched or overcome with an upgrade. The organization that stumbled upon this security loophole has demonstrated that it has the potential to undermine any programs that ask for a credit card number to be typed into a computer. This sort of attack has been demonstrated to defeat the tight RSA encryption security used by Netscape and CyberCash. In reality, those encryption methods weren't cracked at all but the commercially sensitive information was stolen before it was ever sent via the secured messages to the secured server.

Since the computer from which the data is stolen is presumed to be connected to the Internet, at least intermittently, the Internet also provides a safe avenue to convey the purloined numbers into the hands of the thief the next time the computer is plugged into the Net.

There are a number of potential counter-measures that could be employed (and undoubtedly counter-counter-measures to defeat them). For instance, you could interpose a letter or word between the four number groups in the card number or enter the credit card details in a vertical column interspersed with other order information. Of course, if the credit card number or bank details were carried on a smart card (see below), they would never have to be typed in at all.

This type of loophole has been used to compromise passwords in the past and could be used in the future to compromise credit card numbers or bank account details typed in. First Virtual Holdings, the publicizers of this flaw in many Net commerce products, is a company whose Net transaction service does not require a user ever to type in his or her card number and all transactions are confirmed by email. It is impossible to say if this hack has ever actually been exploited to anyone's detriment or if this alert is anything more than an attempt to build business by rubbishing the competition.

http://www.fv.com/

Third-Party Payments

One solution for Internet payments is the introduction of a third-party consolidator: a company that collects and approves payments from one client to another. After a certain period of time, one credit card transaction for the total accumulated amount is completed. This could cut transaction costs for micro-purchases.

This method has several positive attributes. The transaction has all of the convenience of a credit card and the security of an encrypted channel. However, the risk still exists that payment from the card company is ultimately refused because the spending limit has been reached or the card has been withdrawn.

For civil libertarians, the prospect of a person's payment details gathered in one centralized system is frightening. Anyone with access to the system could tell where they buy, when they buy and what they buy. The collation of this data could damage an individual's right to privacy.

First Virtual Holdings

First Virtual Holdings has brought together EDS (Electronic Data Systems – a division of General Motors) and First USA Merchant Services, a rapidly growing USA credit card company, and has created a fast, efficient way to buy information online. Unlike other Internet payment systems, FVH is focusing only on buying information available online; but sellers of offline goods or services have adapted FVH's capabilities to their own businesses.

Spending money has never been easier! You don't have to buy any new hardware or software or use any encryption at all. It works from anywhere – whether you are spending pounds, drachma or dollars. It does, however, require some preparation, an email account and a VISA or Mastercard.

First, to become a buyer you have to register and provide a credit card number (offline). When Internet shoppers find an article or a piece of software they wish to purchase, they request the item quoting their FVH account number. The buyer gets to download the material as soon as FVH verifies the account number for the vendor. FVH then sends an email message to the buyer, who responds in one of three ways: yes, no or fraud. FVH will not debit the buyer's account until it has had confirmation. Abuse by buyers who repeatedly receive information and decline to pay will result in account closure.

To become an FVH seller, you must have a bank account that accepts direct deposit (via the US Automated Clearing House system), complete an application and send FVH a check for the $10.00 registration fee. When you accept an FVH payment the buyer sends a VirtualPIN, which you may easily verify as valid. You then send a message to First Virtual containing the buyer's VirtualPIN and the amount of the sale. First Virtual then confirms the transaction with the buyer and notifies the seller by email. The amount of the sale (minus First Virtual's fees) is later deposited directly into the seller's bank account.

http://www.cybercash.com

While a positive step, FVH's transactions may not be micro enough. Sellers pay a fee of US$0.29 plus 2% for each transaction. They also pay a US$1 processing fee when payments are made to their account. This is fine for an armload of software or a book but nowhere near small enough for the snowstorm of penny transactions that may revolutionize the information economy.

FVH is pushing the boat out with some "virtual" shop space called the First Virtual Infohaus, effectively renting retail space on their system's hard disks. They have a mere handful of merchants up and running (among them a bookshop) but now that they have fulfilled their technical foundations, they are eagerly seeking additional merchants.

FVH's merchants are glad to have the ability to accept payment that their customers can put on their plastic cards. Many of FVH's shops are too small or too new or too insecure to qualify for credit card status on their own. However, FVH holds the funds from a sale for 90 days to decrease their risk of exposure in the case of a chargeback or refund. This can put a strain on the cash flow of small, new and insecure companies.

FVH's system is also very US centric – and the Internet is very international. The buyer's credit card must be able to accept payment in US dollars – almost all do but there are exceptions. For merchants, although opening a bank account in the US is not an insurmountable obstacle for non-resident individuals or companies, it does add a layer of complication to your Net commerce.

CyberCash

Yet another brand of the Internet lucre, the CyberCash payment system, simply seeks to leverage current credit card systems by adding security. CyberCash involves users running a free program on their computer that encrypts their ordinary credit card number so that it will be safe from Net fraudsters. This adds

http://www.digicash.com/

a sense of security to the convenience of using a payment system that is already familiar.

CyberCash transactions move between three separate software programs: one program that resides on the buyer's PC (called a wallet), one that operates as part of the merchant server, and a third part that operates within the CyberCash servers. The merchant and consumer software is free. High-level encryption protects the messages that pass between them.

When a shopper selects items for purchase, he or she fills out the merchant's order form complete with shipping information. The merchant server presents an invoice to the consumer and requests payment. The consumer is given the option to launch the CyberCash Wallet if he or she already has it, or go and get it if not. Depending on which option the consumer picks, he or she is ready in a matter of seconds, or a few minutes, to pay.

When the consumer clicks on the "PAY" button, the CyberCash software on the merchant server sends a special message to the buyer's PC which awakens the CyberCash Wallet. The buyer simply chooses which card to pay with and clicks on it. The rest is a series of encrypted automatic messages that travel between the three parties on the Internet and the conventional credit card networks which are connected directly to the CyberCash servers.

However, CyberCash is still courting merchants, is still much too expensive for micro-transactions and lacks the anonymity of real cash money.

Reinventing Money

DigiCash

Anonymity, an often appreciated attribute of foldable money, is the strong suit of DigiCash, another electronic money hopeful. After a lengthy period of trials, Ecash, DigiCash's "product", has been accepted as a medium for exchange for real money by the Mark Twain Bank in the US, Deutche Bank in Germany and Mertia Bank in Finland. In fact, the bank has reduced its charges to reflect the high volume of transactions that they are handling.

Ecash provides more than impulse purchasing power. Like real paper money, it is anonymous, allaying the fears of users who don't want their transactions monitored by electronic marketing junk email programs or Big Brother. Ecash also offers the same security as cash for both the buyer and seller – it's in your hands when you do the deal.

The software for both paying and receiving payment is free of charge for PCs, Macintoshes and UNIX workstations but the card companies or banks will still take their cut. Charges are levied whenever you move money into or out of the Ecash system. There are no charges when you spend or receive Ecash. You can withdraw digital money from your Internet bank account and store it on your hard disk. Whenever you want to make a payment, you use these bills and coins. The payment is fast and anonymous, and the payer can always prove that he or she made a certain payment – you get an automatic receipt in case of trouble.

Ecash provides more security than even credit cards. Every transaction is for a specific amount of money and good only once – you don't have to worry about being ripped off, now or a couple of months down the line, by an unscrupulous merchant. Ecash provides the highest security possible by applying public key digital signature techniques. Additional security features of Ecash include the protection of Ecash withdrawals from your account with a password that is known only to you; your password is not even known to your bank.

At the moment, the Mark Twain Bank in the US is the only bank offering Ecash so the problem of establishing a US bank account still exists for off-shore buyers and merchants. While the schedule of charges is modest, using Ecash at the moment is far from being a universal cash-value system of monetary exchange. DigiCash has a growing number of merchants that will accept Ecash but it is still in its formative phase.

http://www.mondex.com/mondex/

VISA Cash And Mondex

The lure of cash is strong for ease of use and anonymity. Several other plans to create electronic money are under way. These include a bit of hardware: the much delayed smart card. A smart card is a plastic card the same size, shape and weight as a credit card but it has a chip embedded in its surface. Depending on the use of the card there can be different amounts of memory and even a small processor to provide very strong encryption. The cards are meant to act like a wallet or change purse. You fill it up with money and spend it like, well, money. When it's empty you can fill it again or discard it for a new one.

One example of the use of smart card financial services is VISA Cash. VISA sees typical transactions as the same sort that you now use your pocket money for: pay phone calls, bridge or road tolls, parking fees, or even vending machine goods and services. VISA Cash was specially developed for small purchases

check the

WebExtra

such as a cup of coffee, bus fare, or newspapers which means that the cost of using it will be low. VISA Cash made its first appearance at the 1996 Summer Olympic Games in Atlanta.

Stored value cards have the advantages of cash, the convenience of a card. No more holes in your pockets or not having the correct change for a machine. And just like real money, you can lose it and put it through the wash! Unlike ATM cards, you won't have to remember a PIN.

Mondex, a consortium led by two British banks and British Telecom, has rolled out its smart card-based digital cash system to an estimated 40 000 cardholders in Swindon, England. It is the hope of the sponsors that the system will spread around the world with special phones and electronic wallets used to conduct cash-like, tamper-proof transactions. In addition to pilot trials in Ohio and Minnesota, Mondex has also had some success in Hong Kong.

The smart card route to success is dependent on not just the cards themselves but a proliferation of devices to take the card for payment and refill empty ones. There are lots of machines in the world that can accept magnetic stripe cards but the population of smart card reading machines is still low. For Internet users to use smart card technology, they will need a peripheral device and a bit of software that can recognize the card and put the necessary details through the Net. One company working on this is GIS in Cambridge, England who have been flogging their SmartMouse for some time. Plans are afoot to put smart card readers inside modems, too.

The Business Bottom Line

Businesses and buyers both need secure and simple methods of payment over the Internet with transaction charges in line with the value of the infogoods or services being bought and sold. A variety of companies are vying to provide the necessary technology. You can use conventional credit cards now with no more risk than you have with a telephone order. There are a number of ways to keep card numbers and other sensitive financial information out of the hands of eavesdroppers. Cash is on its way to being introduced to the Net from a couple of different directions. However, no technology has emerged to handle micro-transactions. No clear leader has emerged and it may be the case that several types of Internet payment will be available to suit the different types of transactions possible in the future.

4 Enhancing Business Communication

Electronic mail is often the first experience that users have with the communications capabilities in networks. Practices and policies laid down for intracompany communications, as well as the software and hardware that deliver the services, need tweaking when gateways are opened to the Internet.

The Business Issue

Effective email is a key business tool. Not only does the right email client and server software need to be correctly installed and configured, but it must be used in a way that facilitates communication. The savings in time and money that are attributed to email depend more on the implementation than the technology.

The Email Edge

Today's business has at its command a wide range of communications channels: telephones, fax machines, courier services, telex (still!), the postal service and electronic mail. Each has definite characteristics in terms of speed and cost and suitability for a particular use. Email, the last to arrive on the business scene, combines elements of earlier communications technologies but has some unique attributes.

Email is not quite as immediate as the telephone – as long as you can reach the intended party and don't get their voice mail! Email may take from minutes to hours to reach the desk of the person you are aiming for, depending on the number of gateways that the mail has to traverse. Of course you have to factor in the time it takes the recipient to read it.

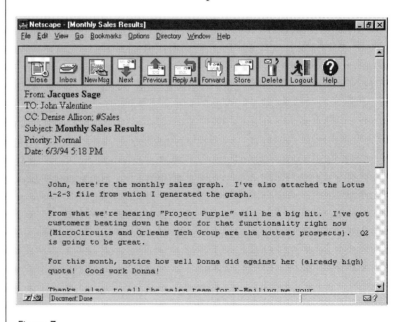

Figure 7

Figure 7
cc:Mail makes it easy to catch up with your mail. While you are reading, all the tools necessary for handling that piece of mail are ready to hand.

While email's lack of immediacy can be interpreted as a deficiency it can actually be used in a positive fashion for asynchronous conversations across time zones. Every time you pick up the telephone it costs money – email is free once you have connected to the Internet. If a person in Europe sends an email to the west coast of the US at the end of the European business day, the reply can be waiting for them when they arrive at work the next morning. From the viewpoint of the European, there has been no time wasted in resolving the matter covered by the email correspondence.

However, as a static medium, ordinary email lacks the emotional impact and rapid statement–response exchanges of a person-to-person conversation. Because the words can lie rather cold on the screen, humor and irony and all the other shades of meaning that are removed with the chance to listen to the cadence, tone and inflection of human speech are being put back in email with emoticons or smileys. Email is catching up with voice communication!

You could use a fax and get the same fast results as an email, too, but the cost of a transatlantic fax is many, many times more than the cost of the same document emailed. Fax documents cost more the longer they are, if there are bad connections that lower their transmission speed and if they have to go a long way. Emails all cost the same: nil.

While it takes minutes or hours to arrive, email is still lots faster than regular mail which can take days to get from one city to another (or even from one side of the road to another!). Courier services are often faster and provide tracking and receipt services but cost far more than an email message. Don't forget, the marginal cost of a single email message is zero.

Email can also be faster to frame than a normal letter, memo or fax. Complex word processors have impeded communication because they allow (and maybe compel) writers to mess about with formats and fonts to put a formal face on the missive. Email cuts through this with its informality. Indeed, when replying to an email, the facility to quote the message you are replying to is built into most email packages.

Of course, if you require formality, a binary word processing file can be attached to an email so that the proposal document or presentation can arrive complete with multiple fonts, colors and diagrams or photographs. To do this you will have to encode the binary document as ASCII text. UUencoding and MIME are two schemes that do this. Many email packages do this automatically when a menu command is given to attach a file.

Because unenhanced email is insecure (it moves through an unknown number of hands between sender and destination and

"Email becomes addictive – which is good from the point of view of harnessing its speed and economy. On the other hand, you have to continually remember that it must be embedded in all your business continuity plans."

can be easily forged) it doesn't have the same legal impact as the original signed copy of a letter. Digital signatures, a Lotus mail feature and available elsewhere, can make email more forgery-resistant than physical correspondence, on the other hand.

Most email is insecure and users take this into account. It is more like a private conversation in a public space than a private exchange of letters. You can be overheard but probably won't be. Depending on the subject matter under discussion you would take appropriate measures to provide confidentiality.

Email is quite useful for person-to-person communication but it can also be used in one-to-many exchanges and can even be the medium for group conversations. It is a simple matter to add additional recipients to an emailed message. And through a device called a listserv, it is possible to make sure that all members of a group receive all copies of correspondence – a many-to-many exchange.

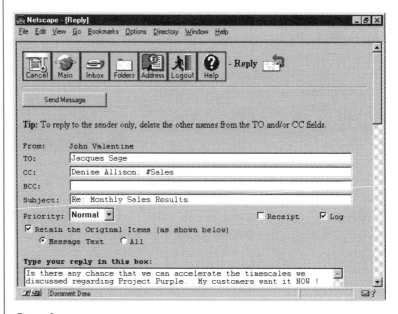

Figure 8

Getting The Most Out Of Email

Here is a compendium of suggestions that will deliver email's promises of faster communication and reduced communications cost and improve the efficiency of your organization. The list is not meant to be exhaustive but is meant to address the most common ways in which email is underused or misused.

Figure 8

The number one faux pas of email is failing to address all points of a message. cc:Mail provides easy to use response tools.

Learn

Before you start using your company's email package, go back to school. Unless you know the capabilities of your software, it is hard to extract all of its value. With a complex constellation of features, cc:Mail deserves a period of familiarization. Whether this includes a training session, a review of company email policies or just some time spent exploring the manual or on-screen Help files, learn sooner rather than later. If you have done this and still have problems you will at least have avoided getting RTFMed by support desk staff or the Lotus help line.

If your business has an email user list, make sure that you are on it. Get your email address on your business cards and stationery – you want the world to be able to find you. While great strides have been taken toward finding information on the Internet, it's still difficult to find people.

Economize

Email is meant to be an efficient means of communications – that means short email messages are often the ones with highest value density. Once you have had the horror of returning from vacation to find hundreds of emails waiting for your attention, you will appreciate the value of succinct email messages.

You can cut down on the volume of your email by carefully editing your signature file to include just the details that are needed. Often signatures are taken as an opportunity to stamp individuality on your messages. There is a limit, however. An extra line or two in every email by every person in a company dozens of times a day could add up to reduced performance, the need for another email server and additional administrative expense.

One kind of unnecessary email that we could all do without is the mis-addressed message. If email goes to the wrong person, not only does it not take the message to the right person but it requires that the erroneous recipient waste his or her time. Often he or she will bounce it back (or it will be bounced back automatically by the system) and you will waste your time dealing with it, too. Use the address book feature of your mail package to cut down on mistyped addresses.

Email should be addressed to the person that needs the information or is required to take some action. Copying your boss, your boss's boss, their secretaries and aunts, uncles and cousins is a good way to dilute the effectiveness of email. By the time five or six disinterested people have read your message, any

" In case you think that cutting one line off an email signature won't make a difference, multiply that line with the thousands of messages you send each year and again by the number of users on the Internet. Fat signature files burn Internet bandwidth."

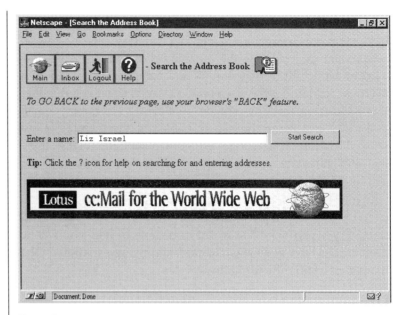

Figure 9

efficiency boost from sending a communication by email has been well and truly dissipated.

Emailed replies should also be a model of efficiency. This means when you are responding to parts of a message that you have quoted, keep the quotes to a minimum. It is a complete and utter waste of email bandwidth to quote a dozen lines of message and add "I think so too."

Use It Appropriately

Email is probably not the best vehicle for negotiation, advocacy or persuasion. Even with emoticons, email is a fairly black-and-white environment. Use email to establish the need for a conference or a conference call or to set the agenda for a meeting. It is not the place for conducting that type of business.

Be sure to read your message before you send it. Most email recipients realize that minor spelling and punctuation slip-ups are all part and parcel of fast email exchanges. However, misspellings can alter meanings. If you are asking for a response, make your questions stand out in the body of the message.

Not everyone will be using the same email reader that you are. Watch your line lengths and keep them between 40 and 60 characters. Beware special symbols that can be turned into garbage by certain mail packages. UKP is understood by all to mean UK Pounds Sterling but £ may come through the mail as gobbledegook.

Figure 9

With the rapidly expanding number of email contacts, a good address database is vital. It needs to be fast to search and easy to use, too.

There is a code of manners about the Internet called Netiquette and typing the term into a Web search engine will get you dozens of different versions of it. It all boils down to the Golden Rule: Do unto others as you would have them do unto you.

Never flame in business correspondence. Never reply to a flaming message. Report abuse to your system administrator.

Leverage The Speed

If email is the most efficient way for you to communicate, express that preference to others. It will avoid piles of post, faxes and voice mail messages. Give email your priority. If you can arrange for your mail to announce itself when it arrives on your desktop, do so. If you have to pick up your mail from the server, do so regularly. The advantages of email dwindle if it is forgotten for days.

Automate

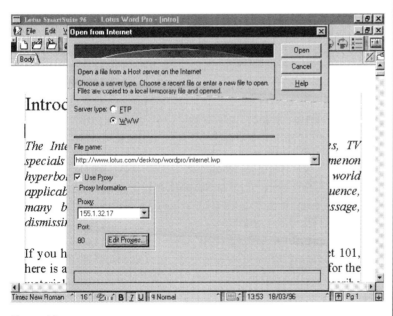

Figure 10

The Role Of cc:Mail

You can't outgrow cc:Mail. How big will your company be in five years? cc:Mail electronic mail contains unique, scalable architecture, which means cc:Mail is a shrewd, and safe, investment. cc:Mail is as big as you are now, and as big as you plan to be. Current cc:Mail customer systems range from five users on a

Figure 10

Document creation used to end in printed copy. Now, however, documents are sent by electronic mail or published at a Web site. Word Pro has integral Internet communication capabilities.

"cc:Mail made it easy for us to extend our internal email system out to the Internet. Because we had invested in email internally, it wasn't hard to move onto the Internet."

single LAN to over 75 000 users on a global wide area network. So you can easily meet the changing messaging needs of a growing company, without overloading the administrator or your resources.

cc:Mail gives administrators the powerful tools they need. To be a viable solution, an email system must: (1) be easy to use to minimize training, (2) feature centralized or delegated administration, (3) provide robust directory synchronization and (4) graphical tools for central monitoring and performance tuning. Proven cc:Mail meets all these criteria now. cc:Mail is the first to give you the big picture. In minutes, an administrator can use the Lotus cc:Mail View for Windows add-on to monitor and manage a worldwide mail system. From a single point administrators can set performance thresholds, receive up-to-the-minute system status reports, and avert problems before they affect users. You can even use this robust tool to chart performance trends and plan for future cc:Mail system growth.

With cc:Mail mobile options, your mail goes where you go. With cc:Mail, users are free to share ideas and information beyond the physical boundaries of a LAN. They can go where the opportunities are, and have up-to-date, 24-hour access to the information they need to do their jobs. The business potential is enormous. Create reliable, immediate links to field operations or branch offices. Empower executives on the move. And communicate efficiently with vendors and consultants. In fact, cc:Mail was the first to offer powerful, time-saving features that allow users to work offline while they're at a hotel, at home or at a customer site. Connect over ordinary phone lines, wireless modems, LAN and wide area network connections. You can even send urgent messages to anyone carrying a pager with the optional cc:Mail Pager Gateway.

Gain worldwide access with optional cc:Mail gateways. Fax without waiting, directly from cc:Mail. Connect to the world's information Autobahn, the Internet. And unify departments on diverse mail systems. With the cc:Mail optional gateways and a rich array of third-party products, you can enhance and extend the reach of your cc:Mail system. Enjoy managed migration to cc:Mail as you phase out an older, less flexible mail system. Or link to subsidiaries or business partners who use different mail systems without sacrificing the quality of communication.

Tight integration means everything works together. cc:Mail works smoothly with virtually every leading software application your organization may be using, which means that cc:Mail can serve as a vehicle to help you plan meetings, route expense

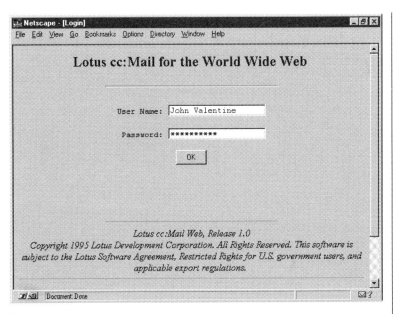

Figure 11

reports, exchange spreadsheet versions, pass on documents, review presentations and more, all without lifting the phone or leaving your desk. For example, cc:Mail works together with Lotus SmartSuite and other Lotus products to help you maximize productivity on every level. cc:Mail integrates with Lotus Organizer to provide group scheduling capabilities, along with personal information management tools. Combine cc:Mail with Lotus Forms, and you've got everything an organization needs to design, route and track electronic forms to automate workflow.

Lotus cc:Mail has won more awards than any other LAN-based email system. While other vendors are playing catch-up, Lotus can provide these proven business solutions now. All cc:Mail products are designed to work seamlessly with the technology you've already deployed.

- cc:Mail LAN System – designed for the enterprise. If you have a large number of users or require communication with off-site divisions, suppliers or customers, this option is for you The cc:Mail LAN System gives you the tools to create a robust cc:Mail system with users on any combination of Windows, DOS, OS/2, Macintosh or UNIX platforms. Requires cc:Mail Router. Available in 10-User and 50-User License Packs.
- cc:Mail Mobile System – for remote sites and traveling professionals. Add mobility to your cc:Mail LAN

Figure 11
Use the simple cc:Mail sign-on for increased security.

System. cc:Mail Mobile System software allows users to send and receive mail messages from remote locations over standard telephone lines, wireless connections and more. cc:Mail currently offers mobile messaging for users on Windows, DOS, Macintosh and HP 200LX Palmtop. Available in 10-User and 50-User License Packs.

- cc:Mail Workgroup System – an ideal entry-level solution. Start here if you're a small company or work-group located at a single site. This cost-effective solution provides for one post office (mail server) and no mobile users. When you need to add more post offices or mobile users, you can easily trade up to the cc:Mail LAN System. Available in 10-User and 50-User License Packs.
- cc:Mail Gateways and Accessories – for open communi-cation. Extend the reach of your cc:Mail system with a rich array of gateways and accessories. It's easy to connect cc:Mail users to fax machines, the Internet, Novell MHS, MCI Mail, alphanumeric pagers and other communications vehicles.

The Lotus Communications Architecture

While cc:Mail provides full-featured email capabilities it is just one facet of a wider communications strategy for business com-munication. Lotus has created a communications architecture to accommodate the advances in technology platforms and func-tionality. Among the factors driving the evolution of messaging are the migration to client/server systems, and the repositioning of email from solely person-to-person communications to group-ware.

The past few years have also seen the separation of the client from the server via industry-standard APIs and the introduction of tiered architectures, in which the variety of messaging com-ponents fall into appropriate technology levels. Businesses, tired of difficult transitions, are demanding managed migration and coexistence. The benefits of new technology and functionality are of little value if they do not exceed the pain of transition.

It's a multi-vendor world, too, and administrators are keen to move to standards-based manageability. The drive toward client/server-based and enterprise-wide messaging increases the need for new management tools.

The Lotus Communications Architecture (LCA) has been

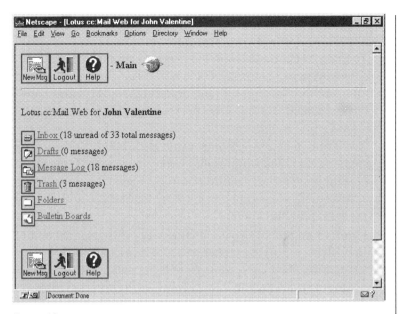

Figure 12

designed to take advantage of client/server technology, fully accommodate file-sharing technology, and provide a path for customer-controlled migration from file-sharing systems to client/server systems.

The LCA is based on the premise that the customer, rather than the technology itself, needs to control the migration from file-share messaging systems to a new open-ended architecture. Additionally, the architecture has implementation lattitude: it provides an easy entry for businesses that are new to messaging as well as those that already use Lotus cc:Mail, Lotus Notes, or both these products.

The separate and sometime antagonistic needs of end users and administrators are catered for under the LCA. With its four-tiered communications architecture, LCA is designed to integrate heterogeneous sets of products and technologies required for different types of customers, including those with the need for email messaging alone, those that have invested primarily or exclusively in Notes groupware, and those with a mix of both.

The LCA is not just vaporware or a marketing scheme. With the delivery of a major new version of cc:Mail (Version 3.0), Lotus' email package provides both a new file-sharing system and a client/server version of the cc:Mail user agent. That happened along with the debut of Notes Version 4, also a major revision, and kicked off the integration of Notes and cc:Mail with common management, directories and administration via the Lotus Notes/cc:Mail Communications Server. It made the two

Figure 12
You can check the status of your in box and out box with a glance with cc:Mail Web.

heretofore separate products mesh for businesses that have evolving communications requirements.

The new software delivers the needed standards-based management systems to monitor Lotus networks, manage alerts and alarms, and provide appropriate reporting, and provides native X.400 and SMTP Message Transport Agents (MTAs) as industry-standard email transports.

The Lotus Communications value proposition is based on customer-demanded features that reduce the cost of owning and operating world-class communications capabilities within a business enterprise and one that is easy to interface with the rest of the world via the Internet.

Lotus' component-driven architecture provides flexibility. Rather than a single, take-it-or-leave-it monolithic product, Lotus communications products will be delivered as components that can be installed and integrated in a variety of ways with third-party products to meet customer needs.

No one wants to get stuck in the proprietary system trap. Lotus customers will be able to install and manage cc:Mail networks, Notes networks and SoftSwitch networks as they have in the past but at the same time, Lotus will provide components integrate these environments to tightly and seamlessly in cases where customers require such integration.

The user is in the driving seat. Customer-controlled migration is the rule. Lotus appreciated the futility of trying to force customers to migrate from file-sharing cc:Mail to client/server-based products. Lotus will continue to invest in all of its products, so that customers can determine the course and speed of their messaging migration.

The result of the foregoing is to reduce cost of ownership. Software licenses represent only a small percentage of the actual cost of operating an enterprise-wide messaging or groupware system. The vast majority of costs lie in the management and support of the distributed environment. Lotus' efforts in reducing total cost of ownership by providing scalable and reliable infrastructure products (post offices, routers, servers, message switches) and by providing standards-based management systems to manage these networks are unparalleled.

The simple view of a business computing infrastructure as the province of a single vendor is dead. It is vital to support heterogeneous environments because reality is full of PCs, Macs, Netware servers and UNIX boxes. Lotus is trying to actually facilitate interoperability rather than just accommodate it or tolerate it. By embracing standard protocols for messaging, management, database access, object containers, and industry-standard APIs, Lotus is making its products a "best fit" for all businesses.

With the architecture in place and established as a safe and secure platform to build business communications, Lotus has committed to deliver a family of products that continue to meet and anticipate customer needs. Improving cc:Mail and Notes environments is not sufficient. They must be, and are scheduled to be, augmented with calendar and scheduling functionality, forms creation and routing tools, programmability tools and companion products.

In large-enterprise environments, a notion of a two-tiered model of client/server computing is too simple. Switched-on businesses almost always seek economies of scale and simplified management by implementing enterprise-scale hub servers in addition to local or departmental servers. Thus, client, departmental and enterprise servers define three distinct tiers that require tailored software and services.

To truly exploit investments in messaging technology, more and more businesses will want to connect their own networks with those of suppliers and customers. This inter-enterprise connectivity evolution will define a separate fourth layer. For external organizations (or remote offices) also using Notes and cc:Mail, this layer provides connectivity through AT&T Network Notes, the Internet, commercial value-added wide area

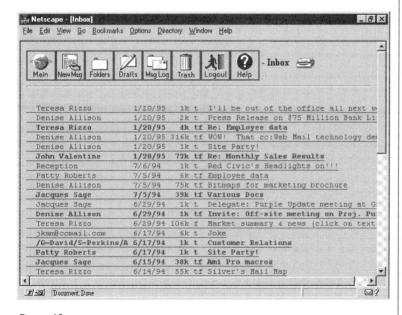

Figure 13

Figure 13

You will be "living" in your email inbox before long. Choosing a comfortable one will be important for efficiency. Being able to read your mail, where ever you are is important. Having a browser-accessible mailbox gives you independence from your office — and even from your own PC.

networks, and SMTP (Simple Message Transfer Protocol) and X.400 protocol compliance.

Operating at the highest tier is likely to be an even more diverse world than that found within a single enterprise. This layer does not assume that an organization has already implemented cc:Mail and/or Notes across an enterprise. That is, a single departmental server can take advantage of inter-enterprise services as well as an enterprise at large.

Messaging: File-Share, Client/Server And Inter-Enterprise

Lotus cc:Mail is the leading LAN-based electronic mail system, with over six million licenses sold worldwide. cc:Mail's ease of use and administration, sophisticated messaging features, and leading-edge support for mobile users have made it a popular communications product for small and large companies alike. The key to the continued success of cc:Mail is improvements in cc:Mail back-end services and tools for administrators and improvements in the cc:Mail front end for end users.

The previous file-sharing version of cc:Mail satisfied the needs of many companies. Consequently, many successful users of cc:Mail have no plans or pressing need to move their systems to a client/server architecture. This installed base has a stake in the continued investment and support of file-sharing cc:Mail. At the same time, the general adoption of client/server technology, and the need of many companies to move their email system to that architecture along with other business-critical applications, makes a client/server version of cc:Mail both necessary and desirable.

Lotus has committed to the ongoing enhancement of the file-sharing cc:Mail client and post office, and is investing in post office/router technology and the cc:Mail user agents that access the post office/router infrastructure, guarding the investment users have made in cc:Mail implementations.

At the same time, Lotus is moving ahead with client/server capabilities for cc:Mail customers in two ways. First, the new cc:Mail client interoperates with Notes servers for client/server-based messaging. Second, cc:Mail users will continue to experience the cc:Mail user interface if they decide to take advantage of an integrated client/server, messaging/groupware environment using Notes and Notes Express clients.

Many Lotus customers will operate mixed environments consisting of cc:Mail file-sharing systems and Lotus Notes servers hosting either or both Notes clients and cc:Mail clients. In these environments, Lotus has delivered complete integration for administration, operation and management of these heterogeneous systems.

Back-End Upgrade

While users are most concerned with the mail client look-and-feel and the feature set available, administrators are concerned with the back ends. Lotus has delivered a new set of back-end tools and services that significantly enhance the functionality of file-sharing cc:Mail. The back-end components will include:

- cc:Mail post office, including a new database (DB8), which is implemented separately from client user agents. The new cc:Mail post office will support 24×7 operation, eliminating the need to shut down the system to conduct system maintenance. For example, the post office reclaim operation will execute while cc:Mail clients are accessing the post office.
- cc:Mail Router 6.0, which will be modified so that it can access both the current and upgraded post offices.
- cc:Mail View, the leading wide area message monitoring tool for a file-sharing mail system, which will support both the current and upgraded post offices.

In addition, Lotus will modify existing cc:Mail clients so that they can access the DB8 back-end post office with virtually no difference in the cc:Mail user interface.

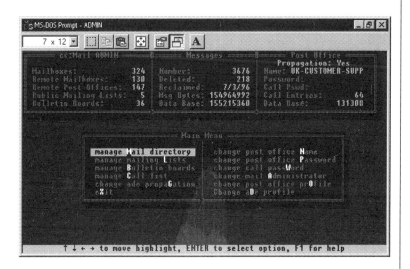

Figure 14

Figure 14

Behind the scenes, the system administrator has to contend with the vast technical workload for any mail system. cc:Mail's administration utilities make it easy. cc:Mail administration is a straight forward, menu operated program. Basic statistics are available at a glance and no rocket science is required to keep the post office running.

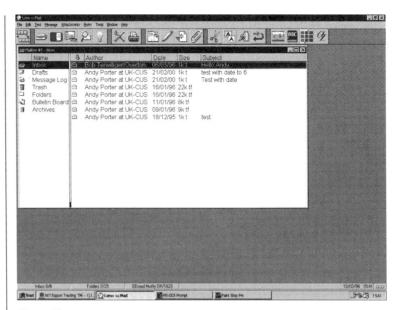

Figure 15

Front-End Upgrade

As depicted above, version 2.5 cc:Mail user agents will be able to access the improved cc:Mail post office. Lotus will deliver a new, enhanced cc:Mail user agent (version 3.0) that will take advantage of the DB8 back-end post office. The version 3.0 client initially supported Windows 95 and Windows 3.1, with other platform support following.

Lotus is committed to an open boundary between the version 3.0 user agent and the DB8 post office. The client will continue to use Vendor Independent Messaging (VIM) to access cc:Mail services on the new cc:Mail post office. In addition, Lotus will deliver a Microsoft Messaging API (MAPI) Service Provider Interface (SPI), which will make the new version 3.0 user agent MAPI-compliant, enabling it to access the DB8 post office as well as other MAPI-compliant post offices or messaging servers, including the Lotus Notes V4 Server and the Microsoft Exchange Server. The MAPI SPIs will also allow the DB8 post office to host other user agents, including the version of Microsoft Mail 4.0 that will be embedded in Windows 95.

Client/Server Messaging

Lotus is delivering messaging technology that takes advantage of the client/server architecture. With the release of Notes V4, Mail can use the Notes object store as a back-end server,

Figure 15

In the latest version of the cc:Mail client, Lotus managed to retain a familiar look and feel but add powerful new features like the Action Bar, heirarchical folders, inbox sorting and other ways to manage a heavy mail flow.

inheriting all the system-level services of Notes. The cc:Mail client uses MAPI and will therefore not support replication.

Mail administrators can begin to take advantage of client/server messaging without requiring a wholesale migration to the new architecture. cc:Mail version 3.0 and later clients will be able to access both the file-sharing DB8 post office and the Notes V4 server because Lotus will provide MAPI SPIs to operate with the Notes V4 server. In addition, because Notes V4 will include this MAPI layer, the Windows 95 mail client and other MAPI-based mail clients will also be able to access both the DB8 post office and the Notes V4 server. Users will not experience any discontinuities, and administrators will be able to migrate users to client/server messaging at their own pace.

Organizations will also have the option of investing in client/server messaging by acquiring Notes Express or other Notes clients. All Notes V4 clients will have the same messaging user experience as the version 3.0 cc:Mail client. In fact, all Lotus messaging clients will conform to the cc:Mail user interface specification, ensuring a consistent user experience across all Lotus messaging user agents.

"We found that 'free' email clients aren't very cheap at all. We went through a period where we used the free client in Windows but we hit the wall with that solution. We will probably save money in the long run because we moved over to cc:Mail now that we are contemplating hooking up to the Internet. The Internet is based on open standards and that meshes well with Lotus email."

Migration To Client/Server Mail: Lotus Vs Microsoft

Lotus understands that the key to a successful messaging strategy is a cogent and realistic migration plan that places as much value on enhancing current systems and coexistence as it does on the benefits of the new technology itself. Lotus has defined four "phases" in the adoption of client/server mail to allow customers to migrate at their own pace.

1. New cc:Mail file-share back end. Leverages user training, familiarity and expertise in the cc:Mail user interface client. Coexists with previous cc:Mail post office.
2. New cc:Mail client. Exploits improved back end. MAPI layer provides access to third-party back ends. Coexists with previous version of cc:Mail.
3. New Notes server for client/server mail. Supports new cc:Mail clients. MAPI layer provides access to alternative clients. Coexists with file-share cc:Mail post office.
4. Introduce groupware using Notes Express or Notes client. Leverages investment in new cc:Mail client. Coexists with messaging-only clients.

Throughout this migration, an organization can choose to continue to use its current desktop and server operating systems.

Lotus messaging products are independent of the operating system.

The Lotus Notes/cc:Mail Communications Server (CommServer)

To make cc:Mail truly an enterprise- and inter-enterprise-scale messaging system, Lotus has released the Lotus Notes/cc:Mail Communications Server (CommServer), technology that was formerly referred to as the Lotus Communications Server, or LCS. CommServer is the Notes V4 server bundled with full-function connectivity to the cc:Mail file-share networks, and optionally hosting native X.400 and SMTP MTAs, which can be configured to meet the specific needs of an organization. CommServer provides four distinct functions:

- cc:Mail Router backbone. CommServer nodes will often be used to replace "hub routers" in cc:Mail networks. A CommServer node will communicate with several cc:Mail routers acting as a hub, and communicate with other CommServer nodes. In this sense, it performs pre-cisely the same router-to-router function as hub routers do today, but will be available on scalable platforms (e.g. UNIX).
- Native X.400 and SMTP connectivity. For those organi-zations with X.400- and SMTP-based constituencies, CommServer nodes can host X.400 and SMTP MTAs, and thus provide this important standards-based con-nectivity for cc:Mail networks. These MTAs can be used as transport between CommServer nodes (i.e., to allow CommServer nodes to operate on X.400 or SMTP back-bones) and for access to X.400 and SMTP user commu-nities. Each of the MTAs is optional.
- Integration of cc:Mail and Notes environments. For those organizations with Notes installed, CommServer nodes provide full integration of cc:Mail and Notes environments, including messaging interoperability, directory interoperability, and integrated management. CommServer Conversion Services will provide high fidelity mapping between cc:Mail objects and Notes objects. CommServer Directory Services will extend the replication of Notes Name and Address Books and the Automatic Directory Exchange function of cc:Mail in order to make cc:Mail directories act like replicas of

Notes Name and Address Books. That is, changes are automatically propagated in both directions.

- High function management is provided by cc:Mail View and NotesView. In an integrated environment, cc:Mail View will act as a proxy agent to NotesView.

Modular Architecture

CommServer is characterized by its modular architecture. While encompassing all the technology and services first articulated in Lotus' announcement of LCS, CommServer presents cc:Mail and Notes customers with a single and flexible enterprise-scale back end. CommServer is a bundled product consisting of the Notes V4 server and the cc:Mail Connector for connectivity to cc:Mail file-sharing subnetworks, and the optional native X.400 and SMTP MTAs. In this way, any Notes server can be deployed as an enterprise messaging server to connect not just other Notes servers but also cc:Mail subnetworks. A CommServer that is first implemented as a cc:Mail hub server can be extended with no additional technology investment to act as a Notes application hub server. CommServer is a true common back end for cc:Mail and Lotus Notes.

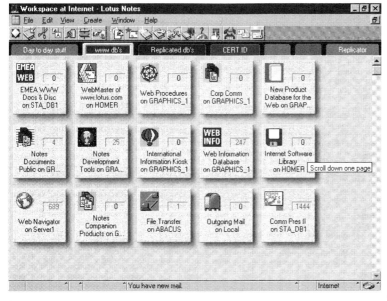

Figure 16

Workgroup Computing

As mentioned earlier, there is a growing trend among organizations to expand beyond electronic mail and message-reliant

Figure 16

Business organizations thrive if smaller units within can co-ordinate their work effectively. Notes is the premier workgroup application because of the way it helps manage the flow of work and information. The Notes 4 workspace has been completely overhauled to facilitate this.

applications by building groupware applications. Groupware applications offer services in addition to messaging, including a distributed object store, replication, document- and field-level security, application development and directory management. By combining these services into a single, unified groupware architecture, every application including electronic mail inherits the services of that architecture. This unified architecture enables an organization not only to build applications that allow teams within and between companies to communicate, but also to collaborate on common projects, ideas and documents, and to coordinate complex business processes.

Communication

The most basic tool for information sharing is electronic mail. Using a mail system, users send and receive notification of events, share timely information on an ad hoc basis, and distribute files and documents. Messaging services are the key to communication-oriented applications.

Collaboration

Whereas electronic mail allows for relatively ad hoc communications, collaboration technologies provide a more targeted and manageable means of information sharing. Specialized databases, such as discussion databases, document repositories and news databases, provide users with a structure in which to manage information, track its history and categorize its content. Collaborative databases and applications make use of client/server-based replication, in which the back-end server is a secure object store. Replication services allow a company to distribute databases across an enterprise and between enterprises, and enable users to make copies of a database for use on a laptop computer, so that their information resources are available to them even when the client is not connected to a server.

Coordination

The strategic applications built on a groupware platform that have helped companies realize unprecedented return on investment are those that coordinate the activities of teams or an enterprise toward meeting organizational goals, often by managing the movement of information and documents through a business process. In addition to using the object store, replication and security services of groupware, these strategic applications, such as customer service, product development and sales tracking, require the complete breadth of groupware services, including a

robust development environment, workflow and agent processing, and integration with relational databases and desktop tools.

Lotus Notes is the industry-standard groupware platform for
developing and deploying applications that help teams communicate, collaborate and coordinate.

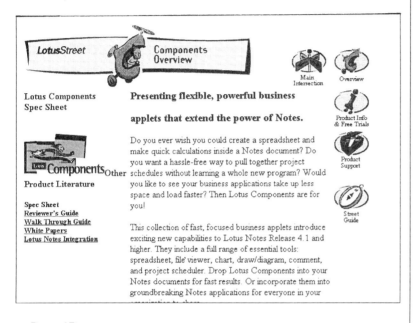

Figure 17

Notes V4

The new release of Notes will continue to support departmental
workgroups with unmatched functionality and flexibility. The
Notes V4 server is Lotus' scalable, reliable client/server platform
for messaging, groupware and application development. The
server provides a distributed, replicated object store, a security
service based on public key cryptography, and programmable
agents. Notes clients provide a user interface for interacting with
local and remote databases, for messaging and for application
development. Lotus is improving the robustness of Notes V4 to
meet the needs of enterprise-wide and inter-enterprise applications.

- Server support. Notes V4 will continue to support the
  breadth of popular servers, including HP-UX, IBM AIX,
  Sun Solaris and SCO UNIX, as well as Microsoft NT,
  OS/2 and Novell NLM.
- Extended client support. Notes V4 clients will include

Figure 17
Lotus continues to add to the Notes portfolio – just as the book went to press, Lotus unveiled Notes Components, a way to add business applets to any Notes Version 4.X server.

Windows 3.1, Windows 95, Windows NT, OS/2, Macintosh and UNIX.

- cc:Mail User Interface. The mail system in Notes V4 conforms to the cc:Mail user interface specification. That is, users will be presented with the cc:Mail client user interface and will experience the same look-and-feel as the standalone cc:Mail product.

- Enterprise scalability. Notes V4 will feature greater scalability and performance. Many organizations choose to implement an enterprise layer of servers to manage large-scale applications. In addition to serving as a departmental server, Notes V4 will be robust enough to allow administrators to deploy it as an applications hub server with no additional technology investment.

- Inter-enterprise connectivity. AT&T Network Notes, allows both intra- and inter-company communication with minimal infrastructure investment. Lotus is also developing technology to allow Notes to act as a server on the World Wide Web on the Internet and to import information from the Internet into Notes databases, which can then be replicated internally.

- Native X.400 and SMTP support. Because X.400 and SMTP are such fundamental transports in enterprise and inter-enterprise messaging environments, the Lotus X.400 and SMTP MTAs can be installed directly on Notes V4 servers, in addition to installing them on Notes/cc:Mail Communication Servers. This provides departmental-level servers with inter-enterprise connectivity.

Lotus Messaging Switch

The Lotus Notes/cc:Mail Communications Server is an integrating element for Lotus components. In large enterprises, Lotus components will typically coexist with legacy systems and messaging components from other suppliers. To help integrate these third-party legacy and messaging systems into the Lotus Communications Architecture, Lotus will be enhancing the Lotus Messaging Switch (LMS), formerly known as SoftSwitch EMX. LMS will provide the following services:

- High-fidelity message switching among X.400, SMTP, IBM SNADS, IBM PROFS, DEC ALL-IN-1 and

VMSmail, as well as among numerous other messaging environments.

- A high function "boundary MTA" acting as the nodes to connect internal networks to external networks for X.400 and SMTP. LMS has access controls, rules, and other features necessary for systems providing this boundary function.
- Directory synchronization among all major environments.
- X.500 support, including native support for the X.500 Directory Access Protocol (DAP), the Lightweight Directory Access Protocol (LDAP) and the Directory Systems Protocol.

LMS is currently available as an integrated hardware/ software solution. In the future, LMS will be available on some of the same platforms as CommServer. LMS will not require a dedicated hardware system, but rather will be able to be installed on the same physical hardware and operating system as CommServer and managed from the same management platform.

Systems Management

No enterprise messaging architecture can be successful without appropriate systems management tools to monitor network traffic easily. As part of the Lotus Communications Architecture, Lotus has developed cc:Mail View, a management tool for cc:Mail, and is working on the development of an SNMP-based (Standard Network Management Protocol) management tool for Lotus Notes networks.

The Notes management tool will be based on Hewlett-Packard OpenView system management technology. Further details of this development project are not available at present.

cc:Mail View provides centralized reporting and status notification and tools to perform in-depth analysis for system planning. This gives systems administrators a detailed graphical display of their cc:Mail email network, alerts them should an exception condition occur and provides charts showing message system statistics. cc:Mail View allows administrators to visualize the status of messaging system components on a wide area network from any location in the world.

A graphical topology manager, called MailMap, displays components such as post offices as icons whose color reflects

"When it comes to upgrading, smooth is cheap. Big jumps wind up costing a lot of money."

their status. By clicking on an icon, administrators can access detailed information regarding message delivery status. MailAlert, an early warning subsystem, notifies administrators of potential error conditions in time to take corrective action before message delivery is compromised. Planning tools based on Lotus Approach help administrators plan growth, identify potential bottlenecks and select optimum network design.

Because SNMP was designed for the management of client/server networks, cc:Mail View is by definition not an SNMP-based product. On the other hand, cc:Mail View will be able to appear as a window within the SNMP-based Notes system management product.

An Evolved Architecture

The architecture and plans presented here represent a significant enhancement to the Lotus Communication Strategy introduced in 1993. The Lotus Notes/cc:Mail Communications Server provides all of the functions which were to be in Release 1 of LCS. The features which were specified for future releases (e.g. PROFS and ALL-IN-1 connectivity) will be provided immediately in the Lotus Messaging Switch. The architectural evolution from the LCS design articulated in 1993 to the design set forth here is driven fundamentally from the mandate to provide a more modular approach to the Lotus Communication Architecture. This component architecture is manifested in the following ways:

- cc:Mail version 3.0 networks can be implemented with or without CommServer nodes (formerly LCS nodes). Administrators can retain and leverage cc:Mail routers and can replace hub routers with CommServer nodes to deploy a high speed backbone at their own pace.
- Notes networks can be migrated to Version 4 of Notes without the need to migrate the Notes servers to LCS nodes. Customers in Notes-only environments can continue to exist in Notes-only environments.
- Notes networks can be enhanced with native X.400 and SMTP MTAs directly without the need to install CommServer or LCS nodes.
- The new cc:Mail version 3.0 client can connect to the new DB8 post office infrastructure as well as to Notes servers because the version 3.0 client, the DB8 post office and Notes servers will all be MAPI-compliant.

Future More Perfect

For email, Internet-based or otherwise, to truly become part of the entire business landscape, there has to be some work done on the problems of directories. Imagine the decreased utility of the system if there were no directories. Imagine the decreased utility of the telephone system if there were no directories. That's just about where we are with email at the present but the future holds the promise of some fairly rapid headway towards a universal directory system.

The Lightweight Directory Access Protocol (LDAP) has been advanced by a cross-industry group of more than 40 companies that announced their support for the system. With wide-based support from computing and Internet luminaries, LDAP may generate enough momentum to ultimately result in comprehensive, Net-wide email directories in the future.

LDAP was originally developed by the University of Michigan and has undergone extensive testing there supporting the university's online database of 100 000 university email addresses and serving five million queries a week. LDAP is a subset of the Directory Access Protocol (DAP) used to build X500-based directories.

You can think of LDAP as X.500 Lite. It is really just a streamlined way to access data from an X.500 directory, an official Internet standard. Complete implementations of the X.500 DAP (Directory Access Protocol) need too much processing power. Besides, DAP only runs atop the OSI protocol stacks which lost out rather heavily to the Internet's TCP/IP standard. LDAP is also simpler for developers to work with and is much more efficient in use.

Essential to its success, though, is the considerable list of industry supporters queued up to implement LDAP in their products. Leading the way is Netscape Communications Corporation, which is putting support for LDAP into its software and server products. Also putting their weight behind the new standard are Lotus, Novell, Banyan, AT&T and IBM. All of the parties have identified interoperability of email directories as crucial for enterprise use of the Internet and intranet.

LDAP will contain name and email address but can also include supplemental data including address, phone and fax. It would be possible also to include a person's public key which can then be used to encrypt messages to ensure privacy and prevent tampering.

Users of LDAP directory services will find a hierarchial struc-

check the
WebExtra

ture that reflects geographic and organizational boundaries. The top-level domain is the "world" and includes all servers. The next level down is individual countries, and then divisions within countries are either geographical, such as by state, or by organization.

For LDAP to succeed, each organization must establish its directory server before email address databases can be relied on globally. Software vendors and even Internet Service Providers may offer products and service to hasten the arrival of LDAP. Netscape has already announces their LDAP-compliant server product.

Lotus is at the forefront of LDAP support with testing under-way for Lotus Pages, an X.500 directory server with LDAP support. Lotus will also offer LDAP links between the cc.Mail address book and an X.500 directory.

LDAP may not be able to solve all directory problems in one fell swoop. Providing a common access method to directories is one thing, but making sense of that directory information is a hurdle that organizations currently supporting multiple directo-ries will still find problematical. There are many users with Novell NDS, Banyan Street Talk and X.500 coexisting uncom-fortably.

But the adoption of LDAP by Lotus, Netscape and others will provide a meanful improvement on the current state of affairs.

The Business Bottom Line

Lotus provides a number of internal and external communica-tions products that can facilitate the movement of information. Using Lotus cc:Mail and Notes, you can create your own intranet and move onto the Internet with ease. Because Lotus products are based on standards, they can be combined with products from other vendors to create a customized solution that fits the unique needs of a growing business.

5 Finding and Using Internet Information Resources

Whether it's support material for your in-house computer systems or marketing data for a new product, the Internet can provide a wealth of resources. As well as being a consumer of information, the Internet is a good way to publicize your own cache of knowledge, either for internal consumption or for the world at large.

The Business Issue

The Internet excels at moving information efficiently and your business can increase its profitability if it can harness the efficiencies that the Internet provides. It is possible to use a computer thousands of miles away to search out a nugget of information in a remote database you can transfer any one of millions of files and programs to your own system and find companies, products and services that meet your needs. However, you will need to become adept at searching out information. If the Internet lacks anything, it is a coherent way for finding what you are after. As the Internet becomes the world's information marketplace, there will be advantages for businesses that set out their own stall.

Introduction

While a great deal of the traffic on the Internet is still from one person to another, more and more information is being made available for transfer, not to a single specified individual, but to anyone with an interest in the content on offer. Although this facility started when the Internet was the exclusive preserve of an academic community eager to share research results and ideas, it has not been outmoded by the commercial orientation of today's online offices and workers.

The Internet has always been a community for computer users and has strong links to the world of software developers. It's not just a world of freeware or shareware, either. Lotus, IBM and others are using the Internet to ship new software to their users, fix problems and provide support for products in the field.

There is an informal global support network waiting to help with problems, too. The Internet facility called Usenet newsgroups is a fantastically efficient way to get the scoop on anything from computer-related ills to the best place for a business dinner in San Francisco.

Here's a personal example: I was installing Insignia's Soft Windows, a package that lets you run Windows software, on a Sun workstation on a Sunday morning in England and I hit a snag during installation. I fiddled about, reread the manual, and was still stymied.

The product had to be up and running for Monday morning so, in desperation, I posted a message to the Usenet newsgroup that I thought would have the right sort of readership. In a matter of hours (this was still the wee hours in parts of the US on a Sunday, don't forget), I had a half dozen good suggestions resolving the impasse. To my delight, I also got a call from Insignia's support department at 9 a.m. on Monday to make sure that everything was all right. The power of the Internet!

While there is a lot of good information available for many business missions (not just MIS issues), it can sometimes be difficult to zero in on what you need. In particular, it is very hard to find people on the Internet. There is much chaff amongst the choice grains. Much of this chapter will be spent describing search tools for locating just what you need.

There are also lessons to be learned herein for information providers. Making it easy for customers to find and evaluate your expertise in a particular field of endeavor should be a goal. There are a number of techniques that can be gleaned from the searching topics that you can employ to make your hard-acquired mastery hard to miss. Experience, as ever, is the best teacher – so start looking!

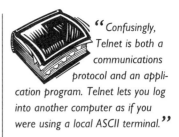

" Confusingly, Telnet is both a communications protocol and an application program. Telnet lets you log into another computer as if you were using a local ASCII terminal. "

Telnet

One of the basic Internet functions is the ability to log into a remote computer, subject to security restrictions, and use it as if it were right by your desk. That is what Telnet does. Telnet is the name of both the bit of software on your computer and the capability for remote operation.

Telnet was an important element of the first computers which made up the Internet which ran on one flavor or another of UNIX. Long before the ascendancy of the graphical windowing user interface, people had to use ASCII terminals that had no or very limited graphical capabilities. Telnet is therefore regarded as fairly primitive because it is restricted to plain text.

There is power in simplicity, however. It takes a fair amount of computer power and communications bandwidth to connect two graphically based computers. Telnet can cram an awful lot of information down a modest telephone connection without demanding a Pentium PC or more at both ends. Telnet is perfect for reading email or conducting simple database queries. As long as you can handle the security implications of allowing remote users to telnet into your system, it can be a very efficient way to meet the needs of traveling or remote workers.

There are a number of public Telnet facilities that allow you to use the power of someone else's computer system to search databases or pass information. You can use text-based Archie or Gopher clients (more about the Archie and Gopher searching aids later) to navigate information resources. You get there by Telnet.

One sterling example of a public Telnet facility has been created by the US Federal Aviation Administration with their DUATS (Direct User Access System). The system enabled the FAA to cut costs and simultaneously improve its vital, safety-related service to pilots. Now pilots can get the latest weather and confirm their navigational calculations without having to talk to a human briefer or wait in a telephone queue for the next flesh and blood person to read the weather to them.

Using Telnet is very easy, no matter if you are using a Windows PC, a Mac or a UNIX machine. At the command line (of a computer connected to the Internet) type `telnet` and the address of the computer you are trying to reach. To get to the FAA's DUAT system you would type

```
telnet duat.gtefsd.com
```

Sometimes, however, you will need to type in the IP address of the site instead of the easier to remember host name:

```
telnet 193.130.228.200
```

You are then connected to the remote computer: your screen will display the same thing as if you were directly connected and your keyboard has sprouted an extension cord miles long. Whether the computer itself is easy or not is in the hands of the designers of the operating system or application you want to use via Telnet.

Generally, after a login prompt and request for a password, you are confronted with a menu system. Although you are on the Internet with a Telnet connection, you can't take advantage of the graphical and other multimedia features of the World Wide Web (although there is a primitive Web browser called Lynx that allows Telnet users to browse in text mode only).

Finding Telnet resources is somewhat more problematic. There is no central listing of Telnet hosts that afford public access. However, when you need to use a public service like a Gopher client or a government system like DUATS, you will be able to find all of the details needed to make your connection. A number of Internet access providers sell Telnet-only access to their host systems – which is fine for email and Usenet news-groups but not much more.

FTP

FTP was also one of the original Internet utilities that got the name of its client software from the protocol used to perform its role in Net life. In the case of FTP, or File Transfer Protocol, there is more complexity than with Telnet to allow for additional functionality. But FTP does what its name says – it transfers files from one computer to another on the Internet (or intranet).

Why would you want to transfer files when you can easily attach them to email? Not all email packages are created equal. There are some email packages that cannot handle MIME binary attachments (like cc:Mail), others can deal with UUencoded attachments and some, like the Mac world, use a scheme called BinHex. There are also mail systems that will not tolerate a multi-megabyte attachment, requiring an emailer to slice his or her file up into digestible chunks. FTP makes it easier to transfer files.

There are also times when you want to go prospecting for software, bug fixes or documents and the transaction won't be between yourself and another person. FTP is the way to get these files. Sometimes you will even use FTP unawares: when you click on a link on a Web page that sends a file to you, you are using FTP.

There are many implementations of FTP, made to fit almost any computer from palmtop to mainframe, so it isn't possible to provide a definitive summary of the commands available. Many

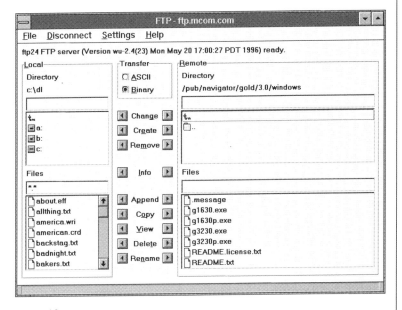

Figure 18

Figure 18

FTP is a way to move files around via the Internet. Once, using FTP required knowledge of a cryptic UNIX command language. Now its "point and click" with highly featured utilities like this component of Netmanage's Chameleon.

" Old-fashioned FTP programs have got to be among the most unfriendly Internet applications. No wonder many vendors are developing Windows FTP utilities! There must be 1001 slightly different implementations – but most of them have a help command."

of the computers that you will be contacting will be running the UNIX operating system. Don't worry, because FTP has a fairly verbose command syntax. You'll have to use the help function built into an FTP client (sometimes accessed by ? or 'help') or dig out the manual for your system or software and read up on it.

FTP isn't fussy about file formats. You can retrieve files generated by UNIX machines or Mac with a PC. But being able to get them isn't the same at all as being able to run programs.

Unlike Telnet, there has been quite a bit of polish applied to the FTP user interface. Instead of typing

`ftp` (starts the FTP client)
`open ftp.lotus.com` (opens the FTP connection)
`cd notes` (changes directory to the notes directory)
`binary` (requests a binary transfer type)
`get notes4.doc` (requests the named file)
`bye` (closes the FTP session)

there are a number of graphical utilities that fit right into the Windows environment and shield you from the ferocity of the UNIX command line. One of the best is the FTP client that comes with Netmanage Chameleon NFS. Instead of using cryptic commands like `cd` and `ls` or `get`, you navigate your way around the remote FTP server using the familiar Windows metaphor of list boxes and control buttons. As mentioned earlier it is possible to use a Web browser as a generalized FTP interface or even use FTP commands that are embedded in HTML pages.

Remote computers like to have you log in because their owners want to know who is using their system. Anonymous FTP allows you access to certain directories on the FTP server without having to register with the system administrator or use a password. Simply type `anonymous` when asked for your user name and give your email address as your password. Some hosts will not allow anonymous FTP and others, while allowing it, will limit the number of concurrent users. You will receive a message telling you if you have permission to use the system.

If you have a system that contains files that you would like your distance workers to have available (documents, spreadsheet files, database table), it is a simple matter to set up your server as an FTP site. However, you must be sure that you have addressed all of the security implications. If you choose not to allow anonymous access, you may marginally improve your resistance to attack. There may be other weak links, though, and only a thorough understanding of the FTP implementation running on your system can make FTP services a safe undertaking.

Additional security can be provided by passwording directories (possible with some operating systems and FTP implementations and not others), using invisible files (that a casual browser wouldn't even know were there) and password-protecting files (an underused capability of the popular Pkzip file compression software package).

FTP is symmetrical which means that you can "put" files into an FTP server as well as "get" them. FTP servers use an incoming directory that allows remote users to write their own files. This, of course, has security implications from two standpoints. Any file that arrives on a system may harbor viruses or other software that can have a negative effect on your system. But even if clean, those files need to be protected from access by inappropriate users on the system.

While you can cut down on the risk of security breaches by FTPing files from reputable sources and making sure that your users' site access privileges are shipshape, the biggest problem with FTP is the thousands and thousands of FTP servers on the Internet, each with dozens, if not hundreds, of directories. How do you find what you are looking for?

This really isn't a new problem but it is reaching new heights with the popularity explosion of the Internet. A bit of common sense combined with Net experience will have you searching out the resources at an FTP site. Some names are easy to guess. If you are looking for a Windows NT bug fix, `ftp.microsoft.com` is the first place to look. Fortunately, FTP has some friends.

" Most of the trouble for businesses that use Usenet newsgroups comes from the alt hierarchy. If you simply ask for this to be deleted from your news feed or employ filtering software, you can rest assured that you have removed a lot of the damaging time-wasting potential for your staff. You could also be missing out on some good information, too. A balance is required. "

Archie

Archie, the Internet's archive file location service that was named after a comic book character, is a system that lets you search file indexes rather than have to search each and every FTP site that might have the file that you want. It's the best (but not the only) place to start a search for a file on the Internet. Archie can find text documents, data files and executable programs with equal aplomb.

You don't even have to know the exact filename for the object of your exploration. You can search for a certain string likely to be in a filename or the file's description. Archie is fairly verbose and has an excellent help facility so it isn't hard to use if you are accessing an Archie server by Telnet. Like FTP, there are a number of Windows front ends available to remove any possibility of interacting with a UNIX command line during your searching quest.

There are thousands of Archie servers and finding a good one is a case of hanging out on the Internet, asking around or hazarding a guess. Archie is often found at universities such as Imperial College in the UK (`archie.doc.ic.ac.uk` – Archie at the Department of Computing, Imperial College, Academic domain, United Kingdom) or `archie.rutgers.edu` in the US or `archie.au`. Going for the Archie server nearest you is always a good idea but not the only good idea. Because Archie servers get busy, sometimes the best thing to do is to go for one that is operating in a time zone that's off-peak.

Other Search Tools – WAIS

The Wide Area Information Server (WAIS) is a powerful way to make databases accessible to users on the Internet. The technology behind WAIS was developed by Thinking Machines, a company that built massively parallel supercomputers as a demonstration of the effectiveness of their products. There are now two different strains of WAIS available, a commercial product and one that is licensed for free.

The heart of WAIS is the indexer which is used to create full text indices of the files that are fed to it. Of more interest to businesspeople that want to find something on the Internet is the fact that there are PC and Mac clients as well as ASCII and graphically based UNIX clients.

The clients provide the parameters for the search engines as single words, text strings or words related by Boolean functions ("car" and "battery" and not "crime"). However, you may wind up using WAIS without firing up a WAIS client. The current crop of Gopher clients and Web browsers can talk to a WAIS database.

Configuring and testing a WAIS installation is a fairly technical process but you should be aware that, even in the free version, there are two ways to safeguard your information. You can limit access to your server to a particular set of hosts and you can restrict access to particular information sources on your server to particular sets of hosts.

While this is not bullet-proof security (spoofing could defeat it), it does offer a relatively fine-grained capability for tuning access to your data in the event that you don't want the entire world stomping around in your databases. Within an organization, it makes it possible for parts of the database (product information, for instance) to be universally available, while holding other parts (availability, costs, production data) accessible to certain individuals or job types. WAIS clients work well with firewalls so your outward access should be unimpeded even if you want to throttle inward contacts.

Other Search Tools – Gopher, Veronica And Jughead

No one seems to know if Gopher was named after the mascot of the University of Minnesota where Gopher was developed or if it was in commemoration of its ability to fetch or "go for" information from the Internet. Both alternatives seem to have some degree of credence.

Gopher, at its simplest, allows you to browse through directories and retrieve files, rather like FTP. However, Gopher is a bit smarter than FTP in that it retrieves files in a fashion that is appropriate for their contents. If you request an image file, Gopher will start the right viewer application. If the file is text, it will be loaded into a text editor. If the file has been compressed, Gopher will fluff it up again. There is lots more user friendliness than you will find in even the best FTP client software. There is a new and improved version, Gopher+, that provides extra user-friendly attributes like forms and abstracts.

Clients for searching Gopherspace (as it is known) run on just about any computer you can fit on your desktop. The best commercial implementation is probably from Netmanage. While the representation is graphical it is more akin to what you may be familiar with in Windows File Manager rather than the all-singing, all-dancing graphical Web interface. This is not a criticism: Gopher directory systems are very efficient to transmit down a wire and contain the minimum amount of verbiage between you and the target of your search.

Gopher servers can be had for free (gn), free as part of an operating environment (Microsoft Internet Information server) or for a fee (University of Minnesota Gopher 2.X). The fee varies according to the size of your organization and the commercial content of your site.

Plan on budgeting for substantial time investment in getting your materials in shape to be published by Gopher. Much thought has to be given to the hierarchical organization of the directories and files and adopting a transparent naming system for various topics and items as well as the length and content of the items. This is not something that you want to rush because you will have plenty of opportunity to rue your oversights in the future. Additional material will have to be generated to provide overviews of the material covered.

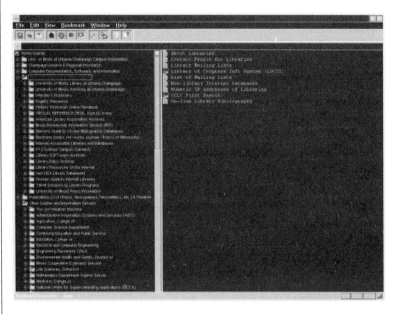

Figure 19

Gophers, like the Web, increase in value to information seekers with the addition of links. Following a link leads you from one Gopher server to another with the same transparency that allows you to navigate between Web sites. In fact, you can link Gopher sites to FTP archives, WAIS databases and, with the right client, to Web resources.

You can find a list of Gophers and a Gopher FAQ at the "mother" Gopher site at the University of Minnesota by Gophering to `gopher.tc.umn.edu`. This is also the address you need for registering your Gopher server. The process is very easy and will result in your server being added to the Master List of Gopher Servers.

If you have anything informational to offer the world, this is a good place to be found.

Archie's Pals

When something gets started on the Internet, it's sometimes hard to stop. When FTP search services got named after the comic book teenager Archie, the Gopher crowd upped the ante with Veronica and Jughead from the same series. Although Veronica is said to stand for Very Easy Rodent-Orientated Net-

Figure 19

While gopher has been pushed into the background by the Web, there are still a lot of gopher resources on the Net. While the Web is chaotic, gopher is much more organised. Gopher clients talk to gopher servers and display a hierarchical, directory view of the world. If you can navigate a hard disk with Windows File Manager, you can find your way around Gopherspace.

wide Index for Computerized Archives and Jughead for Jonzy's Universal Gopher Hierarchy Excavation and Display, many believe them to be the epitome of post hoc acronym formation.

It gets worse: the PERL script that Gopher server owners can use to link their site to Veronica is called maltshop. Thank heavens that the spider and Web-related word games came around and saved us from Internet resources named after 1950's music, cars or comic books.

Veronica is a finding service that provides an index of titles of Gopher items from almost all the Gopher servers in Gopherspace. Only the newest and the voluntarily absented servers are not included. Most Gopher server administrators put a link in their directory tree to a Veronica server. By doing so they not only increase the value of their site to searchers but make it possible for Veronica to automatically find and index their site. Currently it is taking Veronica a bit more than a month to walk through all the servers in Gopherspace.

Jughead is a tool for creating a Veronica-style search facility restricted to in-house resources only. This facility is obviously of interest to companies that have spawned numerous Gopher resources and need to unify them for internal use. Jughead creates an index (partial or complete) of your files and creates a Gopher menu item that permits the usual menu search using keywords.

Usenet And Filters

The Unsung Internet

There are a thousand and one magazine articles and books about the World Wide Web and all its multimedia glory and there are more than a few, too, about the wonderfulness of electronic mail. The Internet is, however, more than flashy Web pages and cheap global messaging.

You may have heard intimations that the Internet is a community. Well, it is if you can drag yourself away from the Web and point-to-point messaging. The feisty, uncensored world and his dog are still hanging out on the Internet despite the recent commercial upswing which is getting all of the press. You will find globally distributed communities of scientific researchers, allergy sufferers, orchid growers, fish fanciers, right-wing nutcases, dirty picture collectors, tattoo artistes and cancer victims. It's all there: the world is reflected in the Internet.

There is a very practical side to Usenet newsgroups, too. You can get free software, fast support on software that you paid

" Most of the trouble for businesses that use Usenet newsgroups comes from the alt hierarchy. If you simply ask for this to be deleted from your news feed or employ filtering software, you can rest assured that you have removed a lot of the damaging, time wasting, potential for your staff."

good money for, find parts for antique cars, discuss pressing political issues or drug side effects and keep your marine aquarium in prime condition. It's not just idle chit chat – unless your business has nothing to do with antique cars, politics, drugs or fish.

A lot of the Internet's genesis arose from various groups needing to communicate with each other, rather than just individuals bantering back and forth. In a way, some aspects of the Internet were the first incarnation of groupware, a term rather overused nowadays by software vendors in search of a new, big-spending class of punter. The first Internet creation to allow this facility was Usenet news.

13161 And Counting ...

Usenet newsgroups are not the Internet although some people think that Usenet is its finest expression. Like much of the Internet, Usenet is run voluntarily and cooperatively by people who care about it. There are no restrictions on who can participate although some newsgroups are moderated and some commercial entities have set up proprietary news servers that you have to pay to access.

A Usenet newsgroup is centered around a discussion topic: `alt.fan.tom.clancy` makes it pretty clear that aficionados of international hugger-mugger, shoot-em-ups and cloak and dagger doings need look no further. Harmonica players will feel right at home in `rec.folk.music`. In most newsgroups, there are a number of discussions taking place at a given time; each one of these is called a thread.

The unfettered Usenet free-for-all can be great – the division bug in Pentium chips was uncovered and publicized in a newsgroup (`comp.sys.intel`) and the company's non-responsive attitude was prosecuted in the newsgroup to the point where the biggest and most advanced semiconductor company in the world had to swallow a multi-hundred million dollar hit to replace duff processors. In the process, Intel became a better company for its customers (and us end users, too).

While Usenet can do wonderful things for companies and individuals, it also troubles some people to an awesome degree. The coppers, for one. Usenet is where you find most of the stuff that makes the newspaper headlines and gets politicians up on their hind legs calling for censorship, control and regulation. While it is true that there are megabytes of stuff that you wouldn't show your mother, there are also many megabytes of useful stuff for people and businesses.

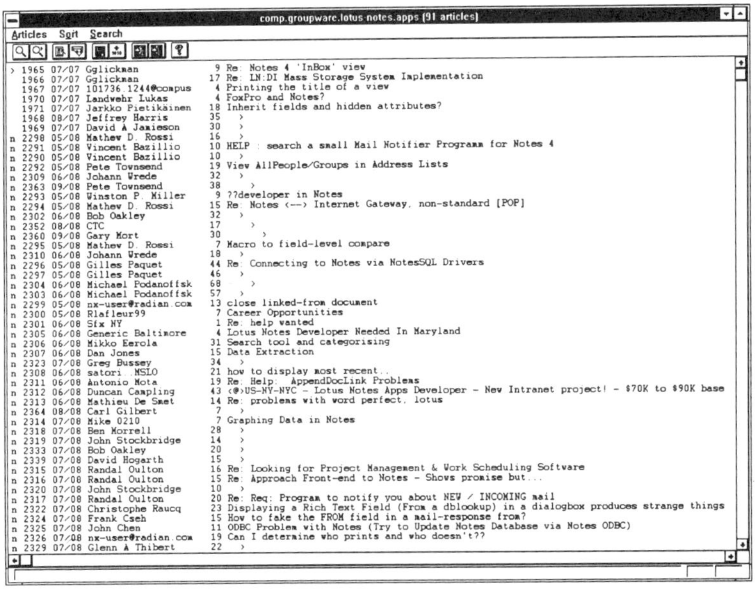

Figure 20

On the news server run by UUNET PIPEX, a UK Internet Service Provider (ISP), there are over 13 000 newsgroups at this writing, some with just a couple of lonely messages, some with over 10 000. The amount of traffic that is run over Usenet news groups is over 100 Mb a day and climbing. This means that most businesses won't be bothered with the technical nausea of building and maintaining their own news archives but will need to connect to someone else's.

Some people think that Usenet is just a jumped-up BBS (Bulletin Board System). While it has some similarities with the FidoNet system, Usenet is on another plane entirely. Most BBSs have a single server that caters to the needs of its local membership. Usenet consists of a global network of servers that are constantly replicating the message base. It's kind of like Lotus Notes on a double espresso.

How It Works

There's a simple explanation and a gruesomely technical one. Here's the simple one: When you post an article using your newsreader software, it is stored as a file on your computer or your local news server. Everyone on your site can read it almost immediately.

In due course, depending on the configuration of your system – a matter of minutes or hours your posting is transferred to a

Figure 20
News isn't just for hobbyists and sports fans. There is a lot of business content in Usenet. A good newsreader application, like WinVN, is essential. WinVN has the added bonus of being free.

You can get a free copy of WinVN at ftp.ksc.nasa.gov.

Usenet site and then along the Usenet backbone. Your article gets circulated around the world, usually in a matter of hours. Once your article hits the backbone, you are global in ten or fifteen minutes, although some backwaters may not get your news for a day or more as in the case of Albania where the Internet connection goes down every time it rains or someone digs up the street.

Once your article has been propagated, anyone anywhere subscribing to that particular newsgroup can read your message, post a follow-up or reply directly to you via email. And it didn't cost a penny more than your local telephone call and your Internet access charge.

How To Get Connected

The cheapest way to get on the Usenet trail is to get an account with your Internet service provider. This is often part and parcel of your monthly fee. You will also need special newsreader software.

If you have a copy of Netscape Navigator, the world-conquering Web browser, you can use it to read newsgroups, too. But there are a lot of other newsreaders out there that do a much better job of threading discussions or downloading multi-part binary files, two key attributes of a well-spec'd newsreader.

My favorite is WinVN which is a freeware product. It's fast, relatively bugless and the price is right. Many commercial TCP/IP packages like Chameleon and OnNet include newsreaders. Others swear by Trumpet's shareware newsreader (and some swear at it). Newsreaders make reading and posting news a point and click exercise.

If you read a news item that demands your response, your reader will take care of creating the header and sending your message back to the news server (and thence the world). Remember to be kind, avoid flaming, and keep it short!

What You Can Do

You don't have to sit there being a Usenet potato. You can create your own newsgroup to support customers or in-house work-groups. Newsgroups can be local or global. Most Internet access providers are glad to accept reasonable requests to create news-groups so long as the hassle-factor is finite. If you have a big (and comprehensively wired) family, small business, social organization or community group, you can take advantage of the public forum aspect of Usenet with a local or global newsgroup as you see fit.

You could also consider running a news server in-house, though this can take an appreciable amount of technical nous and eat up a goodly portion of your Internet bandwidth. There could also be some legal ramifications if users subscribed to some of the pornographic newsgroups.

There is no set procedure to initiating a global alt newsgroup but there is a long and tortuous road to be traveled if you want to add a newsgroup (or modify an existing one) in any of the other umbrella categories. You won't be ready to do this until you have hung out in Usenet-land for six months or more. By then you will be all too familiar with the petty politics, mindless enthusiasm and technical i-dotting required. Check out the news newsgroup for the exact formulae.

While Usenet is a means of conducting global conversations, its value to local discussions should not be dismissed. Usenet may come to play an important part in running democratic governments or bring democracy to places that haven't yet made the jump. Usenet really is the Internet for the people, by the people.

The Internet has spawned a new source of irritation for humans – spamming. Spamming is posting a news article to many different newsgroups, mostly unassociated with the subject of the posting. If you are reading newsgroups having to do with international marketing you may not want to get a news item about a chain letter or telephone sex service. Spamming tends to arouse the ire of Usenet participants because it commits the biggest Internet sin – waste of bandwidth.

The most egregious case of spamming was by a couple of US lawyers who spammed the entire Usenet list with an advert for their immigration counseling services. The combined outrage of Usenet melted down their ISP's mail server and got them thrown off the Net for a while. They are back and say it worked and they would do it again in a minute. Some people just don't get the concept of netiquette.

A Usenet message doesn't take a lot of space but if you multiply it times tens of millions it does represent a titanic waste of communications resource. Rather than send mail bombs (multi-megabyte nuisance messages) to spammers, a short note to their ISP will probably have the desired effect.

A few years back there was a great reorganization of Usenet to make it easier to find newsgroups of interest. A good thing, too, given the extent to which it has grown.

There are a large and growing number of newsgroups but the major categories are:

`rec` – recreational activities

`biz` – business-related groups

`comp` – computers – endless technical discussions and bags of support

`soc` – social issues

`sci` – scientific discussions

`uk` – groups of interest to people in these green and fair isles (de for the Germans, etc.)

`alt` – alternative groups – here there be genital piercers, druggies, and an extensive fringe element (according to one authority, if Madonna were a newsgroup, she would be an alt).

Like electronic mail, Usenet suffers from its text orientation. When you are talking face to face, voice inflection and expression carry as many messages as the words you choose. Misunderstandings are rife in newsgroups. Comparative anonymity also leads many participants to be coarser and less personal than they would be up close and personal.

This communications deficit leads to flame wars where two or more hotheads will egg each other on (and on and on ...), copying messages back and forth and trying to prove who is the cleverest of them all. Stir in a soupcon of racism or chauvinism and you can understand why Usenet is seldom dull. What a waste of bandwidth, though!

To get around this problem, emoticons were invented. The simplest, the venerable smiley :-), can go a long way toward defusing a nascent flame war. There are other, more highly evolved smileys and there is even an eponymous book published by O'Reilly with 650 different shades of expression.

The point of all this is to think about the person you are responding to in a newsgroup and try to meet ignorance with kindness, abrasiveness with understanding. Of course, there are some individuals that consider flaming a sport so an asbestos suit is sometimes de rigueur.

Talk, Talk, Talk

If the organization of Usenet newsgroups is all too deliberate and non-spontaneous, there is a very off-the-cuff rendition called Chat. Chat can be considered to be the CB radio of the Internet! It's like a cocktail party without the drinks.

Groups of people gather to chat about a variety of subjects just like they do down at the pub: business matters, child raising, sports, who is screwing whom, and so on. Just like at the local hostelry, you can wander around and take part in as many conversations as you want. You can even drop out of a larger chat and have a one-on-one talk if the need arises.

Internet Relay Chat (IRC) is a really big party with thousands and thousands of connections happening every day. You don't have to shout to make yourself heard in the crowd (how unlike some parties!) because IRC chats are divided up into so-called channels. Some channels exist all the time and some come and go at the whim of the users.

Each channel must have an operator and that is usually the first person on the scene. In a persistent IRC channel the operator torch is passed from person to person. That's about all of the organization that applies to IRC.

You can join a chat by Telneting to a public chat client running on a server but the best way to chat is to have your own client running locally. (You can read all about IRC by joining the `alt.IRC` newsgroup). Chat suffers from the same signal to noise problems as the newsgroups until you find a channel that has a collection of like-minded individuals. Chat can be addictive once you become a denizen of your favorite channel. There are lots of shareware and freeware IRC clients to choose from.

World Chat is a new, higher-level aspect of Chat incorporating elements of virtual reality. To participate, you have to download the client software from their Web site – that's a multi-megabyte decision to confront. But it is worth it! Installing the client in Windows is no sweat and in terms of communications it offers little more than the private talk and public chat but the environment that it is done in makes a tremendous difference.

To use World Chat you first have to pick an avatar. It can be a fat bespectacled simulacra (if that's what you look like), a svelte blonde or one of a number of fanciful alternatives including fish, penguins or Samurai warriors. This three-dimensional representation (which lives in your machine) gets a big name tag pasted on its head (your name or nickname) and then interacts with the other residents of the World Chat system.

World Chat takes place on a simulated space station and there

" Web sites must change constantly to attract repeat visits. One way to accomplish this is by adding a Chat feature to your Web pages. Your visitors themselves will generate new content with each visit. "

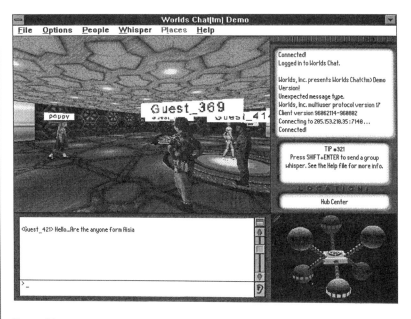

Figure 21

are a number of rooms to focus discussions. You can move around in the simulated 3-D space and chat or talk as the mood strikes you. Considering that you are still just typing in your conversational gambits, it is amazing how much difference this artificial world makes to your relationship with your fellow attendees.

World Chat wants to create artificial worlds for your company and is giving away the above software as a taster. Until we all have ISDN lines sprouting from our walls to permit reasonable dial-up video conferencing, World Chat represents a major move ahead beyond email, newsgroups or just plain old IRC.

Keeping Usenet In A Business Perspective

Opening your business to Usenet is like trying to get a drink from a fire hose. Sure, your thirst is slaked but you can wind up losing your glasses and getting soaked from head to toe if you aren't very, very careful. Even at this early stage in the Internet's development, you can find almost anything you want on the Internet as well as some things that you could well do without.

If you want to get computer system support, survey a market or check out the competition, Usenet can help. For people in business or education, the Internet is a tremendous resource. However, the Internet is made up of millions of people and, as

Figure 21

Internet chat is proof that CB radio will never die! World Chat provides a richer environment for real-time communications than the typewriter interface of ordinary chat. Is this the online meeting environment of the future?

with any collection of souls running to the millions, there are some folks you'd rather not rub shoulders with. In your role as an employer, there are some things on the Internet that you'd rather your employees did not linger over.

In addition to all the worthy U-rated content on the Net, there is a lot of just plain worthless, quirky, and provocative stuff that, if it were a movie, could be rated anywhere from PG to XXX. This can present problems to businesses that don't want to pay their staff for oo-ing and aah-ing at Net porn when there is work to be done.

If you are in a commercial environment there are a number of solutions that can tailor the access of an entire LAN toward Internet access that furthers corporate goals and keeps the time wasters out of `rec.flyfishing`. Firefox's Novix for Netware LANs is one exemplary product. However, if you are trying to steer the efforts of a single wayward worker, there are a number of simple and cheap solutions that can provide some peace of mind.

The Hazards

Aside from the aftereffects of over-eager hobbyists keen on pursuing `alt.manchester.united` or the Doom newsgroups 24 hours a day, the hazards to impressionable and distractable minds comes from the Web and Usenet newsgroups. The Web is especially hazardous given its E-Z to use clickable access. Usenet use needs monitoring because of the sheer volume and depth of depravity to be found therein.

The chances of your employees inadvertently stumbling across undesirable pictorial material in the Internet Usenet newsgroups is pretty slim. It's there, all right, but not in a form that can cause a problem accidentally (intentionally is another matter). Many of the pictures have to be assembled out of a number of parts, decoded from their transmission envelopes and fed to a program that can display them. This takes a bit of technical knowledge and some determination (a large fraction of the dirty pictures is technically corrupted if not morally so!).

A bigger danger to a skiving workforce comes from the newsgroups that feature erotic stories. These can be graphic in the other sense of the word and many would find them distasteful if not downright peculiar. Landing in one of these newsgroups presents no particular technical challenge – clicking on a posting is enough to send the fetish whizzing down the wire to your screen.

The Solution: Filter Out The Naughty Bits

To help restrict your business's access to discussion, forums, or bulletin boards that contain inappropriate material, whether textual or graphic, many of the commercial online services and some private bulletin boards have systems in place for management to block out parts of the service they feel are inappropriate for their employees. If you are concerned, you should contact a number of Internet or BBS services via telephone or email to find out how you can restrict accounts that your employees can access. CompuServe, AOL and UK Online all have fairly high standards in this area but they aren't perfect nor can they accurately reflect your tastes and toleration. But there is a fine line between unacceptable censorship and guarding the unwary. The Net is full of people that put personal liberty ahead of other virtues. There are lots of adult people who just like all that sexy stuff and they have rights, too!

The best way to protect democracy and freedom of the press AND your workforce's efficiency is to exercise management control. Buying and installing Internet filtering and rating software is pretty easy to do and not expensive compared to the number of working hours that can be lost with unhindered Usenet access.

The Software Selection

Screening software works in one of two ways. One is to set prohibitions so that certain Web sites cannot be visited or newsgroups retrieved. This can be a static list or, via subscription, an active one that changes as the Internet changes. The other way to screen relies on a rating service and the cooperation of Web sites to post code that will ward off the attentions of users that have browsers equipped with the right software locks.

There are emerging standards like PICS (Platform for Internet Content Selection) that are trying to get up momentum for a rating system so that the Internet can be what it wants to be without endangering the emotional state of users of any age. It is made up of a voluntary group of publishers, telecommunications companies, Internet and online service providers, and software firms that are working together under the auspices of the World Wide Web Consortium (W3C) to develop an easy-to-use labeling and selection platform that empowers people worldwide to selectively control online content they receive through personal computers. PICS is available royalty-free.

Another rating organization is SafeSurf. You can visit them at `http://www.safesurf.com/wave`.

CYBERsitter

CYBERsitter 1.2 uses a filtering technique that includes blocking of objectionable WWW sites or news groups and intelligent message and email filtering. Program updates are free and automatic update file retrieval via FTP is built right into the program. Just click a button, and updates are performed completely automatically, and at no cost to the user. There is built-in online support, and free upgrades to the Windows 95 version which will be available within a few weeks.

The problem of CYBERsitter is that it blocks access to common types of graphic files, as well as specific files and programs. The bad .gif and .jpg files are kept out but so are the ones of organizational charts and product photos.

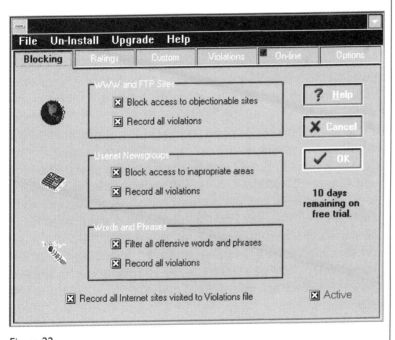

Figure 22

CYBERsitter is also a snitch. This feature will allow completely normal operation of the user's computer while providing information secretly on specific activities. The Alert feature can be combined with the blocking capabilities of CYBERsitter to provide a custom solution to discovering and preventing certain activities from occurring. This may have applications in the workplace!

Figure 22

A number of Internet screening tools have sprung up to protect kids and keep employees from wasting company time. None is perfect, but all provide protection against accidental exposure to the seamier side of the Net.

SurfWatch

SurfWatch 1.0 for Windows claims to reduce the risk of time-wasting surfers. It comes ready to block more than a thousand Web, FTP, Gopher and Chat sites but can be easily switched off for mature browsers after-hours. It also screens for newsgroups likely to contain sexually explicit material.

However, SurfWatch is an Internet-only product. It will not shield anyone from the spicier bits to be found on CompuServe or AOL or private BBS systems.

The only way to keep a program like SurfWatch valid is continual updates – and that's all figured into the cost: $49.95 per copy and a monthly subscription of $5.95. Contact `info@surfwatch.com` for more details

NetNanny

You can check out NetNanny at `http://www.netnanny.com/netnanny` for a free evaluation copy and see for yourself if this Canadian company hasn't created the best way to protect your workplace and free speech on the Internet, online services and BBSs.

NetNanny prevents your address, phone and credit card numbers from being given out on the Internet as well as preventing the loading, downloading and running of unauthorized software or CD-ROMs. A lot of the power of NetNanny comes from its dictionary of user-definable 'Words', 'Phrases', sites, URLs, newsgroups and IRC Chat Rooms that check items being sent from, received by, or accessed by your PC. NetNanny has pre-compiled a fairly comprehensive list including things like bomb making as well as nooky issues. You can screen individual sites you know the name of, like "`Playboy.html`." Or block all gifs or jpgs.

If there is a violation of the restrictions, you can log the access, block the access, shut down the application or lock the PC all the way. The NetNanny safety net extends to keeping your disks and hard drives from being reformatted and files from being deleted or tampered with. There's a full audit trail of the PC's use.

Cyberpatrol

You can download CyberPatrol 2.10, a full copy of the Windows version, for a pre-registration period, but then the blackmail begins. At the end of the pre-registration period, you have the option to register and purchase the full-featured edition, or to register an edition that has limited filtering capabilities which is the Home Edition. After the pre-registration period ends, Internet access from your PC will be obstructed until you register or remove the product.

CyberPatrol is almost too good at what it does. If anyone tampers with it, it obstructs access to the Internet (and that could impair your ability to go get another copy to reinstall! – take a backup!).

The program is extremely configurable. The total time for a given day or week can be set as well as blocking use during set periods (when work is supposed to be done!). If you find something that you think anyone would be wise to avoid, you can send a "Site Inspection Report" to Microsystems Software, and they will check it out and put it on the next update list (called CyberNOT).

CyberPatrol monitors Internet use when you access the Internet through AOL, CompuServe, or other Internet services. However, CyberPatrol doesn't monitor chat groups, email or other activities that are carried on at the Internet service site. The control there is very coarse – controlling time usage only.

You can find out more by sending email to `info @microsys.com`. There is no substitute, however, for a staff that understands what their rights and obligations are toward your business. If you have to devote considerable resources to being a net nanny, then maybe there are more fundamental problems in your business.

http://www.altavista.digital.com

Web Search Engines

With the Web all the rage, it was only a matter of time before someone put a search service together with a Web page front end. In fact, several somebodies have done the job – some for the greater glory of a commercial enterprise (Digital's Alta Vista) and some for the base motivation of making money (Infoseek, which sells not only executive-level search services but also advertising on the search results pages).

Many business-minded Web users will set the home page of their Web browser to go automatically to their favorite search engine. Some Web sites even offer pages that are collections of nothing but Web search engines.

Search engines work by sending software robots out into the Internet that follow every link that they come across. Every page they find is crunched through an indexing process that discards common words like "the" or "and" and lists significant words like "money" or "security" or "computer." It then annotates those words with the URL of the page where they were found.

When you come along and ask for pages that contain the words "computer" and "security," the search engine runs through its lists and finds the pages where the search terms are present. Advanced search engines like Alta Vista also do fuzzy logic searches. If you are looking for "vegetables," Alta Vista will return pages that include "carrot" or "potato" even if the word "vegetable" is absent. Even the meanest search engine takes a great deal of computing power, gigabytes of RAM and very large disk arrays.

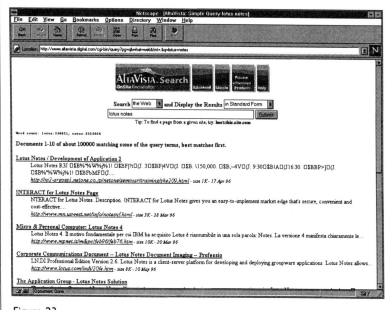

Figure 23

Commercial search organizations like Yahoo or InfoSeek are beginning to extract their investment in computer hardware and software by selling advertising space, charging a fee for searches, or both. Businesses that charge for searching services often include more than just Web pages in their search: Infoseek includes other Internet resources such as Usenet newsgroups; Individual includes many print publications.

It remains to be seen if the advertising-only approach works for search companies. Web advertising is turning out to be an entirely new medium and few of the rules laid down by decades of experience with print media will hold on the Web. It is likely that more Web search engines will turn to subscriptions to fund their efforts in the future.

Figure 23
Alta Vista was originally constructed to demonstrate the power of Digital's hardware and UNIX operating system. It has done so admirably while offering the most powerful search engine available on the Net – something of real value to every business user.

If you are trying to attract attention to a commercial site of your own, it's a good idea to email the person responsible at each of the search engines to get instructions on including your site in their database. Importantly, be sure that the heading and text on your lead pages contain all the hooks necessary to assist even the most inept searcher to find you. If you deal in cameras, for instance, your home page should also contain the words "photograph," "optical," "picture," "film," "lens," etc.

check the
WebExtra

> www.yahoo.com
> www.altavista.digital.com
> www.infoseek.com
> www.lycos.com
> www.excite.com

The ability to find your Web pages is of paramount importance, more important even than snazzy graphics or dazzling Java animation (which will probably consume most of your site-building budget). The text is the key to today's searching technology and your written material needs to be assembled with that in mind.

The Business Bottom Line

The wealth of information on the Internet isn't very well organized so it is important to have a good handle on the various sources and techniques at your disposal. It might even be worthwhile to develop an in-house Internet. If you are trying to make the Internet a place where your business is recognized, some thought in making your Internet sites easy to find will pay dividends. Using the Internet itself to publicize your presence is extremely cost-effective.

6 Surfing the Web for Business

While email, FTP and the other "text"-based Internet capabilities are excellent for cutting expenses and saving time, they are less than ideal conduits for sales and marketing efforts. The World Wide Web delivers an arsenal of business weapons equipped with the full panoply of multimedia elements to attract customers, entertain and inform, and even take orders and deliver info-products.

The Business Issue

The World Wide Web is the darling of business as much for its ability to collect and disseminate information as its capability for being a multimedia advertising hoarding. The era of Web sales is about to begin. There are a few new technologies that make it better than ever before but some business constants still apply to this new medium.

Web Ascendant

The Web is a child of the Internet, hardly more than a toddler. The Web delivers hypertext-linked information "a page at a time." A Web page can be made up of text, graphics, animated images, audio or even live video. As you browse the contents of a page, clicking on a link – a highlighted word or icon – requests another page. The link can take you to the next page in the current series or a related document from another Web server anywhere else in the world.

It is hard to get a tally of the number of Web cruisers now active. While the Internet is often credited with 50 million users, the sterner technical requirements of the Web mean that only a fraction of Internet users can access the Web. However, the servers that provide information for Web browsers are growing at a rapid rate – figures of over ten percent per month are often quoted, adding thousands more each month to the over 300 000 now said to be working.

Today's Web grew out of a project at CERN, a physics research laboratory in Geneva, Switzerland. The National Center for Supercomputing Applications (NCSA) at the University of Illinois provided the first example of graphical browser software in Mosaic for Windows and Macintosh computers (and also the X window system). Mosaic has been distributed free to millions of Internet users around the world and spawned a competitive field now led by NetScape.

How The Web Is Woven

The basic elements of any Web application are universal whether they are deployed internally (as an "intranet" application) or externally over the public Internet. The elements consist of HTML authoring and design tools, a Web server, and a Web browser. Specialized Web programming languages are also being inserted into the equation.

As Web applications increase in functionality, other infrastructure components such as database servers and application servers have been integrated alongside Web servers. Each of these components has evolved in functionality to its current state of the art, and each continues to mature and differentiate rapidly.

Authoring, Design And Management Tools

Authoring tools have quickly graduated from basic text editors to specialized HTML editors, which were typically used by persons responsible for creating Web content or modifying content created by others with different authoring tools. Because anyone who creates a document is potentially a content provider, it was a natural step for standard word processors and other familiar personal productivity tools to become equipped with HTML translation and formatting features. Lotus SmartSuite applications like WordPro and Freelance can perform their historical functions and deliver their documents ready for posting on the Web.

As the number of content providers has exploded to include virtually anyone with a personal computer, it is not surprising that professional Web authoring tools have begun to emphasize document management in addition to document creation. With so many documents becoming Web pages, there is a need for easy management of the hypertext links that are created on a home page or other Web page to lead readers to specific documents.

Since each document may have several links leading to and from it, link verification and management can quickly become time consuming, tedious and error-prone. This means that the task of constantly verifying the validity of links is work that is often shirked in light of other urgent work priorities. It just is no fun checking and rechecking completed work – even if the lines of responsibility are clear, which they often are not.

Web site validation is a task that is usually assigned to one or more Web masters, but which increasingly will become an automated function of the authoring tool (or server) itself as Web sites begin to scale beyond their embryonic stage. Lotus Notes and the InterNotes Web Publisher, which already support link management internally, not only support HTML translation but also Web site creation and management.

Web Servers

The first Web servers were simply HTTP servers that resolved uniform resource locators (URLs) by finding a path to a machine and directory that contained the needed page, and transmitting

" HTML (Hyper Text Markup Language) is a simple, plain text based language that is interpreted by a Web browser to arrange colors, fonts, graphics and multimedia components on a Web page. "

the page back to the waiting browser. A basic HTTPD server is very simple: it can only be used to deliver static pages, though.

To put more pizzazz into Web pages, variability and interactivity were required. Eventually, a common gateway interface (CGI) was introduced, and that provided a standard API by which programs, such as a database query, could be launched. It is important to note, however, that CGI scripts and the actions they instigate are not part of a standard Web server. Thus, as more of the work being performed on the Web is actually taking place on the "other side" of the CGI script, the Web is evolving away from a simple two-tier model of file request and file delivery to a three-tier model of client/server+server. One server provides the basic HTTP services, and the other server provides the actual application-specific processing.

Examples of this second level of server include the large, back-end database systems, such as DB2 and Oracle, which have been augmented by the introduction of CGI script interfaces for access and update by Web browsers. Lotus Notes represents another example of a next-level back-end server for workflow processing that is still accessed by standard Web browsers via a standard Web server.

Web Programming Languages

As the HTTP server changes over time to incorporate widely desired and standardized functions (e.g. full text search), the need for additional programming flexibility and power to craft Web pages will be needed. A critical part of this evolution will be the extension of HTML pages to contain programs in addition to data. Most industry analysts recognize Sun Microsystems' Java as the emerging de facto standard for Web programming for HTML-resident programs (more below), though others, like Microsoft's Internet-enabled Visual Basic, are likely to emerge as well. At present, these languages have focused on client implementation as browser add-ons, but their applicability to server-based functions is obvious.

As a result, vendors of server-based programs are making provisions to fully integrate their products with leading Web-based programming languages. It is Lotus' intention to forge seamless interoperability between Java and Notes and Lotuscript, Lotus and IBM's strategic scripting language.

Web Browsers

Like the rest of the Web infrastructure, Web browsers have improved in functionality at a startling pace. While the first Web browsers such as Mosaic dealt only with HTML, commercial browsers quickly gained the ability to render other native data types such as Adobe Acrobat and VRML (more below) and are now being augmented to include interpreters for executable "applets" contained in Web pages.

Specialized inline viewers have been "plugged" into the current generation of commercial browsers to support such exciting new capabilities as audio, video and animation, like Macromedia Shockwave and Iterated Systems' fractal image compression software.

While browsers are becoming more complex, a trend is emerging toward embedded, function-specific Web access tools. Tim Berners-Lee, the "father" of the Web, believes that browsers are only a temporary phenomenon and will be subsumed into the computer "desktop."

Right now standard desktop applications have begun to include context-sensitive browsing functionality. In this way, users of a desktop tool will be able to click on a Web icon that automatically brings them to a Web site that includes new templates or add-on functions for those products. For example, a user of Freelance Graphics (or any of Lotus' desktop products, for that matter) today from within Freelance itself can easily access a page on Lotus' Web site that makes available any new SmartMasters for use with Freelance. Likewise, a user of a tax preparation product will be able to access the vendor's Web site to access the latest regulations and recommendations from the tax authorities.

One thing is for sure – the future is ahead. The tension between rapidly evolving general-purpose browsers that are acquiring more special-purpose function and special-purpose software products that are acquiring focused browsing services is bound to produce a range of products to suit all requirements. Both Web browsing models will be able to coexist on a single desktop.

In the same way, general-purpose browsers have been adding general-purpose groupware functionality (communication, collaboration and coordination), while at the same time general-purpose groupware products are adding general-purpose browsing functionality. Without a doubt, the former is vastly more difficult to achieve than the latter, though certainly not impossible. Nevertheless, it is likely that the typical user's desktop will include a variety of browsers. It is important to note that this is not to say that groupware competes with the Web itself, but rather that it can effectively assume some of the func-

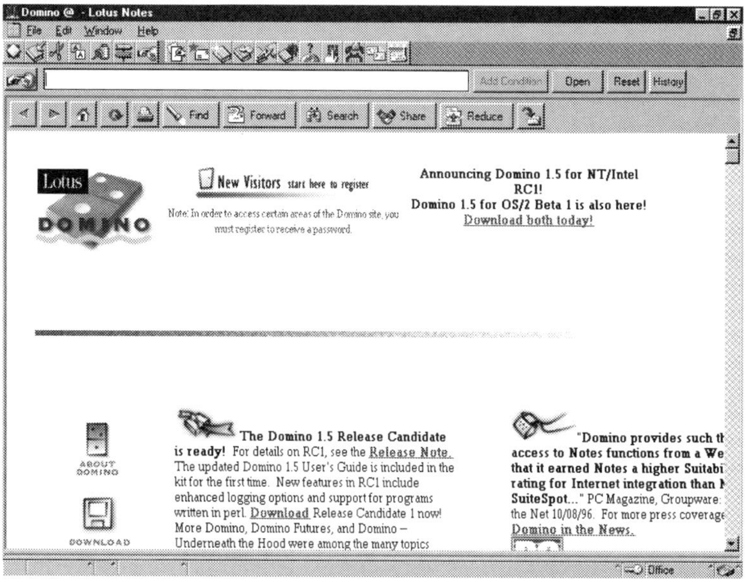

Figure 24

Figure 24

Notes' contribution to the browser wars. Until browsers are integral parts of all applications, all applications must have one.

tionality otherwise performed by traditional Web browsers. By virtue of the InterNotes Web Navigator, Lotus Notes Release 4 includes high-function, groupware-oriented browsing functionality.

Browser Wars Now!

Scarcely more than two years ago, there was no such thing as browser software. But with the ascendancy of the Web, a new battlefront is forming to set the standards for browser software. Browser software and the standards that underlie it are the key to the Internet for users that want exciting multimedia presentations (and businesses that want to deliver them).

The outcome of the browser wars is critical for business. Not only must you equip your staff with software that will allow them to access all the features at all the commercial sites but your own Web site must accommodate the breadth of the browser feature sets, especially security elements. If Web standardization breaks down, then businesses using the Web will be the first to pay through the nose.

Using a browser to view pages on the Web, you can do market research, reserve a hire car or order a pizza on the Internet. Soon other commercial services from banking to personalized horoscopes will be on offer. A host of new software companies, and some old regulars, are busy staking out this new software category. Right now any browser can access any page – but some are more equal than others. The market leader, Netscape, is blazing a trail that is quite alluring but potentially damaging – away from the original Web standard browser: Mosaic.

The thin end of the wedge has appeared already as the powers in the software industry flex their muscles. Sites proudly boast that they are 'enhanced' for Netscape or 'enhanced' for Microsoft's Internet Explorer. If you don't use the proper browser, you don't get the whole show.

In the beginning there was just Mosaic, lashed together by a team of students at the University of Illinois. Mosaic has since gone commercial and is in the hands of Spry, which was in turn bought out by CompuServe. But Mosaic, which got off to a slow commercial start, has taken a back seat to the new darling of the software industry (and the stock market), Netscape. The principles of Netscape were drafted from the student ranks at the University of Illinois who knew a thing or two about this browser business. By poaching most of the talent that created Mosaic, including star programmer Marc Andreessen, Netscape capitalized on its head start to win an estimated 80 percent of the browser market by late 1996.

The big boys have arrived on the scene having been shown up by the new kid on the block. The latest version of IBM OS/2 'Warp' Version 3 comes complete with the IBM WebExplorer browser. Oracle has its database-assisted PowerBrowser. Microsoft has countered with Internet Explorer for its Windows platforms plus the Apple Mac. The new companies joining the fray are sure that browserware will be the next "killer app" to revolutionize our relationship to the computer.

Today most Web browser software is free for the asking. This may change, however, as the Web moves farther away from its academic origins to a commercial marketplace. Free software is wonderful for students or hobbyists, but falls short when there is business to be done.

The primary focus of the new browser contenders, like Netscape Communications Corporation's Netscape Navigator, is increased performance and new features. Once the bugs present in the first-generation freeware were under control, support for paying customers and better performance moved up the list.

Netscape, has been available free on the Internet for over two years on an evaluation basis (and for sale after evaluation). Users have been impressed with the speed, efficient memory use and polished features. An important time-saving feature first introduced with Netscape is the ability to click on a hypertext link

"When Web access becomes part of the portfolio of business tools, users will demand software that you can depend on. That means support and an assured path for future developments. It's great that the world's academic institutions and their talented students have started the Web ball rolling, but the time is rapidly approaching for a more commercialized approach."

before the rest of the page has completed transfer. You can also use more than one browser window open at the same time.

Importantly, Netscape has been able, by virtue of its commanding lead in browser technology, to set the agenda for compatibility for commercially important plug-ins and HTML extensions that deliver useful new functionality.

But it was speed that was Netscape's first claim to user affections. Netscape got some of its speed by using non-standard trickery. While they have been open about documenting their new Hyper Text Markup Language twists, their enhancements are just ignored by other browsers. Microsoft is also "extending and enhancing" the Web to follow its lead so the battle to set the browser standards is now in full swing.

Running second to Netscape with less than a fifth of the apparent market share (18 percent) is Mosaic. Spyglass is the primary licensing contact for the original Mosaic software as developed by NCSA. Microsoft took the Mosaic browser in its first edition of Internet Explorer and built on it for its Version 2.0 and 3.0 product. The "enhanced" prefix comes from the work invested by commercial programmers to increase Mosaic's stability, reduce its system requirements and improve performance.

Even with clever software, page retrieval speed is one of the most significant impediments to widespread popular adoption of the Web as an information resource and commercial conduit. While Web pages containing scintillating graphics, audio narra-

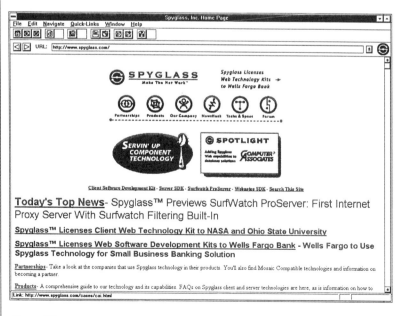

Figure 25

Mosaic was the application that made the rapidly growing Internet phenomenon go ballistic. Many members of the original Mosaic team including Mark Andreesson went on to join Netscape.

Figure 25

tion, and even video clips can be delivered to any current browser, the leisurely pace of most modems can make it a painful, drawn-out process.

Modern modem technology has just delivered 14 400 bits per second (bps) modems at bargain prices but the newer 28 800 bps units are still dear. Even they are really too slow for complex Web pages to snap into existence on your screen at anything like a browsable pace. For really good performance, you need ISDN digital telephone service.

ISDN has been touted as the next breakthrough in communications for so long that many people have stopped listening. ISDN delivers 64 000 bits per second speed and, importantly, call set-up times measured in fractions of a second. The speed of transmission and the speed of connection are perfect for Web browsing – rather than stay connected to save the 30 seconds or so required for a modem reconnection, you can jump in and out, paying for just the time needed to grab the page. The Web may be ISDN's killer app.

Responding to change is the biggest business challenge and to the victor belong the spoils. As fast as they can, more and more businesses are checking out the Internet and the Web for delivering and retrieving information about customers, partners and suppliers. However, managing change is hardest for organizations rooted in public service.

An academic background is particularly unwieldy when it comes to dealing with the explosion of Internet and Web developments. At the first meeting of the World Wide Web Consortium (W3C) in Paris, led by academics, there was evidence that the anointed standards body was well behind the commercial leading edge.

It is in the interests of all parties – private individuals, schools, businesses and governments – to have standards that not only permit but also encourage the growth of the Internet and the Web. This, after all, is going to be the most cost-effective and the most effective way of reaching large and diverse populations. However, I am afraid that the distinguished band of academics that are leading the W3C have their heads full of lofty arguments. While they are worthy of consideration by the standards makers of the Internet, they will not stop the late-arriving commercial denizens from seeking propriety advantages. The result will be divisiveness.

All informed commentators agree wholeheartedly with Tim Berners-Lee, one of the inventors of the World Wide Web and head of the W3C: we need one Internet and one Web. Agreement

http://www.w3.org
The standards organization and talking shop for the movers and shakers of the www.

http://www.sgi.com

on how to ensure that that noble goal is attained is an area of hot dispute, and of keen interest to the business community.

These developments are not just for computer nerds: the same students, small businesspeople, local government agencies that make up the Internet will all gain. But standards are needed; however, the way in which "the" standard is selected is in dire need of turbocharging. Commercial decisions are needed within commercial time frames.

The big challenge for all the companies in the browser market is to make the browser business pay. Microsoft, Lotus and Novell are all adept at turning market share points into big money – and Netscape has certainly done well with its public stock flotation! The Web browser software confrontation, however, is over software that is, for all of its current and many future users, utterly free and has been developed in the Internet culture which is based on voluntarism. It will be a tough transition for the young companies, old pros and users alike.

The 3-D Web Is Coming

There is plenty of substantive capability for businesses in today's Internet but there are a few budding technologies that promise even more in the future. While conventional markets take time to develop because of the physical restrictions on sales, advertising, customer response and so on, the Internet offers a fast on-ramp for new computer-borne capabilities.

Right now the visual Internet is a two-dimensional world of text and flat graphics. Advances in Web technology may be about to change the Internet into a full three-dimensional environment where we can have virtual meetings or even virtual business expositions. While many things in common experience can be modelled on a planar page, the real world is in 3-D with shadows, shapes, textures and physical attributes like inertia and hardness. For retailing and other purposes, hyperlinked, multimedia or not, the Web is, well, a bit flat. Cyberspace, right now, is really a cyberpancake.

A major dimensional change in the Web is in the wings thanks to Silicon Graphics (SGI), a leader in three-dimensional computing. SGI has a browser viewer that will allow users to interact with live three-dimensional World Wide Web pages. Adding the third dimension to Web browsing does not require a high-powered workstation nor a high bandwidth Internet connection, although like with most computer artifacts, it will make good use of all the compute power and bandwidth you have available.

SGI's new WebSpace viewer was co-developed by SGI and Template Graphics Software. Template Graphics will provide WebSpace for Windows and other systems. WebSpace works alongside Mosaic and Netscape Navigator as well as other browsers. With WebSpace coming out on the most popular desktop viewing platforms, it is reasonable to assume that there will be millions of users that can access 3-D Web spaces in the near future.

You have to see it to believe it. On a reasonable-sized PC monitor, you can generate a good 3-D image without the funny bicolored glasses used in 3-D movies so that the image pops out of the plane of the monitor. You don't need Star Trek "eye-phones" or headsets, either. Developments along these lines are natural but you don't need them now to get the benefit of a 3-D Web page.

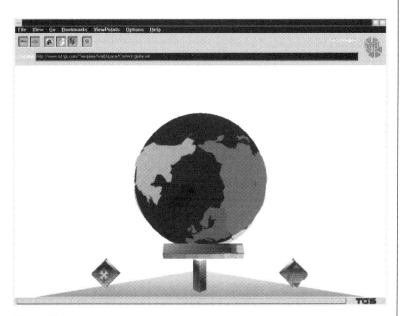

Figure 26

Using WebSpace, users can "fly" through 3-D environments such as virtual shops, libraries, museums, resorts, exhibitions and fantasy worlds. In business applications, remote users can interact with 3-D models of products beckoned from online catalogs. Boy-wonder traders (and their masters) can visualize complex financial information such as derivative trading in Singapore in 3-D. The information can be fed into WebSpace in a

Figure 26
Computer monitors are remorselessly 2D but a number of companies are struggling to make them 3D. The first efforts are impressive…but there is still a long way left to go.

"VRML encodes computer-generated graphics into a compact format for transmission over the Internet. You can actually model a 3-D object, such as a wine glass, with far less data down the wire than a full color graphical picture of the same object. Furthermore, you can rotate, zoom in and fully interact with a VRML image – you can't do much with a flat GIF or JPEG image except look at it.
VRML (Virtual Reality Modeling Language) is an extension of HTML to support simulation and modelling of three dimensional graphics inside a Web browser. These can be rendered as a flat 2-D representation on a computer monitor or, using special hardware, rendered as 3-D images."

"real time" so that you are looking at an up-to-date model of reality.

It's hard to say where WebSpace will take us. Any enthusiastic rendering sounds too much like science fiction but, then again, so does the concept of a global network of computers that can be reached from your own desktop for zero marginal cost.

WebSpace comes from a technology source steeped in open systems ethics. Once the standard is set, companies will compete for the best implementation. The SGI WebSpace viewer is based on Virtual Reality Modelling Language (VRML), an open, platform-independent file format for 3-D graphics on the Internet. If you inspect a VRML document, it is just plain text and numbers. File sizes are relatively small depending, of course, on the complexity of the objects being modeled. VRML is quite similar to the Web's standard HTML that forms the basis for all Web documents.

As with HTML, hyperlinked objects can be used to navigate to other VRML objects or HTML pages. VRML is scalable so that as users navigate through virtual worlds and approach objects, greater levels of detail emerge. It can be made very real indeed.

For VRML to become a usable business standard, there must be widespread support. Thus far 17 companies and organizations support VRML. Early supporters include CERN, Digital Equipment Corporation, Intergraph, NCD, NEC, Netscape Communications, Oki Advanced Products, Spyglass and SGI. Others will undoubtedly follow.

Beta versions of WebSpace for SGI workstations are out as are Windows ports. SGI and Template Graphics Software have chosen a time-honored Internet marketing model by providing non-supported versions of the viewers at no charge. Supported versions and 3-D modeling tools will be the revenue source that will fund the effort.

Meet Me On The Web?

Two nascent conferencing technologies are worth taking a look at although they are both just in the demonstration stage. CU-SeeMe is one-to-one and one-to-many video conferencing over the Internet. It requires a video capture board, a video camera and some free software developed at Cornell University. For effective use, it needs a high bandwidth Internet connection like ISDN or a leased line. Even though the software is only "beta" quality, you can see how it could progress with some additional polish. Video conferencing has always held out a promise to the business community of increased communications effectiveness and reduced travel expenditure. Commercial video conferencing companies are rushing to the Internet. Perhaps the Net is will be the ignition mechanism for this long-delayed technology.

The Internet already has the capability to act like a typewriter connected to a Citizens Band radio with its so-called chat facility. There are even chat "channels" where you can play poker! If you combine that chat capability with graphical representations of offices or exhibitions and populate those cyberspaces with images chosen to represent the attendees then you will have the environment created by Knowledge Adventure Worlds, called World Chat. You can visit a number of "worlds" by download-ing their free software (`www.worlds.net`) with generic "avatars" to represent you and your fellow conversationists. KAW will gladly create a world for you and your business col-leagues to interact in. If it sounds interesting, download the software and try it.

Fancy Some Java?

It has been scarcely more than two years since the Mosaic Web browsing genie was let out of the bottle. We have seen a tremen-dous variety of competing browsers appear to dish up the mul-timedia contents of the World Wide Web for all to enjoy. What has also become apparent is that Mosaic and Netscape are far from the end of the line in terms of Web-harnessing applications.

We have seen features added in profusion to Web browsers, including Spyglass Mosaic, Microsoft's Internet Explorer, Netscape Navigator, and Oracle's PowerBrowser, but there is still more to come. And more features are required if the Web is to reach its full potential as a marketplace for goods and services.

Retailers, and other advanced Web users, have a long wish list of items that must be fulfilled before the Web can be a com-pelling place to shop. To get sales messages across effectively and demonstrate the features of goods and services showcased on the Web, vendors need to have a way to animate their pre-sentations and provide other features to grab the shopper's attention.

To provide the Web extensions needed, Sun is cooking up a cup of HotJava. HotJava, the American slang for strong coffee, is a dynamic, extensible WWW browser that demonstrates the capabilities of Sun's Java language. Java is a new object-oriented programming language developed at Sun Microsystems to solve a number of problems in modern programming practice, including the rapid production of animated Web pages.

Sun has made an early release of the Java language and accompanying browser as a technology demonstration of what is yet to come. There is a version for Windows NT and Windows 95 and a number of other popular operating platforms. Unfortunately, there is little chance of HotJava appearing on the millions of Windows 3.11 screens due to the technical challenges.

The HotJava browser can run executable content downloaded across the Web. These "applets" are programs written in the Java language especially to run within HotJava-equipped browsers. Sun has provided several applets but to see them you have to be running HotJava – it's worth your while to get a demonstration because this is another Internet feature that has to be seen to be believed. The Java-produced code is capable of being run on any platform that supports the HotJava browser so work done on one operating system, say OS/2, can be viewed by users on any other operating system that has a HotJava browser – and that looks likely to be just about all of them!

With the flexibility to run downloadable applets, security is a concern. To provide a security blanket, applets may not write to or change your files in any way. On top of this basic security, you may further restrict the capabilities of incoming content. Simple menu choices are provided which can specify the level of security to be applied to incoming executable content.

The Java language is multi-threaded and therefore requires an operating environment that can handle threads like NT, Windows 95 or UNIX. This means that when browsing, HotJava can fetch multiple images at the same time. You can also start browsing immediately while HotJava is fetching images. You can scroll the demos or even print an applet as it is running. With HotJava, you can elect to load images and applets "lazily" – that is, only when you click on them.

You can never break with the past in computing, even if the sum total of recorded Web history is less than two years. HotJava will support the Web's lingua franca, native HTML, and all of Netscape's HTML extensions with two minor exceptions. Netscape, the current market leader with its browser, has done a deal with Sun to make sure that HotJava is available to all of its users. A joint development, JavaScript, is lowering the technical barriers to the features of Java. Lotus has built Java applet compatibility into its full line of Internet-enabled applications. Even Oracle and Microsoft have had to sign up for Java.

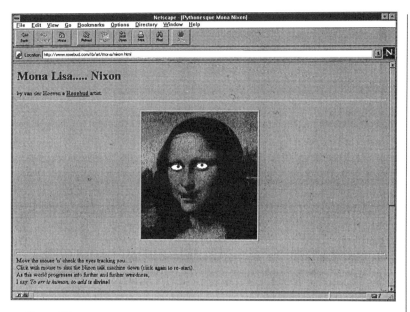

Figure 27

The Internet has the potential to deliver the best sales platform extant. It's convenient, it's only as far away as your keyboard and screen. It's open 24 hours a day (with no additional staff costs) and with HotJava-enabled browsers, you will be able to deliver better interactive, interesting merchandising pitches than anywhere else.

But Java and HotJava-augmented browsers are also ushering in a new world of client/server computing that will not only solve traditional business problems but also create new capabilities to be exploited for delivering information and services. Watch the Java space!

Building Businesses With The Web

It is tempting to address the opportunities for business on the Internet and the Web as just more of what you have been doing all along. The Internet enables businesses to go directly to customers – and there are millions of businesses worldwide that do just that without the golden touch of the Internet. Ingenious businesspeople have been figuring out how to do without middlemen, without expensive information channels, without delays since King Tut built the Pyramids (if not before).

While the Internet can eliminate distribution costs for "info" products, provide easy access to customers, suppliers and business partners anywhere in the world and redefine business boundaries, there ain't no such thing as a free lunch. The Internet

Figure 27

Sun's Java is more than a program-ming language that increases productivity when constructing applications distributed across the Net: it is the embodiment of Net-centric thought about how we (and our computers) should work.

http://www.openmarket.com

"edge" is bundled quite tightly with a brand spanking new set of challenges, among them building relationships in a transaction-oriented environment and charging real money in an online culture that takes free products and services for granted.

Open Market, a marketing technology company, formulated ten rules that they have found helpful for businesspersons to consider before they take the Internet plunge. While the phrase "business process engineering" is quite a trendy concept, it may not go far enough. Open Market proposes nothing short of reinventing your business to get a good grip on what the Internet has to offer.

1. Treat the Internet as a new medium
2. Start with the customer
3. Build relationships
4. Expect change
5. Build a service not a web site
6. Leverage existing business
7. Expect measurable returns
8. Think radically
9. Plan for success
10. Act now

There are few surprises in the list. It's not much different than a list that might be given to someone that is setting up shop in a different country or a different line of business. But because you will be adding the Internet to your business in its current form and in its current location, it is tempting to ignore such advice. The Internet is different and it will be a foreign experience.

1. Treat The Internet As A New Medium

Everything you know may be wrong. Get ready to learn. Create new offerings that exploit the Internet's unique properties. There are a few constants that hold over from terrestrial businesses like branding. The pace of change that will drive your Internet business will be quite different than familiar competitive forces. You will get new feedback – but you have to be ready to analyze it and change.

2. Start With The Customer

Sage advice for any business but the variety of people that use the Internet is daunting. Do you know which ones you want to talk to? And how to find them? And what they want to know?

The challenge is to create services that your audience will find interesting. Open Market recommends that you think of your

Web site as a toll free phone number that you want to get people to call. The Internet exists to move information and the people on it expect to get more than just brochures that advertise your services.

3. Build Relationships

Every business depends on their ability to get customers to come back. Get to know your customers – do some gentle survey work, encourage (but don't demand) registration, truly use email, and don't hesitate to pick up the phone if there is a need. Interact (how long does it take to reply to an email?). Make it easy for your customers to reach out and touch you. When you have a handle on who they are and what they want, redesign your content for them.

Comment forms, special offers, loyalty programs for repeat customers, and other techniques that have proven effective in traditional stores can be used to build relationships with online customers, too. In addition, the Internet provides never-before-attainable methods to track the traffic through the electronic store to study where people went, how long they were there, how many people did the same.

It is tempting to think, however, that a continually changing kaleidoscope of a Web site is all that it takes to keep the punters coming back for more – it is the satisfaction with what you have on offer that is more powerful.

4. Expect Change

There will be new browsers and new versions of old browsers, new technologies, new capabilities, and changes in marketing approaches and business relationships. Once you are on the Internet treadmill you have to keep up with changes. While new technology may offer impressive tricks, stick to standards even if it means that you have to resist offering an interesting feature – at least until you can be sure that a large proportion of your browsing audience can handle it.

Likewise, be ready to change your business. Play upon your successes, and cut out dead wood. The medium positively encourages experimentation – find out what works and track it aggressively.

5. Build A Service, Not A Web Site

This is excellent advice from a company (Open Market) that builds Web sites! Their success in business is contingent on making sure that their customers do what is necessary to succeed. They know that they are only part of the process.

Mastering the technical challenges of managing a transaction environment, creating a secure service network and managing content are necessary but not sufficient to exploit the Internet's business potential. Customers will not return to your site because you run a secure server well (though they may stay away if you don't!). Customers in cyberspace will go to businesses that give them value for their time and money, businesses they trust, businesses that know them, businesses that give them options they cannot get anywhere else.

6. Leverage Existing Business

Are you sure you know what it is that makes you a success now? Leverage the things you do well. The initial payoff for the Internet will probably be the revitalization of your current business. You can use the Internet to build on the assets you have – brand names, operational infrastructure, information, customer relationships.

Then you can explore ways in which the Internet can fill the holes by reducing costs of customer acquisition, reduce churn, reach new markets, fill gaps in your product offerings. One example is to take the assets of a membership subscription service and offer it to new customer segments where customers pay for only the information they use.

7. Expect Measurable Returns

Keep your eyes open and don't abandon your well-honed business attitudes. Expect your investment to justify itself on the basis of returns you can measure – you are spending real money, expect real money in return. You may have to give your Web experiment-time to ripen but start with well-defined business objectives and design the service to meet these objectives. Have you reached new market segments? Reduced churn? Cut lead generation or distribution costs? Generated revenue?

You can measure your Internet success by achieving goals – set your expectations and benchmark your accomplishments.

8. Think Radically

The Internet seems to reward people that are not afraid to obsolete their old business before someone else does it for them. How would you price your product if the marginal cost of what you sold got close to zero? What would your marketing plan look like if you could customize your service for every customer, regardless of size? What level of service would you provide if customer service cost you 90 percent less than it does today?

These suggestions are not meant to be provocative – they are real concerns for real businesses today. Take newspapers and magazines. Shortly they will be competing against a medium that is refreshed continually – not just once a day, that doesn't need expensive presses (or pressmen) or postage, that can be customized to suit the individual reader. While it is true that you can't take the Internet on a train or into the toilet (yet), periodical publishers will feel the impact of the Internet. Financial services, remote retailing and other information delivery businesses will be among the first to feel the cold wind blowing from cyberspace.

9. Plan For Success

Create a system that enables you to attract customers and manage information, one that will help you to build relationships using the efficiency possible on the Internet. A versatile system is required that can handle different ways of getting revenue and providing service. A system that does not force customers to adapt to your needs and a technical architecture that supports any browser, follows standards, and can grow painlessly. With any luck, growth will be your biggest problem!

10. Act Now

You can gain a lot by moving early with real commitment into Internet business. You will be the first to learn the rules in a new medium and, if you are sharp, you will create the business models that others have to follow. There is a limited time to establish your brand in a marketplace that is unique in its ability to force a concentration of suppliers. Most of all, being first will give you time to reinvent your business on your own terms.

It takes more than putting an order form on a Web site and collecting credit card numbers. After you have the technical challenges in hand (squeaky tight security, online payment processing, efficient and personal customer communications channels, integration of current business systems) you still have to have the golden goodie: something that the browsing public can't live without.

You have to prime the pump (to take the expression from a Kingston Trio song). Generating compelling content that attracts traffic gets someone to visit your site once or twice, giving them something they want and need brings them back again and again.

http://cdnow.com/

One successful online CD "store" does more than deliver lists of available recorded material: CD Now provides a comprehensive, free information service about recording artists including discographies and related artists. If you like music, a visit to their site literally pulls the credit card out of your wallet! The only thing lacking is a means to deliver the CDs online (at 650 Mb per CD, there aren't many who would want to download directly at this time!).

Don't forget, you must also deal with customer unhappiness. Every time a customer picks up the phone to dispute a purchase, it costs the merchant real money just to handle the call. If you can put all parts of the transaction online (order or delivery queries, complaint resolution, for instance) you will be further leveraging your Internet investment.

Resist the temptation to let the tail wag the dog. If the Internet portion of your business is to succeed, Internet sales and delivery must be integrated into your existing business models and processes. While it is possible to handle the few orders that are generated today without strong automation or integration into your legacy system, true integration will be critical to the success of businesses in the future as transaction activity grows. Timing is critical – don't run before you can walk. Although Internet business demands up-front investment and constant renewal, be sure that your present business won't suffer from the distractions of the Internet opportunity.

The Business Bottom Line

The Web is a great place for business but it is a new channel that demands fresh approaches. Understanding what is on offer technically is only the first step. To gain the maximum benefit from putting your business on the Web, you may have to reinvent at least a portion of your business to reach and serve cybercustomers.

7 Linking Your Data to the Internet

The Web provides a new communications channel to your employees and also the world at large. Creating interesting and reader-satisfying Web documents is a chore but the results are worth it. However, you may already be sitting on top of a lot of valuable information in your corporate data files that could be useful to your internal audience as well as your customers, suppliers and business partners. Fortunately, there is a way for an online office to move that data from the dusty depths and onto the World Wide Web.

Life is short enough without filling it with repeated attempts to reinvent the wheel. Business pressures make it extremely desirable to use and reuse literature, reports, discussion documents, calendars, catalogs and multimedia presentations in as many ways as possible. Most companies have virtual libraries of data comfortably ensconced in departmental and large corporate databases waiting to be accessed by the right person. That person can be an employee or an outside customer or supplier. The solution is the same – publish the right data where it can be found and used by the people that need it!

Do your employees need to coordinate their holiday leave? Do your customers want to see the latest prices and specs? Does the sales department need to study the latest marketing data? Does the management team need to know the progress of a campaign? Can local government enhance its relations with the community by publishing its operational schedules? All of these communications needs can be satisfied by publishing the contents of databases that already exist, putting them where all that need access can get to them – on the Web. And you can go full circle with this concept, too, by creating databases for the Web that can be reused in other contexts.

The motivation behind the Web's invention and indeed its current popularity explosion is the need to provide a broad spectrum of users with current information no matter where they are geographically. As Web-based interactions become more complex, the next step is to create real-world applications that manipulate, input, modify, analyze and apply this database content to everyday tasks via the Web. As the Internet and the Web ascend in importance to business, those applications will become mission-critical applications so some care is required at the outset. The need for live, online applications, which can manipulate and present dynamic, constantly changing data, will drive the Web into the next phase of its evolution.

In addition to the integration of existing systems with the Web infrastructure and leveraging the investment in current sales tools or internal databases, there is a growing trend of development of an entirely new set of applications specifically designed to take advantage of the Web's reach. These applications will focus on the Internet's ability to establish a direct relationship between a company and its customers, prospects, business partners or suppliers without the need for traditional intermediaries. Electronic commerce is the most obvious example here, although the development of Internet-specific applications such as publishing, customer service, and others are sure to follow.

There is also a trend among users with globally deployed Web applications to improve performance and response times by duplicating the content of one Web server located in one geographical region on a separate Web server located elsewhere. This addresses the issue of latencies and bandwidth restrictions that occur across the varied Internet, whether for internal or external use.

Also, as Web applications are used more and more for business applications that require integration with back-end database and application servers, the stateless connection from a Web browser to a Web server will change. That is, Web servers are highly scalable in their ability to return HTML pages in response to a URL request, so that a Web site typically only requires a single dedicated processing unit. However, as the "transaction" between Web browser and Web server grows more complex, the number of concurrent sessions a Web server can support is constrained. This will naturally lead to the need for multiple, duplicated Web servers to support high volumes of processing. A management and technical challenge if there ever was one!

Lotus provides a way to publish the contents of a Notes database on the Web called, simply enough, Web Publisher. This performs the useful task of transforming your Notes departmental applications into global applications and managing replication chores while heavier corporate data held in relational databases like Oracle 7 can be plugged into the Web using Oracle's suite of Web products. Your choice of method is dictated by the current application platform of your data and the scale of your ambitions. Both approaches are covered in this chapter.

In The Beginning ...

While packaged products from Lotus or Oracle are going to be the preferred way for users of those software environments to get their stuff on the Web, the earliest Web publishers rolled their own software connection (or gateway) between the Internet and their data stores. A brief look at CGI scripts is useful for users that may have applications that don't quite fit the molds offered by Notes or the Oracle WebSystem. The Internet is home to a diverse population and there will always be more than one way to skin the proverbial cat – and a bunch of opinionated Internauts to argue over the best approach.

"*CGI or Common Gateway Interface is a way that you can get a Web page to "talk" to other computer programs. This is often the mechanism used to allow Web pages to be dynamic and respond to user input.*"

Between The Web And Your Data – Common Gateway Interface (CGI) Basics

The Common Gateway Interface (CGI) is a bridge between an internal database and an application – for the purposes of getting your business online that application will most frequently be a Web browser. CGI has become the basic standard for interfacing Web browsers with information servers running HTTPD, the program that turns an otherwise ordinary LAN server into a Web server to push requested documents out to the world at large. However, there are several higher-level, more tailored alternatives becoming available from leading database companies like Oracle or Lotus.

The addition of this bridge between a Web page and your database not only allows you to publish the information that you have already sweated over (sales literature, graphics, reports, and so on) but it also allows you to customize each Web page that is delivered to the browser to conform with the user's indicated requirements or a predetermined plan of action.

For instance, you could quote a cost for a service depending on the reader's geographical area. By clicking on a service map, the user is telling your back-end database where he or she is and what column the fee would need to be read from. Less personal but nevertheless useful, databases can be linked to Web pages to highlight updates – new items could be tagged with a flashy graphic for their first appearance.

An ordinary HTML document that a Web server retrieves from its hard disk and launches across the Internet is utterly static. Everybody gets the same page, whether they (or you) like it or not. The page contains only the fixed elements placed there by the page's author. It can be a rich, multimedia page that was updated only yesterday but it nonetheless exists in a fixed state. No matter when it is accessed or by whom it doesn't change until someone with the right security access edits its fundamental HTML layout.

A page linked to a CGI script or program, on the other hand, can be customized on the spot. The CGI script is a program that is executed when the page is accessed. This can pass information about a database query from the browser to a back-end database in real time or run a pre-written query. When the query results are returned to the CGI script, the Web page that is served to the browser is dynamic. It may have only one variable field or it may be riddled with content that is dredged up from the corporate data files and served interactively to the browser's driver.

Dynamic pages are not only more interesting to readers but

they can more closely tailor the information delivered to readers' preferences – this increases the interest that readers may have in your material by answering their expressed queries directly instead of making them wade through page after page of interim material. CGI-scripted pages also can provide an important novelty element – Web surfers often return to pages that change to find out what's new.

For example, you may want to hook up your Oracle7 database to the Web to allow Web browsers from all over the world to query it. With the Internet, it doesn't make too much difference what that database is running on, where it is physically located, or if, indeed, several databases are involved or what kind of clients are looking in. In this instance, it could be a contact database – your corporate telephone or email directory.

Updating a large number of Web pages without auto- mated help is a big chore and could quickly become a significant portion of the expense required to maintain your Web site. Any auto- mated help that you can avail yourself of is a sound idea. Knowing a little about CGI's capabilities is good for management.

```
<larger><larger>#!/usr/local/bin/perl</larger></larger></fixed>

<fixed><larger><larger>print "Content-type:  text/plain", "\n\n";</
larger></larger></fixed>

<fixed><larger><larger>$remote_address = $ENV{'REMOTE_ADDR'};</
larger></larger></fixed>

<fixed><larger><larger>$referral_address = $ENV{'HTP_REFERER'};</
larger></larger></fixed>

<fixed><larger><larger>print "Hello user from $remote_address!", "\
n";</larger></larger></fixed>

<fixed><larger><larger>print "The last site you visited was:$
referral_address. Am I genius </larger></larger><larger><larger>or
what?", "\n";</larger></larger></fixed>

<fixed><larger><larger>exit (0);</larger></larger></fixed>
```

Figure 28

This could be published on the Web without CGI scripting, of course. You could just enter the names, telephone numbers and email addresses directly onto a static HTML page and get the same result at the browser end, albeit you would have to scroll through the list to find your target. It would be cheap and fast and easy until you had to start making changes. This is where you can save lots of time and effort by linking your Web page to a database with a simple CGI script.

Whenever a database that is linked to a Web server is updated, so is the Web page. With some simple programming, you could even have a list of the people that changed their telephone numbers in the past week presented up front as a special item.

Figure 28
CGI is programming, no doubt about it. Modern Web weaving tools minimize the amount of raw programming, but at one point or another Web sites leave the hands of the sales and marketing departments and enter the realm of the techies.

The more complex scenarios below would be extremely difficult to construct without programatically interfacing with internal databases and would lack that element of interactivity that is so desirable

To deliver the contact information to the world on a Web page, you need to create a CGI program that the Web server will execute to transmit the variable query information to the database engine, and receive the results back again and display them to the browser client. This simple process overview, however, hides some technical complexity.

The contact database example is only a simple implementation where the reader types in a name and the database returns a numeric field (the telephone number) and an alpha field (the email address). Additional CGI powers can deliver video segments, entire documents, or perform calculations and make dependent selections based on the data entered by the reader. There is almost no limit (other than compute resources, Internet bandwidth and ingenuity!) to what you can hook up to the Web. Implementing some of the most novel ideas are a challenge, though.

Here's one that is just about to leap into reality: online shopping. Today, online shopping has yet to take off because shoppers logging onto the Internet and browsing the Web find that the much promoted electronic storefronts use their PC and Internet connection as nothing more than an expensive catalog page turning device. There may be cute graphics, some current information on store hours or special sales but they are essentially static pages little better than a printed catalog but for the hypertext links.

The spark that will light up Web shopping is higher interactivity. How about a personal shopping service? An intelligent system could search the Web for vendors, business terms, product information, independent reviews, discussions in Usenet newsgroups and other related information. This could be assembled and presented to the user, allowing him or her to get far more information than could be available from a simple electronic page turner.

If your business is selling music CDs (one of the more successful Internet-based retail business lines), there could be a considerable business advantage to creating a client-side application for your customers – call it The Music Organizer. This simple database application would help your music-loving customers compile an index of their music collection. When their list is connected to your server application that generates customer profiles, you can dynamically create Web pages that offer selections to fill in any gaps in their library and present new works by their favorite composers or groups. On the back of this service you could also sell hi-fi equipment or even concert tickets.

Remember that while your CGI script is executing and the database is being scoured, the user in front of the Web browser may be getting bored! This poses a practical limit on what you can do with CGI scripting: your reader's motivation.

Additional CGI Issues

A CGI script is an executable program. Basically, when you invite Web browsers to pass variables to your CGI script, you are letting anyone that accesses that Web page run a program on your system. The mere thought of this can cause palpitations in the hearts of any MIS professional.

Clearly some security precautions are in order when you embed CGI scripts in your Web pages. Some are easy and obvious, while others require some awareness of the host operating system, database system and Web server characteristics.

There are other technical issues to consider, including the selection of the authoring environment for the CGI script. A CGI program can be written in any language that allows it to be executed on the Web server system, including: C/C++, Fortran, PERL, TCL, UNIX shell scripts, Visual Basic, AppleScript or any one of a number of other specialized alternatives. There are usually several to choose from. It's a matter of the personal preference of the author, the amount of sophistication that is demanded and the speed of execution required.

Many authors writing for Web servers running on UNIX favor PERL, TCL or UNIX shell scripts because the code can be easily debugged and does not require compilation before execution. While few readers of this book will do their own CGI scripting, some knowledge of the alternative approaches can help when you talk to the people that will be building your Web pages for you.

Whenever an industrial-strength database is involved, there is a need to use SQL (Structured Query Language) to scan the relational tables and return the desired information. Constructing data-mining CGI scripts involves not only programming knowledge but also some expertise with SQL.

Off The Shelf Or Roll Your Own?

Should you try your hand at interfacing your database to the Web using programming tools like Visual Basic to create CGI

"One elementary way to safeguard your security is to give CGI scripts their own special directory, signaling to the Web server that the CGI script is an executable program rather than just another page to display to the browser. Clearly this directory needs to be under the direct control of the Web master alone. On many systems this directory is called cgi-bin and is write protected."

scripts or spend the money for pre-packaged solutions from the likes of Lotus Notes or Oracle? It clearly depends on the depth of your technical resources, the form of your current database and the twin pressures of time and money.

Before you can decide, you need to audit your current database policies and procedures. If you are about to re-architect the whole shebang, there is little to be gained by painstakingly grafting your database onto the Web just in time for transition. Once again, a holistic approach is needed. The Web has the potential to bring creaking databases to their knees and to generate enough additional valuable data to stress a system that is comfortable under internal use only.

If you take heed of the three guiding principles of open systems portability, scalability and interoperability then you won't wind up down too many dead-end streets on the technical end of things. Sound business management is required to keep the Web tail from wagging the dog.

Lotus Notes: A Misunderstood Business Advantage

If you already have Lotus Notes, then you know a bit about what it is for. Now, however, Notes is changing to become more than it ever was – with the addition of tight integration to the Internet – and your conception of Notes is due for an overhaul. With Notes deployed as a departmental or workflow solution, you are closer to the Internet than you might think. Notes is one of the database paths to linking your business data to the Internet (more about the other shortly).

People have been getting the concept of Notes wrong since it was invented. Some of that may have been miscommunication from Lotus as well as a lack of anything to compare it with (which is still a problem!). One reason it is hard for people to understand Notes is because you can use it to do so many things. For instance you can use it to:

- Send and receive email.
- Read the latest industry news or research information about a particular subject.
- Track inventory and automatically generate orders when supplies are low.
- Plan and track progress on complex projects.
- Control the collaboration on a project of people in different locations. You can work together to plan your

work, create reports and databases, and discuss changes you want to make without leaving your office, no matter where the team members are.

- Automatically route forms to those that need to see them. For example, you can create a purchase order and have Notes route it automatically to your manager and then to the Purchasing Department and then to the supplier. This can all take place without you having to leave your office or trying to find your manager, passing (and perhaps mislaying) the paper.
- Discuss and share information without scheduling meetings – Notes can significantly decrease the number of meetings you'll have to attend.
- Take your computer with you and access Notes information from wherever you are.
- Access the Internet.
- Do all of this and more as they say! The use of Notes is limited only by people's imagination. It truly changes the way people work.

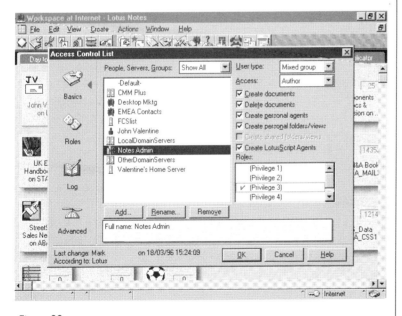

Figure 29

Notes gives you a way to find and share information, to make many tasks easier to accomplish, and to work easily with other people. These people can be anywhere, with your company or outside your company. They can be in your department, state or country or outside your country. They can be anywhere in the

Figure 29
The Access Control List is the key to flexible access with utter security. You can control document access according to group and fine tune the actions that any member of that group can take with a given Notes document.

world, thanks to the inexpensive links that the Internet makes possible.

Some Important Notes Concepts

Notes stores information in databases. Each database contains information about a particular subject, such as "purchasing policy" or "Product information". The person who creates the database decides on the type of information that the database will contain. Databases can even contain forms or reports for you to complete, such as attendance reports or expense reports.

Notes databases usually contain many documents. Each of these documents is about a particular topic. In a Purchasing Policies database, for example, there may be a topic about stationery, one about capital equipment, and one about reimbursement for emergency purchases. Some databases only let you read information, while others let you contribute information of your own.

You create a document by filling in spaces on a form that the database contains – another element set at the creation of the Notes database. While most forms have these spaces, called fields, some forms also have buttons for you to click to perform particular actions.

To add information to the database, you fill in a form and store your complete document in the database. Anyone who has adequate access to the database can read the information that you submitted and can create additional documents in reaction to your information. To read what someone else has written, you just look at the documents in the database.

Databases usually contain so many documents that it can be difficult to find the information you want. Notes gives many different ways to view and store the documents to solve this problem. A view is simply a way for Notes to display documents in a database. A view often shows documents in a particular order and sometimes shows only a portion of the documents in the database. For example, a personnel database that a company uses to store employee information would have a document about each employee. The database could be examined by a view that shows all employees listed in alphabetical order by last name or a view that shows all employees by the department in which they work.

You can also create folders in a database to let you categorize documents to make them easier to find. In the Employee Information database, for example, you could create a folder to store the documents you use frequently, such as those of your boss, department members, and friends. When you open the folder, you would see only those documents you placed in the folder.

You can place the same document in more than one folder, just as documents can appear in more than one view. The difference between a folder and a view is that you can place any document you want in a folder, but a view has a formula that determines which documents it displays.

A more technical definition of Notes would classify it as a client/server Data Base Management System (DBMS) application with messaging elements. It is a DBMS by virtue of its information storage and retrieval capabilities, yet it is very different from most other commercially available DBMSs that are founded on what is known as the relational model.

The differences between Notes and relational DBMSs far outnumber the similarities. Notes was designed to manage an entirely different type of information instead of the highly structured tables typically designed into a relational DBMS. Relational DBMS architecture reflects precise expectations about the data that will be entered. By contrast, the information managed by Notes is semi-structured or even unstructured, including documents, memos, images, and even sound and video recordings. Because these types of information are inherently amorphous, they resist being broken down into rows and columns of data. Notes is built to handle the data that relational DBMSs have difficulty with.

The database model used by Notes is best described as a document model, because the most basic structural component is a document A form determines the number and type of the document's fields, which are roughly equivalent to a relational database's attributes. However, the dependency of a document on a form only exists when the document is created; after that time, the document becomes independent and the form becomes merely one "window" through which the user can view the document. The independence of documents in Notes will be appreciated by the user who attempts to view a document with a form other than the one with which it was created: only the fields defined on the current form will be displayed; any others will remain hidden.

Messaging

Notes is more, however. As a document-based system, it is well suited for messaging-enabled applications. Because they are independent objects, documents can be exchanged between databases. In fact, every Notes user has a personal mail database which allows documents, i.e. email messages, to be sent to and received from other users. With a gateway to the Internet, users can send messages to people outside their own organization's network, even if the recipient is not a Notes user.

Messaging extends beyond email to allow individual databases to send documents to each other automatically. Such functionality is ideal for workflow applications in which documents must pass through many channels before arriving at a final repository. For example, a time sheet application may send a document on the following itinerary: (1) The user fills out a time sheet in the Time Sheets database. (2) The Time Sheets database automatically sends the employee's time sheet to his or her manager's mail database. The manager "signs" the time sheet. (3) Once signed, the time sheet is automatically routed to payroll, where it is approved and processed. (4) After the time sheet is processed, it is returned to the Time Sheets database for archival.

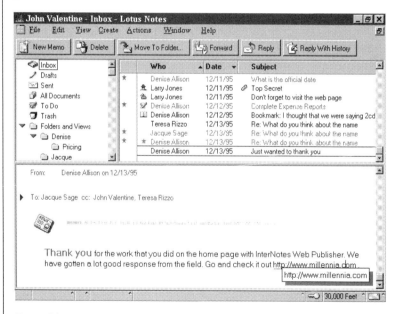

Figure 30

Figure 30

Notes Mail brings the power of Notes and email together to manage communications within organisations and between organisations, too. The three box design puts all the relevant information right in in front of you.

Notes Views

Notes is distinct from relational model DBMSs by having more than one way of representing data: one document at a time, or in summarized form through a view. Notes views are not only different from the views of the relational model: they are altogether incompatible with it.

A view in Notes displays document field contents in columns, with each row representing a single document. A hierarchical organization is imposed on the rows to display parent–child relationships between documents and to categorize documents on certain field values.

A good illustration of a hierarchical structure is a discussion database, like Usenet newsgroups. In such a database, all documents from the same discussion thread are grouped together with the responses to a particular document appearing as children of the parent document. If desired, additional levels can be added to the hierarchy by categorizing documents by general topic, author, date posted, or any other field value contained in the documents.

The hierarchical views used by Notes are structurally incompatible with the relational model. In a relational database, users are looking for specific information and make precise queries toward that goal. In Notes, however, users are generally attempting to keep current by communicating with other users. This calls for a more flexible browsing capability. Users must be able to sift through large amounts of information, often without really looking for anything in particular. Notes views could not be implemented in a relational database.

The hierarchical, categorized views provided by Notes are ideally suited for such browsing. When a user does need to look for something in particular, simple queries can be made against the database's full text index to find documents that meet certain criteria or contain certain words or phrases.

Lotus Notes And The Internet

The Internet and the World Wide Web provide opportunities for intra-enterprise and inter-enterprise communication and co-operative applications that didn't exist just a few years ago. By harnessing standards of the Internet and the Web, companies are able to leverage an inexpensive and commonly available communications architecture to build distributed client/server applications for internal use (called the intranet) and which reach customers, business partners and suppliers via the Internet. Lotus Notes is based on the concepts of a rich document-oriented database, fielded forms and document linking. Therefore, Notes is ideally suited as a development and deployment platform for Web applications. What has been missing in Notes is the direct support of Web protocols.

Lotus has delivered on its promise to provide Web application developers and users with the power of Notes' application development, client/server messaging and distributed object store technology by directly incorporating the key Internet and Web standards HTTP, HTML and Java directly into the Notes architecture. This means that Web developers can leverage Notes groupware functionality to reach non-Notes clients via Internet protocols and formats. The marriage of Notes with Internet protocols represents an enormous opportunity for Lotus' customers and its partners.

By opening Notes fully to Internet and Web standards, Lotus extended the value of the Notes server to support Web browsers as alternative clients. However, it is not a fully symmetrical relationship: The level of functionality that can be shared between any set of clients and servers is determined by the protocol over which the two components interact. Notes clients will continue to take advantage of the native Notes protocol to exploit the Notes compound document (CD) object store, and Web browsers will leverage Notes' native HTTP protocol and native HTML document format which may not be quite as rich as the features enjoyed by a Notes-to-Notes collaboration.

The full support for native Internet and Web standards in the Notes client also extends the value proposition of the Notes client to include end-user and team-oriented Web information management as well as broader utility for research and access to information across the Web. Notes clients extend all of their services to data from Web servers. That is, the Notes client now applies its entire set of functionality (disconnected use, client/server messaging, rich text, security, workflow applications, discussion databases and document libraries) to information published internally and externally on Web servers.

Lotus Notes Internet Directions

With the Internet and the Web on the verge of becoming the central part of any business's computing infrastructure, Lotus is concentrating its Notes development and marketing efforts to take advantage of this new computing paradigm.

Notes will become a complete platform for all Internet applications, including mail, discussions and Web applications. Earlier releases of Notes required an SMTP/MIME add-on to provide standard interoperability with other messaging systems on the Net. Notes Release 4 includes native Notes implementation of the SMTP/MIME protocol for ease of use and administration.

A core function of Notes is its support for group discussions regardless of time or location. The advantages of using Notes in conjunction with Internet-based Usenet news discussions are straightforward: multi-level access management, access for users not connected with TCP/IP, replication to Notes servers not connected to the Internet, support for mobile users, hypertext links to other Notes documents (including mail messages), support for embedded objects.

The World Wide Web needs a full-featured development environment. From its inception, Notes was designed as a powerful development environment built around the efficient management of distributed documents, and has been extended to incorporate data from relational databases.

While the use of a Notes client is not required in conjunction with a Notes application deployed over Web protocols, it nevertheless provides a compelling alternative to traditional Web browsers. The InterNotes Web Navigator is a Notes application that is shipped as an integral part of every Notes Release 4 client and server. It gives the Notes user transparent access to the diverse content that exists today on the Internet.

http://www.lotus.com
Extra! Extra! Read all about Lotus'
Domino Web server for Notes users.

As a groupware product, Notes and the InterNotes Web Navigator naturally exploit Web browsing from a groupware perspective, transforming what essentially has been a personal productivity function into one that is based on such groupware notions as forwarding and routing (communication), shared databases for discussion and reference (collaboration), and custom agents and application development (coordination). Like any other Notes application, the InterNotes Web Navigator also fully supports disconnected use, so that users can make laptop-based replicas of databases and applications that contain Web pages.

There is a lot more that is yet to ripen on the Web. Next-generation Web applications will leverage off ability to connect businesses easily and directly with the great "out there" of customers, prospects, business partners and suppliers, without needing traditional intermediaries. For example, a customer service application extended to the Web can reduce the need for telephone operators (or worse still, voice mail systems) to answer calls while improving customer satisfaction and delivering faster service.

Industries that typically rely on face-to-face or direct telephone contact to establish a relationship with a prospect or a customer (e.g. retail sales, financial services, travel/transportation, etc.) now have a new medium with which to attract and retain customers. Inefficient processes between business partners such as invoice tracking, inquiry status and project

" *SSL is
Netscape's
Secure Sockets
Layer security
protocol that secures
communications. It is proof against
imposters, eavesdroppers and
vandals. SHTTP or Secure HTTP is a
page-based security protocol. At one
time there was serious rivalry
between the two but that is now
history since both are being supported in developers' tool kits.* **"***

management are now subject to automation using the Internet (or private TCP/IP network) and widely available and deployed Web browsers.

Notes Goes Native

While Notes may be a proprietary product, it incorporates the open protocols that make the Internet an almost universal communications medium. Lotus has built upon the support for TCP/IP in Release 3, with Release 4 server features including easier set-up, locations, server pass-through, RAS support and performance improvements.

For example, with the use of Notes server pass-through capabilities provided in Release 4, a Notes client on the Internet can access an enterprise's Notes server on the public side of an Internet firewall, initiate an authenticated session, and then use pass-through to access other Notes servers on the "private" side of the firewall.

To keep communications lines as open as possible to non-Notes or cc:Mail users over the Internet, Notes will include a native Notes implementation of the SMTP/MIME protocol as well as the NNTP open protocol for Usenet news discussion groups through the InterNotes News product. In the future, the InterNotes News functionality will be migrated directly into the Notes client and server.

The lingua franca of the Web, HTML, was supported indirectly through the InterNotes Web Publisher by translating Notes documents, views and forms from Notes format to HTML, and in turn translating HTML forms remitted by Web browsers into Notes document form in Release 3. The functionality of InterNotes Web Publisher was migrated directly into the Notes server. In addition, the Notes R4 server, using the InterNotes Web Navigator, can translate HTML pages from external Web servers to Notes document format. Users can also preserve "raw" HTML text in a Notes compound document.

While Notes Release 3 supported HTTP, the Web publishing protocol, indirectly through the InterNotes Web Publisher, Release 4 supports the HTTP as a native protocol, so that a Notes server will be a native Web server and the Web Navigator provides native HTTP 1.0 support to the server. Eventually, Notes clients will support the native HTTP protocol, allowing it to browse the Web directly.

Notes is built on tough RSA encryption but needs to support the two emerging Internet security protocols, SLL and SHTTP, as well. There is a commitment from Lotus to follow these two initial standards and follow closely any additional work as it appears.

But the Internet is not just the Web. The InterNotes Web Navigator includes full support for FTP and Gopher. The Notes client will also support other emerging Internet protocols and add-ons such as WHOIS, FINGER, Acrobat, Shockwave and VRML.

For Lotus to provide excellent value for Internet-bound Notes users, the need for continual and timely innovation is paramount. New developments like Java have to be embraced. Lotus has announced that Notes will support the execution of Java applets in the Notes client.

This support for open Internet and Web standards is a major step in Notes overall support for industry de facto standards. Customer satisfaction today depends not only on proprietary features and functions but also on the ability to use open protocols. Notes servers have been open to desktop products through OLE, to relational databases through ODBC, to front-end query tools through SQL, and to alternative messaging front ends through support for MAPI. By supporting native HTTP and HTML, Notes servers are now open to standard Web browsers as alternative clients as well. Lotus fully embraces Web browsers and recognizes them as alternatives to standard Notes clients for certain types of Notes applications. Likewise, Notes clients now can access Web servers in addition to Notes servers.

Ease Of Use

While Notes is a powerful business tool, not everyone has it. One of the attractions of the Web is the browsing metaphor employed by Web clients, which lends itself to intuitive, easy use. This metaphor has already become familiar to millions of users worldwide. One of the principal design goals of Notes Release 4 was to improve its ease of use. For end users, work in Notes consists of finding, viewing and creating (or modifying) information. Notes R4 improves the user experience for each of these activities by borrowing (and sometimes using) the browsing metaphor.

Release 4 introduced a multi-pane user interface (at just about the same time that Netscape included such a format in their Navigator browser, coincidentally) that allows users to "surf" through folders and lists of documents, reducing the amount of effort required to browse through a Notes database. Some Notes Release 4 applications actually depart entirely from the standard Notes view, employing navigators, a fully graphical interface that makes use of hotspots to guide users to particular documents or functions. (The InterNotes Web Navigator is only one example of a navigator.)

There has been criticism directed at Lotus (and IBM) for setting Notes on a collision course with the Internet. Contrary to the premise in articles in the *Wall Street Journal* and elsewhere, Lotus does not view Notes and the Internet as competing technologies. Rather, Lotus' strategy and products seek to leverage the Internet, allowing users to take advantage of the unique features of Notes in combination with the wealth of information that exists on the Internet. Their professed goal is to give customers products that help them integrate the resources of the Internet into their core business functions.

InterNotes Web Publisher

The Internet is renowned for the availability of free software, some of excellent quality. Lotus has added to that reputation by releasing InterNotes Web Publisher at no charge to Notes customers (you do still need to buy a copy of Notes, however!).

InterNotes Web Publisher is intended for companies that need to distribute information to internal as well as public audiences (including business partners and customers) and have an appreciation for what the Web can do to further those aims.

While the Web provides a rich, graphical interface, a global

Figure 31
Surfing the lotus.com site with Lotus' own Notes-based browser.

Figure 31

reach and a growing base of clients or browsers, the crunch for most organizations, however, is setting up and maintaining an enterprise Web server. This typically requires significant investments of both personnel and equipment: Web servers where several authors and/or departments are contributing to the information are time-, labor- and resource-intensive because all documents intended for the Web server must be translated into HTML and linked to other documents.

A staff of dedicated HTML and WWW specialists is needed to add pages and maintain both internal and external links. Any time new documents are added and others deleted from the server, all links and pages that refer to those links must be updated. The complexity of creating and maintaining documents and links on a Web server inevitably creates a management bottleneck, making the entire process less than ideal.

Enter the InterNotes Web Publisher, which automatically converts Notes databases and documents into HTML so that they are accessible to popular Web browsers, reducing the staff requirement. Rather than requiring a sustained effort and a considerable staff to convert existing documents into HTML, the InterNotes Web Publisher leverages Notes' distributed authoring and management environment to populate WWW sites. Individual authors can prepare their own information in Notes as an integrated part of their everyday jobs. Using Notes' replication and distributed storage model, authors from geographically decentralized workgroups can conveniently contribute documents to the corporate Web server.

The InterNotes Web Publisher also creates HTML documents of Notes views to provide Web browsers with the rich navigational structure of the original Notes database. Most importantly, as content changes and as contributors submit new material, the InterNotes Web Publisher automatically updates the overview or home pages as well as all links to refer to the new documents, without any manual intervention. No more dead links, the bane of a Web browser's surfing experience.

Notes Full-Text Search is available to anyone with a standard Web browser. They can easily search a site managed with Notes and InterNotes Web Publisher to find the information they need. Users enter their search criteria into an HTML form and submit it. Web Publisher executes a search against a Notes database and returns a list of links to the user. The full range of Notes search options, including a full-search query language, is available to Web browsers.

InterNotes News

InterNotes News is a Notes server application that exchanges Usenet news articles between Notes and news servers using the Network News Transfer Protocol (NNTP), giving Notes users a secure and easy way to access and participate in Usenet newsgroups from the familiar Notes environment. By reading news articles from Notes, users can leverage key Notes functionality, including hierarchical views of discussion threads, full-text search and multiple indexed views of the news articles.

With InterNotes News everyone in your business organization that can reach the Notes server gets access to Usenet newsgroups without a personal Internet connection, and only to those newsgroups deemed useful to the business. Document management capabilities such as Notes macros, full-text search and mail forwarding are provided to enhance the value of Usenet newsgroup articles. With the SMTP gateway, users can post initial and follow-up items from Notes.

InterNotes News offers administrators a way to bring Internet newsgroups into the organization without putting TCP/IP on every desktop. With a centralized Notes configuration database that simplifies configuration and administration of the News service, administrators can subscribe to individual Usenet newsgroups, create customized Notes News databases and control News replication. Notes Access Control Lists also provide selective access to News databases.

Figure 32

lotus.com seen through the Netscape browser. Web standards make the source of the browser immaterial – as long as no one tries to hijack the standard!

Figure 32

InterNotes News gives better control of Usenet's more business-oriented elements and can exclude distracting or potentially damaging material. If there is anything that can bring structure to the amorphous Usenet, InterNotes News is it.

InterNotes Web Navigator

About The Web Navigator

The InterNet Notes Web Navigator is a Notes Release 4 feature that provides Notes users with easy access to information (HTML, FTP, and Gopher) on the Web. The Web Navigator delivers a comfortable way for Notes users to get their feet wet on the Internet by retrieving Internet resources directly into Notes. Then Web Navigator performs the feat of converting Internet content into Notes documents for management in Notes Release 4. What's even better, InterNotes Web Navigator is "free," a bundled feature in Notes Release 4.

The Web Navigator consists of a database and a server task that reside on a Notes server, referred to as the InterNotes server. The InterNotes server stores the Web Navigator database, runs the Web Navigator server task and the TCP/IP network protocol and maintains either a direct or proxy connection to the Internet.

Local and remote Notes users access this database in the same way as they access any other Notes database. With Web Navigator, only one computer (the InterNotes server) needs to

" The Web Navigator database is designed for users to read existing Web pages. If users want to create their own Web pages, they can use the InterNotes Web Publisher which automatically translates Notes documents into HTML pages. "

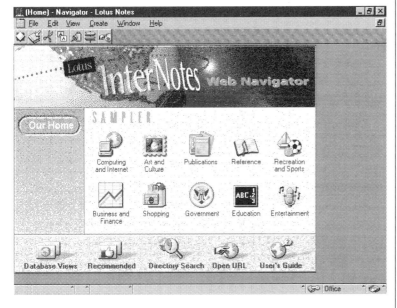

Figure 33

Figure 33
InterNotes Web Navigator delivers a lot of power to Web-aware organizations that have bought into the Notes way of doing business. Combining the Web and Notes creates a powerful business tool.

be connected to the Internet in order to give multiple Notes clients access to the Web. In your organization, you can maintain more than one InterNotes server, each with its own database if you want to provide several places where users can access the Web.

When a Notes user (or Notes action such as an agent or macro) requests a Web page, the Web Navigator retrieves the page from the Internet, translates it into a Notes document, stores it in the Web Navigator database, and displays it to the user. After a Web page is loaded into the database, it does not need to be retrieved from the Internet the next time a user requests it, saving time and Internet connection bandwidth.

If a user requests a page that has not yet been retrieved or if the page is in the database but contains an expiration date that has passed already, the now familiar spinning globe animation appears to indicate that the page is being retrieved over the Internet. Once Web pages are in the database, users can view these pages, copy them into private folders, cut and paste them into other Notes documents, mail them to other Notes users and so on.

InterNotes Web Navigator brings a level of automation and customization to Internet information management. Both end users and corporate developers can use the Notes Release 4 agent builder, the Notes macro language or LotusScript to create useful agents to do tasks such as scanning customers' or competitors' Web sites for new or modified pages and sending daily summaries to users' email files every morning, with Notes doclinks to the complete articles.

Keeping Up With The Neighbors

The Web is exciting because Web pages change rapidly. A Web page stored inside the InterNotes Web Navigator database can become outdated in a short period of time. Even though users can specifically retrieve the latest version of a Web page from its Internet server whether that page is in the database or not, accessing pages directly from the database can be much faster than retrieving them from the Internet.

Therefore, it is important to keep Web pages stored inside the database current. The Web Navigator comes with a Refresh agent that compares the date of each Web page inside the database with the date of the same Web page on its Internet server. If the Web page on the Internet server is newer, the Refresh agent replaces the Web page inside the database.

Web Navigator is transparent to the end user and if you have a lot of Web users in your organization, the database can expand rapidly with use. There is a Purge agent that can be used to keep the size of the database under control.

The Web Navigator database also includes a graphical Home navigator that displays a collection of starting points to browse the Web. It is made up of clickable icons that link directly to the Web pages, display views of Web pages already loaded in the database, display the search form, and open documentation about the Web Navigator. You can use the Home navigator as it is, customize it to suit your needs or create one of your own.

Bookmarks are an important Web researcher's tool. InterNotes Navigator bookmarks are even more powerful because they can be searched and managed with familiar Notes techniques. Personal and corporate bookmark lists can be maintained. You can even rate Web sites on a scale of 1 to 5 for relevance to your company's mission.

Ever find a Web page that you want to send on to an associate? With Web Navigator, users can forward a Web page while browsing the Web. All hypertext links on the page are maintained, so that recipients not only receive a high fidelity rendering of the page, but they can click on any link on the page and be brought back out to the Web for more browsing. Many times important information is discovered on several linked Web pages. The InterNotes Web Navigator keeps track of the route a user took to reach a page, and saves that route as a Web Tour. Notes users can save the tour for future reference or forward the tour to a colleague who can then follow in the same footsteps.

Many Web pages make use of fill-in forms to gather input from readers. These forms range from the simple (with a simple text input field) to the complex (with text fields, option buttons, check boxes and so on). The Web Navigator supports Web forms automatically. When a Notes user opens a Web page in the database that contains a form, the Web Navigator creates a Notes form "on the fly" that the user can fill out and use to submit data back to the Internet server. If the Internet server sends a response document back to the user, that document will be saved in a private folder for the user within the Web Navigator database.

You can preserve precious Internet access bandwidth with Notes Web Navigator because it saves frequently used pages in a cache in the InterNotes database that is accessible to all Notes clients (unlike pages cached in individual users' browser caches). The cache not only improves performance but exposes Web pages to the full breadth of Notes services (agents, full-text search, views, mobile replication, etc.).

Web Navigator maintains confidentiality. Some Internet sites contain pages that requires users to authenticate, or verify, who they are before they can access the pages. The Internet server accomplishes this authentication by requiring the user to provide a user name and password that was chosen (by either the Internet server or the user) in a previous visit to the page. The next time the user attempts to open that page from the Internet server, access will be allowed only after supplying the user name and password. After the user has accessed the page once, Notes encrypts that page to protect confidentiality and then saves it in a private folder in the database.

Notes Newsstand And The net.app

To prime the pump, Lotus is creating a series of "network application frameworks" or net.apps to allow Notes users to roll out Web-enabled business applications without lengthy custom development. net.apps provide a set of building blocks designed for publishing, marketing, customer service or electronic commerce applications.

Lotus Notes:Newsstand is the first completed net.app. It is a network-based publishing medium for users that want to provide their workers with business publications in Notes formats but it can also be used by publishers or other information providers that want to reach the Notes user community via the Web.

Figure 34

Newstand is both an example of the power of Notes on the Internet and a working application that can deliver electronic subscriptions to users.

Figure 34

Access to Lotus Notes:Newsstand publication databases is subscription-based, with subscription fees established by the individual information providers. All network users have access to the Guide to Newsstand electronic catalog, where they can find a list of publications they want and instructions on how to subscribe to them. Subscription requests are routed to the information providers.

After agreement to terms, the subscriber simply replicates the publication from the server and distributes it in accordance with the agreement for use by using the Notes infrastructure in their organization.

Lotus Notes: Newsstand helps deal with the need for published information throughout a business in an efficient way. Why subscribe to paper journals and magazines that are often inconveniently located or inaccessible to computer search techniques? Notes: Newsstand can also combine print media sources with publications on CD-ROM or even journals that exist only online.

Customers enjoy access to favored business and trade publications in Notes format, including ability to use Notes indexing, searching and retrieval features. Notes:Newsstand also helps customers manage connection fees, using replication to minimize connection time and avoid multiple subscriptions (the old left hand/right hand problem).

A developers edition of Lotus Notes:Newsstand provides product development and automation tools for publishers. Newsstand also creates a distribution channel designed for dependability and security, access to the customer and simplified subscription management. Not to be underestimated is the opportunity to leverage the technology and gather critical market data. With InterNotes Web Publisher and the forthcoming Notes WebServer, information providers can translate their Notes documents to HTML format for publishing to the World Wide Web.

Other net.apps are set to follow with a marketing communication framework that allows the fulfilment of customer requests for publications, documents, account status updates and customer demographics. The customer service net.app will consist of templates and secure bi-directional capabilities that will allow Notes to be used as the back-end engine for customer support databases. The commerce net.app will provide a secure way for customers to order and buy products and services over the Internet.

Each of the net.app frameworks will be built from one or more of eight different building blocks:

- Catalog consists of forms and fields designed to help create and manage product information for publication on the Web in traditional catalog presentation. Tools are included that enable users or "shoppers" to flip through the catalog and place items in their "shopping trolley." When they have finished shopping, the cost of the items is automatically totaled. Catalog also includes tools to enable specific information or content to be viewed only by authorized users.

- Interactive extends the Notes document/response model to the Internet for better management of threaded discussions. Interactive also allows documents to be composed or responded to by either a Notes client or a Web browser. Interactive also supports forms. For example, a user can complete an order form on the Web that will automatically be submitted into a Notes database.

- Order Processing interfaces with catalog and payment building blocks to facilitate transactions and create an order history database. By adding this building block, any of the frameworks inherit commerce capabilities. For example, by adding this building block to the Customer Support framework, a user can take orders for maintenance contracts, support plans or product documentation.

- Publishing includes SmartMasters and ready-to-use Notes templates, with built-in formatting for publishing in Notes or on the Web. Users can preview how their publication will look using a particular SmartMaster before publishing their data.

- SmartMaster includes formats that create more sophisticated-looking Web pages than could be produced using the Lotus InterNotes Web Publisher. Notes templates provide a consistency of functionality, look-and-feel and support for security between Notes and Web versions of documents. The templates also support the automatic conversion of RTF and ASCII content into Notes and HTML formats.

- Subscription Management leverages Notes' workflow and approval mechanisms to process subscriptions. It also includes a security module to ensure that material is made available by those authorized to receive it.

- Security enables Web browsers' security information such as registration, name and password to be stored in a Notes database. When a user attempts to access information on the Web or in Notes using a browser, the user's password and ID will be verified in the Notes database before access to the information is granted.
- Payment supports secure transmission of credit card data over the Web. When credit card information is entered for payment, a message for approval is sent to a credit card clearinghouse which sends back a message either approving or denying the purchase. Lotus plans to integrate support for SEPP (Secure Electronic Payment Protocol), the open method of secure credit card payments supported by IBM, into the Payment building block.
- Legacy Integration allows companies to tie data from mainframe systems into Web-enabled applications. Legacy Integration will support most standard databases including DB2, Oracle and Sybase.

Notes, and especially the new Release 4, has tremendous utility for any business that wants to get wired. Notes adds convenience as well as security and manageability to any Internet effort. With net.apps, a lot of the work is already done! No longer can you consider Notes to be just a departmental solution – your department can span the world.

Putting Corporate Data On The Net

Despite the strengths of the new Notes, there are still lots of relational databases that need to be connected to the Internet (or you may not yet have Notes or be fighting shy of the upgrade to Release 4 with all the Internet goodies). Oracle is the de facto high-end database because of its architecture and aggressive cross-platform support. Any heavy corporate data that needs to get wired will find Oracle's Web migration path of interest.

Oracle WebSystem

Oracle is almost synonymous with large-scale databases and their market domination extends from PC LANs to mainframes. Oracle recognized early on that the Web presented special opportunities and challenges to the use of business data in new areas. Their comprehensive WebSystem is a modular and

Oracle's WebServer Option pre-packages the elements that any Oracle customer and would-be Web publisher needs to put their data on the Web. One of its major strengths is its close integration with an existing Oracle 7 enterprise database.

complete Web extension kit for database publishing from top to bottom, bringing their Oracle7 flagship products to the Web.

The Oracle WebSystem consists of Web server and client products that provide integration with existing corporate data and enable the development of Web-based client/server applications. There are currently three products in the Oracle WebSystem: Oracle WebServer Option, Oracle WebServer and Oracle PowerBrowser.

The Oracle WebServer Option

The Oracle WebServer Option combines with your existing Oracle7 database and couples it to the global publishing power of the Web, giving data access to a broader range of users than possible before. With its built-in safeguards, you can open portions of your database to the public while keeping other parts strictly for internal consumption.

The WebServer Option is made up of two components: the Oracle Web Listener and the Oracle Web Agent. The Listener is an Oracle-developed HTTP Web server and the Agent is an enhanced CGI interface especially for Oracle servers.

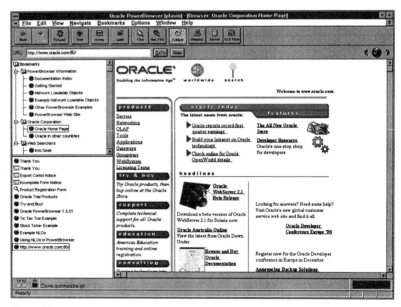

Figure 35

Figure 35
The Oracle WebServer architecture provides products and functionality at all levels from browser to enterprise databases.

The Oracle Web Listener is more than just a Web server – there are literally dozens of others to choose from dozens of software houses. Database applications are extremely complex and getting them to run right requires a lot of knowledge and expertise. Tuning can make a tremendous difference. The same is true of Web servers. Given that Listener is going to spend its life serving up pages delivered hot from an Oracle7 database, it stands to reason that some of that database tuning skill when applied to Web serving should yield good results.

Web Listener supports imagemaps natively. This feature allows you to use parts of an image as hyperlinks, e.g. click on a part of an image of the globe and get information on the respective country. The native processing of imagemaps gives considerably faster response than an unenhanced Web server running standard CGI imagemap coding.

In the Web's multinational environment, Oracle Web Listener makes it easy. There is support for type negotiation which enables the server to deliver different versions of the same object according to each client's preferences (for instance returning the user's national flag as part of the page makeup) as well as national language negotiation which returns the same document in different translations at the client's request.

Like any Web server, attention is paid to industry standards. The Oracle Web Listener can talk to any browser (though there are special capabilities available when it talks to Oracle's PowerBrowser) using the standard HTTP protocol. The Web pages returned to the browser can be static pages or dynamic documents constructed on the fly using Oracle Web Agent.

The Oracle Web Listener provides a Security Framework which supports two common authentication mechanisms: Basic

WebServer Architecture

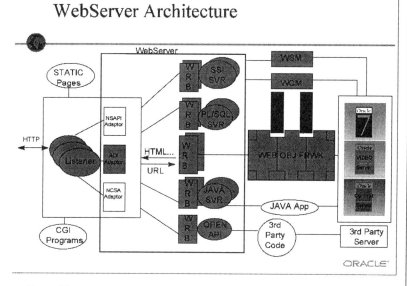

Figure 36

Figure 36

The Oracle WebServer has a broad range of modules that cater to all of today's Net needs but allows for future developments to be slotted in.

and Digest Authentication. Both mechanisms allow certain directories to be protected by user name and password combinations. However, Digest Authentication transmits encrypted passwords, while Basic Authentication does not, and is included only to support third-party Web browsers not capable of Digest Authentication.

With the fast pace of change in Web technology, flexibility is critical. Oracle Web Listener is an open-ended design with provision for future security extensions. Any HTTP-based security scheme can be added as and when it become available or desirable. The next release of Listener will be ready to support any security mechanism or mechanisms standardized by the World Wide Web Consortium which currently has before it SHTTP (Secure HTTP – a page-based security system) and SSL (Secure Sockets Layer – a data encryption system proposed by Netscape).

The Agent Of Change

The Oracle Web Agent is a generic procedural gateway that invokes Oracle stored procedures with an object-oriented, user-extensible framework. It is the Agent that provides the requisite CGI for managed, transparent and optimized access to data used to create dynamic Web pages. The Web Agent uses a specialized Developers Toolkit (bundled with WebServer Option). This is what generates HTML using Oracle's PL/SQL; the resulting page is delivered to the Web Listener which then serves the waiting client. CGI version 1.1 is fully supported to support work already done or those few operations that fit better under the basic CGI framework..

The Oracle Web Agent Developers Toolkit answers two challenges that the Web poses to any business that wants to harness its publishing power: rapid application development and data management. For a few static Web pages, these two nettles can be comfortably handled by human diligence alone but once dynamic pages fed by a database are contemplated, serious thought must be given to the difficulties in managing high volumes of data and quickly creating flexible connections to Web pages to meet changing business requirements.

Oracle's Developer Toolkit and the Oracle7 WebSystem are designed to overcome the difficulties of file-based storage. Web servers usually deal with static HTML documents and image files. As the Web site grows, managing the exploding sets of information becomes difficult and extreme care is required to modify old content entirely without destroying links. The data

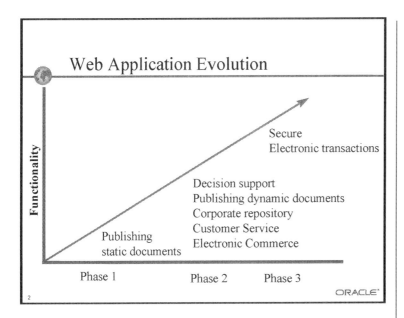

Figure 37

management techniques available with production-quality databases are well employed for managing growing Web sites.

The Toolkit is HTML 2 compliant and ready for the changes contemplated for HTML 3. Using PL/SQL to develop Web applications enables them to be ported across any operating system supported by Oracle (and their support list is nearly encyclopaedic) so there are no dead ends if your Web success requires more scalability than your current platform permits.

There is much to be said for automating as much as you can on a Web site. With the Oracle WebSystem, entire multi-screen applications can be packaged and treated as single Oracle7 database objects allowing Oracle's dependency checking, scaling, parallelism and replication features to be used.

The Oracle WebServer

The Oracle WebServer contains the same components as the WebServer Option but adds an Oracle7 database server (Workgroup or Enterprise Server depending on the platform used). It is intended for organizations that either don't already have an Oracle7 database or don't want to deploy a Web server extension to their existing database for security or operational reasons. This makes WebServer much more of a Web-in-a-box solution than the WebServer Option, limiting further the chances for haphazard implementation of Web publishing plans.

Both the WebServer and the Option include an administration utility that allows you to manage the WebServer components

Figure 37
The Web is on the move at many levels of business organisation. What is optional today is certain to be tomorrow's mission critical element.

Oracle WebServer has everything needed to publish data on the Web including the Oracle7 Workgroup or Enterprise server database.

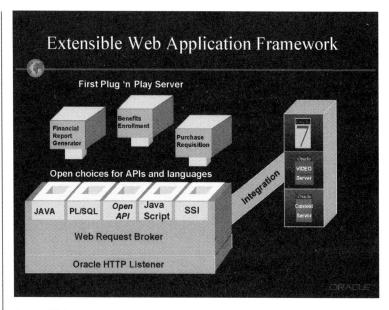

Figure 38 from page 6 WebSystem Product Briefing

from a browser screen (with the right access rights, of course!). The Oracle WebSystem has been constructed so that you can administer the Web Listener, Web Agent and the Oracle Enterprise server entirely using standard Web protocols. This de-skills many of the Web site maintenance operations, divorcing common housekeeping chores from a need to become adept at UNIX (or NT or …) file system commands.

Oracle PowerBrowser

While Oracle's WebServers can be accessed by any standard browser, Oracle has created PowerBrowser to extend the usefulness and capabilities of Web applications. It is also more than just a browser. It includes a BASIC programmable browser, an HTML authoring environment and a personal Web server.

PowerBrowser toes all the current standards lines, is fully HTML 2 compliant and supports the newer HTML extensions for tables, frames and backgrounds. Bookmarking, a vital browser function, is done with nested folders to make return visits easy. PowerBrowser also includes integrated email and Usenet newsgroup clients.

A lot of PowerBrowser's attraction comes from the Oracle BASIC engine which allows users to execute customized BASIC scripts directly on the client. This engine has its roots in Oracle PowerObjects, the database application development tool.

In addition, PowerBrowser incorporates an integrated

Figure 38
The benefit to business of the Oracle WebServer architecture is what you can plug into it. This isn't just a browser for surfers or a Web server for publishing marketing glossies – it's a way to use the Internet to run your business more efficiently.

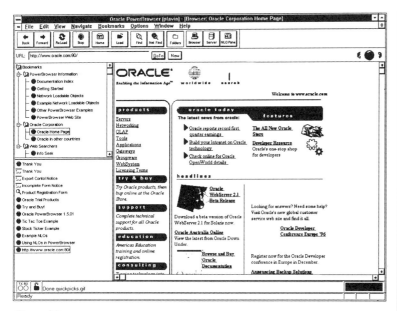

Figure 39

personal database, Blaze, that can effectively multiply your Web bandwidth with local storage of application-based data. Blaze is SQL92 compliant and any Web-based application that needs to store or manipulate data can use Blaze.

Almost every Web user has a need to publish certain information, if not to the world, at least to their colleagues and associates. PowerBrowser's Personal Server is a small-footprint Web server that runs on the same computer as the browser and let's coworkers share, peer-to-peer, in workgroup environments.

Going hand in hand with the Personal Server is the Personal Publisher which provides a WYSIWYG HTML page authoring environment. Users don't have to know the nitty-gritty of HTML with Personal Publisher – page creation is a drag and drop exercise for buttons and text boxes.

PowerBrowser also incorporates the Java technology introduced by Sun which lets users execute mini-applications or applets within PowerBrowser. In addition, Client-Side Processing, an Oracle load-sharing technology, allows developers to create operating system-specific applications running on the client computer (usually a PC).

The extensibility of PowerBrowser is ensured with the incorporation of Network Loadable Objects (NLO) which allow new document types to be displayed and executed within the browser. For instance, instead of loading a viewing module like Adobe Acrobat to view a high resolution document encoded with Adobe's Portable Distribution Format technology, using

Figure 39
The Oracle Power Browser is designed for the corporate desktop and incorporates a number of features missing from the headline-grabbing Microsoft and Netscape offerings. An internal, personal database and authoring capabilities make it a leading candidate for intranet use.

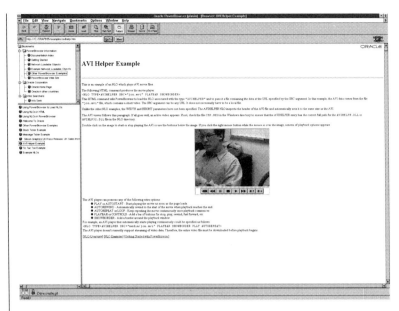

Figure 40

NLO you can view those documents natively within the browser with faster performance and increased security.

Why Oracle?

Obviously if you are already running an Oracle database, the choice is easy. No one else's tools are going to fit as well and integrate as completely as Oracle's even given the open system principles that form the foundation for most database vendors including Oracle. The benefits of using a well-integrated development and delivery system are fast application development times and fewer security lapses.

Performance in a large application is an issue. With Oracle7 components interfacing directly to Web Agent rather than through CGI, both performance and scalability will be improved. Backwards compatibility with CGI ensures that content created earlier will still function.

Portability will be a big issue for business Web publishers in the future. The growth rates exhibited so far in the Web mean that if you have a popular site or application, everyone will be knocking at your door. That in turns requires that you be able to ramp up your communications and Web serving capabilities at a fast pace, as well. It could be expensive and frustrating to develop a hot Web application only to see it melt down because you could not quickly move it to a bigger, faster computing platform.

Figure 40

Oracle's Net Loadable Objects are another way to animate and automate Web pages.

While it is early days for the Oracle PowerBrowser, it does point the way to the extended capabilities that will be needed in business-grade Web utilities in the future. Other browsers are passive viewing appliances not unlike TV. PowerBrowser promises to bring more intelligence and interactivity to the client end of the Web. Oracle is following the lead of other browser-ware authors and eliminating price as an objection to trying out its capabilities: it's utterly free for the asking.

The world is also waiting for the Network Appliance tale to unfold. It is being pushed hard by Oracle's entrepreneurial leader, Larry Ellison. Needless to say, if the inexpensive Internet terminals being developed are successful (each carrying a copy of PowerBrowser) it may make the extensions in PowerBrowser a necessity in the future for all Web cruising platforms. Microsoft has recognized the utility of the PowerBrowser already and has signed up for the technology for their own Internet Explorer browserware.

The Business Bottom Line

Getting your database wired with Internet technology can pay off. While the cost of integration is not negligible, the improvement in internal communications between individuals and groups can produce measurable benefit. For the outside world, the ability to browse your database contents can lead directly to sales. Increasingly, those sales orders can be taken directly from the Internet without any mediation. Information products can be delivered from your database directly to the buyer. If you can cut sales expenses and increase sales volume with the Internet, the technology is ready and waiting.

check the
WebExtra

8 Doing Business on the Internet – Legal Issues: Copyright, Contracts, Torts and Crimes

As far as the law is concerned, the Internet is a frontier, more like the Wild West of one hundred years ago than a modern, high-tech environment. Businesses need to consider the arrow-filled backs that sometimes result from pioneering. The Internet touches every single legal jurisdiction on the planet but you can't say that all of the laws apply simultaneously. When you use the Internet for your business, there is very little legal precedent to say what law protects you or what your liabilities are for Internet-triggered events on the other side of the world. Rather than a list of dos and don'ts, this chapter is meant to trigger discussions between businesspersons and their legal counsel.

> *"Business involves risk, sure, but we had no idea about some of the facets of risk that we assumed when we started our Web site. Fortunately, none of our lessons were learned the hard way. While we have learned that there are few hard and fast rules, guidance from our lawyers minimized the chances of an expensive error."*

Doing Business On The Internet: Business Issue

The laws that guide and protect us in our personal and professional lives have evolved over hundreds of years and are intimately tied to the geo-political space where we live. The Internet, by its newness and its transnational span, make it a very different sort of place, indeed, to transact business.

Someone living in the US, for example, can have a certain amount of detachment when considering the laws of the United Kingdom. Traditionally, only if they did business directly with a UK company in the UK or sent representatives to the UK would they ever come under the jurisdiction of its laws. The Internet, however, makes it easy for someone to trip up on a legal system that exists thousands of miles away from their PC keyboard or Internet server.

Want to sell religious pictures? You might be contravening the laws of Saudi Arabia. How about an Internet gambling casino? It's illegal to wager by wire in the US but it's OK (if you have a license) in Belize! Certain pictures are illegal in the UK but legal in the comparatively liberal Netherlands.

This chapter is not meant to be a definitive legal guidebook but seeks merely to sensitize businesspersons to the issues that may confront them when they venture to do business on the Internet. If you are going to use the Internet as an integral part of your business, you should have a talk with your legal department or counsel. They will be best placed to give you firm advice (or as firm as it can be given the state of change in the Internet's legal status).

Choice Of Law And Conflict Of Laws

Whenever the laws of two jurisdictions overlap on a business transaction, you have a problem that is referred to as a conflict of laws. This situation is very easy to envisage in an Internet marketplace. Party A is in New York in the US and Party B can be in California, the UK or China. The agreement that may come into force between them may be governed by one set of laws or the other or both.

There is no universal panacea for the confusion that this can cause except to provide for a choice of law in your contract documents. Even then it is no sure remedy: some legal jurisdiction somewhere may take the view that regardless of your stipulation, their law applies to the transaction.

A vendor in the UK can state that the laws of the United

Kingdom apply to the contract and, in fact, this is often done with maritime contracts due to the UK's strong naval heritage and the high regard for its maritime dispute resolution. But there is as yet no jurisdiction in the world that has excelled in its ability to deal with the important differences between traditional businesses and transactions conducted over the Internet.

It may well happen soon, though, and it may not be one of the big economic powerhouses. Internet law may become a "race to the bottom" like the choice of Delaware for a US-based company because Delaware has more corporate freedoms than many other US states. If you look at the offshore banking industry situated in places like Bermuda, the Cayman Islands, the Channel Islands and so on, you may see a parallel soon for Internet business law.

At this very moment, the laws that exist on the statute books and in cases decided in the past are being pulled, stretched and molded to fit the commercial reality that is coming into existence on the Internet. While many legal principles can be distorted to cover new areas, the Internet is proving to be a challenge.

Legislative recognition of the problems unique to computers and the Internet are slow in coming, perhaps due to the innate conservatism of law makers (and their electorates). In many cases new Internet-related laws are prohibitory – trying to set limits as to what you can and cannot do. The US's most recent attempt at this was the Communications Decency Act – an attempt to regulate Internet and online service content.

An appreciation of the Internet is slowly dawning on governments. Business flourishes where there is a stable legal framework for commercial relationships. As new laws are introduced, material for this chapter is likely to be a hot area on our WebExtra extension.

Contracts And The Internet

Like all the other legal issues that beset an Internet transaction, the details of forming a contract will vary from place to place. Common-law jurisdictions like the United Kingdom, the US (with the exception of Louisiana) and most English-speaking countries have fairly similar basic contractual elements.

A contract is generally considered valid if: there is an offer, an acceptance, and some form of consideration to support the contract; it is made by parties with legal capacity to contract ; it is about a legal subject matter; and the contract takes a specified form, if required (e.g. reduced to writing in the case of an interest in real estate). Just what constitutes each of these elements in every possible jurisdiction served by the Internet could fill many volumes.

An obvious example: if a book shop in Amsterdam, Netherlands agrees to sell a book of photographs to a 17 year-old in Florida, can the shop sue if they are not paid? It depends on whether the purchaser was of legal age (in Florida? the Netherlands?) and if the book was "legal subject matter." You may perhaps be aware of some books that are legal in the Netherlands but not in the US. (In some cases, there might be criminal liability attached to selling goods via the Internet where the transaction is legal in one place but illegal in another.)

Of course an Internet transaction will be largely negotiated by email or via a form in a vendor's Web site. Unless both parties are using something like Public Key Encryption it will be hard to prove that the agreement had not been modified in some way between dispatch and receipt. You may even have difficulty in proving that it was sent by one party or received by another and the timing of the messages. Is an electronic signature proof in court? Which court?

Common sense should prevail. Small-value transactions won't prove too difficult to swallow if they go wrong. If you are conducting high-value transactions, however, the Internet is at its most useful and least risky if you use it only for supplying information or perhaps negotiating details. For the moment, you are better off formally completing your contracts in the age-old way – on paper and signed in ink.

Your Relationship With Your IAP

One contract that every Internet-enabled business is likely to be involved in is the relationship with your Internet Access Provider. This, at least, is one agreement that is fixed to a particular body of law. This document covers what could be an important element of your business communications and deserves careful reading and perhaps negotiation.

While all and sundry are promoting the Internet as tomorrow's vital business communications conduit, there are pitfalls that exist today if your Internet business communications are interrupted – you may not have Internet access for some period of time or important email messages, sent by you or addressed to you, vanish into the ether.

While it is a fundamental principle of common law that any harm must have its redress, there is little so far that an Internet user can do, as a matter of practicality, about the quality of Internet communications. In the sweet bye and bye, once law

Figure 41

makers cotton onto the importance of the Internet in commerce, there may be statutory law to lay out the legal minutiae but that is unlikely to be settled in the short term.

Your legal relationship with your Internet service provider is governed by the terms and conditions (Ts and Cs) of your contract with them. Typically this is a pre-printed document, often in impressively small type and couched in the sort of language that have kept lawyers busy since contracts were invented. Given the inevitable slant that these contracts have in favor of the IAP and against the Internet user, it is important to check the level of service and the business reputation of your IAP before you sign.

UUNET PIPEX, a business-oriented IAP in Europe, has fairly typical Ts and Cs for any IAP anywhere. That means that they are largely written by the vendor's lawyers with careful attention to the business relationship from PIPEX's perspective. A careful perusal of your own contract is in order.

An Internet Access contract with PIPEX says that any condition or warranty which might be implied or incorporated within their contract by reason of statute or common law or otherwise is expressly excluded as far as the law permits. In plain language, they aren't promising anything above what is in the contract and what is required by law.

This is standard wording for a contract between two business parties. However, in contracts between individuals and a business, there may be statutory protections. Most IAPs will attempt to make their contracts as narrow as possible.

Figure 41

While the law is a pretty staid field of endeavour, the changes in the law and the Internet move much quicker. Any Net-bound business will need the guidance of a law firm that understands what the law is now and what it is likely to be in the not too distant future.

"You may not have much choice of terms with an Internet Service Provider – those sharp-dressed salesmen get very nervous if you want to make exceptions to their small print. You do , however, have a choice of which ISP you give your money to – that may be the most meaningful choice you have over terms.**"**

PIPEX promises to use all reasonable endeavors to provide a prompt and continuing service but it will not be liable for any loss of data resulting from delays, non-deliveries, missed deliveries or service interruptions caused by events beyond their control. Experience will prove whether or not PIPEX or indeed any other IAP fulfills this promise. The converse of this is that any interruptions that ARE within their control should entitle the customer to compensation. Proof, however, may be impracticably difficult.

Commercial contracts often contain standard language of limitation of liability. In no circumstances whatsoever (their words) will PIPEX be liable for economic or consequential loss. By this they are seeking to limit any damages that can be recovered by you to no more than the value of the service that they are charging you for. And PIPEX specifically excludes any warranty as to the quality or accuracy of the information received via PIPEX Internet services.

Although bluntly worded, the above-cited clause is fair because PIPEX obviously can't take on the obligation to insure that the Internet works every time, all the time, for every one of their customers from one end of the Earth to the other.

However, when your IAP is providing some other service, such as a maintained Web site, you should insist on performance guarantees. How many hits per hour can their installation sustain? How fast will they post upgrades to the site material? What happens if their server is offline?

No receipt or non-delivery of email may be the most frequent cause of complaint. Here's what you can do to ensure delivery of email that even the best IAP cannot guarantee: If you want to use your Internet connection for vital business correspondence, insist that the recipient confirm receipt of the message immediately. If you don't hear from them right away, you will know that something has gone awry.

Follow up crucial email with faxes or snail mail or telephone calls as appropriate in instances where absolute certainty of receipt is required. Make printed copies of your vital email just as soon as you have sent it, for the previous reason as well as for your filing clerks' continued employment.

The probative value of an email in court proceedings in any jurisdiction is not well settled but don't count on it being universally high for some time – it passes through too many hands and is too easily altered. Getting the contents of email admitted as evidence in a legal tussle will take the cooperation of the other side in the suit – and that is something you can't really count on.

If the misdirection or non-receipt of valuable email is the fault of your service provider, then you are stuck with the terms and conditions you signed. For that reason, make sure that any terms and conditions that YOU wish to include are made known to the Internet service provider when you sign up in writing. With the amount of competition going on between service providers, somebody is bound to take you up on any reasonable conditions that you request as part of a big ticket deal.

A reasonable T and C, at least from the point of view of an Internet subscriber, would be the application of liquidated damages in the event of a documented service interruption. Rather than trying to figure out how much each service interruption actually costs, you and the Internet service provider could agree on an amount that would be fair.

For instance, if the interruption was less than an hour, it would be worth a modest sum but if it lasted more than two hours it would be the equivalent of the daily rate you are paying for service. This is probably only going to make sense for leased line connections that cost a fair amount of money and also have more riding on them, so to speak. It is pointless to try to impose conditions on many IAPs, though, because most small and medium sized businesses do not have the necessary leverage.

The best Internet insurance is awareness of the limitations of service providers and the Internet in general. You can still enjoy the pluses if you take the minuses into consideration.

Intellectual Property And The Internet

The Internet is full of copyright material and almost equally full of violated copyright material. You can't access a Web site without copying its contents to your local machine where the copy will persist in your browser cache for some days. Is this a violation of copyright? What if you systematically copied everything in a competitor's site for purposes of competitive analysis?

While this kind of copying is causing relatively little economic damage (compared to the size of the computer industry as a whole or the national economy), knowing the basics of copyright, the rights and obligations that arise, is key to any business use of Internet resources like the Web, FTP or even email.

The photocopier machine began ringing the death knell of copyright protection. It made it easy and cheap to copy text and graphical material that was ostensibly covered by copyright. The owners of the copyright could scarcely be aware of the theft of their property every time it was photocopied. The personal computer has also been branded as delivering another lethal blow to copyright, in fact it has been likened to attaching a filing cabinet to a photocopier.

The Internet goes even further than that in slicing away at the protections that copyright affords authors, illustrators and businesses that are copyright holders. Because copyright material can be easily and cheaply transported around the world in large quantities, you could say that the Internet is like combining your corporate filing cabinet with a fax machine attached to a free telephone line.

Copyright law seeks to protect originality in a person's (or company's) expression. Under the UK's Copyright, Designs and Patents Act 1988, copyright extends to any literary, dramatic, artistic or musical work, sound recording, film, photograph, broadcast or typographical arrangement. While the Act doesn't specifically include materials sent zooming around the Internet in email, binary files or as World Wide Web pages, it is safest to assume that the Act will be extended to these transmission vehicles in due course. Clearly, at some point, the overworked legislators in Westminster or Brussels will have to address the unique characteristics of the Internet. Don't hold your breath, though, while they deliberate.

For a work to become copyrighted, it must be original and a substantial work. The courts have held that some work or effort must have gone into creating the material, but even the selection and arrangement of material that is not under copyright can lead to copyright rights for an originator or publisher.

Copyright is an enduring right. It can last for up to 70 years or 50 years after the death of the author or for other durations depending on where the copyright was established and the recognition of foreign copyright laws (governed by treaty, etc.). If copyright is violated, injunctive relief, civil damages and criminal prosecution can result. The former two are much more likely for small infringements; the latter is usually reserved for commercial copyright theft. In other jurisdictions around the world, copyright can last for longer or shorter intervals and differ in the sort of remedies available to wronged copyright holders.

Copyright can be contracted away. An author is often required by the terms of an employment contract to assign the copyright. Copyright material may be published under license, the terms to be agreed by the parties. Once again, the trappings of this aspect can differ in individual jurisdictions: French photographers will always retain copyright for their work regardless of their employment situation.

If you are publishing your company's Web pages, make sure that you own or are licensed to use any text or images that you incorporate. NB: Freelance photographers retain copyright to any photographs they take unless there is agreement to the contrary in the UK at least and probably in other jurisdictions as well. Those shots taken for the annual report should not be republished on the Web without subsequent agreement if all rights were not secured originally.

If you want to link to some other company's Web pages, the copyright of material on those pages is not your concern. The liability for violation of copyright lies with the publisher, in this instance the entity that put the material on the Web. Linking in does not result in liability for you, any more than would mentioning a book that contains purloined material in some business correspondence. However, there may be other pitfalls for you if you link to pages that contain defamatory material.

Of course, the Internet presents additional complications for copyrighted material. Not all national jurisdictions have similar copyright protections and, even if intellectual property laws are on the books, they may not apply the same degree of diligence to the prosecution of claims for violation of the law. Microsoft's recent software theft experiences in China by state-run duplication factories are a case in point.

It is the jurisdictional wrangles that make Internet copyright thieves feel that they are above the law. If a picture is taken from an American copyright source, placed into the Usenet in Holland and downloaded to a news server in the UK and then retrieved in France, who is going to chase whom? And where? For small, infrequent violations, expediency will win every time. *De Minimus Non Curat Lex* means that the law does not concern itself with trifles, and this is a legal concept often applied to copyright violation.

Piracy On The Cyber Sea

Larger publishers have been known to clear their legal throats in the direction of persistent offenders. There is much apocrypha about Playboy's lawyers having a word with posters to the `alt.binaries.pictures.erotica` newsgroup if their Playmate posting activities are excessive. There is no known instance of an actual prosecution, undoubtedly for the above-stated reasons.

When mass copyright violations occur against substantial

http://www.eudora.com

commercial interests (i.e. stolen applications program binaries), the copyright holder will attempt to act either alone or in concert with organizations like FAST (Federation Against Software Theft) to squash the offenders like bugs. Software piracy is big business even if you discount the obviously inflated figures bandied about by FAST and others that have a PR as well as an enforcement role in software theft cases.

Ignoring the obviously ripped-off commercial software from Microsoft and the other major publishers that you can sometimes download from clandestine bulletin boards or the Net (and use at your peril), the Internet is a source of a large volume of legal software of all qualities and functional levels.

However, there are at least two kinds of "free" software on the Internet. One is software that is there for the taking with licensing terms that allow for free usage and distribution. And then there is the so-called "free" software that is actually not free at all but something known as shareware. In all cases, the usage and distribution of software FTPed from servers on the Internet is governed by the licensing conditions that accompany the software.

The seminal newsreader for the PC, WinVN, has been placed in the public domain by its authors and can be freely used, copied and distributed by anyone for any purpose. The authors have even placed the source code in the public domain so that you can make alternations in its functioning to suit your particular purpose. It is an excellent piece of software, and few would quibble about the price (free).

An example of a more restrictive license for genuinely free software comes from Qualcomm which distributes a version of Eudora, their electronic mail application, via the Internet. They also sell a separate, more full-featured version. The "free" version is essentially a try-before-you-buy promotion. However, Eudora's licensing is still quite restrictive.

"This PC Eudora Software is owned by QUALCOMM Incorporated. QUALCOMM grants to the user a nonexclusive license to use this PC Eudora Software solely for its internal business purposes. The user shall not commercially distribute, sublicense, resell, or otherwise transfer for any consideration, or reproduce for any such purposes, the PC Eudora software or any modification or derivation thereof, either alone or in conjunction with any other product or program. Further, the user shall not modify the PC Eudora Software, other than for its own internal business use."

Beware if your Internet Access Provider gives you a "free" copy of Eudora – you may have an illicit copy of the software. There are a number of IAPs that are playing fast and loose with the distribution of software like Eudora. Would you want to do business with a service provider that promiscuously violates software copyright by illegally distributing software?

Honest IAPs pay tens of thousands of pounds in license fees to provide users with legal copies while they have to compete with others that don't pay a penny. Honest IAPs are angry ... but if you think they are angry, you should talk to the shareware authors that are being stolen blind by unprincipled Internet providers. Apparently, the problem runs from the very smallest to near the top.

The most popular browser of the moment, Netscape Navigator, is freely available by FTP download. However, one suspects that many tens of thousands of users are in violation of the licensing:

"GRANT. Subject to the provisions contained herein, Netscape Communications Corporation ("Netscape") hereby grants you a non-exclusive license to use its accompanying proprietary software product ("Software") free of charge if (a) you are a student, faculty member or staff member of an educational institution (K-12, junior college or college) or an employee of a non-profit organization; or (b) your use of the Software is for the purpose of evaluating whether to purchase an ongoing license to the Software. If you do not fit within the description above, a license fee is due to Netscape and no license is granted herein. If you are using a free version of the Software, you will not be entitled to support or telephone assistance."

The final sentence may be of some consequence to business users. However, the Netscape license terms continue:

"RESTRICTED USE. You may not copy the software, except for backup or archival purposes. Any such copy made by you shall be subject to this Agreement and shall contain all of Netscape's notices regarding copyrights, trademarks and other proprietary rights as contained in the Software originally provided to you. You may not lend, rent, lease or otherwise transfer the Software."

Netscape is quoted as having near 70 percent of the browser market which would require rather a lot of extended evaluations being conducted. On the other hand, if the Netscape browser is being distributed illegally by unscrupulous or ignorant IAPs, then you must take care where you place your business.

It is incumbent on businesses and their managers to make sure that the software installed in their PCs and servers is appropriately licensed for their use. Failure to heed this almost common-sense business precaution can lead to corporate embarrassment, at the least, and to fines or imprisonment for directors in egregious cases. The downside risk is not worth the cost of complying with software licensing. FTP to your heart's content but READ THE LICENSE.

Copyright And The Web

While there is likely to be little comeback for minor misuse of copyright materials, companies that are using the WWW as a marketing vehicle can little afford the opprobrium that would occur if they were seen to be flouting copyright conventions.

Make sure that you own what you publish on the Web as well as make it crystal clear to anyone browsing your Web site that you are the owner of the material that is found there and that they are free to copy it for whatever stated purposes you allow. Where you are offering free, "free," or limited-use software or information, make sure that the user is aware of their legal rights and obligations.

Usually, this is done by a notice page that must be traversed before access can be gained to copyright-protected material. Sometimes an email form must be completed so that the copyright holder knows the identity of individuals and businesses viewing the protected material.

As in most legal matters, that apocryphal ounce of prevention is worth a pound of cure. When you commission work, make sure that you use written contracts assigning the appropriate rights to your company for the duration of your use. Any potential future question can be resolved by negotiating an "all rights" deal. It may cost more to secure all rights and written contracts are always more hassle than a handshake, but they are worth it as litigation insurance.

Torts And The Internet

A tort is a harm caused to a person, his or her property or reputation. Tort liability is an Internet pitfall waiting for the unwary.

Mail-bombing, maliciously sending numerous or large email objects to someone, can be considered an intentional tort. So would sending someone a virus hidden in a file on purpose. But you don't even have to intend the harm for tort law to apply – the courts are full of cases where the harm was caused negligently.

In the US, products can give rise to a particularly nasty form of tort called strict liability. This legal doctrine can have profound effects: the light aircraft industry in the US almost disappeared because of the liabilities imposed on manufacturers.

One clear danger to a business using the Internet is an action for negligent harm due to improper professional advice. Lawyers, accountants, doctors and other professionals must guard against the contents of their email, FTP archives or Web pages giving advice where none is intended. If something goes wrong, there could be liability.

Perhaps this is too obvious – the law can deliver up some very well-camouflaged dangers. For instance, did you know that pages on the World Wide Web can give rise to liability for defamation? But the defamatory language doesn't even have to be on your own pages. Merely pointing to other pages that contravene defamation laws can create a liability for the owner of pages bearing the link.

Putting aside the thorny issues of jurisdiction, the disparate wording of diverse defamation statutes and practicality, wherever there is a publishing medium, someone's laws of defamation will apply. Anyone in a publishing capacity must seek to avoid making defamatory statements. Unfortunately, no concise definition of defamation that applies to all cases has been created.

However, defamatory statements are those that generally tend to expose the complaining party to hatred, ridicule or contempt, cause him or her to be shunned or avoided, lower him or her in the estimation of right thinking members of society generally or disparage him or her in his or her business, trade, office or profession. Judges often instruct juries that a statement is defamatory if it was capable of bearing a defamatory meaning and was also used in a defamatory manner.

Where the law is a bit murkier, however, is in the liability of anyone that provides Web hypertext links to a defamatory page.

Probably the last thing aspiring Web weavers want to fear are potential liabilities on their pages. Clearly, you should not include libellous material at all for altogether obvious reasons. But, less obviously, you need to consider whether linking to another page could make you responsible for what is on that other page that is beyond your control.

There is no precedent in law that establishes that this is the

http://www.twobirds.com/

case at the moment. However, it is very likely that under English law you could be sued if you link to a libelous page, based on an old precedent, according to Graham Davies of Bird & Bird.

An analogous case, decided in 1984, suggests that a court might find liability when faced with a Web page linking to libelous material. The old case established that drawing attention to existing libelous material can constitute the necessary "publication" to found liability for defamation.

Mr Hird, who lived in a village called Worth, obtained an injunction against two boilermakers nearby in the village, putting them out of business. Some people, including a Mr Wood, sought to arouse local sympathy for the boilermakers and a local gala provided an opportunity to raise donations for the destitute boilermakers. Someone (there was no evidence who) wrote a sign and put it up near the gateway leading to the gala; the sign referred to the boilermakers having been "ruined in their business and their living taken away by the animosity of one man." Mr Hird sued Mr Wood for libel.

Testimony showed that Mr Wood took up a position near the sign and continually pointed at the sign with his finger, thereby attracting it to the attention of all passers-by. He did this for a long time. The court held that this was evidence of publication, so that there was a case to answer.

The hypertext links of the Web provide a rather more sophisticated method of pointing at defamatory material but the analogy with Mr Wood sitting on his stool, pointing at the sign, is clear. If you include a pointer to someone else's defamatory material on your Web page, you could be said to have published it and thus be exposed to libel proceedings.

It is impossible to say if today's courts would apply century-old case law or seek some new interpretation that springs from an understanding (or misunderstanding) of the current publishing realities of the World Wide Web. It may well be found that Mr Wood was the precursor to a hypertext link.

Certainly, the facts of a modern case would clearly have an impact if, for instance, the contents of the selected pages had crossed the line into defaming speech after the link was created. This could happen if the link were to a Web periodical that changed its content frequently.

Apparently, there is no escape in adding a disclaimer on Web pages akin to the ones that adorn many email messages nowadays; disclaimers are ineffective in matters of defamation. It may be vital to your continued legal health to use disclaimers elsewhere in your Internet transactions, though. For instance, if you are providing software, you would not want become liable if it were to damage someone's computer, data or business relationships. Nor do businesses want employees' personal comments to create liability, in contract or tort, for the business.

Effective disclaimers are best derived from a first-hand knowledge of local practice and procedure. This is one area where you should talk to your lawyer rather than risk using an impressive-sounding but ineffective disclaimer.

Criminal Law And The Internet

While most businesses focus on commercial arrangements and seldom trespass into the realm of criminal law, the Internet makes it much more likely that you will do something that offends some criminal jurisdiction. Driving is a perfectly legal activity for a licensed individual almost anywhere in the world but recall that women are forbidden to drive in Saudi Arabia.

Most illegalities that involve the Internet today are likely to concern material defined as obscene or indecent by a local jurisdiction. Just what crosses the line is highly variable: a bare female face could cause offense in some Middle Eastern countries while a bare everything else may not in others.

A recent development that has attracted the criticism of many Internet users in the US is the Communications Decency Act that was made law in early 1996. Although commentators have found many shortcomings in the bill, it will remain US law until it is found to be unconstitutional by the United States Supreme Court.

The Act, according to analysts, dramatically restricts the First Amendment (free speech) rights of Internet users. Paradoxically, the very same materials and language which are legally available today in book stores and libraries would be illegal if posted on World Wide Web sites or in Usenet newsgroups. In the eyes of many Internet users, this bill transformed the Internet overnight from the freest communications medium to the most heavily regulated medium in the United States.

The Communications Decency Act, a small part of a massive telecommunications reform, imposes $250,000 fines and prison terms for anyone who posts "indecent" material, including the so-called "seven dirty words" that are barred from TV and radio broadcasting.

The Act renders publishing the text of classic works of fiction, such as *The Catcher In The Rye* or *Ulysses*, images of nudes such as Michaelangelo's Sistine Chapel ceiling, or rap lyrics, a criminal act if posted on the Internet forum.

While the stated aim of the bill was to protect minors from adult material on the Internet, the over-broad terms of the Act could potentially land organizations counseling breastfeeding of infants in hot water. Informational material concerning abortion, while legal if printed on paper, becomes illegal if published on the Internet. Pictures of naked infants gamboling at the beach in family Web pages could expose parents to arrest, fines and imprisonment. Surgeon-instructors posting instructional material will need to exercise caution if they want to show before and after photographs of post-mastectomy breast reconstruction. The legal standard applied by the Communications Decency Act takes no notice of the context of the image or text.

Undoubtedly, until legal tests are completed, the effect will be for US online and Internet access providers to remove pages and links from their Web sites that might contravene the Act, in effect "dumbing" down the Web to avoid any potential indecency, a heretofore legally undefined standard.

A multinational company in Milton Keynes, UK that is linked to the Internet was recently involved in a run-in with the Obscene Publications Squad of Scotland Yard. The case concerned 40 obscene photos that were stored on the company's computer by a 23-year-old male employee. The company blew the whistle for the police to come in. Their former computer graphics expert was in correspondence over the Internet with another individual in Birmingham who was also recently accused of using Birmingham University's computer system to store thousands of pornographic images.

Images held on a computer in digital form are the equivalent of photographs or negatives or printed material, according to police. There is little comfort for computer users or owners in the fact that unlawful images stored on a hard disk are not directly viewable. If the images are encoded or password locked, they are still unlawful but the problem for the authorities is one of access to evidence.

Any clued-in police force acknowledges that the Internet carries just about all of the varieties of human expression through hundreds of countries and legal jurisdictions and that police everywhere are powerless to stop one string of binary digits or another in email or Usenet newsgroups. The entré for the UK police is when the information is stored in Britain and contravenes the Official Secrets Act, the Obscene Publications Act, the Protection of Children Act or contains material that is otherwise unlawful (pilfered proprietary data including copy-righted material, defamatory matter, seditious tracts or whatever).

In discussing the matter of a company's exposure to prosecution with Scotland Yard, a police source compared an Internet server with an automobile. If a car is stolen and breaks the speed limit, the owner cannot be prosecuted for the offense. However, if the owner conspires with the driver to commit a crime then there may be a chargeable offense.

In the absence of clear-cut legal precedent or guidelines, common sense is the bottom line for company officials anywhere, according to the men in blue. A company policy should be created that makes downloading or storing material likely to be deemed unlawful a dischargeable offense. It is not up to a systems administrator, manager or director to interpret the finer points of the law so no further specificity is required in your employment policy.

If you are unlucky enough to find such material on your system you have several courses of action – delete the material, discharge the employee or call in the police. Recognize that you may be creating headlines for yourself, however, if you opt for the last alternative. An ounce of prevention may be worth a pound of cure. There are a number of products that will prevent access to newsgroups that are likely to harbor questionable material which, if used properly, could keep a company's computer resources from being misused and avoid uncomfortable interviews with lawmen.

The Business Bottom Line

The interaction between the law and the Internet is almost as complicated as the technical underpinnings of the Internet itself. However, while the techie bits remain constant throughout the world, the law that applies is vastly more variable. The only effective repellent for legal problems is care and knowledge so finding an Internet-aware counsel is vital. It may seem facetious but – "Good luck."

Appendix A
Getting Connected

If you have weighed up the pros and cons of bringing the Internet into your business, and reached the conclusion that it would be a good thing, one burning question remains: how does my business get connected? This appendix is not meant to be a definitive guide for every business, anywhere in the world but rather a practical approach to the issues for businesses confronting a first-time connection.

Business Issue

It costs a considerable amount of money in terms of hardware, software, telecoms, Internet access provider fees and training for your users to make the Internet part of your business. Getting wired isn't a decision to be taken lightly – it costs money even if your decision to use the Internet is motivated by overall cost savings or even revenue enhancement.

Choices, Choices

You will probably need at least two kinds of Internet access: A number of dial-up accounts for remote or traveling workers and a reasonably high bandwidth connection for your main site. And that may mean you may need more than one Internet access provider. While some businesses can get along with dial-up accounts only, if you are interested in putting your business on the Web you will either have to have your own dedicated connection or lease space on a commercial Web server.

If you have truly peripatetic staff, you may find that one of the national Internet access providers like PIPEX in the UK or UUNET in the US is going to give you the best coverage. PIPEX has a string of affiliates that can be pressed into service on a European basis, too. If you have international concerns, you may find that CompuServe or the Microsoft Network can reach farther. The IBM Global Network may be the best provider for very distributed businesses.

An Assortment Of Connections

At the bottom of the rung are online services and BBSs. They are lumped together because they have traditionally provided less than full Internet service. They may offer advantages of locale, ancillary services or cost but they are seldom good for more than an email gateway or sporadic access to Usenet newsgroups or perhaps just terminal connectivity to resources like Gopher or FTP. They are almost always accessed by modem which makes them fairly slow for anything other than individual use.

There is another, lower, class of Internet service, the UUCP connection, but this has been all but taken over by other, more efficient methods. UUCP Internet connections are not full connections (no Web access, for instance) but are capable of handling mail and news traffic.

CompusServe, America OnLine and the Microsoft Network

used to be classed as online service providers with just mail gateways but they have undertaken ambitious Internet upgrades so that you can reach their services via the Internet as well as use them to access the Internet itself. As a result they have become Internet access providers with unique strengths as long as you are interested in dial-up access only.

You can sometimes get better service, however, if you opt for Internet access from a dedicated provider. This type of service uses SLIP or PPP as the communication protocol that can put your PC or small LAN directly on the Internet. This type of access is again by modem and is restricted to no more than 28.8 Kbps – too slow for multiple simultaneous users, especially when you take into consideration the 30 second to one minute call set-up time. Also you are only on the Internet when you are dialed up and connected – SLIP and PPP connections are useless for Web or FTP serving. On the other hand, SLIP and PPP access are relatively cheap.

There are some service providers that, for a premium, will dedicate a modem at their central office for your use. Most Internet service providers have banks of modems and struggle to maintain a 20:1 or 30:1 ratio between users and modems. During peak times, busy signals and dropped lines are not infrequent with some Internet access providers that are strained to meet demand.

ISDN connections, which are increasingly available in the US and Europe, are an important alternative to leased line connections as they are much faster than dial-up connections. ISDN goes just as fast (64 or 56 kbps depending on your telephone company) as a leased line but is billed like an ordinary telephone call. Unlike modem dial-up connections, ISDN call set-up times are in fractions of a second. Internet service providers that have ISDN service can often provide inbound service for you.

To decide whether ISDN is a viable alternative for you requires a careful examination of the call and Internet access tariffs in your locale (as well as availability). It could wind up more expensive than a leased line, depending on your intended use and call charges. Many businesses use ISDN as a backup for their leased line: you only pay for it if you have to use it and if your leased line goes down, you can carry on with ISDN virtually unimpeded.

If you intend to offer interactive services, highly graphical presentations or attract a lot of callers, a 64 Kbps leased line may not suffice. Depending on where you are the alternatives may be a T1 or 2 Mbps or 'Megastream' service. Your telecoms provider can

" The single greatest determinant of success on your first Internet foray is setting your priorities and goals. This then informs many later decisions about platforms, budgets and so forth. "

" By far the thorniest problem faced by Internet novices is whether to have their Web site hosted by another organization or to do it in-house. The cheap way is obviously via a commercial host but it won't stay cheap or be satisfactory for other reasons for long. It's best to set a trigger point for bringing your site in-house for optimal control once you are on your way towards your initial goals. "

tell you what is available and how much it costs. Another important consideration is the lead time needed to install the service.

Installing and managing a leased line requires more than just familiarity with PC technology. Some kind of in-house support structure is vital because after the Internet service provider and the telephone company have verified that the service arrives at your router, you are on your own. Although a dedicated connection is at first blush the most expensive way to get wired, it provides an unimpeded presence on the Internet with full access to all services.

Leased line Internet access may even wind up being the cheapest way to go if your outbound usage is heavy. It is the only way to go if you want to establish a Web presence.

Be Size Wise

If your only Internet experience thus far has been through a dial-up connection (or none at all), it can be pretty difficult to estimate the size of Internet connection and the amount of server horsepower you will have to dedicate to feeding it.

It is true that you can take a notebook PC and hook it to a router and use it as an email host, FTP site AND Web server on a 64 Kbs leased line. The notebook may have advantages in its size and independence from mains electricity but if the notebook Web site gets busy at all or there is a lot of FTP traffic or many emails arrive with large binary attachments, its strengths will pale beside its weaknesses.

While there is a big temptation to put as much functionality as possible in a single box, there are reasons why you might want to dedicate separate machines for each Internet function. You want your email to arrive and leave unfettered by updates to the Web server configuration or security breaches on the FTP server. There is also the temptation to use the server as a cc:Mail SMTP gateway, router and firewall, too. While it is technically possible to build all of this into a single box, prudence suggests that putting all of the eggs in one basket is asking for it.

For anything except the most tentative initial Internet experiments, your budget needs to encompass a number of functional building blocks with a degree of independence. Routers and firewalls fit well together, as does FTP and email access under some circumstances. Some consolidation can be helpful to balance the load and reduce the statistical probabilities of failure.

As well as administrative efficiency, you have to consider the sources and type of Internet traffic. It basically comes down to the number and sizes of requests and replies. Requests for files and information are generally small and the replies can be small or multi-megabyte. Demand forecasting is a black art and you can be sure that there will be peaks and troughs in your server operation.

Although some books are tempted to provide what appears to be a mathematically rigorous method for calculating server size, the truth is you will never know until you stick your toe in the water. If you can get a feel for the approximate size of your Web pages and the size of files on your FTP site and combine this with a stab at your anticipated traffic level, you can get an indication of how many bits per second will be flowing over your Internet connection. Web and FTP servers may require the most bandwidth but mail, if used with list-serving features, can consume a lot of outgoing bandwidth.

Mail is the least CPU-intensive activity and Gopher, FTP and Web activity consume CPU power in proportion to the number of queries that they receive and the size of their replies. Web servers, because of inline graphics, can get intensive, as can any Web application that requires database access. If you want to plan for the future, putting your server on a hardware platform that supports CPU upgrades or additional CPUs would be a smart move. While it is possible to just "add another server" if the going gets hot, it will save administrative time and effort if your critical Internet server is scalable.

Historically, Sun enjoyed dominance in the Internet server market in part because of the ease with which the hardware and the software could be scaled up. Silicon Graphics, HP, IBM, DEC and other RISC-based UNIX systems are also popular. Windows NT on Intel Pentium and Pentium Pro platforms is emerging as the inexpensive, but as yet unproven, alternative.

Disk budgets are secondary to CPU sizing but still important. There are a plethora of log files that grow in proportion with the popularity of your site. Unless managed, they will cover your disks with information of marginal utility. It is important to select a disk architecture that will allow graceful upgrades and a measure of failure resilience. If you are hoping to conduct commercial transactions, then nothing less than a RAID (Redundant Array of Inexpensive Disks) that provides mirroring and striping and possibly hot swapability will do.

" The Net really brings home the point that the various UNIX vendors have been banging on about for years: the best platform is the one that delivers scalability, portability and interoperability. It's essential not to get locked into one vendor's product plans or capabilities – no matter how attractive the brochures are or how pervasive their presence in other parts of the computing world. "

Service Quality Is Paramount

The next major hurdle after sorting out the means of connection that suits your plans and trying to estimate the size of the server required is choosing the right Internet access provider. The business of providing commercial Internet access has seen significant growth over the past few years (it is almost keeping up with the Internet explosion) and the scope and range of services provided by one supplier may be totally different than those provided by another – a situation not dissimilar to the PC boom of the early 80s with garage-based manufacturers competing with Big Blue.

When looking for an access service provider, it is important to evaluate the quality of service they provide down the wire as well as beyond the connection itself. Draw up a list of questions that includes the following:

- How reliable is the network connection? Do they offer any guarantees?
- Does their network perform? Ask for graphs of throughput.
- Are there any restrictive access provisions? How will your traffic be routed?
- What other value-added services does the provider offer? Web space? Security?
- Is the access provider accessible? When you have a problem can you get through to the right people?
- Is their connection secure? Ask about their peering arrangements and system redundancy as well as data protection.
- And, always the bottom line, what does it cost and what does that cost include?

Choosing The Internet Access Service Provider

Open any computer-related magazine and you will see evidence of the rapid growth in the number of advertisements for Internet access service providers. More than 100 have started up in the UK alone in the past two years – in the US they now number in the hundreds. While there is a lot of hype in the press about different browsers and other Internet tools, reviews of access service providers tend to take a back seat because of the difficulty of establishing objective measures. It is up to the individual user or appointed employee to research the service provider and make recommendations based on the local market and your business's particular needs.

What To Look For

Reliability

Will I always have a network connection that works? That is always a useful starting point because the Internet has enough uncertainties without using a dodgy provider. The most important feature of a good connection is that it connects when you want it to, it stays connected all the while you want it to, and it is ready and available at any time. Stability in service is very important. If constant network outages or equipment downtimes are problems, you will not be happy with the service offered. Ask your prospective supplier to show you reliability data and talk to other customers. Word of mouth is often the best recommendation.

Troubleshooting

Even the best network in the world can suffer from lapses and outages. The critical factor here is not that the network is down but how quickly the provider can recognize the problem and fix it. Complacency or downright misdirection are all too common. Ask about the provider's network monitoring tools, ask about downtime and ask about what measures they take to solve problems so that disruptions to customers are imperceptible.

Your work practices may differ from those of the access service provider – you may need to be online at odd times of the day and night. Check with them to make sure there is 24-hour support coverage. If you are in the middle of a mission-critical data transfer at 3.00 a.m. and you experience a technical network problem, you need support and a procedure for solving problems right then. Tomorrow may be too late.

Performance

While performance may be at an acceptable level today, ask your potential access provider about their plans to keep abreast of new technology and improve network facilities for their customers. Ask about planned hardware and software upgrades, modem upgrades, new technology implementations. If their expansion plans or upgrade strategy doesn't seem aggressive, is this the one for you?

Restricted Access

Network performance is related to the access service provider's own network configuration – who is connected to whom, how

"There's no one best Internet Service Provider. They all have feet of clay. Spreading the risk is the smart thing to do. If the Net is important to your business, pick more than one even though it might mean added expense. Leased line customers should have ISDN backup and some dial connections. If they are with different ISPs all of your eggs won't be in one basket."

they are connected, and where. The access provider's connection to the Internet can determine if certain kinds of traffic are subject to restriction. If you are using a connection primarily for business and commercial transactions, it is important that the provider allows, supports and encourages commercial use and has at least one commercial gateway.

Some of the networks do not allow direct user connections. There are many networks, and larger network providers will generally have multiple routes to other networks. If you have a particular need, you may want to try to research the networks you will cross to make sure that there aren't any strange Acceptable Use Policies in place, holdovers from the pre-commercial Internet.

Since the Internet works by a chain of connections, you should look at where the slowest link in the chain is. You may have the fastest connection in the world but if you encounter slower connections between you and your important contacts, an expensive fast connection is of no value.

Value Added – Support And Service

With a competent MIS staff or in-house gurus, you may not think you require any technical services from your provider. However, Internet developments are moving very quickly and it may be helpful to take advantage of knowledgeable staff. Newsletters, bulletin boards, announcements, dedicated help lines and online archive facilities all add to the services offered by the provider. A quick check of their FTP server will show if they are making the "Best of the Net" easily accessible to their subscribers.

If a company is standardizing on one access service provider who makes it easy for their customers to access Internet applications using a common interface, look to see if the provider organises specialized training courses, not only on how to access the Internet but how to effectively use all of its various components to a business advantage. A Lotus specialist can provide added value to cc:Mail and Notes users. A little training can increase productivity.

Customer Relations

Remember, the access provider is working for you and trying to help you or your business be successful. As with any business supplier, establish a good relationship with the service provider. Make sure that there is a representative there for you whenever you need assistance.

References

Talk to other customers who have similar business issues. Ask how the service provider helped them. If you are uncertain about the financial stability of the provider, do a credit check on them. Treat them like any other supplier.

Security

This is a big issue. Both small and large businesses alike should work with their access provider to understand what kind of preventative measures are appropriate and what kind of problems have occurred recently. In addition to securing the connection, ask about the provider's own security measures – is data held on their servers secure? Is it being viewed, disseminated without your permission or accessible to unauthorized personnel? If you are happy with the access service provider's own security measures, you can be reasonably confident that your business is safe in their hands.

"A good security consultancy is worth its weight in gold. Their outside perspective makes it easier to spot the chinks in your armor – and make uncomfortable suggestions regarding internal policies."

The Business Bottom Line – What Is It Going To Cost My Business To Get Connected?

Individuals and small businesses may want a dial-up connection or ISDN whereas medium-sized to large businesses will want a leased line. Prices vary enormous from one supplier to another but the most expensive does not necessarily mean the best. Neither does the least expensive necessarily mean that you are getting a good deal. Shop around and get quotes and compare the features offered and their prices.

Do not be tempted by offers of a free connection – there ain't no such thing as a free connection. What may appear on the surface to be a great deal may be fraught with problems. If you can find such a thing as a free connection, it may be fine for an individual for a limited time span but how long can you tolerate inefficiency and being put last because you are not a paying customer? This should not be considered for any serious business user.

Some sites may offer to sell a piece of their link, in other words a shared connection. This again may appear like a good deal, especially to a business which is not totally convinced that a full-blown Internet connection is the way forward just yet, but there are so many other considerations to ponder and a cheap link is false economy.

Don't forget – your place on the Internet has a lot in common

check the

WebExtra

with your physical business premises. What conclusions do you draw about a business that is constantly changing its address, not open at the advertised times (which on the Internet is 24×7) or can't deliver the goods?

While every business may have minimal hardware to get connected, startup costs for additional hardware like dedicated servers, routers, installation of extra telephone lines, and so on may add an extra dimension to the budget. Budgeting for an Internet connection is essential. An Internet connection itself is not that expensive but taking into consideration all the attendant components, it soon ramps up and will become a significant item in the accounts.

A hidden cost may be in the contractual obligation with your access service provider. What happens if you wish to change – are there any financial penalties involved? As with any business agreement, look carefully at the terms and conditions.

Once you have made the decision to get connected, what happens if you want to change your provider for one reason or another? Maybe another provider is offering better value for money, maybe another one is more technologically advanced. Maybe it just didn't work out. For whatever reason, it can be expensive to change access service providers. For individuals and small businesses using a dial-up account, it is rather like moving offices and change of address notices will have to be sent out, assuming that you can get reconnected in good time. Medium and large organizations will have to face considerable cost in moving suppliers, greater administrative overhead, and inevitably some disruption to business.

Choose carefully.

Appendix B
Getting Started with
Dial Trial

What is PIPEX Dial Trial?

Your CD-ROM includes a copy of the popular and easy to use PIPEX Dial software, together with a 28 day, unlimited Internet account with the PIPEX Dial service. Netscape Navigator is provided enabling you to browse the World Wide Web, send and receive email and participate in Newsgroups. Internet access is available throughout the UK for the cost of a local telephone call.

What You Need

- A PC with 486 DX-33 processor (or better)
- Modem running at V.32 (9600 bps) or faster. Faster modems may need a 16550 serial port to operate at top speed. Modem speeds up to 33.6 kbps are supported.
- A minimum of 4Mb of memory (8Mb is recommended)
- 8Mb hard disk space
- Windows 3.1, 3.11 or Windows 95

PIPEX Dial is intended for use on standalone PCs only.

Installing PIPEX Dial

Before installing PIPEX Dial, you should have the following information to hand:

- The number of the COM Port to which the modem is connected
- The PIPEX Dial Registration Card with your unique Product Code and Serial Number (if this has not been included with your CD-ROM, please call 0500 474739)
- The make, model and maximum speed of your modem

To connect your modem and install PIPEX Dial:

1. Ensure that the modem – whether it is an internal card or connected to an external COM port – is installed and switched on. Plug the modem's phone cable into a nearby telephone socket.
2. Prepare the modem to use the"factory default" settings.
3. Switch on the computer and start Windows.
4. Close down fax or other communications software running on your computer.
5. From Program Manager Win3.1/3.11 or Start menu Win95, select the Run option. From your CD-ROM drive go to sub-directory PIPEX and run Setup.exe.

At the end of the installation, the setup program will automatically restart your PC.

Configuring PIPEX Dial

When running PIPEX Dial for the first time after installation you will need to select the appropriate COM port and modem type from the drop down boxes. If your modem speed is not included in the list provided, select the next higher speed rather than the next lower. If you are using an internal exchange and need to get an outside line, select a Dial-out prefix from the Phone Configuration box.

Registering PIPEX Dial

Full Internet access is not possible until you have registered as a PIPEX Dial user. Clicking the Connect button connects you to the PIPEX Dial registration service. To register click the Register button and follow the instructions given. Enter your Product Code and Serial Number, together with your personal details. A Username and Password will be automatically assigned to you. It is very important to keep a note of these for future reference. Finally, click on the Webpage link to complete the software installation process.

The first time you run PIPEX Dial as a registered user, the Phone dialogue box appears again to allow you to select a point of presence. UK users should select London if the area code of the line you are calling from is 0171 or 0181 and All UK all areas outside London (including the Channel Islands and the Isle of Man).

You will now have unlimited Internet access for a period of 28 days. After this time, you will be able to subscribe to the PIPEX Dial service by following the on-line instructions or by telephoning FreeCall PIPEX Dial on 0500 474739.

Uninstalling PIPEX Dial

PIPEX Dial is supplied with a program which can be used to remove the product entirely from your computer.

PIPEX Dial Support

If you have a question not covered here, there are many ways to obtain technical support for your PIPEX Dial Trial.

Support Web Pages

If you can connect to the Internet start by reading the PIPEX Dial Support Services Web pages at `URL http://www.dial.pipex.com/` These pages contain a wide variety of useful information and answers to commonly asked questions.

Email

If your question is not answered, please email `support@dial.pipex.com` with full details. If your problem is related to your PC or software please include information about how your PC is set up and attach to the message any configuration files you feel are relevant.

Telephone

If you cannot connect to the Internet or are having problems using your email program you can telephone 0541 50 60 67.

Glossary

56K	US ISDN service. A 64 kbps digital telephone circuit with 8 kbps used for signaling. Also called DDS or AND.
64K	European and US ISDN service. A 64 kbps digital telephone circuit (DS). "Clear Channel" is 64 kbps where entire bandwidth is used.
Archie	A system for locating files that are publicly available by anonymous FTP.
ARPANet	An experimental network established in the 1970s where the early Internet implementations were tested. No longer in existence.
API	Applications Programming Interface.
ASCII	American Standard Code for Information Interchange. Seven-bit ASCII has 128 characters – sometimes referred to as 'plain text'.
Backbone	A high bandwidth access point to which other networks are connected.
Bandwidth	The carrying capacity of a data communications connection. It is generally measured in (kilo or mega) bits per second.
Baud	The number of state changes per second in a data transmission. For example, a 28 000 baud modem changes the signal it sends on the phone line 28 800 times per second. However, each change in state can correspond to multiple bits of data so the actual bit rate of data transfer may exceed the baud rate. See bits per second.
BIND	The UNIX implementation of DNS. It stands for "Berkeley Internet Name Domain."
BinHex	A file compression standard used in the Macintosh world.
Bits per second (bps)	The speed at which bits are transmitted.
Browser	A program that interprets and displays HTML documents; the viewer for Web documents.
BTW	An abbreviation used in email and news for "By The Way."
Byte	A set of eight bits.
Cache	A temporary storage area designed to increase the apparent speed of operation when data is stored remotely.
CGI	Commm Gateway Interface.

Chat	See IRC chat.
CIX	Commercial Internet Exchange; an agreement among network providers that allows them to exchange commercial traffic.
Client	A local software application that works in conjunction with software on a server on the local network or Internet.
Cracking	Breaking into a computer system.
Cryptography	The science of using mathematics to encrypt messages.
CSU/DSU	Channel Service Unit/Digital Service Unit. Interfaces the telephone company's line with a V35 or RS232 connection to your router or other network equipment.
DBMS	Database Management System.
Decryption	The transformation of encrypted text into plain text.
Dedicated line	See leased line.
Dial-up line	(i) A fairly slow method of connecting to a computer by calling it up on the telephone. (ii) A port that accepts dial-up connections.
DNS	The Domain Name System; a distributed database system for translating computer names (like www.itcpmedia.co.uk) into numeric Internet addresses (like 123.456.123.456) and back. DNS allows you to use the Internet without remembering long lists of numbers.
Email	Electronic mail; a system which allows a user to compose, transmit and receive messages through a computer network, including the Internet.
Encryption	The transformation of plain text into unintelligible text using numerical methods for security purposes.
Ethernet	A local area network standard that incorporates several types of wiring and speeds from 2 to 100 million bps. Computers using TCP/IP are frequently connected to the Internet over an Ethernet.
FAQ	Either a frequently asked question or a file of frequently asked questions. Many Usenet news groups maintain FAQ lists so that participants won't spend a lot of time answering the same questions.
Finger	A tool that helps provides information about other Internet users.
Firewall	A system that isolates or protects a site's computers or networks from external access, as through the Internet. Firewalls screen all traffic, allowing some to pass through that has been security checked and disallowing the rest.
Flame	A virulent and (often) personal attack against the author of a Usenet posting. "Flames" are unfortunately common. People who write flames are known as "flamers." Flamers often have other personality defects.
freeware	Software that you can download from the Internet freely and use or redistribute freely.
FTP	(i) The File Transfer Protocol; a protocol that defines how to transfer files from one computer to another. (ii) an application program which moves files using the File Transfer Protocol (FTP).
Gateway	A computer system that transfers data between incompatible applications or networks, allowing two incompatible applications to communicate over the same network (like email systems with different formats).
GIF	An image file format that is common on the Web.

Gopher	A menu-based system for exploring Internet resources.
Helper	An application that helps a Web browser by displaying an image, playing a sound recording or performing some other subsidiary task.
HTML	Hyper Text Markup Language.
HTTP	Hyper Text Transfer Protocol; the standard protocol used for communications between servers and clients on the World Wide Web.
HTTPD	Hyper Text Transfer Protocol Daemon; the process that actually does the serving on an HTTP server.
Hypermedia	A combination of hypertext and multimedia.
Hypertext	Documents that contain links to other documents; selecting a link automatically displays the second document.
IAB	The Internet Architecture Board; the council that makes decisions about Internet standards and other important issues.
IETF	The Internet Engineering Task Force; a volunteer group that investigates and solves technical problems, and makes recommendations to the IAB.
Internet	When capitalized, the global "network of networks" that are connected using the IP protocol. When lower case, the connection of any two networks.
Internet Access Provider	An IAP is an organization that provides connections to the Internet. Anyone that wants to connect a network or single PC to the Internet has to work through an Internet (access) service provider.
Internet Service Provider	An organization that provides connections to the Internet. Anyone that wants to connect a network or single PC to the Internet has to work through an Internet (access) service provider.
Intranet	A network inside the firewall that uses Internet applications and utilities to deliver information to employees.
IP	The Internet Protocol; the most important of the protocols on which the Internet is based. It allows a packet to traverse multiple networks on the way to its final destination.
IRC	Internet Relay Chat; an Internet-based application that allows users to interact in real-time, unfortunately more like a Citizens Band radio than is comfortable.
IRC chat	A service that allows large group conversations over the Internet.
ISDN	Integrated Services Digital Network; a kind of dial-up connection offering higher speed connections than you can get with a modem.
ISO	The International Organization for Standardization; an organization that has defined a different set of network protocols, called the ISO/OSI protocols. The ISO/OSI protocols were to eventually replace the Internet protocols. Wrong.
ISOC	The Internet Society; a membership organization whose members support a worldwide information network. It is also the governing body to which the IAB reports.
JPEG or JPG	An image format defined by the Joint Photographic Experts Group; common in Web documents.
LAN	Local Area Network.
LCA	Lotus Communications Architecture.

LCS	Lotus Communications Server.
Leased line	A permanently connected private phone line between two locations. Leased lines are typically used to connect a moderate-sized local network to an Internet service provider.
Link	A highlighted bit of text (or graphic) on an HTML page that can take you to other HTML pages or Internet resource (such as an FTP site).
MAPI	Messaging API.
MIME	Multipurpose Internet Mail Extensions; a standard that allows graphics and multimedia information to be included in Internet documents such as email messages.
Modem	A contraction of modulator/demodulator. A modem connects a computer to a telephone line and then to another modem. Modems transfer data at speeds ranging from 300 bits per second (bps) to 28.8 kbps. Modems also provide higher speeds and support other media than ordinary telephone lines.
Mosaic	The first browser for the World Wide Web that supported hypermedia.
MPEG or MPG	An image file format defined by the Motion Pictures Experts Group.
MTA	Message Transport Agent.
Multimedia	Documents that include different kinds of data; for example, plain text, audio, graphics, moving images (animation or video) or a "live"spread-sheet.
NIC	Network Information Centre, usually means the InterNIC; an important administrative role in Internet coordination.
NFS	The Network File System; a set of protocols that allows you to use files on other network machines as if they were local.
ODBC	Open Database Connectivity.
OLE	Object Linking and Embedding.
OSI	Open Systems Interconnect; another set of network protocols.
Packet	A bundle of data. On the Internet, a data stream is broken up into packets; each packet travels the network independently of any others. Depending on technical factors, packets can vary from 40 to 32 Kbytes, but are usually less than 1500 bytes.
PGP	Pretty Good Privacy; a freeware program written by Phil Zimmermann which performs public and private key cryptography and key manage-ment.
Ping	A command used to help network managers or users identify problems. Ping is a command that sends Internet Control Message Protocol (ICMP) echo requests and echo reply messages.
Plug-in	Applications that enhance the functionality of Web browsers. They are faster than helper applications.
POP	(i) Point of Presence for network services or (ii) Post Office Protocol for email services. The two are unrelated.
Port	(i) A number that identifies a particular Internet application. The "port number" identifies the application. (ii) One of a computer's physical input/output channels (i.e. the plug on the back).
POTS	Plain Old Telephone Service.

PPP	Point to Point Protocol; protocol that allows a computer to use the TCP/IP (Internet) protocols with a standard telephone line and a high speed modem. PPP is a new standard for this which replaces SLIP. Although PPP is less common than SLIP, it is increasing in popularity.
Protocol	A protocol is just a definition of how computers will act when talking to each other. Protocol definitions range from how bits are placed on a wire to the format of an electronic mail message. Standard protocols allow computers from different manufacturers to communicate; the computers can use completely different software, providing that the programs running on both ends agree on what the data means.
Proxy server	An Internet server that provides indirect access for an internal network, part of a security firewall.
RFC	Request for Comments; a set of papers in which the Internet's standards, proposed standards, and generally agreed upon ideas are documented and published.
RISC	Reduced Instruction Set Computer.
Router	A system that transfers data between two networks that use the same protocols. The networks may differ in physical characteristics (e.g. a router may transfer data between an Ethernet and a leased telephone line).
RTF	Rich Text Format.
RTFM	A common abbreviation used in email and news, referring the reader to the software or hardware documentation. It stands for Read The F****** Manual.
SATAN	Security Administrator Tool for Analyzing Networks; a probing tool that probes a system from outside, just as a cracker or attacker would.
SANTA	Security Administrator Network Tool for Analysis; if you don't like the name SATAN, use a script called repent and change all references from SATAN to SANTA.
Search engine	A program that provides a way to search for specific information on the Web or on different servers.
Server	(i) Software that allows a computer to offer a service to another computer. Other computers contact the server program by means of matching client software. (ii) The computer on which the server software runs.
shareware	Software you can download from the Internet and evaluate subject to license restrictions.
Shell account	Also known as a terminal account. A dial-up connection where you log in to a host computer that is on the Internet (you, in fact, are not).
Signature	A file, customarily no more than five lines long, that people often insert at the end of electronic mail messages or Usenet news articles. A signature contains minimally a name and an email address. Signatures usually also contain postal addresses, and often contain silly quotes, ASCII pictures and other things.
SLIP	Serial Line IP; a protocol that allows a computer to use the Internet protocols (and become a full-fledged Internet member) with a standard telephone line and a high speed modem. SLIP is being superseded by PPP but it is still in common use.

Smiley	Smiling faces used in news and mail to indicate humor. The most common smiley is :-). There is also :-(which is frowning. There are many variations on the smiley theme.
SMTP	Simple Mail Transfer Protocol.
SQL	Structured Query Languages.
T1	1.54 Mbps service.
TCP	Transmission Control Protocol. One of the protocols on which the Internet is based. A connection-oriented reliable protocol.
TCP/IP	Transmission Control Protocol and the Internet Protocol, the common networking language for all computers on the Internet.
Telnet	(i) The terminal emulation protocol that allows you to log onto another computer system on the Internet. (ii) An application program that allows you to log in to another computer system using the Telnet protocol.
URL	Uniform Resource Locator; a system of standard addresses for different types of Internet resources that can be reached through a Web browser.
Usenet	An informal collection of systems that exchange "news." Usenet operates in a similar fashion to "bulletin boards" on other networks. Usenet existed before the Internet but today uses the Internet to carry its traffic.
UUencoded	A method of encoding binary data for transmission over the Internet.
UUCP	UNIX-to-UNIX copy; a utility for copying files between the UNIX systems on which the core mail and Usenet news services are built. While UUCP is still useful, the Internet provides a better way to do the same job.
Veronica	A service similar to Archie, which is built into Gopher. Veronica allows you to search all Gopher sites for menu items (files, directories, and other resources).
Viewer	An auxiliary application that helps a Web browser display a data type.
WAIS	Wide Area Information Servers; a system for looking up information in databases across the Internet.
WAN	Wide Area Network.
WWW	World Wide Web; a hypertext-based system for publishing information and accessing Internet resources.

Bibliography

!%"@:: Addressing & Networks	Donnalyn Frey & Rick Adams, O'Reilly & Associates, 1994
Building Internet Firewalls	D.Brent Chapman & Elizabeth Z. Zwicky, O'Reilly & Associates, 1995
Computer Crime: A Crimefighter's Handbook	David Icove *et al.*, O'Reilly & Associates, 1995
Connecting to the Internet	Susan Estrada, O'Reilly & Associates, 1993
Doing Business on the Internet	Mary J. Cronin, Van Nostrand Reinhold, 1994
Internet: Getting Started	April Marine *et al.*, PTR Prentice-Hall, 1994
Internetworking with TCP/IP, Vol. 1	Douglas E. Comer, Prentice-Hall International, 1991
Managing Internet Information Services	Cricket Liu *et al.*, O'Reilly & Associates, 1994
Navigating the Internet with Windows 95	Ned Snell, Sams.net Publishing, 1995
Netscape Navigator	Jason J. Manger, McGraw-Hill Book Company, 1995
PGP: Pretty Good Privacy	Simson Garfinkel, O'Reilly & Associates, 1995
Practical Unix Security	Simson Garfinkel and Gene Spafford, O'Reilly & Associates, 1991
Spinning the Web: How to Provide Information on the Internet	Andrew Ford, International Thomson Computer Press, 1995
Teach Yourself Web Publishing with HTML	Bruce Morris, Sams.net Publishing, 1995
The .net Bible	Richard Longhurst, Best Boy, Future Publishing, 1995
The .net Directory	Andy Lowe, Editor, Future Publishing, 1995
The Mosaic Handbook for MS Windows	Dale Dougherty and Richard Koman, O'Reilly & Associates, 1994
The Usenet Handbook	Mark Harrison, O'Reilly & Associates, 1995
The Whole Internet: User's Guide & Catalog	Ed Krol, O'Reilly & Associates, 1994
The World Wide Web Handbook	Peter Flynn, International Thomson Computer Press, 1995
Using E-Mail Effectively	Linda Lamb and Jerry Peek, O'Reilly & Associates, 1995

Index

Childbirth and Tradition
in Northeast Thailand

Childbirth and Tradition in Northeast Thailand

16080l

Forty Years of Development and Cultural Change

By Anders Poulsen

Edited by Pernille Askerud
Ritual texts translated with a commentary by
Supranee Khammuang and Pernille Askerud

NIAS – Nordic Institute of Asian Studies
NIAS Monographs, 109

First published in 2007 by NIAS Press
Leifsgade 33, DK–2300 Copenhagen S, Denmark
Tel: (+45) 3532 9501 • Fax: (+45) 3532 9549
E–mail: books@nias.ku.dk • Website: www.niaspress.dk

British Library Cataloguing in Publication Data

Poulsen, Anders
  Childbirth and tradition in northeast Thailand : forty
  years of development and cultural change. - (NIAS
  monographs ; 109)
  1. Birth customs - Thailand, Northeastern
  I. Title
  392.1'2'09593

ISBN: 9788776940034

Design and layout by Sirisak Chaiyasook
All photographs by the author

Printed and bound in Thailand by M.C.D. Printing (Thailand) Co., Ltd..

Digital versions of related materials, including photos and recordings of the chanting of the rituals, have been deposited at the Princess Maha Chakri Sirindhorn Anthropology Centre. Interested readers can see further details of the archived materials on the centre's website www.sac.or.th which is available both in Thai and English.

*This book is dedicated to
the village of Baan Phraan Muean
– a worthy representative of the Isan culture*

Contents

Foreword

Anders Poulsen's study of the traditions and beliefs associated with childbirth and pregnancy is a very thought-provoking study, building on the seminal work in the field by Stanley Tambiah. Poulsen's work is particularly important due to the longitudinal methodology used and the opportunity it gives to observe the changes and continuities in the Isan region of Northeast Thailand in relation to modern development processes. Especially interesting is Poulsen's observation that there are two distinct and separate traditions, the *khwan* ceremonies and the *mae kamlerd* ceremonies, which influence local customs and beliefs related to pregnancy and birth. This work illustrates how in-depth research can reveal layers of meaning and identities in behaviour and belief that may otherwise be ignored.

The documentation and translation of the ritual texts are very strong points of this monograph, providing an important contribution to further study of these traditions and their origins, knowledge which is in danger of disappearing totally. Recording of the ritual chanting is an especially important feature of the monograph. In coming years, further research into these local traditions will provide a better understanding of the diversity of Thai cultures and aspirations. In addition, the elegant translation of the ritual texts provides non-Isan speakers a rare impression of the diversity and vividness of the oral imagery used in the rituals – imagery which is reproduced visually in design details and wall paintings in Buddhist monasteries well-known throughout Northeast Thailand. The ritual texts in the various forms as well as the glossary at the back will give this monograph a long academic shelf life.

The monograph demonstrates an interesting parallel to the evolution in the area of UNESCO's and other international organizations' programmes since they were established half a century ago. In the 1960s, Anders Poulsen was part of a UNESCO team working in Baan Phraan Muean to collect information that would form the basis for the development of education institutions and programmes in the years to come. At that time, it was commonplace for teams of anthropologists and educators to work in many villages like Baan Phraan Muean throughout all the world's developing countries in order to help formulate UN programmes of development assistance. The focus of these inter-disciplinary studies was to document the living conditions of the target populations and to analyse the inter-relationship between a variety of economic, environmental, social and historical factors, particularly those that affect children's well-being and upbringing with emphasis on the improvement of health, hygiene, and basic education. In those days cultural programming focused primarily on the fine arts and tangible cultural heritage. Since then, UNESCO's culture programmes have greatly extended to emphasize cultural rights and cultural development as inalienable components of sustainable development, with notions such as cultural diversity and the importance of oral and intangible heritage taking centre stage.

Oral traditions reflect many aspects of community life, from the spiritual legacy of ancestors through to the current politics of local society. However, many of the traditional forms for transmission of this knowledge are disappearing, being replaced by increasingly literate lifestyles and institutions. Responding to warnings that global cultural diversity is under threat due to the pressures of globalization and the promotion of national cultures, and that especially intangible cultural expressions such as oral traditions and literature, music, visual arts, and performing arts, are fragile and easily lost, the General Conference of UNESCO adopted the 'Convention for the Safeguarding of the Intangible Cultural Heritage' in 2003.

In Thailand, there is also a growing awareness of the value of cultural diversity and wealth that is expressed in oral traditions and the important role they played – and continue to play – in society and culture. The awareness is accompanied with a recognition of the need to ensure that the oral traditions are documented and do not slip into oblivion.

> These oral traditions ... come from the hearts, minds, memories, skills, beliefs and performance of people in each community from birth to death. In Isan ... oral tradition represents a whole community life, the daily communication between all villagers and between parents and children. ... In former days, the disseminators of oral heritage in Thailand were three groups of people. They were the monks, elders, and entertainers who taught, performed the ceremonies and entertained people. Monks learned religious texts, local literature, and some were also healers. Buddhist monks spent time studying sacred literature, meditating and preaching. The respected elders presided over or performed many of the ceremonies and festivals and *lakhon* (Thai performance actors) entertained people on special occasions. [1]

Anders Poulsen's work is an invaluable contribution to the safeguarding of the oral culture that is so determining a component of Isan culture. At the same time, it documents aspects of that culture which is seldom the subject of research and documentation. The more private nature of the *mae kamlerd* rites and the graveness of the issues involved have perhaps contributed to the fact that the rites have remained widely unknown and undocumented outside the society where they are still very much alive. On the basis of documentation done by Anders Poulsen and his team, future researchers now have a chance to study these texts and traditions in depth and unveil layers of meaning that continue to make these rites so relevant and meaningful today.

Richard A. Engelhardt

UNESCO Regional Advisor for Culture in Asia and the Pacific

---

1   Chaveelak Boonyakarnchana, Surithong Srisa-ard, and Pornpimol Manochai: *Preservation of the Thai Oral Heritage in Libraries in Thailand,* published by the Thai Library Association www.tiac.or.th/thailib/Ifla99_TOC.htm

Preface

The material for this book about pregnancy and childbirth in Baan Phraan Muean has been collected over a period of more than forty years. Throughout these years, I received invaluable support and assistance from innumerable people and institutions.

It began in 1961, when UNESCO entrusted to me a position at the *International Institute for Child Study* in Bangkok, whose directors at the time were the late Professor Hugh Philp and the late Professor Lamaimas Saradatta. I am deeply grateful to them both for a great many things including life-long friendships; above all I am grateful because it was their wish that I should take part in a research programme in a village. This took me to Baan Phraan Muean in Northeast Thailand (also known as Isan) in the company of a multidisciplinary team of predominantly Thai professionals. During the stimulating working period there, strong bonds were formed both within the group and between this group and the village. Although either everybody or nobody should be mentioned, Professor S. J. Tambiah must be an exception because his scholarly works have been of inestimable importance to what I present here.

My UNESCO employment was finished in 1962 but at the end of 1967 the *Danish International Development Agency* (DANIDA) gave me the opportunity to go back and stay one month in the village. On this occasion great practical assistance was given by the *Bangkok Institute for Child Study*, as it was now called, and its Director, Professor Lamaimas Saradatta. The Institute placed the late Mr Niyom Kamnuanmasok at my disposal as a highly competent associate and interpreter.

After this, the better part of a decade passed during which I was unable to spare any time for this project, which always had to be cultivated after long working days. At the end of 1977 and again in late 1988, DANIDA enabled me to make follow-up visits to the village. The *Behavioural Science Research Institute*, as my former place of work is now called, was peerless in its readiness to help and give support. Its then director, Professor Chancha Suvannathat, my friend and associate from 1961 onwards, and her assistants have shown my work a limitless degree of concern and helpfulness over the years.

During all my visits to the village from 1977, Associate Professor Mrs Supranee Khammuang, herself from Udorn in the Northeast, was my extremely talented and capable associate and interpreter. Her insight in and understanding of the Isan culture and its traditions, combined with her linguistic skills, have contributed greatly to the present book. Especially, she is to be given credit for translations and notes in the Part 2, which I consider an important part of this book. Mrs Supranee is simply unique and she possesses all thinkable abilities needed for obtaining qualified and reliable results in research of this type.

The provincial (Changwat) authorities, too, were very supportive and many people there ought to be thanked for the good-will they demonstrated towards my project. However, it will hardly be misinterpreted if this is personified in a single man, the late Superintendent Khun Satuern Ouppa-Bongse. In 1961, he was a well-loved headmaster at the Baan Phraan Muean School and very supportive of our UNESCO team in its relations with the villagers. In his succeeding positions in the school administration of the province he was indefatigable in his readiness to help, and so also after his retirement.

My gratitude and thanks must be directed, above all others, towards the villagers of Baan Phraan Muean. I was met there with nothing but warmth and obliging kindness. Particularly, I must mention three people. Phor Tuu Phan, who died in 1970, was in 1968 an extremely helpful, knowledgeable and wise source of knowledge of everything related to the local customs and traditions. More than anyone else Phor Jampii Naakdong was of importance to me. He was in all respects a fine man with exceptional personal qualities: deeply and earnestly involved in the village's religion, culture and tradition, and at the same time a pioneer regarding education, the supply of good water, and hygiene. He had the capacity to combine the old and the new ways. In 1980, he died of a liver disease that is one of the scourges of the district. The village lost someone vital – I lost a friend and a tutor. He was engrossed in my work and keen to ensure that everything was understood correctly and documented properly to be preserved for future generations. It was his expressed wish that the knowledge and traditions of his culture be published. The old ways were to be preserved. Together with Phor Jampii, his son Khun Jan must be mentioned. During all my stays in the village from 1968 and until this day, he capably and efficiently organized all details connected with the smooth planning of our work in the village. He arranged everything so well that the limited time available to me was used with an efficiency which is exceptional for projects of this type.

In the initial phase of preparing my material for publishing I was fortunate that Mrs Pernille Askerud by mere chance came across my manuscript. She has been living 15 years in Thailand working as international consultant and editor for UNESCO and other agencies. This gave her a particular insight in the context of the present study. Mrs Askerud helped me pull together the present manuscript out of a very large material collected and drafted over a period of over 40 years. In addition, she and Mrs Supranee Khammuang committed themselves to a renewed study and translation of the ritual texts the result of which contributed to a more comprehensive understanding of the rites. The readability of the text presented here owes considerably to Mrs Askerud's patient and thorough editing. I am extremely grateful for her work and support.

I owe thanks to many others, among them the Ministry of Education, Bangkok; Thailand's National Research Council; the Danish Embassy, Bangkok; and to my publisher Gerald Jackson of NIAS Press who trusted in this manuscript and helped to make it available to a wider audience thereby ensuring that the knowledge of these oral traditions may not disappear altogether. Thanks are also due to Khun Sirisak Chaiyasook for the elegant book design and layout, and to Senior Editor Leena Höskuldsson of NIAS Press who finalized the typesetting and prepared the book for print. I am so grateful and pleased by the result of their work. For financial support I owe thanks to DANIDA (1968, 1978, 1988) and to VELUX FONDEN of 1981 (1998).

January 2007

Editor's Introduction

Over the last decade there has been growing recognition of the need to consider culture seriously as an inherent component of sustainable development. In such discussions, the human ability to aspire has become a key to understanding the development process. This ability to aspire is inextricably linked to culture – or in other words, to our consciousness of past and present, as well as to ideas of future possibilities. It has proven very difficult to operationalize this insight and make projects in which culture is an integral part of the development process. This is partly because the process of cultural change and the role of culture in societal change is very poorly understood.

In *Notes Toward The Definition Of Culture* from 1948, T. S. Eliot argues that there are three different dimensions or senses of the concept of culture. Hence, 'the term culture has different associations according to whether we have in mind the development of an individual, of a group or class, or of a whole society.' Eliot also points out that though we always will focus on one of these three dimensions when we use the term, the other dimensions are always underlying silent references in the statement. It is this evasiveness of the concept of culture that can make it difficult to fully determine the factors that influence cultural change and indeed to describe such change itself, unless it is done over a longer period of time.

Anders Poulsen's study of customs and beliefs related to pregnancy and childbirth describes an area of life and culture that is central to people's life no matter what stage of development. He describes how these customs and beliefs have changed over almost half a century in a small Isan village, for the villagers individually and collectively, and how the wider appreciation of these customs (for example in terms of international research) have changed as well. Hence, the study is a rare documentation of how the development process affects customs and beliefs in a society, and so manages to capture the interdependency between the different aspects of culture and cultural change. Based on Anders Poulsen's description of customs and beliefs in this Isan village we can identify contours of a more complex, general discussion of culture and development.

Longitudinal studies are particularly useful to more accurately map cultural and societal change. However, being humans with a limited lifespan, only very few such longitudinal studies have been undertaken. Over and above the specific topic of this study, it is therefore of wider interest because it provides a more general opportunity to analyse both the process of cultural change itself and more specifically the relationship between cultural and societal change.

More specifically, Anders Poulsen's study discusses the Thai belief in a dual soul, the *khwan* and the *winyaan*, and the widespread belief in good and evil spirits within a psychological and socio-therapeutic framework that provides the basis for a wider understanding of why some traditions maintain their importance while others fade away.

The text is a work of high-quality descriptive ethnography. His descriptions reflect a willingness to put himself in the villagers' place and to be faithful to the villagers' own voices, without prematurely injecting and interposing analytical or theoretical concepts that belong to a different discourse. The text portrays the villagers over time and their efforts to find a place and identity in a world increasingly dominated by development, globalization, and modernization.

In addition to the descriptions that make up the core of the study, the texts refer to a wide range of international research – much of it undertaken when the academic interest in these areas of research was more pronounced than it is today. This is of course also a perspective of the longitudinal studies; they tend to outlive the focus, preferred methodologies and frame of interpretation characteristic of a specific period. The inevitable shifts in scientific discourse and methodology that occur over such a long period of time threaten to make the studies appear dated and out of touch with current academic approaches and research interest, not to mention the academic jargon. Nevertheless, the findings of such studies are still very valuable for the perspective they give.

The concept of culture and its relation to the development has changed since the 1960s when the village study that Anders Poulsen was part of, was only one of many such studies aimed at overcoming the 'backwardness' of these places and achieve better living conditions for children and adults. The subject matter of the study is today covered by different areas of research including women's studies, social development studies, oral heritage research, and, not least, Isan studies. Today ethnic minorities (in this case a very numerous minority) are increasingly claiming their cultural integrity and rights, and efforts are made to preserve and keep alive the oral traditions that are such a fundamental characteristic of Isan culture. This must please researchers such as Anders Poulsen who perhaps never saw the need to abolish these traditions in the first place and who at least in this respect is as modern in his view as anybody. As he once wrote : 'By participating in the everyday life of the village I realized that one cannot, by force of power or in any other radical way, abolish all the old ways, however inexpedient they might be. Were this attempted, progress might well appear to be made in this respect, but, at the same time, a process would be started that would contribute to making man rootless, and out of harmony with himself and his surroundings.'

The longitudinal approach applied by Anders Poulsen makes his study particularly interesting because it contributes to a more holistic analysis of the subject matter. It also documents that some of the assumptions we hold based on short-term studies may be false and that the relationship between customs, belief, and the modernization process is more complex than previously described. In this way, Anders Poulsen contributes with significant new findings to the anthropological literature on Northeast Thailand and the neighbouring regions.

The most interesting finding of Anders Poulsen's research is perhaps the documentation of the cult of *mae kamlerd* which appears to be absolutely unknown in other parts of Thailand. In his analysis of the rites that are related to pregnancy and childbirth, Anders Poulsen convincingly distinguishes

two separate traditions, namely the *khwan* rites and the *mae kamlerd* cult that in other research have been treated as parts of the same tradition. Anders Poulsen argues that the *mae kamlerd* cult is not part of the *khwan* rites but a separate cult aimed at protecting the baby from the evil influence of the 'old mothers'. His argument is supported by the translation of the ritual texts themselves, which clearly refer to different traditions. Hopefully, someone will feel inclined to make a more thorough analysis of these texts which here have been preserved for future studies.

The *khwan* rite *suukhwan maemaan* was closely related to ease the minds of the mother vis-à-vis the perceived dangers of the childbirth. Perhaps not surprisingly, with modernization and better healthcare this danger has significantly diminished and Anders Poulsen documents that so has the importance and prevalence of this rite among the villagers. Interestingly, the fear of *mae kamlerd* appears to survive despite the changes in society. Other researchers may be able to study the origins of this cult and explain why these beliefs are so rooted in the villagers' world-view.

Another interesting finding of the study also relates to the pervasiveness of the traditions. Anders Poulsen documents how the tradition of *yuu fai* – a period just after the birth when the mother is lying next to a fire – is not only still very much observed in the Northeast but also practised much more widely than previously documented. What he found was that the custom of confinement is not, as sometimes believed, totally abandoned in modern society; on the contrary, there seems to be a re-evaluation of the benefit and importance of this custom. It is interesting to read how this tradition – for long referred to as 'mother roasting' by international research and much despised – may be up for a re-evaluation.

All in all, what Anders Poulsen has documented is that the ritual practice – then as well as now – provides the villagers with a system of social therapy that helps them deal with sorrows and problems encountered in their lives in a manner that is often superior to the kind of psychological support systems found in our more modern societies.

Many of the popular traditions and beliefs in Thailand remain unrecorded and research done by Thai- or Laotian-speaking researchers has not been translated. In this respect, the situation is very different in Asia than it is for example in Europe where great interest and efforts have been devoted to the documentation of traditional belief and knowledge.

Anders Poulsen could still find people in the village who understood and could explain the background and meaning of the rites and the texts – albeit they, too, did not understand everything. However, it is getting increasingly difficult to find people who have the knowledge and training to continue the function as ritual masters – and without that their knowledge will disappear. In spite of the fact that there still is an interest for the rites, it is therefore conceivable that the deeper knowledge of the belief that lies behind them may disappear as the villages are increasingly integrated in modern Thai society through closer contact and the modern media.

Anders Poulsen's study is therefore a significant contribution to the understanding of these traditions and rituals in their social and cultural context and provides a basis for further study of these traditions. As such it provides an important key to the aspirations of the Isan people.

Bangkok February 2007

Pramille Askvind

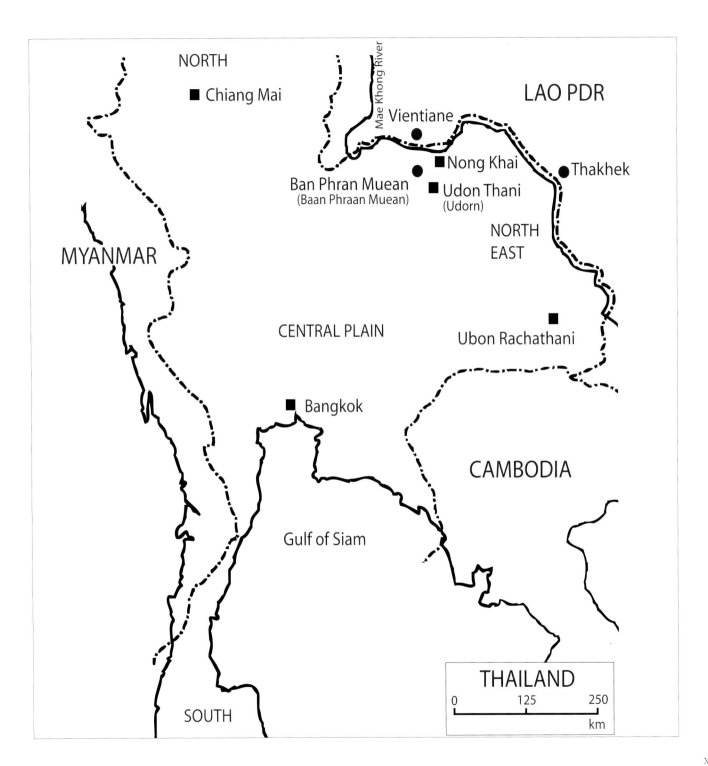

NORTH

■ Chiang Mai

Mae Khong River

LAO PDR

Vientiane
●

MYANMAR

■ Nong Khai
●
Ban Phran Muean
(Baan Phraan Muean)

Thakhek
●

■ Udon Thani
(Udorn)

NORTH
EAST

CENTRAL PLAIN

Ubon Rachathani
■

■ Bangkok

CAMBODIA

Gulf of Siam

THAILAND

0   125   250

km

SOUTH

xvii

Part 1

Customs of Pregnancy and Birth
– Then and Now

Suukhwan Maemaan
(1962)

Prologue

In the early 1960s, the International Institute for Child Study, established and run jointly by UNESCO and the Thai Government, undertook extensive studies in typical villages focussing on the social influences on the development of Thai children. From October 1961 to April 1962, I was fortunate to take part in the Institute's fieldwork in the village of Baan Phraan Muean in the Udorn province of Northeast Thailand – an area often referred to as Isan.

Although our team was to concern itself with almost everything that happened in the daily life of the villagers, some limitations to our studies were necessary, and we had to refrain from areas that had no direct relevance to our project. One of these areas concerned the customs and traditions related to a woman's pregnancy and the childbirth itself. Nothing of what we in the West would consider necessary was available in the village, and we witnessed how the villagers tried to make themselves secure by whatever means available to them. I found it of personal interest to study this particular area. And so I have done now for more than 40 years. Four times since my first stay in the village I have been able to return for month-long systematic studies. Besides this I came for shorter stays on many occasions, each time adding bits of information to the material presented here. As the details of the whole research process and the methodology of the study are quite extensive these are placed in an Appendix in Part 3 of this book. I only want to mention here that the Grade 1 children in the local school who originally (in 1961–62) together with their parents were our basic sample have continued to be so, although successively supplemented with younger families.

The main purpose of my work is above all to document, and thus to preserve traditional knowledge and traditions relating to pregnancy and childbirth that have not previously been illuminated systematically in English. I have sought to describe and understand the customs and traditions related to pregnancy and birth both as they were in the 1960s and as they are today in relation to the social and economic conditions then and later. I have also aimed at seeing some of the traditions and customs in their cultural context on the basis of available literature about Thailand and the neighbouring countries. I have endeavoured to present my material as solidly as possible, so that it may be of use to others who are interested in the village culture of Isan and in how these traditions have changed and developed over the years.

To place my studies in the proper context, much more could be written about daily life and activity as it unfolded in the village at the beginning of the 1960s, and about the changes I have been able to observe during the more than 40 years that have passed since then. However, I have limited myself to deal only with those details I consider most important to understand the context within which these customs and rites have been functioning.

What is mentioned and what is omitted, is naturally coloured by what my foreigner's eyes found most important as a background for the chapters that follow. The faith of the villagers, the temple and all formal as well as informal aspects of their religious life ought perhaps to have been explained in more detail.

I have aimed to draw a course over the period of the beliefs, rituals and practices relating to pregnancy and

childbirth in Baan Phraan Muean, and to describe how the villagers progressively experienced, reacted, and participated in some of the forces of 'development', 'modernization', and 'globalization'.

To make the material as useful as possible my study is presented in three parts:

Part 1 is an introductory description and analysis of the village and its people and a detailed description and analysis of all the traditions, beliefs, and rituals associated with pregnancy and birth, and the changes in this respect over the years.

Part 2 contains a critical edition of the ritual texts in Thai and English of the three most important rites (as well as some minor texts); this part also includes information on the recipes for various 'medicines' used by the villagers in connection with pregnancy and birth.

Part 3 includes a chapter on research methodology, a glossary and notes on the Isan language and the tran-scription of Isan Thai into English, and a bibliography.

Anyone interested in further text-based studies of these traditions may access the original recordings of the ritual texts and a picture gallery accessible through the Princess Maha Chakri Sirindhorn Anthropology Centre (www.sac.or.th) which graciously has accepted to function as repository library for these materials.

I am now close to formulating the very last sentences before publishing the outcome of my many years of interest in this particular aspect of Isan village culture, and I feel a personal need to share some of the reflections I made rather early during my first stay in the village.

In 1961, it was an amazing experience to me so immediately to feel at home in this distant village community. Everything was new to me and so different, and yet there was something I recognized and felt agreed with me in the company of these farmers. They seemed to have much in common with the farmers amongst whom I had grown up in the 1930's, in a relatively poor and isolated village in Denmark.

They were, in the same way, a little reserved and shy of strangers, and to a degree also of each other. What a person really thought and felt was never expressed particularly clearly or explicitly but was concealed as far as possible. Their curiosity towards the stranger was as I had known it in my childhood. When you had been sized up and found reasonably acceptable, goodwill and helpfulness flowed towards you. Their forbearance with the cultural blunders that you, being a stranger, inevitably committed, was obvious. Their humour in the face of human folly was well-known to me. We could delight in the same things, and together feel humble about the indisputable facts in life and in nature.

In a way we knew each other.

This is perhaps not astonishing. We are all human beings. But it was, all the same, at the time most amazing to me. It would not have been surprising if easily observed differences in our personalities and their modes of expression should have been found. I did not immediately see such differences. All I had read about

heredity and environment, about how biology and socio-cultural conditions work together and balance each other out, were brought up for reconsideration.

Another factor also intrigued me.

In my country, I had grown up during a period when it, among educated people, was indisputable that superstition, magic and prejudices often were decisive to the way poor people quite passively came to terms with their situation.

I arrived in this distant village with this traditional 'western academic' attitude to man and his existence. By participating in the everyday life of the village I almost from the beginning developed doubts about whether such problems were of major importance in this place. Was it necessary here, too, to abolish all the old ways in order to obtain what we call progress? While some of the old practices were potentially harmful and ought to be abolished, other old ways were at least harmless and would not create obstacles for development, and some traditions appeared to be more meaningful still, even when evaluated from a modern point of view. How to approach this in a proper manner? I witnessed how the villagers tried to make themselves secure with whatever means were available, including magic and superstition. Above all, I became very soon aware that one should not, and could not, know what was good and what was not so good based on ready-made ideas brought in from another world but that any analysis and action must be based on studies of the local culture.

In a commentary relating to research on Northeastern village societies Charles F. Keyes wrote in 1975: 'Yet, it is not merely more research which is needed, for in fact, troops of researchers, both Thai and Western (…) paraded from village to village during the 1960s.' Keyes pointed out that little of this research 'penetrated beyond the superficial level of socio-economic characteristics of village life' and considered that there was still a need for research that will give an insight into 'what life in the Northeastern community means for those who live there' (Keyes 1975: 206).

I would be most gratified if my studies were to be seen as a contribution to our insight in the life of the Isan villagers.

Top: Net-fishing in the dry season (1962)

Bottom left: Paddy to barn (1961)

Bottom right: Palm sugar ready for sale in the market (1962)

CHAPTER ONE

Village Life and Economy in Isan, 1961-2005

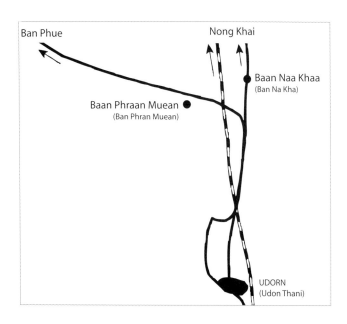

Baan Phraan Muean – a Village Community

Baan Phraan Muean means 'the hunter Muan's village'. Local tales tell of the origin of this name, and together with Buddha images and old stone structures found in the temple ground, these tales indicate that people have lived here for a very long time, most likely several hundred years. The village lies in the Northeastern part of the country, about 600 kilometres from Bangkok. The administrative centre of the province, Udorn, is about 17 kilometres south of the village. The small trading town of Nong Khai lies 45 kilometres north of

the village on the river Mae Khong, which here forms the frontier with Laos.

The Northeast of Thailand is mainly populated by people we will describe as 'Laotian Thai'. Linguistically these people are closer related to the population on the Laotian bank of the river Mae Khong than to people further south in Thailand's central area around Bangkok. The Isan language is often considered a Thai dialect but it is not very easily understood by anyone who has grown up in Bangkok. The pronunciation is different for many words, and it contains many words not found in the Central Plain.[1]

Traditionally, the population here has first and foremost subsisted by growing rice. The soil is poor and infertile as for example described by Pendleton: 'most of the topsoils in the Korat Plateau are almost entirely sandy', and 'in many places in the region the surface of the sandy soil shows an efflorescence of salt'.[2]

This is also the case in Baan Phraan Muean. There is no possibility for irrigation and the villagers are completely dependent on the monsoon. It is only possible to grow one crop a year and in some years the monsoon comes so violently that it causes crop-destroying floods, in other years so scantily or late that the harvest fails. In 1961 and at least in the first of the succeeding years, the yield was so modest that the income from the sales of rice was very limited. The villagers did make a little money by raising poultry and by producing palm sugar. For many years, several of the younger men and girls had taken paid jobs in the nearest towns or even as far

away as in Bangkok for some months after the harvest in October, thus putting a bit of cash into their hands. But in the early sixties they did not have much money.

There was only one small, simple shop in the village; besides cultivating his few rai[3] of rice-fields, the proprietor did a little sewing for people, sold detergent, cigarettes, matches and a few other items. What we consider ordinary consumer goods hardly existed here. There was one solitary radio receiver, and only one person in the village had a bicycle. Of course there was no electricity, and during the dark hours a primitive torch would break the deep darkness here and there. On the whole this was a subsistence economy that hardly provided a basis for a money economy.

The villagers made most of their day-to-day utensils from bamboo, straw and other natural materials. Even salt was washed out of the topsoil, which in certain places was far too salty for cultivation. The traditional Northeastern glutinous rice was the staple of their diet. There was rarely any meat, but some small fish were caught during the rainy season. The villagers rarely went hungry, and they were not undernourished either, but the diet was no doubt deficient in many nutrients.

Baan Yai and Baan Nory

Like most of the villages in the region, Baan Phraan Muean had always been a clustered village. In 1961, a total of 932 people lived there in 149 households and 182 families (Tambiah, 1970). In a way, Baan Phraan Muean was divided into two: *Baan Yai* (the big hamlet) and *Baan Nory* (the small hamlet). *Baan Yai* was the old core where the houses lay close together in an almost square structure. The other part of the village, *Baan Nory,* consisted of a row of houses along the road towards Udorn. Here lived mostly young families who had been unable to find rooms in their parents' compounds within *Baan Yai.*

Threshing (1961)

Everybody made their living almost exclusively from rice farming. Their fields lay in the large, open countryside around the village. Practically all families owned land, or would come to own land at some time when their parents' land would be divided up through inheritance. They were small freehold farms of an average of 18.82 rai[3] of rice fields and, as stated by Tambiah, 'there is very little renting-in or renting-out of land, and landlord/tenant categories are not important in village economy.'[4] It was obvious to anyone who knew the place that the differences in the families' financial circumstances were very modest. In spite of slight variations in the quality of the houses – some were of slightly better material or a little bigger in size – the villagers were all almost equally poor and their daily living standards almost the same. This did not imply that there were no differences in status, esteem, and influence. Such matters were just not based on financial circumstances but to a greater degree on factors that I, too, tend to consider more reasonable: age, involvement in the welfare of the Buddhist temple, abilities and experience as ritual masters, and really also on 'wisdom and intelligence'. In other words, a man who was considered worth consulting for advice and guidance in life's many difficult situations would hold a higher status in the village.

Already in 1961, several of the village elders were concerned about how the village would feed itself in the future. Previously, the young had been able to bring new scrub-land under the plough but changes in legislation, population increase, and the lack of suitable land meant that this practice would not be possible in the future. Following the inheritance system, the land available was divided into smaller and smaller plots when it changed hands from one generation to another, and this practice would soon make the already small plots of land so tiny that no family could live from what could be grown on them. At the time, the village elders could only acknowledge the problem but they did not see any possible solution.

In everyday life they had practically no communication with the outside world. They attended religious and civil festivals in the nearest villages. A lorry would occasionally pass by, during the dry season blanketing everything in a cloud of reddish dust. Now and then, a trader came on foot or on a bicycle, offering charms, clay goods, various 'miracle' medicines and such. Many of the older people had never been further afield than the very closest villages; most saw their first film when our UNESCO team gave a screening at a temple festival. They could see and hear the train connecting the Northeast with Bangkok, but the nearest station was Udorn. In fact, unless one was particularly lucky, Udorn could be reached only by walking the 17 kilometres along a road, which during the dry season was covered in red dust and which was almost impassable in the rainy season because of churned-up mud.

They liked to go to Udorn, of course; especially the young. This large town which then had 30,000 inhabitants and shops where everything from the whole big world could be bought, be it advanced electric equipment, cosmetics, or all sorts of medical products. In Udorn there was an airport, technical colleges, a teacher-training school, a hospital, fine people in uniforms and modern clothes. There were hotels, and even a couple of nightclubs housed in simple wooden sheds, mainly for the benefit of the American military personnel.

To us outsiders Udorn at that time was a cosy, peaceful, and a little untidy and unkempt township, that had no telephone connection to any place outside the town. Seen from Baan Phraan Muean, however, Udorn was distant, big, rich, and tempting, offering goods and a lifestyle that in every aspect was in stark contrast to life in the village only 17 kilometres away.

Health and the treatment of illness

Although there is no data on well-being and health in the village, it is safe to surmise that the situation for the whole population was not much different from what our UNESCO team found in 1962 among the children who then were attending 1st Grade (*prathom* 1) in the local school. 42 children in the age groups 7.6–9.5 years were on average 3.6 centimetres shorter than a corresponding age group in Udorn. The average weight of the village girls was significantly lower than that of girls in Udorn, while the boys on average weighed only about one kilogram less than a corresponding group in Udorn, a difference which was not significant. 44 village children examined had a haemoglobin percentage that was significantly lower than the Udorn children's.[5]

The team of physicians established that 45 of the 47 children in the class were in such poor state of health that they 'were in need of treatment', and nine of them even 'in urgent need of treatment'. Of the 25 children examined for internal parasites only five were free of these; 11 had tapeworms, 10 hookworms, and 15 liver flukes. Seven of the children had two of these parasites, and two of them had all three. Further comments regarding these 7- to 9-year-old children's terms of life are hardly necessary.

It must also be mentioned that the team found that 43 of the children were not very clean and that, among other things, 28 had lice or their eggs in the hair. This finding could be interpreted as an indication that the villagers had no tradition or desire to keep themselves clean. But this is far from being the case. Here, as everywhere else in Thailand, in all places people were seen pouring buckets of water over themselves at all times, and every day towards sunset one would see – as everywhere in Thailand – the women going to the few scattered wells to fetch water, where at the same time they would have a wash.

Every fortnight, the school in our village would arrange a communal bath for the youngest children in the pond that had been dug to collect rainwater. The pond was situated next to the assembly hall (*saalaa*) in the temple compound where the children were taught. The youngsters had to bring a bucket or a watertight basket, soap, and clean clothes. They rarely brought any clean clothes, and if they did have soap it was most often some harsh detergent. It was wonderful to witness how they were anyhow rubbed and scrubbed and the great delight with which they helped pour buckets of water over one another. Personal cleanliness in Thailand, as everywhere on the earth, depends on many factors, among these whether one can afford to buy soap, whether one has the reserve of vigour needed to attend to such things, and not least on how easy or difficult it is to get access to water.

In 1961, the lack of water was a considerable problem for the villagers. There were only four or five wells in total. Apart from one, several hundred metres north of the village, all the wells dried up during the dry season. Only during the peak of the rainy season was there no need to economize on water. The quality of the water was poor, as evidenced by the result of an analysis made on 24 November 1961, when the water from five sites in the village was examined. Only the well that was located north of the village had potable water. The water at the school was the worst: 46,500 bacterial colonies per cubic centimetre flourished here and of these bacteria more than 39 per cent were coliaerogens!

Almost all treatment of the sick was in the hands of persons who were not in any way trained to do this. The 'treatment' was done by ritual experts and herbal 'doctors', and this was supplemented with various Chinese and Thai 'miracle medicines' sold by itinerant traders who visited the village. During military service, the teacher had learnt to give injections and so he was a little more advanced in his approach. Consulting the catalogue of a

Every fortnight the head teacher arranged a bath for the younger children in the pond next to the school (1962)

large pharmaceutical firm, he would suggest modern 'Western' medicine according to the extent of one's purse. Every imaginable item of these medicines could be bought in Udorn without prescription. Much of this local treatment was not bad at all; some of it probably very good.

It has to be said that it was not superstition and prejudice that deterred the villagers from consulting a qualified physician, but rather a lack of practical opportunity and of money to pay for it. A public district health system already existed in 1961 and it had a centre about seven kilometres from the village. The centre was tended by a single person, a trained nurse (*mor tambon*); the medicine prescribed there had to be paid for by the patient. For economic reasons alone, the doctors in private practice in Udorn were outside the reach of the villagers but a few patients went to the hospital in Udorn where the outpatients' department made a very great and praiseworthy contribution under difficult conditions. In 1961, it was, however, extremely difficult to get to Udorn not least if one was really ill. The waiting-time at the outpatients' department was long and the poor, uneducated villager did not always (and possibly not unjustly so) feel himself treated decently and respectfully by the hospital's white-coated personnel.

The school

Baan Phraan Muean then held school in the approximately 11 x 18 metres large *saalaa*, the meeting hall, which almost everywhere goes together with the site of the village's central ritual, religious and social activities: the Buddhist temple (*wat*). The *saalaa* was a traditional building erected on stilts, with a wooden planked floor about 1.5 metres above the ground. There was a tiled roof over the entire building, but only an outer wall towards the North. The whole building was one large open room. There, three teachers taught the four obligatory classes with a total of 152 pupils. Only the head teacher had any training as a teacher – the other two teachers only had two to three years' lower secondary schooling in addition to their four years in primary school. The two male teachers owned some rice-land which they and their families cultivated to sustain life.

The 1st Grade, which was our study-group, kept to a corner of this *saalaa*, where the 47 children had available to them a floor area of about three by five meters. Like all other children in the school they sat on the floor, and a few of them had a little stool on which to lay their books or slates. The sole teaching aid in the school was a wall-map of Thailand, made by the teacher on a piece of cardboard. Each of the four grades into which the children were divided had a blackboard of about a square meter in size, made by the teachers. The head teacher taught the 3rd and 4th Grades simultaneously, a total of 64 pupils.

The pupils were obliged to purchase their own textbooks and few of them had the two text books required for Grade 1. Of the 47 pupils in 1st Grade, 23 children did not have a single textbook. They wrote on small slates, which they also had to get for themselves. Only 17 children in the 1st Grade possessed whole slates, and of these, five or six would usually not have a slate pen. The remainder either had no slates or had to make do with pieces of a broken slate that were big enough still to be usable. Pencils and paper to write on did not exist. However, everybody worked incredibly hard and dutifully to create a 'school' from nothing, and the parents devoted greater attention and interest to their children's schooling than could be expected in the circumstances.

The majority of the children were able to read after the four years of compulsory school attendance, but many forgot it again as there were neither books nor any other reading matter available in the village. In 1968, I had the opportunity to test the reading ability of some of the pupils who had attended the school's 1st Grade in 1961. They had left the school no later than 1965, so at the time of the test they had been without formal education for approximately three years. Only about half of them could be described as literate.

The 152 pupils in the school were all sitting on the floor (1962)

Like in many other villages in the district, in 1961, the school did not have its own building but used the *saalaa* belonging to the Buddhist temple

The group of young men who for a time was admitted to the local temple as monks (at the age of about eighteen) systematically renewed their reading skills and some tuition was also given during military service. The final result was that most of the younger men were functionally literate, while the women's reading abilities ranged somewhat lower.

In addition, there was also a large group of elderly and old men who could read and write. To the stranger who came to this place for the purposes of study it was striking how great a knowledge, insight and understanding of traditional culture and religion many an elderly or old villager had gleaned through his reading ability.

Change and Development

Forty years is a long time. It has been a period that has seen radical changes throughout the world. Everything has changed. Let us for the moment call it 'development', a term most often used to indicate and signal positive changes, but forgetting that 'development' is not without its costs. Sometimes these costs are not foreseen at all, and sometimes they are calculated incorrectly in cost-benefit analyses. It is everywhere and at any time a very difficult balance, especially where the consequences of a possible 'stagnation' and 'decline' are to be considered as well. How does this relate to our Northeastern Thai village?

During my month-long stay in the village in December–January 1967–68, practically no change could be traced in comparison to 1961–62, except for the new school that was constructed in 1965 with support from Denmark. However, when I came back for the New Year 1977–78 very many things were markedly different. The changes were similar to those described by Klausner in the Ubon region, another part of the Northeast, and were dominated by 'the inexorable shift from a barter to a cash economy'.[6] New – and considerable – changes were noted during all later visits.

The houses in *Phor Tuu Phans* compound were all constructed of solid timber and were the very best in the whole village (1961)

In 1961 the total population in Baan Phraan Muean was 932, most of them living in the older, central part of the village (*Baan Yai*) and some younger families in *Baan Nory*. Today almost 800 are living in *Baan Nory*, which after a yearlong conflict with *Baan Yai* in 1980 officially got permission to form an independent administrative unit under the name of Baan Noon Ngaam ('the beautiful small hill'). Part of the disagreement was about the temple; Baan Noon Ngaam now have a beautiful temple of their own while they still share the school with Baan Phraan Muean. Baan Phraan Muean has also seen some population growth over these years with a little more than 1,200 living there in 2001. In total, the population in the two hamlets has doubled over the whole period. The growth must be considered in connection with a lower infant mortality rate (which on the other hand is balanced by a much lower number of children in each family). The extended life expectancy is another factor in the population growth. Also, by 2001, several young families had moved from isolated villages in the hinterland to Baan Phraan Muean, which lies by a main road.

As we recall, in 1962, the village elders were seriously troubled regarding the future because of the already then slightly increasing population. Their worries have so far been groundless, as the considerably larger population has not only been able to survive but also to increase their standard of living. How this has been possible, will be reported to later. However, the villagers still consider themselves poor, and are made to feel so when they compare their own life with the impressions they get from the street-life when they visit Udorn. They feel poor, too, because they still have nothing at all in reserve when difficulties with crops, work, health, and old age hit them. But the outsider who has been visiting regularly over these many years must add: they are still poor but in a different way. Those of the village elders, who are old enough to remember 'the old days', recognize a marked increase in the standard of living. Much good has happened, and though some things have had negative results – in the end, the development is more good than bad, they conclude.

More concretely the changes are reflected in easily observable changes in the village. There are so many different aspects of a living standard but housing no doubt is a principal issue. Although several of the farmhouses in 1960s were constructed of solid timbers most had walls and roofing of various types of materials that did not last very long. There was not any doubt that the village was poor – and the evidence was to be seen everywhere and in everything. The first improvements seen during the 1970s were new walls made from boards of weather-resistant compressed sheets, and roofs of corrugated galvanised iron. During the 1980s and especially in the 1990s this all changed.

In the 1960s, most houses had walls and roofing of materials that did not last very long

Today's paved lanes with the well-constructed houses make you think of the middle-class dwelling areas in the outer parts of Udorn

Today, you see a number of well-constructed houses made of a combination of brick, concrete, and wood. Today, the houses are rarely built on stilts as they used to be. Doors and windows are well made and of good materials. Of course there are also some newer houses that are more cheaply built, but all are remarkably better than previously. Only a few of the old houses are still there, looking more or less deserted and inhabited mostly by old people who are no longer able to take care of the houses. Centrally situated is a recently built community hall, constructed of lasting materials and furnished with equipment for its function as the place where the villagers can meet to discuss and decide on matters of joint concern. Also very recently, the unpaved, earthen lanes in the village itself have been paved with concrete, and designed so that they are passable also during the rainy season.

These paved lanes with their well-constructed houses make one think of some of the lanes in the recently developed middle-class dwelling areas in the outer parts of Udorn.

The introduction of electricity into the village in 1971 was another decisive step towards improved everyday life quality. By 1981, 12 households had refrigerators, 15 had television sets, and radios were everywhere. Today everybody has a colour TV and of course a refrigerator.

On the other hand, an adequate, reliable water supply continued to be a problem until recently. With financial aid from Denmark, a bore was drilled at the new school in 1967. At first, this yielded a good supply of potable water and plans were made to install more taps at various sites in the village. Unfortunately, after two years, the water from this well became salty, a prevalent problem throughout the district. Soon thereafter, the school and the families in the village established facilities to store rainwater, and almost all families made a well in their own compound, normally about six metres deep and

lined with concrete. Today, the villagers find that they have reasonably good and sufficient water all year round. Today they also know that the water from the well in their compound is not safe for drinking, and prefer to use rainwater for this purpose. Finally, in 1999 water began to be delivered once a week to the school by a water tanker from the Department of Water Supply.

As previously mentioned, in 1962 there was only a solitary, modest little shop in the village. Today there are many shops though they are still small and their stock does not exceed a few hundred *baht* in value. There are also small restaurants, and several hairdressers and tailoring shops for men as well as for ladies. Still very few shopkeepers, if any, have trade as their sole livelihood. In almost all cases, it is the wife who runs the shop while the husband looks after the farming or goes out to a paid job – perhaps both.

Very recently – beginning in 1999 – daily delivery of mail to a 'post office' was introduced. The post office is really just a table and a shelf in the house of one of the villagers looked after by the wife of the house who also has a little stock of stamps for sale. Outside her door is a new public telephone box.

Top: In 1962, there was only a solitary, modest little shop in the village.

Bottom: Today there are many, though they are small and the stock does not exceed a few hundred *bath* in value

The new school

A new school was built in 1965; a typical Thai-style school, constructed from wood on concrete stilts. This was a joint venture between the Thai Ministry of Education and the school children, their parents and the municipal school authorities in the suburban community of Gladsaxe in Denmark, where I was then working. The official name is the 'Thai-Denmark Friendship School'. It has in every respect been well looked after and tended by the parent-elected school committee and the teachers. The villagers are proud of their school, which during its years of existence has been honoured more than once as the best school in the district. It has been enlarged several times to suit legislative changes, such as the extension of compulsory education to six years of schooling (*prathom 1-6*). Classes for lower secondary (*mathayom 1-3*) level have also been introduced, and so far about two-thirds of the children are attending these classes. Today there are even two well-attended kindergarten classes, one for the three- and four-year-olds and one for the five- and six-year-olds. A language laboratory was established in 1999. It is overwhelming and astonishing to have witnessed how the Thai authorities have managed to develop a basic educational system in this distant part of the country. However, the curriculum seems very theoretical for children in this village, and there is a need for considerable further education of the teachers.

A typical Thai-style school, constructed from wood on concrete stilts was built in 1965

The school has been enlarged several times to suit legislative changes and the increasing number of pupils

The old *bood* was rotten and heavily damaged by termites (1961)

The new bood

The villagers' biggest joint project has been the building of a new, imposing 'holiest house' (*bood*) in the temple compound, as a replacement for the simple, rotten, wooden house they had before. The plans were made in 1963, commenced in 1966, and it was estimated then that completion could not be expected for another ten to fifteen years. Still it took longer than that as the *bood* was finished only in 1985. The villagers may have planned to build their *bood* bigger and more luxurious that they were able to afford. More importantly, it was not part of the original plan that during the construction process the *Baan Nory* part of the village would abandon their support for the original joint project and decide to build a temple of their own. Nevertheless, the *Baan Yai* residents persisted, and there is no doubt that the successfully completed project accrued much 'merit' for many individuals, and for the village as a whole. It was their pride then. In spite of a year-long conflict between

The new *bood* under construction (1980)

the Lord Abbot and the temple committee, the construction of a new *kuti* (dwelling quarters for the monks) and a large, new *saalaa* has been commenced but not yet finished.

Even so, it must be noted that the regular visitor senses that the temple does not play the same vital role in the life and thinking of the villagers today as it did fifteen or twenty years ago. The village elders confirmed this in 2001, saying that this is more or less a general trend underlined by the fact that not so many young men as previously enter into the monkhood for a period of their life. The tendency may be somewhat more marked here than in neighbouring villages because of the conflict between the Lord Abbot and the temple committee. Observed by an outsider, however, it is notable that the assembly facilities constructed in connection with the school and most recently the community hall right in the centre of the village have added to or been a consequence of an increasingly mundane village life.

Let me not omit to emphasize the joint care of the new school and the common project of the constructions in the *wat* compound as both concrete and quite convincing examples of a community economy that contradict the rather common descriptions of the village communities in Thailand as 'loosely structured' and 'economically inefficient'.[7]

Baan Khaaw public health centre

A Health Centre was built in the village in 1987 by the Ministry for Public Health, which had been establishing such centres all over the country. By 1987 most villages in Thailand already had such centres but the Northeast, in this as in many other respects, had lagged behind in this general development. The Centre covers a '*tambon*', an administrative unit that (in this case) serves ten hamlets; the name of this *tambon* is Baan Khaaw. Our

village, Baan Phraan Muean, had then just recently been designated as the main village in this particular *tambon*, a fact of some importance when we are trying to give a description of change and development in this place over the number of years we are considering. Of course, such a centre (though periodically understaffed) has been a catalyst for tremendous improvement not only in relation to pregnancy and childbirth, but also for the general health care for all villagers, independent of age. Two of the three-to-five staff-members always have had training as midwives on top of their basic training as nurses. Every one of these '*mor tambon*' has been a delightful person with great understanding of local problems. They all have had a good sense of educating and teaching without prejudice or condescension and have often proven their ability to introduce and develop 'the new and modern' as a natural continuation of 'the old', and to let 'the old' continue where and when it did not harm anyone or anything.

A health centre that serves all hamlets in the *tambon* was established in Baan Phraan Muean by the Ministry of Public Health in 1987

Economic development

The descriptions of change in Baan Phraan Muean over the last forty years also reflect the tremendous changes that have occurred in the surrounding economy.

Despite the poor quality of the soil in Baan Phraan Muean some increase in the yield from the fields has been obtained through the introduction of fertilizers, new seed varieties, and lately through modern machinery that has replaced the traditional water buffalo in the cultivation of rice-fields. However, the improved output from farming is not the decisive factor in the economic development that has taken place in the village. Economic changes have also occurred in nearby town communities, for instance Udorn and Nong Khai. The Vietnam War and the civil war in Laos led to an economic boom in the towns, which were bases for the USA's military activities. The presence of military personnel on Thai territory brought with it business opportunities and investments in public buildings, hotels, restaurants, roads, bridges, and so on.

After the end of the Vietnam War, a serious stagnation set in. However, for a variety of political and social reasons vast amounts of public money continued to be directed to the Isan provinces. The war period, as well as what happened thereafter, gave many young villagers the opportunity for paid work in the towns. The pay was not high but town work earned more than farming at home, and it up-graded the youngsters' skills for various types of semi-professional jobs, mainly related to building and road construction. During one of my stays in the village in the early 1980s, I found that about one hundred people resident in Baan Phraan Muean earned full-time wages by working outside the village: in furniture making, electricity supplies, roadwork, building construction, forestry, and tailoring. Young women found employment mainly as servants in private

homes, in restaurants, and some in shops. About half of these were employed outside the hamlet all year round, and the other half followed the old, traditional patterns and had 'winter-jobs' after the harvest as a supplement to farming. In the same period in the early 1980s a few in the village owned small, very old and run-down automobiles, and they made their living by transporting goods and passengers in the towns. Some of these people lived throughout the week near their places of work and came home only for weekend visits, but most lived in the village and went away every morning and came back in the evening. This was now possible, as the transport system had improved considerably. A gravel road passing through the village was built around 1950. Around 1970 some regular goods and passenger services were established. In 1977, the road was paved with asphalt, and from around 1980 regular transportation services for goods and passengers were passing the village eight times a day in both directions.

The economic boom all over Thailand contributed much to the further development of the local economy. At the moment, it is impossible to say what the long-term consequences of the recent recession in the national economy will be, but during my stays in the area in 1999 and later some serious local consequences were reported, such as the forced sale of houses and farmland.

All of the above have contributed to changes in everyday life and to the development of a lifestyle based on money instead of on self-sufficiency and the exchange of goods and services. Nevertheless, relatively lowly paid jobs outside the village cannot possibly explain how the villagers have been able to afford the tremendous improvements of their houses. More likely we have to turn to a fully new trend beginning when the oil prices increased dramatically after 1973, followed by an economic boom in the oil states in the Middle East. There, they were short of manpower willing to do the

dirty, hard, and often dangerous work in all types of construction. The poor young men from Isan who traditionally went to Bangkok or to the local towns to earn a bit of cash during the dry season were more than willing to listen to the smart commission agents offering jobs in Saudi Arabia for a much higher pay than the unskilled local young men had ever dreamed of. If they were lucky, they could send back home a monthly amount three times the size of the salary for a teacher at the local school. To obtain a contract they had to pay the commissioner a considerable sum of cash. The sum varied, but it was more than they ever could get together without raising a loan on the family land. Now and then the commissioner cheated the young men: there was no job, or it was lower paid than promised. Many a family lost its rice land in this way, when they could not pay back the bank loan. There was no way to sue the commissioner, and this, too, is Thailand in a nutshell.

Many young men[8] went away for a year or more; some went overseas several times, and countries other than Saudi Arabia also became golden goals for them. Although they acknowledged that there were risks, they were used to gambling, and there was much to win if they succeeded. Three years savings and a good, well-constructed house would be paid for! The first results of this were obvious in the village during the late 1970s and quite remarkable during the 1980s and 1990s. When I visited in February 2001, about 40 young men from the village were abroad indicating that overseas labour contracts were still an attractive proposition.

Many things other than new, well-built houses have resulted from this change in the village economy and employment situation; some very positive, and some negative. It is very good that the villagers now can afford to buy well-made clothes for their children, medicine, nutritious baby food, and a number of modern appliances for their homes – things most townspeople have regarded as daily necessities for decades. Also, they now

have small motorbikes that are a boon for daily travel inside and outside the village. On the other hand, it would appear that some young wives of the far-away husbands spend a lot of money on sweets and poor-quality toys for their children and fancy things for themselves; and that they do not cook for themselves but take their meals together with their children at small local food shops. It seems as if all types of traditional crafts, such as basketry and weaving have ceased.

The grandparent generation does not understand today's life at all. It sees the younger generation as lazy, spending more money than it earns, spoiling its children totally, and so on. These are universal complaints often heard between two generations but in this village it is obvious that traditional family patterns are undergoing considerable and very rapid changes, and perhaps greater changes than in a neighbouring village, where not so many of the young people have been working abroad. It also worries the older generation that money lenders from the town today own some of the arable land in the hamlet, leaving it lying fallow just as an investment or renting it out to either the former owner or to other people in the hamlet.

The questions of the longer-term mental and social impact of these changes must be left open here in order to concentrate on the not un-important aspect of life and welfare of the families in our Northeastern Thai village that is the focus of this study. What happened to the traditional customs and rites related to pregnancy and childbirth during a period when so many other things changed in the life situation of the villagers?

The following chapters will focus on these issues, based on the findings and data collected from 1961–2005 as illustrated in the table on next page. For more information about these families and the research methodology, please refer to Part 3.

List of interviews and data collection 1961–2005

1961–62	Preliminary survey of the subject obtained in connection with a UNESCO study on education and social development in a village in Northeast Thailand – the children themselves and the families of the 47 pupils in the local school's Grade 1 were the research sample.
1968	Interviews with 33 of the initial sample families.
1978	Interviews with 27 families, of which 19 were from the initial sample families, supplemented with 8 of the youngest families in the village at that time.
1979–82	Supplementary data obtained during shorter visits in 1979, 1980, 1981 and 1982.
1988	Interviews with 34 families – of which 25 of the 1978 sample, supplemented with 9 of the youngest families in the village at that time. Additional interviews in 30 villages from a large areas around Udorn.
1991–97	Supplementary data obtained during shorter visits in 1991 and 1997.
1999	Interviews with 5 young families and 7 female teachers.
2001–05	Supplementary data obtained from Baan Phraan Muean and neighbouring countries: Cambodia (2001), Myanmar (2003), Yunnan in People's Republic of China (2004), and Laos (2005).

The teachers have recently somehow got hold of two old computers; they may be slow, but they work, and now the older pupils can be taught at least some basic principles of computer literacy (2005)

(1962)

CHAPTER TWO
Faith, Belief, and Birth

In the beginning of the 1960s, three aspects of the villager's world of faith were, according to the villagers, of special importance to and directly influential upon the pregnancy and a fortunate course of the childbirth:

- the fleeting soul called the *khwan*;

- the belief in 'old' or 'previous' mothers: the belief that 'old' or 'previous' mothers (*mae kau mae lang* or *mae kamlerd*) may want to take back the child during the birth or after it has been born;

- the two dreaded spirits *phii phraay* and *phii porb*.

In the following we shall look a little closer at each of these beliefs. We will listen to descriptions given by village elders, ritual masters and midwives, and report their opinions and evaluations. We shall also see how families actually conduct themselves in these matters, and we shall observe the changes that occurred over the years that this study was undertaken. As the world of faith in Baan Phraan Muean is well described elsewhere[9] we shall here only give the most essential background to enable what follows to be seen and understood in its wider context.[10]

Village Belief

Most of people in Thailand are Buddhists, as are those in the neighbouring countries of Burma, Laos, and Cambodia. All of the villagers in Baan Phraan Muean are Buddhists but they are plain ordinary people and their faith, their interpretations and explanations of how things hold together, will possibly cause discussion on many a detail based on doctrinaire theological viewpoints.

This is not particular to this village or to Thailand but is so everywhere. The villagers' conceptions of things are of interest to us as a basis for an understanding and evaluation of what they do in different situations.

Had this been a book primarily about religion I should be obliged to enter into deliberations about which elements of Thai faith belong under the umbrella of Buddhism and which do not. Many books have been written that classify and analyse this. The majority of authors introduce 'animism' as an aspect of Thai religious practice, implying that two religious systems exist side by side. This discussion is in itself both interesting and important from many points of view. However in my context, it is without meaning and I shall therefore leave the matter entirely alone. Instead I shall merely say that the villagers operate with a coherent system of beliefs that, in practice, does not have any built-in contradictions and conflicts. To them it is *one* system even though they know very well that part of it, strictly speaking, does not reflect a direct concern of the temple and the monks. To the villagers of Baan Phraan Muean it is, however, more natural and fruitful to see the relationship between these different traditions, as does Tambiah, as 'a field of religion in which various cults are arranged according to principles of complementarity, hierarchy, and linkage'.[11]

The Buddhist religion in a more restricted sense has hardly any relevance to the subjects we are dealing with in this book. The Buddhist temple and its monks have no function at all in our context. However, some of the fundamental principles of Buddhism have great influence on the villagers' whole outlook on life and their behaviour and they play an essential role in their day-to-day activities and beliefs – including those that belong to a different tradition.

Central in the world of the villagers is the idea of merit (*bun*) and demerit (*baab*). The simple man and woman consider that the amount of merit one has gathered for oneself throughout life has determining significance for the life into which one is later to be reborn. The person who has gleaned much merit will be reborn in happiness and wealth. Not only that, merit-making also gives satisfaction here and now as it gives gladness in the mind. And so merit-making protects one from mishaps and accidents in everyday life.

The conduct or actions of the individual gaining merit (*bun*) or demerit (*baab*) much occupies the villagers; that is understandable because one's amount of bun and baab at the time of death are balanced against each other, determining what will happen to your soul.

It is essential for our understanding of the rituals we are studying to keep in mind that in Thailand we find what some define as a belief in a 'dual soul', the *winyaan* and the *khwan*, and that these two parts are of widely different nature. Both are parts of man; indeed, together they could be what constitute human beings equipped with spiritual essences. *Winyaan* leaves man and can only leave man when death occurs, and it is its fate afterwards that one is concerned with because it is of importance for the cycle of rebirth.

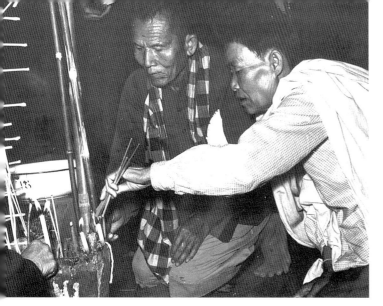

Worshipping in the *wat* (1962)

The *khwan* also leaves man at death and is then irretrievably lost, for which reason one is then no longer concerned about it. In contrast to the *winyaan*, however, the *khwan* can leave man at any time throughout his lifetime. When this happens it always does so for a reason, and there are unavoidable consequences resulting from this departure. The *khwan* can be so ill at ease, or so afraid, that it must leave man. This happens, for instance, when man is anxious, or ill, or in other ways in difficulties. Hence, the separation takes place when man's general condition is not good, and this condition deteriorates even further when the *khwan* has left. Many efforts in everyday life in the village must be directed towards preventing the *khwan* from leaving man. If the damage is done, one must do whatever possible to get the *khwan* back to its owner again. So the *khwan* is clearly tied to man's well-being, his mental condition, strength, his will to live, and his vital power. In our Western understanding, subjects such as these are closely connected to the world of psychology. We shall return to this shortly.

The village elders were of the opinion that when a person dies, the soul (*winyaan*) becomes an invisible spirit (*phii*). If one has a great excess of merit, one's soul will go to heaven to be reborn on this earth later when the amount of merit has been used up. In the case of approximate balance between *bun* and *baab*, *winyaan* must go to hell and not until the amount of *baab* has been expiated will it proceed to heaven, there to use up the acquired *bun* before the soul is again being reborn on earth. Of course it is quite dreadful if one has spent life on earth being a bad person and so has accumulated a large excess of demerit. In such cases, the *winyaan* is reduced to an existence as a freely-itinerant spirit (*phii*) on earth, or will be committed to hell until it will be reborn some time.

In another part of heaven a certain type of super naturals, the (male) angels, *theiwadaa*(s), reside. Man cannot become a *theiwadaa* at death, and a *theiwadaa* is never reborn.[12] To the ritual masters, and in the mind of ordinary people, spirits (*phii*) and *theiwedaa*(s) are opposites, in a way. *Phii*(s) may have their origins in people and can be benevolent but are most often malevolent. *Phii*(s) exist virtually everywhere – in trees, hills, water, animals, and in the earth. *Theiwadaa*(s) are of divine nature and are good angels.

As some *phii*(s) have their origin in people, this is a good explanation for their ability to be most different. They can be good and helpful if they are treated well. Capriciousness and spite, however, are much more commonly found in them. *Phii*(s) can punish people and can bring about mishaps, accidents, grief, distress, and illness. Good and divine *theiwadaa*(s) can help man against the activities practised by *phii*(s). For this reason they are invited to be present and to assist in many village rituals.

So, in our village, *theiwadaa*(s) are understood to be gods or angels of non-human origins, while most of the *phii*(s) are beings that have their origins in now-deceased humans. The most malevolent, powerful and dangerous *phii*(s) come from people who have suffered violent or unnatural deaths, including women who have died in childbirth (*phii phraay*). A much feared *phii* that may appear at childbirth is the *phii porb*, which is believed to have permanent existence.

We shall later return to the above in more details.

Khwan Rites

The villagers have the belief that the 'fleeting soul', the *khwan*, remains with man for as long as he has good health, has vigour and strength and is altogether comfortable with himself and his environment. But, they say, the *khwan* is inclined to leave man when his state of mind is not good. If man is left by his *khwan*, his already poor state of mind will be aggravated. The general condition will be bad and the result can be a real state of ill health. If this condition is not remedied it may lead to the death of the person affected. So, it is necessary to take action to prevent it if there is a possibility that the *khwan* might leave a person. If the condition is such that the *khwan* has already left, it must of necessity be called back (*suukhwan*) as a condition of recovery and the restoration of physical and mental vigour, strength, and well-being. There are many situations in which there is a danger that man can run into problems, and when the *khwan* may be inclined to vanish.

In a more Western secular understanding, many of the concepts underlying the *khwan* rites are connected to the world of psychology. In fact, I would argue that with the *khwan rites* we are faced with a well-developed

system for treatment of what may be called minor psychological miseries. As this system was functioning in the 1960s, it contained elements that are clearly comparable with what we, in the modern Western world, would describe as psychotherapy. To that extent, I would not hesitate to call it better suited for its purpose than anything we have been able to achieve, faced with

Suukhwan maemaan for two pregnant women (1962)

parallel groups of citizens in our countries. We in the West must acknowledge that practically all our psychological forms of therapy are best suited to people who are relatively well educated. In this village in Thailand the *khwan* rites, seen as a therapy, have reached a group of very ordinary people with very little educational background.

The *khwan* rites in this village in Thailand may well be directed towards an individual person and his/her problems but we are wrong if we call it 'individual therapy' as it draws in the person's surroundings; the family in the case of *suukhwan maemaan*. In other types of *khwan* rites, neighbours and friends (and at times the entire immediately surrounding community) are included. In

fact, the *khwan* ceremonies are all therapies where the social surroundings of the person – their 'network' – are drawn in as support. It is in this way in perfect agreement with what we in the Western world today consider most essential in order to achieve good results of psychotherapy. One is tempted to say that the villagers have practised for generations what we are only now approaching in theory, and what we are almost incapable of accomplishing in practice.

Through the *khwan* rites, Isan villagers have a very valuable and singularly good therapeutic tradition that, in their context, must be considered well-suited for minor neurotic conditions which may arise (or be thought to arise) in situations where people may suffer from fear, loss of courage, or the will or strength to live. These are situations in which dread can arise because of uneasiness with regard to mastering one's own personal situation or one's relationships in a social context.

The temple and the khwan rites

Let it be mentioned again that there is no connection between the Buddhist religion and the rites for *khwan* (and nor for the *mae kamlerd* rites). S. J. Tambiah explains that these ceremonies have their roots in Brahmanism but that in Thailand they are accepted under the roomy umbrella of Buddhism.[13]

Nevertheless, the two belief systems co-exist seamlessly and there is even a *khwan* ritual (*suukhwan naak*) directly connected with the young men's admittance as monks into the temple. As the Lord Abbot in Baan Phraan Muean expressed it in 1978, the *khwan* ceremonies are very important for the villagers' psychological and physical well-being, wholesomeness, and health. The harmonious co-habitation of traditional beliefs and Buddhism is also illustrated in the fact that the temple's assembly hall (*saalaa*) can be used for certain types of larger *khwan* rites when it is only there possible to accommodate all the participants. The monks' dwelling (*kuti*) can also be used. I have been present there for a *suukhwan thammadaa* several times in connection with celebrations of the New Year. On certain occasions, the monks also participate in *khwan* ceremonies (*suukhwan thammadaa*) in the village school.

'Suu khwan' – calling the khwan

Each time I visited the village I witnessed one or another *khwan* rite. To me, there is no doubt that they were always taken seriously by all those present. These rites are not just ceremonial traditions that merely live on in an outward form without an obvious meaning for those participating. However, the types of *khwan* rites in actual use are today somewhat limited compared with earlier times.

In the *khwan* ceremonies that I have personally witnessed and which I have described below, it was almost self-evident that the rites must have had a relieving and anxiety-releasing effect on the person's mental and psycho-social condition. Let us look at some examples:

Two youngsters had been to prison for a time because of a brawl during a temple festival. To ensure that their *khwan*(s) accompanied them home and would not leave them after their arrival home a suukhwan thammadaa was performed after they were released. The rite was attended by family, friends and neighbours, and was concluded by a large common meal and cosy, prolonged togetherness. Tambiah mentions the same situation and records: 'The youths were not condemned or in any way ostracized; rather, the ethos of the village was such that they were greeted, accepted and reintegrated. This is an object lesson in rehabilitation, and an impressive demonstration of the community ethos.'[14]

Another example concerned a popular head teacher who had been employed in the village school for many years and who, against his own wishes and contrary to the wishes of the villagers, was transferred to another village where the school was neglected and needed a capable leader. This man was in a situation that could have caused considerable personal uneasiness, insecurity and anxiety, one in which his *khwan* might be inclined to leave him. His successor as head teacher was, in reality, in the same situation. He had been selected by the provincial authorities to be the leader of the school. He was from the same province but he hardly knew anybody in the village and nobody knew anything much of him.

I witnessed the common *suukhwan thammadaa* performed for these two men in January 1981. More than one hundred adults in the village took part, among them, of course, all formal and informal village leaders. The teachers were there, as were the monks from the temple led by the Lord Abbot. All the school children were there, not as direct participants but as interested observers. The *khwan* ceremony in itself, the subsequent common meal, the spontaneous dancing as the rice whisky began to have effect, the likewise spontaneously-performed popular, local, and somewhat daring 'folk opera' (*mor lam*), left no doubt that there was a warm fellowship between the celebrants and the audience. Both school leaders' *khwan*(s) must have been strengthened! And so were also the *khwan*(s) of the UNESCO team by the *suukhwan thammadaa* the villagers performed by the conclusion of the field-work in 1962. (See photos to the right, of Prof. S. J. Tambiah [top] and the author [bottom].)

The social-psychological and individual-psychological effects of the supporting fellowship are of substantial importance for the prophylactic and therapeutic effect that is doubtless a consequence of many a *khwan* cere-

mony. However, while the coming together of the participants in the ceremony is an important element in the *khwan* rites, there are other elements which, according to local understanding, are just as important: the ritual objects, the ritual text, and the person performing the rite – the ritual master ('*phaam*' or '*mor khwan*'). Certain ritual objects belong in every *suukhwan* ceremony, and they must be manipulated in the correct manner and in the correct sequence. Broadly speaking, the ritual elements are common and almost the same for all types of *khwan* ceremonies.

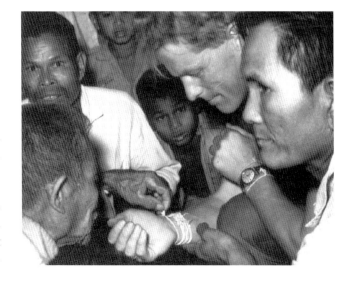

When our study began in the 1960s, the *khwan* was considered very easily affected in connection with pregnancy and childbirth and was therefore the object of much attention.

The *khwan* ceremony for the pregnant woman is called *suukhwan maemaan*. The literal meaning of the name of this rite is to call (*suu*) the *khwan* of the pregnant woman (*maemaan*). The word '*khwan*' itself in the literature is tentatively translated as the 'life spirit' and 'morale' – indicating a state of peace of mind, harmony, the will to live, or the vigour of life – which is the situation when a person's *khwan* is 'at home' and is well.

The declared purpose of *suukhwan maemaan* is to give the mother strength and an easy delivery. The *khwan* rite aims to ease any anxiety and to give the mother peace of mind about the coming event. If the pregnant woman is well psychologically she will also feel better physically, and indirectly that will help her to an easy delivery. The concept encompasses a sprinkling of magic – it is believed that the *suukhwan* has the power to *make* the delivery easier which is a key concern of the villagers. Childbirth may be considered a natural thing but in this village it has been seen often enough that a birth can be a serious matter for the mother as well as for the baby. The mother may also be anxious about the pains involved, and above all about complications that may arise. The villagers have seen so many cases in which they were helpless bystanders while the birth ended in illness or death.

The same train of thought comes to the fore if the mother is poorly or has lost courage. It is then believed that the khwan has left her and that it must be called back.

The purpose of the *suukhwan maemaan* is, therefore, partly to prevent a mental state of unbalance, and partly to treat such a condition should it already have arisen.

The *suukhwan maemaan* as a ceremony in Baan Phraan Muean is so well described, comprehensively discussed and evaluated by Tambiah (1970) that it would be meaningless for me to go into details here.

I will therefore merely describe a few elements as a background for the following description. The very esteemed ritual master, Phor Jampii had the following ideas about the *suukhwan maemaan* which he dictated to me shortly before his death in January 1980: 'The rite of *suukhwan maemaan* should be performed in the 5th to 6th month of the pregnancy. The purpose of it is to help the mother have an easy delivery and give birth to a healthy child. It also has a certain prolonged effect for the baby which will be a happy child, not sickly, and easy to bring up. Generally, the rite should be performed before noon on a day the astrologer (*mor duu*) has identified as an auspicious day.'

As with all *suukhwan* rites, people gather around an offering to the *khwan*, a carefully and beautifully

The carefully executed flower decoration (*phaa khwan*) is intended to attract the *khwan* to come and be present at the rite

executed decoration (*phaa khwan*) standing on a tray. There is also an offering of food, usually a boiled egg, bananas, a lump of sticky rice, and some beautiful flowers. All this is intended to attract the *khwan* to come and be present at the ceremony. The *khwan* takes its place in this lovely *phaa khwan* which is really considered a symbol for the *khwan* itself.

A long thread of good fortune (*faay mongkhon*), spun from cotton, is tied to the *phaa khwan* and passes from there to all who are participating in the ceremony, symbolizing their support and involvement. The participants sit with their hands in the traditional Thai *wai* position, the palms of the hands held together at chest to lower face level. Everyone holds the thread in the grove between the thumb and the index finger.

As the most important of the 32 *khwan*(s)[15] that resides in man's body is the *khwan* of the head, the pregnant woman carries a ring of thread or bamboo trimmed with small pieces of white cotton on her head. A specially produced wax candle burns during the entire ceremony. This candle (*thian wian hua*) is formed around a wick the length of which is adjusted to reach round the head of the pregnant woman, measured at the forehead.

The effect of the ceremony is enhanced and supported by the persons who participate in the ceremony together with the mother-to-be. These are first and foremost elder, close female relatives, and at times, elder male relatives. Highly esteemed elderly female neighbours are often witnesses to the ceremony as well. The husband is most often there but according to the tradition his presence is not absolutely necessary.

There are several steps in this ritual, most importantly the reading of the text itself. The ceremony is concluded (as are all rites of this kind) when the ritual master (*mor khwan*) ties a cotton thread round the woman's wrists and symbolically ties the khwan, which is now definitely domiciled, firmly to her. In turn, all other participants in the ceremony now tie these 'powerful' cotton threads around the woman's wrists, all the time mumbling magic incantations with wishes for her and her baby.

After the ceremony, everybody gathers around a large and lengthy common meal, which has been prepared during the ceremony by younger relatives and neighbours.

The *suukhwan maemaan* is the khwan rite that is clearly directed towards the period of pregnancy, and it is performed without first having consulted a *mor sorng* (diagnostician). It is customary, as prevention and treatment, in the situation in which the woman finds herself. If the pregnant woman feels well it may not be necessary to perform the ceremony. However, if someone sees a

Today the *phaa khwan* is much more elaborate than before

Other khwan rites related to pregnancy and birth

The *suukhwan luang* ceremony is performed during evenings and nights. It is intended for adults suffering from an illness diagnosed to have been caused by the absence of *khwan*. If a pregnant woman intended to perform the *suukhwan maemaan* ceremony but did not manage to do so in time before the childbirth, this rite can be performed after the birth. In such cases the woman may not display any symptoms of ill health but she has the feeling that her *khwan* may have gone lost after the birth. The ceremony starts at night after the woman has fallen asleep. After reciting the ritual text for this rite, the ritual master ties a cotton thread to one of the woman's wrists. This is to be repeated for three evenings in succession. It is believed that after this the woman will get her *khwan* back and will be freed from the effects that loss of *khwan* might have had on her. If this does not happen, or if the ritual master during the night following one of his recitals of the *suukhwan luang* text has an ill-boding dream, the rite must be repeated every night until his dreams are again well-omened.

Another ceremony, called the *suukhwan kong khau*,[16] also takes place in the evening. The name refers to the fact that the ceremony includes the use of a plaited container used for the local sticky rice, an ordinary household item (*kong*: container; *khau*: rice). The *suukhwan kong khau* ceremony is used for children up to the age of around ten years who are ill because their *khwan* has left them. The symptoms are often that the child does not thrive, will not take its mother's milk, loses weight, or sleeps restlessly. The child does not have to be present when the rite is performed. The mother must decorate the above-mentioned *kong khau* with flowers and candles and take it to the ritual master in his home by herself or the child's father must do so. For three successive evenings the master recites the special text required for this ceremony. During the recitation,

rainbow (an omen of a difficult birth) the *suukhwan maemaan* must be performed for all who were pregnant at the time. Whether this in fact happens cannot be stated definitely but several people in our research groups spontaneously mentioned this special occasion.

In addition, there are a couple of special *khwan* rites that can be performed for the mother and for her child that should be mentioned briefly.

the *kong khau* is standing open in front of him. After having done this, he must at least one of the nights have dreams that bode well, and none that bode evil. If the ritual master has good dreams he will put the lid on the container on the third evening and the child's *khwan* is then considered to have returned to the child. If the master does not have the appropriate dreams he must continue the recital for more than three evenings.

If the right dreams continue to be absent, it is assumed that a wrong diagnosis has been made and that the child's problems have other causes than the loss of the *khwan*.

When the rite is concluded successfully, the mother (and in exceptional cases the father) brings the child to the ritual master who ties a magic cotton thread round the child's wrist in order to tie the *khwan* to the child. The mother then takes the closed *kong khau* home with her.

Extension of the suukhwan maemaan rites

A concept of the *khwan* that is largely reminiscent to the *khwan* we know from Baan Phraan Muean is probably known throughout Thailand. Besides Tambiah, however, only two references mention a *khwan* rite performed especially for the woman during pregnancy: Sparkes from a village close to Loei, and Whittaker from a village 60 km North of Roi Et, both in the Northeast. None of them provides any details.[17]

My 1988 interviews in 30 villages in an area mainly north and east of Udorn indicated that the *suukhwan maemaan* ceremony was known in 20 of the villages but that it was not performed very often in 11 of these.

A few interviews made in 1968 around Saraburi, the region bordering the Central Plain, indicated that a *suukhwan maemaan* ceremony most probably was unknown in these parts of the country.

My own (few) interviews in Laos in 1968 showed that a ceremony was performed there, which in its details resembles the *suukhwan maemaan* ceremony from Baan Phraan Muean. This was confirmed by my interviews in the surroundings of Vientiane in February 1999, and again in February 2005 on the Plain of Jars and in Luang Prabang.

In an attempt to demarcate how widely the *suukhwan maemman*, which in Baan Phraan Muean is performed **before** the birth, is known we have consulted existing collections of ritual texts from Northeast Thailand. These collections of ritual texts are the standard references for ritual masters.

Interestingly, the collections only include *khwan* rites related to birth and pregnancy that should be performed for mother and child **after** the birth and after the confinement (*yuu fai*); the names of these *suukhwan* rites are *suukhwan mae yuukam* and *suukhwan deknory*. Oliver Raendchen has also published lists of *khwan* rites both from Northeast Thailand and from Laos.[18] There is no *khwan* rite for the mother included here either that is to be performed before the birth.

My conclusion in relation to the extension of a *khwan* rite performed for the woman <u>before</u> the birth has to be that it is only documented by my own findings in a rather large area mainly north and east of Udorn, and supported by two references from the same geographical area, Sparkes and Whittaker, and by my own findings in a few places in Laos. This result surprises me greatly because the rite, as I know it, is very elaborate and various versions of the ritual text are locally known.

I could hope that my findings in this respect would challenge researchers engrossed in the Isan oral village culture to study this further.

Relating to other neighbouring countries, I have found nothing that seems comparable to the *suukhwan maemaan* we know from Baan Phraan Muean.[19]

Mae Kamlerd

Tambiah divided the *khwan* rites into six groups.[20] Of these only the *suukhwan maemaan* mentioned in the second group relates to pregnancy and childbirth. However, in these six groups he also includes (in groups 2 and 5) some rites addressed to super naturals pictured as the 'old mothers' or the former spiritual mothers, who may want to fetch back the child right at birth or after it has been born.

My studies of these traditions, however, have led me to question this categorization and the inclusion of these rites among the *khwan* rites. I find that the rites related to the belief in the rites 'old mothers' or 'previous mothers' – *taengkae maemaan* and *taengkae mae kamlerd*, often just called *kae kamlerd* – are totally different from the *khwan* rites and the concepts related to these, and that they must be considered as an entirely independent group of rites.

Besides a brief mentioning by Tambiah (1970), it has not been possible for me to find any references to this group of rites. We shall therefore look somewhat more detailed into this whole topic.

In the 1960s, the village elders and 'ritual experts' described and interpreted the background for these rites as follows. Every child that is to be born comes from the great creator, *puu thaen yaa thaen. Puu thaen*[21] means 'paternal grandfather in heaven'. He lives in remote zones of the heaven, or perhaps just somewhere in the air. *Yaa thaen* correspondingly means 'paternal grand-mother'. *Puu thaen yaa thaen* is understood to be the supreme of all gods and goddesses, belonging in *mueang thaen* that lies above the heavens.

Puu thaen yaa thaen is responsible for every child that is born. It is he who sends the child. One must pray to him to persuade him to allow the child about to be born to be a healthy child, so that it will be 'born well'. It is possible that it is in fact too early for this child to be born, that something has happened so that the child must be taken back. By praying to *puu thaen yaa thaen* one tries to achieve that he, in this very pregnancy, will act in such a way that it will not be necessary for him to take the child back.

In reality, the villagers sometimes think of *puu thaen yaa thaen* as the child's father with the implication that conception has taken place without the assistance of the husband but instead by the 'Great Creator'. As it is his child, he will sometimes not let it live as a human after all but will try to take it back to himself again. He does not consider that the time has yet come for the child to be born into this family. *Puu thaen yaa thaen* can cloak himself in many forms and appear both as a man and a woman. If he wants to take his child back, he always appears in the shape of a woman and is then called *mae kau mae lang*. Literally, this name refers to the mothers in the child's former lives and by some she is understood to be the one who was the mother of the child during its immediately previous life. *Mae kau mae lang* also appears under the everyday name of *mae kamlerd* because she represents a series of ominous symptoms in the tiny baby, under one heading described as *kamlerd*. The child may appear to be sickly if, for example, it cries and screams unnaturally, or it is unable to suck its mother's milk, or there are inflammations in the throat. *Mae kamlerd* is the 'mother', the cause of these symptoms. She is interpreted as a person with evil intentions, sent by *puu thaen yaa thaen* to take back the child. It is the case, it is said that in all life's circumstances, there will always be somebody or other, something or another, attempting to ruin the good thing about to happen. In this instance *mae kamlerd*. The great creator must think that it is too early for this child to be born into this family after all. Its previous mother still considers that it belongs to her and will endeavour to take it back. In this

way the *mae kau mae lang* (or the *mae kamlerd* as she is also called) is interpreted as the child's previous mother or in any case her representative, who has been sent to fetch the child at the request of *puu thaen yaa thaen*.

The explanations above were given to me by some of the local ritual masters – and where they originated I do not know – may be in India? To most people the reality was that there is danger afoot at childbirth, and that this is due to *mae kamlerd*. She is therefore quite definitely the one they must endeavour to prevent from carrying out her intention. A rite must be performed to make *mae kamlerd* allow the child to remain in peace where it is now to be born. As the outcome is uncertain, the rite includes elements of both bribery and trickery. Hence the offerings to *mae kamlerd* include a 'symbolic' child that she may be satisfied with and so leave the newly-born alone.

The rite must be performed as closely to the birth as possible as *mae kamlerd* can be relied upon to appear just around the time of birth.

The whole ceremony is called *taengkae maemaan* and means an action (*taeng*) that is to deliver (*kae*) the pregnant woman (*maemaan*). At times the rite achieves the desired result, at other times not. Even if everything at first looks alright and the rite apparently has been successfully performed it may later happen that the *mae kamlerd* discovers the fraud of the symbolic child, or that she is otherwise dissatisfied with the offering made. She may therefore return at any time after the child has been born.

Two of the ritual masters, who were our consultants in this rite in the 1970s, thought that the *mae kamlerd* could return right up to the time when the child is 12 years old while another thought that she could succeed in harming the baby only during the first two to three months after the birth. They agreed that at all times throughout childhood one must pay attention to any symptoms in the child that could have been caused by the *mae kamlerd*.

Whether she is responsible for an actual illness the child suffers from can be ascertained only by approaching a *mor sorng* (the 'expert' who can 'search' and find out by 'seeing'). A *mor sorng* belongs to the large group of ritual specialists in our village that are a very important link in the thriving and feeling of security in everyday life. The *mor sorng* is at the same time adviser, diagnostician, and prophet. But he does not, under any circumstances, occupy himself with healing whether by medicine or by magic. He identifies the cause of the symptoms and will then make suggestions as to what ought to be done.

In the 1970s, there were three or four *mor sorng* in Baan Phraan Muean. They employed various methods for their diagnosis including looking through an egg while a lit candle was held behind, or looking through a cone made from a leaf, or using a mirror. At that point in time, everyone would respect that one had to seek out a *mor sorng* to sort out properly what was wrong. Even in the village, a correct diagnosis was considered an essential condition for qualified treatment!

If a *mor sorng* finds that the symptoms are caused by *mae kamlerd*, one then is informed about what to do. If the child is only slightly ill it may be sufficient to perform the *pau kamlerd*. The villagers will often start with this, the least-demanding rite. If the child does not get well, or perhaps worse, the more comprehensive and 'stronger' *taengkae mae kamlerd* ceremony must be performed.

The purpose of *pau kamlerd* and *taengkae mae kamlerd* is the same, namely to free the child from the symptoms caused by the *mae kamlerd*. It is understood that if the illness is caused by *mae kamlerd* it is to be taken seriously.

It is *mor sorng*, and only he, who can make a diagnosis. The illness may be due to many things other than the *mae kamlerd* – for example the evil influence of a spirit (*phii*). If this is the case, the *mor sorng* will also play a role in the treatment by helping to identify which *phii* is involved so that the villager can approach the *mor phii* who knows the treatment for that particular case. The sick child might also have symptoms connected with its *khwan*. If so, the *mor khwan* must be consulted. If the symptoms are not due to any of these supernatural things at all (which *mor sorng* can also tell), it is necessary to approach a *mor yaa*, a herbal specialist who can cure illnesses that do not have their root in the spirit world.

It is important to mention that there is a further step that has to be taken between the 'diagnosis' and the 'treatment' itself. Hence the treatment will only have its proper effect if it is enacted on the right day and at the right time for the person involved. Both the day and the time of the ceremony must bode well. Here enters the astrologer (*mor leik* and *mor duu*) as an inevitable link who must also be consulted in the majority of cases. The astrologer knows that there are certain basic principles to be observed. While the *suukhwan maemaan* ceremony can be performed on all days except Thursdays, the *taengkae maemaan* must always be performed on a Saturday. The astrologer can sort out which Saturday it ought to be and at which hour of the day. The *taengkae mae kamlerd* and *pau kamlerd* can in principle be performed on any day but only during the late hours of the afternoon.

Only when the astrologer has established the most auspicious day and the time can one take the required action. When a condition is acute it may not be possible to wait until the day determined by the astrologer. If the ceremony thereafter has not produced the proper effect it is often understood to be due to this very fact.

Let us end this description of the village elders' interpretations of the rites for *mae kamlerd*, with a summary:

The *taengkae maemaan* should be performed before birth but as closely to it as possible. It has the purpose to free the mother from the dangers that might arise during delivery as the *mae kamlerd* might try to prevent the child from remaining in the family into which it is now born.

In the case of a sudden childbirth there may not be time to perform the *taengkae maemaan*. In such cases it is possible to perform a special rite with the same purpose soon after the birth. In both cases the rite has prophylactic aim. After the birth, the rite is called *taengkae mae kamlerd*, or often just *kae kamlerd*. The name means an action (*taeng*) that is to deliver from, or banish (*kae*), *mae kamlerd*. Besides the prophylactic aim the *taengkae mae kamlerd* can also be performed if the child has (often rather severe) symptoms which the *mor sorng* attributes to *mae kamlerd*. It can therefore be performed throughout childhood.

If the symptoms are less alarming it may not be necessary to perform this very strong and rather complicated rite. In these cases, the situation is often initially addressed through a minor rite that is easier to arrange for and which does not require as much time. This smaller ceremony is called *pau kamlerd*. The intention is the same, to treat and remove symptoms caused by *mae kamlerd*. The ritual master 'blows' or 'puffs' (*pau*) magic words onto the child whereby the *kamlerd* symptoms vanish.

The above describes the beliefs and tradition of the villagers in Baan Phraan Muean during the 1960s and 1970s. However, we must not forget that only some kilometres away was a district health centre and in Udorn a hospital. In Udorn, too, all sorts of medicine were available at the pharmacy. In addition, one of the

teachers working in Baan Phran Muan in the 1960s had been a nursing orderly during his military service and therefore had a certain expertise that he passed on. There were in other words, certain limited alternatives to the traditional treatments even in the 1960s and 1970s. We shall later look into the extent to which these alternatives were employed at the time.

Over the years, I have been present at various *taengkae maemaan* rites. The first occasion was in 1961 and though the ceremony on following occasions were not performed by the same ritual master, the different performances of this rite were practically identical, perhaps because the new ritual master were trained by the older master. The following is a description of the course of the whole ceremony as it happened in 1961.

Taengkae maemaan – a case history

Around 3 p.m. the ritual master, Phor Tuu Phan, arrived at the house. He, the pregnant woman, and her husband, sat down on the roofed veranda outside the main room of the house. The husband had previously cut a number of sticks of the banana plant – green sappy stems as thick as an arm. He had also cut a good number of banana leaves, and a lot of thin, split bamboo slivers of different lengths. In addition, a large lump of soft clay and cotton threads of various colours had been prepared for the ceremony.

Phor Tuu Phan could not count the number of times he had conducted this ceremony, and it was obvious that he was master of his role as leader and performer of the ceremony. He immediately began to produce the items that were to be used as ritual objects, assisted by the woman and her husband. He prepared all the more complicated objects, and put these in their correct places.

First he made a *krathong*, a sort of box or tray that is made for many special purposes and shaped accordingly.

In this case, it can best be described as a 40 x 40 cm square, low box with nine compartments made of banana rods and folded leaves. The box rested on four legs, one in each corner, also made from banana rods. The rods that formed the legs extended upwards above the rim of the box and were tied together, so that the whole *krathong* took on the shape of a pyramid. The rods were joined partly by using thin bamboo splinters as 'needles', and partly by tying them together with plant fibres.

Phor Tuu Phan then formed eight little clay animal figures, one for each of the traditional eight points of the compass. The figures were laid in the eight compartments along the edges of the *krathong*. There was a tiger, a naga, a rat, an elephant, a cow, a garuda, a cat, and a lion.

After this, small lumps of differently coloured sticky rice, *khau dam* (black rice), *khau daeng* (red rice), *khau lueang* (yellow rice) and lastly, plain rice (*khau khaaw*) were formed and scattered randomly into all compartments.

As the whole rite is connected with the great creator *puu thaen yaa thaen*, the instruments needed for him to create a child must be present. For that reason, small models of the blacksmith's tools – hammer, anvil, a pair of bellows, tongs, mould, etc. – were formed from clay, bamboo, and banana leaves. These were put into a certain compartment in the *krathong*. Then Phor Tuu Phan made an 'infant', coarsely cut from a bit of banana rod. It was given a scrap of a loincloth around the waist and was laid into the centre compartment of the *krathong*. With it were a 'bundle of silver' and a 'bundle of gold', also made from the banana plant. Into all the compartments were then scattered little models of all sorts of utensils, baskets, the ladder up to the house, a yoke, etc. – all crudely made on the spot from available materials. Then, on each of the *krathong*'s four legs were placed nine thin sticks of split bamboo, stuck into the banana plant rods. They bristled

like ships' masts above the whole stand. Each of them was equipped with nine bits of thread in red, black, yellow, and white, with no definite number of colours on each 'mast'. Many of these details are mentioned in the ritual text (see Part 2).

Finally a candle was made. A cotton thread was laid around the woman's forehead. It was then cut off so that its length matched the circumference of her head exactly. This thread was rolled in a soft wax. When finished, the candle (*thian wian hua*) was a little thinner than a pencil.

The preparations had by then progressed so far that the ceremony itself could commence. It began with the pregnant woman and Phor Tuu Phan showing respect

(1961)

(1961)

and reverence to 'the higher powers' in the customary manner: kneeling, with arms stretched halfway forward, the palms of the hands together, they *wai'* ed – bowing several times towards the *krathong*, the forehead almost touching the floor.

A white cotton thread was tied between the *krathong* and a small clay jar (*khaay*) in which lay the presents to the master of the ceremony. In this case the presents consisted of vegetables, two boiled eggs, a washed-out cotton cloth, in size corresponding to a man's loincloth (*phaa khaumaa*), five small wax candles, a little cotton thread, and two *baht* (which then was worth about ten American cents). The cotton thread between the gift jar and the *krathong* symbolized the connection between the ritual master and the beneficiary.

The following is the sequence of the various steps in the ceremony:

1. Phor Tuu Phan first took a small lump of ordinary, boiled, sticky rice and formed it into a little ball. Moving this ball of rice (*khuad khau*) forwards and backwards near the woman, he then mumbled magic words. With the *khuad khau* he would draw out all illnesses from the woman. Subsequently the lump of rice, and with it all illnesses, were tossed into a random compartment in the *krathong*.

2. The long, thin candle was lit. It was fastened to the rim of the *krathong*. Only a short piece extended above the edge, so that the long, limp end lay along the floor. This very candle, because of the way it had been made, indicated that all of this was about this particular woman and the child she was expecting. For this reason the candle burned all the time during the whole ceremony, and as soon as the short piece above the *krathong*'s edge burned down to the rim, Phor Tuu Phan

moved it up a bit. It had to be done many times to avoid that the candle would extinguish its flame.

3. Phor Tuu Phan then invited all *theiwadaa*(s) (guardian angels) to come and witness what was happening and protect the woman against all dangers. He indicated that the *theiwaadaa*(s) could know whom it was all about from the burning candle and the way it was made. While inviting the *theiwadaa*(s) to attend the ceremony Phor Tuu Phan was throwing rice grains over his shoulder and down into the *krathong* inviting them to accept the offering in the *krathong*. The *theiwedaa*(s) were to assist in keeping all illnesses and dangers away from the woman, and protect against the dangers that could threaten the mother and the child from *puu thaen yaa thaen*.

4. Phor Tuu Phan then made *nam mon*, magic water, reciting magic words in Pali, while melted wax from the long candle dripped down into the water.

5. A short wax candle, *thian khuu aayu*, also attached to the edge of the *krathong*, was lit.

6. Phor Tuu Phan then sprinkled the magic water by hand over the *krathong* as an offering (*yaad nam*) to *mae kau mae lang*.

7. The young mother then took some of the magic water in her hand and applied it to her hair. She would then sweep the drops that had settled in her hair down into the *krathong* with her hand. Thereby illnesses were removed.

8. Phor Tuu Phan then tied white cotton threads around the woman's wrists. First he tied around her left wrist while requesting her *khwan* to come home if it had left her, and then to her right wrist while he beseeched the *khwan* never to leave the woman.

9. With some words in Pali, Phor Tuu Phan asked for everything good for the woman.

10. Then, finally, could he begin to recite the text of the *taengkae maemaan* (for the text, see Part 2).

When the long recitation ended, the *krathong* with its content of sacrificial gifts inclusive the 'child' was taken away, usually by the husband. It had to be placed in such a way that the 'previous mother' whenever she might approach the house after the mother had given birth to her child inevitably must come across the offering. Phor Tuu Phan informed us that the 'previous mother' would arrive from the corner of the world corresponding to the pregnant woman's year of birth. In this case, the *krathong* was therefore placed to the North of the house on a site outside the land belonging to this family but not on any other person's property – i.e. on the boundary line. Hence it is hoped that the 'previous mother' would be deceived and satisfied with the offering, and that she would leave the mother and her newly born baby in peace.

This was the conclusion of the ceremony. There were no guests, no family or friends participating in a *taengkae maemaan*, so there was no meal or anything else expensive connected to this rite. Phor Tuu Phan did not take all that was laid out as a gift for him in the little *khaay*. He was content with one of the eggs and the two *baht* in cash. When asked afterwards, he said that the family would probably have felt slightly offended, had he taken it all.

During the course of the rite, the mother sat devoutly and listened and was obviously intensely engrossed in what went on. Nevertheless, she also had to keep an eye on her toddler who could not leave her or the items alone. The mother appealed several times to a daughter of about ten to take care of the boy but she could not make him behave. The husband was sitting behind. He took no part in the ceremony and, typically, it did not occur to him to take charge of the restless youngster!

The *taengkae mae kamlerd*, which is performed after the birth, follows almost the same pattern as in the rite described above. Some masters, however, shape the *krathong* differently as I recently had occasion to observe. (See photos on pp. 45 and 60.)

This ceremony directed at preventing the 'old mother' or 'previous mother' from taking back the new-born (*taengkae maemaan*) is highly respected by the local monks, and so are also the other *kamlerd* rites mentioned. Hence the monks even told how the old or previous mother (*mae kau mae lang*) had sought to do harm in one or another family.

Please note that the ritual texts and comments to these are reprinted in Part 2.

Extension of the mae kamlerd cult

Apart from the works of Tambiah, I have only succeeded in finding two references[22] that probably have to do with the *mae kau mae lang/mae kamlerd* ceremonies; unfortunately none of them provide any details. Stephen Sparkes writes: 'Another ritual was held for the pregnant woman called "bargaining with the maternal grandfather".' Sparkes' work is from a village close to Loei, about 150 km northwest of Baan Phraan Muean. Whittaker writes about a village close to Khon Kaen: 'Kamlert is usually a fatal condition in neonates, and it is believed that only the action of a 'mor pow', a traditional 'blowing' doctor can cure (…).'

Both correspond well with my own findings in 30 villages in an area around Udorn in 1988, which proved that the ceremony was very well known in 26 of these localities – a few of these not far from Loei. Further, I have information from Sakon Nakhon indicating that the cult was known there about 200 kilometres east of Udorn (personal communication with Mrs Supranee).

In the boundary areas between the Northeast and the Central Plain provinces, more accurately in villages around Saraburi, in 1968, I found just one informant who had vague ideas about *mae kamlerd*. She seemed to identify it with '*mae suee*' known in the Central Plain as a cult concerned with the survival of the infant child. All other informants in this area only knew of the *mae suee* and the nomenclature around this cult.

It seems that there might be a basic concept corresponding to *mae suee* or *mae kamlerd* underlying the rites for *phau-koed mae-koed* (birth-father and birth-mother) mentioned by Kingshill[23] and Viggo Brun[24] and the *padkae maemarn* rites,[25] as well as the Father Thaen and Mother Thaen mentioned by Davis,[26] all from the North of Thailand. However, the information is not comprehensive enough to state anything definite about a possible relationship.

As mentioned above, I documented in 1988 that *mae kamlerd* and the rites for her were very well known in 26 out of 30 localities in a rather large area around Udorn. I therefore expected to find this reflected in the printed collections of ritual texts existing in Thailand. Surprisingly, none of the published compilations of ritual texts include any rituals related to the *mae kamlerd*: neither *taengkae maemaan* nor *taengkae mae kamlerd*. In fact, the texts found in these compilations do not mention *mae kamlerd* – not even in relation to the rites performed after the birth or in connection with *yuu fai*. As a further investigation of this, we approached research institutions and libraries that specialize in or study Isan culture.[27] None of these institutions could refer me to any research, nor had they ever heard about the *mae kamlerd* or the rites used to protect the mother and the young child from her.

I find it most surprising that the concept of *mae kamlerd* should be so absent in the research that in practice it appears not to be documented and registered anywhere. This is even more puzzling as the cult is so important an element in the world view of the Baan Phraan Muean villagers, that it still survives today when other parts of traditional belief has disappeared.

During the survey we discussed with the ritual masters and some villagers why it is that the *mae kamlerd* rites are not documented anywhere. According to them, one possible explanation why the *mae kamlerd* rites have remained undocumented may be the fact that these rites are performed as a very private affair, often in a context of considerable mental strain and sorrow. In contrast, the *suukhwan* rites are always performed in public and often center around more joyous transitions and occasions such as weddings, housewarming, homecomings, the beginning of a new project, etc. In any case, the matter deserves further investigation.

A medical doctor has not been able to improve the health of this 6-week-old baby. The family has now seen the local diviner (*mor sorng*), who found that *mae kamlerd* has caused the baby's rather serious symptoms why a *taengkae mae kamlerd* rite must be held for the baby. Khun Jan is today the most reputed *mor kamlerd* in the district (February 2003)

In a last effort to evaluate the extension of the rites connected to *mae kamlerd*, we made a survey in December 2005 among the seven ritual masters who are currently working in our area. The survey gave some indications on the extension of the *mae kamlerd* cult in the area, which are presented in the table on next page.

It is interesting to note that the task as ritual master has often passed from father to son. Of our seven ritual masters, only Khun Jan and Khun Sukan (who are our primary informers) have been trained by the same ritual master, namely Phor Jampii. The survey confirmed that ritual masters that have been trained by different ritual masters all use a different text.

The survey may also indicate something about the perceived strength of the *taengkae* (*mae kamlerd*) rites – it was said about Mor Toey, a cousin of Phoor Jampii who trained together with him under the same ritual master, that he did not perform the *kamlerd* rites as he was not considered as 'powerful' as Phor Jampii; even after Phor Jampii's death he did not start to perform these rites.

Today, Khun Jan only performs the *taengkae* rites (*mae kamlerd*) having let his younger cousin take over the performance of the *suukhwan* rites. As Khun Sukan is becoming more experienced and more accepted he is increasingly also performing the *taengkae* rites. This

may indicate that the ritual master needs to be a strong and charismatic personality to successfully perform the *taengkae* rites.

The survey also illustrated that the demand for the *taengkae* rites is higher in Baan Ngory than it is in Baan Phraan Muean. According to Khun Jan, the reason for this is likely that access to the hospital in town is more difficult from Baan Ngory than it is from Baan Phraan Muean.

During the survey, it was confirmed that the rites for *mae kamlerd* are known in the area around Khon Kaen. However, we did not manage to contact the ritual masters there and so there is no information about how widely it is performed.

Below a survey of the extension of *mae kamlerd* rites:

Neighbouring countries

With respect to the neighbouring countries, in 1968, I recorded a description of *taengkae maemaan* in Laos, about 30 kilometres north of Vientiane. The description was analogous to what I knew from Baan Phraan Muean. I found rites for *mae kamlerd* again during my visit to Laos in 1999 and in 2005. Knowledgeable people in Laos assured me that these rites are known by almost the identical names as in Baan Phraan Muean, on the Lao side of the Mae Khong, emphasizing that close cultural bonds have spanned the river since olden days.

I assumed that references to this cult would be found in the literature about Laos but I have not succeeded so far in finding any such references. In other neighbouring countries no certain relationship to *mae kamlerd* can be proved because the descriptions that exist are not sufficiently detailed.

Name of *mor phaam*	age	Location	Knowledge of *mae kamlerd* (December 2005)	Performs *taengkae* rites	Times per year
Mor Jan	72	Baan Phraan Muean	He learned how to perform the rites from his father, Phor Jampii, as part of his training (text)	Yes	6
Mor Sukan	64	Baan Ngory (located Northeast of Baan Naa Khaa)	He learned how to perform the rites from his uncle, Phor Jampii, as part of his training (text)	Yes	10
Mor Wan	57	Baan Khaaw (located just North of Baan Phraan Muean)	General knowledge – but he did not learn how to perform the rites	No	n. a.
Mor Sii	60	Baan Khaaw	He learned how to perform the rites from his father as part of his training (text)	Yes	4
Mor Bua	66	Baan Khaaw	General knowledge – but he did not learn how to perform the rites	No	n. a.
Mor Toey (no longer active)	90	Baan Khaaw	He learned how to perform the rites from his father as part of his training (text)	n. a.	n. a.
Mor Nuu	57	Baan Thorn (located near Baan Naa Khaa – East of Baan Phraan Muean)	He learned how to perform the rites as part of his training, from his father (who studied the text while he was monk)	Yes	10
Mor Thorng Rak	72	Norng Khorn Khwaang (located near Udorn – in direction towards Khon Kaen)	He learned how to perform the rites from his teacher as part of his training – they did not have/ use any written text but knew it as oral tradition	Yes	12

In some works 'special' spirits are mentioned that appear to have a certain similarity to the concept of *mae kamlerd*. These special spirits appear to be the subject of a particular cult, which separates them from the treatment of spirit symptoms altogether, and which does not deal with the 'fleeting soul', the *khwan*.[28]

What is the nature of mae kamlerd ?

To summarize, I have found that a *mae kamlerd* cult exists in areas of upper Northeastern Thailand and in some places of Laos with which the upper Northeast traditionally has had cultural connections.

According to rather sparse literature, there are in Thailand, at any rate in certain areas, concepts with features reminiscent of *mae kamlerd* in Baan Phraan Muean under the name 'mae suee'. The *mae suee* is mentioned only in a few works about Thailand. Hanks mentions the following local belief from the village she studied in the Central Plain: 'The child is not fully human the first three days. This period was under the supernatural control of Mother Sü, for babies never died during the first 3 days after birth.' And so does also Attagara: 'a new-born baby (...) has a guardian spirit called Mae Sue.'

Rajadhon has more comprehensive deliberations about *mae suee* but does not give information which would make it possible to establish geographical limits.[29]

However, she seems to be a type of a 'guardian spirit' which *mae kamlerd* certainly is not. Rajadhon names her 'the purchasing mother'[30] and calls her elsewhere *mae sü*.[31] From his deliberations and considerations based on old descriptions in Wat Po, there appears to be a relationship between this older type *mae sü* in Central Thailand and the present day *mae kamlerd* in the Northeast, despite the differences.[32]

Today, in a village in Northeastern Thailand, *mae kamlerd* is seen as the exponent of something supernatural that can be very dangerous to a child's welfare and to its survival. The same has previously been the case with *mae suee* in other parts of Thailand. Both have power; both appear to have a certain right to interfere. Both have to be paid in various ways, and both may be defrauded with a 'trick child'. A great deal of information points in the direction that *mae suee* and *mae kamlerd* have the same roots, presumably in Brahmanism. Today they appear different, with completely different names for various reasons.

Hanks and Attagara (1963, 1967) regard and describe *mae suee* as a 'guardian spirit'. Tambiah (1970) places the rites for *mae kamlerd* in the group of *khwan* rites. Rajadhon (1961) comes no closer to a category for *mae suee* than to class her in the group of evil spirits.

According to what has earlier been told about her and her doings, the *mae kamlerd* must be described as evil and malevolent. But the village elders did not have her clearly defined in their minds. They came no closer than to say that she must be 'a kind of spirit'. When they talked of her, they wavered between considering her a child's previous mother during the child's last completed existence on earth, and a concept that she acts as a messenger on earth for *puu thaen yaa thaen* and the whole long series of 'previous mothers'. As a messenger she could be regarded as belonging to the group of 'ancestor spirits'. There may well be traits in her doings that resemble actions the villagers attribute to these spirits[33] but she has been regarded with a greater seriousness and respect than these, a regard which is given a clear expression in her cult. She is malevolent, not because one has transgressed prohibitions or specific directions of any kind, and not because she is to maintain law, order, and morality. In a way she is malevolent to

obtain her own gains. She is no ancestor spirit in the general sense, and she is more dangerous than they, and also more dangerous than most 'ordinary' spirits.

As mentioned earlier, the two 'strong' *kamlerd* rites can be placed parallelly to the highly esteemed *khwan* rites as regards the ritual text, the elaboration of the ritual itself, and the qualities the ritual performers must possess.

All the same, they are widely different in their purposes. The *khwan* rites for the pregnant woman aim to support the mother's peace of mind and, indirectly, her psycho-physical well-being. The ceremony will help her remain completely intact, so that nothing vital, especially her *khwan*, should leave her. The *mae kamlerd* rites before the birth, on the other hand, are directed against something coming from outside that may possibly attack the mother so that she does not deliver a sound, healthy, living, and viable child. In the words of the villagers, the *taengkae maemaan* ceremony before the birth is intended to 'loosen and untie' the mother and the child. It thus may be seen as an intention to affect the mother physically so that the delivery proceeds as it should. Interpreted in this way both the *khwan* rites and the *kamlerd* rites performed before the birth are directed towards two aspects of equal importance: the mental and the physical condition of the mother, respectively, with regard to a successful delivery.

The above is an outsider's attempt at interpretation and evaluation of these rites. To the villager the *kamlerd* rites, both before and after the birth, have the clear purpose of pacifying and possibly rendering harmless the *mae kamlerd* and the threat she constitutes. There are distinctive elements of magic in this, for in a series of cases of physical illnesses in an infant the *kamlerd* rites by themselves cannot have any adequate effect on the ills they aim to cure.

In the village context, this part of the intention of the *kamlerd* rites is in reality fully comparable with that practised by the group of *mor phii*(s), who as intermediaries free the person that has been exposed to an attack from some *phii*. The attack can very well manifest itself as some kind of organic illness, something comparable also to what the *mae kamlerd* can cause. But the group of *mor phii*(s) is not nearly as highly esteemed as the group of *khwan* and *kamlerd* practitioners. The *kamlerd* rites have hereby placed themselves steps higher than the exorcists of ordinary *phii*(s), including the group of ancestor spirits. The content of the texts used for these rites seems to give some support for reflections like these.

As the cult stands, *mae kamlerd* cannot be classified as an ordinary 'evil spirit', and certainly not at all as a guardian spirit. I have not been able to find any good arguments for her being included in the group of *khwan* rites as Tambiah did. She seems rather to approach what Rajadhon calls 'aristocratic' spirits.[34] In other words, she stands perhaps closer to the '*devas*', the gods, than does the general group of spirits. With this concluding open question, the *mae kamlerd* is left for further elucidation and evaluation to those who may be interested in pursuing this intriguing issue.

The Spirit World and the Birth

The belief in spirits – *phii*(s) – played in the 1960s a vital role for everyone in the village and occupied the villagers as a very real part of their world and their daily existence. This is still the case today for most elder and many younger people.

Many spirits are man's protection. If they are dealt with properly they help and assist people in their lives. The spirits may, however, also act in a punishing and reprimanding way, and they have the power to provoke illnesses. Some spirits can possess a human being with very serious consequences. Some are malicious spirits whose actions are erratic; against these it is difficult to protect oneself.

The whole spirit world in Baan Phraan Muean has been treated extremely ably and competently by S. J. Tambiah[35] and placed by him in its natural context in this village; so also the two dreaded spirits, *phii phraay* and *phii porb*, who are seen as very dangerous in connection with the childbirth and the time immediately after.

In the ordinary family, fear of these two sprits or *phii*(s) makes it necessary to take precautions and prevent them from harming the mother and the child. How this is done will be described in a following chapter dealing with the delivery itself. In order to understand the extent and the meaning of the fear that the villagers had for these spirits we will, however, briefly look at the nature of these two spirits and the risks that they represent for the mother and the child.

Spirit belief and the temple

I discussed the beliefs and manifestations of *phii phraay* and *phii porb* with the monks of the temple in the village several times, most recently in 1988. The monks not only accepted that the population had this strong belief in and fear of these evil spirits. They even related their own experiences with these spirits and thus had no doubts about their existence. There is, then, no basis for conflict between temple and village. The world of faith has been a functional entirety for them all.

Phii phraay

In the village, a distinction is made between a 'natural' and an 'unnatural' death. It is normal to die when one reaches a certain age and when specific illnesses occur. In these cases, the deceased is cremated and the usual funeral rites are performed with the participation of the Buddhist monks. In this way the soul (*winyaan*) of the deceased is guided onto the right road, and it becomes what is known as an ancestor spirit.

However, in the cases of unnatural death – when people die suddenly and in an unnatural way before a normal life cycle is completed, for example as a result of accident, murder, epidemics, or in childbirth, there is a risk that the *winyaan* may become a very dangerous *phii taay hoong* (spirit after accidental and sudden death). It may also happen that elderly people die in a unnatural manner but the risk of *phii taay hoong* is first and foremost present when a young, strong, and vigorous man is torn away, or when a woman dies in childbirth. Such people have not lived through a normal life span and their spirits may, if nothing is done to prevent it, rampage on earth and among people because they still feel strongly tied to life on earth. If such a death occurs there is no time to perform the normal funeral rites and the cremation does not take place as it normally would. Instead. the deceased must be buried immediately without ceremony of any kind, so that the soil can absorb the impurity that has arisen.

In April 1980, a man of about forty years of age was shot and killed, presumably in an attempted robbery,

during a temple festival in the village. Before two hours had passed he was interred, without a coffin or ceremony of any kind in the burial place on the Northwestern perimeter of the village. People who have been buried in this way can be disinterred later and cremated with the participation of monks from the temple. The ceremony should, however, not take place until two months after death at the earliest, and in some cases not until one to two years have passed.

The *phii taay hoong* that may come into existence in connection with a death in childbirth is called a *phii phraay*. It is believed that it is really the child that becomes a *phii phraay* who then, so to say, sucks the mother's blood. The risk is present also when a woman dies in childbirth before the baby is delivered and when both mother and child die immediately after the birth. If the child is unborn when the mother dies it must be removed from the mother's womb by an operation. In such a case a particularly powerful person must immediately be called from the village of Baan Naa Khaa, about seven kilometres away. He is considered very competent, and his power is seen as the reason why there appear to be fewer *phii phraay* now than in past times.

A *phii phraay* is very dangerous and not easy to protect against. It will roam around, especially during the night, and will adopt the shape of some animal and its young one. It often appears as a hen and her chick, but it may also take the form of a bitch and her puppy. The peculiar and odd aspect of *phii phraay* is that it vanishes at once if one becomes aware of its presence. It is lucky that this is so as it makes it a little easier to take care of it. *Phii phraay* will seek out places where there are human impurities, above all blood. There is a risk every time a human bleeds: even a cut finger may be enough. If the bleeding cannot be stopped it is taken as a sign that a *phii phraay* is present and sucking the blood out. The risk is by far the greatest during childbirth as especially this blood attracts *phii phraay*.

If the woman is particularly drowsy and if it is difficult to make eye contact with her, it will be thought that a *phii phraay* is present. If she bleeds more than usual it is a sure symptom that *phii phraay* has possessed her and is sucking her dry. Then nothing much can be done, and she will faint and become unconscious. An attempt will of course be made for a *mor phii phraay* to exorcise the spirit but if he does not succeed, she will die. Because of this there is every reason – as we shall see later – to do as much as possible to prevent *phii phraay* from getting an opportunity to attack the mother.

In February 1999, I discussed the beliefs around *phii phraay* with a group of ritual masters from Baan Phraan Muean and its neighbouring villages. They all agreed that many of the young generation do not believe in the existence of *phii phraay* and so do not do anything to prevent attacks by these spirits. The discussion revealed that Khun Jan, my close associate among the villagers since 1968, did not believe in the *phii phraay* and never had done so, nor did he believe in any other *phii*, being the modern and very rational man that he is. One of the others declared a strong belief in *phii phraay* and reported that in his village many people still did all the traditional things to prevent being attacked by these spirits.

Extent of the belief in phii phraay

The idea that there are particularly serious consequences arising from a violent death at an early age, including confinement, is not peculiar to Baan Phraan Muean. I have not found references that occupy themselves in depth with this aspect but several authors mention, without giving details, spirits that in significant respects reminds one of the belief in *phii phraay* in Baan Phraan Muean.[36] It is worth recalling that Irwin at the beginning of the previous century points to the fact that the same spirit has different qualities attributed to it in various parts of Thailand, and that people from the same region

and village may have varying conceptions of the same *phii*.[37] Referring to the above, one can add that spirits with relatively uniform qualities can appear under different names in various regions of the country.

Spirits that in terms of prevention, effects, and consequences resemble the *phii phraay* known in Baan Phraan Muean are found also in references from other cultures in the region.[38]

My own interviews in 1988, which covered a rather large area to the north of and around Udorn established that the belief in *phii phraay* was then known in at least 20 out of 30 localities, and that both the name by which these spirits were known, their most important qualities, and the special arrangements for protection against these spirits were very similar. In addition, in February 1999 and again in 2005, I found that people on the Laotian side of the Mae Khong river believed in spirits that were identical to the *phii phraay* known from Baan Phraan Muean.

Phii porb

In general conversation about the dangers of childbirth, everyone in the village in the 1960s mentioned the spirit *phii phraay* together with another very dangerous spirit, *phii porb*. From the following description of *phii porb* and its origin, victims, and mode of operation, it will be seen that it may represent a certain risk for the woman giving birth. But it may also be presumed that the ordinary villagers mix up the two spirits in their world of ideas.

In the village, there is an understanding that *phii porb* belongs to the group of malevolent spirits but that it has a special status within this group. The *phii porb* is above all characterized by being able to have a living person as its host in contrast to other spirits who are disembodied spirits of deceased humans. A living person may then also be a *phii porb*, which means that with these spirits we approach a concept of what may generally be described as a 'witch'.

Women as well as men may be hosts, or agents, for *phii porb*. The person possessed may be quite an ordinary person and those around will not be aware of the true state of affairs until the *phii porb* possesses another person and is disclosed in connection with the treatment of the one attacked. Other kinds of spirits may be persuaded to desist from troubling the person in question through placation techniques, where one first asks the spirit to go away, and then pays it a fee in the form of an offering. In contrast to the treatment for ailments caused by ordinary spirits, the treatment for possession by *phii porb* is 'exorcism'.

Everyone in the village feared *phii porb*. During our conversations with the families in the 1960s and 1970s, *phii porb* was always mentioned at one time or another. It may have been with a trace of humour, so that one could get the impression that the villagers did not take this *phii* very seriously. But it should not be misinterpreted. Digging a little deeper during the conversation would reveal that everybody had a real dread of this *phii*, even the very youngest mothers in the 1978 group. By 1988, however, the fear was almost gone among the younger people, as it was in 1999, but the reality of *phii porb* was nevertheless still recognized by all.

The following is a brief account of *phii porb* as it was described by village elders and *mae tamyae*(s) with special regard to dangers in connection with childbirth:

It is thought that a new *phii porb* can arise in two ways. Firstly, it can be caused by a person who is a *phii porb* before his death transferring *phii porb* to one of his children. It is usually the oldest, if the 'heir' is of the same sex as the person who transfers the *phii porb*. Second, a new *phii porb* may emerge if a person (be it

man or woman) who has been taught by a master to perform magical arts (e.g. protective magic, love magic or magic to control epidemics) does not live according to the rules imposed on him/her in this respect. For example, if the expert in magic, *mor wichaa*, is tempted to contravene the food restrictions that are imposed on him/her. More often and with more serious consequences, the *mor wichaa* may behave unethically in the practice of the acquired art. He or she might be tempted to misuse his/her magic ability to harm people, rather than help and benefit them. Should this happen there is a very grave risk that *mor wichaa* will become a *phii porb*. A relatively recent example was reported in 1978 of a woman that turned out to be a *phii porb*. She was learning the art of performing love magic so that she could help women to be more sexually attractive to their husbands. She did not follow the ethical rules, but exploited her knowledge to enter into love affairs with the women's husbands herself.

It is believed that *phii porb* is especially dangerous for weak persons. It will launch an attack on such people and invade them, often through the mouth. The victims are most often women, married or single but usually quite young. Children of both sexes are similarly at risk whereas adult men are seldom exposed to attacks by *phii porb*.

This *phii* also likes to consume blood as well as the inner organs of a weak person. The spirit is therefore particularly dangerous to women who are giving birth. Should a *phii porb* succeed in possessing a woman in childbirth and it cannot be removed, there is no doubt that the woman will die.

People who are *phii porb* will in most cases know that they are so. The neighbours will often sense who is a *phii porb* and will endeavour to take their precautions against their influence. Fortunately, there has been a decline in recent years in the number of possessions by *phii porb*. The villagers were not able to give any reason for this.

The most significant symptom of a *phii porb* having a grip on a mother is that the possessed will stare fixedly at anyone coming near. She will scream out, break into loud bursts of laughter for no reason, and during these outbursts she will often hide her face. The description indicates what Western professionals normally would consider hysterical symptoms.

Most often the villagers are in no doubt as to whether it is *phii phraay* or *phii porb* who has attacked the mother or the child, or possibly both. They will then call the *mor phii* who can make the correct treatment. However, the symptoms are not always of only one interpretation, and in such a case the villagers must of course have help to get the correct diagnosis.

As in other similar contexts, the villagers will consult a *mor sorng*. He will assess whether one or the other of these two spirits has caused the symptoms, or whether the cause of the symptoms is entirely different. When the diagnosis has been made, the treatment must be undertaken by a skilful person, a *mor phii porb*, who belongs to the group of village experts named *mor tham* (exorcisist of malevolents spirits).

Each *mor phii porb* has his own method for exorcising the spirit. According to the villagers' descriptions, the exorcism is sometimes very violent because the aim is literally to scare off the *phii porb*, to make it afraid. To achieve this, some *mor phii porb* will strike or kick the patient so that the *phii porb* will dare do nothing but answer the exorcist's question: 'Who are you? Tell me who you are.' When the patient answers – often in a loud and distinct, almost screaming voice, she (or he) will give the real name of *phii porb*. It is in other words not the possessed himself/herself who responds but the

phii porb who answers with the voice of the possessed. So it becomes known who the *phii porb* really is. When *phii porb* has been disclosed in this way it will leave the person who is then cured.[39]

In the village, descriptions of *phii phraay* possessions appeared to be related to symptoms of physical problems associated with the childbirth. In the descriptions of *phii porb* possessions, we found that almost all the symptoms belonged to the world of psychology and psychiatry. This is also the finding of the more systematic research data and descriptions by the psychiatrist Dr Sangun Suwanlert who divides the *phii porb* possessions into three categories:[40]

- the once-only possessed, who has presumably had psychological problems prior to the possession,

- the several times possessed and each time cured (spirit possession neurosis),

- the cases in which the exorcist does not succeed in driving *phii porb* out of the patient (spirit possession psychosis).

Dr Suwanlert's information about *phii porb* and his description of the associated symptoms correspond fairly accurately to the descriptions we have from Baan Phraan Muean both from the findings of the present study and from the description given by Tambiah.[41]

It is worth noting that Suwanlert is of the opinion that only a minority of *phii porb* possessed people are in need of treatment by a qualified physician. He acknowledges the treatment practised by the local *mor phii porb* who is a healer and exorcist by virtue of his being an integral part of the local culture. Because of his closeness to the environment and the villagers the *mor phii porb* has an excellent ability to help most of the people who are possessed by this interesting spirit, or, I should say, show symptoms that traditionally relate to a person's being 'possessed' by *phii porb*.

Suwanlert's deliberations and conclusions thus agree well with the ideas about psychological and psychiatric therapy and therapists, for whom Fuller Torrey, among others, acts as a spokesperson in *The Mind Game, Witchdoctors and Psychiatrists* (1973, 'Preface', p. xiv): 'This book will focus on the healer, the therapist. It will attempt to show how much of his effectiveness comes through his sharing of a common world-view with the patient, through certain personality characteristics, and through expectations that the patient has of him. It will then show how another source of his effectiveness, the techniques of therapy, are basically the same whether they are used by a witchdoctor or a psychiatrist'.

Extent of the belief in phii porb

As already mentioned, Suwanlert is the only source known to me that provides a thorough report on the *phii porb*.

This dreaded *phii* is, however, mentioned by many authors and they all attribute to it largely the same qualities as described above from Baan Phraan Muean.[42] *Phii porb* are found in both older and relatively recent references. It is therefore interesting to quote Seidenfaden for a remark he made on the belief in this spirit amongst the Thai Lü in Laos almost 50 years ago, that this 'absurd idea reminds one of the phii pop superstition <u>formerly</u> [my underlining] widespread in Northeastern Thailand, where the evil eye of the possessed person may do harm'.[43]

For the sake of entirety it should be mentioned that Hanks in her work on the Central Plain of Thailand refer to a *phii krasüü* that have qualities reminiscent of our *phii porb* in the Northeast, and that Attagara mentions a *phii pob* who does not, according to the brief description, appear to have qualities resembling ours in Baan Phraan Muean.[44]

Finally, it must be reported that Milne[45] mentions a Buddhist group that she studied from 1907 in the Shan States of Burma. These people are related to the Siamese. Milne describes a *bre* that in all essential respects is entirely parallel to the *phii porb* as this spirit is described in our references from Northeastern Thailand and Laos.

In the context of the present study, however, it is most interesting to note that none of the references mentions that *phii porb* is considered a particular threat to the woman giving birth. Not even Sangun Suwanlert who gives the most systematic and thorough descriptions of *phii porb* based on his research findings from the area around Ubon. Of my other references only Bastian in a study from 1866 mentions that the pregnant woman is especially exposed to attacks by 'Phii Phob and Phii Praj'.[46]

My interviews and conversations, however, established as late as in 1988 that *phii porb* in fact was feared in connection with childbirth in considerable areas of the upper Northeast. Our study found the same beliefs prevalent in February 1999, in villages around Vientiane in Laos. It should also be mentioned that the young people in Baan Phraan Muean seemed not to bother about the *phii porb*. My February 1999 discussions with local ritual masters confirmed this – but most of them still believed in the *phii porb*, even though no one has been attacked locally for many years.

Phor Long was well-known as a *mor phii* (1961)

CHAPTER THREE

Ritual Practice Surveyed, 1961–2005

It is important to keep in mind that in any culture, the ordinary men or women are rarely aware of the reason for actions performed according to common practice. Nor was this the case in Baan Phraan Muean. Only a small group of village elders (especially men) were conversant with the reasons behind many of the ritual practices, and several of these indeed only with narrow aspects of the larger whole. No more than a handful of men had sufficient insight and knowledge of traditions to enable them to present and argue a general view of these subjects.

Like Terweil[47] in Ratchaburi, oouthwest of Bangkok, in Baan Phraan Muean we also experienced a large difference between the young and the old with regard to insight and coherent interpretation of tradition and religion. The same tendency can probably be found everywhere in the world. In Baan Phraan Muean, an important condition for the 'transfer' of traditional behaviour and belief was that young wives during the first years of married life live with their parents or, at times, with their parents-in-law. Even though very young women might have appeared to have only a little insight into tradition, it did not necessarily indicate that they were about to lose their faith in the value of tradition. Perhaps they had just not been 'trained' yet! In Chapter Two we looked at the principles of pregnancy rites as described by the most esteemed ritual masters. We shall now turn to a closer description of how the village families practised these rites.

How did they relate to these things and what were the major changes related to this from the 1960s until today? In parallel, we shall also listen to points of view and opinions from *mae tamyae*(s) (midwives), village elders, and ritual experts and compare their opinion with the actual practice as it was over the years among the women in this village.

Khun Jan is today the only person in Baan Phraan Muean who has an extensive knowledge of the non-Buddhist traditions

Everyday Practice of the Pregnancy Rites

Let us turn to some concrete information given by people in the village during visits in the 1960s and the 1970s.

Those most tradition-bound said that both *suukhwan maemaan* and *taengkae maemaan* ought to be performed prior to every birth, but added that if the woman wanted to perform only one of them, it ought to be the *taengkae maemaan* as this was the most powerful and important ceremony. A couple of our *mae tamyae*(s) and some of the village elders were more liberal in their views. Their opinions can be summarized by saying that the mother must decide for herself, in every case based on how she feels during the pregnancy, how well she could afford the ritual, and how well she was coping with it all.

The general belief in the village in the 1970s was that there was no reason for performing the *suukhwan maemaan* if the pregnant woman felt that she was well and mentally balanced. On the other hand, as the dangers to the mother and the (unborn) child posed by *mae kamlerd* were always present, this ceremony was more often performed than the *suukhwan maemaan*.

It may be relevant here to remember that in my group from 1968 the mothers were all relatively old – none of them less than 30 years of age and a few close to 60 – and that they all had born quite a number of children. Most of them – if not all – had by then established their basic patterns of behaviour and attitudes relating to most everyday things in their lives, and presumably also their general attitudes to the rites we are concerned with here. In contrast, my 1978 group was young: no one older than 25 years of age and thus not nearly as experienced as the mothers of the 1968 group. But when I revisited this younger group in 1988 they had become experienced mothers. In order to try to evaluate the changes over time as accurately as possible, I included in 1988 a small group of the nine youngest mothers in the village.

The replies to the question: *'Did you have any rites performed during your pregnancies?'* were the following:

Rites during pregnancy	1968 (no. of mothers: 33)		1978 (no. of mothers: 27)		1988 (no. of mothers: 27)		1988 (no. of mothers: 9)	
	no.	%	no.	%	n..	%	no.	%
No rite of any kind during pregnancy	5	15	13	48	11	41	3	33
Both rites (*suukhwan and taengkae maemaan*) for all children	10	30	5	19	3	11	2	22
Never *suukhwan* but *taengkae maemaan* or *taengkae mae kamlerd* for all children	8	24	9	33	10	37	4	45
Suukhwan for some children, *taengkae maemaan* for all children	2	6						
Suukhwan for all children, never *taengkae maemaan*	3	9						
Other variations	5	15			1	4		
Moved away from the village					2	7		

These data give no clear picture but some tendencies may be identified on the basis of these figures:

- In 1988, more women than 20 years earlier had no rite at all;
- Fewer had both rites than previously;
- An increasing number of the mothers had a rite made as protection against *mae kamlerd*.

It is evident that the *suukhwan maemaan* ceremony was performed less frequently than the *kamlerd* ceremony. However, as the sample of very young mothers in 1988 was only nine we have to be careful not to conclude too much from their replies although it is worth noting that both rites still were in use.

How ingrained the fear for *mae kamlerd* was as late as in 1988 is evident from the replies to a hypothetical question I asked the same group of mothers in 1978 and again in 1988: 'What do you think you would do in the future regarding the pregnancy rites?'

The replies in 1988 underlined again that the *taengkae maemaan* is considered more important than the *suukhwan maemaan*, as about half of the total group would consider having the *taengkae maemaan* performed, while only two mothers mentioned *suukhwan maemaan*. It is, however, interesting to note a very new trend: out of the 27 older mothers in the 1988 group, 13 were by then sterilized so they would not have more children, and consequently there would be no need for any rites!

A real, important, and very positive sign of change in everyday life from 1978 to 1988 appeared in the replies to our next question which was also asked of the same group of mothers with an interval of ten years.

The question was: 'What would you do first of all if your baby were to become ill?'

Actions taken if the baby falls ill	1978 number of mothers: 27	1988 number of mothers: 27
Consult the *mor sorng*, follow his advice; most often *kamlerd* rite + local medicine	15	2
Consult the *mor sorng*, follow advice + local medicine + medical doctor in Udorn	4	1
Consult medical doctor/ Health Centre/ hospital + may supplement with herb medicine. Not seeing *mor sorng*	8	22
Moved away from village	-	2

In 1978, there was a widespread fear for *mae kamlerd* in the replies. Many had the preventive rite, *taengkae maemaan* performed before the birth. In their thinking, the concept of the *mae kamlerd* came up as soon as the little child became ill. There was a perceived danger that she would take the child from them. Fortunately, in the course of the ten years that had passed, the arrival of modern medical practice and facilities had made it possible for the mothers to find more adequate help. But the fear had not gone at all! In our very little group of the nine youngest mothers in the village, in 1988, more than half would first of all see the mor sorng, and if he told them that *mae kamlerd* had caused the illness, the rite would be performed. They found this rite a good thing to do – just to play safe! However, these mothers added that they would also visit the local health centre.

To sum up the importance of those two rites in the 1970s and 1980s, it is obvious that village families broadly speaking were in agreement with the active *mae tamyae*(s) and village elders in their views and evaluations of the two pregnancy rites. The *suukhwan maemaan* is performed foremost to strengthen the mother but it has also a certain effect for the child. Here they thought primarily, as we have seen above, of the mother's mental

welfare, her balance of mind and, as a consequence, also of some influence upon her physical condition. For the mother the rite was thought to promote an easy and uncomplicated delivery, and thereby help the child to survive. The effect of the *suukhwan maemaan* on the child is primarily that its *khwan* becomes 'good': an easily managed child with a kind mind and heart.

Everybody seemed a little less clear in their views on the main principles around the ceremony of *taengkae maemaan*. The purpose of this ceremony was first and foremost to protect and assist the unborn child against the *mae kau mae lang*, and help it to be 'well born', i.e. alive, healthy and well. The ceremony should be performed before the birth so that the mother can be 'loosened and freed' physically, which will assist in an easy and uncomplicated delivery and the survival of the child. It is the fear of giving birth to a stillborn child, a child that will not survive, that lies behind this view. Experience of uncomplicated deliveries of healthy and strong children, who are developing well, may make mothers decide not to have this rite performed. Part of the perception of an easy delivery means that the mother quickly will regain her physical strength after the birth, and that there will not be complications of a physical nature for her after the childbirth. As late as the 1980s, there was no doubt among the women that very many of the illnesses after the birth were caused by the *mae kamlerd*, and that the appropriate treatment of these illnesses is the performance of a *kamlerd* rite.

During the 1968 fieldwork in particular, we discussed these circumstances thoroughly with the mothers. We ourselves were confused about the *kamlerd* rites with respect to their performance before and after birth, an uncertainty that illustrates how careful one must be in fieldwork of this kind where both linguistic and cultural barriers are present. We knew of the *taengkae maemaan* ceremony from our 1962 work in the village, and had

then understood that this rite could be performed before as well as after the childbirth. My interview questions in 1968 were based on this assumption. As previously told, the *kamlerd* rites are known only in Northeastern Thailand and not at all for example in the Bangkok area. My interpreter and highly-qualified professional co-worker during the 1968 work in the village was a Bangkok Thai who did not know anything about the *kamlerd* rites in the Northeast of Thailand. The result was that we had progressed a fair way with the interviews in the village before we fully realized that behind slight linguistic nuances were hidden three rather diversified rites in connection with the cult around *mae kau mae lang*, more often known as *mae kamlerd*. Fortunately, we were in time to correct the errors in our data arising from these misunderstandings. The ceremonies that we identified – the *taengkae maemaan* ceremony which is performed <u>before</u> the birth, and the *taengkae mae kamlerd* ceremony (also named *kae kamlerd*) and the *pau kamlerd* ceremony which both are performed <u>after</u> the birth of the child - fully and completely covered the real practice in Baan Phraan Muean.

When during pregnancy ought the rites to be performed?

Key people in the village in the 1970s were of the opinion that the *suukhwan maemaan* should be performed in the 5th-6th month of pregnancy and the *taengkae maemaan* as late as possible in the pregnancy - in any case, not earlier than the 8th month. If both rites were performed, the *taengkae maemaan* should be performed after the *suukhwan maemaan* ceremony. Moreover, they agreed with previously-reported information on which day and at which hour the various rites should be performed in order to have their optimal effect.

While the majority of the families knew very well that this was how things ought to happen if they were to

conform entirely to manners and customs, they did not take these details seriously. Hence we found that what they had done in practice was as follows:

1968: Seven families had the *suukhwan maemaan* ceremony performed after the *taengkae maemaan* ceremony. The majority had the *suukhwan maemaan* ceremony performed in the 7th or 8th month, a few in the 3rd to 4th month, and one in the 5th to 6th month of the pregnancy. The majority would have the *taengkae maemaan* performed as closely as possible to childbirth, but a few had it already in the 5th–6th month.

1978: The young people did not take seriously which rite should be performed before which. Apart from a single *suukhwan maemaan* ceremony, which was performed in the 2nd month, and a *taengkae maemaan* ceremony in the 5th month, all others were, however, performed in the 8th–9th month of the pregnancy.

Varied opinions were found in later research groups, indicating clearly a *mai ben rai* ('never mind') attitude among the villagers in this matter.

Development and Changing Customs

By the end of the 1970s and up through the 1980s, the social and cultural changes occurring generally increased and impacted also on the traditional life of the villagers. This is illustrated in our 1981 interview with 16 female teachers in three village schools, one of these in Baan Phraan Muean. The ages of the teachers ranged from 25 to 56 years; all were born and had grown up in the region, 12 in towns and 4 in villages.

Of these teachers, only one had both the rite for the pregnant woman (*suukhwan maemaan* and *taengkae maemaan*) performed at all of her seven childbirths. One had had *taengkae maemaan* performed at the first two of six childbirths. Besides, one had had a *khaa saang* (local dialect 'to kill the worm'). 14 out of the 16 had none of these rites performed. This was not because they did not know the rites from their homes and whilst growing up. But their education, social status, and most importantly the increased opportunities for modern medical aid had made the rites obsolete. These teachers' circumstances were such that they could obtain more adequate help and assurance from the medical centre for their physical problems and uncertainties in connection with childbirth, than any rite could give the mother and the baby.

My open question was then whether this development eventually would extend also to the ordinary families in the villages? And would it happen without qualified medical assistance available in the village itself? Or will the community be able to prioritize and manage so wisely that a primary health service will be available for those living and working in the villages?

In 1982, I made a note in my drafts: 'It would give me a great satisfaction if it should be possible for me to follow the change and development in the village, in these respects, for yet a considerable number of years.' I have been fortunate enough to have had the opportunity to do so. Several times during the 1990s and after the turn of the century, I met with village leaders from Baan Phraan Muean and from other neighbouring villages to systematically discuss the changes in belief and customs related to pregnancy and birth that may have occurred in recent years.

Their evaluations and information related to the ritual side of everyday life can be summarized as follows: All types of ritual masters are still available and functioning, but almost all are elderly and hardly any young persons are entering into the art. In addition, some of the rites are not much in demand any more.

It is interesting though, that especially many of the *khwan* rites still are practised widely, almost as much as many years ago. Only the *suukhwan maemaan*, the rite aimed at strengthening the pregnant woman was on the decline. The ritual masters found this very natural as the health centre and the systems for medical care had improved so much over the years. They reported that the changes within this area were common to all the villages in the district.

The *kamlerd* rites were performed much more often than the *suukhwan maemaan* but even so the frequency was less than previously. This change was seen as a sign of a positive development and as a natural consequence of better education and the improvements in medical and other services that had occurred in the village.

The changes found in February 1999, a decade after the latest systematic collection of data related to the ritual practices in 1988, reinforced the tendency already identified. None of the five mothers in our little 1999 sample (average age 25 years) and none of the seven female teachers (average age 46 years) from the local school had had performed any *suukhwan maemaan* in connection with their pregnancies. This underlined what the ritual masters told us in the 1970s: namely that there is no need to perform this rite if the mother generally feels well and is mentally well balanced. It is understood that this is generally the case today because there is now easy access to nurses in the local health centre and to medical services in Udorn.

Still, the old fear of the well-being of the baby and what could happen to the new-born lingered: three of the five mothers had had a rite performed to protect against the *mae kamlerd*, and one of the female teachers had this rite made for all her four children. It is still the case: in February 2003, I happened to pass by Baan Phraan Muean, and that very afternoon a *taengkae mae kamlerd* ceremony was just to be performed for a mother and her very sick child.

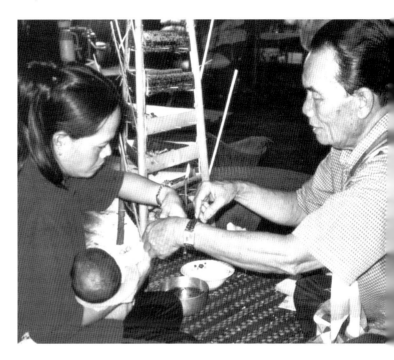

At the *taengkae mae kamlerd*, Khun Jan ties the protective threads to the baby's wrists

CHAPTER FOUR

Pregnancy and Birth Surveyed, 1961–2005

In order better to understand how the traditions and beliefs work within the village and understand also why some beliefs abate while others persist, we shall now turn to a description of the course of a pregnancy and the birth and the actions taken on this occasion. Each single action and step will first be detailed on the basis of what our local advisory group in the 1960s considered to be normal and traditional.

Picking up the thread from Chapter 3, we shall then look at how the families in fact conducted themselves in these matters in 1968, 1978, 1988, and in 1999 to determine the kind of change that may have occurred in these matters.

(1962)

(1961)

Attitudes to Pregnancy

Nobody who has lived and worked closely with Thai people can have any doubts that they love children, and are as good and loving towards them as circumstances allow them to be. So it was also among the Isan villagers in the early 1960s. However, giving birth to many children in close succession, as was the practice then, could become a burden to the mother, whose everyday life was poor and most often filled with a considerable workload. No wonder children therefore outwardly might have seemed neglected and under-stimulated. But very, very rarely – if ever – did I observe that any child, even in a large family of siblings, got the feeling of being unwanted.

In our 1968 group, who at that time had borne an average of 7.9 children, almost half of the sample expressed that father and mother both had been 'pleased' each time they could establish that a new child was on its way. The remainder thought that they had enough children and stated that either both or one of the spouses during several of the most recent pregnancies had had 'mixed feelings'.

It comes as no surprise then that our young 1978 and 1988 families expressed – almost without qualifications – that they were 'pleased' when a child was expected. The fathers had no reservations whatever, while some of the mothers had 'mixed feelings', either because they felt that the child came a little too soon after the latest one, or because they were afraid of a difficult and painful birth.

The same basic attitude was mirrored in their reaction to the question of what they would feel, and possibly do, if they had been unable to bear children at all, because either the wife or the husband was infertile. Around 70 per cent of the 1968 group would have been very unhappy if they had been unable to bear children, and

of these, three-quarters stated that in such case they would adopt one or more children. The remainder (around 30 per cent) would either accept childlessness as 'their fate' or intimated an attitude of unconcern. Importantly, for the majority there was a clearly formulated wish to have children. However, not a single person mentioned the possibility of seeking qualified professional assistance to find out if anything could be done, should they not become pregnant and bear children. Furthermore, none stated that they would seek aid in the case of childlessness through either religion or magic.

The same subject was brought up with the 1978 and 1988 groups.

The 1978 reactions to the possibility of not having children, and what they might do, can be summarized thus:

A very considerable majority considered that it would be unfortunate if they could not have children, and half of them felt that something could be done about this, and that they would seek a qualified medical opinion. This latter attitude markedly separates this 1978 group from that of their mothers' generation of 1968, and is undoubtedly an indication of the changes that had taken place in this community during just one decade.

This change was reinforced by the responses of our 1988 group, and during later visits the question was not raised in our conversations at all as by then medical advice was sought as a matter of course in a childless situation.

Preference for sons

In many cultures the world over – in the past as well as the present – there is a tendency to prefer male rather than female children. In our 1968 group, almost two-thirds of the mothers expressed a clear wish to have

male children, one-fourth preferred daughters, and the remainder had no preference. During their pregnancies, only three mothers had sought a fortune-teller to have an advance indication of what sex the unborn child might be expected to be. All three predictions were stated to have been correct.

For the 1978 group, there was also a clear tendency to prefer sons, at any rate as the first child. That cultural tradition was then still strongly prevalent. None of these young families had consulted a fortune-teller to have an advance indication of the child's sex. But three mothers told us that they had received omens from dreams. It was claimed that if one dreamt about a watch or a knife it would be a boy; if one dreamt about a bracelet or a necklace the baby would be a girl. A young woman of 21 who wanted girls related how she had learnt from an older relative how she could, prior to a pregnancy, influence the sex of the subsequent child by magic. This was to happen by means of a special treatment of the afterbirth at the immediately previous childbirth. If one wished for a girl the next time, according to customs and habit, the afterbirth was laid in a section of bamboo with the umbilical cord uppermost. If one wished for a boy, the afterbirth was turned so that the umbilical cord lay at the bottom of the container.[48]

In contrast, our very young families in the 1988 group, and also those we met during later visits, were ready to accept either sex equally well. Some mothers mentioned that during a pregnancy, for some reason or other (such as dreams), they had felt sure of the sex of the child, and they had been correct!

Health

In 1962, about one-fifth of the 47 mothers stated that on the whole they had gone through their pregnancies entirely without health problems. These findings were

(2001)

repeated in 1968. The remainder had suffered only what they called ordinary pregnancy complaints during the whole period or parts of it (headaches, vomiting, dizziness, poor appetite, irritability, fatigue, etc.). None of them had consulted a qualified doctor, nurse, or midwife, during any pregnancy. Many of them, however, had taken a 'patent medicine' (*yaa kamlang*) that could be bought in Udorn or from itinerant traders. The medicine was said to have good effect for practically everything, including headaches, hang-overs and tiredness.

In the 1978 group, well over half stated that they had not had any health problems at all. Two had had some trifling matters that they considered normal for their

condition. Many had taken the above-mentioned *yaa kamlang* from time to time. Information from nine persons in our group clearly reflected a change since 1968:

- Four had visited *mor tambon's* clinic (the district health service) situated in a larger village some seven kilometres away;
- Four had visited the out-patients' department of the hospital in Udorn;
- The last of the nine had consulted a doctor practising in Udorn.

None of those nine had symptoms, which according to the description were serious but they had felt it reassuring to seek the best possible help.

The new and more modern times with better facilities and possibilities were so much more marked and clear by 1988 when all the mothers reported that they had consulted the local health centre. This had opened in their own village just the year before, with three full-time working nurses in attendance. Visits after 1988 found that this centre continued to work well in relation to pregnancy and birth health services.

Work

Two-thirds of the 1962 group (repeated in 1968) stated that they continued their usual work in the house and in the fields during practically the entire pregnancy. Only a few intimated that they had to work a little less hard at the very end. The remainder mentioned greater or smaller changes in their daily tasks during almost the total period of pregnancy.

More than two-thirds of the young 1978 mothers also worked completely as usual during all nine months. They talked about it in such a way that we got the impression that it was rather a point of honour for them

to be able to manage the daily routine, apart from short periods when they had felt a little unwell. They let us understand that they had received offers of relief from close relatives, with whom they lived, who wanted to help and relieve them, but they themselves saw no reason to accept the offers, for they were, after all, physically well. But we cannot be quite certain how things really were. When their mothers' generation or younger/older sisters were present during the conversation, these women indicated on several occasions that they felt that they (perhaps a bit on the quiet) had lent a relieving hand.

No changes to this general picture were observed either in 1988 or later.

Food

More than half of the 1968 group (17 out of 33) informed us that they did not change their eating habits during pregnancy. The 16 who had adhered to certain food taboos all felt that they should not eat fatty things as these would cause a difficult delivery and/or could be physically harmful to the embryo. Some added other restrictions – eggs that had been kept for a long time; meat from pregnant animals, grilled glutinous rice, sweet potato or taro – all reasoning that such consumption would cause a difficult delivery. Several mentioned *luuk-bok*[49] as a particularly fatty fruit to be avoided. Whether the mothers had more or fewer taboos regarding food during pregnancy did not appear to be connected with their ages but maybe rather with how strong and healthy their first babies were as the fact is that almost all mothers who had not lost any of their children (in either childbirth or later) did not observe any food taboos during their pregnancies.

There was no change in this respect for the group of young mothers in 1978; again about half of them did not mention any real food taboos. The remainder had

(1962)

one or more taboos of the same kind as the older one, and for entirely the same reasons.

For these two groups there was the common belief that the embryo must not grow too big or too fat, for then it would be difficult to bring it into the world without complications.

This seems to have changed considerably in the following decade. By 1988, our young mothers all said that they could eat everything during the period of pregnancy, although one did mention a few things she did not like to eat because they did not taste good. Generally they no longer seemed so pre-occupied with the size of the baby and the influence this could have on the birth.

Health and Nutrition – an Evaluation

In 1978, the District Health Nurse (*mor tambon*) stated that in her evaluation the population of the villages around Udorn was both incorrectly and deficiently nourished. She found that the large majority of mothers observed one or more food taboos during their pregnancies. The taboos were not in themselves very serious, but could contribute to an exacerbation of a negative effect on the mother and the embryo of deficient and incorrect nutrition. According to *mor tambon*, the nutrition problems were not due to cultural taboos. They were to some extent caused by lack of knowledge but mostly upon the nature of nutrition that was available to them under the given naturally-conditioned and economic circumstances.

In 1988, the nurses at the local (then recently-opened) health centre in Baan Phraan Muean agreed with the above evaluations. Related to the food of the pregnant mother – and not less important the nutrition of the baby – the nurses found it very difficult to introduce necessary changes, as they were dealing with old beliefs and some superstitions then still prevalent among the older generations who were very influential in matters of this kind.

The nurses underlined that they found a vicious circle at work that consisted of poverty, lack of knowledge, and the fact that insufficient funds were available to cope with this problem. In 1999, the head nurse in the Baan Phraan Muean Centre found that general nutrition for mother and baby on the whole had improved during the previous decade. The women were now better educated. Though still relatively poor most were able to buy supplementary food of good quality. The very good educational programmes broadcast by the Government's TV channels had contributed to the women's greater awareness of nutritional needs.

In reality, however, no detailed information about the state of health of the women in Baan Phraan Muean is avaiable. When I first went there I had the feeling that the state of health for some was such that it could seriously influence the mother and subsequently the development of her baby physically as well as mentally as described in general terms for Asia by UNESCO in 1982.[50] Today, I do not observe anything that brings that thought to mind but it should be noted that the latest period of economic recession has brought some of the families rather severe financial problems.

Magic and superstition connected to eating and food habits

All conversations with the mothers in this village in the 1960s and the 1970s inevitably touched on the fear of a complicated and difficult birth, and the fear that perhaps both the mother and the child would not get through it well and safely. Also there was a general fear that the baby would not be healthy and quite normal in all respects.

These fears were also articulated during the conversations about food habits; many mothers expressed the possibility of working towards an uncomplicated childbirth by observing special rules and customs surrounding eating and food habits. Importantly, by observing such rules they sought to allay the fear that they to a greater or lesser degree all felt about the approaching delivery.

Many of our 1968 mothers said things like:

- One must eat nothing that is tough to chew, e.g. the rind of fruits, or dried meat, as it causes a difficult delivery;
- The peel must be picked completely off the banana before one begins to eat it;
- One must be careful to finish one's meals faster than the rest of the family.

How widely these rules were observed was not investigated.

The 'midwives' were also engrossed in these matters. Those functioning in the 1960s and 1970s mentioned more rules to be observed by the woman:

- A pregnant woman must not eat while standing up; if she does so, mishaps and accidents of many kinds might occur at the birth.

In 1968, 30 out of 33 observed this rule; in the 1978 group, 23 out of 27; in 1988, 7 out of 9. But the reasons differed. If one did not observe this rule, it would cause:

- Involuntary bowel evacuation during the birth, (the same will happen if she eats whilst walking);
- A delivery that is too quick or too slow;
- Premature childbirth.

Interestingly, our little group of 1999 mothers all believed that they should not eat standing up; while only one of them thought it influenced the birth others thought it was just tradition and something the elders were telling them (not) to do.

Other types of fear-allaying practices

Some mothers had still other rules they observed. Some of these had really nothing to do directly with meals or food taboos but as they are indirectly connected with this topic they can appropriately be mentioned here:

- If a pregnant woman is out catching frogs or crabs, she must not gather them in her skirt (*phaa sin*). If she does, the baby will produce far too much saliva. Two-thirds of the young mothers in 1978 observed this taboo though not all for the mentioned reason. They just observed the rule because it was the proper way for a pregnant woman to behave!
- The pregnant woman must not pick fruit. It causes a too easy delivery, possibly far too early. Most of the women in the 1978 group did not observe this restriction. However, the rule was still known to most 1988 mothers and observed by a few of them;
- The pregnant woman must not walk across the rope with which the water buffalo is tethered. If she does, the child will eat more than is normal. By far most of the 1978 group knew this taboo well, and about two-thirds of them obeyed it. Some of them had an additional reason for not stepping across this rope, such as that the child would 'cry without a sound' like the mute water buffalo. But most of them

admitted that they had no clear idea of what would happen should they go against the rule. They observed it merely because it was an ancient custom and habit. Interesting enough, the rule was still observed by half of the young mothers in our 1988 group, and they mentioned the same reasons; some believed in it and some did not.

The 'midwives' who were functioning in the 1960s told us that the pregnant woman ought not to sit down on the threshold, or at the top of the ladder leading up to the house. The reason is that these two places mark the way out of the house, and if the mother blocks this way, the baby will also have difficulty in 'getting out through the door', that is, it will be a difficult childbirth. 31 out of 33 mothers observed this rule in 1968, and 22 out of 27 did so in 1978. Out of the 9 young 1988 mothers, 7 observed this rule. Again, in 1999 our sample followed this taboo, but only one said it was because it would make the birth difficult. The others did so just because of tradition, and with no thought that not following the taboo could have any consequences. But some in all three samples said that they had never heard of this custom.

Already in 1968, conversations with respondents made clear that many more particular rules and customs existed and were observed in the families within this special area. We did not systematically go into these but noted around 20 other practices, which were observed with the purpose of promoting an easy and safe childbirth.

In Baan Phraan Muean we found only one single general taboo observed in all our families and this taboo is still observed today: No family of a pregnant woman would slaughter any domestic animal during the pregnancy. If one does that, there is a very serious risk that the baby and/or the mother will die during the delivery. It is also considered a very bad omen if a domestic animal is unintentionally wounded during this period and it is believed that the wound-mark will be found again in the baby. In Baan Phraan Muean, it was generally agreed that the same concept was prevalent in all the nearby villages. In the literature on Thailand, this taboo is found mentioned only from the Ratchaburi area.[51]

The ritual texts refer to many superstitions and omens that we did not find articulated by the villagers. The more general literature from other parts of the world gives many examples of food taboos and sympathetic magic, both imitative and contagious, during a woman's pregnancy, and I dare say that Baan Phraan Muean (and Thailand generally) are today not among the areas where the most, or the most severe, taboos are to be found.

Generally, several of the above-mentioned taboos are still observed, but almost all respondents now say that they do these things because the elders tell them to do so. Beliefs have really changed, and in many cases correspond to practices adhered to by many allegedly non-superstitious people in my own country, such as not buying the pram until the baby is well and truly born!

Fear of childbirth

The above descriptions and statements illustrate convincingly that fear and uncertainty were present in almost all families before nearly all childbirths.

Not until at the end of our conversations with the mothers were they asked questions where the word 'fear' was used in direct connection with the matter of impending childbirth.

Their fears can be summarized as the

- fear that the mother or the baby, perhaps both, should die;

- fear that the child might not be healthy and well; 'normal';
- fear that the childbirth might be very difficult and painful;
- fear that spirits – *phii*(s) – might attack the mother and/or the baby.

Fear of birth	1968 (%)	1978 (%)	1988 (%)
Not fearful at all before any childbirth	6	15	34
Very fearful prior to all deliveries	58	51	22
Fearful before all childbirths, but mostly for the first one	33	30	0
Only fearful at the first childbirth	3	4	44

The few, who in 1968 and 1978 did not refer to any fear before any childbirth, gave the reason that it was, after all, a perfectly natural thing to give birth to a child, and that the family was supportive of them. So it was also in 1988, but it was added that support from the clinic/hospital/health centre helped them to feel safe and not afraid.

During later visits we found only what is inherent in most mothers in any culture: a very natural concern about the coming event.

Midwives[52]

In the local dialect a midwife is *mae tamyae* (i.e. 'the mother who receives'). In 1968, there were two women in the village who functioned as midwives. Neither had received any kind of training to perform this function; they were just highly respected women who were generally trusted, whom first relatives and then later also other people had asked to assist at childbirth.

One of the women was then 59 years old. She had married when she was 18 years; shortly after that people began to approach her for help. She could not count the number of children she had helped into this world but it was high.

The other midwife was about 60 years old and had for the past 20 years or more functioned as a delivery assistant. She was employed somewhat less often than the first one; she thought that she had assisted at about ten childbirths a year. This woman had a daughter who was a nurse in Udorn, and through her she had received some guidance regarding what she was to do when a delivery was not completely free of complications.

Both these midwives had modern and sound attitudes towards many things. They were aware that hygiene played a part in a successfully conducted childbirth, and they knew something about the significance of nutrition, both during pregnancy as well as after the child had been born. They did not promote the prejudices that otherwise stamped the conception of the pregnant woman's sayings and doings.

Both these women had in 1978 quite recently ceased to function in their roles. They felt that they were now too old. New midwives had come onto the scene. Two women in particular were often employed to assist at births. One was 55 years old, and the other thought she was somewhere between 60 and 65 years old. They had not had any kind of training for the job, and had not been in contact with the district health service, which was under the management of a nurse who was also a qualified midwife and who had her clinic some seven kilometres away.

The younger of the two had worked as midwife only three to four years. It started when she helped one of her own daughters, and by 1978, she had become a midwife who was in great demand. The older of the two women had functioned for about one year. She had never thought that she should engage in such work but

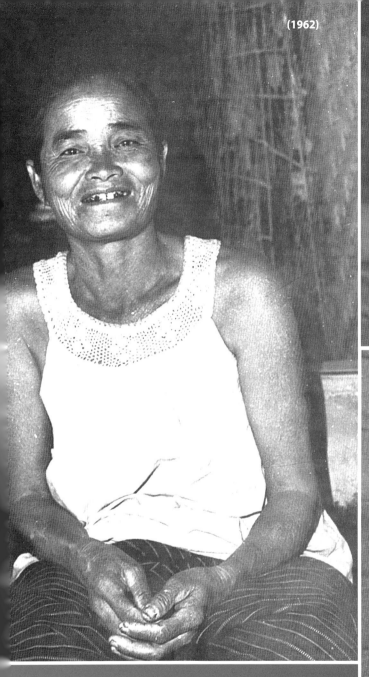

(1962)

(1978)

(1962)

The women who in the 1960s and 1970s were functioning as birth assistants (*mae tamyae*) had no training in this function but they were highly esteemed and respected, and also delightful to talk to

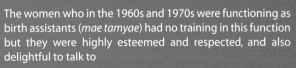

a neighbouring woman had asked for help, and she had since assisted in a total of more than 20 deliveries.

These were two highly esteemed women; two delightful women to talk to, as were also their predecessors. However, it must regretfully be recorded that they – in contrast to their predecessors – were full of all sorts of ancient prejudices regarding all possible circumstances concerning the pregnant woman. Restrictions such as we have already described, during and after childbirth must be observed, or the worst would happen. Also, they held that confinement ought to be for as long as in the olden days when lying-in was for up to a month, sometimes longer. And they promote many more of that sort of practices.

If the changes in the village during the intervening years – the development so to speak – were taken into consideration, it was more than a little amazing to find more prejudiced and less progressive midwives than ten years previously. Perhaps it should be seen in connection with the following: in 1968, the very progressive head teacher lived in Baan Phraan Muean itself. He was married to the daughter of one of the midwives. He took a very active part in all aspects of what was happening in the community, and was generally highly respected and well liked. He possibly also had influence on the midwives' attitude and understanding. By contrast, in 1978, none of the schoolteachers lived in the village and none was part of the village by birth or marriage. Their association with the village population was in fact rather limited.

In the 1960s and the 1970s, the *mae tamyae* generally had no contact with the pregnant woman prior to the childbirth itself, although sometimes a pregnant woman would approach her if she was not feeling so well and had not been able to get help in other ways. All that the midwife could do was to investigate whether the embryo might be lying incorrectly. If that were the case she would by means of a special massage, try and get it turned the right way round. The pregnant woman would not be charged any fee for such a visit but she would normally, of her own accord, give the midwife a few baht.

Ordinarily, the midwife would come into the picture only when the labour pains began. The husband, or a close relative of the pregnant woman, would fetch her. One of the midwives (1968) also said that the night before the birth she would nearly always have a warning that she would be called out. A *phii* would bother her all night through, giving her a stabbing pain in her legs so that she could get no peace in her sleep.

For assistance at a delivery the *mae tamyae* usually would receive about 10 baht in 1968, and 20–25 baht in 1978, both amounts corresponding to a day's wages for farm work in the region. The amount was sometimes paid immediately after the birth but most often in connection with the following New Year celebrations. The mother would then go to the midwife's house, and kneeling, show her respect and gratitude and hand her the money together with perfumed water (*nam horm*), some small candles, flowers, and perhaps a piece of fabric or a blouse.

As mentioned previously, the midwife and her function was regarded with the greatest esteem and respect in Baan Phraan Muean. The general public's evaluation of the profession did not, therefore, correspond to the description by Rishøj and Rajadhon ('People detest the word midwife') but on the contrary, agreed with Hanks: 'Though living like other elder citizens of the community, in their social role they were more respected, known as selfless donors of energy for the sake of others (...)'.[53] However, unlike the midwives in her observations our midwives were not relied upon to master magic.

In Baan Phraan Muean there was not the least indication that there was anything 'unclean' in the midwife's function; consequently, no ritual cleansing of the midwife took place after the childbirth as Rishøj found in her studies.[54]

Conversations were held with our research groups on the basis of the questions: Were you in contact with the midwife prior to your childbirth? Did you, during the pregnancy, contact anybody outside the circle of family and friends for advice and guidance?

Both in 1968 and in 1978, the mothers confirmed the midwives' information that they did not normally have contact with *mae tamyae* during the course of the pregnancy period. But it was a clear trend that the younger group of mothers were more often than the older group of mothers in contact with mae tamyae before the birth itself.

Significant in this context was the mothers' information that while none of the older ones had done so, one-third of the younger group had sought advice, guidance, and perhaps treatment, outside the village from people with adequate training for the purpose (clinic, hospital, *mor tambon*).

However, the large majority of about 75 per cent of the young 1978 mothers preferred to be confined at home, for a multitude of reasons. First and foremost, at home the woman had the family around her and that gave her both confidence and a real peace of mind. There you could also give birth in the manner that was the custom and habit, kneeling and not lying on your back (see later). At home it was also possible to observe customs and habits as they would like to do. Furthermore, a particular anxiety about the hospital asserted itself with considerable strength: namely the risk of having to lie in a bed where people had died and dangerous *phii*(s) therefore were assumed to be present in great numbers.

The changes found in 1978 were so great that we presumed a beginning modification of previous practices. New and better roads were without doubt of importance in that as many as one-third of the young people were seeking advice outside the village. At that stage, however, this outside, qualified, advisory service had far from the capacity to accept everybody for consultation. In our discussions, we found it locally agreed that if real improvements in advice and guidance were to be achieved, both during the pregnancy and in connection with the birth itself, it would best be obtained by an expansion of the *mor tambon*'s clinic (the district health service).

That was in fact what happened. By our visit in 1988, a Village Health Service Centre had been functioning right in the village itself for about a year. Our 1978 mothers, by then ten years older, had all been in contact with the centre and the nurses there for their latest births, and by far the majority preferred to give birth in a clinic or hospital even though about one-quarter of them still preferred to have the confinement at home. The trend was even clearer among our new, young group of 1988 mothers, which we will return to. In 1999 we found that every pregnant woman in the village, consulted the local health centre during the pregnancy as a natural course of action, and that all gave birth at the hospital in Udorn.

This fact indicates a tremendous change and achievement over a relatively short period of time.

The Birth of a Child

Who is present during the delivery?

When the contractions occur in such a way that one must assume that the birth is imminent, the midwife or others who are to be present as delivery assistants are brought in. In principle anyone (except children) may stay in the room where the birth takes place as 'the mother during the childbirth turns her front side towards the wall'. It is considered customary that the husband should be present and take part in the practical tasks.

Data showing actual practice in 1962 and 1978:

Birth assistants	1962 (mothers: 47)	1978 (mothers: 27)
Nobody present at all	1	0
The husband only	10	1
The midwife only	0	5
The husband + older relatives	24	1
The husband + midwife + relatives	6	12
Relatives	5	2
Relatives + midwife	1	4
Delivery in hospital/clinic	0	2

If we look specifically at the attendance of the midwife and the husband, we get this result:

Midwife/husband present	1962 (%)	1978 (%)
Midwife present (incl. hospital delivery)	15	85
Husband present	85	52

There is a marked increase in the employment of a midwife between 1962 and 1978, and at the same time the husband is not present as often as in 1962. It may be a coincidence in the studied groups, but most likely it reflects a trend. It may be presumed that by 1978 a number of men had permanent employment outside the village. Times had changed, which was even more obvious according to data from 1988. By then, more than half of the mothers gave birth at the hospital/clinic in Udorn, and in 1999 only those very few where birth came very suddenly gave birth at home; all others gave birth a the hospital/clinic in the town.

Delivery position

In this part of Thailand the mother traditionally gives birth in a kneeling position, initially sitting back on her heels with her knees apart. Often she will be sitting with her back against a post for support. When the labour begins she will lift herself up to give room for the baby by holding on to a rope tied to a rafter in the ceiling of the house.

After the water has broken, the midwife or another female helper will position herself behind the mother and give her abdomen a kind of massage to speed up the birth. The mother sits on a piece of fabric, usually one of her own loincloths (*phaa sin*).

All 'hanging things' are to be removed from the house, or at any rate from the room where the birth is taking place. That includes items of clothing, household implements, jars, baskets, fishing tackle, etc. If this is not done 'the baby will remain hanging too long in the mother, and that is not good'.

This custom was widely observed both in 1968 and in 1978:

Objects removed	1968 (%)	1978 (%)
Removed everything for diverse reasons	94	89
Removed everything because it promotes an easy delivery	85	56

According to tradition it is also important that doors, windows, baskets and jars with lids be opened to promote 'that the mother opens up and the baby has an easy way out'.

Even in 1968, the villagers were far from being faithful to this custom and just barely half conformed for the original reason. This tendency was considerably strengthened by 1978:

Jar/basket lids opened	1968 (%)	1978 (%)
Opened for diverse reasons	64	52
Opened for the reason of an easier delivery	46	19

Both the above customs were in 1988 only observed at very few of the home deliveries, and the young mothers themselves did not know why the assisting older relatives would remove the items.

Nam mon – magic water

As soon as the childbirth seemed to be underway, the woman should drink *nam mon* (*nam*: water; *mon*: magic spell formula). Several of the villagers, among others some of our 'midwives', were able to prepare it. They were just to recite the right magic incantation over the container with the water.

Mae Mai used the following text (approximate translation): 'We show the very greatest respect through body, speech and soul (*khwan*) towards the supreme God, who is the purest, who is free from all defects and through his own strength liberated from all prejudices, omniscient.'

This is repeated three times. Anyone who knows such an incantation can produce the 'magic water' (for more information see Part 2).

Nam mon is the same designation as that applied to 'sacred' or 'purifying' water prepared for use at many ritual occasions, Buddhist as well as non-Buddhist. To drink *nam mon* also helps to further an easy and uncomplicated delivery. Most complied with this tradition:

Women who drink *nam mon*	1968 (total: 33)	1978 (total: 27)
Drinks *nam mon*, diverse reasons	73%	81%
Drinks *nam mon*, reason: easy delivery	70%	74&

It was understood that *nam mon* is considered good '*for all good purposes*'. The tradition was still observed among almost all mothers giving birth at home in 1988, but was fully gone by 1999 as no one any longer gave birth at home.

Prayer for an easy delivery

One further tradition should be observed whilst the childbirth goes on. One should show respect and pay homage to someone/something that is particularly revered and honoured by the family involved. This should be done kneeling in the traditional Thai manner, with the arms stretched halfway forwards, and the palms of the hands together (*wai*). There is no definite rule as to who should do it. It could be the pregnant woman herself but most often it is her husband or one of her parents. The 'homage' – a plea for aid – can have a religious direction (towards the Lord Buddha, or 'the Three Gems'),[55] but may also be directed at other non-Buddhist 'supernatural beings' (e.g. *phii faa*,[56] *Taapuubaan*,[57] or the ancestor spirits).

Traditionally, this address was intended to ask for support or blessings to make the delivery easy and uncomplicated, and in general ensure that all goes well for the mother and the baby.

Paid homage	1968 (% of total 33)	1978 (% of total 27)
Tradition observed	73	44
Tradition observed explicitly to promote an easy delivery	48	22

Almost three-quarters of the 1968 group observed this tradition, and almost half of the total group did it for the obvious purpose of promoting an uncomplicated delivery. The custom and the traditional reason were clearly declining in 1978 and had almost disappeared by 1988.

After the Birth

In connection with the delivery itself, there are a series of things that ought to be done immediately to protect against the previously-mentioned, very dreaded *phii*(s), *phii porb* and *phii phraay*.

At the moment the birth begins somebody – usually the husband – should place branches with stiff thorns on the ground under the house, in particular below the room where the birth occurs. Any type of thorny bush can be used. Most common in our region is the *maak than*.[58] The thorns themselves and the place where the branches are laid are what are important for the effect. The branches are put on the ground beneath the confinement room to prevent that the *phii phraay*, for example in the shape of a hen and its chick (or in the form of another animal and its young), in getting to blood and other liquids from the birth, which may have dropped onto the ground. If this should anyway happen, the mother will faint, perhaps lose consciousness, and die.

It is generally agreed that the *phii phraay*'s special characteristics are no different from those of *phii porb*, and that the branches have the purpose of protecting against both of these *phii*(s). Both, as mentioned, attack weak persons and like their blood, and if they can get hold of some from the weak mother, the prospects are very poor for both the mother and the baby.

In 1968 and in 1978 we asked the group the following questions: 'Were special things placed underneath the house in connection with the childbirth? What things? Why were they put there?'

Thorny branches under house	1968 (% of total 33)	1978 (% of total 27)
Thorny branches placed for various reasons	100	92
Thorny branches placed as protection against *phii*(s)	88	74

The figure from 1978 should in fact have been 100 per cent as well since the two who gave birth at the clinic stated that at a home-delivery they would definitely have placed *maak than* under the house to protect against the two *phii*(s).

It was thus a custom which had survived and was observed with a very high degree of awareness about its purpose and which was only slightly weakened in the young generation in 1978. But the picture was different in 1988. Of those still giving birth at home only half observed the custom, and a lower percentage had any idea about why the thorns were placed there. Ten years later, in 1999, most of the youngest generation of mothers had heard about these *phii*(s), but did not believe that they are of any threat at all. 'Now we are "protected" by the qualified people surrounding us from the Health Centre', was their comment.

Scattering of rice grains

At the same time as the thorny branches are placed under the house to protect the mother and her baby, rice grains or something similar should be scattered around perhaps inside the house itself, to prevent the spirits, *phii phraay* and *phii porb*, from attacking the mother and the baby. While this is done, magic invocations are recited. This is called *kan phraay, kan porb* (*kan*: to protect against).

Anyone who knows the magic incantations can perform this invocation. It may be the husband though particularly knowledgeable neighbours or family members more often perform such a magical and powerful thing. Most often a male person performs it but a few women were also mentioned as practitioners.

According to the local understanding, the rice grains have a connection with the fact that *phii phraay* most often takes the form of a hen and its chick and will be attracted to the rice grains and will be discovered while eating the grains. If the chickens are discovered, they immediately disappear without anyone being able to say where they went.

Scattered rice grains	1968 (total 33)	1978 (total 27)
Rice grains scattered, diverse reasons	28 (85 %)	26 (96 %)
Rice grains scattered, as protection against the *phii*(s)	28 (85 %)	24 (89 %)

As seen from the table above, this custom was very widespread in 1968 and appeared even strengthened in 1978. And this custom was still strong in 1988. Almost all had scattered rice grains, even those who gave birth at the clinic/hospital, in which case the family would scatter the grains when the mother returned home. The custom still prevailed for many in 1999, but not even all of the elders who did the scattering had any idea about the original reason for doing so. By then it had just become a 'tradition' to do so – a way of celebrating the mother and child.

The umbilical cord

According to the local tradition, the way mother and baby are separated and the placenta is dealt with is quite significant. In the 1960s, the 'midwives' stated that under no circumstances must anything be done to the navel cord before the afterbirth has come. The birth assistant should, by massaging the mother's abdomen, seek to push or squeeze the afterbirth out.

When that has happened, again according to local custom, a cotton thread is tied tightly around the umbilical cord in three places, each knot a short distance apart and close to the baby. No particular reason was given why there had to be three knots. It was merely stated that an uneven number brings luck and progress and is therefore better than an even number.

The cord will then be cut through between the second and third knot, counting from the newborn's navel. In many cases, the birth assistant will just do this but some mothers hold the firm belief that the baby's disposition will be like that of the person who cuts the navel cord and will therefore prefer a particular person to do so. In the 1960s, the umbilical cord was most often severed with a small, sharp knife, perhaps a pocketknife or a razor blade. The knife must first be cleansed in boiling water. But there were some who observed an old custom believing that iron must not be used for cutting the navel cord and instead used a sharp split of bamboo.

As a base for the cut the midwives use the root of *khamin*,[59] which in the district is regarded as an effective medicinal herb against, among other things, prickly heat and open wounds.

The midwives informed us that some prefer to use a piece of charcoal as a base. They, however, disassociated themselves from this practice as in their opinion the child would become 'black' in its soul, i.e., merciless. The midwives would sprinkle ordinary baby powder on the umbilical wound. One of them would supplement the powder with the mudwasp's powdered nest, grilled in a frying pan.[60] Another would supplement it with the dust from a mat that has lain on the floor for some time. Each thought that her supplement would assist the navel to dry up completely and nicely.

The midwives and the village elders agreed that there were no special traditions with regard to what happened to the things that were used in connection with cutting the new-born baby's navel cord. The base was simply thrown away, and the cutting tool was not to be regarded as an object of particular attention either.

The above descriptions of the circumstances are based on the midwives' more general concept of how affairs then ought to be conducted. In the following we shall look at the actual practice.

Almost all the 1968 mothers followed the tradition of tying three knots on the umbilical cord. They could not give any reason for this practice; it was just a custom and a habit. The large majority stated that whoever cut the cord had influence on the child's personality. It was also found that 30 out of 33 thought that even left-handed fathers ought to use the right hand when cutting the umbilical cord. By so doing, one would work towards the child becoming right-handed, which was seen as somewhat important as the left hand is considered unclean because it is used to wash the body after visiting the toilet.

The 1978 mothers followed a similar pattern. Only the two who had given birth at the clinic could not, naturally enough, maintain that the cord should necessarily be tied tightly in three places.

It was thus a matter of a very strong tradition to tie three knots on the umbilical cord and an equally strong tradition to assume that the child will be influenced by the personality of the person who cuts the navel cord.

By 1988, however, these beliefs were almost unknown, and where they were known it was not thought that these matters could have any influence on the child whatsoever.

The tool and base for the cutting

In around 80 per cent of the cases in both 1968 and 1978, one or another type of iron knife was used to make the cut, and it was not thought that this practice would have any significance for the child's later personality development. The old, in Thailand wide-spread belief that iron ought not to be used for this purpose had practically disappeared in this village, and had been gone for many years, we were told. But many knew about the old sayings, such as the following: 'A bamboo splinter ought to be used; it has the effect that the child will be calm but not cruel as if iron were used.' The use of a special mussel shell was also mentioned by a few.

The use of the traditional *khamin* root as base for the cutting was the most common in 1968 and 1978, mainly because it was found to be a strong medicinal herb with antiseptic properties.

As described above, the midwives mentioned that there were no special traditions in regard to the cutting-tool and the cutting-base after the cut was made. Practice within families, both in the older group of mothers in 1968 and the younger mothers in the 1978 group showed otherwise. About one-third of the families in 1968 stated that after use, the cutting tool was just taken back into general use, and that the cutting base was thrown away. The remainder (22) gave no less than nine

different procedure-patterns established within individual families. What each family did was a good example of the many variations found in the performance of the traditions within even as narrow an area as a single village. Rich in tradition the community at the same time striving for strength to be itself, individualized.

In the 1978 group about a third would pay no attention to either tool or base after use whilst the remainder had traditions as varying as those in 1968. It was, however, characteristic for both groups that they had only vague ideas about what might be of special significance in doing what they did with the things: keeping them in specific places, burying one or both things together with the placenta, and so on.

The afterbirth

Both the midwives and the village elders told us that the birth assistant must always rinse the afterbirth in warm water. Then salt should be added to it. The elders agreed that salting the placenta has indirect effect on the child: the child would less easily fall ill and it would in particular keep the child free of inflammations of the throat (some said larynx). The afterbirth should then, according to the local custom, be laid in an internode of bamboo that it is open at one end (a bamboo section approximately 20–25 centimetres long and 8–10 centimetres in diameter) – a 'natural' container used for many purposes in the village). On top of it, salt should be sprinkled with some *khaa* leaves – a plant that is of the ginger genus.

To ensure that the child will be right-handed, the husband should then carry the container out of the house, using his right hand.

All of the 1968 mothers were found to have used the traditional bamboo section for this purpose, whilst the plastic bag gradually began to gain admittance in the 1978 group. In both groups it was in all cases the husband who carried the container with the placenta out.

In 1968, more than two-thirds of the women stressed that the placenta ought to be brought out of the house with the right hand, and all for the reason that the child would then presumably be right-handed. In 1978, well over half were of the same conviction.

A very large part of the mothers in both groups added the further proviso that the placenta ought not to be carried out until all children in the house were in bed and asleep. This would have the effect that the new-born would become a calm child and sleep well.

The container with the placenta should be buried in the soil. It was understood from the midwives and village elders that it is not unimportant where the placenta was placed. While all agreed that the location was significant, opinions varied widely on where and the meanings of different locations.

Some said it should be buried in the ground by or under the ladder leading up to the house. Most could not give any reason for this location; however, a few said that it had the effect that the child would not move away from the home too early or too far away when growing up. This was considered a valuable practice, especially for the girls.

Two older women mentioned the following as rules from 'olden times':

• The placenta by, or under, the ladder, then the child remains at home;

• The placenta by a bamboo plant, then the child will, when adult, be brave, serious and firm, and will go out into the world to earn a living.

Therefore the former site should be used for girls, and the latter for boys.

Others had different beliefs:

The placenta ought to be buried in 'rising ground' or in the highest place in the grounds, because the child would then develop into becoming 'unselfish and well gifted'. Several were of the opinion that the container should be buried deeply to make the child strong and healthy.

Whatever was said about the burial site by the elders and the midwives, the families' replies showed that 'by or under the ladder' was the preferred place, both in 1968, 1978, and 1988, irrespective of whether the child was a boy or a girl. By 1978, only a few thought that the place had some influence upon the child's development. Later, almost all children were born in the clinic and the mothers had no influence upon what happened to the placenta. Luckily they no longer cared at all.

According to tradition, the hole in the ground where the placenta container is buried must be so deep that the upper rim of the container will be level with the surrounding soil surface. The husband should then make a red-hot fire on top. Anything may be used as fuel, any sort of wood or perhaps rice husks. The fire should burn day and night until the entire contents of the container has dried up.

Rajadhon[61] mentions that the custom of lighting a fire on top of the buried placenta is known only in Northeastern Thailand. He adds that he is unable to give any reason for this custom.

In our village and in all the villages in this area, there was a clear and easily understandable reason for maintaining this fire. The reasoning was identical for all 47 mothers in the 1962 investigation, repeated by 33 of them in 1968, also given by all 27 mothers in 1978, and found again in 1988, with the few still giving birth at home: the drying up of the placenta by fire has the magic power to dry out the baby's navel, and the wound will heal as rapidly as the placenta in the container dries up. This took approximately seven days. Interestingly, the same notion was found in most of the 30 villages we visited in the upper Northeast in 1988.

So in the popular belief there is a clear connection between the drying-out of the placenta and the healing of the navel, and this is probably the answer to the question raised by Rajadhon in 1961.

After about seven days have elapsed, the remnant of the umbilical cord situated between the first and the second knots should be so dry that it drops off. According to the local tradition one ought not to throw away this little piece as various qualities are attributed to it.

In 1968 and 1978 about half of the mothers kept this piece of the navel cord, and most of those who did, did so because they thought the remnant possessed 'a power'. In 1988, a follow-up on the 1978 sample showed that this group still had the belief that there was some 'power' in this piece. But the belief had almost disappeared completely from the group of the youngest mothers in our new 1988 sample, and in 1999, the question was no longer relevant as all were giving birth in a place where neither they nor their older relatives had control over such matters.

What qualities did they attribute to it? Varied, indeed, and of magic as well as medical nature.

- It should be saved in a cloth bag near the infant's head. This would have the effect that the baby becomes healthy, strong, and easy to raise. It brings general good health, and the baby will not cry so much;

- Laid in rice whisky, a tot of this will be good for an inflated stomach, both for the child and for the adults in the family;

- If the baby has stomach aches the mother should rub the remnant against a stone lying in a bowl of her own milk. This mixture should then be rubbed onto the baby's stomach;

- If the growing child gets an itchy rash around the mouth, it helps if the mouth is moistened with water in which the navel cord remnant has lain for a while;

- If the remnant is put in the children's food or drinking water, they will not bicker among themselves and the younger will respect the older;

- It is saved so that the son can take it with him, should he be sent off to war. As a charm it will provide protection ('bullet-proof');

- Used as a charm, the child will become 'co-operative', some said, while others held the belief that the charm would protect the child against all dangers. As a charm it will make the child remember his home and his parents. Some mothers actually showed us the remnant, encased in a little plastic heart with a chain, meant to be worn around the neck.

Protecting the Mother

Traditionally, when the childbirth is over and the mother has been washed, and before she commences her lying-in, she should walk three paces in the room where the delivery has taken place. In her hand, she should have an ordinary 50 to 70-centimetre-long knife, which should be rammed hard into the floorboards at each of the three steps. After that she should stab the knife blade down between the plain planks (not tongue and groove) near the confinement couch and its adjacent bonfire site. One can imagine that certain words would have to be recited, perhaps an incantation, whilst the action is performed. However, that is not demanded.

The traditional house was built on poles and underneath the house there was thus an open space, taller than a man, used for all sorts of activities. Here, the long knife-blade is now visible, and that is the intention. According to popular belief, the noisy action itself and the visible knife blade helps in keeping *phii phraay* and *phii porb* away from the mother and her baby. When asked why spirits are afraid of knives the answer was quite unanimous from both village elders and mothers: as human beings are afraid of knives (weapons) so, too, are spirits.

To what extent did the mothers over the years adhere to this tradition?

There was a marked slide in this tradition over the years. In 1968, 88 per cent of our sample group observed the custom totally or almost totally in its traditional form, and all of them thought that it protected against the two dreaded *phii*(s). In 1978, almost as many observed the custom (85 per cent) but only one-third for the reason of protection against the *phii*(s). They still observed the custom in its outer form but the reason for doing it was unknown to them.

In 1988, the youngest mothers – those of them who gave birth at home – were still walking the three steps

and ramming the knife hard into the floorboards in the traditional way, but they had no idea why they should do so. They were told to do so by their mothers and/or grandmothers! By February 1999, this practice had completely disappeared from our hamlet. However, in 2001 and 2003, I still observed a knife near the confinement couch, placed there by the mother's helpers of an older generation. Just to play safe, one never knows!

The mother herself must be guarded from all imminent dangers, especially those posed by the evil spirits, *phii phraay* and *phii porb*. To do so, after the placenta has been delivered, a cotton thread must be tied around the mother's neck, then around both wrists, and lastly around both ankles.

This is called *kan haay* – to 'give protection against'. Usually a magic incantation is recited whilst the threads are being tied. Mae Mai, one of the mid-wives, used this: 'I protect you from all "giants", the one-footed spectre, the one-eyed ghost, and all other spectres and ghosts beneath the heavens, and within a distance of 30,000 kilometres they will be conquered by me.' Other midwives and many of the village elders had their own powerful spells to be recited on this occasion (for the texts see Part 2).

The powerful cotton threads can be produced by 'someone who knows about it'; this is done as part of the preparations for the childbirth. Anyone may tie them and it is not strictly necessary to recite an accompanying strong incantation. The threads are protective in themselves, because magical and powerful incantations are recited whilst they are made.[62]

It is important that a string is first tied around the mother's neck as the *phii porb* and *phii phraay* invade a person through the mouth.

To what extent and for which reason *kan haay* was observed by the mothers is seen from this summary:

Kan haay performed	1968 (%)	1978 (%)
Had threads tied in the prescribed manner	100	100
Reason: Protection against *phii phraay* and *phii porb*	97	96

In the 1968 group *kan haay* was in all cases performed by men (such as the grandfather, older brother, husband, neighbours). In 1978, apart from the male relatives, 15 different male 'masters' were mentioned who were able to conduct this ritual, but only two women.

The belief in, and fear of, these *phii*(s) and their unpredictable, serious, and perilous actions in connection with the birth of a child were, according to the just described *kan haay*, as evident in 1978 as ten years previously. Pregnancy and childbirth were still dangerous matters in this part of the world and naturally, a 'safety net' had been developed so that mortal illness and death possibly could be averted.

In 1988, all the then very young mothers in our group had *kan haay* made, even those who gave birth in the clinic, but by then only half of them knew the reason for tying the threads. In 1999 and in 2001, there were still some of those who had the ritual made that knew it had to do with protection against some *phii*(s) and felt it could be important to follow the practice.

The Infant in the Kradong

According to tradition, a baby in this village should spend its first three nights in a *kradong morn*, something that can best be described as a plaited tray. It is not completely flat-bottomed, but slightly concave, with a low rim and round in shape. In this basket-tray is placed a little mattress, filled with kapok. The tray need not be new. It is all right to borrow one if you do not have one. The tray is the type that is normally used for breeding silkworms.[63] Almost all village elders and midwives in 1968 were in agreement that it must be exactly this type of basket, for the reasons mentioned below.

The tray is of the same shape and size as the basket-tray used when the villagers separate rice grains and husks – dextrously tossing rice and husks up in the air catching the grains again while the husks blow away. The basket for silkworms is just a little less sturdy in construction. According to tradition, the basket for winnowing rice must not be used as a bed for the baby as it could have a harmful effect. It is said that this basket has moved about far too much which could have the effect on the baby in that he/she will suffer from epilepsy or in other ways 'be sick in the brain'.

There are other basket-trays, in construction and shape reminiscent of the *kradong morn*. They are used for many things in the village including for drying fish and palm sugar. But these cannot be used for babies either. They are used for edible things and ought therefore not to be used for something as 'unclean' as a newborn baby.

During conversations about this, we found in 1968 that it was in fact a problem to provide the correct basket-tray. Silk was no longer produced in this village, and the existing *kradong morns* eventually wore out. But so far they managed, so they saw no reason to consider seriously what to do when the day came for the last *kradong morn* to fall to pieces.

We got no unanimous reason for the baby being laid in a *kradong*. Two explanations recurred from village elders and midwives. One was practical: it is convenient. The baby was easily moved about when lying in such a tray.

The other was magical: it protected against *phii*(s). The midwife most frequently employed in 1968 informed us that when she laid the infant in the basket she would raise it up and move it in calm, circular movements from right to left saying: 'Come here, *phii phraay, phii porb,* and *phii nok khau.*[64] If this child is yours, take it now. If that does not happen here and now, from now on it belongs to me.' Then she would tie a cotton thread round the child's right wrist as protection against *phii*(s).

Nor was there agreement as to why the baby must lie in the *kradong* for exactly three nights. We got answers like:

- 'One night for each of the Three Gems';[65]

- 'Three is better than any other figure';[66]

- 'It is just tradition';

- 'Any number of nights is satisfactory, but at least three, because three – like other uneven numbers – is considered a good number'.

Uncertainty is mirrored clearly in the mothers' information about the practice itself and the reason to follow it, as seen in this summary:

Use of *kradong*	1968 (%)	1978 (%)
The baby in *kradong*, various types	85	81
The baby in *kradong morn*	85	44
Reason for *kradong*: protection against the super naturals	33	4
Three nights	82	70
Three nights or longer	100	100

The 1968 mothers who did not use a *kradong* all said that the baby 'ought to be' in a *kradong* but as they did not have the correct one they used instead a mattress on the floor. At the same time they had not yet gone as far as to imagine using another type of *kradong*. The majority of this group used a *kradong* either because it was practical, or because it happened to be tradition.

In the 1978 group, the greater majority continued to use a *kradong* but a very large percentage of them used a *kradong* of a type other than that which, according to tradition, was the only one usable.

This did not bother the young but to some degree it did concern their mothers for the reasons explained above. Practical people as they were the mothers tolerated it by saying: 'Perhaps when all is said and done, it means nothing.' A great deal fewer of the young than the older connected the lying in a *kradong* with protection against super natural beings. But from this we should not be misled into believing that the fear of *phii*(s) was dying out. This fear was mirrored with great clarity in what, according to custom and usage, was to take place next.

But before going on, just a few words about the time after 1978 in relation to the above: a *kradong* was still in use in 1988 though most of the mothers would just place the child on a mattress right on the floor, and whatever was done had no magical or any other influence, as they commented. Their replies in 1999 and in 2001 were the same.

Life and health alone do not suffice. According to local tradition, immediately after the birth of the baby one should not only consider the mere physical survival of the child. The little one needs also to develop into a human being with good personal qualities, and live in as secure circumstances as at all possible.

The villagers were quite aware that one's influence through the upbringing and the things to which one exposes a child during its growth are of extraordinarily

great significance for the child's development. They also held a strong belief that personal qualities and the building of possibilities into the child could happen in various supernatural and magic ways. We have seen examples of this earlier. That it is considered possible to transfer qualities to the child is also mirrored in several of the things the villagers do when the infant is to be laid on the bed next to the mother.

A good, secure, and safe future in adulthood depends, among other things, on being adept at the things one has to deal with in everyday life. The girls should be good in sewing and at handicrafts, plaiting, weaving, etc. and the boys at using heavier tools, above all, the large knife used for innumerable tasks. By the 1960s, it was also considered important for both boys and girls to do well at school. They should be able to read, write, and do sums – a first condition for them to have a chance in the future to move beyond the economically insecure daily life of the parent generation. In 1968, the eldest, most knowledgeable, and respected of our village elders, Phor Tuu Phan, stated the following: 'In the olden days they used to place a knife and a sickle under the mattress for both girls and boys for the three nights they spent in the *kradong*. By so doing, they would become diligent and adept at working with these implements that are made from strong iron and are the most important in the work we must perform. Nowadays, the most important is to do well at school for which reason we lay paper, a book, and a pencil (slate pencil) under the child's mattress.'

Now, what happened to this practice? Was the custom about to disappear?

Families that placed something under the child's mattress	1968 (%)	1978 (%)
At all childbirths	58	89
At some childbirths	42	0
Never	0	11

Directly evaluated, it may appear that the custom was more widespread in 1978 than in 1968, and therefore actually had been strengthened during the time elapsed. But this interpretation is probably going too far. The mothers in the 1978 group were young and did not yet have many children, and there is no guarantee that they would continue this custom at all future childbirths. It is important to note that in contrast to the 1968 group, in the 1978 group there were three mothers (11 per cent) who explicitly stated that they placed nothing under the baby and did not intend to do so for later childbirths because they did not believe it had any significance.

Yet the custom had far from vanished. The very act of placing things under a newborn could perhaps just be contingent upon observing a sweet old custom without attaching any importance to it? As seen from the following this was far from being the case:

Purpose of placing items under the baby	1968 (%)	1978 (%)
Magic purpose clearly formulated	55	82
Magic purpose not clearly formulated, but lies indirectly in the given reason	42	0
Not convinced of a magic purpose	3	0
Absolutely no magic purpose	0	2
Nothing under baby; do not believe that it means anything	0	11

It is clear that in 1978, a very large group of the young still had a clear magic purpose in placing things underneath their newly-born though some, in contrast to the findings in 1968, definitely did not think it meant anything. In effect a change had taken place but as yet this change was not particularly marked.

What parents in fact placed under the baby varied tremendously in both groups. 'Knife' was listed less frequently in 1978 than in 1968 whilst 'book and pencil', and also 'coin, money', were mentioned more often in the younger group. This is hardly incidental but presumably an expression of real alterations in the conception of the significance of the listed items.

In 1988 and also during later visits, we found mostly books, pencils, and coins placed under the infant. The mothers explained that their mother or grandmother/grandfather did it. 'Maybe it means something', some of them would say.

The health of the new-born infant

All the mothers in the 1968 as well as the 1978 group stated with pleasure that most of their babies were well and healthy when delivered and that they immediately cried out.

Of the older women who between them had been through many childbirths, nearly all related instances where the baby was very weak at birth, or became so in the course of a few hours or days. A few of the quite young mothers had also already been in the same situation. When this occurred, the whole family would engage itself in the illness and weakness of the newly-born and the parents would seek the help of different rituals, as directed by *mor sorng*. This was the case for both the older and the younger generation of mothers. However, one marked difference became evident in the two groups' statements about what they would do in such cases. No one in the 1968 group stated that they would seek help at the hospital, from the physician, or from the district health service (*mor tambon*), while just over half of the 1978 group, besides finding ways and means to help the baby through the traditional and already-mentioned precautions, also spontaneously mentioned that they would draw on the professional competence from the various medical services.

Hence, in 1968 and 1978, the villagers would almost surely first and foremost think of *mae kamlerd* or a *phii* as the reason for the child's problems. The diagnosis had to be made, and they would call upon the diagnostician – *mor sorng* – and they would follow his directions.

Most were quite certain that they would not, regardless of the age of the patient, be content with only one form of treatment. 'You can never be quite sure, and it can do no harm to try different things!'

In this, as in other contexts, the attitude in Baan Phraan Muean corresponded – and still corresponds – extremely well with the deliberations by Ingersoll (1966). He writes, for example: 'When the augury is unfavourable (…) they generally react not with resignation but with determined efforts to avoid the predicted misfortune. If, despite all their attempts to cope, disaster still befalls them, only then do the villagers take refuge in explaining their evil lot as fate. (…) They tend to accept events as their fate only after the fact.'[67] Terweil relates the same experience. He who takes no action 'is a sort of gambler trusting his luck'.[68]

Our 1978 group was re-visited in 1988. Obviously changes had occurred in these ten years during which the whole society had changed rapidly. The first reply to the question, 'What would you do if your very young child should become ill?' was now from more than 80 per cent of the mothers that they would 'visit the hospital/health centre/clinic', adding, 'and maybe also visit one of the local diagnosticians' – just to play safe! The remaining 20 per cent said that would they first and foremost use the local and traditional ways, partly because they found them good enough and partly because they could not afford to buy the modern medicine prescribed by a real doctor. Nor had the new group of very young mothers included in our research in 1988 fully given up on the local and traditional

diagnosticians and their various ways of treatments and inclusive rites.

Even in 2005, some of the old traditional medicine remained but better economic conditions, better and easier bus connections to town, a well respected local health centre, and probably also better basic education of the new generations is bringing most of it to an end.

Concluding Remarks

This positive development well reflects the observations by Phraya Anuman Rajadhon in 1961. In the introduction to his dissertation about 'Customs Connected with Birth', he stressed that the 'beliefs of some people of any given age or any locality are always suited to the life and needs of the period or that locality'. He continues: 'Any custom which is appropriate to one age but perhaps not appropriate to later ages declines and disappears, or is altered to make it appropriate', but mentions at the same time that people will not infrequently adhere to customs 'even though the usefulness or necessity is gone. (...) People dare not change.'[69]

This leads Rajadhon towards some deliberations about a people's (group's) adherence to customs 'that are harmful or that obstruct or delay progress' and to saying that a people (a group) at times 'cast away everything old because they regard it as out of date, and seize upon new things which are not suited to the mentality or lives... Both these methods result in damage.'[70]

Similar thoughts also occupy Terweil when he writes: 'Since the culture is in constant flux, a norm should be interpreted in its contemporary context: in relation to the whole cultural situation of the particular time.'[71]

How do childbirth customs as we have now had them described from Baan Praan Muean fit in with these points of view? If we avoid using 'our own measuring

basket to measure other people's rice'[72] it seems justified to summarize thus:

The local traditions in connection with childbirth have been very strong in this area of Northeast Thailand. Assessed on the basis of the villagers' circumstances, the large majority has had a sensible reason directed towards, to the best of their ability, helping the mother and her baby through the delivery, by protecting and assisting both after the childbirth, and finally by giving the child the best possible opportunities during its lifetime.

Until a few years ago there was still a need, to some extent, to live according to tradition even though some of the customs had been vanishing and others only upheld in an outward form without the youngest mothers making themselves aware of their significance.

One could note that while the customs in principle were the same for everyone, considerable variation existed in the performance of these customs. Local cultural tradition has been very strong but so is the individuality of each woman and her family.

None of the customs found can be said to have been harmful. It is my evaluation that none of them directly or indirectly took part in obstructing or delaying the development of a qualified health service that could provide better help, greater confidence, and safety during childbirth. There was every indication that all women in our various groups from 1968 and up to 2001 would be ready and willing to seek adequate help and assistance, were there a possibility to obtain it.

In conclusion, some remarks should be linked to a few of the customs previously mentioned in this chapter.

Delivery position

The village women's traditional kneeling delivery position was discussed with both the District Health Nurse and with the obstetrician at the hospital in Udorn. When a delivery took place at one of the mentioned institutions the mother lay on her back. The staff had learnt that this is the right way and had got used to it. Equipment, etc., was arranged for this. Both stated that they found the kneeling position safer for both the mother and the baby when the childbirth took place in her house in the village where no special help was available. The reason given was that this position is more natural in order to advance a rapid delivery, and it thus assists in the best way possible to avoid childbirth injuries.

This keeling position is used in wide areas of Northeast Thailand and is mentioned from Laos.[73] Other variations of kneeling–sitting positions are known from other parts of Thailand and also in other cultures, e.g. the Shan States,[74] Buganda,[75] Mexico,[76] and among Netsilik Eskimos,[77] and also in Denmark right up until the end of the 18th century,[78] and probably in many more places around the world.

Judging by the frequency of its mention in books from widely different regions of the country,[79] a sitting position appears to be the most often adopted position in Thailand. Ploss[80] and de Young[81] mention that lying on the back is a common delivery position in Thailand but I believe we may consider this a misstatement.

The umbilical cord

Almost all references describing childbirth – regardless of how few details they give – have remarks about special circumstances that must be observed when the mother and her baby are separated by cutting the navel cord. They talk about the number of knots, the length of the bit that is to remain, about the cutting tool, about the cutting base.

It is also significant that the dried-up remnant of the umbilical cord has both magical and medicinal power attributed to it. An investigation would show that there is considerable uniformity in the concepts people all over the world have formed, and are still forming, about the meaning of the various details.

Frazer mentions that people world-wide appear to have considered the afterbirth and the umbilical cord in 'sympathetic union with the body'; so intimate is the connection understood to be 'that the fortunes of the individual for good or evil throughout life are often supposed to be bound up with one or other of these portions of his person, so that if his navel string or afterbirth is preserved and properly treated, he will be prosperous, whereas if it be injured or lost, he will suffer accordingly'. [82]

Among the many references only four circumstances will be mentioned here:

1. References relating to Thailand seem to show that in many parts of the country, the sharp edge of a bamboo splinter has, until recently, been considered the most correct tool to use for the cutting.

2. This goes together with 'iron' making 'hard'. But change has occurred, as both Suvannathat[83] and Mougne[84] mention that now, as already for quite some time in Baan Phraan Muean, a knife made of iron or a pair of scissors is used most often.

3. No reference is found to the fact that using either right or left hand to cut the cord should influence the child's right- or left-handedness but it was believed to be so among most people in Baan Phraan Muean in the 1960s and the 1970s.

4. In my own country, Denmark, there are references to the umbilical cord. Møller mentions an example from 1894 where the pulverized remnant of the child's cord had been used for a medical purpose and was administered to the child. He also refers to an instance from the provincial town, Viborg, where as late as in 1908, it was used as a medicine against, amongst other things, cramp, St. Vitus's Dance (Chorea), and colic in the abdomen. [85]

The afterbirth

Concepts corresponding in principle – and at times right down to every detail – to the descriptions from Baan Phraan Muean are found in all those of my references mentioning this aspect of the delivery progress from other parts of Thailand. This applies to both earlier and more recent references. A sympathetic connection between the treatment of the placenta and the child's subsequent existence is found also in most of my references that relate, not only to Thailand's neighbouring countries, but also to more distant cultures.

If we look at older Nordic descriptions, it is cited from Finn Magnussön[86] that in olden times, the afterbirth was considered sacred in Iceland. The child would lack his guardian angel if the afterbirth was thrown away or burnt. It should instead be buried by the threshold where the mother would pass to and fro. A series of concepts, in principle corresponding to those applying in Baan Phraan Muean, are for example found in references from Denmark where a midwife, born as late as 1846, has given descriptions containing the same elements. [87]

A few special circumstances from the references must be brought to light:

1. From Baan Phraan Muean the treatment of the placenta is mentioned to possibly influence on the child's right-or left-handedness. This concept is found only in one other reference, that of Rajadhon. [88]

2. Apart from Northeastern Thailand, nowhere is a fire lit directly upon the afterbirth. In several locations the afterbirth is placed near the lying-in fire. According to Rajadhon, this is done 'in order to cause the umbilical cord of the child to dry rapidly'. [89]

3. It is noted that from Baan Phraan Muean no concepts are described to indicate that the placenta itself would have any medicinal use. Nor are such qualities found in references relating to other parts of Thailand though they are mentioned in references from Vietnam where this understanding is extensive in Sino-Vietnamese medicine. [90] In my own country, Denmark, there are several examples from the past of the afterbirth having been used as a remedy for epilepsy. [91]

The child's bed immediately after its birth

The use of a flat basket-tray, presumably almost like that used in Baan Phraan Muean, as the infant's first bed after its birth appears to be very widespread in Thailand both in the past and in the present time. Numerous references, both old and recent, mention such a tray including Bock from 1884, and more recently Terweil in 1975 and Whittaker in 2000. [92] The same bed is described from the neighbouring country of Laos by Berval (1959, p 134); notably, only he mentions that the tray is understood to provide protection against spirits.

Many references mention for how long (one to seven days) the baby must lie in the basket-tray; to take a couple of examples: Rajadhorn's (older) and Whittaker's (more recent) references. [93] Also, magical ideas about being able to influence the child's development by placing things under the new-born baby's mattress are

intimated in many references, and are known in many countries which have no affinity to Thailand. In Denmark, they would, among other things, put a hymnal in the cradle so that the child would have a good singing voice. The same source informs us that as late as in the 1890s it was not unusual to place a knife in the cradle as protection against 'underground creatures'. [94]

(1981)

CHAPTER FIVE

The Confinement – Yuu Fai

When the childbirth is over and everything has been put in order, the mother will begin her lying-in. Older people call it *yuu kam*. Rajadhon[95] sees a linguistic connection between *yuu kam* and to 'be in karma' while Mougne[96] gives the meaning 'to observe prohibitions, or be in a state of restrictions'. This does not fit the linguistic content of *kam* in the Isan language. According to Ass. Professor Supranee Khammuang *kam* corresponds to 'bother', 'inconvenience', closest to the term of multiple interpretations: 'in trouble'. However, younger people have adopted the term *yuu fai* – 'to lie by the fire', corresponding to the vernacular of the Central Plain.

The traditions of the confinement are described to me as follows:

In the room where the woman is to have her childbed her husband will make a site for a fire directly on the wooden floor. Four planks are set on edge to form a quadrangle, and strong banana plant rods are laid at the bottom of this quadrangle. On top of these is laid a layer of clayey soil. The fireplace is made immediately beside the low couch where the woman is to spend her confinement. During the lying-in, the intention is that she will turn over and around on the couch at suitable intervals so that both her back and her front are warmed through. Above the fire, a large pan or tin tub filled with water and various herbs simmers all the time producing a liquid that is assumed to have a medicinal effect. The mother will use this to wash herself in. In a smaller vessel or kettle another herbal decoction is boiled which

the mother is supposed to drink. After every birth, a number of days (from over a month down to seven or five days) are spent this way. All mothers in both the 1968 and 1978 samples went through a confinement in this quite traditional form.

During the decade from 1978 to 1988, very rapid changes took place in very many aspects of rural life in the Northeast of Thailand. Modern contraception came to the villages, and it was no longer unusual to give birth at the hospital in town. In this period, too, it became customary to be sterilized when no more children were desired, and the sterilization was made at the clinic/hospital in connection with the birth of the last child. After sterilization it was believed that a *yuu fai* was not needed after the birth.

These new patterns are reflected in our findings in 1988, when we revisited the mothers of our 1978 sample. Half of them still wanted more children and had a *yuu fai* after all their births in the period. The other half had a *yuu fai* at all their births in the period except the last one when they were sterilised. In 1988, we also had a new sample of the very youngest mothers. All of them went through a traditional *yuu fai* including those who gave birth at a hospital/clinic which was about half of them. Their reasoning for the practice was unanimously: 'We are young and wish to have more children.'

Also in 1999, in 2001, and in 2003, our young mothers had a *yuu fai*, some of them using a charcoal stove instead of an open fire.

Similarly, in our 1988 interviews in thirty villages in an area of the upper Northeast, we found that *yuu fai* was known and still in use all over. The tradition of *yuu fai* is so strong a part of the local custom that there is hardly any woman in Baan Phraan Muean and very few, if any, in villages in that part of the country who have not had a *yuu fai* in connection with their childbirths. In some places, mostly semi-urbanized areas, it has been given up in its traditional form with the open fire, but everybody finds that heating is an important element of the confinement, and a charcoal stove or in some more advanced places an electric heating pad or hot-water bottle, have replaced the traditional open fire.

Wood for the yuu fai bonfire

The traditional *yuu fai* as it was performed in this village in the 1960s and 1970s proceeded as follows:

Traditionally, the husband must procure the wood for the fire. This is usually done one to two months before the expected childbirth. There does not appear to be any particular superstition connected to the actual obtaining of the wood. Of course, fresh wood should be gathered rather early so that it will be dry enough. Wood from trees already dead can wait somewhat longer. The husband can choose any day and time to fetch the wood.

Most people prefer the very strong and durable *mai tiw*[97] for several reasons. First, it does not spark so much; second, it does not throw out so much heat and does not cause the mother (and possibly the baby) heat rashes so easily. Other species can be used. Several of those mentioned have tart fruits; it is presumed that this wood prevents poisoning and inflammation in the mother. One particular kind of wood must, however, never be used. This is *mai khaam pom*,[98] a member of the same family as the tamarind tree. This wood is used for cremations.

When the husband has found the wood, he will cut it into pieces of about an arm's length and stack it to dry somewhere inside the fences around the grounds of the house, in a place where it will not be in the way. It was observed that branches with stiff thorns covered some of these stacks of wood. This practice is aimed at preventing the evil spirits, *phii phraay* and *phii porb*, from getting access to the wood. How generally this belief prevailed was not investigated.

As mentioned earlier, it is the husband who builds the fireplace. Usually he will also place three stones, large enough to form a suitable base for quite a large cooking pot, in the fireplace. The pot is either a clay jar or a square paraffin drum with the top cut off. This latter cooking vessel is most often given a handle so that it can hang rather than stand on the fireplace.

Anyone may set the *yuu fai* bonfire alight, and it appeared that there are no special rules or customs in respect of this. Generally, however, certain verbal restrictions apply during the *yuu fai* period – for example should words like 'hot' or 'heat' not pass one's lips.

There are no rules stipulating that the mother must lie or sit in any particular way, nor that her couch must point towards any special corner of the world. The location of her bed seems to depend solely on the size and site of the room. Nor are there any established regulations governing where in the house the confinement must be done. It can be the place considered most convenient for all.

To kill the heat – praab fai

Most of the year the outdoor temperature is so high that is a difficult matter to lie for many days by a red-hot burning fire that one must keep as close to as possible. It happens that the women develop rashes and feel really unwell. There is therefore a need to prevent the most unpleasant side effects of the heat, and for this

A typical *yuu fai* situation from 1978. As always, two vessels with decoctions are heated on the fire, one for washing her body and the other one for drinking

purpose a small rite *praab fai* ('to kill the heat') may be performed.

In 1968, everybody had this ritual performed immediately after the confinement had begun with the intention 'to kill the heat from the fire' as much as possible. There were no definite rules as to who must perform this magic action. Anyone who 'knew about it' could do so.

There were many different ways of doing this but in all cases salt is involved. About three-quarters of all would perform this little ritual by standing facing the fire, then bending the knees slightly and throwing a handful of salt from behind between the parted legs into the fire.

The two most frequently employed performers of *praab fai* gave the reason that the salt must be tossed between the legs thus: 'There the sexual organs are, and that is strong stuff, which will make the ritual more effective.'

One of our midwives, Mae Mai, performed her *praab fai* by first kneeling and showing respect to Lord Buddha; then she threw salt between her legs whilst she repeated three times: 'I blow on the hard iron in the evening. I puff at the glowing iron in the morning. I will blow and puff until it turns white as powder and dry as lime.' (For more information on the texts used in the *praab fai* see Part 2).

All of the 27 young women in our 1978 group had *praab fai* performed in exactly the same fashion as the older group in 1968. The tradition was still followed by the 1978 group when they were revisited in 1988. Our new and very young group of 1988 mothers also followed this tradition, and so did the 1999 mothers. These findings and the fact that many mothers reported rashes, as well as burning and smarting sensations of the skin caused by the *yuu fai*, are a strong confirmation that the *yuu fai* is unpleasant.

Herb decoctions used during the confinement

Two containers with herb decoctions were standing on or possibly suspended above the fireplace during the confinement. One was a large jar or tub with the contents intended for washing the body. The other was smaller, possibly a kettle, for a decoction to be drunk. These potions were considered to have a medicinal effect. The ingredients of the two decoctions were different, each adapted to its purpose.

The content of the vessels was to be prepared by 'someone who knows about it'; a man or woman in the village with knowledge of herbal medicine.

Within the subject treated here I shall beware of making any judgments whatsoever. I have wished – possibly for use in such judgments – to give recipes with which I have become acquainted. The names of herbs and plants are given in the local Isan language. Mrs Supranee Khammuang, who is herself from Isan, has done her utmost to search out their Latin names. There is, however, uncertainty with regard to the identification of some of the plants. But, pointing out this uncertainty, I have chosen to include them as additional material in Part 2 of this book.

I have used the term 'herbal decoction' deliberately in place of 'herbal medicine'. There is no doubt that the mothers use it for the purpose of treatment, therefore as a remedy, or a means of improving their health. As to its factual effect, my immediate attitude to the practice performed by the local herbal specialists corresponds very well with the points of view presented by a former Minister of Health in Laos, Dr Oudom Souvannavong, when he describes how modern medical science and old local tradition are practised peacefully side by side, and states that this should give no cause for concern, quite the contrary. Most often it is harmless, and 'if they do not always cure the patient, at least they do not make his condition worse and that is already something'. [99]

On the confinement couch the mother must turn so that both her back and her front are warmed through. The ablutions must be as hot as at all possible. She washes herself with a rag wetted in this decoction, and she must do this as often as she can – at least three times daily. Also she must drink as much as possible of the drinking decoction, and drink it as hot as she can.

All 33 mothers from 1968 followed this custom in the way described here; the 27 young mothers in the 1978 sample did likewise, although one of them had only one vessel with herb decoction. Its contents were used both for washing and drinking. Ten years later, in 1988 this group still continued this practice after a birth. Also the new, very young 1988 group of mothers attended to this custom in the traditional way, and so did the 1999 and 2001 mothers, though one of them had only plain water for drinking and for washing her body.

Additional treatment during yuu fai

The midwives were of the opinion that, apart from the presumed medicinal effect of the hot herbal decoctions, no medical treatment was needed after the birth. One might take one or another of the 'patent medicines' of

Notice the little knife in the centre of this *yuu fai* situation from 1988. The young mother told us that her grandmother suggested that the knife be placed there, because it would protect her against 'some *phii*(s)'. She herself was doubtful whether or not to believe in *phii*(s), but found it a good thing to 'play safe'.

which several were on sale, made to either Thai or Chinese recipes.

The data in 1968 showed that the majority of this older group did not take anything else than the herbal decoctions that accompanied any proper confinement. The young from 1978, who were undoubtedly better off

than most people ten years previously, supplemented this with one or more 'patent medicines'. So also in 1988, but in 1999 most of the women said that they would first of all follow the advice given by the local health centre although they still listened to the advice given by their mothers and older relatives.

The duration of the confinement

There were various opinions about how long one must lie by the fire, and also about other details in connection with the confinement. Broadly speaking, these issues are illustrated, in the case of our 1968 group of mothers, by the following summary:

Always a decreasing number of days, and always odd number of days:

First child 25, 23 or 21 days and youngest child 13, 11 or 9 days	4 mothers
First child 19, 17 or 15 days and youngest child 13, 11 or 9 days	7 mothers
First child 19, 17 or 15 days and youngest child 7 or 5 days	3 mothers
First child 13 or 11 days and youngest child 11 or 9 days	4 mothers

Always decreasing number of days; for some an odd number of days, for others an even number of days:

First child 40 days and youngest child 5 days	1 mother
First child 20 days and youngest 16 days	1 mother
First child 21 or 20 days and youngest 13, 11 or 9 days	3 mothers
First child 19, 18, 17, 16 or 15 days and youngest 13, 11 or 9 days	4 mothers
First child 15, 14, 13, 12, 11 or 10 days and youngest, 8, or 7 days	3 mothers
At some births, irregular number of days	3 mothers

The great majority of the mothers in 1968 thought that one must be confined for the longest time for the first child, and for ever fewer days for the subsequent children. The majority of the women also attached

significance to the fact that the duration had to be an uneven number of days.

They had difficulties in giving explanations as to why one must always lie-in for the longest for the first child, and thereafter for a decreasing number of days until a certain minimum below which one does not go. Around half of them gave as the most important explanation that one gets weary of lying for so long and therefore one cuts down each time. Among the other explanations were:

- everything is so unaccustomed the first time one gives birth that longer time is needed to get over the first birth than over later births;

- a decreasing number of days means that the younger siblings will respect the elder siblings;

- a decreasing number of days has the effect of extending the interval between the pregnancies;

- it is tradition (the response given by a group who had no particular reason to express).

Everybody appeared to think that the longest possible confinement was good for the mother, and that it was conductive for her recuperating quickly and regaining her full strength.

In 1968, it would seem that no special factor (such as the age of the mothers) influenced the attitude as to whether the confinement ought to be of particularly long duration, or whether it might be a little shorter without causing any harm.

Two-thirds of the mothers felt that it was best to lie-in for an odd number of days in connection with childbirth. Most of them gave as their main reasons for this that an 'odd' number is better than an 'even'. That has to be seen within context of beliefs of 'life and death'. As an example, in the case of a death in the family an even number of monks are invited but on all other occasions an odd number are invited. Similarly, if a child is still-born or has died immediately after birth or during the *yuu fai* period, all would lie-in for an even number of days.

Some of the mothers who thought that they really ought to be confined for an odd number of days nevertheless gave examples of having had to stop lying-in with one or more children at an even number, due to an unusual event, such as the house catching fire or a natural catastrophe. In no case had this given rise to adverse consequences for either the mother or the baby.

Yuu fai and the younger mothers

The younger mothers in the 1978 group had a somewhat curtailed confinement compared to the first-born of the 1968 mothers. All the young indicated that they would not go below five days, regardless of how many children they might have. They thought, furthermore, that one must absolutely lie-in for the longest time during the first childbirth, and thereafter shorten the confinement for the subsequent births. That was just the custom, they said, having no other reason to offer.

It is worth noting, however, that many of them mentioned that a decreasing number of days had the clear significance of making the younger children obey the elder siblings; a belief also implied by the older generation from 1968.

Two-thirds of the younger mothers also felt that they definitely must lie-in for an odd number of days for the same reason as that given by the older generation, namely that 'odd is better than even'. The remaining one-third either had no opinion about whether it ought to be even or odd number of days, or felt that one could be as good as the other. In this there was also no change in relation to the findings of 1968 when exactly one-third expressed indifference in this matter.

It is reasonable to summarize the data of 1968 and 1978 research in this way:

At this *yuu fai* from 2003 a large knife is also seen, placed there again by the older generation to protect the young mother against *phii*(s). Notice the traditional two cooking vessels with decoctions which are seen more clearly on the picture p. 98

- all went through with a complete, traditional *yuu fai*, including the young who had given birth in hospital or clinic;

- all but one had two kinds of herbal decoction, one for washing and the other for drinking;

- other details were almost totally consistent;

- the reasons for taking their actions were almost totally consistent.

The only real difference between the 1968 and the 1978 mothers was the duration of the confinement. The young were not confined for as long as the older group.

The 1978 group of mothers was re-interviewed in 1988 and no changes were found in the patterns described already. The same was the case with the new group of very young mothers included in our 1988 sample. As already mentioned the biggest change in respect of the *yuu fai* was that the mothers who were sterilized in connection with a birth would not go through confinement as 'this is not necessary'. In 1999, 2001, and 2003, the above patterns were still found in this village although with a slight tendency to a little shorter confinement.

Food during the confinement

The untrained midwives in the village in the 1960s and 1970s did not agree on what one ought to eat during the lying-in.

Two of those much employed in the 1970s maintained that it was essential for the mother's recuperation that she sticks to *khau jii* with salt. *Khau jii* is the villagers' ordinary steamed glutinous rice that has been grilled. A little while later during the confinement, it is all right to eat a bit of chicken or pork, also grilled. Both these midwives had a long list of things the mother definitely could not eat. A number of things were considered almost pure poison to a mother who had just given birth, and other food items were prohibited because there were beliefs attached to them in relation to both the mother's and the baby's subsequent health.

What the mothers in fact did in 1968 and in 1978 showed that most held very strong prejudices related to food during the confinement.

The mothers in both the older and the younger groups commented that more up-to-date acquaintances such as the teachers, tried to make them eat food of a greater nutritional value during the confinement. However, most of them persisted in their own ways as illustrated on opposite page.

Food during the confinement	1968 (total 33)	1978 (total 27)
Only *khau jii* with a little salt, perhaps a little garlic	17	10
Khau jii and *plaa haeng* (dried and salted fresh-water fish, grilled before eating), perhaps supplemented with *kluay nam waa* (the flower of a very common 'finger-banana', boiled, supposed to assist lactation)	14	15
Only *khau jii* + dried crabs	1	0
Only plain glutinous rice with a little chicken grilled with ginger	0	1
For the first child only *khau jii*, for the subsequent babies also boiled fish	1	0
All ordinary food as advised by the hospital	0	1

Granted, around a third of the mothers gave no clear reasons for limiting themselves to eating mainly *khau jii*. To them it was first and foremost a question of following the tradition but they had a firm conviction that it was beneficial and necessary for both themselves and their babies. The remaining two-thirds gave reasons that can be summarized as follows:

• It is good for the blood and will make the mother strong;

• It will help the abdomen to 'dry-out' quickly and to stop the discharge;

• It is beneficial for the baby's digestion.

As seen from the figures given above, only one single mother would eat everything 'advised by the hospital'. She was the village headman's young daughter-in-law. She and her whole family on both sides stated with strong conviction that after childbirth one must eat especially nutritious food, out of consideration to both the mother and the baby.

But traditions die hard. Our 1978 group was re-interviewed in 1988, and at that time still more than half of this group found that *khau jii* should be the major part of the diet during confinement. It is noteworthy, however, that one-quarter of them had adopted more modern food habits in connection with their latest childbirths.

In 1988, when we also interviewed a small group of very young mothers, we found a major change in practice and attitude: only one of them found that the only safe diet during the confinement was *khau jii* supplemented with a little pork. All others were taking a varied diet according to the advice given by the health centre and/ or the hospital.

Because of the above data from 1988 it was unexpected and disappointing in 1999 to find a resurgence of food taboos: three out of our little sample of five mothers stuck to the belief that the mother should only eat *khau jii* during the time of the confinement. The head nurse at the local health centre claimed that this was not the current norm for mothers in the hamlet, but at least we may conclude that by 1999 negative, old beliefs and traditions had not yet fully disappeared from Baan Phraan Muean.

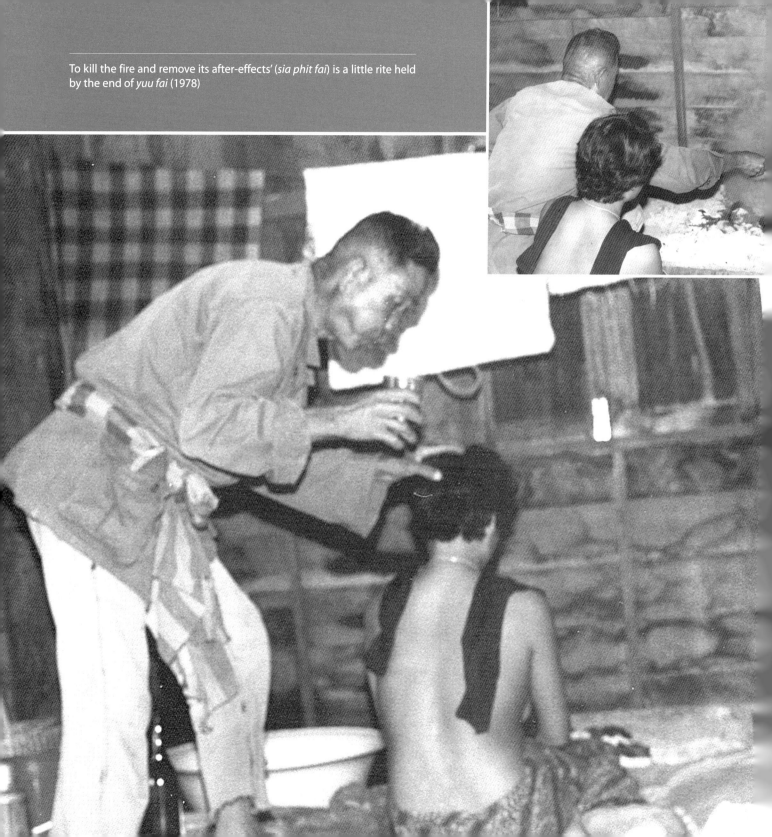

To kill the fire and remove its after-effects' (*sia phit fai*) is a little rite held by the end of *yuu fai* (1978)

The confinement ends

Towards the conclusion of the *yuu fai,* tradition stipulates two small rites to ensure that all is well for the baby and the mother.

A modest little rite must be performed in connection with the mother's leaving the fireplace and the fire being extinguished. The flames can be 'killed' with water but at the same time something else must be done to ensure that the mother can escape the after-effects from having lain by the hot fire for a long time. If this custom is not observed, she might continue to feel the heat in her body in unpleasant ways for quite a long time, and might feel dizzy and sluggish.

The midwives had varying ideas about how this ought to be done. One thought that it was best performed by a *mor yaa* (herbal specialist), a man who knows about such things. Standing behind the woman's back, he would take a draught of strong spirits in his mouth and, blowing, spray the spirits onto the woman's back and into the fire. Another midwife did not consider the use of strong spirits necessary; instead lime-water (a special type of liquid used in the preparation of betel quid) could be blown onto the fire and the woman's body. The midwife thought that anybody other than the husband could perform this ritual, the only condition being that the person knows the magic incantation that must be recited at the same time (for the text see Part 2).

One of these incantations goes like this: 'I will take you in my mouth and keep you there. I will hold the mouth of April's heat, the evening sky's firebrand, the night's hot iron and the daytime hours' white-hot steel. I will blow (puff) until you become as white as powder and as dry as lime.'

This little ritual is locally called *sia phit fai,* which means to kill the fire and remove its after-effects.

In 1968, a little more than half of the mothers followed this custom, but in 1978 it appeared to be declining as a little less than half of our group observed this tradition. However, it had not disappeared completely, as, in 1988, more than one-half of the group of the very young mothers observed this custom. In 1999, it was not found in our little group of mothers but was still mentioned together with the *praab fai* ceremony by several of the female teachers in the local school.

After the performance of the *sia phit fai* ceremony, the mother can leave the fireplace in complete compliance with tradition. However, according to the interpretation of one of our 1960s midwives, she ought also to make 'an offering to the fire' called *suay dork.* She should thank the fire and show it respect because of the help it had been to her, and ask for forgiveness for having been 'unclean' for a time because of the blood that flowed from her.

The designation *suay dork* has perhaps a double meaning. While *suay* means 'beautiful' in Central Thai it means 'tapering' in the Isan language; *dork* means 'flower'. In other words: 'something tapering – a cone with flowers'. *Suay dork* can consist of three small cones made from banana plant leaves. In each of these are placed two flowers and two small wax candles. It is stated, that the husband should prepare the offering but that the mother herself then puts it very close to, or between, the three stones that were placed for the cooking vessel to stand on. The mother, kneeling, then must bow to the fireplace three times.

For both the 1968 and the 1978 groups, less than a third went through with this offering but still in 1988, a few of the very young mothers observed this sweet little tradition.

According to the older people in the village, in the past the great majority of women would make the *suay dork* offering and it was thus apparent that here was a

tradition, which had been declining but had not yet totally vanished from the village. In 1999, none in our little group knew about this old tradition, which by then had possibly disappeared.

Preventing new pregnancies

Still, according to tradition, the mother is not yet quite ready to return to her daily life. If she now takes a specially prepared 'medicine' – *yaa kam* – she will not become pregnant again so quickly! This should be taken shortly before leaving the fire, or when she does so. It should be prepared by 'someone who knows about it'. *Yaa* means 'medicine'; *kam* here corresponds to 'trouble'. So, this is medicine for the woman who wants to avoid 'new trouble'.

The preparation largely follows the same pattern in all cases: certain herbs and roots are used – the exact recipe differs from person to person 'who know about it'. The ingredients are boiled, usually in three measures (or cupfuls) of water. The cooking vessel is covered with a leaf of the banana, *kluay tiib*, and the mixture boils until reduced to only one measure (cupful). The decoction is then poured into a drinking vessel, and the cooking pot turned upside down. The woman drinks the medicine, and must then quickly put down the drinking vessel with the bottom upwards. One wishes, so to say, to 'close the aperture'. The recipes for this *yaa kam* vary in ingredients. We collected as many as eight different recipies, which we interpreted as a sign that *yaa kam* was indeed taken seriously (see Part 2).

In Baan Phraan Muean, apart from those I knew of, there were presumably a few others who made the *yaa kam*. This widely held tradition for the avoidance of too-frequent pregnancies was openly talked about and generally known among the villagers. It should be noted that Hanks, Rishøj Pedersen, and Mougne, all state that such entirely local methods to attempt birth control did not exist in their investigation areas.[100]

The above is the tradition as explained to us by the village elders and midwives; now we will turn to what the mothers told on these issues in 1968 and in 1978. A summary of our findings below shows quite interesting changes:

Reasons for taking *yaa kam* (%)					
Took *yaa kam* on ending *yuu fai*:	1968	1978	Did not take *yaa kam*:	1968	1978
• as a means of birth control	45	22	• did not believe it helps as birth control	4	19
• as a means of birth control and for other reasons	15	19	• no reason given	0	18
• for reasons other than birth control	24	22			
• only because of tradition	12	0			

These figures clearly show that considerably more of the mothers in 1968 took *yaa kam* than in 1978. Also, whereas the older group saw it as a contraceptive measure the younger women doubted this effect to a greater extent. Modern methods and attitudes were then already becoming known and accepted, even though the new methods were expensive and far beyond the financial means of many of these women.

In 1988, we returned to our 1978 group and inquired about the same matters. The differences from 1978 were striking: in 1988, about 98 per cent of either the wife or the husband had been sterilized, as they did not want to have more children. The rest either used the pill or got a regular contraceptive 'shot'. In 1988, the new, young group of mothers were all aware of modern ways of protection, and used these methods. Still, some of them said that they could hardly afford to buy contraceptives. There is no doubt that the old *yaa kam* has completely disappeared nowadays.

The very young generation of 1999 had not even heard about *yaa kam* and was as familiar with contraception as are modern women in Denmark.

According to the above, attempts were made over the years to limit the number of pregnancies but nobody had ever tried to encourage pregnancy. Some women who had such problems were said sometimes to try to find help from a very powerful Buddha-image, *Ongtuee*, near the town of Tha Bo not far from the river Mae Khong.

Yuu Fai – an Evaluation

We have now in some detail described how women in Baan Phraan Muean have conducted their confinements over a period of more than forty years. Now we shall look a little more closely at two of the elements in this tradition: the fire and the decoctions for drinking and ablution of the body.

From the descriptions given by the women, it is evident that the effect of the fire and the two herbal decoctions formed a whole in which the significance of each element could not be explained more exactly. What was known was that

- the mother *must* lie by this fireplace;
- the mother *must* wash herself and drink as much and as often as possible.

The women did not agree on the meaning or the effect of this practice. The predominant reason given was that it cleansed the abdomen of 'bad blood' and impure fluids, and that the practice prevented the women from getting 'bad blood'. Practically everybody also mentioned the practice as conducive to putting the abdomen in order so that the inner and the outer organs would 'fall into their right places' and adopt the proper shape. Some also mentioned that after this kind of confinement one

could eat all kinds of food without ill effects; that it aided lactation; and that one got a lovely clear skin by following the custom. Clearly everybody recognized elements of both 'cleansing' and actual treatment as part of the regime, centering its importance around the mother and not on the newborn child.

Sir James Frazer discusses the uncleanness of the woman in childbirth very comprehensively and stresses that in many cultures women who have just given birth are 'supposed to be in a dangerous condition which would infect any person or thing they might touch.'[101] The diverse ways of cleansing these 'unclean' women is the subject of the great mass of literature covering practically all cultures, past and present.

However, it is only when we approach cultures with direct or indirect connection to Southeast Asia, that we seemingly get support for the thesis that the fire's 'purificatory virtue'[102] has direct application in connection with the woman in childbirth, in a form that is roughly reminiscent of the description from Baan Phraan Muean.[103]

My own interviews and observations confirmed in 1968 and in 1999, respectively, that in and around Vientiane in Laos the fire was an established part of the confinement. This was reconfirmed when I, in 2005, visited a Lao village on the Plain of Jars and Luang Prabang.

Furthermore, in February 2001, I visited women in childbed with an open fire in villages around Siem Reap, Cambodia, as well as in the town itself, and our local, very knowledgeable informant told us that he believed this was the custom all over Cambodia. In February 2003, I made interviews in Myanmar (Burma) and established that several of the ethnic groups in this country are still practising a confinement and using either an open fire or sweatbaths.

In January 2004, I found that some of the Dai villages in Yunnan, China, still practised a tradition of resting by a fire after the childbirth.

In large parts of Thailand, the fire has been a part of the confinement since time immemorial. This can possibly be verified right back to the thirteenth century through Marco Polo's accounts which included a description 'from hearsay' of the country of *Caugigu*, which is assumed to cover, among other areas, the Northern parts of present-day Thailand.[104] Ploss mentions that Marco Polo reported that in Siam confined women 'for four whole weeks must sit by a well-maintained fire and turn now to this side, now onto that'.[105]

In the nineteenth and early twentieth centuries, we find a series of authors who mention *yuu fai* in Thailand.[106] All these describe a long confinement of up to 40 days. The fire itself is described in such a way that one understands it to be larger (and therefore to give off more uncomfortable heat) than the fires used today. Ablutions are also mentioned, and the effect explained as both related to the cleansing of the unclean woman and as a treatment to allow her to recuperate more rapidly.

A characteristic common trait of these descriptions is the strong disassociation from the custom as reflected in the choice of words used, most strongly, by Curtis: 'The term roasting is entirely correct, for the flesh is actually cooked upon the abdomen and back. [...] Often the woman dies before the fire.'[107] Bowring calls it a 'torture'.[108]

The past centuries' Europeans – travellers, missionaries, and advisers – presumably did what they could to let the Siamese understand that *yuu fai* was one of the many signs of how primitive and backward they found their culture.

Twentieth-century writers continue in the same vein: Le May considered the custom more wide-spread in the Southern regions than among the Lao people (whereby he means Northeastern Thailand) and after a brief description he says: 'If this gruesome custom is not observed many people firmly believe that the woman will both see and hear "badly" throughout the rest of her life.' He thought himself able to find an explanation for the custom in the fact that 'the mother is in her most acute state of receptivity, and as there are always malignant spirits lurking about [...] every effort must be made to guard the mother.' He had, however, no doubt that *yuu fai* indeed had an effect, namely that the attractive and well-built girl would probably during the course of only 'seven or eight years suddenly collapse and become old, haggard and lined'.[109]

Wales remarks among other things: '[...] that of lying by the fire, which Western science has shown to be definitely harmful, has been discontinued in most upper-class families.' He continues: 'Western physicians in more recent times having rightly not failed to denounce it as exceedingly prejudicial to the health of both mother and infant.'[110] Unfortunately, for the latter claim he gave no evidence.

De Young follows up on this by writing: 'Within the past thirty years "roasting" has been practically swept away except in isolated villages of Central Thailand', and he found that the reason for a lower infant mortality rate was among others, 'the abandonment of certain childbirth customs – for example "mother-roasting" – which both directly and indirectly affected the newborn child.'[111] Blanchard similarly observes that the *yuu fai* custom had almost disappeared, 'at present being practised mostly in Central Thailand, and there only for at day or so'.[112]

What caused these authors to state that the tradition of *yuu fai* was about to vanish completely in Thailand I am unable to discover. But the *yuu fai* had definitely not generally disappeared at the time when these authors wrote. Kaufman describes *yuu fai* in villages not very far from Bangkok but adds that not everybody practised it. Hanks has no reservations regarding the extent of it in Bang Chan. Attagara describes *yuu fai* in a village southeast of Bangkok, and Rishøj Pedersen in a Lao Song Dam village 24 kilometres west of Ratchaburi.[113]

This last author, by the way, took exception to the designation 'mother-roasting' and found 'mother-drying' much more to the point as it was the fire's warming and drying qualities the women believe in. *Yuu fai* was so strong a tradition in the Lao Song Dam village that Rishøj Pedersen could write 'that very cogent arguments are required to convince the women that this period which they themselves also consider a hardship is not merely unnecessary but directly harmful, – not only to themselves but also for the babies.'[114] Any reason why women ought to be induced to discontinue *yuu fai* was not explained more fully; reference was merely made to de Young's earlier, unsupported, views.

Even in Bangkok's city areas, two investigations show that *yuu fai*, in one form or another, was practised in 1962 by 59 out of 60 mothers (30 middle-class, including lawyers, architects, university professors, primary-school teachers, and 30 lower-class, including unskilled labourers, dock-workers, bus-drivers, peddlers, small shopkeepers), all representatively selected from the group to which they belonged.[115]

On the other hand, there are some serious studies that find that *yuu fai* was no longer generally practised in Thailand. Terweil states that *yuu fai* was considered to be 'old-fashioned and not worth the trouble (…) can now be regarded as a kind of elaboration' in a village

in the Ratchaburi area.[116] I have also found two investigations where it is directly stated that *yuu fai* was not practised in the area of research, both from Northern Thailand.[117]

I have no doubts that there is research on *yuu fai* that I have not uncovered. For this reason there may be circumstances around *yuu fai*, such as its extent, reasons for aversion to it and so on, of which I have no knowledge.

According to what is available to me at least three areas of uncertainty can be set out:

1. On the basis of the sources that I have used it is impossible to evaluate the extent of the practice of *yuu fai* in Thailand as a whole, whether in the past or more recently. No investigation known to me from a limited geographical area gives a definite reply to the question of how generally *yuu fai* is or was practised in that area.

2. The reasons why the mothers are going through with *yuu fai* is not clarified exactly, and the more profound motives for maintaining the custom are not very well elucidated.

3. In the literature, there have not been found any convincing explanations regarding what positive or negative effects *yuu fai* in reality might have on the mother after a childbirth.

Let us now look a little closer at these three findings. On the basis of my own fieldwork in a village chosen at the time rather randomly in Northeastern Thailand, I have established that all the women with whom I was in contact, whether older or quite young, until recently went through with a traditional *yuu fai*. I dare add that until very recently there was hardly a woman in this village who had not carried out a traditional *yuu fai*. The new trend is that women who do not want more children

and are sterilized following their last birth do not have a *yuu fai* as 'this is not necessary for her', a notion interesting in itself, and one to which we shall return.

Yuu fai is a very strong tradition in this part of the country. Interviews from January 1981 with all the female teachers in three village schools in the Udorn area confirmed this. These 16 women, of age 25–56, of whom seven were born and had grown up in the town of Udorn, five in other town communities in Northeastern Thailand, two in villages around Udorn, and two in other villages in different parts of Northeastern Thailand, had *all* in one form or another gone through with *yuu fai* after the births of their total of 48 children. Of these, seven were totally traditional *yuu fai*(s) by an open bonfire like the village women; seven replacing the open fire with the more modern charcoal-basin. Two had traditional *yuu fai* for their first child but for the later confinements used only charcoal-basins.

In my 1988 interviews in places around Udorn, along main roads and small dirt roads and in little townships (a total of thirty different localities), and in talks with more than one hundred women, I did not meet one single woman who had not gone through a *yuu fai*. In more urbanized areas, attitudes were found to be in the process of change and in many of these places it was by then the common concept that after sterilization a *yuu fai* was not a necessary 'treatment'.

Again, in February 1999, interviews with the seven female teachers in the Baan Phraan Muean school established that all of them had had a *yuu fai* with their total of 13 children, and again we were told that they had no *yuu fai* in connection with a childbirth followed by a sterilization. Some of their *yuu fai*(s) were still by an open fire but most of them had used a charcoal stove.

I find that all the above and my findings in Baan Phraan Muean itself provide a well-founded assumption that the *yuu fai* custom has been followed quite traditionally,

and presumably by all village women in rather extensive parts of upper Northeastern Thailand. In fact it would surprise me if this is not still so.

Turning towards the reasons why *yuu fai* has been practised since time immemorial and the motives for continuing to do so, I refer to Phya Anuman Rajadhon and Jane Richardson Hanks. Both occupied themselves in depth with this subject, the former more widely and generally for the cultural territory as a whole, and the latter more narrowly in Ban Chan in the Central Plain.[118]

Rajadhon proves that the custom must have had its origin in a belief that it was 'cleansing impurities that arise from childbirth more than matters of care and treatment.' Though *yuu fai* has been considered by many to be a kind of treatment for the mother so that she can recuperate after the delivery, he considers that this belief gradually has gained credence only as the original cleansing purpose was forgotten. He emphasizes that 'for removing impurities there are two methods, namely cleansing with water or with fire'. In fact they employ both, he observes, as in addition to the fire the mother sprinkles herself with holy water at the conclusion of the lying-in.[119]

Jane Richardson Hanks describes how the inhabitants of Bang Chan attached a many-sided importance to *yuu fai*. She finds confirmation that besides 'care and treatment' it is also to be regarded as 'one of the series of rites of the life-cycle which marked the course of an individual from birth to death'. It was said that through *yuu fai* the woman attained 'full maturity', making her fit for her role as a woman. Hanks also mentions four purposes for which the sacred fire is the key: 'it perfected her as a compassionate being; restored and strengthened her body; improved her capacities as a nourisher; and strengthened her own *khwan*.'[120]

The woman in Baan Phraan Muean understands herself, and is understood by others to be in need of cleansing somehow, both internally as well as externally. It is strongly emphasized in the attitudes of all the women that the fire and the two herbal decoctions for ablution and for drinking, respectively, serve to cleanse. So it is here a matter of cleansing both by fire and by water, and in a more lucid mode of expression than described by Rajadhon.

However, to separate 'cleansing' and treatment does not reflect the popular conception of what really happens. According to the people in Baan Phraan Muean, cleansing and treatment together form a whole. By being cleansed, and here they think definitely in terms of 'bad blood', 'evil-smelling discharge' and such things, there is a 'treatment' in *yuu fai* that helps the mother to recuperate after a childbirth and to be able to resume an everyday existence quickly. Everything 'falls into place', externally as well as internally.

It might be expressed thus: In Baan Phraan Muean, *yuu fai* and what it incorporates is today not understood as a 'ritual cleansing'. However, with its firm structure and homogenous performance based on local tradition, the practice has the character of a ritual but with an aim uniformly conceived of as a sort of medical treatment – including the improvement of the mother's capacity as a nourisher.[121]

In Baan Phraan Muean, I did not find attitudes toward *yuu fai* to indicate that a woman understands herself – and is understood by her environment – to be properly mature and adult only when she has had a *yuu fai* as indicated by Hanks.

Nor was anything implied by the woman herself or her surroundings in terms of an influence of the *yuu fai* on the woman's *khwan* in the sense which is the pervasive feature in Hanks' descriptions and evaluations from

Bang Chan. No one in Baan Phraan Muean made any statement indicating that *yuu fai* was considered to have a hand in strengthening the woman's *khwan*. That could only be done by performing the ceremony intended for that purpose as described earlier. As an outside observer, I believe that *yuu fai* may have such a calming influence on the mother's psychological well-being that it actually has a therapeutic effect. In this context, it could be expressed briefly by saying that *yuu fai*, in fact, strengthens the mother's *khwan*.

Finally, let us now turn to the third question: What effects, positive and/or negative, do the *yuu fai* in fact have on the mother?

In much of the literature there is no doubt: 'mother-roasting'. The term alone has negative connotations. Rajadhon and Hanks represent exceptions to this prevalent attitude.[122] They describe and competently provide a picture of the cultural context to various customs and, significantly, do not pass judgements.

Is the practice of *yuu fai* altogether bad?

I have not succeeded in finding literary works that deal seriously with the effects of *yuu fai* from a medical point of view. Therefore it is possible here only to record evaluations and opinions as they have come to light through many conversations during more than 40 years with people – Thai as well as foreigners – whose education and experiences in Thailand have given them the background to enable them to speak professionally about the subject.

Their evaluations can on the whole be separated into two groups:

One group has no doubts at all: the heat is directly harmful; it induces haemorrhaging, causes burns and heat rashes, and the long confinement increases the risk of blood clots. Statements from this group can be

summarized as follows: *yuu fai* is a tradition from which one must dissociate oneself. All that is possible must be done to make the women stop going through with *yuu fai* or at least to curtail its duration.

Another group says that the heat itself is considered harmless though of course there is a certain risk of heat rashes and burns, and too prolonged a confinement can increase the risk of blood clots. On the other hand, the *yuu fai* doubtlessly has a psychological effect and is for this reason of assistance to the woman. Furthermore, the *yuu fai* period gives the woman a pause to rest; during this time – in a life of hard work – she is being waited on. If the woman did not observe *yuu fai*, a reasonable period free of hard work after a childbirth would hardly be respected. In other words: while the fire/heat is hardly of any benefit from a medical point of view it is not in itself harmful, and the whole experience of *yuu fai* includes many positive elements that may improve the general condition of the woman; consequently the practice of *yuu fai* should not be discouraged.

It is not without interest to note that the negative evaluation is based on statements which all originate from the 1960s while the more neutral, even positive, viewpoint reflects evaluations of a more recent date. Could a change in attitude among the professionals have happened in this period? If so, it is interesting from a cultural and socio-psychological point of view that the change occurs in a period when non-Western cultures have become more self-confident in expressing their views and the West is no longer as self-assured as it once was.

However, it should also be noted that although the evaluations recorded here in all cases were propounded by people of esteem and competence within the medical field, it is a random selection of people and what they state are their personal opinions and not proved in any scientific sense.

We therefore lack a real answer to what the positive and negative medical effects are of lengthy exposure of the body, particularly the abdomen, to heating after childbirth in a tropical climate, and under hygienic conditions that, in the village at any rate, may give rise to all imaginable infections. Furthermore, it has not been possible to ascertain more exactly whether there is any positive or negative effect on the newborn baby who finds itself for a period in surroundings that have a higher temperature than the already rather high natural temperature.

In my conversations about *yuu fai* and through search in available literature on the subject I have tried to find a professionally competent evaluation of the herbal decoctions used by the mother for external and internal purposes, as well as of the fact that the woman washes her body with a hot liquid and drinks hot liquid. There is both the question of the possible medical effects of the herbs used, and of raising the body temperature. It has not been possible for me to find analyses of the herbs' medicinal effect, and unfortunately I do not know whether or not competent professional evaluation has been made in Thailand of the various recipes used. Nor has it been possible to get consistent answers about the consequences of increasing the body temperature further through ablutions and the drinking of hot liquids.

CHAPTER SIX

The Young Baby

Many peoples the world over, probably most people, know of diverse ceremonies during the period of a child's growth. Many authors report on these from Thailand's neighbouring countries and also from Thailand itself. In Baan Phraan Muean no ceremonies of this kind take place throughout childhood. In Baan Phraan Muean this period of life is today, for both boys and girls, completely free from actions of ritual character, apart from those already mentioned in connection with illness.

Not until the time when a young man decides to be admitted as a monk in the Buddhist temple are ceremonies again performed. So there is no ceremony in connection with the giving of a name to a child, and according to the oldest people living in the 1970s there had not been any such ceremonies during their lifetimes. Neither are there today firm traditions that a child must be named after relatives. The name-giving in Baan Phraan Muean is, then, a rather uncomplicated matter. Many authors report from other regions of Thailand that they there allot the infant a 'loathsome' nickname, like 'frog', 'pig', 'dog', in the intention of deceiving the evil spirits into leaving the child in peace. In Baan Phraan Muean this tradition is not known of at all. The parents most often give the child a pet name shortly after the birth, very frequently of a poetic nature: little flower, jasmine, rose, etc. According to regulations in force the parents must approach the village headman after the child has been born and have a birth certificate made out by him. Years ago this did not happen in all cases, and often it was so that a child was not officially registered, with its real name, before it was to start the school.

As there are no special customs, traditions, or ceremonies throughout childhood in Ban Phraan Muean we shall instead, as a kind of conclusion, look into a few – to us important – aspects of a child's early life, and examine how these aspects may have changed over the years.

It is well known that early care, including nutrition in the first years of life, has a lifelong impact on the child physically as well as psychologically. Mental development, health, and in fact the whole personality are to some extent influenced by a number of things that happen in the important period of early childhood.

The most important issue related to the baby's nutrition concern the quality of the food and the habits surrounding eating. All the mothers in the 1968 group breast-fed their children, and this was also the case in the groups from 1978, 1988, and 1999. Further, less than a handful of mothers in these four groups had any wish to introduce certain regularity in the nursing, or to try to limit the number of daily feeds. Those who tried did not succeed; other adult women around them reproached them for their attitude, and they themselves could not bear to hear the baby whimper without putting it to the breast. It is therefore practically impossible to get the mothers' estimates about how many times during a twenty-four hours period the infant ought to be fed, and how many times it was actually nursed. 'Demand feeding' seems to be the only description covering practically all babies' nourishment in this village.

(1962)

At the same time we must note that all mothers – older as well as younger – stated that the best way to calm a little child was to put it to the breast. Every sign of discomfort – be it whimpering, crying, or other forms of unrest – would almost inevitably lead to the child being laid to the breast.

Hence satisfaction of hunger and calming by contact with the mother and her body cannot be separated. This means that infants in the village were often held and were often seen asleep with a nipple in the mouth.

The mothers from 1968 and up to 1988 introduced supplementary feeding very early. Around half of them did so almost immediately after birth, about a third at approximately the conclusion of the lying-in, and the remainder between that time and, at the latest, when the baby was a couple of months old. But in all our research groups there were a few who did not introduce the supplement until the child was 2–3 years old.

They all gave the same reasons for introducing supplementary nourishment. One of these was that the mother must necessarily go away from home to work in the fields or go to market in town where she could not take the baby along with her. Certainly, several of them had female relatives or women neighbours who would willingly nurse the baby during the mother's absence, as long as they had enough milk for two. More importantly therefore, the mothers did not consider the mother's milk sufficient. According to them the milk is digested so quickly that the infant does not get enough nutrition, and besides, the baby does not get a proper feeling of being full on milk alone.

The mothers held definite beliefs concerning a number of things that may be dangerous if fed to young children. The only thing almost all considered wholly safe was *khau yam*,[123] their local steamed, sticky rice chewed by the mother and mixed with a little banana and then roasted in a banana leaf. This mixture is thereafter mashed with a little water and stirred to a paste-like consistency. A few of the young mothers from 1978 and 1988 added that they bought condensed milk when they could afford it, and talked about it with a choice of words showing their belief that this kind of milk was richer in nourishment, and better than breast milk.[124]

There is no doubt that the mothers considered it correct and beneficiary for the children to breast-feed. It was considered necessary, and good, but not sufficient, so for this reason and because of their work duties they gave the child supplementary food early.

The mothers nursed their babies for a long time (2–3 years or longer unless they stop because of a new pregnancy) for very complex reasons. Partly, because they thought that there were good things for the child in the mother's milk, and partly because they had the opinion that children must be quite big before ordinary food agreed with them. At least two additional aspects went into the quotation as well:

• The difficulties that arise in weaning the child before he stops by himself are avoided; 'permissiveness' is often an expression used about Thai parents' attitudes towards their children. Here, I feel, is an area where it is not unjustified to introduce this term in the village context;

• The mother's milk is free. They are poor and one must use this source of nourishment for as long as possible. For many in the village, this was a quite significant reason for the late weaning.

The nutritive value of mothers' milk supplemented with only *khau yam* has been evaluated by experienced experts as by far the most serious problem for the favourable physical development of the village child in the Northeast. The district health nurse (*mor tambon*) who

already in 1978 was very popular and highly respected by the village women, said that she was unable to make the mothers follow her advice about the infants' nutrition. Sticky rice was in no circumstances sufficient as a dietary supplement. The mothers said that the babies got intestinal worms if they gave them varied and ordinary food. The *mor tambon* regretfully acknowledged that this could be true, taking into consideration the unsanitary conditions in which food was generally prepared in the village.

In 1978, the *mor tambon* also stated that she had many mothers coming to her with their 1–1½-year-old children because they were ailing, weakly, and tired and in general not thriving and developing. They were not really ill, and though they had food enough they suffered from mal-nourishment. Paediatricians in Udorn expressed similar views on the same problem, and a larger-scale investigation confirmed that in most villages in the Northeast sticky rice and bananas were practically all that babies were given as supplement to their mothers' milk.[125] The same was found in Baan Phraan Muean in 1988 and in the 30 villages visited the same year in a rather large area around Udorn.

Physicians and health personnel in the Udorn region informed me that they saw a connection between these nutritional problems and the differences found and described in Chapter One between the physical development of children in Baan Phraan Muean and in Udorn. Very many of these things have luckily changed over the last two decades, at least in Baan Phraan Muean. Today, the young mothers seem on the whole to follow the advice given by the nurses in the health centre, and the Government TV broadcasts very good and informative programmes about such problems. The mothers are all still breast-feeding their babies and most will do their best to find the money to buy what is needed for the best possible supplementary nutrition.

While we may therefore conclude with considerable certainty that up to very recently there have been nutritional deficiencies during a child's earliest life, it seems justified to emphasize that other and very important aspects of the child's total situation appear to be exceedingly favourable.

The babies are all nursed and the mothers do so lovingly maintaining close bodily and emotional contact between the baby and the mother. These are factors that internationally are considered to be fundamental to the child's feeling of security and of long-lasting importance for the youngster's emotional development and the adult personality.

There are other factors concerning the young baby's feeding and care that are favourable from a developmental point of view.

What is understood by the so-called 'nuclear family' did not exist in any of our research groups. There were always older relatives and the father's or the mother's siblings in the immediate vicinity. The divorced mother did not live alone with her children but were surrounded by relatives. No mother implied that she alone was responsible for such things as feeding the child, keeping him/her clean and washed, dressing him/her or for carrying the baby around. The father was mentioned as having joint responsibility for such things, as were several (first and foremost female) relatives. This did not shake the principle that the mother was the one who had the predominant responsibility, and with whom the baby had the closest contact, but from a very early age the child was also in other (often many) responsible hands.

Researchers from varying professions and with widely differing theoretical observances have contributed to the illustration of basic factors for the little child's development. I consider Bronfenbrenner as a reasonable

exponent and summarizer of what must be regarded as fundamental in this context. He says: 'During the first years of the child's life the psychological development is furthered by having continual and ever more extensive forms of mutually influencing interaction with persons with whom the child has developed a lasting mutual emotional tie.' If we look at the child's development during childhood as a whole, Bronfenbrenner concludes that 'children need human beings in order to become human'.[126] These circumstances still exist for children growing up in this Northeastern environment.

The little child's circumstances in the village context should, however, be neither idealized nor romanticized. In the first decades of my visits, contraception and sterilization were not known, and the families would normally have many children. In terms of daily care and close contact with the mother the child's world would therefore fundamentally alter when the next baby was born. There was not always sufficient time or strength to take close care of all the children in the family, and it often seemed that when siblings were born too close after each other, the older child did not get sufficient attention and the care that he/she needed.

However, before the arrival of the new baby, the child would without doubt have forged ties to closely related adults other than the mother. Also, throughout early childhood there was natural and relevant stimulation through daily observation of and participation in all the everyday duties of the family's existence, and cultural activities in relation to customs and religion. Today, the families usually have only two children (three, at the most) and though they still are (and feel) poor, their situation is fundamentally different from the situation 40 to 50 years ago and what was the reality for the babies and their mothers then.

(1962)

113

Epilogue

Though I only visited the village now and again, I still remember clearly how things were a few decades ago. Let me therefore bring the reporting of my study of childbirth and its traditions, and the changes and development in this area, to an end by stating simply that it has been a great pleasure and very impressing to be able to observe the 'modernization' of the birth and the caretaking of the little child in recent years in this village.

My studies were possible only because the entire village over time opened not only their homes but also their hearts to me. It is touching that I, as a *farang*,[127] have been met with so much confidence that I was allowed to question the families as closely as my study required. I am profoundly grateful for this and direct this gratitude also to those key persons inside and outside the village that helped and supported me throughout.

As we discussed, we came to share the desire to publish and thus safeguard the knowledge of this small but significant component of Isan culture, as no systematic and coherent record seemed to be available in any language.

Personally, I regard what is presented here as an inspiring example of humankind's ability and striving towards ensuring, to the best of his or her ability under the given conditions, the development of a sensible socio-cultural support system that meets a universal need for emotional security, well-being, and peace of mind, in a variety of situations.

Magic and rituals were natural components in such a system and did not prevent the villagers from embracing changes that the development processes brought to

them. In this book, I have aimed at presenting the villagers world-view and their wisdom without adding more or less sophisticated interpretations of my own.

After consulting libraries of Isan culture and Isan cultural institutions I am surprised to find that the cult and fear of *mae kamlerd* appears never to have been documented in detail and be virtually unknown to scholars of Isan culture, even though we have documented that is it well-known and still alive in a larger area around Udorn.

The cult of *mae kamlerd*, and the elaborate rites around her appear to survive better than most other rituals connected to childbirth. New research is required into the origins and extension of this belief in the North-eastern areas, and into the possible reasons for the firm rooting this belief seems to have among the villagers.

Also the *khwan* rite held for the mother before the birth, the *suukhwan maemaan*, invites to further study. Though we have documented its existence not only in Baan Phraan Muean but in a rather large area around Udorn, it appears to be unknown in existing compilations of Thai, Lao, and Isan *khwan* rites.

Finally, I cannot omit pointing to the interesting and surprising documentation that our study provides about the custom of confinement by a fire, *yuu fai*. Already 40 to 50 years ago, most studies about Thailand reported that this custom was no longer practiced by most women throughout the country. Our study, on the contrary, documents the pervasiveness of this custom in a large area around Udorn where it is as a tradition followed, I believe, by every woman so to say up to the present day. In the light of this, the harmful or valuable benefits

from the fire and possibly from the decoctions used during the confinement need to be studied further.

During my close association with the young families and with the village elders, we discussed many things other than those immediately within the scope of my study. Not least did we consider the consequences for the rural family of the very rapid and radical general changes in the Thai society that have taken place during the years of the study. It is tempting to include reports and evaluations about the young families' thoughts and attitudes to these social changes but I shall limit myself to what I consider a fair summary.

The changes have in some aspects meant easier and better circumstances for the villagers. At the same time and to an increasing degree, these changes have made the villagers dependent on an urban economy, which is alien to them and often beyond their grasp. The arrival of a modern, more contrast-filled society is, however, a reality. It lures and challenges but it also frightens. In part, it emphasizes the poverty and makes the villagers realize that they have no reserves to fall back on when special problems arise. The changes have brought about new life styles and changes in family patterns. All of this has left many in a state of confusion and concern about the future. There are good reasons to ask what in fact will happen as new and probably very large changes are implemented, including the nation-wide reforms to decentralize educational and administrative decision-making. With these changes, much more local responsibility is foreseen for the conduct of public affairs. No doubt these reforms (if implemented as intended) will have a major impact on almost everything in the everyday life of the villagers. How will they be able to cope with the changes? How will the changes impact on the traditional culture and its values? And how will all of this influence the views and attitudes of the villagers towards the upbringing of their children?

These are open questions but my evaluation is that a strong social and cultural background and the Isan sturdiness will allow also future young generations in Baan Phraan Muean to bring up their children to match the needs of the future.

Professor Chancha Suvannathat stated a similar belief in an article on the inculcation of values in Thai children: 'From this generation, the transition of old and new values to the next generation will continue.'[128]

Should this process not succeed, the reasons will not be found in the people of this farming community. The ability, the will, the power to carry forward the best of the old, and to accomplish a renewal in a spirit of social justice, are potentially present.

Notes to Part 1

1. See also *Principles for the Transcription of Isan Names and Words in* Part 3, Appendix III.

2. Pendleton (1943, pp. 25, 40).

3. *Rai*: the common measurement for land in Thailand. One *rai* is approx. 0.40 acres or 0.16 hectares meaning that 1 hectare is about 6.25 rai.

4. S. J. Tambiah (1970, p. 24).

5. This was measured using the Tallquist-Adams method.

6. Klausner (1981, p. 103ff.).

7. Embree (1950), and among other writers Phillips (1963 and 1965).

8. Though in the case of Baan Phraan Muean it was almost exclusively men that went to the Middle-Eastern countries to work, it was not unusual in the neighbouring villages that also women went abroad.

9. Hardly any village in Thailand is better and more thoroughly described with regard to the collective religious universe than Baan Phraan Muean, as it forms the core in several of the quite outstanding works of Professor S. J. Tambiah. Above all one must refer to *Buddhism and Spirit Cults in North-East Thailand* (1970). It was my privilege during the original fieldwork in the village in 1961–62 to work with Professor Tambiah in Baan Phraan Muean. Our UNESCO team as a whole was responsible for the collective work in the village but we were split up into sub-groups that were each responsible for individual subjects. Tambiah's was among other topics 'faith' in all its shades, inevitably also covering aspects in connection with the subject of this book. The child, and the child in the family, was one of my topics.

10. The following descriptions are based on information and data collected in 1961–62. Some aspects will then be treated more extensively depending on the importance they have for our subject. Here, too, the basic material is the original 1961–62 data but these data were later substantially augmented in several respects.

11. S. J. Tambiah (1970, p. 326)

12. S. J. Tambiah (1970, pp. 59–60).

13. S. J. Tambiah (1970, pp. 252ff.)

14. S. J. Tambiah (1970, p. 225).

15. Phya Anuman Rajadhon explains in 'The Khwan and its Ceremonies' (*Journal of Siam Society*, L.1962, p. 124): 'Traditionally a person has 32 khwan(s). This tradition is known among the Thai of Thailand particularly in the North and the North-East, also among the Laos and perhaps to the Shans, (…).'

16. In central Thai: *suukhwan kong khaaw* while the tone is different in Isan: *suukhwan kong khau*.

17. Sparkes (1993, p. 180), and Whittaker (2000, p. 127).

18. Raendchen (2002).

19. Porée-Maspero (1951, p. 161) mentions an example from Cambodia describing a simple rite connected with a *khwan*-like soul in which: 'Powerful' threads are tied round the pregnant woman's waist, wrists and ankles shortly before the childbirth. The rite thereby seeks to prevent the *pralin* (~ *khwan*) from leaving the woman, and obstructs *prāy* (: *phii phraay* ?) from attacking her.'

20. S. J. Tambiah (1970, p. 224):
    - Rites of passage (marriage and ordination into monkhood);
    - Pregnancy (*suukhwan maemaaan*). In this group he also includes the rite *taengkae maemaan*, which is addressed to super naturals pictured as 'old mothers';
    - Threshold ceremonies;
    - Ceremonies of reintegration;
    - Rites for those suffering from prolonged illness. In these he includes a rite, *kae kamlerd* to dispel sickness in children caused by 'former spiritual mothers';
    - Rites dispelling bad luck betokened by inauspicious happenings.

21. In the Thai and Isan languages, there is only one word for 'he', 'she', and 'they'. To a Thai or Isan speaker, the term *puu thaen yaa thaen* therefore refers to a male-female couple or the 'ancient parents'.

22. Sparkes (1993, p. 78), and Whittaker (2000, p. 81)

23. Kingshill (1960, p. 155).

24. Viggo Brun (1976, p. 107).

25. Suvannathat (1971).

26. Davis (1984, p. 270).

27. We contacted, among other places, the Sirindhorn Isan Information Center at Mahasahakhram University, the Isan Cultural Center at Ratjabhat University Udornthani, the Center for Research on Plurality in the Mae Kong Region at Khon Kaen University, Naraisuan University, Pitsanulok University, and the Princess Maha Chakri Sirindhorn Anthropology Centre. In addition, we contacted the Chetawan Center, a newly started training school for ritual masters in Ubon. Khun Chetawan Bun-ngok, the founder of the school, had never heard about *mae kamlerd* and, logically, it follows that it is not part of the curriculum taught there.

28. Please refer to Burma (Bernot, 1967b, '*The Seven-Sister-Spirits*'; and Nash, 1966, '*Anauk Mèdaw = Lady of the West*'); Vietnam (Hart et al., 1965, '*Ba Co, the parental great-aunt spirit*'); and China, Western Valley of Sining (Frick, 1951, *Five-Way-Spirit*). In 2004, I found in Dai villages in Yunnan a belief in a *mae geb*. *Mae geb* is seen as a former mother who comes to 'tease the baby', preventing the baby from falling asleep and causing it to cry a lot.

29. Phya Anuman Rajadhon (1961).

30. Phya Anuman Rajadhon (1961, pp. 159–171).

31. Phya Anuman Rajadhon (1952, p. 253). 'The female supernatural being is called in Siamese *Mae Sü* a purely Thai word which means 'Purchasing Mother'.

32. Phya Anuman Rajadhon (1961).

33. S. J. Tambiah (1970, p. 313ff.).

34. Phya Anuman Rajahhon (1961, p. 165).

35. S. J. Tambiah (1970, p. 312–326).

36. Irwin (1907, p. 24); Rajadhon (1961, p. 118); Terweil (1975, p. 48); Klausner (1981, p. 298); Phongphitt (1990, p. 70); Sparkes (1993); Whittaker (2000, p. 135).

37. Irwin (1907, p. 19).

38.   Bernot from the frontier area between Burma and Bangladesh (1967b, vol. 2, p. 511); Hart from the Philippines (1965, p. 50); Coughlin from Vietnam (1965, p. 262); Porée-Maspero from Cambodia (1951, p. 145).

39.   Detailed descriptions by S. J. Tambiah from Baan Phraan Muean and information by S. Suwanlert show something about the extent of variations in the methods of treatment.

40.   Dr. Sangun Suwanlert (1968, 1969, and especially 1976).

41.   S. J. Tambiah (1970, p. 318ff.).

42.   All the following references confine *phii porb* geographically mainly to regions in the present Northeastern Thailand and to Laos: Bastian (1866, vol. 3, p. 274); Berval (1959, p. 184); Bowring (1857, vol. 2. pp. 5–6); Henderson (1971, p. 160); Irwin (1907, p. 31); Klausner (1981, p. 299); Lebar (1960, p. 46; 1964, p. 220); Rajadhon (1961, p. 119); Seidenfaden (1958, pp. 44, 119); Phongphitt (1990, p. 70); Whittaker (2000, p. 135).

43.   Seidenfaden (1958, p. 44).

44.   Jane Richardson Hanks (1963, p. 80) and Attagara (1967, p. 27).

45.   Milne (1924, pp. 260–261).

46.   Bastian: 'Schwangere Frauen sind den Nachstellungen der Dämone (*Phii Phob* und *Phii Prai*) besonders ausgesetzt' (1866, vol. 3, p. 279).

47.   Terweil (1975, p. 41).

48.   This belief is reflected in the ritual texts for both *suukhwan maemaan* (verse 84-85) and *taengkae maemaan* (verse 185–186).

49.   Central Thai: *kra-bok.* Latin: *Irvingia malayana*, wild almond.

50.   *Bulletin of the UNESCO Regional Office for Education in Asia and the Pacific,* No 23, 1982 (p. 260-268).

51.   Rishøj Petersen (1967, p. 62; 1968, p. 137).

52.   Whenever the word 'midwife' is used it means a person who is functioning as a birth helper without having any training to function as such. The exception is the persons employed at the Health Centres who are all professionally trained.

53.   Phya Anuman Rajadhon (1961, p. 166); Rishøj (1968, p. 152); Hanks 1963 (p. 82 ff).

54.   Rishøj Petersen (1968, p. 149).

55.   'The Three Gems' are 1) Phra Phut: Lord Buddha ; 2) Phra Tham: Buddha's dogma; and 3) Phra Song, or in other words, Buddha's disciples, monks, and priests.

56.   *Phii faa*: According to our village elders *phii faa* is understood to be a special form, which the great creator *puu thaen yaa thaen* can assume. He can also in this connection appear in both female and male form. In reality it is understood that he will at times be teasing and a little 'naughty' towards certain persons. He will then enter into this person. That will appear as a long-lasting feeling of being unwell. The person will ail, feeling off-colour and weak without any specific symptoms. When *phii faa* takes possession of an individual, the possessed will often have a particular dream. If a woman dreams that she has intercourse with someone other than her husband, and a man dreams that he has intercourse with someone other than his wife, it is a sign that *phii faa* may have possessed this person. The person must then visit a *mor sorng* who can investigate whether or not it is a case of *phii faa* possession. If it is, the person must visit the *mor phii faa*, who can

exercise this *phii*. In our village the *mor phii faa* was a very old woman who was considered best at it. This woman functioned as a 'midwife' in her heydays.

57. *Taapuubaan*: a protecting spirit, understood to be the real owner of all land in the village.

58. Isan word corresponds to *poot-saa* in Central Thai. Latin: *Zizyphus jujuba* – Chinese date or Indian jujube.

59. *Khamin* (*Curcuma longa L.* reminiscent of ginger).

60. Mudwasp: *Maa-raa*.

61. Phya Anuman Rajadhon (1961, p. 156).

62. Phya Anuman Rajadhon mentions (1961, p. 140) that the 'protective' or 'magic' thread relates to various important aspects of Buddhism.

63. Local dialect: *kradong morn* (*kradong*: basket of this type. *morn*: Indian mulberry).

64. *Nok khao*: either Horsfield's Scops owl (*scops lempifi*) or collared pygmy owlet (*glaucidium brodici*). Some of the locals believed that a sick and perhaps weak person would die if the screech of this owl was heard.

65. 'The Three Gems' are 1. Phra Phut: Lord Buddha ; 2. Phra Tham: Buddha's dogma; and 3. Phra Song: Buddha's disciples, monks, and priests.

66. The mothers had no real opinion about the reason for at least three nights in the *kradong*. It may have to do with the Three Gems mentioned above, but it may also be connected to the belief that the *phii phraay* and *phii porb* are especially dangerous for the baby the first three days of life. From many parts of the country is reported a belief that a newborn belongs to the spirit world the first three days, and may be taken back.

   First on the fourth day is the baby regarded as human. Rajadhon (1961, p.133 and 171) deliberates about this, and it is with variations reported also by Rishøj (1968, p. 145); Kaufman (1960, p. 144); Attagara (1967, p.75); and Hanks (1963, p. 66); Whittaker (2000, p. 147).

67. Ingersoll (1966, pp. 210 and 215).

68. Terweil (1975, p. 47).

69. Phya Anuman Rajadhon (1961, p. 107).

70. Phya Anuman Rajadhon (1961, p. 108).

71. Terweil (1975, p. 37).

72. Phya Anuman Rajadhon (1961, p. 107).

73. Lebar (1964, p. 220).

74. Milne (1924, p. 280).

75. Jelliffe (1963, p. 135).

76. Whiting (1963, p. 637).

77. Rasmussen (1931, p. 258).

78. Møller (1940, p. 147).

79. See for example,: Kaufman (1960, p. 142), Kingshill (1960, pp. 178–87); Rajadhon (1961, p. 124); Hanks (1963, p. 45); Attagara (1967, p. 72); Rishøj (1968, p. 139); Mougne (1978, p. 75).

80. Ploss (1887, vol. 2. p. 175).

81. de Young (1958, p. 49).

82. Frazer (1971 edition, p. 51).

83. Suvannathat (1967).

84. Mougne (1978).

85. Møller (1940, pp. 155–156).

86. Faye, 1885 (p. 754) cited in: *Edda-Lære*, vol. 4, p. 35.

87. Møller (1940, p. 150 ff).

88. Phya Anuman Rajadhon (1961, p. 157).

89. Phya Anuman Rajadhon (1961, p. 132).

90. Coughlin (1965, p. 241).

91. Møller (1940, p. 153).

92. Bock (1884, p. 223); Terweil (1975, p. 47), Whittaker (2000, p. 147).

93. Phya Anuman Rajadhon (1961, p. 131), Terweil (1975, p. 47) and Whittaker (2000, p. 29).

94. Møller (1940, p. 186 and p. 266).

95. Phya Anuman Rajadhon (1961, p. 146).

96. Mougne (1978, pp. 77–78).

97. *Mai tiw (Cratoxylon Pluniflorum).*

98. *Mai khaam pom (Phyllanthus emblica).*

99. Dr Oudom Souvannavong in: Berval (1959, p. 301).

100. Jane Richardson Hanks (1963, pp. 16–17); Rishøj Pedersen (1968, p. 153); and Mougne (1978, p. 82).

101. James Frazer (1971 ed.).

102. Sir James Frazer (1971 ed., p. 851).

103. See for example, Okinawa (Whiting 1963, p. 458); the Philippines (Whiting 1963, p. 810; Hart 1965, p. 66); Vietnam (Hart 1965, p. 243; Hickey1964, p. 108); Burma (Foll 1959, p. 551; Smart 1931, p. 53; Nash 1966, p. 110); and besides from some tribes and groups, e.g. Thai Yai (Seidenfaden 1958, p. 115); Mon-Khmer in Burma, Khmer in Cambodia, Muong in Vietnam, and Malay Muslims (Lebar 1964).

104. However, according to le May (1926, p. 41), Marco Polo never reached so far south of China that he reached Northern Siam.

105. Ploss (1911, vol. 1. p. 390): '... vier Wochen lang an einem wohlunterhaltenen Feur sitzen und sich bald auf diese, bald auf jene Seite wenden müsse.'

106. Bastian (1866, p. 29); Bowring (1857, p. 120); Bock (1884, pp. 224–25); Young (1907, p. 48); Curtis (1903, p. 169).

107. Curtis (1903, pp. 169–70).

108. Bowring (1857, p. 120).

109. Le May (1926, pp. 103–104).

110. Wales (1933, pp. 442, 447).

111. De Young (1958, pp. 50, 180).

112. Blanchard (1958, p. 436).

113. Kaufman (1960, p. 143), Hanks (1963), Attagara (1967, p. 74), and Rishøj Pedersen (1968, p. 143ff.).

114. Rishøj Pedersen (1968, p.148).

115. Rasmussen (1968, pp. 31 and 42).

116. Terweil (1975, p. 51).

117. Suvannathat (1971, p. 9); Mougne (1978, p. 80).

118. Phya Anuman Rajadhon (1961, p. 146); Jane Richardson Hanks (1961).

119. Phya Anuman Rajadhon (1961, p. 147).

120. Jane Richardson Hanks' (1963, pp. 71, 73).

121. Jane Richardson Hanks (1963, p. 73).

122. Phya Anuman Rajadhon (1961); Hanks (1963).

123. Although written /y-/ it is pronounced as /-gn/ as in French 'campagne'. Most of the /y-/ in Isan are pronounced in this way.

124. However, condensed milk consists mainly of sugar and palm oil.

125. Varaswapati, (1977).

126. Bronfenbrenner (Danish edition 1980, pp. 95, 104).

127. *Farang*: a word used in Thai to refer to Caucasian foreigners.

128. In the article *'The Inculcation of Values in Thai children'* (1979), Professor Chancha Suvannathat discusses the requirements for ensuring the necessary balance between tradition and the introduction of new ideas that is a pre-condition for stable social and economic development. Professor Chancha points to the following issues as determining for successful development in this respect:
    • to provide the child with certain values basic to the distinctiveness of Thai society;
    • to help children to adjust to new values arising from the rapid socio-cultural changes;
    • to carefully review traditional cultural values; and
    • to ensure that while the co-operative effort between different socializing agents will introduce socio-cultural changes they will also conserve and enhance Thai cultural tradition.

Part 2

The Ritual Texts

In this part of the book, I have collected examples from Baan Phraan Muean of the texts of the rites that are connected with pregnancy and childbirth.

I have chosen to include the full texts in their Isan versions – which is the text used by the ritual masters now – and the English translation and recreation. The two texts are presented synoptically verse by verse so that each line in one text corresponds to the same line in the translation. Please note that the Isan version of the texts in the following reflects accurately what the ritual master chants. Hence the text is in Isan and the spelling is accordingly different from standard Thai.

The texts were translated from their original versions into Isan by Phor Jampii and his son Khun Jan, a task that they undertook with pleasure hoping thereby to preserve their cultural heritage for future generations by making it known and available to a larger audience. Their translations were then translated into English by Mrs Supranee Khammuang and Mrs Pernille Askerud. Khun Jan helped in this translation, too, by clarifying many details of the text.

Also reproduced here is the original palm-leaf manuscript of the *suukhwan maemaan*. It would probably be possible to find palm leaf manuscripts in the village for the other rites as well but because of the small variations found from text to text they would not be exactly the same texts as the ones we have.

The transcription of the original texts follows the rhythm of the spoken text and reflects Isan pronunciation. All the main texts can be downloaded as sound recordings at www.sac.or.th.

Phor Jampii and his son Khun Jan translating the
ritual texts from their original versions into Isan
(1978)

(1961)

(1978)

Phor Tuu Phan (left) and Phor Jampii (right) were, for many years, the most employed and esteemed ritual masters in the village

Introduction

The Ritual Masters

The involvement and support from the surrounding community is an extremely important aspect of the prophylactic and therapeutic effect of the *khwan* rites discussed in Part 1, while this is not at all important in the *kamlerd* rites. However, in the local understanding, the ritual objects, the ritual text, and the integrity and force of the person performing the rite – the ritual master (*phaam* or *mor khwan* or *mor kamlerd*) – are just as important.

Etymologically the word *phaam* points to Indian Brahmanism and to cultural and religious relations between India and Farther India. On the other hand, the term *mor khwan* or *mor kamlerd* is used just as often, and it is a term used in Thailand also to refer to a series of other persons that have special functions or expertise in the village. The word *mor* is used as a title of courtesy (of which there are very many in Thai) and its meaning is close to 'expert', one who masters something. *Mor yaa* is the designation for local physicians and experts in herbal medicine. *Mor duu* is the astrologer, *mor sorng* the diviner and diagnostician, *mor lam* the expert who can perform the local folk opera, *mor tham* the exorcist of malevolent spirits, *mor tambon* the everyday name for the nurse in the health centre of the district (*tambon*), and *mor khwan* the expert in *khwan* rites.

The ritual masters of the two 'strong' *kamlerd* rites are highly esteemed men, who must possess all the same qualities as the masters of the *khwan* rites. The *mor kamlerd* as well as the *mor khwan* must have obtained their skills through apprenticeship with an older ritual master who has found him ethically suited to become a master. In Baan Phraan Muean, the two most respected practitioners of *khwan* rites in the 1960s and 1970s were also the most employed and esteemed practitioners of the two 'strong' *kamlerd* rites.

It is a different matter for the 'weaker' *pau kamlerd* rite. This rite does not involve ritual objects and the short magic invocation differs from one of its performers to another (*mor pau kamlerd*). The *mor pau kamlerd* have also undergone training in a teacher/apprentice relationship but not nearly with the same expectations with regard to their personal background as in the case of practitioners of the 'strong' *kamlerd* rites. All in all, being *mor pau kamlerd* does not carry the same prestige as being *mor kamlerd* or *mor khwan*. The *pau kamlerd* rite rates in every respect lower in the minds of the people, and so do its practitioners.

Great respect, honour, and reverence surrounded the village elders who performed the *khwan* rites and the *taengkae maemaan*. In 1968, all mothers except one had made use of only two different masters for their *suukhwan maemaan* rites. At that time, the same two masters were also in charge of the main part of all the *taengkae maemaan* rites performed in the village, but the oldest of the two, Phor Tuu Phan, then about 75 years old was regarded by some as the best and most competent. These two masters, Phor Tuu Phan and Phor Jampii, were both farmers and as regards income or wealth they did not differ greatly from most of the other villagers. Both were highly esteemed and respected, above all because of their personal character. They both

had quite extraordinary qualities with regard to integrity, and were strong and gentle men with exceptional charisma. They were highly gifted and had great insight in religion and tradition. They knew of the human nature and possessed the wisdom that induced natural confidence and trust into their environment. Both had been monks in the local temple in their younger days and could read and write the languages in which both religious and ritual texts were available. Both were members of the temple committee. The elder, Phor Tuu Phan, was also a respected herbal specialist (*mor yaa*) and Phor Jampii had been the headman (*phuu yai baan*) elected by the villagers.

Phor Tuu ('grandfather') Phan was invited by an older relative to learn to perform the rites when he was about 50. About ten years later, when he himself wished to pass on his art, partly to share some of his workload and partly to have a proper and well-qualified successor, he proposed to train Phor ('father') Jampii, a distant relative living in the village.

He was definitely the right heir for Phor Tuu Phan and when Phan died around 1970 Jampii was already undisputedly the most esteemed and valued *mor khwan*, and *mor kamlerd*, in the village and in the neighbouring villages.

Phor Jampii could not quite make up his mind whom to select as his successor. He regarded his eldest son as a potential successor and heir. This son, Khun Jan, was almost at the right age – 45 – in 1979. Admittedly, he had not been a monk and while he was fully literate in Lao script he could not read the *nang suee tham*, the language in which some of the ritual texts were written. He was, however, much respected in the village for his diligence and ability. He was a modern man who first and foremost had asserted himself in village politics; he was then the elected headman but had in this capacity acquired certain opponents. He had assisted his father in the rites so often, that, with his great talents, he was fully familiar with these ceremonies and their performance.

But his involvement in politics might indicate that he was not the very best choice as successor to his father. For this reason, a younger cousin of Khun Jan who lived in another village of the district was also considered. He was then only about 37 years of age but had already proved to have the personal qualities which Phor Jampii considered essential for selecting him as his successor. As late as January 1979, I discussed this matter with Phor Jampii and with his son, Khun Jan, and it was understood that although the final decision was not yet made it was most likely that both cousins would be announced as Phor Jampii's successors.

In January 1980, Phor Jampii died unexpectedly, 71 years old, and neither Khun Jan nor his cousin, Khun Sukan, were by then well-established among the villagers as respected and powerful ritual masters. The villagers were in a situation corresponding to Tambiah's discussions with village elders quite some years earlier:

Q: What are the implications for traditional ritual and medicine of the fact that in recent years there have been hardly any young men in the village who can read the traditional manuscripts, both because of the government's educational policy of teaching children only in Thai language and because the novices and monks today need not, and in the main do not, master the Tham script?

A: Village elders are very much aware of this as a problem, for the number of *mau khwan* and *mau ya* is dwindling, but not, as yet, the public demand for their services... Already, the death of elderly specialists is causing a visible shortage.'[1]

Tambiah presumably wrote these lines around 1966–67, and his discussions with the village elders on this question had taken place earlier. When we keep in mind the very extensive development and the many changes that had taken place, and also the more modern attitudes of large groups of younger people in the village by then,

it could be anticipated that these rites were about to outlive themselves and that the young and younger would merely take the death of Phor Jampii as an opportunity to stop having these old rituals performed. Not so. In the years immediately after 1980 there was no sign of this as a large proportion of the local villagers, young as well as older, as a matter of course expected Phor Jampii's son, Khun Jan, to take over his father's role and function as *mor khwan* and *mor kamlerd*. He was expected to possess his father's knowledge of tradition so that he could successfully perform the ceremonies and everything related to this.

Khun Jan took on the role. albeit with hesitation. The first year he was not considered a powerful ritual master, and he felt that himself. He did not have the charisma that is necessary to release the 'power' of the texts. But he grew with the task laid upon him.

Already by 1982, he was a highly respected *mor kamlerd*, and his cousin, Khun Sukan, had taken over the role as the most respected and powerful *mor khwan* in the district, also performing the rites connected with *mae kamlerd*. Since then I have had the opportunity to follow up on this many times both in discussions and by being present on occasions where one or the other of the two have performed some rite, latest in January 2004. Although many villages in the district still have local practising masters who perform the various types of rituals, Khun Jan and Khun Sukan have without doubt a particularly good reputation for the 'strong' and powerful results of the rites they perform, not only of the pregnancy rites but also of various other rites. For this reason they are much in demand in the many villages around, and even in the township of, Udorn.

Khun Jan (2001)

Khun Sukan (2004)

Ritual Texts

In Baan Phraan Muean and the neighbouring villages, as far as we were able to determine, there were no ritual texts in modern print, neither for the *khwan* nor for the *kamlerd* rites, and only few written in Indian ink on paper.

Originally, the texts used were palm-leaf manuscripts (*bai laan*), a traditional form of books. In these, the characters were first scratched with a sharp instrument on the dry leaves of a particular suitable palm. Then soot mixed with oil was rubbed into the scratches which made the writing appear clearly. A cord was pulled through one end of the narrow, oblong pieces of leaf to make a continuous 'book'. These books had mostly been copied from existing texts while the owner had been a monk in the local temple in his youth. The used language depended on the text available for copying and of course to a certain degree on the person who did the copying.

Before the Thai alphabet and language were introduced as the language of instruction in schools, the people of Isan would use the Lao alphabet (*tai noi*) when writing ordinary text.

In Baan Phraan Muean, the palm-leaf books for the *khwan* and the *kamlerd* rites were written in both the *nangsuee tham* and in *tai noi*. In some 'books' the two languages were mixed.

Most of the books still in use were made quite a long time ago. Owing to a series of alterations in temple practice in more recent times, palm-leaf books are no longer produced in Baan Phraan Muean, and only in few if any other places at all. In Baan Phraan Muean, it was estimated that no palm-leaf books had been produced for almost one hundred years. However, these palm-leaf books are incredibly durable. In the village we found books that had been stored in conditions where

they were not protected from damp, dirt, or insects, and still the books were entirely legible, supple and strong, even though they were about one hundred years old.

The ritual master recited the text in the local Isan language, reading it from the palm-leaf book that was entrusted to him by the master who taught him his art. More recently, the ritual masters have begun to make written copies of the texts in Isan, using the Thai script. This is the case for Khun Jan as it was for his father, and for the texts that we have translated in the following.

Most of the words used in the texts and the contents as such are intelligible to the villagers. Occasionally, the texts contain Pali words or sentences that are not commonly understood. Similarly, the references to the many gods, spirits, and other supernatural beings, which appear in the text, are not always fully understood by the villagers. In general, however, the 'message' in the texts is understandable, and what is not easily understood just adds to the authority – the importance and power of the text.

The ritual master's power and ability are evaluated partly from the text he employs. The text works by the 'power in the word' so the chanting must correspond exactly to that written on the leaf in order to have its full effect. He must adhere closely to the words of the text and improvisations are not accepted. Hence, the message in the text and the power of the words are entirely decisive for a successful outcome and depend to a great extent on the status and personal qualities of the ritual master.

Not all texts for the same rite are considered equally powerful but there is no doubt that the ritual master, the person behind the words (and the public respect and trust that he enjoys) is rated with regard to whether or not the villagers consider him to be in possession of a 'strong and powerful' text.

There is nothing secretive in or about the texts, and there is really nothing standing in the way of ritual masters being able to borrow texts from each other.

The text itself differs in the various types of *khwan* ceremonies; it is adapted in content and message according to its purpose. Even for the same kind of ceremony, the ritual masters use slightly different texts. Certainly, all *suukhwan maemaan* texts contain the same main elements – just as the *kamlerd* rites do – but each text may differ in linguistic construction, in poetic expression, and figurative language.

The variations in these texts for the same rite appear to have been introduced during repeated copying or when the copier made alterations to augment the beauty of the text and perhaps also its power, and to fit his personal linguistic sense. The same variations in style are also found, for the same reasons, in the *kamlerd* rites.

The texts that are translated here are beautiful and poetic, and characteristic by their complex and vivid imagery. The original texts as well as the Isan version are composed with attention to both rhythm and rhyme – which is more difficult to render in the English translation. When the texts are recited, the sound of the words is rhythmic and melodious. For more information on the style and language please refer to Appendix II.

Ritual texts presented in the book	Original language	Handwritten copy of the Isan Thai version of the manuscript	English translation	Recording
Suukwan Maemaan	Nangsuee tham	Yes – This version is typed out and reproduced in Poulsen, 2007	Yes – (Khammuang and Askerud, 2004)	Yes – Chanted by Khun Sukan (new recording 2004) This is a recording of the text that is used by Khun Sukan and Khun Jan and which we have translated
Taengkae Maemaan	A mixture of the sacred *Tham* script and the secular Lao script	Yes – This version is typed out and reproduced in Poulsen, 2007	Yes – (Khammuang and Askerud, 2004)	Yes – Chanted by Phor Jampii (1968) This is a recording of the text that Phor Jampii and now Khun Jan uses, and which we have translated
Taengkae Mae Kamlerd	The original palm leaf was written mainly in Lao with some words and sentences in the *Tham* script	Yes – This version is typed out and reproduced in Poulsen, 2007	Yes (Khammuang and Askerud, 2004)	Yes – Chanted by Phor Jampii (1968) This is a recording of the text that Phor Jampii and now Khun Jan uses and which we have translated
Small ritual texts included in the book	Local dialect	No	Yes – (Khammuang and Askerud, 2004)	Only a few recordings – Unfortunately, some of the recordings of these rites have been lost

Original Palm-leaf Manuscript of the *Suukhwan Maemaan* Rite

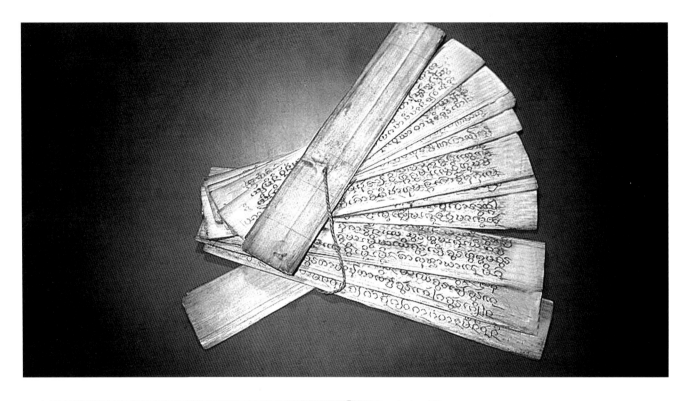

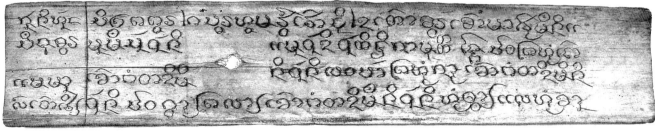

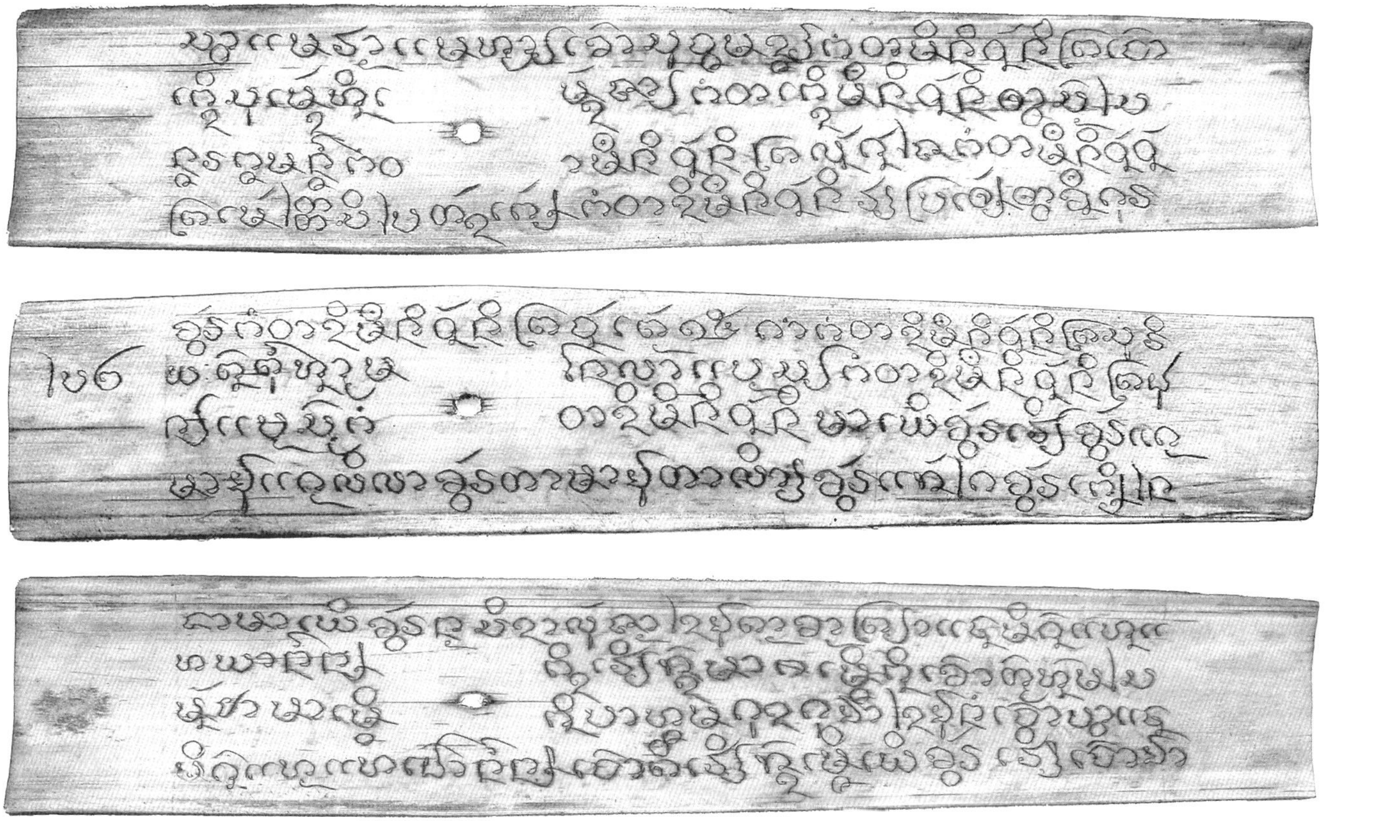

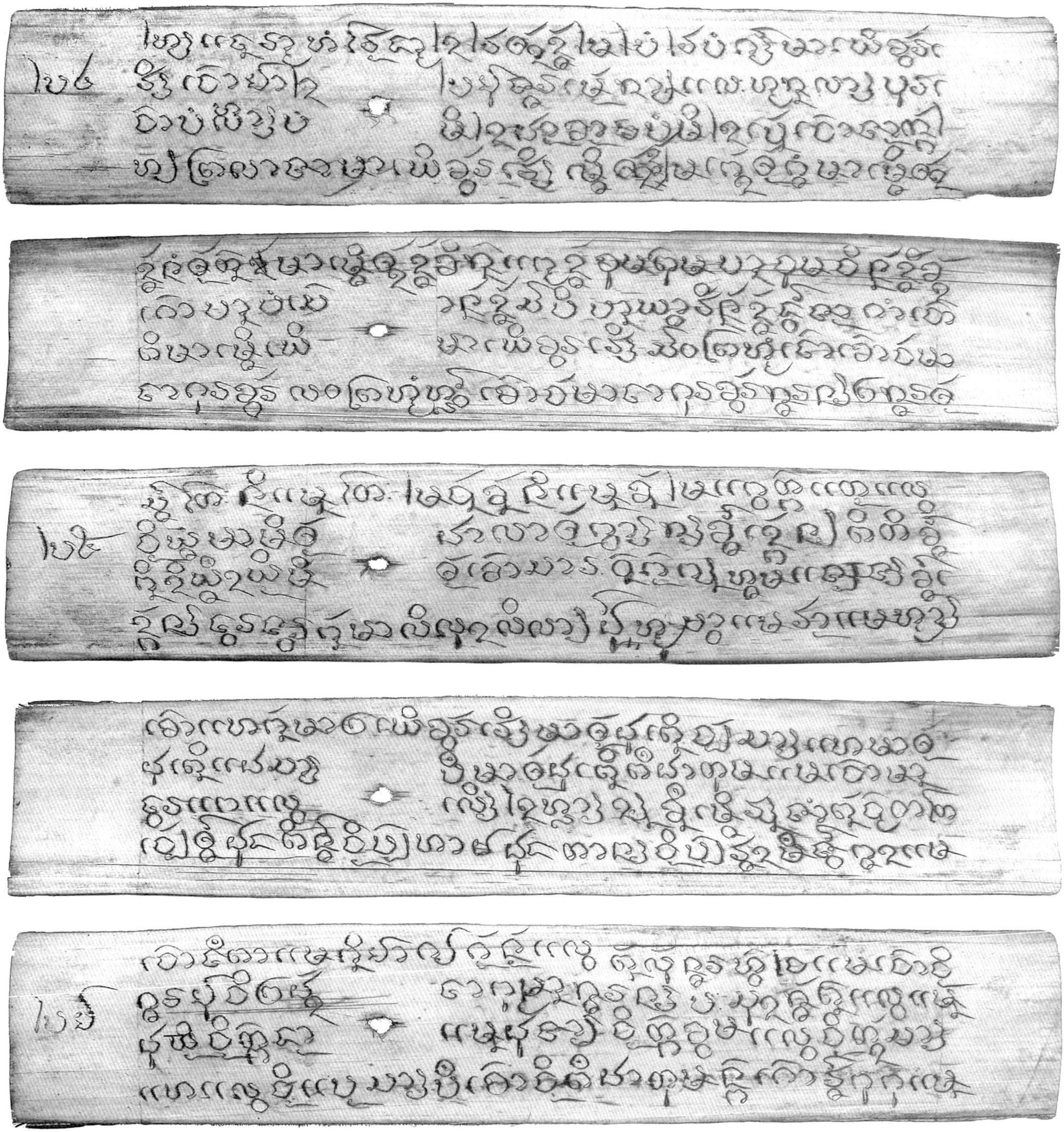

Original Palm-leaf Manuscript of the Suukhwan Maemaan

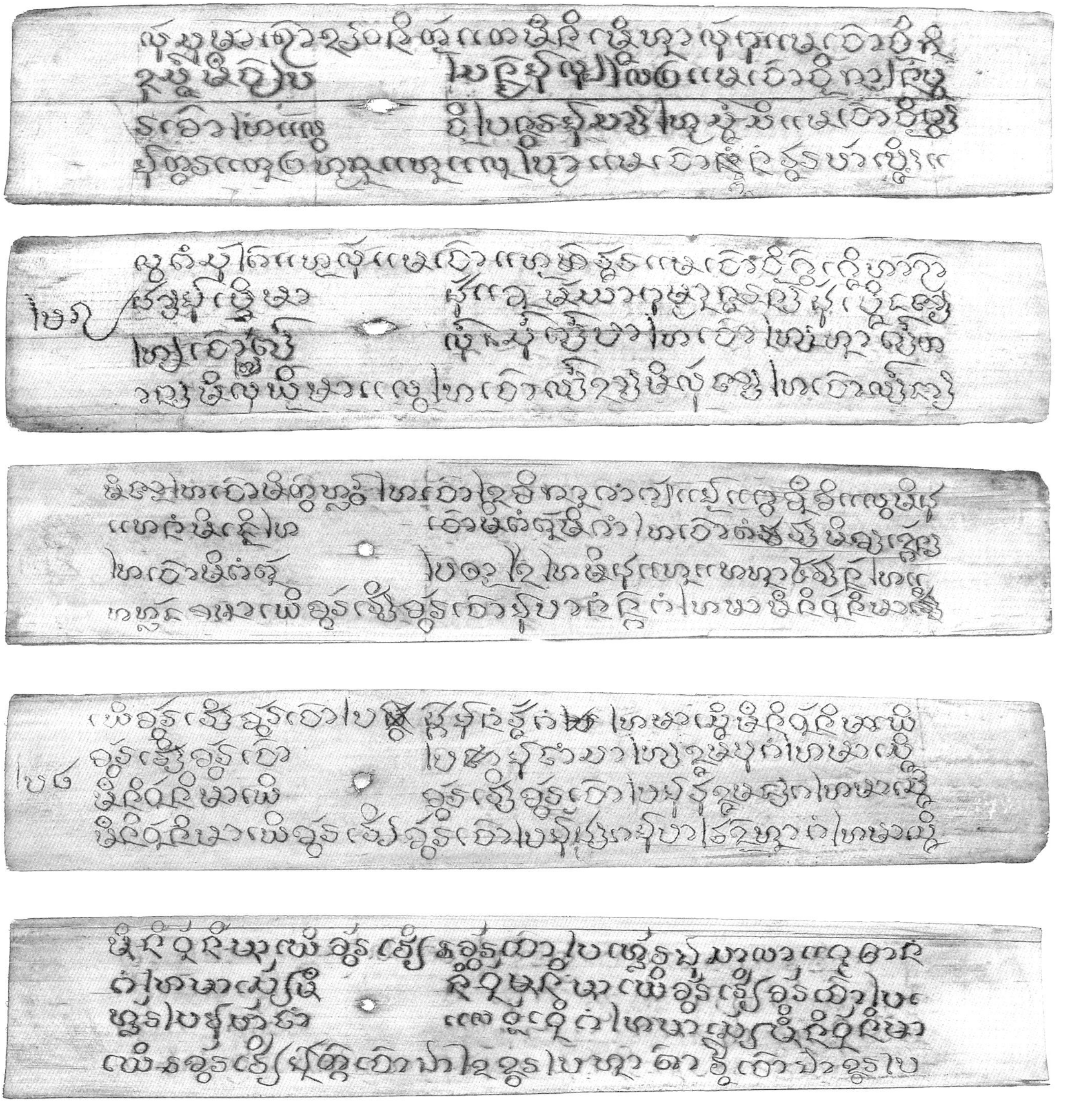

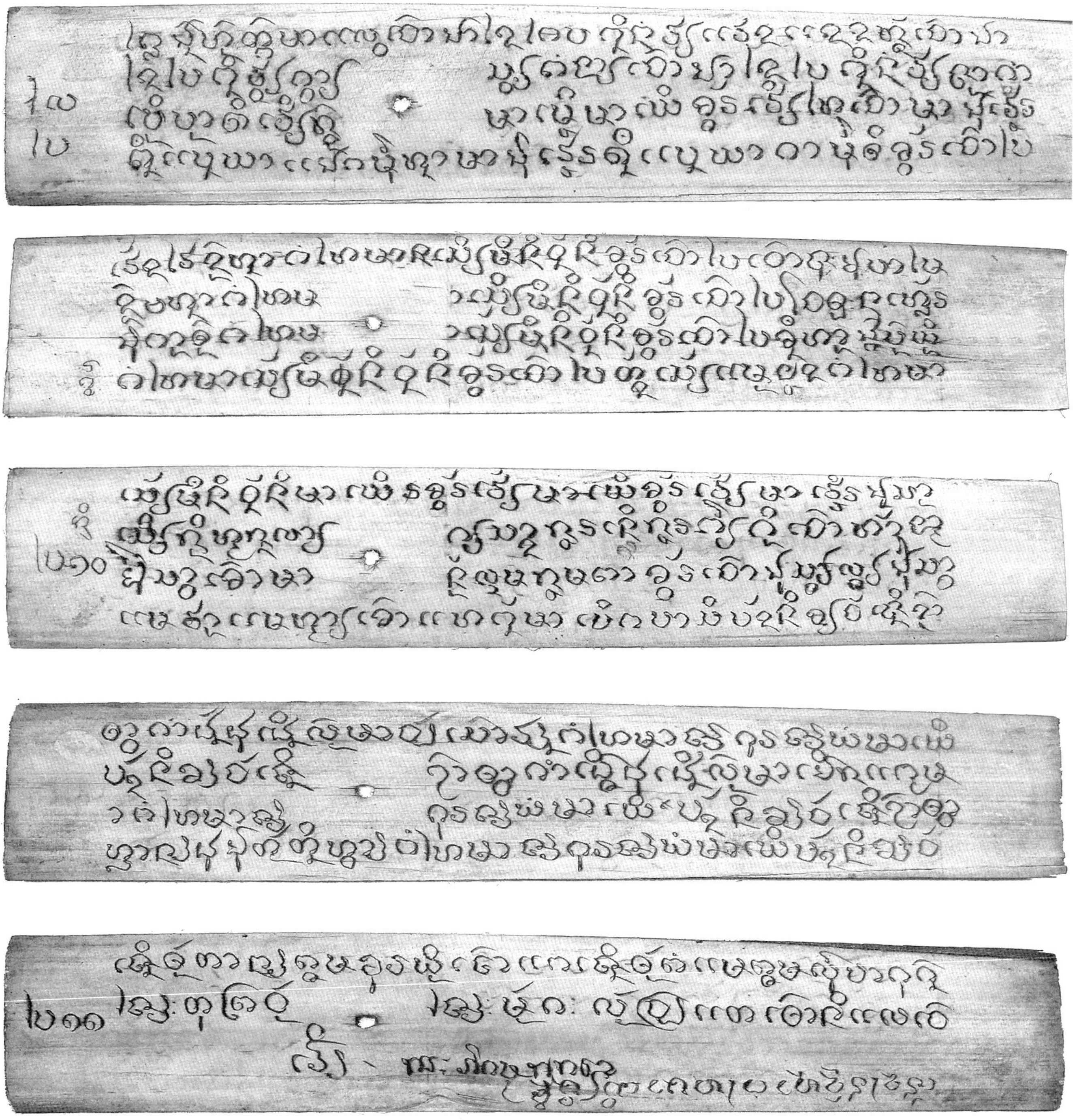

Original Palm-leaf Manuscript of the Suukhwan Maemaan

Khun Jan Somnuek was 92 years old when he was photographed in 1961. His memory was surprisingly good. He had much to narrate about his youth as a monk in the wat of Baan Phraan Muean. During that time he copied a large number of palm-leaf books of which 40–50 were still in his possession. Some were holy Buddhist scripts, and many Isan non-Buddhist texts of rituals, herbal medicine, and love potions. There were also love stories used by the *mor lam* singers. In 1978, I happened to pass by his house where a son was now living. His father's non-Buddhist palm-leaf books were in his possession, and he entrusted to me the palm-leaf with the *suukhwan maemaan* text (reproduced on pp. 131–135).

1   สีสีพระสิทธิพรไกรสรหอมเฮ้า

2.   จึงได้เต้าขวัญเข้ามาโฮม

3.   มื้อนี้แม่นมื้อสัน วันนี้แม่นมื้อดี วันดิถีอะมุตตะโชค

4.   30 พระหมอเฒ่าเขาก็ว่าดีมื้อนี้วันนี้

5.   90 ปากพระหมออามเขาก็ว่าดีมื้อนี้วันนี้

6.   30 ความพระลายเขาก็ว่าดีมื้อนี้วันนี้

7.   หมอทวยและหมอขานเขาก็ว่าดีมื้อนี้วันนี้

8.   หมอฮูฮาผู้เขาเคยคูณลึกเมืองเขาก็ว่าดีมื้อนี้วันนี้

9.   พือพระอยู่ในเมืองเขาก็ว่าดีมื้อนี้วันนี้

10. พระบุญเรืองขึ้นนั่งแท่นเขาก็ว่าดีมื้อนี้วันนี้

11. แอ่นแก้วขึ้นแปงฮังก็ว่ามื้อนี้วันนี้

RITUAL TEXTS

Suukhwan Maemaan

As already mentioned, there are some variations in the texts used for the *suukhwan maemaan* in the village. Tambiah[2] has a translation of the text used by Phor Tuu Phan and Phor Jampii. The ritual text reproduced and translated here is from Dorn Saang Kwaay, a hamlet next to Baan Phraan Muean. The owner, Khun Jan Somnuek copied it during his time as a monk in the *wat* of Baan Phraan Muean in the 1890s. It is written in the *nangsuee tham* script and is now translated into Isan.

The *suukwan maaemaan* is intended to ensure that the 'fleeting soul', the *khwan*, remains with the pregnant women so that she will remain healthy and strong and is altogether comfortable with herself and the approaching birth; or it is intended to call back the *khwan* (*suu khwan*) in the case that it may have left the woman so that she can again become strong and healthy.

The declared purpose of *suukhwan maemaan* is to give the mother strength and an easy delivery. The *khwan* rite aims to ease any anxiety and to give the mother peace of mind about the coming event. If the pregnant woman is well psychologically she will also feel better physically, and indirectly that will help her to an easy delivery. The concept encompasses a sprinkling of magic – hence it is believed that the *suukhwan* has the power to make the delivery easier.

1. *On this auspicious occasion, with fragrant flowers,*

2. *I, thus, humbly request the khwan to come hither.* [3]

3. *Today is a happy day. It is a good and lucky day.*

4. *Thirty old mors say that this is an auspicious day.* [4]

5. *Ninety mouths of Mor Aam say the same thing.* [5]

6. *Thirty statements of Phralaay pronounce it a good day,* [6]

7. *Fortune-tellers and ritual masters say that today is an auspicious day.*

8. *Mor Huuhaa who did the fortune telling for the town says so, too.* [7]

9. *All the monks in town say, too, that it is a good day.*

10. *From the throne the monk Bunrueang says this is a good day.* [8, 9]

11. *The delicate swallow making its nest also says this is a good day.* [10]

12. เขียงคำขึ้นเกี้ยวค้างก็ว่ามื้อนี้วันนี้

13. สาวแม่ฮ่างแม่หม่ายเข้าสู่จอมดอยก็ว่ามื้อนี้วันนี้

14. พระเจ้าเกิดสู่เม็ดหินทรายก็ว่ามื้อนี้วันนี้

15. ท้าวสงสัยก่อมน้องก็ว่ามื้อนี้วันนี้

16. พระลั่นฆ้องคันไชก็ว่ามื้อนี้วันนี้

17. พระเมตไตยสลิไปตัดเกษก็ว่ามื้อดีนี้วันนี้

18. ฮ้อยประเทศท้าวขึ้นคูณขวัญก็ว่ามื้อดีนี้วันนี้

19. พระจันทร์เพ็ง 15 ค่ำก็ว่ามื้อดีนี้วันนี้

20. พระสุริยะพันพุ่งหน่ามาก็ว่ามื้อดีนี้วันนี้

21. มะโนราแปงสร้อยก็ว่ามื้อดีนี้วันนี้

22. พระผู้น้อยแปงสมก็ว่ามื้อดีนี้วันนี้

23. มาเยอขวัญเอย

24. ขวัญแคงให้มาอยู่แคงลีลาลีลา

25. ขวัญขาให้มาอยู่ขาลีล่าย

26. ขวัญแอกไค่นางเกิดในงามาเยอ

27. ขวัญนางสีดาลูกช้างอย่าได้พ่างข้างพญาแถน

28. มีคนแหนแห่ยานางนาถพี่เอย

29. อดมาเมือกินเข่าต้มหนมไส่มันงา

30. มาเมือกินปลาแห้งคุดคู้

31. อย่าได้อยู่นำเจ้าบ่าวแถน

32. มีคนแหนแห่เฝ้า นางนาถเจ้าพี่เอย

33. อดเมือเยอขวัญเอย

34. เจ้าอย่าได้ไปอยู่ค้างฮั่วไฮ่ดอมสวน

35. ยาเพินเนอ

36. เจ้าอย่าได้ไปอยู่ค้างฮั่วนาและสวนห่อมเพินเยอ

37. อ้ายกล่าวแล้วน้องพื่อดมาเมือ

38. มาเยอขวัญเอย ขวัญหัวพร้อมขวัญอ่อนตีนแดง

39. ขวัญจอมแพงคั่วเมือเมืองฟ้า

40. ลูกหล่าย่าแถนมีคนแหน่แห่ยานางนาถพี่เอย

41. อดมาเมือมาเยอขวัญเอย

42. มาเมือมาผัวเจ้าบ่าวน้อยงามละห่อยเฝ้าหา

12. *The golden vine rambling around the poles says this is a good day.*

13. *The separated and divorced women say this is a good day.*

14. *The gods residing in the soil and the sand declare it a good day.*

15. *Thaaw Songsai lulling his younger brother to sleep says it is a good day.*[11]

16. *The monk beating the gong for luck declares it a good day.*

17. *Phraa Meit Trai who comes to have his haircut says so, too.*[12]

18. *The kings of a hundred countries coming to this khwan rite say this is an auspicious day.*

19. *The full moon of the fifteenth night says it is a good day.*

20. *The sunrise with its shinning rays says it is a good day.*

21. *Manooraa, in her disguise, says it is a good day.*[13]

22. *The young monk, dressing himself neatly, says it is a good day, too.*

23. *I request the khwan to come.*

24. *Khwan of the shin, please stay with the shin.*

25. *Khwan of the leg please stay with the leg.*

26. *Khwan of Aekkhai, lady born in the elephant's husk – please come.*[14]

27. *Khwan of Siidaa, daughter of the elephant, do not linger beside Baaw Thaen.*[15, 16]

28. *Though there are many attendants around you, my lady,*

29. *Come to sample this khau tom – stuffed with sweet potato and sesamee.*[17]

30. *Come and taste the beautifully arranged dried fish.*

31. *Do not linger with the young Thaen*

32. *Though surrounded by many attendants, my lady.*

33. *Oh, khwan, do try to come.*

34. *Do not wander to the fences of the plantation, lingering in the garden;*

35. *Be not fascinated by it.*

36. *Do not remain by the fences of the rice-field, enjoying the fragrant garden.*

37. *I have said it out loud, my young lady, try to return.*

38. *Please come, and bring with your own khwan and the khwan of the little baby.*

39. *My beloved khwan, wandering towards the sky.*

40. *Youngest child of Yaa Thaen, with your many attendants,*

41. *Khwan, please come, please come back.*

42. *Come and take pleasure of your longing husband.*

43.   ปานนี้ผัวเจ้าบ่าวน้อยให้เช็ดน้ำมูกน้ำตาอยู่ลีลาลีลา
44.   ปานนี้ผัวเจ้าเช็ดน้ำตาอยู่ลีไล่ลีไล่
45.   นางแอกไค่นางเกิดในงานางสีดาลูกช้าง
46.   เจ้าอย่าได้ไปอยู่พ่างข้างพญาใหญ่แถน
47.   ฮามหอโฮงงามบ่อได้ไฮ้
48.   ทัดดอกไม้บ่อไฮ้บ่อเคียง
49.   มาเยอขวัญเอย
50.   เจ้าอย่าได้ไปอยู่ซ้อนเมงอาจและหมอนลาย
51.   บุญเจ้าบ่อหลายบ่อได้มีผ่างข่าง
52.   บ่อมีได้เป็นเจ้าช้างเอกใหญ่ราชา
53.   มาเยอขวัญเอย
54.   เมือทัดดอกไม้เกดข้างกอ
55.   เมือทัดดอกยอทั้งต้น
56.   เมือทัดดอกขี้อ้นแกมดอกขูมพูม
57.   บานจูมจีนั้นดอกคัดเค้า
58.   บานบ่อเศร้านั้นดอกสามปี
59.   บานยาวฮีนั้นดอกงวงช้าง
60.   คำเจ้าพี่มาเมือเยอ มาเยอขวัญเอย
61.   สามสิบพระหมอเฒ่าเขาจักมาถ่าคูณขวัญ
62.   สามสิบพระหมอหลวงเขาจักมาถ่าคูณขวัญอ่อนน้อยๆ
63.   โตกนี้ แม่นโตกไม้จัน
64.   ขันนี้ แม่นขันไม้แก้ว
65.   ตกแต่งแล้วจึงยอมา
66.   มีทั้งผาลาทั้งกล้วยอ้อย
67.   ของเด็กน้อยพีตี้ของกินดียอดยิ่ง
68.   มีทั้งเข่าสาละวนกงเกวียนหอมแชมช้อย
69.   ของเด็กน้อยชวนกันมาลีลุดลีล่าย
70.   ฝูงหมู่สาวแม่ฮ่างแม่หม่ายเขาแห่กันมา
71.   มาเยอขวัญเอย
72.   มาทั้งผู้เพิ่นจับสายแฮ
73.   มาทั้งผู้เพิ่นจับสายบือ

43. *Until now, he has been busy wiping his tears.*

44. *Until now, he has been weeping.*

45. *Aekkhai, born in the elephant's husk and Siidaa, the elephant's daughter,*

46. *Do not remain at the side of the great Thaen.*

47. *That beautiful hall is not for you.*

48. *It is not right to adorn your head with flowers.*[18]

49. *Please come back.*

50. *Do not lie with him, do not share his bed and his pillow.*

51. *You do not have such luck as to be with him.*

52. *You will never be of prime importance to him.*

53. *So please come back.*

54. *Come and decorate your head with flowers from the kaed bush.*[19]

55. *Come, arrange instead the flowers from the beautiful yor tree, behind your ears.*[20]

56. *Place the khii-on and the khuum phuum flowers behind your ears.*[21, 22]

57. *Blooming beautifully are the flowers khad khau.*[23]

58. *Blooming, knowing no sadness, are the flowers saam pii.*[24]

59. *Blooming, long and tapering, are the flowers nguang chaang.*[25]

60. *Please come back, my beloved.*

61. *Thirty old mor have been waiting to perform this rite.*

62. *Thirty great mor have been atteding the rite for this tender little khwan.*

63. *This phaakhwan is made of sandal wood.*[26]

64. *This bowl is made of the finest wood.*[27]

65. *Beautifully adorned, they are carried here,*

66. *Full of fruits – bananas and sugarcane.*

67. *Healthy for the children, delicious food.*

68. *There is also sweet-smelling rice,*

69. *Attracting many children here.*

70. *Groups of young girls come; separated and divorced women, too.*

71. *Dear khwan, please come.*

72. *She who cuts the umbilical cord will come.*

73. *She who carries the placenta will come, too.*

74. มาทั้งผู้เพิ่นจับพือผ้าตุ้ม
75. แม่เจ้ามานถ้วนแก่แล้วเลยได้หลายเดือน
76. ขึ้นเมือเฮือนชำผั้นจ่มว่าโตเจ็บท้อง
77. ฝูงพี่น้องจึงปบมาหา
78. ฝูงตานายจึงปบมาฮอด
79. มือทรวงกอดแม่เจ้าถือพา
80. แม่กินยาคอยคั่งนั่ง
81. แล้วผั้นลุกลุกแล้วผั้นนอน
82. หัวใจแม่เจ้าจึงคอนอยู่จีจี
83. บัดท่ากุมมารอ่อนน้อยประสูติออกพ้นแล้ว
84. เป็นผู้หญิงตกหงาย
85. เป็นผู้ชายตกข่วม
86. แล้วจึงตัดสายแฮ
87. แล้วจึงแผ่สายบือ
88. เขาจึงพือผ้าตุ้ม
89. นกเค้าฮ้องกูกกูกกู
90. แมนลูกสูมาเอาเดี่ยวนี้
91. ตั้งแต่มื้อนี้เมือหน้าแมนลูกกู
92. แม่เจ้าจึงอิดสองมือจับเจ้าใส่นมอยู่ลี่ไล่ลี่ไล่
93. แม่เจ้าจึงอาบน้ำป้อนเข่า
94. แล้วจึงไปนอนอู่สายไหม
95. สองมือแม่เจ้าจึงกวยอยู่ต่อนแต่นต่อนแต่น
96. หมอนแหนแล่นไปมา
97. แม่เจ้ากินน้ำฮ้อนปากเปื่อยโพงสุก
98. ไฟแฮงลุกแม่เจ้าแฮงฮ้อน
99. แม่เจ้าจึงคั่วเคียหาเอาฝ้ายอยู่เปียมาผูกแขน
100. มัดสากุมมารอ่อนน้อย
101. ผูกเบื้องซ้ายให้เจ้าใหญ่เพียงลุง
102. ผูกเบื้องขวาให้เจ้าสูงเพียงป้า
103. ให้เจ้าใหญ่หน้าเพียงตานาย
104. มีลูกยิงมาแล้วให้เจ้าเลี้ยงดาย

74. *As will she who who folds the diaper.*

75. *Your mother is at full pregnancy.*

76. *Returning home, she complains of pain.*

77. *All the relatives then come.*

78. *Your grandparents are here.*

79. *Your mother is ready for the delivery.*

80. *Taking the medicine, she sits,*

81. *Then stands, then lies down.*

82. *Your mother's heart is shaking.*

83. *Now the baby comes.*

84. *With the navel up, it is a girl.*

85. *With the navel down, it is a boy.*

86. *The umbilical cord is cut.*

87. *The navel is unfolded.*

88. *The diaper is wrapped around it.*

89. *An owl cries kuuk kuu, kuuk kuu.*

90. *If the baby is yours, come and take it now.*[28]

91. *Otherwise, it will be forever mine.*

92. *Your mother, with her two hands, carries you to breastfeed.*

93. *She bathes you and gives you rice,*

94. *She puts you in a cradle made of silk strings.*

95. *She swings it with her two hands.*

96. *The pillow moves to and fro.*

97. *Drinking hot water, her lips are swollen and burnt.*

98. *The higher the fire burns, the hotter she feels.*

99. *Your mother hurriedly looks for a thread from the spinning reel to tie around your wrists.*

100. *To tie the tiny baby.*

101. *Around the left, to make you grow as big as your uncle.*

102. *Around the right, to make you grow as tall as you aunt.*

103. *To make you become as great as your grandparents.*

104. *Having a daughter, she will be an easy child.*

105. มีลูกชายให้เจ้าเลี้ยงง่าย

106. มีช้างให้เจ้ามีตัวหลวง

107. ให้เจ้าได้ขี่อานคำและแย่งแก้ว

108. ขึ้นขี่แล้วมีผู้แห่นำ

109. มีเงินให้เจ้ามีพอพัน

110. มีคำให้เจ้ามีพอฮ้อย

111. มีข่อยเด็กน้อยให้เจ้ามีพอพัน

112. ไปทางใดให้มีผู้แหนแท่หน้า

113. ห้าฮ้อยนั้นให้แห่หลัง

114. มาเยอขวัญเอย

115. ขวัญเจ้าอยู่ป่านานกก็ให้มาสามื้อนี้วันนี้

116. มาเยอขวัญเอย

117. ขวัญเจ้าไปผกอยู่นำฮอกก็ให้มาเสียมื้อนี้วันนี้

118. มาเยอขวัญเอย

119. ขวัญเจ้าไปอยู่นำถ้ำสระใหญ่ดอมปูก็ให้มาเสียมื้อนี้วันนี้

120. มาเยอขวัญเอย

121. ขวัญเจ้าไปอยู่สู่นำเงือกก็ให้มาเสียมื้อนี้วันนี้

122. มาเยอขวัญเอย

123. ขวัญเจ้าไปอยู่นำเผือกอยู่ป่าใหญ่ดงหนาก็ให้มาเสียมื้อนี้วันนี้

124. มาเยอขวัญเอย

125. ขวัญเจ้าไปเล่นอยู่ศาลาแคมท่าน้ำก็ให้มาเสียมื้อนี้วันนี้

126. มาเยอขวัญเอย

127. ขวัญเจ้าไปเล่นอยู่ปากน้ำและวังเวินก็ให้มาเสียมื้อนี้วันนี้

128. มาเยอขวัญเอย

129. ฝนตกเจ้าอย่าได้ด่วนไปหน้า

130. ฟ้าฮ้องเจ้าอย่าได้ด่วนไปไกล

131. ฝนตกมาโฮ่งแล้วเจ้าอย่าได้ไปกินน้ำฮอยแฮด

132. แดดออกเจ้าอย่าได้ไปกินน้ำฮอยควาย

133. สวยพองายเจ้าอย่าได้ไปกินน้ำฮอยช้าง

134. คำเมืองนางพี่เอย

135. อดมาเมือมาเยอขวัญเอย

105. *Having a son, he will be easy to raise.*

106. *Having an elephant, you will have a grand elephant,*

107. *You will ride in a golden saddle and a bright seat.*

108. *Riding on it, many will be in the procession.*

109. *Having money, you will have up to a thousand.*

110. *Having gold, you will have up to a hundred.*

111. *Having young attendants, there will be up to a thousand.*

112. *Wherever you go, many will lead the procession.*

113. *Five hundred people will follow you.*

114. *Please come back.*

115. *Khwan who is lingering in the forest among the birds,*

116. *Please come back.*

117. *Khwan who is away watching the squirrels,*

118. *Please come back.*

119. *Khwan who is in the cave and in the big pond with the crabs,*

120. *Please come back.*

121. *Khwan who is in the hole with the snakes,*[29]

122. *Please come back today.*

123. *Khwan who is with the taroes in the large, thick forest,*

124. *Please come back today.*

125. *Khwan who is playing in the shelter by the river,*

126. *Please come today.*

127. *Khwan who is playing at the entrance to the cave and the whirlpool,*

128. *Please come back today.*

129. *When it rains, do not hurry ahead.*

130. *When it thunders, do not hurry farther away.*

131. *When it pours down, do not go to drink water in the footprints of rhinocerous.*

132. *When the sun shines brightly, do not go to drink water in the footprints of buffaloes.*

133. *When it gets late, do not go to drink water in the footprints of elephants.*

134. *My beloved lady.*

135. *Try to come back.*

136. ให้เจ้ามาอยู่เฮือนพื้นเป็นหญ้าแฝกมุงหนา

137. มาอยู่เฮือนพื้นเป็นหญ้าคามุงถี่

138. ขวัญเจ้าไปเฮดไฮ่ดงหนาก็ให้มาเสียมื้อนี้วันนี้

139. ขวัญเจ้าไปโจนทะนาเล่นอยู่กลางท่งก็ให้มาเสียมื้อนี้วันนี้

140. ขวัญเจ้าไปขึ้นห้างผกป่งยิงกวางก็ให้มาเสียมื้อนี้วันนี้

141. ขวัญเจ้าไปตัดเสียงแมงงอดก็ให้มาเสียมื้อนี้วันนี้

142. มาเยอขวัญเอย

143. มาเฮือนอยู่ส้างเสื่ออิงหมอนลาย

144. คอยสะออนเนื้ออ่อนเกี้ยงคิงเจ้าหากงาม

145. ผู้สาวเขามานั่งล้อมอ้อมพาขวัญเจ้าอยู่ซอนลอน

146. ผู้สาวแม่ฮ่างแม่หม่ายเขาแห่กันมาเบิกษาศรี

147. บักนี้ข่อยจักเชิญเอาท้าวคำฝั่น

148. ผู้เพิ่นมาจับเสาเฮือน

149. ก็ให้มาช่อยคูณซ่อยยอ มาเยอ

150. บัดนี้ข่อยจักเชิญเอาท้าวคำเฝือผู้เพิ่นมาเยือแคมม้า

151. ก็ให้มาช่อยคูณซ่อยยอ มาเยอ

152. บัดนี้ข่อยจักเชิญเอาท้าวหล่าน้อย

153. ผู้อยู่ตั้งตีนหงาย

154. ก็ให้มาช่อยคูณซ่อยยอ มาเยอ

155. บัดนี้ข่อยจักเชิญตานายพร้อมผู้ยิงเฒ่าแก่

156. เชิญทั้งพ่อแม่พร้อมลุงป้าซู่คน

157. *ชัยตุภวังชัยมังคลัง*

158. ความสุขสมบูรณ์ จ่งให้มีแก่เจ้าเฮือนฝูงนี้

159. และแม่มานผู้นี้ให้มากๆ ทุกพวกทุกประการผู้ข้าเทอญ

136. *Come to stay at the wooden house, the roof is thickly thatched.*

137. *Stay at the wooden house whose roof is closely thatched.*

138. *Khwan who is planting in the thick woods,*

139. *Khwan who is adventurously playing in the midst of the field,*

140. *Khwan who watches the salt lick from the shelter, waiting to shoot deer.*

141. *Khwan who is out to still the noise of the scorpions,*

142. *Please come back today.*

143. *Return home to weave the mat and sew the patterned cushion.*

144. *Everyone looks forward to admire your beauty.*

145. *Many young girls sit conspicuously around the phaa khwan.*

146. *Young girls, separated and divorced women swarm in to join the rite.*

147. *Now I should like to invite Thaaw Khamfan,* [30]

148. *Who comes to raise the house poles.*

149. *Please help raising this phaa khwan, please come.*

150. *Now I should like to invite Thaaw Khamfuea who stays around the horses.* [31]

151. *Please assist in the raising of this phaa khwan, please come.*

152. *Now I should like to invite Thaaw Laanory* [32]

153. *Who is on the seat with beautifully curved legs,*

154. *Please assist in raising the phaa khwan, please come.*

155. *Now I should like to invite the grandparents and the elderly ladies.*

156. *I also invite the parents, every uncle and aunt.*

157. *Chaiyatuphawang chaiyamangkhalang* [33]

158. *May blessings and good fortune follow the members of this family,*

159. *And this pregnant lady.*

(1961)

1   เทวบุตร เทวดา พญาอินทร์ พญาพรหม พญายมนา นาคครุฑ เจ้าทั้งหลาย

2.   มื้อนี้มีเหตุจั่งขาน มีการจั่งเฮียก

3.   จึงได้แต่งขัน เข่าตอกดอกไม้

4.   และธูปเทียน

5.   มาขอตั้งสักเคกล่าว

6.   เอาเทวดาเจ้าลงมาเป็นสักขีพยาน

7.   สิได้แก้ท้องแม่มานคนนี้แหละ

8.   ขอให้ได้จักความมักความหมายของข้าพเจ้าทั้งหลายผู้ข่าเทอญ

9.   นโมตัสสะ ภควโต อรหโต สัมมาสัมพุทธัสสะ

10.   นโมตัสสะ ภควโต อรหโต สัมมาสัมพุทธัสสะ

11.   นโมตัสสะ ภควโต อรหโต สัมมาสัมพุทธัสสะ

12.   อมส้มป่อย กูบ่อว่าส้มป่อย

13.   กูว่าแม่นส้มสะลันตา

RITUAL TEXTS

Taengkae Maemaan

The original palm-leaf manuscript was written in a mixture of the sacred *nangsuee tham* script and the secular *tai noi* script. Phor Jampii and his son Khun Jan made the translation into Isan and this is the text now used by Khun Jan. It is also the text rendered here.

The *tangkae maemaan* is performed closely before the birth to protect the mother from the dangers that might arise during delivery as the *mae kamlerd* might try to take the child back.

Note that the *taengkae maemaan* text has many explicit references to both Thai and Indian Gods, and that the text is addressed to these rather than to the *khwan*(s) as the *suukwan maemaan* is.

1 *Theiwadaa(s), Indra, Brahma, God of the Rivers, Naga, and Garuda –*

2. *On this occasion I have special reason to call your names,*

3. *Adorning a bowl with roasted un-husked rice and flowers,*

4. *Incense sticks and candles,*

5. *I shall pay my respect requesting*

6. *You to be present and bear witness to this rite.*

7. *I shall kae the pregnant mother*[34]

8. *May my intention be successful.*

[this incantation is followed by a prayer in Pali:]

9. *Namotassa bhagavato arahato sammasam buddhassa*

10. *Namotassa bhagavato arahato sammasam buddhassa*

11. *Namotassa bhagavato arahato sammasam buddhassa.*[35]

12. *Om – sompory, I do not call it sompory*[36, 37]

13. *I call it som salantaa.*

14. *กูว่าแม่นส้มสาหัว*

15. *กูจักสาหัวท้าวท้าวก็หาย*

16. *กูจักสาหัวนางนางก็ผู้ดีอ้อนแอ้น*

17. *กูจักสาหัวช้างช้างจักเกิดเป็นช้างเผือกแลไพวัน*

18. *กูจักสาหัวควายควายจักเกิดเป็นควายเขาแก้ว*

19. *กูจักสาหัวม้าม้าจักเกิดเป็นม้าพนละหก*

20. *กูสิมนหดไม้ไม้ก็เกิดเป็นต้นเป็นลำ*

21. *กูจักสาหัวสาวสาวจักเข้ามาสู่*

22. *กูจักสาหัวชู้ชู้ก็เข้ามาหา*

23. *อมพุธทา มหาพุทธา*

24. *กูจักสาหัวพญา*

25. *พญาจักได้นั่งแท่นแก้ว*

26. *กูจักสาหัวช้างช้างก็เป็นช้างแก่นควน*

27. *กูจักสาหัวนางนางก็ผู้ดียียิ้ม*

28. *อมอินทา มะหาอินทา*

29. *ให้เจ้าลงมาแก้*

30. *อย่าได้แพ้คิงบาง*

31. *อมพรมมา มหาพรมมา*

32. *ให้เจ้าลงมาแก้*

33. *เพิ่นใส่หว่านก้านหนา กูแก้กูสา*

34. *เพิ่นใส่ยาก้านก่ำ กูแก้กูสา*

35. *เพิ่นใส่ฮุ่นเอาฮอย กูแก้กูสา*

36. *นกเค้าฮ้องกูกเอาขวญ กูแก้กูสา*

37. *ไข่ผอมเหลืองเป็นพยาด กูแก้กูสา*

38. *เคราะห์คาดเข้าอยู่ในคิง กูแก้กูสา*

39. *ลางหมาและลางฟานเห่า กูแก้กูสา*

40. *พายหลวงแห่งเทียวมา กูแก้กูสา*

41. *หนูฮ้องอยู่ในเฮือน กูแก้กูสา*

42. *ลางงูและหนอนไต่ กูแก้กูสา*

43. *เลือดฮ้ายตกกลางเฮือน กูแก้กูสา*

44. *ลางฮ้ายและหามผี กูแก้กูสา*

14. *I think it is the plant used for washing hair.*

15. *Washing the hair of a man, he will get well.*

16. *Washing the hair of a woman, she becomes a beautiful high-class lady.*

17. *Washing the hair of an elephant, it becomes the white elephant in the forest.*

18. *Washing the hair of a buffalo, it will grow horns like jewels.*

19. *Washing the hair of a horse, it will be born vigorous and healthy.*

20. *Watering a plant, it will grow a huge trunk.*

21. *Washing the hair of a young girl, she will come to me.*

22. *Washing the hair of a lover, the lover will come to me.*

23. *Om, Buddha, Maha Buddha –* [38]

24. *I shall wash the hair of Phayaa* [39]

25. *He will be entitled to sit on a jewel throne.*

26. *I shall wash the hair of an elephant; it will become the pride of its owner.*

27. *I shall wash the hair of a woman; she will become a high-class lady.*

28. *Om, Indra, Maha Indra –*

29. *I request your presence.*

30. *Do not surrender to having a skinny body.* [40]

31. *Om, Brahma, Maha Brahma –*

32. *I request your presence.*

33. *Should anyone add herbs with coarse stems: I shall wash and kae it.* [41]

34. *Should anyone add herbs with black stems: I shall wash and kae it.*

35. *Should anyone add a trace pattern:, I shall wash and kae it.*

36. *If owls are to call out for the khwan: I shall wash and kae it.* [42]

37. *If there is fever, parasite worms – anyone who is skinny and pale:* [43] *I shall wash and kae it.*

38. *Any unexpected bad luck dwelling in the body: I shall wash and kae it.*

39. *The bad omen of dogs and barking deer: I shall wash and kae it.* [44]

40. *Huge spirits that haunt more frequently: I shall wash and kae it.*

41. *Mice squeaking in the house: I shall wash and kae it.*

42. *The bad omen of snakes and creeping worms: I shall wash and kae it.*

43. *Poisonous blood dropping in the middle of the house: I shall wash and kae it.*

44. *The bad omen of carrying a corpse: I shall wash and kae it.*

45. *หนึ่งเข่าเหลืองเป็นเลือด กูแก้กูสา*

46. *กูจักสาเมือภูเขาข่วม*

47. *กูจักสาเมือน้ำเขาเขียว*

48. *กูจักปัดป่าป่าก็หาย*

49. *กูจักปัดผีพายพายก็เว้น*

50. *สานัง สาเน ภันเต สัพพะเคหังทุละตะจิตตา สามาคันทสันตุ*

51. *อมหูนลูฯ สั่วหายยะ*

52. *อมเครือเขากาดหมากน้ำเต้าตายพาย*

53. *ก่ออู่ท่อเก็ดหอย*

54. *ก่อเมืองก่อนาท่อฮอยไก้*

55. *เครือ ๑ ถ่ายเมือเมืองแถน*

56. *เครือ ๑ ถ่ายเมือเมืองฟ้า*

57. *เครือ ๑ ถ่ายเมือเมืองผี*

58. *เครือ ๑ ไปเวียนอ้อมขอบจักกะวาน*

59. *ย่าง่ามเจ้าตกแต่งลงมา*

60. *ทาง๑นั้นงัวควายเกิดแวนมาก*

61. *อันนี้กะย่าง่ามเจ้าตกแต่งลงมา*

62. *ทาง๑นั้นเด็กน้อยเกิดเหลือหลาย*

63. *อันนี้แถนเถ่าเจ้าตกแต่งลงมา*

64. *ทาง๑นั้นคนเกิดมาแวนมาก*

65. *อันนี้กะแถนเถ่าเจ้าตกแต่งลงมา*

66. *ปั้นฮูปเผิ่งให้เป็นควาย ก็ว่าแม่นมื้อนี้วันนี้*

67. *บักไม้ให้เป็นคนก็ว่าแม่นมื้อนี้วันนี้*

68. *หมอหนลงมาจากฟ้าก็แม่นว่ามื้อนี้วันนี้*

69. *อมสั่วหาย*

70. *อมสีฯ สิทธิไชยะ มังคะลังปะวอละสีวิมน อมสาคะลาชา*

71. *เทวดาเจ้าตน๑ ชื่อว่าพระอาทิตย์*

72. *ตนหนึ่งชื่อว่าพระจันทร์*

73. *ตนหนึ่งชื่อว่าพระคาร*

74. *ตนหนึ่งชื่อว่าพระพุธ*

75. *ตนหนึ่งชื่อว่าพระหัส*

45. *Steaming rice that turns yellow and bloodlike: I shall wash and kae it.*

46. *I shall wash, driving all these omens back yonder the mountains.*

47. *I shall wash, expelling them all to the water and the green mountain.*

48. *I shall wipe away the forest, and the forest will disappear.*

49. *I shall wipe away the Phii Phaay; they will be stopped.*[45]

50. *Saanang saanei phantei sappha kheihang thulatajidtaa saamaakhanthasantu*[46]

51. *Om – hunlu hunlu – evils be gone.*[47]

52. *Om – rambling vines; withering gourd, dead before its time.*

53. *Cradle as tiny as the husk of a shell.*

54. *Town and rice fields as tiny as the trace of kai.*[48]

55. *One of the vines climbs back to the town of Thaen.*[49]

56. *One of the vines climbs back to the town in the sky.*[50]

57. *One of the vines climbs back to the town of ghosts.*

58. *One of the vines circles around the edge of the universe.*

59. *Grandmother Ngaam has made this decoration.*

60. *On one path, buffaloes and cows were born.*

61. *This path is decorated by grandmother Ngaam.*

62. *On one path, several children were born.*

63. *This path is decorated by the old Thaen.*

64. *On the other path, several people were born.*

65. *This path is also decorated by the old Thaen.*

66. *Today is the day to mould the wax in the shape of buffaloes.*

67. *Today is the day to cut the wood in the shape of human beings.*

68. *It is the day that the fortune-tellers come down from heaven.*

69. *Om – all evils be gone.*

70. *Om – sii sii sit thi chaiya mangkhalangpaworlasiiwimon omsaakhalaasaa*[51]

71. *Theiwadaa named Phathit (Sun),*

72. *Theiwadaa named Phajan (Moon),*

73. *Theiwadaa named Phakhaan (Mars),*

74. *Theiwadaa named Phaphut (Mercury),*

75. *Theiwadaa named Phahat (Jupiter),*

76. *ตนหนึ่งชื่อว่าพระศุกร์*

77. *ตนหนึ่งชื่อว่าพระเสาร์*

78. *ตนหนึ่งชื่อว่าพระราหู*

79. *ตนหนึ่งชื่อว่าพระเกตุ*

80. *ทั้ง ๙ พระองค์นี้ก็ดี*

81. *คือว่า*

82. *ปู่ทิ้นขึ้น*

83. *ย่าทิ้นลง*

84. *ถือหม้อยาและถาดฮ่าง*

85. *ตกต้นไม้*

86. *และควายชน*

87. *เสือกิน*

88. *และงูตอด*

89. *ป่วยไข้และช้างแทง*

90. *หนังแข็งเป็นพยาดเกิดเหลือหลาย*

91. *ผอมเหลืองแลคิงส่ม*

92. *ทาดฮ่อนปานไฟเผา*

93. *ก็ให้เจ้าลงมาแก้*

94. *เทวดาผู้ปั้นฮุ่น ก็ให้เจ้าลงมาแก้*

95. *ผู้ปั้นเบ้าหล่อคน ก็ให้เจ้าลงมาแก้*

96. *แม่มดผู้ป้อนข้าวม่าม ก็ให้เจ้าลงมาแก้*

97. *ผู้เจ้าหล่ออูปผี ก็ให้เจ้าลงมาแก้*

98. *นางนีผู้ตัดสายแฮ ก็ให้เจ้าลงมาแก้*

99. *แม่เลี้ยงผู้แผ่สายบือ ก็ให้เจ้าลงมาแก้*

100. *เทวดาเจ้าตนอยู่ภูผาและป่าไม้กะให้เจ้าลงมาแก้*

101. *เทวดาเจ้าตนอยู่ปากถ้ำและเมืองผีกะให้เจ้าลงมาแก้*

102. *เทวดาเจ้าตนอยู่ดอยหลวงและคอกช้างกะให้เจ้าลงมาแก้*

103. *เทวดาเจ้าตนอยู่ดอยก่วงและชมพูกะให้เจ้าลงมาแก้*

104. *ขออัญเชิญเทวดาเจ้าทั้งหลายให้ลงมาพร้อมกันช่วยล่วย*

105. *มาแก้เคราะห์เข็นให้แก่คนผู้นี้เสียเทียวพลันเทอญ*

106. *หมากแข้งสุกคาเคือ*

76. *Theiwadaa named Phasuk (Venus),*

77. *Theiwadaa named Phasau (Saturn),*

78. *Theiwadaa named Pharahuu (Pluto).*

79. *Theiwadaa named Phakaet (Earth),*

80. *I request the presence of these nine virtuous theiwadaa(s).*

81. *The following bad omens:*

82. *Grandfather pushing up,*

83. *Grandmother pushing down,*

84. *Carrying an old herbal pot and a broken tray,*

85. *Falling from the trees,*

86. *Being hit by the buffaloes,*

87. *Being bitten by the tigers,*

88. *Being bitten by the snakes,*

89. *Plagued by fever and being stabbed by the elephants,*

90. *Plagued by rough skin and many worms inside,*

91. *Being skinny, with pale and yellowish skin.*

92. *Physical elements, hot like being burnt by fire,*

93. *I request your presence to assist in this ritual.*

94. *Divine spirit, who makes the pattern, please come down to this kae.*

95. *You, who moulds the pattern, please come down to this kae.*

96. *Witch who feeds us nuggets of rice, please come down to this kae.*

97. *The moulder of the pattern of phii, please come down to this kae.*

98. *Naang Nii who cuts the placenta, please come down to this kae.*[52]

99. *The wet nurse who cuts the umbilical cord, please come down to this kae.*

100. *Divine Spirit, who resides in the mountain and in the forest, please come down to this kae.*

101. *Divine Spirit, who resides in the mouth of the cave and the town of phii, come to this kae.*[53]

102. *You, who reside in the soaring mountain and the elephants enclosure, come down to this kae.*

103. *God, who resides in the spacious peak of Chomphuuthawiip, please come down to this kae.*[54]

104. *I humbly request all divine spirits to gracefully come down here,*

105. *And immediately kae the bad luck of this person today.*

106. *Maak khaeng, left ripe on its stems,*[55]

107. หมากเขือสุกคาขว่น
108. ก็ให้เจ้าลงมาแก้
109. กล้วยอ้อยเหี่ยวเหลืองแดง
110. ก็ให้เจ้าลงมาแก้
111. กล้วยแนนสุกเหลืองหลอด
112. ก็ให้เจ้าลงมาแก้
113. อยู่ฟากน้ำดอยภู
114. ก็ให้เจ้าลงมาแก้
115. ให้เจ้าทั้งหลายพร้อมกันลงมาเสวยยังเครื่องกิยาบูชาฝูงนี้เทอญ
116. *จัตตะโร ธรรมาวุทธิ ศรีสวัสะดี*
117. คิงอ่อนให้เจ้าลงมาสาง
118. คิงบางให้เจ้าลงมาแก้
119. อย่าได้แพ้คิงบาง
120. ให้เจ้าฮาบปานหน้าเขียง
121. ให้เจ้าเพียงปานหน้าต่าง
122. คิงส่มให้เจ้าสง
123. คิงขมให้เจ้าแก้
124. พยาดเกิดเหื่อในคิง ให้เจ้าลงมาแก้
125. ในขันทะสันดานและธาตุไม่ ให้เจ้าลงมาแก้
126. อย่าได้แพ้คิงบาง
127. ให้ฮาบปานหน้าเขียง
128. ให้เพียงปานหน้าต่าง
129. *อมไชยะยันตุทันทะละนา ลันทะเทวดา ปาวิมะตะนีสีมา*
130. ฝ่ายยอดขิดยอดตัดต่อค่อฟ้าค่อเมือง
131. ปูกพูให้เป็นฮาก
132. ปูกหมากให้เป็นใบ
133. กล้วยอ้อยเหี่ยวเหลืองแดง
134. ก็ให้เจ้าลงมาแก้
135. แถนเถ่าผู้ว่าเฝ้ากกแนนให้เจ้าลงมาแก้
136. แถนเลิงและแถนตื้อผู้เจ้าเป็นย่า
137. ก็ให้เจ้าลงมาสืบชาตาให้อ่อนน้อย

107. *Egg plants, left ripe on their twigs,*

108. *Please come down to this kae.*

109. *Withering bananas and sugar cane, red and yellow,*

110. *Please come down to this kae.*

111. *Naen bananas, tiny but yellow and ripe,*[56]

112. *Please come down to this kae.*

113. *Though you are beyond the river, the hill and the mountain,*

114. *Please come down to this kae.*

115. *I am requesting all of you to come down and take this offering.*

116. *Jat taroo thammaa see sawat dii*[57]

117. *I request you to kae this weak body.*

118. *I request you to kae this skinny body.*

119. *Please do not surrender it.*

120. *Make it as smooth as the board of the chopping block.*

121. *Make it as orderly as the windows.*

122. *I request you to wash off the pale skin,*

123. *And to kae the coarse skin.*

124. *I request you to kae the disease that causes the body to perspire.*

125. *I request you to kae the elements of human nature and the elements on fire.*

126. *Do not surrender to being skinny and pale.*

127. *Make the body as smooth as the board of the chopping block.*

128. *Make it as orderly as the windows.*

129. *Om chai ya yantu than thalana lantha theiwadaa paawimatanii siimaa*[58]

130. *Cotton thread, cut and connected to the sky.*[59]

131. *Beetle trees planted but growing only roots.*

132. *Areca trees planted but bearing only leaves.*

133. *Bananas, sugarcane – withering, yellow and red.*

134. *I request you to kae them.*

135. *Old Thaen who guards the birth tree naen, please come down to this kae.*

136. *Thaen Lerng and Thaen Tuee who are the grandmothers,*

137. *Please come down to lengthen the life of this baby,*

138. ให้ค่อยหมั่นเทือละคา

139. แถนลอและแถนตื้อผู้เป็นเจ้าย่า

140. อย่าได้เว้นคะไค

141. ให้เจ้าลงมาสืบชาตาหลานน้อย

142. ให้อิ่นอ้อยในเมืองคน สนละวนฮ่ำฮ้อง

143. เมือเมืองบนเจ้าใหญ่หน้า

144. เมือเมืองฟ้าเจ้าลืมหลัง

145. กกนิ่งเจ้ายังไปแคน

146. กกแนนเจ้าไปซ้าย

147. เมือหลังเจ้าแบกฟ้า

148. เมือหน้าเจ้าแบกขอ

149. เจ้ามาเมือเกิดเมืองฟ้า เจ้าว่ายามบ่อดี

150. เจ้าจึงหนีมาเกิดที่หน้า

151. ผู้อยู่ถ่ายย่อมคองหาเจ้าละนา

152. งัวควายอยู่เต็มคอก

153. สาวชอกใช้เต็มเฮือน

154. ใจเจ้าอย่าได้เบือนทางใหม่

155. ไก่กะตากเทิงเฮือน

156. ลางบ่อดีเจ้าจึงหนีมาเกิด

157. คิงส่มให้เจ้าย้อมฝาง

158. คิงบางให้เจ้าย้อมคั่ง

159. แถนหลวงเจ้าผู้หล่อฮูปคน

160. ฝนตกเจ้าอย่าได้กล่าวเถิงหน้า

161. ฟ้าฮ่องเจ้าอย่าได้กล่าวเถิงหลัง

162. แม่เจ้าอยู่เมืองคนคองถ่าเจ้านา

163. แม่เจ้าปลูกกล้วยอ้อยเป็นหนามแม่นา

164. แม่เจ้าปลูกตานเป็นกิ่งเป็นหมาก

165. แม่หน้าเจ้าว่าชัง

166. แม่หลังเจ้าว่าบ่อดี

167. เจ้าจึงหนีมาเกิด

168. เมืองเพียงอ่อนแอ่น

138. So that he may grow up year for year.

139. Thaen Lor and Thaen Tuee who are the grandmothers,

140. Do not neglect to visit him regularly.

141. Please come down to lengthen the life of your little grandchild,

142. So that he may enjoy the human town, playing and crying.

143. If you go back to the upper town, you will become great in the future.[60]

144. If you go back to the town in the sky, you will forget the past.

145. Your ning tree is swaying.[61]

146. Your naen tree is leaning to the left.

147. Going back, you carry a big knife.

148. Going ahead, you carry a big hook.

149. Born in heaven, you think the time is not auspicious.

150. Thus you decide to be born in the human town.

151. People, waiting, are longing for you.

152. Many buffaloes and cows in the pen.

153. Many young girls in the house.

154. Do not change your mind.

155. Hens cackling inside the house.

156. The bad omens make you flee down to be born.

157. If you look pale, dye your skin with faang.[62]

158. If you look skinny, dye your skin with khang.[63]

159. Thaen Luang, the moulder of human beings.

160. When it rains, do not mention the future.

161. When it thunders, do not mention the past.

162. Your mother in the human town is looking forward to be with you.

163. She grows bananas and sugarcane, but they turn thorny.

164. She grows sugar palms, but they turn out as areca palms, full of twigs.

165. Your stepmother says she hates you.

166. Your previous mother says you are no good.

167. You flee down to be born,

168. In this beautiful and orderly town.

169.	คิงเจ้าอ่อนปานเทา

170.	คิงเจ้าเบาปานนุ่น

171.	กล้วยอ้อยสุกคาเคือ

172.	หมากเขือสุกคาข่วน

173.	ฟ้าใหม่เป็นปีใหม่

174.	ปู่แถนจึงปั้นเบ้าหล่อ

175.	ให้เป็นคนละงอก

176.	ให้เป็นฮูปละแงก

177.	เจ้าจึงแบกเอาลิงเอาลาย

178.	เจ้าจึงไปบายเอาดอมพ่อหมอเฒ่า

179.	เจ้าจึงลงมาดอมพ่อหมอหลวง

180.	แถนจึงยกเอาในเนื้อในเสื้อแถนมา

181.	แล้วจึงลงมาเอาปติสนธิในท้องแม่มัน

182.	ได้ ๒ เดือน ๓ เดือน ๔ เดือน จึงตุ่มหน้า

183.	ได้ ๕ เดือน ๖ เดือน จึงเป็นละงอกละแงก

184.	ได้ ๙ เดือน ๑๐ เดือน จึงออกมาจากท้องแม่มัน

185.	ตกข่วมเป็นผู้ชาย

186.	ตกหงายเป็นแม่ยิง

187.	ถือชื่อเป็นผู้ชาย

188.	ถือสายเป็นแม่ยิง

189.	จึงฮู้แจ้งเมื่อยามมันออก

190.	จึงบอกแจ้งเมื่อยามมันมา

191.	เจ้าจึงลงมาดอมพ่อหมอเฒ่า

192.	เจ้าจึงลงมาดอมเจ้าพ่อหมอหลวง

193.	ว่าเจ้านี้เกิดมาบ่อถึกปี

194.	บ่อถึกเดือน

195.	บ่อถึกยาม

196.	บ่อถึกวัน

197.	บ่อชอบ

198.	คอบผีฮ้ายมาเถิง

199.	ผีเหิงชิงแหนแล่นมาใกล้

169. *Your body is as delicate as watery seed.*

170. *Your body is as light as cotton wool.*

171. *Bananas and sugarcane are neglected, ripe on the branches.*

172. *Eggplants are left ripe on their stems.*

173. *A new sky means a new year.*

174. *Thaen, the grandfather, then moulds the pattern,*

175. *To shape it human*

176. *To reshape it – little by little.*

177. *Thus you carry the pattern.*

178. *Thus you go to the old mor.*

179. *Thus you come to the great mor.*

180. *Thaen bestows you with his flesh and genes.*

181. *In your mother's womb, you are eventually fertilized.*

182. *After 2, 3, 4 months, your grow a face,*

183. *After 5, 6 months, the other parts grow,*

184. *After 9, 10 months, you are delivered.*

185. *If the navel is up, you are male.*

186. *If the navel is down, you are female.*

187. *If the umbilical cord is straight, you are male.*

188. *If the umbilical cord is long, you are female.*

189. *These are known when you are delivered.*

190. *These are known when you arrive.*

191. *Thus you come down to the old mor.*

192. *Thus you come down to the great mor.*

193. *Saying that you were born in the wrong year,*

194. *In the wrong month,*

195. *At the wrong time,*

196. *On the wrong day,*

197. *You are not satisfied,*

198. *The evil ghosts arrive,*[64]

199. *Phii herng runs near.*

200. *ผีไม้แล่นมาตาม*

201. *ผีลักลานแล่นมาหลอก*

202. *ผีนอกบ้านแล่นตูมตาม*

203. *ผีหามเสียป่าช้า*

204. *ผีหน้าก่ำตาเขียว*

205. *ผีเทียวเมืองเมือค่ำ*

206. *ผีหม่ายฮ้าง*

207. *ให้มาเอาเครื่องแก้*

208. *อย่าได้แพ้คิงบาง*

209. *เดือนหกคนหาแอก*

210. *เดือนแปดคนหาไถ*

211. *ลายมือเจ้าเป็นช่าง*

212. *แต่พิจาระนาแล้ว มีฮูปท้าวแลกตา*

213. *มีฮูปหมาแหนแฮฮ้อง*

214. *ทางบกนกเขียนฮ้อง*

215. *ทางฟ้าไก่กะตาก*

216. *เมือกางคืนบ่างลั่วฮ้องเฝ้า*

217. *นกฮูกกูกเอาขวัญ*

218. *แม่เจ้าอยู่เมืองคนคอยถ่า*

219. *ฟ้าฮ้องแผดเสียงวอน*

220. *น้ำถ่วมท่งแวนหนา*

221. *เฮดนายามเดือนเก้า*

222. *แถนเถ่าเฝ่ากกแนน*

223. *นางจันทาผู้เป็นเค้า*

224. *ให้เจ้าลงมาแก้*

225. *เจ้าแม่เลี้ยงผู้แผ่สายบือ*

226. *แม่นมผู้ป้อนเข่า*

227. *ยังอยู่เฝ้าย่อมคองหา*

228. *อาสังสะละกังหุนลูฯ สัวหายยะไชยยันตุโพนโต วุระสาลีสาลอด*
    (ยายเข่าตอก)

229. *ยอดติดยอดต่อก่อฟ้าก่อแนน*

200. *Phii mai runs after.*

201. *Phii laklaan runs to haunt.*

202. *Noisy Phii(s) outside the house,*

203. *Phii(s) in the cemetery,*

204. *Phii with the red face and green eyes,*

205. *Phii(s) frequently coming to town at night,*

206. *Phii(s) of the divorced,*

207. *Please come to take this offering.*

208. *Do not surrender to being skinny and pale.*

209. *On the sixth lunar month, people look for yokes.*[65]

210. *On the eighth lunar month, people look for ploughs.*

211. *Your palms say you are an artist.*

212. *After consideration, however, a pattern of Thaaw Laek Taa appears.*[66]

213. *There is a pattern of a dog snarling.*

214. *On earth, the khian birds are calling.*[67]

215. *In heaven, hens are cackling.*

216. *Coming back at night, the big bats are keeping watch and crying.*

217. *Owls are threatening the khwan.*

218. *Your mother, in the human town, is waiting.*

219. *Thunder rolls unceasingly.*

220. *Flood overflows the rice fields.*

221. *On the ninth lunar month, it is the ploughing time.*

222. *The old thaen who watches over the naen tree,*

223. *Naang Jantha who is the prototype,*

224. *Please come to this kae.*

225. *The midwife who cuts the umbilical cord,*

226. *The wet nurse who feeds the baby,*

227. *They are still waiting for you.*

228. *Om sangsalakanghunluuhunluu suahaayya – chayyayantuphoontoo wulasaaliisaalord.*[68]

   [Not pausing in the chant, the ritual master scatters the roasted un-husked rice.]

229. *Tops after tops connected to the sky and to the naen tree.*[69]

230. ให้เจ้าลงมาแก้ยังชาตาอันนี้

231. คิงอ่อนให้เจ้าสาง

232. คิงบางให้เจ้าแก้

233. ไก่กะตากหนีเห็นให้เจ้าลงมาแก้

234. เคราะห์เข็นมีในเนื้อกะให้เจ้าลงมาแก้

235. พยาดเกิดเหื่ออยู่ในคิงให้เจ้าลงมาแก้

236. ผอมเหลืองและคิงส่มให้เจ้าลงมาแก้

237. เคราะห์ฮ้ายแลลางงูให้เจ้าลงมาแก้

238. ลางหนูและฟานเห่าให้เจ้าลงมาแก้

239. นกไซฮ่องเป็นลางให้เจ้าลงมาแก้

240. ในขันทะสันดานแห่งเจ้าชาตาอันนี้จักมา

241. เป็นฮ่างเป็นหม่ายในเนื้อในคิง

242. ฮาฮ่างแขนท่อคันจ่องให้เจ้าลงมาแก้

243. ผอมเหลืองเป็นพยาดให้เจ้าแก้

244. ให้แก้ดวงชาตาอันนี้

245. *จัดตาโร ธรรมะวุดธิสีสวัสดี ลุกขาธรรมะเตลาสุกขังพุทธัง ธรรมัง สังมัง สั่วหายยะ*

246. *อมลิทธิการปัดหน้า เจ้าฟ้าใหญ่แถนลอเทิงแถนตื้อ*

247. ผู้ชื่อว่าแถนหล่อแถนลอ

248. ให้เจ้าลงมาติดต่ออันยอดชาตาอันนี้

249. ให้หมั่นปั้นเบ้าหล่อเป็นฮูปคน

250. ก็ว่ามื้อนี้วันนี้

251. แถนเถ่าเจ้าทายแนน

252. แถนหลวงเจ้าทายนิ่ง

253. ก็ว่าเสียมื้อนี้วันนี้

254. เลี้ยงลูกฮู่หลอดตาย

255. ก็ให้เจ้าลงมาแก้สามื้อนี้วันนี้

256. ผีตานายฮู่มากวดกินไก่

257. ก็ให้เจ้าหนีเสียมื้อนี้วันนี้

258. ผีฮู่ไล่กินกา

259. ก็ให้เจ้าหนีเสียมื้อนี้วันนี้

230. *Please come to lengthen the life-line of this person.*

231. *If the body is fragile, you should comb it out.* [70]

232. *If the body is skinny, you should kae it.*

233. *Frightened hens cackling, trying to escape the hen – please kae these.* [71]

234. *Bad luck existing in the flesh – please kae it.*

235. *Disease that causes the body to perspire – please kae it.*

236. *Sickly and pale body – please kae it.*

237. *Omens of bad luck and snakes – please kae it.*

238. *Omens of rats and barking deer – please kae it.*

239. *Bad omen of the bird sai crying – please kae it.* [72]

240. *Elements of human nature of this life – please come.*

241. *Separated, divorced in flesh and body.*

242. *If the arms, separated, are as big as the handle of the ladle – please kae it.*

243. *Skinny, pale, and plagued by worms – please kae it.*

244. *For the sake of the owner of this life.*

245. *Jattaloo thamma wuthisiisawatdii lukkhaathammateilaasukkhang phuthang thammang sangkhang suahaayya.*

246. *Om – king of Thaen, Thaen Lor, and Thaen Tue*

247. *And you who are known as Thaen Lor and Thaen Lor* [73]

248. *Please come down to connect the birth line today.*

249. *To mould industriously the pattern of human beings,*

250. *Please do it today.*

251. *The old Thaen who must interpret the naen tree,*

252. *The great Thaen who must interpret the ning tree,*

253. *It should be done today.*

254. *Raising an easy child who dies prematurely;*

255. *Please come down to kae it on this particular day.*

256. *Phii Taanaay, knowing, coming to eat the chickens;*

257. *On this particular day you will be chased away.*

258. *The ghost, knowing, hunting for crows;*

259. *On this particular day you will be chased away.*

260. ผีอยู่นาฮู่ให้เจ็บท้อง

261. ก็ให้เจ้าหนีเสียมื้อนี้วันนี้

262. ผีพี่น้องฮู่มายาม

263. ก็ให้เจ้าหนีเสียมื้อนี้วันนี้

264. อมสั่วยะสั่วหาย

265. บัดนี้ข่อยจักเชิญเอาหูละมาน

266. ผู้มีลิดทีมาก

267. ให้มานาบเคราะห์หนี

268. ให้มาตีเคราะห์แล่น

269. ไปอยู่ฟากน้ำคุงคาพุ้นเยอ

270. กูบอกแล้วศรแก้วกูจักยิง

271. ฆ้อนสั้นกูจักตี

272. ฆ้อนฮีกูจักฟาด

273. ให้สูล้มลอดตายกองกันไป

274. เป็นดั่งทรายไหลแล้ว

275. สูบ่อหนี

276. กูจักจับเอาแม่กำเลิดมาใส่คอกทอง

277. ให้สูปองหนีบ่อมีได้

278. ให้สูฮ่องไห่อยู่ลีลันลีลัน

279. หนีเนอ

280. ให้สูหนีเมือเมืองบนดั่งเก่า

281. ให้สูเต้ากันสู่เมืองหลัง

282. แกงส่ม

283. กูสิไปวาน

284. แกงหวาน

285. กูสิไปผอก

286. มีทั้งเหมี่ยงและส่อมช้อนกูก็มี

287. น้ำหอมและเหล้าใส่กระบอก

288. ของกูก็มี

289. เป็ดใส่ข่องจ่องแจ่ง ไก่ใส่กระบอก

290. ของกูก็มี

260. *The ghost in the rice field, knowing, and causing pain in the stomach;*

261. *On this particular day you will be chased away.*

262. *The ghosts of the relatives, knowing, coming to visit;*

263. *On this particular day you will be chased away.*

264. *Om - all evils be gone.*

265. *On this occasion, I humbly request the presence of Huulamaan*[74]

266. *Who possesses supernatural power,*

267. *To drive away the bad luck,*

268. *To strike away the bad luck,*

269. *Beyond the Khongkhaa river.*[75]

270. *I have stated that my shiny arrow will shoot,*[76]

271. *My short hammer will hit,*

272. *My oblong hammer will strike,*

273. *To massacre you, scattering you in piles*

274. *Like sand in the dry season.*

275. *If you do not escape,*

276. *I shall catch Mae Kamlerd and put her in the golden cage.*

277. *To make you unable to escape as intended,*

278. *To make you sob and cry.*

279. *Run away now.*

280. *Return to the upper home where you lived.*

281. *Return to your previous home.*

282. *When I cook the sour curry,*

283. *I shall ask for your favour.*

284. *When I cook the sweet curry.*

285. *I shall bestow it to you.*

286. *Both miang, forks and spoons I have here.*[77]

287. *Scented water and whisky in a bamboo jar,*

288. *I have, too.*

289. *Duck in the swaying basket, chicken in a bamboo rod,*

290. *I have, too.*

291. อันนี้แม่นแตงและเต้า

292. อันนี้แม่นกะเช่าและกะบุง

293. อันนี้แม่นทุงและพัด

294. อันนี้แม่นสาดและวี

295. อันนี้แม่นปลีและกล้วย

296. อันนี้แม่นถ่วยและหมากเขือ

297. อันนี้แม่นเทียนและธูป

298. อันนี้ปั้นฮูปไว้ตางตน

299. อันนี้ปั้นฮูปคนไว้ตางชื่อ

300. อันนี้แม่นแพรตางเนื้อ

301. อันนี้แม่นเสื่อตางคิง

302. ให้มาเอาเยอ

303. ของกูมีทุกสิ่ง

304. ซิงๆหน่าน่างแถน

305. แหวนตันและต่างโค่ง

306. ของกูก็มี

307. ทงหอและขั้นใดแก้ว

308. ของกูก็มี

309. กูแต่งแล้วจึงยอ

310. เอามาถวย

311. ซวยเงินเลียงพาน

312. บ่วงปิ่นแก้วและหวีพันทอง

313. ของกูมีพรั่งพร้อม

314. ขออย่าให้คนผู้นี้อย่าได้เดือดฮ่อนนอนตาย

315. กายฮ่อยปี สูอย่ามาพ่อ

316. สูลงมาพ่อ

317. น้ำบ่อแก้วกูแช่ด้วยหมากส้มป่อยและหมากส้มดง

318. กูปงลงใส่หัวสู

319. บัดนี้ อมสั่วฮับสั่วหาย

320. บัดนี้กูจักเชิญเอาแถนใหญ่เจ้าทั้งปวง

321. ให้ลงมาปัดขอด

291. *Here is a cucumber and a gourd.*

292. *Here is a small basket and a bigger basket.*

293. *Here is a flag and a fan.*

294. *Here is a mat and another fan.*

295. *Here are the bananas and their cluster of flowers.*

296. *Here are the cups and eggplants.*

297. *Here are incense sticks and candles.*

298. *Here are the replicas representing the human self.*

299. *Here are the replicas representing the human name.*

300. *Here is the cloth representing the flesh.*

301. *Here are the clothes representing the body.*

302. *Please come to take them all.*

303. *I have everything.*

304. *All fresh and good in front of Naang Thaen,*

305. *Solid rings and earrings,*

306. *I have them.*

307. *This lofty container with its bright stairs,*[78]

308. *I have it.*

309. *I have decorated it and carry it*

310. *To bestow it to you.*

311. *Well-arranged, money on the tray,*

312. *Spoons, beautiful pins and a gold-plaited comb,*

313. *I have everything ready.*

314. *I simply demand that this person be no longer in trouble.*

315. *During these hundred years and more, do not come across.*

316. *If you dare to come,*

317. *In the water of this glassy well, I have put both sompory and somdong.*[79]

318. *I shall pour it over your head.*

319. *Now, all evils be gone.*

320. *On this occasion, I shall invite all the great Thaen*

321. *To wipe away the bad luck,*

322. ลงมาลอดชั้นกลาง

323. ลงมาปะติสนธ์ อนตาย เชิญอ่อนน้อย

324. ให้เจ้าลงมาแก้

325. พยาดเกิดเหื่ออยู่แฮมปี

326. ให้เจ้าลงมาแก้

327. ถือหม้อยาและถาดฮ่าง

328. ให้เจ้าลงมาแก้

329. ฝันฮ่ายแม่นนอนกลางคืนกลางวัน

330. ให้เจ้าลงมาแก้

331. คิงเหลืองปานกล้วยบ่ม

332. ให้เจ้าลงมาแก้

333. นมสี่เต้าฮูปเขดขวง

334. ให้เจ้าลงมาแก้

335. เป็นปานดำปานแดง

336. ให้เจ้าลงมาแก้เสียมื้อนี้วันนี้

337. สายเข็ญตกกลางท่อง

338. สายฟ้าต้องกลางนา

339. ให้เจ้าแก้เสียมื้อนี้วันนี้

340. แก้ทั้งนมเป็นงา ฮู่แท่งลูกหลอด

341. แก้เสียมื้อนี้วันนี้

342. แก้ทั้งตะแหล็วหลวงจับหน้าผาก

343. เพิ่นว่าคนขวง

344. แก้เสียมื้อนี้วันนี้

345. แก้ทั้งได้เฮียนมนยำยาแฝก

346. แก้เสียวันนี้

347. แก้ทั้งยาแฝกช้างและนางนี

348. แก้เสียวันนี้

349. อมต่อฮับต่อหาย

350. อมหมากน้ำเต้าปุงหน่วยท่อเล่า

351. เค่าฮากมันท่อเขาสุเมร

352. เครือมันท่อเขาสีนีโนลาด

322. *To walk under the middle tier.*[80]

323. *Many are still born.*

324. *Please come down to this kae.*

325. *The disease causing fever for over a year,*

326. *Please come down to this kae.*

327. *You with the broken herbal pots and the old tray,*

328. *Please come down to this kae.*

329. *The bad dreams of day and night,*

330. *Please come down to this kae.*

331. *Skin as pale as ripened bananas,*

332. *Please come down to this kae.*

333. *The bad breasts with four nipples,*

334. *Please come down to this kae.*

335. *Birthmarks, black and red,*

336. *Please come down to this kae.*

337. *Weaving thread dropping in the middle of the room;*

338. *Flash of lightning striking in the middle of the rice fields;*

339. *Please come to kae it on this particular day.*

340. *Husk-like breasts, miscarriage, and premature birth,*

341. *Please kae it today.*

342. *The whorl in the forehead,*

343. *Said to be the mark of a troublesome person,*

344. *Please kae it today.*

345. *The learning of black magic and spell throwing,*

346. *Please kae it today.*

347. *And the black magic of the elephants and that of Naang Nii,*[81]

348. *Please kae it today.*

349. *Om – connect and disconnect.*

350. *The gourd bearing fruit as big as a barn,*

351. *Its root as big as the Sumein mountain,*[82]

352. *Its creeping stem as large as the Siiniinoolaat mountain.*[83]

353. ย่าง่ามเจ้าผู้ปลูกกกแนน

354. ขอให้เจ้าลงมาติดต่ออย่าช้า

355. ยังยอดชาตาหากมาขาด

356. ให้ย่าง่ามเจ้าสืบให้ดี

357. ให้เจ้าไปเอาน้ำเต้าแก้วนำพญาอินทร์

358. ยอหลั่งหดคนเถ่าสำปานเล่าเป็นสาว

359. นมจูมจาวใส่ส่อง

360. หดคนหลังค่อมกะให้เลาคืนดี

361. ขอให้ย่าง่ามเจ้าลงมาแก้เยอ

362. แก้ทั้งเคราะห์เข็นนอนตายทุกสิ่ง

363. ฟ้าวตาลมิ่งกกแนน

364. ให้ย่าง่ามเจ้าลงมาแก้

365. หมาสวงเฝ้ากกนิ่ง

366. ให้ย่าง่ามเจ้าลงมาแก้

367. หนึ่งเข่าเหลืองเป็นเลือด

368. ให้ย่าง่ามเจ้าลงมาแก้

369. เลือดฮ่ายตกถึกคิง

370. ให้ย่าง่ามเจ้าลงมาแก้

371. ลางงูและปิงไต่

372. ให้เจ้าลงมาแก้

373. เคราะห์เกิดใหม่เห็นหนอน

374. ให้เจ้าแก้

375. ย่าเจ้าเหงานอนอยู่ถึกดิน

376. ก็ให้เจ้าลงมาแก้

377. ป่วยเฮื่ออยู่ฮามปี

378. ให้เจ้าลงมาแก้

379. นอนกลางคืนฮู่เขี้ยวปาก

380. ให้เจ้าลงมาแก้

381. เอาหน้าผากเป็นฮูปูงชวง

382. ให้เจ้าลงมาแก้

383. ขวัญหัวเจ้าคืนไปกินเหล่า

353.   Grandmother Ngaam, grower of the naen tree,

354.   Please come immediately to ensure the connection.

355.   If the line of birth is broken,

356.   Please re-connect it with care.

357.   Please go to the god Indra, and take his beautiful pot.

358.   Pour from it over the old; the old will become young,

359.   With blooming and shining breasts.

360.   Pour from it over the hunchback; so he will become normal.

361.   Please, Grandmother Ngaam, come to this rite.

362.   Of all the bad luck causing death,

363.   Coconuts and sugar palms disturbing the naen tree,

364.   Please, Grandmother Ngaam, come down to this kae.

365.   The dog suang watching the naen tree,[84]

366.   Please Grandmother Ngaam, come down to this kae.

367.   Steamed rice turning yellow and bloodlike,

368.   Please, Grandmother Ngaam, come down to this kae.

369.   Bad blood dropping on the body,

370.   Please, Grandmother Ngaam, come down to this kae.

371.   Bad omens of snakes and creeping leeches,

372.   Please come down to this kae.

373.   Bad luck of the newborn baby seeing worms,

374.   Please kae it.

375.   Your grandmother being drowsy and falling to the ground,

376.   Let it be kaed.

377.   Continuing illness through many years,

378.   Please come down to this kae.

379.   Grinding teeth at night,

380.   Please come down to this kae.

381.   Having the shape of a snake suang on the forehead,[85]

382.   Let it be kaed.

383.   The khwan of the head going back to drink whisky,

384. ดอมผีแม่เก่า

385. ก็ให้เจ้าแก้

386. ช้างน้ำแล่นแทงเงา

387. ให้เจ้าแก้

388. หนูซิ่งฮู่เลียปาก

389. ให้เจ้าแก้

390. แม่ไส่แห่งลงมาสูน

391. ให้เจ้าลงมาแก้

392. *พุทธคุณนัง ธรรมคุณนัง สังฆคุณนัง อมสัวหายยะ*

393. บัดนี้ *อมสิทธิการ*

394. ครูอาจารย์กล่าวไว้ให้กู

395. บัดนี้จงมานั่งเหนืออาสนา

396. ด้วยยศศักดิ์บริวารทั้งสองประการ

397. ตามอาจารย์กล่าวไว้แต่ประถมมะหัวที

398. อาราทนาเทวดาเจ้าทั้งหลาย จงมาเอาเครื่องสักกาละบูชา

399. กล้วยอ้อยสดของดี

400. ราทนาทั้งมหาลักษมีเจ้า

401. ขออาจารย์เจ้าผู้แก่กวดเญาหมาย

402. ให้ฮู่ว่าแก้หูลาสาดและตับบอละเมสวน

403. เจ้าตนองอาจ จงมาฮับเอาเครื่องบูชานี้

404. ให้หายเคราะห์โศกอันมาเถิง

405. ค่ำหงำเพิงตามกูแต่ง

406. ว่าตามพรหมชาติอายุขาดเขินบางทุกขนาด

407. เคราะห์มิ่งอย่าเข้ามาแขน

408. เคราะห์แนนอย่าเข้ามาช้าย

409. เคราะห์เจ้าชาตาผู้นี้เฮียวแห่ง

410. ไฝคอแดงบ่อชุ่มบาน

411. ฮดบ่อหอมหวานฮ่วงเฮ้า

412. กกมิ่งเล่า

413. ฮากเข่าบ่อขึ้นดี

414. เคราะห์หลวงหลายปีมีมากในตน

384. *To be with the ghost of your previous mother,*

385. *Let it be kaed.*

386. *The water elephant playing, stabbing its shadow,*

387. *Please kae it.*

388. *The tame sing mouse, licking your lips,*[86]

389. *Please kae it.*

390. *Mae Sai Haeng coming down to make people upset,*[87]

391. *Please come down to this kae.*

392. *By the merits of the Three Gems, all the evils be gone.*

393. *On this occasion, Om Sidthikaan,*[88]

394. *The teachers who have taught me,*

395. *On this occasion, please come kindly to sit on the throne,*

396. *Surrounded by honours and attendants*

397. *As described in the old writings.*

398. *I invite all mighty gods to take this offering.*

399. *Fresh bananas, sugarcane and all excellent items,*

400. *I invite the great goddess Laksaamii.*[89]

401. *I invite my teacher who is experienced in legal knowledge.*

402. *To let him know that everything is in accordance with the wisdom of astrology and Borlameisuan*[90]

403. *Mighty gods, please come and take this offering.*

404. *To be rid of the bad luck among us*

405. *Hiding in nooks and corners decorated by me.*

406. *According to Phommasaad, the age is short and thin in any way.*[91]

407. *The bad luck of ming, do not hang around.*[92]

408. *The bad luck of naen, do not come near.*

409. *The luck of this life owner is withering.*

410. *The red disagreeable spots in the throat,*

411. *Neither the taste nor smell is sweet.*

412. *The ming tree is sad.*[93]

413. *The roots of the rice do not grow well.*

414. *Great bad luck residing in the body for years*

415. ใจกางวนเดือดฮ่อน
416. โพยพยาดข่อนหากเถิงตน
417. เหตุว่าเทวดาเจ้าทั้งหลายยังทั่วละเทียวไปใน 12 นทีลาด
418. พยาดจึงได้เกิดเถิงถอง
419. เคราะห์ไต่ตองในตน
420. เพื่อว่าชีวิตบ่อยืนยาว
421. แนนใบเหลืองเหี่ยวแห้ง
422. ไฟคอแดงบ่อชุ่ม
423. ขอแก่เทวดาเจ้าทั้งหลาย
424. จ่งมาฮูดสงเจ้าชาตาผู้นี้
425. จิ่งให้มีแนนชื่นบานล้ำเลิศ
426. ประเสริฐกว่าท่านทั้งหลาย
427. เหมือนดั่งพระจันทร์เพ็งงาม 15 ค่ำ
428. บ่อต่ำจากรัศมี
429. เทวดาเจ้าตนอยู่เทิงอากาศทั้งหลาย
430. จงกูนายังชาตาผู้นี้
431. ให้สืบยาวนานอย่าได้ขาด
432. เคราะห์ฮ้ายให้กวดหนีเสียวันนี้
433. เพิ่นใส่ขื่อลำหนา
434. เพิ่นใส่คาลำตั้ว
435. กูจักแก้เสียมื้อนี้วันนี้
436. ทางหน้าเพิ่นใส่กัง
437. ทางหลังเพิ่นใส่แฮ่ว
438. กูจักแก้เสียมื้อนี้วันนี้
439. ฝนตกเจ้าอย่าได้ปิ่นหน้า
440. ฟ้าฮ่องเจ้าอย่าได้อ่าวคะเนิงเถิง
441. อมสัวหายยะ
442. *อมสิทธิมหาไชยะ ทำโมอิติปิโสภะควา นาลังนาลา อิติปิโสภะควา สัมพัง สัมพะทุทะทุทัง ทุนังสัพเพ เวโลวินาสันตุ กุสาเลเม มายา ทุละจิตตะ ปริตเดไชยะวะลุกขามุเลวะ ธัมมัสสะวะสาฯ วะเตวะนาทุเต อิติปิโสภะคะวา อาระหัง สัมมาสัมพุทโธ*

415. *Worrying and troubling the mind.*

416. *All diseases, if there are any, in the body.*

417. *The fact is that all the gods are still wandering around the twelve spacious rivers.*

418. *Many diseases occur in the body.*

419. *Bad luck swarms in the body.*

420. *Life is not meant to be long.*

421. *The leaves of the naen tree turn yellow and withering.*

422. *The throat is red and parched.*

423. *May all mighty gods*

424. *Come to water the owner of this life.*

425. *To make the naen tree cheerful, superior,*

426. *More prosperous than any other tree.*

427. *Like the full moon of the fifteenth night*

428. *That has never been beneath the rays of the sun.*[94]

429. *Theiwadaa(s) who are in the sky above,*

430. *May you come to the life of this person,*

431. *To everlastingly lengthen it.*

432. *Let the bad luck be chased far away.*

433. *Chained to a thick piece of wood,*

434. *Shackled to a beautiful piece of wood,*

435. *I shall kae it on this particular day.*

436. *In the front, there are traps.*

437. *At the back, there are snares.*

438. *I shall kae it today.*

439. *When there is rain, keep your face straight.*

440. *When there is thunder, suppress your yearning.*

441. *May all evils disappear.*

442. *Om sidthi mahaachaiya thammoo itipisoo phakhawaa naalang naalaa itipisoo phakhawaa samphang sampha thuthathuthang thunangsamphei weiloowinaasantu kusaaleimei maayaa thula jidta paritteichaiya walukkhaa muleiwa thammatsawasaa thammatsawasaa wateiwanaathutei itipisoo phakhawaa aarahangsammaasamphudthoo*

443. *อมสิทธิการ*

444. *กูกู่แม่นแถนหลวงฟ้าก่อเค้าก่อแนน*

445. *ให้เจ้าลงมา*

446. *ย้ายนิ่งย้ายแนนให้แก่สองผัวเมียนี้*

447. *กูเฮียกหาท้าวพญา เทพดา นาคา เทพบุตร ครุฑา*

448. *พระอาทิตย์ พระจันทร์ พระคาร พระพุทธ พระหัส พระศุกร์ พระเสาร์ พระราหู พระลัคณา เทวดาเจ้าทั้งหลาย*

449. *เทวดาเจ้าทั้งหลาย จ่งพร้อมกันลงมา*

450. *เสวยเครื่องบูชาแห่งเจ้าชาตาอันนี้ให้แล้ว*

451. *ขอนใหญ่ล้มทับทาง*

452. *ให้เจ้าลงมาเกิดเมืองเพียงดังเก่า*

453. *จัตตาโร ทัมมา มังคะละ หูลู*

454. *เทวดาตนอยู่ภูเขาและป่าไม้*

455. *ปากถ้ำและเมืองผี*

456. *ลุกขาเทวดาเจ้าทั้งหลาย*

457. *เทวดาหกหมื่นเทวดา*

458. *ภุมมาเทวดา ลุกขาเทวดา นาโมนาโถ นาคาครุฑา*

459. *ปากห้วยและลาวเขา*

460. *ให้พร้อมกันลงมาเสวยยังเครื่องทิพย์บูชาเจ้าชาตาอันนี้*

461. *ให้เคราะห์เข็ญผูกนี้ ให้หายเสียทุกเมื่อเทอญ*

462. *บัดนี้ข่อยขออัญเชิญแถนหลวง*

463. *เจ้าผู้แก้แฮธาตุเหลืองแต่น้อย*

464. *ให้มาแก้เคราะห์เข็ญอันนี้ให้หายเสีย*

465. *แก้ทั้งเคราะห์สองผัวเมียเลี้ยงลูกยาก*

466. *เลี้ยงลูกยิงให้ลอดตาย*

467. *เลี้ยงลูกชายให้เจ้าใหญ่หน้า*

468. *เลี้ยงลูกหล่าให้ใหญ่เพียงลุง*

469. *ให้สูงเพียงฟ้า*

470. *บาดเฮดนาให้หมานเข่า*

471. *ทั้งพ่อแม่ลูกเต้าและหลานเหลน*

472. *ให้งามล่วยช่วย*

443. *Om – all the success.*

444. *I call the presence of the great thaen who makes and builds the naen.*

445. *To come down*

446. *And move the naen of this husband and wife.*

447. *I call the presence of the great gods, nagas, theiwadaa(s), and Garuda.*

448. *The Sun, the Moon, Mars, Mercury, Jupiter, Venus, Saturn, Pluto, and the Earth*

449. *Theiwadaa(s), please come down all*

450. *To take the offering bestowed to you by the owner of this life.*

451. *Though a huge log is blocking you the way,*

452. *Please come down to be born in this orderly town as intended.*

453. *Jadtaaroo thammaa mangkhala huuluu*

454. *Theiwadaa(s), who reside in the mountain and forest,*

455. *In the cave and the town of ghosts.*

456. *All the theiwadaa(s), living in the trees.*

457. *Sixty thousand theiwadaa(s).*

458. *The earth god whom one can depend on, Nagas and Garudas,*

459. *The beginning of the stream and the strip of the hill,*

460. *Please come down to take the divine offering of this life owner.*

461. *To make disappear forever the bad luck of this person.*

462. *On this occasion, I request the presence of Thaen Luang*

463. *Who kae the placenta, the yellow element of birth.*

464. *The bad luck will be chased away today.*

465. *The bad luck of the husband and wife raising the child with difficulty will be chased away today.*

466. *Having born a child, it will not die at birth.*

467. *Having born a son, he will be healthy.*

468. *Having born the youngest among siblings, he will be as tall as his uncle,*

469. *As tall as the sky.*

470. *If planting rice, the harvest will be abundant.*

471. *Parents, children, grandchildren and great-grandchildren,*

472. *May they all be good-looking.*

473. *บัดนี้ให้พร้อมกัน*

474. *ปลูกกล้วยนิ่งอย่าได้แคน*

475. *ปลูกกล้วยแนนอย่าได้ช่าย*

476. *ปลูกกล้วยตีบแม่น่าว่าหน่วยลีบก็ให้หวาน*

477. *ให้มีอาจารย์เจ้าผู้ฉลาด*

478. *คองธรรมเป็นพี่น้องอ้อมเฮือน*

479. *ให้มีงัวควายหลายลื่นเก่า*

480. *ให้มีเยียเข่าเปลือกเข่าสารหลายแสนเล่า*

481. *ขออัญเชิญแถนหลวง เจ้าผู้ใหญ่*

482. *ลงมาแก้เคราะห์ฮ่างหม่าย สองผัวเมียเจ้าเฮือนนี้ให้หายเสีย*

483. *ทุกคนทุกคนผู้ข้าเทอญ*

484. *อิมัสะมิง กาเย เกษา ผม โลมา ขน นขา เล็บ ทันตา แข่ว*
    ตะโจ หนัง มังสัง เนื้อ นะหะลู เอ็น อัตถี กระดูก มิงสัง สมอง
    หากัง หมากไข่หลัง หัตถะยัง หมากหัวใจ ยะกะนัง ตับ
    กิโลมะกัง ผังผืด ปิหากัง ม่าม สัพพะสัง ปอด อันตัง ไส้ใหญ่
    อัดทะคะยัง ไส้น้อย อุตาริยัง อาหารใหม่ กาลิดสัง อาหารเก่า
    ปิดตัง น้ำดี เสมหัง น้ำเสลด ปุปโพ น้ำหนอง โลหิตตัง น้ำเลือด
    เสโท น้ำเหื่อ เมโท น้ำใค อัดดูลู น้ำตา อัดสา น้ำมันเหลว
    เขโล น้ำลาย สิงคายิกา น้ำมูก ระสิกา น้ำเหลือง มุตตัง น้ำมูด
    มัตถะเก กระโบงหัว มัตถะลุงคัง กระหมอง ขันติ ติงทวด ติงสาคะลัง

485. *อายุวัฒโก ธนวัฒโก สิริวัฒโก พละวัฒโก วัณณวัฒโก สุขวัฒโก โหตุสัพพะนา*

473. *Now please come all.*

474. *Growing a banana tree, it will not grow on a slant.*

475. *Growing a naen tree, it will not sway to the left.*

476. *Growing the tiip banana, tiny as they are, but sweet.*[95]

477. *May you have a knowledgeable teacher.*

478. *Morally upright are your relatives.*

479. *May you have more buffaloes and cows than ever before.*

480. *May you have ten thousand barns of rice, husked and unhusked.*

481. *I humbly request the greatest among the thaen*

482. *To eliminate the bad luck, the broken luck of this couple*

483. *And of us all.*

484. *The uncertainty of physical organs: hair, skin, body hair, nails, teeth, skin, muscles, tendons, bones, cerebrum, testis, heart, liver, lung, intestine, small intestine, old food, new food, bile, sputum, pus, blood, sweat, tears, fat, saliva, nasal mucus, vomit and skull.*

485. *May everyone be blessed.*

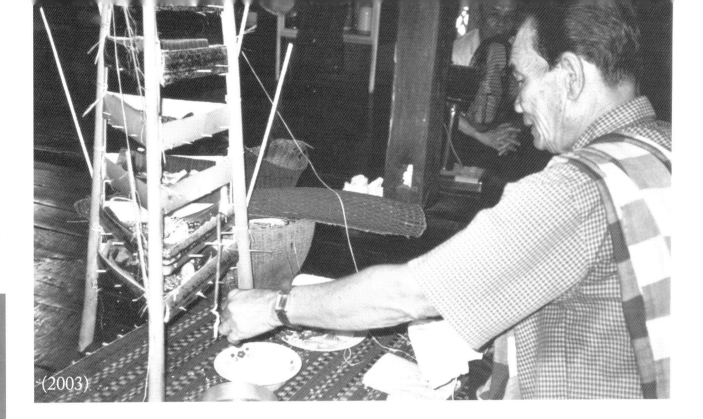

(2003)

สักเค กาเมจะรูเป สิริสิขารัตตะเต จันตะลิเข
วิมาเน ทิเปรัตเถจะคาเม ตะลูวะนะคะหะเน
เคหาวะตุงเห เคเต พรหมาจะยันตุเทวา
สะละทะละวิสะเมยะขา คันทะยะขาปะนาคา
ติดทันตาสันติเก ยังมุนีวะละวะจะนัง
สาทุโวเมสุนันตุ
ธัมมะสะวะนะกะโล อะยัมปะทันตา (3 ครั้ง)

นโมตัสสะ ภควโต อรหโต สัมมาสัมพุทธตัสสะ
นโมตัสสะ ภควโต อรหโต สัมมาสัมพุทธตัสสะ
นโมตัสสะ ภควโต อรหโต สัมมาสัมพุทธตัสสะ

1.   เทวบุตร เทวดา พญาอินทร์ พญาพรหม นาค ครุฑ
2.   มื้อนี้มีเหตุจั่งขานมีการจั่งเฮียก
3.   จั่งได้แต่งขันข้าวตอกดอกไม้

RITUAL TEXTS

Taengkae Mae Kamlerd

This palm leaf manuscript belonged to Phor Jampii. He had inherited the book from his father. The original palm leaf was written mainly in *tai noi* with some words and sentences written in *nangsuee tham*.

In the case of a sudden childbirth there may not be time to perform the *taengkae maemaan* before the birth. In such cases, it is possible to perform a special rite with the same purpose soon after the birth. After the birth, the rite is called *taengkae mae kamlerd* or often just *kae kamlerd*. The name means an action (*taeng*) that is to deliver from or banish (*kae*), *mae kamlerd*. Besides the prophylactic aim, the *taengkae mae kamlerd* can also be performed if the child has symptoms which the *mor sorng* attributes to *mae kamlerd*. It can therefore be performed throughout the childhood.

Like the *taengkae maemaan*, this rite starts with a summons to all *theiwaadaa*(s) to come and attend the ceremony, followed by a prayer in Pali:

I humbly request the presence of all deities who reside in any level of Heaven;
The theiwadaa(s) who reside in the mountains, in the air, in the country, in the house,
in the trees and the jungle, who reside in the house compound and the plantation;
The spiritual beings who reside in the water or on land,
whether in places that are far away or near, gather here.
May the virtuous listen to the words of the Supreme Sage.

Now is the time to listen to the Teachings.[96]
Now is the time to listen to the Teachings.
Now is the time to listen to the Teachings.

Namotassa Bhagavato Arahato Sammasambudhtassa[97]
Namotassa Bhagavato Arahato Sammasambudhtassa
Namotassa Bhagavato Arahato Sammasambudhtassa

1.   *All theiwadaa(s), Indra, Bhrama, God of the rivers, Naga, and Garuda.*

2.   *On this occasion, I have a special reason to call your names.*

3.   *Decorating a bowl with roasted unhusked rice and flowers*

4. ฮ้องป่าวกล่าวสักเค

5. เอาคุณเทวบุตรเทวดาเจ้าทั้งหลาย

6. ลงมาย่ำง่ำค่ำซู

7. มื้อนี้ผู้ข่าจะได้แต่งแก้กำเลิดให้เด็กน้อยผู้นี้แหละ

8. เกิดเย็นเห็นฟ้ามาแล้วแม่เก่าแม่หลังเขาบ่อลืม

9. ผู้ข่าจึงได้แต่งเครื่องสักการะบูชา มาขอถวยแก่เทวดา แล้วสิได้แต่งแก้ให้เด็กน้อยผู้นี้

10. ขอให้ส่วงหายไว

11. ไข่หายเสียแต่มื้อนี้วันนี้ผู้ข้าเทอญ

12. *นโมตัสสะ ภควโต อรหโต สัมมาสัมพุทธตัสสะ*

13. *นโมตัสสะ ภควโต อรหโต สัมมาสัมพุทธตัสสะ*

14. *นโมตัสสะ ภควโต อรหโต สัมมาสัมพุทธตัสสะ*

15. *สิทธิการ ครูบาอาจารย์ ให้กูไปจ่มมนอยู่เทิงฟ้า*

16. ๓ คืนน้ำจึงบก

17. ๖ คืนน้ำจึ่งแห้ง

18. เมื่อเห็นน้ำแห้งแล้ว อยู่เมืองฟ้าว่าบ่อแก่น

19. แล่นเมืองฟ้าว่าบ่อเพียง

20. เจ้าจึงตกลงมาเมืองลุ่ม

21. หาแม่เกิดเอากำเลิดดอมตน

22. เอาปะติสนธิ์ในท้องแม่น้อยหนึ่ง แล้วจึงหายเลือด

23. ได้เดือนหนึ่งจึงละงอก

24. ได้สิบเดือนจึงออกมา

25. ตกข่วมเป็นผู้ชาย

26. ตกหงายเป็นผู้ยิง

27. ถือชื่อเป็นผู้ชาย

28. ถือสายเป็นผู้ยิง

29. *โอม ติงๆ ตังๆ*

30. กูจักเชิญแถนหลวงลงมาช่อยแก้ดอมเยอ

31. แถนหลวงเจ้าผู้ปั้นหล่อฮูปคน

32. ให้เจ้าลงมาช่อยแก้ดอมเยอ

33. แถนเลิงผู้ต่อมไคให้เป็นหน้า

34. ก็ให้ลงมาช่อยแก้ดอมเยอ

4.   *To announce to all, in prayer and worship.*

5.   *I should like to draw on the merit of all deities*

6.   *To support and assist in this rite.*

7.   *Today I shall perform this rite in order for this baby to live happily.*

8.   *After being born, it is not forgotten by its previous mother.*

9.   *I bestow this offering as a sacrifice to the theiwadaa(s) to taengkae for this baby.*

10.   *So that it may quickly recover from sickness.*

11.   *So that it may recover from the fever it is suffering from now.*

12.   *Namotassa Bhagavato Arahato Sammasambudhtassa*[98]

13.   *Namotassa Bhagavato Arahato Sammasambudhtassa*

14.   *Namotassa Bhagavato Arahato Sammasambudhtassa*

15.   *Sidtikarn – my teachers had me pray to the sky above.*[99]

16.   *At the end of the third night, the water had lessened.*

17.   *At the end of the sixth night, the water had run dry.*

18.   *Seeing the water dry, Heaven was no longer a proper place to live, you thought.*

19.   *Neither was Heaven an orderly place.*

20.   *Thus you decided to come down to the lower town,*

21.   *To your new mother, to be born human.*

22.   *Fertilized, staying in your mother's uterus for a while – until the blood all has gone.*

23.   *After one month, you start to grow.*

24.   *After ten months, you are delivered.*[100]

25.   *If the navel is down, you are a boy.*

26.   *If the navel is up, you are a girl.*

27.   *If the umbilical cord is straight, you are male.*

28.   *If the umbical cord is long and linear, you are female.*

29.   *Om, ting ting tang tang.*[101]

30.   *I humbly request the assistance of Thaen Luang;*[102]

31.   *Thaen Luang who moulds the pattern of human beings,*

32.   *Please come.*

33.   *Thaen Lerng who molds an egg to shape a face,*

34.   *Please come down.*

35. *แถนฟ้าผู้เจ้าต่อคอ*

36. *ก็ให้ลงมาซ่อยแก้ดอมเยอ*

37. *แถนลอผู้แปงแขนขัวและแขนซ่าย*

38. *ก็ให้ลงมาซ่อยแก้ดอมเยอ*

39. *แถนผ่ายเจ้าผู้แปงปากและหูตา*

40. *ก็ให้ลงมาซ่อยแก้ดอมเยอ*

41. *แถนพิจารณาผู้แปงแขนขาเพียงฮาบ*

42. *ก็ให้ลงมาซ่อยแก้ดอมเยอ*

43. *แถนผาบเจ้าผู้แปงสม*

44. *ก็ให้ลงมาซ่อยแก้ดอมเยอ*

45. *แถนลมผู้สูบจิตให้เป็นท้าวเป็นนาง*

46. *ให้ลงมาซ่อยแก้ดอมเยอ*

47. *แถนห่าวผู้สูบจิตให้เป็นคน*

48. *ก็ให้ลงมาซ่อยแก้ดอมเยอ*

49. *กูจักแก้ทั้งแม่ตอบซอบนมยาน*

50. *กูจักแก้ทั้งแม่พานลานนมหย่อน*

51. *กูจักแก้ทั้งแม่ก่อนกี้แต่ภายหลัง*

52. *กูจักแก้ทั้งแม่สะลังงังแห่งเที่ยวมาหลอก*

53. *กูจักแก้ทั้งแม่กอกซอกเที่ยวมาหลอกกลางคืน*

54. *กูจักแก้ทั้งแม่นมลืนเหลือกตาใส่*

55. *กูจักแก้ทั้งแม่ใหม่นมยอคอ*

56. *กูจักแก้ทั้งหม่อยาหน่วยเข็ดขวง*

57. *กูจักแก้ทั้งฮากไม้บาดเป็นแสง*

58. *กูจักแก้ทั้งผ้าอ้อมแขงใหลหลอก*

59. *กูจักแก้ทั้งผ้าอ้อมออกเป็นขี้ไก่ขาง*

60. *กูจักแก้ทั้งกางและเม่า*

61. *กูจักแก้ทั้งก้อนเส้าหน่วยแบน*

62. *กูจักแก้ทั้งสะแนนหน่วยแขนห่อย*

63. *กูจักแก้ทั้งหีดคะเยอไอ*

64. *กูจักแก้ทั้งฝดไฟและหมากไม้*

65. *กูจักแก้ทั้งผีไข่และหนาวเลิง*

35. *Thaen Faa who connects the neck,*

36. *Please come down.*

37. *Thaen Lor who builds up the left and right arms,*

38. *Please come down.*

39. *Thaen Phaay who adorns the face with lips, ears, and eyes,*

40. *Please come down.*

41. *Thaen Phijaranaa who reshapes the arms and legs,*

42. *Please come down.*

43. *Thaen Phaab who is responsible for the finishing touches,*

44. *Please come down.*

45. *Thaen Lom who blows at the mind making it a man or a woman,*

46. *Please come down.*

47. *Thaen Haaw who blows at the mind to make it human,*

48. *Please come down.*

49. *I shall kae also Mae Torbsorb, with her drooping breasts.*[103]

50. *I shall kae also Mae Phaanlaan, with her sagging breasts.*

51. *I shall kae also all the mothers in the past.*

52. *I shall kae also Mae Salang Ngang who haunts more frequently.*

53. *I shall kae also Mae Kork Sork who haunts at night.*

54. *I shall kae also Mae Nom Lueen, her unbalanced breasts and her eyeballs upside down.*

55. *I shall kae also the new mother whose breasts are full and bouncing.*

56. *I shall also perform this rite to kae the bad herbal pots.*

57. *I shall also perform this rite to kae the sharp plant root that cuts.*

58. *I shall also perform this rite to kae the diaper so stiff that it makes you talk in your sleep.*

59. *I shall also perform this rite to kae the diaper so rotten that it turns mouldy.*

60. *I shall also perform this rite to kae the diaper spread or wrapped around the baby.*[104]

61. *I shall also perform this rite to kae the poor stove rock.*[105]

62. *I shall also perform this rite to kae the bamboo bed that is stowed away.*

63. *I shall perform this rite to kae asthma and coughs.*

64. *I shall perform this rite to kae prickly heat and shivering fever.*

65. *I shall also perform this rite to kae fever spells and shivering coldness.*

66. *กูจักแก้ทั้งทางเทิงและทางลุ่ม*

67. *กูสิจักเชิญเอาแถนหลวงและแถนงึ่มลงมาช่อยแก้*

68. *ทางลุ่มนั้นกูจักเชิญเอาแถนตื้อและนางธรณินลงมาช่อยแก้*

69. *กูจักแก้ทั้งแฮบ่อตก*

70. *กูจักแก้ทั้งพกบ่อหลอด*

71. *กูจักแก้ทั้งลูกอ่อนน่อยคาดมาตาย*

72. *กูจักแก้ทั้งผีพายกุมกินเลือด*

73. *กูจักแก้ทั้งฮ้อนเดือดในขัน*

74. *กูจักแก้ทั้งไข่ดิ้น*

75. *กูจักแก้ทั้งตาเหลือกปิ้นขึ้นเมือเทิง*

76. *กูจักแก้ทั้งผีเขมรและผีห่อ*

77. *กูจักแก้ทั้งย่อและผียวง*

78. *กูจักแก้ทั้งผีพวนและผีม่าน*

79. *กูจักแก้ทั้งผีขาก่านแห่งเทียวมาหลอก*

80. *กูจักแก้ทั้งตานายแหงเทียวมาเยี่ยม*

81. *กูจักแก้ทั้งผีเสียมดวงมันขุดฝังแฮ*

82. *กูจักแก้ทั้งมีดน้อยๆดวงมันแผ่สายบือ*

83. *กูจักแก้ทั้งสะพือหน้าง้ำ*

84. *กูจักแก้ทั้งสะพ้าง้ำตา*

85. *กูจักแก้ทั้งสายสะพายแขนอยู่ฮ่อน อุดอยู่นอนตาย*

86. *กูจักแก้สามื้อนี้วันนี้*

87. *หรือว่านมแม่มันลายเป็นฮูปผีเป้า*

88. *กูจักแก้สามื้อนี้วันนี้*

89. *นมแม่มันเส่าเป็นฮูปผีโพง*

90. *กูจักแก้สามื้อนี้วันนี้*

91. *นมเข็ดขวงเป็นงาช้างเผือก*

92. *กูจักแก้เสียมื้อนี้วันนี้*

93. *นมเป็นเหลือกงูชวง*

94. *กูจักแก้เสียมื้อนี้วันนี้*

95. *นมเป็นคางแลบลิ้น*

96. *กูจักแก้เสียมื้อนี้วันนี้*

66.   *I shall perform this rite to kae both the above and the underneath.*

67.   *And I shall request the presence of Thaen Luang and Thaen Nguem to come down to assist.*

68.   *From below, I shall invite Thaen Tuee and Naang Thoranin, the goddess of Earth, to come.*

69.   *I shall kae, too, the umbilical cord that does not come out with ease.*

70.   *I shall also kae, too, the placenta that is too big.*

71.   *I shall kae the baby who dies unexpectedly at birth.*

72.   *I shall kae the Phii Phaay that greedily sucks the blood.*

73.   *I shall kae the heat boiling in the water bowl.*

74.   *I shall kae the convulsion.*

75.   *I shall kae the eyeballs that turn upside to the above.*

76.   *I shall kae the ghosts of Khmer and of Hor.*[106]

77.   *I shall kae the ghosts of Yor and Yuan.*[107]

78.   *I shall kae the ghosts of Phuan and Maan.*[108]

79.   *I shall kae the ghost with tattooed legs that comes around more frequently.*[109]

80.   *I shall kae the Phii Taa Naay coming here more frequently.*[110]

81.   *I shall kae the ghost of the spade that is used to dig the burial site of the placenta.*

82.   *I shall kae the tiny knife that is used for cutting the umbilical cord.*

83.   *I shall kae Mae Saphuee whose face is jutting out.*[111]

84.   *I shall kae Mae Sapham whose eyes are jutting out.*[112]

85.   *I shall kae even the strings of the cradle with the heat inside and the rash it causes.*

86.   *I shall destroy them on this particular day.*

87.   *Or, if the mother's breasts have the shape of Phii Pau,*[113]

88.   *I shall kae it on this particular day.*

89.   *The sad breasts of the mother that have the shape of Phii Phoong.*[114]

90.   *I shall kae on this particular day.*

91.   *The unlucky breasts that look like a white elephant's husks,*

92.   *I shall kae on this particular day.*

93.   *The breasts that have patterns of the snake suang*[115]

94.   *I shall kae on this particular day.*

95.   *The breasts that look like chins with tongues drawn out.*

96.   *I shall kae on this particular day.*

97. ขวนนมปิ้นเป็นตา

98. กูจักแก้เสียมื้อนี้วันนี้

99. นมยอคอตอดลูก

100. กูจักแก้เสียมื้อนี้วันนี้

101. กูจักแก้ทั้งนาค ๓ หัว

102. กูจักแก้ทั้งสองผัวเมียเลี้ยงลูกยิ่งยาก

103. กูจักแก้ทั้งผากผีเฮด

104. กูจักแก้ด้วยคาถาพระยาแถนแม่นตาทอกว่า

105. *อะๆ วะลุงลังมัดชัง สวาหม อมวะๆ อมวันๆ มะตังละตัง*

    (ให้ยายเข่าตอก)

106. ตั้งเกี้ยวซ้ายแห่งเทียวมา

107. กูจักแก้เสียมื้อนี้วันนี้

108. ผีตานายแห่งเที่ยวมาหลอก

109. กูจักแก้เสียมื้อนี้วันนี้

110. แขนแม่ก่ำเป็นงา

111. กูจักแก้เสียมื้อนี้วันนี้

112. แขนแม่ชาปักง่อน

113. กูจักแก้เสียมื้อนี้วันนี้

114. กูแก้แล้วสูอย่าสุมา

115. ทางไฮ่นั้นกูจักใส่ขวกหนามคา

116. ทางนานั้นกูจักใส่เฝือกเก้าล้าน

117. ทางบ้านนั้นกูจักใส่หลาวคันเหล็ก

118. ทางผักตูเฮือนกูจักใส่ขวกหลวง

119. ขวนฟ้าผ่าหัวผี ให้ทลายให้กองกันตายอเนกนอง

120. ป่องเอี้ยมนั้น กูจักใส่หลาวเพ็ดบ่วงบาดพญาอินทร์

121. ทางหลวงกูสิใส่หน่วงบ่วงน้อยๆฮัดคอผี

122. ผีย่าแห่งเทียวมาเยี่ยมหลาย ก็ซ้ำสิถึกตาย

123. ผีตานายแห่งเที่ยวมากินเข่าก็ซ้ำสิถึกตาย

124. ผีตัวมันแห่งตอมกินเลือดก็ซ้ำสิถึกตาย

125. กูจักแก้ทั้งเดือดฮ้อน นอนอนละหนในเมืองคนทะแหล่งหล่า

97. *The nipples that look like eyes,*

98. *I shall kae on this particular day.*

99. *The breasts that look like necks raised to nibble at the baby,*

100. *I shall kae on this particular day.*

101. *I shall kae also the three-headed Naga.*

102. *I shall kae the married couple who bring up their children with much difficulty.*

103. *I shall kae all the phii that haunt.*

104. *I shall destroy them with the magic words of the great Thaen just like Grandfather Thork:*

105. *A a walunglangmatsang sawaahom omwa omwa omwan omwan matanglatang.*[116]

[chanting and scattering the roasted unhusked rice]

106. *Scattering this rice to the left, the phii that wanders even more frequently,*

107. *I shall kae on this particular day.*

108. *Phii Taanaay who comes more often to tease us,*

109. *I shall kae on this particular day.*

110. *The mother's arms that have become black like sesame,*

111. *I shall kae on this particular day.*

112. *The mother's arms that become numb, painful up to the nape,*

113. *I shall kae on this particular day.*

114. *Now that I have performed this kae, shall you dare to come?*

115. *The path to the plantation, I shall obstruct with thorns.*

116. *On the path to the ricefield, I shall put nine million rods.*[117]

117. *On the path to the house I shall put pointed metal pikes.*

118. *On the doors, I shall put huge barbs,*

119. *And the heavenly axe I shall use to chop off the phii's heads so that they may die in piles and piles.*

120. *On the windows, I shall put the diamond spear and the loop of Indra.*[118]

121. *On the main path, I shall put tiny loops fastened to strangle the phii's heads.*

122. *Phii Grandma coming here more often to visit will be trapped to death.*

123. *Phii Taanaay coming here more often to eat rice will be trapped to death.*

124. *The phii swarming more frequently to suck blood will be trapped to death.*

125. *I shall kae all the trouble, the turmoil overall in the town.*

126. *เคราะห์อันจักมาต่อหน้าและภายหลัง ก็ให้หายเสียมื้อนี้วันนี้*

127. *เคราะห์คิงไฟใหม่ย้าว ก็ให้หายเสียมื้อนี้วันนี้*

128. *เคราะห์หมากพร้าวหล่นจากแขง ก็ให้หายเสียมื้อนี้วันนี้*

129. *เคราะห์เข่าดำเข่าแดงจักเกิดเป็นเลือด ก็ให้แก้เสียมื้อนี้วันนี้*

130. *เคราะห์ขำเขือกและลางงู ก็ให้หายเสียมื้อนี้วันนี้*

131. *เคราะห์หนูกัดเสื้อผ้า ก็ให้หายเสียมื้อนี้วันนี้*

132. *เคราะห์อันจักเป็นก่ำพร้าพัดแม่อยู่นอนเคียง ก็ให้หายเสียมื้อนี้วันนี้*

133. *เคราะห์สอยวอยผ้าขาด ก็ให้หายเสียมื้อนี้วันนี้*

134. *เคราะห์อนละหนในเนื้อ ก็ให้หายเสียมื้อนี้วันนี้*

135. *เคราะห์สองผัวเมียหมั่นผิดข้อง ก็ให้หายเสียมื้อนี้วันนี้*

136. *เคราะห์งัวควายถึกแอกและบ่วงน้อยยักขาคา ก็ให้หายเสียมื้อนี้วันนี*

137. *เคราะห์ไปมาเห็นเหตุ อุบัติเหตุเป็นลาง ก็ให้หายเสียมื้อนี้วันนี้*

138. *เคราะห์หมั่นคางป่วยไข่ ก็ให้หายเสียมื้อนี้วันนี้*

139. *เคราะห์ทุกข์ยากไฮ้บ่อมีสัง ก็ให้หายเสียมื้อนี้วันนี้*

140. *กูจักผาบหมู่เคราะห์กำเลิบให้เพิก*

141. *กูจักแก้หมู่แม่กำเลิดให้หนี*

142. *ให้สูหนีเมือภูตกข่ามพู้นเยอ*

143. *ให้สูหนีเมือน้ำตกเขียวพู้นเยอ*

144. *สูเหลียวมาให้สูตาแตก*

145. *ยามฝนสูอย่าได้มาถึกบ่วงหนังแห่งกูเยอ*

146. *ยามแล้งสูอย่าได้มาถึกบ่วงทองแห่งกูเยอ่*

147. *ให้สูกองกันตายเต็มท่องท่ง*

148. *กูส่งแล้วสูอย่าสู่มาเท่าวันเทอญ*

149. *อม สมเด็จเจ้าตนฉลาด ผู้ข่าทั้งหลายจักขออัญเชิญเจ้าตนฉลาดมาลักสา*

150. *ขวัญอ่อนสีไวได้ไปอยู่เมืองม่อย*

151. *ก็ให้มาสามื้อนี้วันนี้*

152. *ขวัญอ่อนน้อยผู้คิงแดง*

153. *ก็ให้มาสามื้อนี้วันนี้*

154. *ขวัญจอมแพงผู้คิงก่ำ*

155. *ก็ให้มาสามื้อนี้วันนี้*

156. *ขวัญเจ้าถึกกะต่ำเมืองแถน*

126. *The bad luck of the future and the past, let it be gone on this particular day.*

127. *The misfortune of a house on fire, let it be gone on this particular day.*

128. *The misfortune of the coconuts falling from the trees, let it be gone on this particular day.*

129. *The misfortune of rice, black and red, turning bloodlike, let it be gone on this particular day.*

130. *The bad, poisonous luck and omen of snakes, let it be gone on this particular day.*

131. *The misfortune of mice ruining the clothes, let it be it gone on this particular day.*

132. *The misfortune of orphanage, separating the baby from its parents sleeping nearby, let it be gone.*

133. *The misfortune of exhaustion and torn clothes, let it be gone on this particular day.*

134. *The misfortune of turmoil in the human flesh, let it be gone on this particular day.*

135. *The bad luck of frequent arguments between husband and wife, let it be gone on this particular day.*

136. *Bad luck of buffaloes and cows yoked and fastened by the feet by snaring loops, let it be gone.*

137. *Ominous luck of seeing an accident while traveling, let it be gone on this particular day.*

138. *The misfortune of moans and fever, let it be gone on this particular day.*

139. *The misfortune of extreme poverty, let it be gone on this particular day.*

140. *I shall banish all the current misfortune.*

141. *I shall banish all the Mae Kamlerd.*

142. *Make them escape to the yonder mountains.*

143. *Make them escape to the water in the green mountain over there.*

144. *If you dare look back, your eyes will be broken.*

145. *During the rainy season, please do not come to this leather trap of mine.*

146. *During the dry season, please do not come to this golden trap of mine.*

147. *Die in heaps scattered all over the rice field.*

148. *I have driven you away, do not ever return.*

149. *Om, sages, we invite your protection.*

150. *This delicate young khwan, who went to the town of Mory,* [119]

151. *Please return on this particular day.*

152. *Delicate young khwan of the red skinned baby,*

153. *Please return on this particular day.*

154. *Beloved khwan of the dark skinned baby,*

155. *Please return on this particular day.*

156. *Khwan that has been under the spell in the town of Thaen,*

157. *ก็ให้มาสามื้อนี้วันนี้*

158. *ขวัญเจ้าไปยามป้าอยู่เมืองเสลายน*

159. *ก็ให้มาสามื้อนี้วันนี้*

160. *ขวัญเจ้าไปดอมคนอยู่เมืองลุ่ม*

161. *กะให้มาเสียมื้อนี้วันนี้*

162. *ขวัญเจ้าไปถึกสุมอยู่กางหนอง*

163. *กะให้มาเสียมื้อนี้วันนี้*

164. *ขวัญเจ้าไปชมซอนหาคู่*

165. *กะให้มาสามื้อนี้วันนี้*

166. *ขวัญเจ้าไปยามปู่อยู่เมืองมัดตะบอง*

167. *กะให้มาสามื้อนี้วันนี้*

168. *ขวัญเจ้าลงไปตีกองอยู่เมืองนาค*

169. *กะให้มาสามื้อนี้วันนี้*

170. *ขวัญเจ้าทุกข์ยากฮ้ายไปเที่ยวขอกิน*

171. *กะให้มาสามื้อนี้วันนี้*

172. *ข่อยจักเชิญเอาขวัญอ่อนสี่ให้มาอย่าช้า*

173. *ข่อยจักเชิญเอาขวัญอ่อนหล้าให้มาโดยพลัน*

174. *ขวัญหัวเจ้าขึ้นเมือยามแม่เก่าแม่หลัง*

175. *เจ้าผู้ชื่อว่าแถนตื้อ*

176. *บัดนี้ข่อยไถ่ชื่อเอาแล้วหมื่นแปดพันคำ*

177. *ทางฮกฮ้ายเป็นป่าคาก็ให้เจ้าบุ๊ลงมา*

178. *ทางเป็นน้ำให้เจ้าขี่เฮือทองลงมา*

179. *ทางเป็นหนองให้เจ้าขี่เฮือไม้ลงมา*

180. *ลงบ่อได้ให้ไต่หลังฮุ่งลงมา*

181. *เจ้าบ่อมานมแม่เจ้าเบื้องซ้ายเขาสิยาดกันกินอยู่ลีลาลีลาแลนา*

182. *เจ้าบ่อลงมาผ้าฮ่มเจ้าสิหมองแลนา*

183. *เจ้าบ่อลงมาบ่อนนอนเจ้าสิเส่า*

184. *แม่เจ้าจี่ชิ้น เหน็บฝาไว้ถ่า*

185. *แม่เจ้าจี่ปา เหน็บหญ่าไว้ถ่า*

186. *เจ้าหล้าน้อยแม่น้อยลงมาเที่ยวปะลันเทอญ*

157. *Please return on this particular day.*

158. *Khwan that has visited the aunt in the town of Seilayon,*[120]

159. *Please return on this particular day.*

160. *Khwan that has been with the people of the plain,*

161. *Please return on this particular day.*

162. *Khwan that was caught in the fishing net in the middle of the pond,*

163. *Please return on this particular day.*

164. *Khwan that has been staying amorously with the lover,*

165. *Please return on this particular day.*

166. *Khwan that has visited the grandfather in the town of Mudtaborng,*[121]

167. *Please return on this particular day.*

168. *Khwan that has been down to beat drums in the town of Naga,*

169. *Please return on this particular day.*

170. *Khwan that has been wandering in poverty, begging for food,*

171. *Please return on this particular day.*

172. *I shall invite this fine young khwan to come without delay.*

173. *I shall invite this delicate young khwan to come in a sudden.*

174. *Khwan that has been up to visit Mae Kau Mae Lang,*[122]

175. *Please, god whose name is Thaen Tuee,*

176. *Now, that I have paid a ransom of eighteen thousand pieces of gold to you.*

177. *If the path is covered with tall grass, please struggle down.*

178. *If the path is flooded with water, please sail down here in the golden boat.*

179. *If the path leads through swamps, please sail down here in the wooden boat.*

180. *If you cannot walk down, climb on the back of rainbow.*

181. *If you do not come down, your mother's milk of the left breast will be shared by other greedy babies.*

182. *If you do not come down, your blanket will lose its colour.*

183. *If you do not come down, your bed will be sorrowful.*

184. *Your mother, waiting, has grilled pieces of beef and put it up in the wall for you.*[123]

185. *Your mother, waiting, has grilled fish and put it up in the thatch for you.*

186. *Beloved tiny one, please come down immediately.*

Phor Torng Dii is a farmer as everybody else in the village. Besides this, he is a many-sided and inventive talent. In the 1960s he made a primitive bellow and forged sickles and knives. He also repaired the old muzzle loaders in the village, and was very creative making various utensils from buffalo horn. Also, he is a reputed herbalist and was for years a master of various rites. In 2004, at 75 years of age, he was still active from early morning. Now his main interest is astrology and he also helps some ritual masters by making the krathong(s) used in various rites

RITUAL TEXTS
Smaller Rites

The following texts are not to be found in the palm leaf books or in any other written format. Hence, the texts are all transcriptions and translations based on tape-recordings made in the village and published here with the villagers' permission.

A. The Pau Kamlerd Rite

The *pau kamlerd* rite is a smaller and less demanding rite than the *taengkae mae kamlerd* (also just called *kae kamlerd*) but the purpose is the same, namely to free the child from the symptoms caused by the *mae kamlerd*. If the child is only slightly ill it may be sufficient to perform the *pau kamlerd* ceremony. In the ceremony, the ritual master 'blows' or 'puffs' (*pau*) magic words onto the child whereby the *kamlerd* symptoms vanish.

The *pau kamlerd* rite does not involve ritual objects and the short magic invocation differs from one performer to another. While the stronger *kamlerd* rites must be performed by a *mor kamlerd*, who has obtained his skills through apprenticeship with an older ritual master who has found him ethically suited to become a master, the 'weaker' *pau kamlerd* rite is performed by *mor pau kamlerd*. A *mor pau kamlerd* has also undergone training in a teacher/apprentice relationship but not with nearly the same expectations with regard to their personal background and insight.

Text A1 - Informant: Phor Thorng Dii

The second line of the verse is obscene. Like in the following texts, the purpose is to drive away the *kamlerd*. The use of dirty language and rude expressions as well as the references to scary situations is intended to distract the interest of the *mae kamlerd* and make her want not to come near or stay. The text is very difficult to translate.

In this version, the introduction is made up of fragments in Pali, which Phor Thong Dii remembered from his time as a monk in the local temple. After this, words in Phor Thorng Dii's own dialect followed:

1. *Om – blow out, blow out – the causes of kamlerd.*
2. *The cause that makes the woman's cunt feel like it was made of toad's skin.*
3. *Dead phii(s) go towards the above.*
4. *Dead people go towards the sky.*[124]
5. *The baby's step-father is called Chiang Ling.*[125]
6. *Its real father is called Chiang Ngae.*[126]
7. *My real father is called Yae Long Huu.*[127]
8. *My bonfire (my knowledge) is called Phaya Long Lueem.*[128]
9. *Om – blow away, blow away.*
10. *My real father is called old Sii Son Sai.*[129]
11. *Because our penises are inserted into many cunts.*
12. *Om – be gone.*

Text A2 - Informant: Phor Mun

1. *Om – Phii Kam dies in the saalaa,*[130]
2. *Grandfather Khai is in the town of Thua,*[131]
3. *Grandmother Khai is in the town of Thua,*
4. *Om – be gone.*

Text A3 - Informant: Phor Phan

1. *I will blow away the kamlerd,*
2. *Whether she originated in the town in the sky or on this earth.*
3. *I will blow to disperse poisons of every kind.*
4. *Om – be gone.*

B. Spells for Nam Mon (Magic Water)

Various types of spells are used in the preparation of *nam mon* (magic water) that the mother must drink just before the birth. These are some examples of the texts used. Other villagers who were also preparing *nam mon* informed that they would chant fractions of Pali prayers as a kind of spell.

Text B1 – Informant: Phor Pia

1. *Here is the mighty worship*
2. *Whose power eliminates all illnesses and all difficulties.*

These words are repeated several times interspersed with fragments of Pali prayers.

Text B2 – Informant: Mae Mai

1. *Om ------*
2. *Stems of saang phai bamboo.*
3. *Ghosts tell us to leave paths for buffaloes.*
4. *Om ------*

Text B3 – Informant: Phor Lory

1. *Om ------*
2. *I recite this spell to make elephants drop their babies at birth.*
3. *They do drop them, consequently.*
4. *I recite this spell to make women drop their babies at birth.*
5. *They drop them, consequently.*
6. *Performing this sacred rite, bamboo strips are scattered.*
7. *Om ------ run as eel oil,*
8. *Flow as sesame oil.*
9. *Om ------*

C. Spells Used in Connection with the Kan Haay

The following are examples of the spells used by some of the village elders either while they produce the *kan haay*, the powerful magic thread used in the ceremonies – or while tying them to the mother just after the birth for protection against evil.

Text C1 – Informant: Phor Mun

1.   *Om - with these magic words,*
2.   *Om - with these magic words and the five Lord Buddhas*[132]
3.   *Om - I should like to pay my obeisance*
4.   *and make this request to all theiwadaa(s).*
5.   *Om - you Mighty, I shall pull out the heads of the ghosts,*
6.   *the so-called phii faa and naang thaeng,*[133]
7.   *I shall destroy them all.*
8.   *I shall destroy phii paa and the phii kaa.*[134]
9.   *Om - you Mighty,*
10.   *Om ------*

Text C2 – Informant: Phor Phorng

1.   *All mighty and superb wishes,*
2.   *Crystallized thread born in Heaven,*
3.   *Scented thread born of the sky,*
4.   *The excellent Heaven of Dusit.*
5.   *This perfect crystallized thread of Heaven,*
6.   *Divided and delivered to seven areas by the God Indra.*
7.   *Put in the spinning wheels, and woven in a fine thin thread.*
8.   *Delicate thread presented by one thousand eyed Indra.*
9.   *The physical uncertainty –*
10.   *Coughs, brain, bone joints, and necks,*
11.   *Eye-sickness and stomach ache, excretion, fever, and colds.*
12.   *A charm that will never be defeated,*
13.   *This thread worth ten hundred thousands nuggets of gold, deserves to be kept.*
14.   *From the South, people come to help.*
15.   *From the North, people come to construct.*
16.   *May people walk behind you.*
17.   *May people help carrying silver and gold flowers after you.*
18.   *Om ------* [followed by a few words in Pali]

Text C3 – Informant: Phor Phrom

1. *Lord Buddha protects everything.*
2. *His teachings protect everything.*
3. *His successors protect everything.*
4. *They are powerful.*
5. *They protect the five sensational paths of human beings.*[135]

Text C4 – Informant: Phor Tuu Phan

1. *Om ------*
2. *I shall select a phii porb or a phii phraay.*
3. *Phii naay, do not look.*
4. *I shall pronounce these magic words*
5. *To the elephants in their enclosure.*
6. *I shall pronounce these magic words*
7. *To the people in their homes.*
8. *Surrender to me as crows to a trap.*[136]

Text C5 – Informant: Phor Lory

1. *Om ------*
2. *I shall select phii porb and phii phraay.*
3. *May you surrender to me as crows to a trap.*
4. *May you come to me cowardly as crows come before eagles.*
5. *I say these magic words to elephants, they will roam in the jungle.*
6. *I say these magic words to people in their homes, they will cry.*
7. *Tell them to young female elephants, they will sob.*
8. *You cannot resist, but will cross thirty paddy fields to come to me.*
9. *You cannot resist, thirty rice fields, you cross to come to me.*
10. *You cannot stay, you cry for me.*
11. *Om – be gone.*

D. Spells Used in Connection with Praab Fai

As described in Part 1, a small rite is observed at the beginning of the confinement in order to *praab fai* – to kill the heat from the fire as much as possible. There were many different ways of doing this but in almost all cases salt is involved. Most would perform this little ritual standing and facing the fire, then bending the knees slightly and throwing a handful of salt from behind between the parted legs into the fire.

Text D1 – Informant: Phor Thorng Dii

Phor Thorng Dii uses a Pali prayer, repeating the words three times for this small ceremony:

1. *Namo tassa*
2. *Bhaga vato*
3. *Namotassa, bhagavato, bhagavato*
4. *Namotassa, bhagavato*

Text D2– Informant: Phor Mun

1. *Om ------*
2. *Red iron during the fifth lunar month.*
3. *Om ------*
4. *Evening sky.*
5. *Om ------*
6. *Red iron to be perfectly red.*
7. *Om ------*
8. *Evening sky to be bright as daytime.*

Text D3 – Informant: Phor Pia

For this ceremony Phor Pia needs a 'five item bowl' (*khan haa*) which is in fact a bowl filled with the following: five flowers – preferably white, five candles, and five incense sticks. The bowl is placed near the fireplace. Phor Pia then takes a mouthful of whisky and blows it onto the fire while he chants:

1. *sa–sa–sa–sa–sa–sa–sa sahaay …..wa*

The Pali text means 'wash away and disappear'. Phor Pia is the only person we know of who is not using salt as part of the *praab fai*. For him the procedure is the same for *praab fai* as for *sia phit fai* (a small ceremony which is used to 'kill the fire' at the end of the *yuu fai* period (see further below).

Text D4 – Informant: Phor Phrom

Phor Phrom also brings a 'five item bowl' (mentioned above) and one and a half *baht* (Thai coins) as offerings, then he throws the salt and he chants :

1. *Do not lay eggs in pus.*
2. *Swell not in blood.*
3. *Stretch out as flatly as (vegetable) beds.*
4. *Dry out as lime.*

Text D5 – Informant: Midwife Mae Daa

1. *Keep in the mouth, the unclear water to blow out the fire,* [137]
2. *Keep in the mouth, the clear water to blow at the charcoals,* [138]
3. *I shall extinguish it – turn the ashes as fine as powder, as dry as lime.*

Text D6 – Informant: Phor Tuu Phan

1. *Defeat the fire of the fifth lunar month.* [139]
2. *Defeat the thunderbolt of the dry season.*
3. *Defeat the bright red iron.*
4. *Defeat in the day time and in the night time.*
5. *Be gone.*

Text D7 – Informant: Phor Lory

1. *Keep in the mouth, the fire, in the fifth lunar month*
2. *Keep in the mouth, the sky, in the evening*
3. *Keep in the mouth, the red iron, at night*
4. *Keep in the mouth, the dark iron, in the daytime.*
5. *I will blow it as if it was powder,*
6. *May it become dry as lime.*[140]

E. Spells Used in Connection with Sia Phit Fai

Sia phit fai is a ceremony that takes place at the very end of the *yuu fai* period. It is aimed, literally, at 'killing the fire and removing its after effects' discussed in Part 1.

Text E1 - Informant: Phor Tuu Phan

1. *Om ------*
2. *I shall eliminate all disease.*
3. *I shall flush out all the poison.*
4. *May my words be powerful*
5. *As a medicine.*
6. *Blow away the poison, the rashes*
7. *Om ------*

Text E2 - Informant: Phor Phrom

Phor Phrom uses a Pali prayer related to the Three Gems of Buddhism. He repeats this prayer three times.

Text E3 - Informant: Phor Lory

Phor Lory uses the same wording for this ceremony as he uses for *praab fai*.

RITUAL TEXTS
Traditional Recipes

A. Recipes for Herb Decoctions for Hot Ablutions during Yuu Fai

Note: *Bai* means 'leaf', and it is therefore in all cases the leaves of the plants that are used.

A1 – Informant: Phor Tuu Phan

Phor Tuu Phan, the village's most esteemed herbalist (*mor yaa*), recommended the use of the following herbs:

- *(ใบหนาด) [bai naad]* : *Blumea balsamifera* (L.) DC., *Compositae*
  It has a scent of menthol. In the villages, it is often mixed with tobacco and the inhalation of this is considered beneficial against nasal congestion and disease. When taken orally, it is considered a treatment for excess stomach acid.

- *(ใบข่า) [bai khaa]* : *Alpinia galanga* (L.) SW., *Zingiberaceae*
  Of the gingerfamily. Galanga is also used for the treatment of flatulence.

- *(ใบตะไคร้) [bai takhrai]* : *Cymbopogon citratus* (DC.) Stapf, *Poaceae*
  The roots of lemon grass are also used in the village for the treatment of gallstone and urinary tract problems.

A2 – Informant: Midwife Mae Mai

Mae Mai uses only *(ใบหนาด) [bai naad]*.

A3 – Informant: Midwife Mae Bua

Mae Bua uses *(ใบหนาดและใบข่า) [bai naad and bai khaa]*.

B. Recipes for Herb Decoctions for Drinking during Yuu Fai

Note: The word *raak* means 'root'.

B1 – Informant: Phor Tuu Phan

The *mor yaa* recommends using:

- *(รากชะมด) [raak chamot]: Abelmoschus moschatus* Medik., (syn. *Hibiscus abelmoschus* L.) *Malvaceae*
  Varied use as medicinal plant in the village. Besides the roots for the *yuu fai* decoction, other parts of the plant are used, too:
    - the leaves and the root: against skin diseases, hair problems and dandruff
    - the flowers: against intestinal worms
    - the fruits: against boils

- *(รากกระชาย) [raak krachaay]* probably Zingiberacea Boes Embergia Rotunda Mons F. (Linn.)
  In the village the plant (of the ginger family) is also used as a remedy against dry lips and infection in oral passages. The burnt roots mixed with limejuice are thought to be good against dysentery. The shoots of the plant are regarded a component in the treatment of impotence.

- *(รากเอ็นอ้า) [raak en-aa]: Caesalpinia bonduc* (L.) Roxb. *Leguminosae*
  The leaves are also used to treat flatulence; the fruits against urinary problems, bladder, and kidney diseases.

B2 – Informant: Mae Mai

All of the following ingredients are boiled together in the water:

- *(โกฐน้ำเต้า) [kood nam tau]* : *Rheum palmatum* L., *Polygonaceae*
  It is supposed to treat indigestion and is used as a laxative. Also used as a treatment for eye sickness and haemorrhoids.

- *(รากขี้แรด) [raak khii raed]: Caesalpinia digyna* Rottler, *Leguminosae*

- *(รากเอ็นอ้า) [raak en-aa]: Caesalpinia bonduc* (L.) Roxb. *Leguminosae,* see above.

- *(มะขาม) [ma khaam]: Tamarindus indica* L., *Leguminosae (tamarind)* for this decoction she uses a piece of the core-wood of tamarind.

- *(มะเฟือง) [ma fueang]*: probably *Averrhoa carambola* L., Oxalidaceae, Artemisia, Compositae
  She also uses a piece of core-wood of this tree. *Ma fueang* is also used in the treatment of fever.

B3 – Informant: Mae Bua

Mae Bua uses a simpler but similar recipe that includes:

- A piece of the core-wood of *(มะขาม) [ma khaam] (tamarind)*

- A piece of core-wood of *(มะเฟือง) [ma fueang]*, see above

C. Recipes for Yaa Kam

Yaa kam is considered to be a contraceptive; it is a decoction that is taken by the end of *yuu fai* to prevent pregnancy. Some - perhaps all - of the masters who were able to prepare *yaa kam* have a magical spell that they use either when collecting the herbs or when mixing them.

C1 – Informant: Phor Thorng Dii

To make *yaa kam* Phor Thorng Dii uses a herb of the *Compositae* family *(Artemisia)* that has many different medicinal uses. Unfortunately, I do not know the Thai name of this woody herb, which is very common in Southeast Asia. Most likely it is the plant *Triumfetta bartramia*, which is part of the lime family (not the lemon family).

While mixing and boiling these herbs, Phor Thorng Dii recites:

1. *At this moment I shall defeat Phayaathorn[141]*
2. *Whose white hair can be seen from far away.*
3. *My hammer will knock on the head of Phayaathorn.[142]*
4. *Om – I shall awaken these herbs.*
5. *I shall make them get up and get up.*
6. *Your trunks are not permitted to wander away.*
7. *Your trunks stand in the sand.*
8. *Your tops point to the sky.*
9. *I request the presence of the old Thaaw Laa at the sacred*
10. *Mixing of this yaa kam.*

C2 – Informant: Phor Phorng

Phor Phorng is married to the midwife Mae Bua. While collecting herbs for the *yaa kam* he says:

1.   *Om - wake up, wake up.*
2.   *I shall wake up these herbal roots.*
3.   *The herbs that have wandered away, please come back.*
4.   *The herbs that have returned, belong to me and stay with me.*
5.   *Om ------*

The herbs he uses are the roots of two plants from the same family:

- (เข็มขาว) *[khem khaaw:* probably *Chasalia curviflora* Thw., *Rubiaceae*
  a shrub with fragrant white flowers that belongs to the *Rubia* family. This shrub is also used for the treatment of eye sickness and to stimulate the appetite.

- (คัดเค้า) *[khad khau]:* probably *Randia siamensis* Craib, *Rubiaceae*
  of the same family *khad khau* is a climbing vine with white flowers. The plant is also used to treat anemia, and to drive out waste fluid from the uterus after the birth.

C3 – Informant: Phor Tuu Phan

While collecting the herbs Phor Tuu Phan says:

1.   *Om - Phayaathorn*[143]
2.   *My hammer will knock thy head*
3.   *Om ------*
4.   *I shall wake up these herbs,*
5.   *Up, up, up, ..*
6.   *I shall wake up these herbs,*
7.   *Up, up, up, ..*
8.   *Awake, the herbs flock to me.*
9.   *Three thousand herbs run to me.*
10. *Nine thousand herbs gather around me.*

The ingredients he uses are:

- A type of Boraginaceae, probably *Cordia myxa* L., *Boraginaceae*.
  It is a herb with rough leaves.

- A piece of root from a large tree, (หมากหวด) *[maak huad]*: probably *Lepisanthes rubiginosa (Roxb.) Lennh* (Syn. *Erioglossum rubiginosum* (Roxb. Blume) *Sapindaceae*

- A piece of root from (กระบก) *[kkra-bok]*, ((หมากบก) *[maak-bok]* in Northeastern dialect*)*: probably wild almond, *Irvingia malayana* Oliver, *Simaroubaceae*

C4 – Informant: Phor Pia

Before picking the roots that he needs for the *yaa kam*, Phor Pia buries an offering consisting of flowers, candles, a cigarette, and a mouthful of spit from a betel quid on the site. The plants he uses are:

- The root of (เล็บแมว) *[leb maew]*: probably *Ziziphus brunoniana* C.B Clarke ex Brandis, *Rhamnaceae*

- The root of (คอม) *[khorm]* (not otherwise identified)

C5 – Informant: Phor Sau

- The root of (หัวหวาย) *[hua waay]*: *Palmae* (not otherwise identified)

- The root of (นมวัว) *[nom wua]*: *Artabotrys harmandii* Finet & Gagnep., *Annonaceae*

- The vine (เขากาบ) *[khau kaab]*: *Ventilago calyculata* Tul., *Rhamnaceae*

- Root of (ผักทุง) *[phak thung]*: *Ocimum teniflorum* L., *Labiatae*

- Root of (เอ็นอ้า) *[en-aa]*: *Caesalpineae bonduc* (L.) Roxb., *Leguminosae*

- The vine (หมากแตก) *[maak taek]*: *Celastrus paniculatus* Willd., *Celastraceae*

C6 – Informant: Mae Thorng Bai

The following items are buried close to where the plant that she uses grows: flowers, candles, one cigarrette, and one mouthful of betel.

The name of the plant is (ต้นเงี่ยงปลาดุก) *[ton ngiang plaa duk]*. The plant is named after its shape, which looks like the pectorial fins of the fresh-water cat fish. It belongs to the *Labiatae* family.

C7 – Informant: Phor Chuay

The ingredients Phor Chuay used are:

- The root of (รางจืด) *[raang jueed]*: *Milletia kityana, Leguminosae*

- The root of (แข้งขม) *[khaeng khom]*: *Solanum trilobatum* L., *Solanaceae*

- The root of (หมากนาว) *[maak naaw]*: *Citrus aurantiifolia* (Christm.) Swingle, *Rutaceae*

While collecting the plants, he, too, buries candles and flowers nearby while he chants:

1. *Om – white haired Phayaathorn*
2. *I shall knock thy head with my hammer.*
3. *Om – white haired Phayaathorn*
4. *I shall knock thy head with my hammer.*
5. *Om – white haired Phayaathorn*
6. *I shall knock thy head with my hammer.*

In addition, Phor Chuay informed that the woman has to be naked while she is drinking the *yaa kam* and she must not talk to anyone until she has drunk everything in the cup.

C8 – Informant: Phor Pan

Phor Pan uses the following plants:

- (คัดเค้า) *[khad khau]* : probably *Randia siamensis* Craib, *Rubiaceae*
  of the same family. *Khad khau* is a climbing vine with white flowers. The plant is also
  used to treat anemia, and to drive out waste fluid from the uterus after the birth.

- (ต้นเล็บแมว) *[ton leb maew]*: *Ziziphus brunoniana, Rhamnaceae*

- (ต้นชายเต็น) *[ton saay ten]*: *Diospyros variegata* Kurz, *Ebenaceae*

Notes to ritual texts

1. S. J. Tambiah, 1970 (p. 136) – please note that Tambiah uses a different norm for transcription than applied here. Hence we would write *mau khwan*: '*mor khwan*', and *mau ya*: '*mor yaa*'.

2. S. J. Tambiah, 1970 (p. 248).

3. In this case the *khwan* implies the multitude of *khwan*.

4. For the meaning of *mor*, see Glossary.

5. The name of a man; it means that he said it 90 times.

6. The name of a monk; it possibly refers to *Narai* in Ramayana.

7. The name of a fortuneteller. *Huuhaa* is an unsual name which denotes that the person is very well reputed.

8. The *throne* is the elevated seat which the monk sits on when he preaches.

9. *Bunrueang* is a common name that has a good meaning. *Bun* means merit and *rueang* is progress.

10. The word used here is *glassy*, an adjective that is used to express that something is good, bright, delicate, or clear.

11. *Thaaw* means 'Mister'. *Thaaw Songsai* is, in other words, a man.

12. The name of the next Lord Buddha. According to the scriptures there were three Lord Buddhas before the current Buddha. The fifth Lord Buddha (called *Phra Meit Trai*) will appear during a coming time of utopia.

13. *Manooraaa* is a leading female character in Thai literature. Originating from India, the character is half human, half bird. When she wants to swim she sheds her wings and turns into a beautiful woman.

14. *Aek khai* is a female leading character in a Northeastern folk tale.

15. *Siidaa* is a character in a folk tale. *Siidaa* is also the name of the wife of the God *Narai* in Ramayana but this *Siidaa* is another woman.

16. *Baaw Thaen* is the king of a town who falls in love with *Siidaa*. Baaw means young man.

17. *Khau tom* - sticky rice cooked with coconut cream (often stuffed with banana) and wrapped in banana leaves.

18. Meaning the flowers of Heaven.

19. The *kaed* is a bushy plant, *Pandamas tectorius Bl., Pandanaceae*.

20. The *yor* tree - *Morinda Citrifolia Lin. Rubiaceae*. Its common name is *noni*.

21. *Khii-on* is an annual plant, *Xantium strumarium Linn., Compositae*.

22. *Khum phuu* is a kind of climbing plants that are usually found in the rice-field. It is similar to *dork leb muee naang (Quisqualis Indica Linn., Combretaceae)* in Central Thai except that the flowers of this plant are light green while the flowers of the latter are red and white.

23. *Khad khau - Randia saimensis Craib, Rubiaceae*.

24. *Saam pii - Gomphrena globosa Linn., Amaranthaceae*. The literal translation of *saam pii* is 'three years' – referring to the long blooming of the flower.

25.   *Nguang chaang - Heliotropium indicum R. Br., Boraginaceae.*

26.   The *phaa khwan* is the container that is used in the rite.

27.   See Note 10.

28.   See explanation in the main text.

29.   The Isan word *ngueak* means 'mermaid' in Central Thai. Here it is a kind of legendary snake, not very big, but black with a red comb.

30.   *Thaaw Khamfan* is a name.

31.   *Thaaw Kamfuea* is a name that rhymes with verse.

32.   *Thaaw Laanory* is a name.

33.   A Pali blessing.

34.   *Kae* is the main verb used in this and other rites. It means 'to dispel and chase away something'.

35.   The words of the prayer means: *We worship the Blessed One, Arahat, Supreme Lord Buddha.* (Source: Tambiah, 1970, p. 244)

36.   *Om* is a magic word used at the beginning of an incantation; it equals the long *Oom* in Central Thai.

37.   *Sompory* is a herbal plant of the acacia family. The fruit is very aromatic, especially when roasted and is used to purify the water used in this ceremony. In every-day life it is used as hair shampoo.

38.   The Great Lord Buddha.

39.   *Phayaa* denotes the high rank of courtiers in the old days. It is also the rank/title used to address the highest of all. In Central Thai the same word is pronounced *Phrayaa*.

40.   The notion of skinny is used repeatedly in this text as another word for sickly, unhealthy, weak.

41.   The coarse stems (line 33) refer to plants that are not proper for the ritual as the only proper plant to use is *sompory*.

42.   Line 36 refers to the figures of a man and a woman prepared by the family as part of the items in the ritual container, and the undesirability of using any other pattern or models.

43.   Line 37 refers to a bad omen. If such a thing happens and the *khwan* of someone in the family were to follow the call of the owl, he or she might fall ill.

44.   In the Thai text, it refers to a kind of ruminants, *Muntiacus Muntjak* of the *Cervidae* family. This kind of deer is widely known in Thailand.

45.   *Phii phaay* is the same as *phii phraay* – an evil spirit. See also Part 1.

46.   Words of blessing in Pali.

47.   Originally, the expression in Pali *'sua haaya* is used to end the magic chanting. When pronunced in Northeastern dialect Isan it sounds like: 'evils be gone' – and this is how it is used and understood here.

48.   *Kai* is the smallest ruminant of the *Tragulidae* family.

49.   *Thaen* means 'God in the Northeast'. There are many *thaen* with different capabilities and responsibilities. The greatest of all is named *Thaen Luang* or *Phaya Thaen*.

50.   The sky here refers to the Heavens.

51. Words of blessing in Pali recited in the Isan language.

52. *Naang Nii* is a female spirit who resides in a particular kind of banana tree (*Musa balbisiana Colla*, of the musaceae family). She is a lovely young girl who possesses some magical power, and so is a spirit who is ready to help good people. She is named after the tree in which she resides.

53. The town of *phii*(s) refers to the place where *theiwadaa* who have not collected sufficient *bun* to reside in heaven live. The town of *phii*(s) could for example be a place where people have been dying of the plaque and these lower *theiwaadaa*(s) also live here.

54. One of the legendary continents, *Chomphuuthawiip* is believed to be the present-day India.

55. *Maak khaeng* is a plant that is commonly grown in the kitchen garden - the *solanaceae* family. The name of this plant rhymes with aubergine (in Isan *maak khuea*) mentioned in the following verse.

56. The name must be derived from a birth tree called *naen*. *Ning* and *naen* are names of the birth trees in Heaven. It is also the name of a local, wild sort of bananas.

57. Blessing words in Pali.

58. Blessing words in Pali.

59. This is a reference to the *phaa khwan*.

60. The following verses are directed at the baby.

61. *Ning* and *naen* are names of the birth trees in Heaven. The lines to climb down in order to be born are known as s*aay ning* and *saay naen*. It is unclear whether *ning* and *naen* are the same tree or whether there are in fact two birth trees.

62. *Faang* is a small tree of *Caesalpinia Sappan Linn* of the *Leguminosae* family. Besides using the leaves and sprigs as a herb, the wood is used for colouring and dyeing.

63. *Khang – Laccifer Lacca, Lacciferidae* – in Central Thai: *khrang*. It is used for dyeing.

64. The spirits mentioned in the following verses are different kinds of evil ghosts but not as dangerous as *phii porb* and *phii phraay*.

65. It is simply a reference to everyday farming life and is used here to rhyme with the following verse.

66. *Thaaw Laek Taa* is male spirit. Its name signifies bad luck – an exchange for eyes. The spirit comes to take your eyes (i.e. to make you blind).

67. *Khian* is a kind of bird.

68. Blessing in Pali.

69. A reference to the *krathong* and the thread that are used in the ceremony.

70. To 'comb it out' is a Thai expression that fits in this context.

71. A *hen* is a mammal of the *viverridae* family.

72. A *nok sai* is a kind of pecking bird.

73. These are two different gods. One name is pronounced with the low tone while the other is pronounced with the common tone.

74. *Huulamaan* – the monkey king in the Ramayana. The name slips from *Hanumaan* in Central Thai.

75. *Khongkhaa* is the Ganges river.

76. From line 270, 'I' refers to the ritual performer.

77. *Miang* is a dish that consists of different ingredients that are cut into tiny pieces (for example lime, ginger, dried shrimp, green banana, fried coconut, peanuts) – when eaten, all the ingredients are wrapped together inside a leaf. It is interesting that forks are mentioned here: they are a relatively recent implement in Northeastern culture.

78. This line and the following make reference to the *phaa khwaan* and the other items that are part of the ceremony.

79. The literary meaning of *somdong* is wild orange.

80. The middle tier of the *phaa khwaan*.

81. For *Naang Nii*, see note 51.

82. *Sumein* is the name of the mountain where a high level heaven is located.

83. *Siiniinoolaat* is another name of the *Sumein* mountain. In Central Thai, it is called the *Sineiru* mountain.

84. The dog *suang* is guarding the birthtree, *naen*.

85. The shape refers to the long, snakelike black pattern that is the symptom of shingles.

86. *Sing* is a species of mice commonly found in the houses.

87. *Mae Sai Haeng* is a female spirit whose stomach is empty.

88. Introductory expression used to ask for a successful outcome.

89. *Laksaamii* is the goddess of fortune and the beautiful wife of *Narai* also known as *Vishnu*, one of the Brahman gods.

90. *Borlameisuan*, Isan pronunciation corresponding to the Central Thai *Porrameisuan*, refers to the great *Siwa* – Shiva, a Brahman god.

91. A reference to the life-line of the hand – a short and thin life-line is a sign in fortune-telling of a short and uncertain life. *Phommasaad* is a text that is used in fortune-telling.

92. *Ming* is here the same as *ning* – it is probably a slip by the ritual master. *Ning* and *naen* are birth trees.

93. See note 92.

94. The full moon has never been beneath the rays of the sun – when the moon is waning it falls beneath the rays of the sun.

95. *Kluay tiip* is a kind of bananas of the family *Musa Sapientum Linn*. As the name implies the bananas are tiny and less sweet than other bananas and therefore not well liked. Anyhow it grows among many other kinds of bananas.

96. The words are in Pali. Buddhists commonly know this prayer as 'the worship to deities (*theiwadaa*)'. Here it is written and recited in the Northeastern Isan language pronunciation. The introductory part is called *paaw sak khei; paaw* means to announce, *sak khei* is the first word of the incantation.

97. The words of the prayer mean: '*We worship the Blessed One, Arahat, Supreme Lord Buddha*"(Tambiah, 1970 (p. 244)).

98. See note 97.

99. *Sidtikarn* is an introductory word used in prayers to ask for success.

100. Note that in Thai tradition counting age or duration start from 1, not from 0.

101. Poetic expression with magic power.

102. *Thaen Luang* – the greatest of the Gods (*thaen*).

103. *Mae* means mother. Therefore, the spirits are female. These spirits are not really bad but they come to 'tease' people. The names listed reflect their peculiar feature and character.

104. Two different ways of wrapping a diaper around the baby.

105. The text mentions the stove rocks that are flat or falling down – i.e. that cannot support the pot.

106. *Khmer* and *Hor* are two different minority tribal groups in Thailand.

107. *Yor* and *Yuan* are two different minority tribal groups in Thailand.

108. *Phuan* and *Maan* are two different minority tribal groups in Thailand

109. The Lao *Phuan* often tattoo their legs. The mentioning of the tattooed legs is a kind of abuse as ordinary Thai people do not tattoo their legs and consider this practice ugly.

110. Some ritual masters said that the *phii taa naay* were the *phii taayaay*, the ghosts of the grandparents.

111. *Mae saphuee* is a female *phii* or spirit.

112. *Mae sapham* is a female *phii* or spirit.

113. *Phii pau* refers to the spirit of a woman who studies black magic. At night her spirit will leave the body to look for food, i.e., fish in the pond.

114. The *phii phoong* is the spirit of the big, black cat.

115. The snake-like pattern on the body that is a symptom of shingles, cf. note 85.

116. A Pali prayer and blessing.

117. The nine million rods refer to a kind of fish trap – the rods are plaited or woven into a mat that obstructs the water flow and catches the fish – the mat is made from the 'nine million sticks'.

118. The loop is a rope used by the god Indra as a weapon (like a lasso).

119. *Mory* is most likely a legendary town.

120. *Seilayon* is a legendary town in a Northeastern folk-tale.

121. *Mudtaborng* – the same as Battambang in Cambodia.

122. *Mae kau mae lang* – a more proper name for *mae kamlerd*.

123. For keepsake the meat is stuck between the rafters of the house.

124. The point is that the thought of dead *phii* and dead people trying to go to heaven is frightening and this is exactly why it is mentioned here.

125. The name of the baby's step-father is *ling*, which is not a nice name as it also means monkey. *Chiang* is a title used for a man who used to be a Buddhist novice.

126. The father's name, *Ngae* is not a nice name either – it has associations to the sound of a baby crying – a different child of his. Chiang is a title used for a man who used to be a Buddhist novice.

127. 'My' refers to the ritual master himself but here it is more likely a case of poetic license. The name *yae long huu* has the following components: *yae* – a large lizard that lives on the ground and which is most hated or feared by the people; *long* – to come down or enter; *huu* – a hole. In Northeast Thailand the name roughly translates: *the lizard comes down into its hole* – an expression used to describe a coward, always hiding himself in the hole. It has also an obscene connotation because of the words *long* (to enter) and *huu* (hole).

128. According to Khun Jan, 'bonfire' is another word for knowledge. *Phaya long lueem* is another unpleasant name. *Phaya*: the title of a high-ranking courtier; *long lueem*: forgetful.

129. *Sii Son Sai* is a name with good connotations but it indicates that the real father is old. The meaning of these lines may be that the mother has been sleeping around with the so-called 'stepfathers'.

130. The meaning of the text may be: 'Grandma and Grandpa are not here – and there is a dead *phii* in the *salaa* [*kam* means "black" – here it is a reference to a black ghost] – therefore do not come here – this is not a good place to be.'

131. *Thua* is the name of a town – nobody knows where it is.

132. According to the scriptures there were three Lord Buddhas before the current Buddha. The fifth Lord Buddha (called *Phra Meit Trai*) will appear during a coming time of utopia.

133. Both *phii faa* and *naang thaen* are ghosts.

134. *Phii paa*: the fish ghost; *phii kaa*: the crow ghost.

135. Eye (sight), ear (hearing), nose (smell), tongue (taste), and body (touch).

136. This expression is used in several versions of the text; it may be an allusion to a Thai saying.

137. Rice whisky.

138. Another kind of rice whisky.

139. The fifth lunar month is the hottest month of the year.

140. It is the wound caused to the womb during the birth, that needs to become dry as lime.

141. *Phayaathorn* is the same as *Withayaathorn* who in the folktales is known to secretly make love to *Kaakii*, the wife of king *Phrommathat*. He is mentioned here because of his adultery as the rite is also about restoring sexual potency and interest to the woman after the birth and pregnancy.

142. See note 141.

Part 3

Appendices

From above: Tuan, Prawong, Sawang and Koon from the research sample, photographed in 1962, 1978 and 1988

APPENDIX I

Research Process and Methodology

In the early 1960s, the International Institute for Child Study[1] in Bangkok conducted extensive studies in typical villages in Thailand focusing on the children and their living conditions.

The studies aimed to provide answers to questions such as: How were the children and their living conditions in those village communities where 90 per cent of the population then lived? To what influences were the children exposed? What did parents do for and with their children? How did their school function? And how should an educational system be organized and perhaps adjusted to better respond to the realities of life in the villages, and in such a way that it, at the same time, would support and promote a positive development?

I had the good fortune from October 1961 to April 1962 to take part in the Institute's field-work in the village of Baan Phraan Muean – at the time a typical village in the Udorn province in the Northeastern part of Thailand.

Our team was to concern itself with everything that took place in the village. In fact nothing was irrelevant because everything that happened had some influence on the children who were the target of our study.

Our many and long interviews and conversations in the home, weeks of systematic work directly with the children and the teachers in the school, and our presence at all forms of social activities during these six months gave us much insight as well as understanding of the subjects that we were to study and describe.

Essential parts of the material from the project have gradually been utilized.

Professor S. J. Tambiah, who was a member of our team, described the field-work within his professional area in detail in one of his main works and also utilized data in several articles.[2]

The Institute has published the results from the interviews with the families in a large work in Thai. A summary of this is available in English.[3] Results from the study inspired the Institute to make several subsequent country-wide curriculum studies.

In 1965, I produced an educational film 'A Village in Thailand' for Mellemfolkeligt Samvirke (The Danish Association for International Co-operation). The film has been used widely in teaching in Denmark, first and foremost in the higher grades of the elementary school for whom it was intended, but also in higher education and in several University departments.

Generally speaking, the Institute completed this research project in a manner that created respect for its activities.

During our period of work in the village, questions arose that we never had thought to include in the research. Unfortunately, we were not able to devote our time to everything we wanted to study. Financial and other constraints forced us to limit the area of research and to refrain from studying areas with no direct relevance to our project. We noted in passing, however, that these areas might deserve attention if a possibility should later be found.

Among these areas were the customs and traditions related to a woman's pregnancy and the childbirth.

During our time in the village, we witnessed the important role played by traditions and customs based on faith, superstition, prejudice and magic, and how these were expressed in daily life as well as through various ceremonies.

At that time, nothing that the modern world found necessary and important to ensure the health and well-being of a pregnant woman was available. It was intriguing to witness the measures by which the villagers tried to help themselves and to meet the need for support and the feeling of confidence in this situation. My curiosity made me search for literature about Thailand in Western languages but I found no studies that dealt systematically with this important aspect of a family's life. However, reading increased my interest for pursuing the subject, not least because I also found obviously incorrect information related to the topic even in then very recent books. It had to be at least of folkloristic importance to have this area properly described, as the ongoing development in Thailand would most likely change these old traditions and customs totally over a relatively short number of years. Radical changes were to be expected for every woman, and these changes would influence the social and cultural life of the family as well as that of the village.

I found it of personal interest to be able to follow the changes and the variety of their consequences. My absorption in the Northeastern Thai family and the traditions related to impending childbirth has been a fascinating and enriching commitment to me for more than four decades. As the years passed, I realized that I had become eye-witness to a radical transition of cultural patterns in a topic of importance to families world-wide. I felt it almost an obligation to study and document this process and the related traditions thereby contributing positively to the understanding and appreciation of the Isan village culture.

The material presented in this book is based on data obtained as described below.

1961–62 and the follow-up in 1968

In the extensive and comprehensive study undertaken in 1961–62 by the team from the International Institute for Child Study in Baan Phraan Muean our basic sample consisted of the 47 children (23 boys and 24 girls) in the local school's Grade 1, and their parents. The preliminary information gained during this fieldwork formed the basis of my studies of pregnancy and its customs and rites. In 1968, the sample was the same as in 1961–62. However, in 1968 only 33 families were included. These mothers were not in their first youth. None of them was under 30 years old: 14 were between 31 and 40, 11 between 41 and 50, and eight between 51 and 60 years old. Seventeen of the mothers did not know their exact ages but through conversations with older relatives we agreed to an estimated age for each of the women. The 33 women had borne a total of 260 children (3–13 children each with an average of 7.9 children), and of these a total of 209 were alive (an average of 6.3 per family). Nine of the mothers had all their children alive in 1968.

The original interviews with the families in 1961–62 were based on a schedule ad modum Sears, Maccoby & Levin: *Patterns of Child Rearing* (1957), adapted to the Thai culture during some pilot interviews in a village about one hundred kilometres East of Bangkok. From these we had obtained a certain but rather superficial knowledge about customs, faith, prejudice, rites, etc. connected to pregnancy and childbirth.

Hence, we knew enough to be able to ask the relevant questions of those who were experts in the area: the women functioning as midwives in the village, the village headman, and the three most respected and knowledgeable ritual masters among the villagers. The

head teacher, a long-time resident of the village, was included in the interviews as well. Based on this, the final interview schedule was developed. The interviews were made jointly by the author and a Thai staff-member from the Bangkok Institute for Child Study (previously the International Institute for Child Study) during January 1968.

By the very end of the 1968 work period, every question of doubt that had arisen was placed before a joint meeting with the above-mentioned advisory group. Such a group of the most competent and respected villagers has continually been functioning as an advisory team, and has also over the years been consulted by letters. Throughout they have been extremely supportive also in terms of collecting ritual texts, etc.

For me, this work has fully emphasized the basic fact that one condition of getting to know something of importance is to be able to ask the right question in the right manner. In a foreign culture, this is of course even more difficult than in your own culture. Getting detailed information of and insight into the area that we were interested in was not without problems. As the work in all its phases and over all the years was carried out with very capable and knowledgeable Thai colleagues, and in so close co-operation with the village elders that they were, in reality, regarded as particularly competent co-workers, I believe that there is very little that we did not examine and about which we have not obtained detailed knowledge.

The 1978 follow-up

Many changes took place in Thai community from 1968 to 1978, resulting in considerable changes to the daily life of the population.

In the district around Udorn, the change was drastic and rapid. The town and the area were then estimated to be a politically sensitive region where large investments were made. During the Vietnam War, the USA had large military forces stationed in Udorn from where bombers were dispatched over Vietnam. When I visited Udorn in 1968, the town itself was entirely different from what it had been in 1962. The lifestyle of the many foreign troops and the consequent economic boom had made imprint. The population of the town had almost doubled from 30,000 inhabitants to around 60,000 by 1970. Employment opportunities of many kinds attracted young villagers, both men and women, to the town.

With all these changes, what was the influence in terms of our particular interest in the village of Baan Phraan Muean, some seventeen kilometres from Udorn? What was the attitude of the young people to the customs and traditions that were maintained in a group of rather old mothers in 1968? As in 1968, DANIDA was willing to support my return to the village during December/January 1977–78 to gain more information about this aspect of our study.

Our 1961–62 sample were the pupils of Grade 1 who were all born during 1953 and 1954, and who, in 1978, were 24–25 years old. Some had married and had their own children. Considered as a group they were possibly not representative of the entire younger generation of the village as they were 'their mothers' children', and therefore to some extent bearers of certain customs and traditions more so than other young people from the same village. For that reason it was desirable also to include families from outside our original sample.

Hence, our 1978 sample consisted of 12 girls and seven boys of the village school's 1961–62 Grade 1 pupils who had children of their own and who lived either in the village itself, or in villages not too far away, or in the town of Udorn. These 19 young people from the original sample were supplemented with eight of the youngest

mothers in the village. In this way, the 1978 research sample came to consist of 27 young families in total.

The families were visited several times during the month of January 1978. The interviews were made in close cooperation with Mrs Supranee Khammuang from the Teachers' College in Udorn. The interviews were conducted as conversations based on the same questions as those we had used in 1968. Of course, the young person in our sample had to be present. If this was a married young man, his wife also had to be there to complement the information. If it was a married young woman, we endeavoured to have her husband present but in this we did not always succeed. Often he was present only during parts of the conversation, and some husbands we never saw at all. They worked far away from home, or they were doing their military service, or they simply had left their wives. On the other hand, small children were sure to take part in the interviews and very often one or more of older relatives with whom the young people lived. Sometimes good friends or neighbours and their children were also present, and naturally all took part in the conversation. One might assume that the resulting jollity – always on the open veranda – would distract from the professional gain of the conversation. Perhaps the interviewees under the circumstances might have been a little more shy and reticent in answering many of the slightly special questions that we wished to have cleared up. This was, however, never the case. First and foremost, we were welcome acquaintances who had come to visit. Second, the villagers had since long become familiar with my particular interest. They eagerly told me of anything I wanted to know. In 1968, it had been the same. One just had to be prepared for a visit to take its own time and to arrange matters accordingly.

During my month-long 1978 stay in the village, I recorded few more ritual texts, magic spells, and medical recipes, and in this form the texts were entrusted to us by the villagers in the understanding and hope that, if at all possible, they would be published together with my findings at a later time.

Reporting the results

During shorter visits in 1979, 1980, 1981, and 1982, I updated my interviews and had discussions with the villagers about matters of doubt. I felt that my material was complete by then – that not much was missing – and that it was time to make an honest, sensible, and comprehensive representation of an aspect of everyday life in rural Thailand that is important to the villagers and that, to my knowledge, had not yet been described systematically in English.

By early 1983, I accomplished this goal with a 269-page report to DANIDA entitled: 'Pregnancy and Childbirth – its Customs and Rites in a Northeastern Thai Village'.

After the writing of this report, it was in one way my intention then to end my systematic study of this area of rural Isan life. But it turned out differently. Personally, I could not let go of my interest in seeing, how the fast moving modernization in Thailand would affect this particular area of village life and culture.

International colleagues and some in the village urged me to continue as they, too, found it of interest that this part of family life and Isan folk culture be followed through a time of transition.

And so, I visited the village again to follow up on my systematic studies in 1988, supported financially by DANIDA, again in February 1999, this time supported financially by VELUX FONDEN.

1988

Again, the decade following 1978 was a period in which all areas of life in Thailand underwent many changes.

Our research sample, the pupils from Grade 1 in the local school in 1961–62 were now 34–35 years old, and of such age that they could be regarded as fully integrated adult persons within their local cultural setting.

How did this group relate to the subject under study? Further, what was the relationship of a group of very young mothers to the traditions we had been dealing with since 1961–62?

My intention was to make a follow-up on all the 27 families from the 1978–79 sample (see above). We almost succeeded as only two families from this group had moved away from the village. The 25 families were supplemented with the 9 youngest mothers, who had recently given birth, to give a total of 34 families as our sample in 1988.

During this visit, I was able to extend my study to a wider area outside this specific village. I had, for a long time, felt uncomfortable at not having any kind of documentation for the traditions from outside this village. Was what I had found here narrowly restricted to this and nearby villages only? Or was the information more or less representative for a larger area of the Northeastern region? For years it had been my strong wish to visit villages in as large a geographical area as possible. This time my wish was realized.

I shall dwell on the approach to this part of the study, as it tells so much about Northeastern rural Thailand at the time. Our considerations and experience are also very informative in terms of what 'research' is and can be, and still in my best opinion very reliable and trustworthy. We considered many ways in which to perform this part of the study in a reasonable, un-complicated fashion, and at the same time feel assured that the information obtained was reliable. How best to contact local people in often very isolated places, and question them about their personal things? How to make them respond openly and freely when a foreigner turns up in their village? I felt sure that it would be no good to arrive together with Government officials in their uniforms, and yet an introduction was needed in a place where I was a total stranger.

We decided to try the following: the former headmaster of the school in Baan Phraan Muean, by then a retired superintendent of primary education, and his wife, joined me and my wife. So did the headman of Baan Phraan Muean village, who was a very capable local man who knew Isan people and their way of socializing with one another. Of course, my highly qualified inter-preter, Mrs Supranee, herself from Isan, also helped us. All in the group were people who easily established open and direct contact with other people in full respect for their integrity. But how to find the people who would be able to inform us in detail about the local cul-ture and traditions in this area?

The first strategy went wrong: we stopped at the school in the villages and contacted the headmaster but found that his knowledge about the families in his village was very limited because he rarely lived in the village himself.

Taught by this experience, we tried another strategy: driving slowly through a village lane we found a place where we could stop. In just a few minutes a group of people, mostly women of all ages and children, gathered around us. Then we introduced ourselves and started talking with them about the issues that concerned us. This proved to be completely uncomplicated, and I feel sure that we got a good and reliable overview of the local traditions in the total of 30 localities where we made a stop. In some places a family also invited us inside, where we conducted detailed interviews similar to those in Baan Phraan Muean.

We drove more than one thousand kilometres in the three *changwats* (provinces) of Udorn, Loei, and Nong

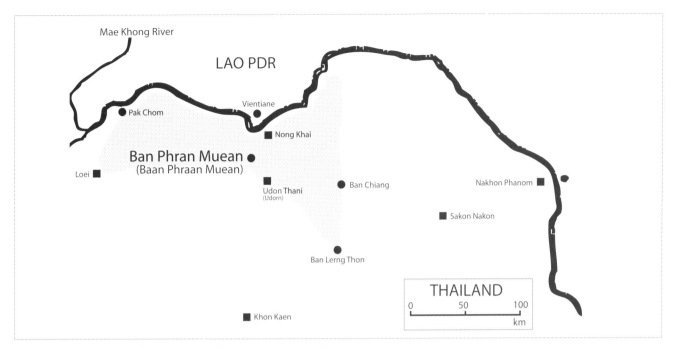

Mae Khong River

LAO PDR

Pak Chom

Vientiane

Nong Khai

Ban Phran Muean
(Baan Phraan Muean)

Loei

Udon Thani
(Udorn)

Ban Chiang

Nakhon Phanom

Sakon Nakon

Ban Lerng Thon

THAILAND
0   50   100
km

Khon Kaen

Khai (highlighted in the above map). After about each thirty-to-forty kilometres we made a stop. Every second time we wanted to make a stop, we turned away from the road and followed a narrow wheel-track to its very end. Here, amongst a little group of primitive farm-houses, we made our stop. From these experiences we gained much, not only about the subject under study, but about rural people and their life in general in outlying places in this fraction of the upper Northeast Thailand.

1999

A decade had passed since the last systematic follow-up of the study. Short visits to Baan Phraan Muean in 1991 and 1997, and information received through the exchange of letters, indicated that considerable changes had occurred in the intervening period. The follow-up in 1999 concentrated first and foremost on interviews with village elders, local health persons, and the most respected ritual masters in the village and in two other

Group-interviews were made in 30 localities within the area highlighted in the map above

villages in the neighbourhood. The five very young mothers and the seven female teachers in the local school were included as well, as were a few mothers from neighbouring villages. I found it important also to try and obtain updated information from Laos, which by then welcomed visitors crossing the border from Thailand. In Laos, we had discussions with people who had insight into the local culture and visited mothers in childbed, but unfortunately only in Vientiane and in its closer outskirts.

2000–2005

In February 2001, I again spent a few days in Baan Phraan Muean to follow-up on older data and to obtain new data. During this tour I also visited women in childbed in and around Siem Reap in Cambodia.

224

Forty years had passed since I designed my research project and started collecting and analysing my first data about customs and rites connected to pregnancy and childbirth. Now it was time to make a status report for the whole period!

In 2003 and again in 2004, I went back – this time as part of the process of preparing my material for publication. We were especially interested in checking certain information and in obtaining copies of the texts for the different rites. In the aftermath of this trip, we recorded the *suukhwan maemaan*, which we did not have on tape and translated anew.

I was particularly gratified to be able to observe this time, too, both a traditional *yuu fai* and a *taengkae mae kamlerd* (*kae kamlerd*) rite for a almost new-born sick child, that took place during the few days we were in Baan Phraan Muean.

In 2003, 2004, and 2005 I also visited the neighbouring countries of Myanmar, Yunnan (China), and Laos.

Notes

1. The International Institute for Child Study in Bangkok was established by and until 1963 jointly run by UNESCO and the Thai Government. Today the Institute is named *Behavioral Science Research Institute.*

2. S. J. Tambiah: *Buddhism and Spirit Cults in North-east Thailand* (1970), – various professional articles (among other: 1968a, 1968b, 1968c, 1973).

3. C. Suvannathat (ed.) (1971): *Summaries of the Study of Social Influences on the Development of Thai Children in the Villages of Ban Pranmuen and U-Meng.*

Both Khun Supranee and Khun Jan are very special persons.

Khun Supranee's insight in the Isan culture and its traditions, combined with her linguistic abilities is unique, as is Khun Jan's critical, but detailed familiarity with the local culture and traditional beliefs.

Since the late 1970s, their positive co-operation and their respect for each others particular qualifications have contributed greatly to bring forth the material presented in this book.

I am deeply indebted to both of them.

APPENDIX II*

A Note on the Isan Language

The Northeast region of Thailand is also referred to as Isan. The large area, which covers 160,000 square km, has been part of Siam since the 17th century. The treaties between the French and the Siamese from 1893 and 1904 made Isan the border area between Siam and French Indochina.

The language that the people of Isan speak at home is also called Isan. It is a language linguistically closer related to Lao than to Central Thai.[1] The estimated number of people who speak Isan is 23 million. Though Thai, Lao, and Isan are substantially mutually understandable, Isan is not easily understood for a person who speaks Central Thai: the pronunciation is quite different, and so is the meaning of many words, many of which are the same as in Lao.[2]

According to Professor Suwilai Premsilat from Mahidol University, there are almost 70 indigenous languages in Thailand but generally Thailand has promoted Central Thai as the only official language: only Central Thai has officially been used as the language of instruction in the schools.[3] Hence over the past many years, Isan has been considered a dialect of Central Thai.

In recent years, there has, however, been a trend to emphasize the need to maintain the diversity of cultures and languages as a tool for social development and sustainable economic growth. This new recognition was, among others, expressed by His Majesty King Bhumibol in 1989: 'Languages are a tool of humanity. They are a way to express opinions and are things of beauty, for example in the form of literature. It is necessary to carefully preserve languages.'[4]

Today Isan is not used often as a language of written communication but when it is, the Thai script is used.

Before the Thai alphabet and language were introduced as the only language of instruction in schools, the people of Isan would use the Lao alphabet, *tai noi*, when writing ordinary text. Another script, *nangsuee tham*, was originally used for the writing of religious texts, and was an important medium of education when monks were in charge of education in these areas.[5] While the *nangsuee tham* alphabet is that of the ancient Lao language mixed with the ancient language of the Mon-Khmer sub-group (in Thai known as *aksorn khorm*) and today only used in the religious manuscripts, the *tai noi* script is the current script used in Laos.

Most of the texts in the palm leaf manuscript reproduced in this book are written in the *nangsuee tham*. But according to Khun Jan, there are also passages in the original manuscript that are written in *tai noi*.

---

* Appendix II was written by Mrs Supranee Khammuang and Mrs Pernille Askerud

Poetic Techniques in the Ritual Texts

When discussing literary techniques in Isan poetry, the most important thing to keep in mind is that contrary to English, Isan and Thai are monosyllabic languages, i.e., each word consists of only one syllable. Because English is not monosyllabic it is impossible to make a translation that reflects the rhyme pattern in Isan and Thai. When listening to the chanting of the ritual texts it is, however, possible – even for those who do not understand the language – to hear these rhythmic patterns and get an impression of the energy and beauty that they render the texts.

For the benefit of those who are able to read Thai we have, after the description of each of the different rhyme patterns, listed one or more examples from the Isan versions of ritual texts discussed in this book. In each of the examples, the literary technique applied has been highlighted in the verses themselves with contrast colour which can perhaps also help the non-Isan speaker to understand the principles described. As a translation would not make any sense in this particular discussion, we have not reprinted it here.

Description and narration

The main literary techniques used in the ritual texts are description and narration, both of which reflects the way of life in the village and the villagers perception of the world, as illustrated in the following verses:

เดือนหกคนหาแอก	*On the sixth lunar month, people look for yokes.*
เดือนแปดคนหาไถ	*On the eighth lunar month, people look for ploughs.*

(*Taengkae Maemaan* – Verses 209–210)

แม่เจ้าอยู่เมืองคนคอยถ่า	*Your mother, in the human town, is waiting.*
ฟ้าฮ้องแผดเสียงวอน	*Thunder rolls unceasingly.*
น้ำถ่วมท่งแวนหนา	*Flood overflows the rice fields.*
เฮดนายามเดือนเก้า	*On the ninth lunar month, it is the ploughing time.*

(*Taengkae Maemaan* – Verses 218–221)

Raay rhyme patterns

Most parts of the ritual texts employ the rhyme pattern known from traditional Thai poetry that is called *raay*. In the traditional *raay*, every line has eight words – or syllables. (Note however, that the rule concerning the length of each line is not always observed in the ritual texts discussed in the book.) In this rhyme pattern, for every two lines the last word or syllable in the first line must rhyme with one of he five initial words or syllables in the following line, as illustrated in the diagram below.[6]

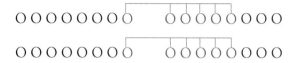

Occasionally the rhyme pattern will even be applied between the two-line segments to provide additional variation and melody to the verses.

เมือทัดดอกไม้เกดข้างกอ
เมือทัดดอกยอทั้งต้น
เมือทัดดอกขี้อ้นแกมดอกขูนพูม
บานจูมจีนั้นดอกคัดเค้า
บานบ่อเศร้านั้นดอกสามปี
บานยาวฮีนั้นดอกงวงช้าง
(*Suukhwan Maemaan* – Verses 54–59)

Repetition and emphasis

There is only one example in our texts where the last word of a verse rhymes with the last word of the following verse (see below the first example – *Taengkae Maemaan*, Verses 300–301) – though this is a rhyming pattern often used in other Isan poetry and also is often used in European poetry.

When the regular *raay* rhyme pattern is not employed, the texts make use of repetition of lines, as a kind of refrain, to create rhythm and emphasis, as illustrated in the continuation of the *Taengkae Maemaan* text (verses 302–304) and in the other examples on the next page.

อันนี้แม่นแพรตางเนื้อ
อันนี้แม่นเสื่อตางคิง
ให้มาเอาเยอ
ของกูมีทุกสิ่ง
ซิงๆ หน่านางแถน
(*Taengkae Maemaan* – Verses 300–304)

ปานนี้ผัวเจ้าบ่าวน้อยให้เช็ดน้ำมูกน้ำตาอยู่ลีลาลีลา
ปานนี้ผัวเจ้าเช็ดน้ำตาอยู่ลีไล่ลีไล่
(*Suukhwan Maemaan* – Verses 43–44)

ของเด็กน้อยชวนกันมาลีลุดลีล่าย
(*Suukhwan Maemaan* – Verse 69)

หัวใจแม่เจ้าจึงคอนอยู่จีจี
(*Suukhwan Maemaan* – Verse 82)

นกเค้าฮ้องกูกกูกูกกู
(*Suukhwan Maemaan* – Verse 89)

สองมือแม่เจ้าจึงกวยอยู่ต่อนแต่นต่อนแต่น
(*Suukhwan Maemaan* – Verse 95)

แม่เจ้าจึงคัวเคียหาเอาฝ้ายอยู่เปียมาผูกแขน
(*Suukhwan Maemaan* – Verse 99)

This technique is widely used throughout the texts. Repetition is a distinctive characteristic of the Isan language even in everyday usage. As noted by Chaakrit Ananthrawan: 'Word play is used to emphasize the holiness of the text. The repetition of certain phrases and words underlines this and is at the same time a reference technique for meditation practice.' This is particularly seen (or heard) in the *Taengkae Mae Kamlerd* text, which is full of such repetitions.

เคราะห์อันจักมาต่อหน้าและภายหลัง ก็ให้หายเสียมื้อนี้วันนี้
เคราะห์คิงไฟใหม่ย้าว ก็ให้หายเสียมื้อนี้วันนี้
เคราะห์หมากพร้าวหล่นจากแซง ก็ให้หายเสียมื้อนี้วันนี้
เคราะห์เข่าดำเข่าแดงจักเกิดเป็นเลือด ก็ให้แก้เสียมื้อนี้วันนี้
เคราะห์ขำเขือกและลางงู ก็ให้หายเสียมื้อนี้วันนี้

เคราะห์หนูกัดเสื้อผ้า ก็ให้หายเสียมื้อนี้วันนี้

เคราะห์อันจักเป็นกำพร้าพัดแม่อยู่นอนเคียง ก็ให้หายเสียมื้อนี้วันนี้

เคราะห์สอยวอยผ้าขาด ก็ให้หายเสียมื้อนี้วันนี้

เคราะห์อนละหนในเนื้อ ก็ให้หายเสียมื้อนี้วันนี้

เคราะห์สองผัวเมียหมั่นผิดข้อง ก็ให้หายเสียมื้อนี้วันนี้

เคราะห์งัวควายถึกแอกและบ่วงน้อยยักขาคา ก็ให้หายเสียมื้อนี้วันนี้

เคราะห์ไปมาเห็นเหตุ อุบัติเหตุเป็นลาง ก็ให้หายเสียมื้อนี้วันนี้

เคราะห์หมั่นคางป่วยไข่ ก็ให้หายเสียมื้อนี้วันนี้

เคราะห์ทุกข์ยากไฮ้บ่อมีสัง ก็ให้หายเสียมื้อนี้วันนี้

กูจักผาบหมู่เคราะห์กำเลิบให้เพิก

กูจักแก้หมู่แม่กำเลิดให้หนี

ให้สูหนีเมือภูตกข่ามพู้นเยอ

ให้สูหนีเมือน้ำตกเขียวพู้นเยอ

(*Taengkae Mae Kamlerd* – Verses 126–143)

Alliteration and assonance

Finally, the use of alliteration and assonance also appears throughout the texts as a successful literary and narrative technique.

เคราะห์คิงไฟใหม่ย้าว ก็ให้หายเสียมื้อนี้วันนี้

เคราะห์หมากพร้าวหล่นจากแซง ก็ให้หายเสียมื้อนี้วันนี้

เคราะห์เข่าดำเข่าแดงจักเกิดเป็นเลือด ก็ให้แก้เสียมื้อนี้วันนี้

(*Taengkae Mae Kamlerd* – Verses 127–129)

Though the translation is quite literal and cannot reflect the rhyme patterns and other stylistic characteristics of the texts, the translations will hopefully give the reader an impression of both

the form and the beauty of the texts in their original version, as well as of the complexity of the universe they spring from.

Because the Isan language is monosyllabic, it leaves more room for variations in the recital than for example an English text does. The way the metre falls on any word, or the use of cadences and breathing pauses, all depend on the skills of the individual ritual master. Phor Jampii was such a recognized authority not least because of his ability to recite the text in a masterful way – as can still be heard in the recordings. His art, or his ability to do this, made the text more powerful. Hence the texts only really come to life when they are recited.

Notes

1. For more information on the Isan language, see for example http://en.wikipedia.org/wiki/Isan_language or Ethnologue: *Languages of the World* available at www.ethnologue.com

2. See also Suwilai Premsilat et al. 2004.

3. Mrs Suwilai Premsilat is Professor at the Institute for Language and Culture for Rural Development (ILCRI) at Mahidol University where she has been spearheading a programme for minority languages in development for the last 30 years. Other institutions, including Khon Kaen University, the most influential university in the Northeast, are also working to promote the recognition and wider use of Isan language.

4. Translation of a quotation from the preface of *The Isan–Central Thai Dictionary*, Khon Kaen University & Sahawittayalai Isan, 1989, here quoted from Draper, John (2004) *Isan: The Planning Context for Language Maintenance and Revitalization.* In SLLT, vol. 4, 2004-www.usq.edu.au/opacs/sslt/4

5. Saan Saarathasananan, 1986 (p. 53) and Jarubut Ruangsuwan, 1977 (p. 13).

6. Chaakrit Ananthrawan: *Bot Suud Khwan (Changwat Loei).* Odeon Store Press, Bangkok 1995 (p. 53).

APPENDIX III*

Principles for the Transcription of Isan Names and Words

Several different systems for transcribing Thai letters to English are currently in use in Thailand, as easily observed in traffic signs and maps. Furthermore, there are distinct differences between Thai and Isan pronunciation of the same words. The principles used for transcription in this book aim at rendering the pronunciation as close to Isan pronunciation as possible.

Some notes on the principles followed in this book when transcribing Isan names and words into English script are presented below. In order to facilitate the reader's understanding of the text we have compiled a pronunciation guide as well as a glossary of the Isan terms used in the text when no easy translation was identified.

Please note that there are distinctive differences between the Central Thai and the Isan language that go beyond the lexical differences. The following are a few examples of such differences that are important when one reads the book or wants to study the matter more deeply.

1. There is no /**r-**/ sound in Northeastern dialect. The /**r-**/ sound in Central Thai will be pronounced as /**h-**/ in Northeastern dialect, for example:
    *   '**bad**' in central Thai is /**raay**/,
    *   in Northeastern dialect it becomes /**haay**/.

2. There is neither an /**l**/ nor an /**r**/ cluster in the Northeastern dialect, for example:
    *   **praab fai** in Central Thai will be pronounced
    *   **paab fai** in Northeastern dialect.

3. The /**w**/ cluster in the Northeastern dialect is pronounced differently, for example:
    *   the word /**khwan**/ in Central Thai
    *   will be /**khwuan**/ in Northeastern dialect**.**

4. Some words (not every word though) with the high tone in Central Thai tend to be pronounced in the low tone in Northeastern dialect, for example:
    *   the word rice /**khaaw**/ (high tone) in Central Thai
    *   in Northeastern dialect it is /**khau**/, shorter and in the low tone.

---

* Appendix III was written by Mrs Supranee Khammuang and Mrs Pernille Askerud

5. There is no /**ch-**/ in the Northeastern dialect. The /**ch-**/ of Central Thai is pronounced as /**s-**/ (if it appears in a word with the same meaning of Northeastern dialect and Central Thai), for example:

- The word /**mor wichaa**/ in Central Thai
- in Northeastern dialect is pronounced /**mor wisaa**/.

In writing, however, one might see more often /**ch-**/ pronounced as /**ch-**/ by educated people and when it is used in a formal context. The fact remains that in everyday life ordinary villagers will normally pronounce it as /**s-**/.

The Isan versions of the ritual texts printed here reflect these general differences between Central Thai and Isan. However, as there is no standard for Isan spelling and usage, the texts are not always absolutely consistent. Please note that the Isan versions of the ritual texts rendered here follow the writing and spelling of the ritual master.

Guidelines for Pronunciation and Transcription

CONSONANTS

THAI/ISAN	ENGLISH		EXAMPLES	
			words used in the present book	
	Initial	Final	Thai script	English transcription
ก	k-	-k	แก้	**k**ae
			หมากบก	maak bo**k**
ข, ค, ต	kh-	-k	ขวัญ	**kh**wan
			ควดเข่า	**kh**wuad **kh**au
ง	ng-	-ng	แต่ง	tae**ng**
			งาม	**ng**aam
จ	j-	-t	จำปี	**j**am pii
			เข่าจี่	khau **j**ii
ฉ, ช, ฌ	ch-	-t	หมอวิชา	mor wi**ch**aa
ย, ญ	y-	-y	ยากำ	**y**aa kam
			พราย	phraa**y**
ด, ฏ	d-	-d	ดอก	**d**ork
			กำเลิด	kamler**d**

CONSONANTS

THAI/ISAN	ENGLISH		EXAMPLES	
			words used in the present book	
	Initial	Final	Thai script	English transcription
ต, ฏ	t-	-d	กุฏิ	ku**t**i
			พ่อตู้	phor **t**uu
ถ, ท, ธ, ฐ, ฑ, ฒ	th-	-t	แถน	**th**aen
น, ณ	n-	-n	น้ำมนต์	**n**am mon
			โนนงาม	**n**oon ngaam
บ	b-	-b	โบสถ์	**b**ood
			ผีปอป	phii por**b**
ป	p-	-p	ผีปอป	phii **p**orb
			ปราบไฟ	**p**raab fai
ผ, ภ, พ	ph-	-p	ผีพราย	phii **ph**raay
ฝ, ฟ	f-		อยู่ไฟ	yuu **f**ai
ม	m-	-m	แม่มาน	**m**ae**m**aan
ย	y-	-y	อยู่กำ	**y**uu kam
			ผีตายโหง	phii taa**y** hoong
ร	r-	-n	--	--
ล, ฬ	l-	-n	แถนหลวง	thaen **l**uang
			ตำบล	tambo**n**
ว	w-	-w	หมอวิชา	mor **w**ichaa
			ไม่ติ้ว	mai ti**w**
ศ, ษ, ส	s-	-t	เสียพิษไฟ	**s**ia phit fai
ห, ฮ	h-	–	หอม	**h**orm
อ	–	–	--	--

VOWELS

THAI/ISAN		ENGLISH	EXAMPLES words used in the book
		Thai script	English transcription
อะ, อา	a,aa	ขวัญ	khwan
		พาขวัญ	phaa khwan
อิ, อี	i, ii	เสียพิษไฟ	sia phit fai
		ผี	phii
อึ, อือ	ue, uee	หนังสือ	nang suee
		แม่ซื้อ	mae suee
อุ, อู	u, uu	สู่ขวัญ	suu khwan
เอะ, เอ	e, ei	เอ็นอ้า	en - aa
		เทวดา	theiwadaa
แอ	ae	แต่งแก้	taengkae
เออะ, เออ	oe, er	กำเลิด	kamlerd
โอะ, โอ	ɔ, oo	ตำบล	tambon
		โบสถ์	bood
เอาะ, ออ	or	หมอส่อง	mor sorng
เอียะ, เอีย	ia	เสีย	sia
เอือะ, เอือ	uea	พรานเหมือน	phraan muean
อัวะ, อัว	ua	กล้วย	kluay
ไอย, อัย	ai	อยู่ไฟ	yuu fai
เอา	au	เป่ากำเลิด	pau kam lerd

Names of places and locations. Besides the names of the target province, Udornthani, the other proper names of provinces and places are spelled in the book according to the current official spelling – Isan, Chieng Mai, Nakhon Phanom, Loei, Pak Chom, Sakon Nakhon, Ubon, Nong Khai, Tha Bo, Khon Kaen, Saraburi, and Ratchaburi – even though this is not always consistent with the transcription rules otherwise applied.

For the target province, the names are transcribed in line with the Isan-Thai transcription used otherwise in the book. Both Udornthani and Udon Thani are acceptable transcriptions though the latter is gaining in popularity. In this context we have chosen the more traditional transcription /**Udornthani**/ or it's shorter form /**Udorn**/.

The place names used in the book include the following:

Official transcription	*Our Isan transcription*
Udon Thani	Udorn Thani (Udorn)

Names of locations in Udorn province:

Ban Phran Muean	Baan Phraan Muean
Ban Non Ngam	Baan Noon Ngaam
Ban Yai	Baan Yai
Ban Noy	Baan Nory
Ban Na Kha	Baan Naa Khaa
Ban Khaw	Baan Khaaw
Ban Phue	Baan Phuee
Ban Chiang	Baan Chiang
(Menam) Kong [the Mekong]	Mae Khong (River)

Names of locations in Laos:

Thakhek	Thaakhaek
Viangchan	Vientiane
Luang Prabang	Luang Phrabaang

APPENDIX IV

Glossary

A / B

Baab	บาป	Disadvantage (opposite of merit)
Baan Noon Ngaam	บ้านโนนงาม	The 'small hamlet' in Baan Phraan Muean grew over the years and was accepted by the authorities in 1980 as an independent administrative unit under this name, which means 'the beautiful small hill'
Baan nory	บ้านน้อย	'Small hamlet', the extension of the village along the road to Udorn
Baan yai	บ้านใหญ่	'Big hamlet', the largest and oldest core part of the village Baan Phraan Muean
Bai laan	ใบลาน	Palm leaf manuscript
Bood	โบสถ์	The name of the holiest house in the temple compound
Bun	บุญ	Merit *Bun* and *baab* are verbal categories frequently used by the villagers. They are essential in their everyday thinking about how to 'make merit' (*tam bun*)

C

Changwat	จังหวัด	Province, e.G. Changwat Udorn

D

Deva	เทว—	God, Sanskrit word; from the Indian world of god. In Thai these gods or divine beings are called *theiwadaa*(s)

E / F

Faay mongkhon	ฝ้ายมงคล	'Thread of good fortune' – the cotton thread that is attached to the *phaa khwan* and connects this with the officiant of the ceremony (*mor khwan*) and the audience

Farang	ฝรั่ง	Caucasian foreigner – a word which denotes white-skinned foreigners; the word is derived from 'français' (*farangseit*) – the French

G

Garuda	ครุฑ	A mythical sky bird, in Thai called *khrut*

H / I

Isan	อีสาน	Thai name for the region covering the Northeastern Thai provinces – today it is often transcribed Isan but it is also found as Isarn, Esarn, Isaan, Esaan

J / K

Kae	แก้	*Kae* is the main verb used in the rites. It means to dispel and chase away the evil – or to deliver someone from that evil
Kae kamlerd	แก้กำเลิด	A rite performed to dispel sickness in children caused by 'former spiritual mothers' (*mae kau mae lang*)
Kae mae kau mae lang	แก้แม่เก่าแม่หลัง	To dispel *mae kau mae lang*
Kan haay	กันฮ่าย	An Isan word - *kan* means 'to protect', *haay* means 'evil' or 'danger'; to give protection against any evil
Kan phraay kan porb	กันพรายกันปอบ	To 'protect against' the two spirits mentioned
Khaa saang	ข่าซาง ไทยกลาง : ฆ่าซาง	Local dialect 'to kill the worm', a small rite performed to kill *saang* – the sickness that makes you pale, weak and skinny. *Saang* must refer to intestinal worms
Khaay	คาย	A small container or jar in which a present (or payment) to the ritual master is placed
Khamin	ขมิ้น	The root of *Curcuma Longa L.* – reminiscent of ginger, in the Northeast it is called *khiimin*
Khan haa	ขันห่า ไทยกลาง : ขันห้า	A small bowl (*khan*) filled with five (*haa*) flowers, preferable white, five candles, and five incense sticks
Khau daeng	เข่าแดง ไทยกลาง : ข้าวแดง	'Red' rice – rice mixed with (brown) palm sugar to make it red

Khau dam	เข่าดำ ไทยกลาง : ข้าวดำ	'Black' rice – naturally black (or purple) rice, or white rice mixed with black sesame to make it black
Khau jii	เข่าจี ไทยกลาง : ข้าวจี่	Steamed and grilled glutinous rice
Khau khaaw	เข่าขาว ไทยกลาง : ข้าวขาว	Plain rice
Khau lueang	เข่าเหลือง ไทยกลาง : ข้าวเหลือง	'Yellow rice' – rice mixed with egg yolk to make it yellow
Khau yam	เข่าหย่ำ	An Isan word referring to the local steamed sticky rice chewed by the mother, then mixed with banana and roasted in a banana leaf, to make a supplementary food for babies
Khuad khau	ควดเข่า ไทยกลาง : คดข้าว	The ceremonial master will use a lump of sticky rice (*khau*) to pull out (*khuad*) all illnesses
Khun	คุณ	Common title of courtesy used for both sexes in front of the name instead of Mr or Mrs
Khwan	ขวัญ	One half of the dual human soul, the *khwan* connotes a kind of 'spirit essence' or 'life soul'
Kradong	กระด้ง	The general name for the flat plaited tray used for all sorts of purposes in the village
Kradong morn	กระด้งหม่อน, กะด้งมอน	A special basket tray used in the breeding of silkworms
Krathong	กระทง	A word that covers many kinds of containers – in the context of the book it is used for ceremonial purposes
Kuti	กุฏิ	Monks' dwellings or residence
L		
Lao tham	ลาวธรรม	A script, often just named *tham*; the language in which (all or most) sacred or ritual literature in the village is written Locally it is referred to as *nangsuee tham* (see below). According to Tambiah (1970, p. 119), the word *tham* derives from the Pali word Dhamma, which means Buddhist doctrine and is used to refer to the corpus of Buddhist sacred texts

Lord Abbot	เจ้าอาวาส	The head monk in the temple
Luuk bok	ลูกบก	Local name for wild almond, in central thai called: *kra-bok*

M

Maak than	หมากทัน	Dialect, corresponding to *phutsaa* in central thai: chinese date or Indian jujube
Mae kamlerd	แม่กำเลิด	See: *mae kau mae lang*
Mae kau mae lang	แม่เก่าแม่หลัง	The name of the 'former spiritual mother(s)' who allow children to be born as humans. In everyday language she also appears under the name *mae kamlerd*, because she represents a series of symptoms in he baby described as *kamlerd*
Mae suee	แม่ซื้อ	'The purchasing mother'
Mae tamyae	แม่ตำแย	'The mother who receives' is the everyday name for the local woman who assists in childbirth and who functions as midwife though she does not have any formal training to do so. However, the trained midwives from the newly established district health centers are also called *mae tamyae*
Mai ben rai	ไม่เป็นไร	A commonly used comment in Thailand which indicates a 'never mind' attitude to the subject under discussion
Mathayom	มัธยม	Grades 7–12 of secondary school
Mor	หมอ	Title used in front of a qualifier to indicate a specialization in something – an expert; it doesn't necessarily relate to any formal qualification
Mor duu	หมอดู	Astrologer, fortune-teller
Mor khwan	หมอขวัญ	Lay officiant performing *khwan* rites. *Phaam* is colloquially used by the northeasterner; in central thai this person is called *phraam*
Mor lam	หมอลำ	Performer of a 'folk opera'. The content of these performances are often somewhat daring
Mor leik	หมอเลข	Astrologer, fortune-teller
Mor pau kamlerd	หมอเป่ากำเลิด	Performer of the *pau kamlerd* rite

Mor sorng	หมอส่อง	Diviner; the expert (*mor*) who can 'search' and find by 'seeing' (*sorng*)
Mor tambon	หมอตำบล	The local people's name for the head nurse in the District Health Clinic
Mor tham	หมอธรรม	exorcist of malevolent spirits
Mor wichaa	หมอวิชา	'Expert in magic', especially in love magic and protective magic, such as making amulets
Mor yaa	หมอยา	Herbal specialist, herbalist

N

Naen	แนน	Birth tree – see *ning* below
Naga	นาค	The water-serpent. The symbol of a Buddha who preceded the historical Gotama Buddha
Nam horm	น้ำหอม ไทยกลาง : น้ำหอม	Perfumed water
Nam mon	น้ำมนต์ ไทยกลาง : น้ำมนต์	'Magic' water
Nam maak	น้ำหมาก ไทยกลาง : น้ำหมาก	Betel or lime water, produced by chewing a betel quid (a combination of areca nut, betel leaves, and lime) and mixing this in the mouth with water
Nangsuee tham	หนังสือธรรม	The language most often used in Buddhist texts in the Northeast of Thailand. In addition, some of the ritual texts for *khwan* and *kamlerd* are written in *nangsuee tham*. The language is also called Lao *tham*
Ning	นิ่ง	Birth tree The birth tree(s) contains both good and evil qualities and are the source of this in human nature. The child is said to come down – to be born on Earth – by the line going from Heaven to Earth called *saay* (line) *ning saay naen* It is unclear, whether both *ning* and *naen* refer to the same tree and are used as reduplication, or there are indeed two trees and not one

Pali	บาลี	The Indian literary language in which the holy texts of the Buddhists are written; closely related to Sanskrit
Pau kamlerd	เป่ากำเลิด	A smaller rite aimed at removing symptoms in the child caused by mae kamlerd. *Pau* means to 'blow' or to 'puff'
Phaa khau maa	ผ่าเข่าม่า ไทยกลาง : ผ้าขาวม้า	A man's loincloth
Phaa khwan Phaa khwuan	พาขวัญ พาขวัญ	Conspicuous ritual item in all *khwan* ceremonies. It is a tiered conical structure build on a tray, often a beautifully executed decoration. On the tray are placed a boiled egg, bananas, flowers and a lump of rice. Placed on the tray are also the short 'sacred threads' that will be bound around the wrist of the celebrant after the rite to 'bind the *khwan*' *phuuk khaen* to the body. In Isan often called *phaa khwuan*
Phaa sin	ผ่าสิ่น ไทยกลาง : ผ้าซิ่น	Woman's skirt
Phaam	พ(ร)าหมณ์	See *mor khwan*
Phii	ผี	Spirit
Phii faa	ผีฟ้า	A special form which the great creator *puu thaen yaa thaen* can assume
Phii nok khau	ผีนกเค้า	An evil spirit who appears in the form or shape of a *nok khau* – an owl
Phii phraay	ผีพราย	A malevolent spirit who is particularly dangerous for the woman in childbirth – the spirit possibly comes into existence in connection with a woman's death in childbirth
Phii porb	ผีปอบ	An evil spirit considered particularly dangerous for the woman in childbirth. This spirit can be/is hosted by a living person
Phii taay hoong	ผีตายโหง	The soul (*winyaan*) may become this very dangerous spirit if the death is unnatural and sudden, brought about by e.g. child birth, accidents, homicide and sudden virulent disease, before a normal life-cycle is completed
Phor	พ่อ	Father

Phor tuu	พ่อตู้	Grandfather, commonly preceding the name of elderly and respected male persons
Phuu yai baan	ผู้ใหญ่บ้าน	The elected village headman
Plaa haeng	ปลาแห้ง	Dried and salted (fresh water) fish
Praab fai	ปราบไฟ	To 'kill the heat'; a rite that is performed in order to minimize the unpleasant side-effects of lying by a fire after the birth
Prathom	ประถม	Name of the grades of the elementary school
Puu thaen yaa thaen	ปู่แถนย่าแถน	Paternal grandfather and paternal grandmother in heaven; connected to the *taengkae maemarn* rite

Q / R / S

Saalaa	ศาลา	The assembly hall in the temple compound
Sia phit fai	เสียพิษไฟ	'To kill the fire'; a rite held by the end of *yuu fai* to remove the possible unpleasant after effects of having been exposed to the heat of the fire for some time
Suay dork	ส่วยดอก	'Something pretty with flowers', offering to the fire by the end of *yuu fai*
Suukhwan kong khau	สู่ขวัญก่องเข่า	A *khwan* rite for sick children up to the age of about ten years
Suukhwan luang	สู่ขวัญหลวง	Ceremony for adults suffering from absence of the *khwan*
Suukhwan	สู่ขวัญ	*Suu* ('to call') – *suukhwan* ('calling the *khwan*'). In Isan often procounced *suudkhwan*
Suukhwan maemaan	สู่ขวัญแม่มาน	Rite for the pregnant woman, calling the *khwan* of the mother and of the child in her womb
Suukhwan thammadaa	สู่ขวัญธรรมดา	'Ordinary' *khwan* ceremony performed on a number of occasions, e.g. before a man goes on a trip or a youth into military service
Suukwan naak	สู่ขวัญนาค	A rite that is performed when a (young) man enters the monkhood

T

| Taapuubaan | ตาปู่บ้าน | Guardian spirit, understood to be the real owner of all land in the village |

Taeng	แต่ง	An action
Taengkae mae kamlerd	แต่งแก้แม่กำเลิด	Often called just *kae kamlerd*: it can be performed as a treatment throughout childhood if the child has symptoms attributed to *mae kamlerd*
Taengkae maemaan	แต่งแก้แม่มาน	An action (*taeng*) that is to deliver (*kae*) the pregnant woman (*maemaan*). Addressed to supernaturals pictured as 'old mothers' (*mae kau mae lang*) who allow children to be born as humans
Tambon	ตำบล	An administrative unit or district consisting of a number of villages
Thaen	แถน	The divine beings or gods, part of the Northeastern universe. There are many *thaen*(s) and all have different capabilities and responsibilities. Within this hierarchical system the greatest of all is named *thaen luang* or *phaya thaen* who is close to a concept of the great creator. The *thaen*(s) of lower rank under him are responsible for the creation of humans with the involvement of the 'birth tree(s)' – called *ton ning ton naen*. Hence the *thaen*(s) form or shape human with different components from the birth tree(s) The place where the *thaen*(s) reside is called *mueang thaen* – this is heaven
Theiwadaa	เทวดา	Guardian and divine beings, benevolent in nature. The word refers to a wide range of beings of more and less importance of which some are god-like, some like angels, and some are guardian 'spirits'. While many *theiwadaa*(s) resides in the different levels of heaven, some live on earth as illustrated in the ritual texts. The word *theiwadaa* is derived from the Pali *deva*
Thian khuu aayu	เทียนคู่อายุ	Short wax candle prepared for a purpose in connection with a rite
Thian wian hua	เทียนเวียนหัว	A special wax candle used in various village ceremonies; has the length of the circumference of the head of the celebrant
Three Gems	พระรัตนตรัย	Refer to *Phra Phut*: Lord Buddha *Phra Tham*: Buddha's dogma *Phra Song*: Buddha's disciples, monks and priests

U		
Udornthani	อุดรธานี	also transcribed into English as Udonthani. Today most often called Udon
V / W		
wai	ไหว้	a customary Thai greeting and a manner of paying respect to someone
wat	วัด	Buddhist temple
winyaan	วิญญาณ	the part of the dual human soul that only leaves man when he dies
X / Y		
yaa kam	ยากรรม	a herbal decoction that the mother drinks at the end of *yuu fai* to prevent another pregnancy from coming too soon. In Baan Phraan Muean, *yaa kam* is drunk at the end of the *yuu fai* while in other areas it is being drunk during the period of *yuu fai*
yaa kamlang	ยากำลัง	this is a patent medicine that is sold by itinerary traders. *Yaa* means medicine and *kamlang* means energy and strength and so the mothers take this medicine to feel stronger and more energetic
yaad nam	หยาดน้ำ ไทยกลาง : หยาดน้ำ	the sprinkling of magic water (*nam mon*) by hand over the *krathong* as an offering
yuu fai	อยู่ไฟ	'to lie by the fire'
yuu kam	อยู่กรรม	a more original Northeastern designation for *yuu fai*

APPENDIX V
A Brief Survey of Literature

Few scholarly works have pregnancy and childbirth in Thailand as their main subjects.

Phya Anuman Rajadhon's *Customs Connected with Birth and Rearing of Children*, originally published in Thai in 1949, was, on publication in English in 1961, immediately considered as a classic; the well from which one could draw when this aspect of Thai folklore was to be elucidated. Professor William J. Gedney wrote of Rajadhon in his preface to Rajadhon's *Life and Ritual in Old Siam*, part of which was about birth customs: 'He has a position in the field of Thai letters and scholarship which is unique and paradoxical. Though he is not an academician by training, his scholarly attainments have placed all younger teachers and students at his feet and made him one of Thailand's most highly respected university professors.'

Rajadhon's sources are first and foremost oral legends but his unique insight into the classical literature, both from Thailand and from neighbouring countries, contributes significantly to the whole that his dissertation constitutes.

His basic material did not make it possible for him to state anything decisive as to whether this or that custom is general for Thailand, or to which extent it is observed in given regions or by population groups. In this respect, how he himself evaluated his material is evident from a quotation: 'There are some that are still observed in certain localities, and some that have been given up. Even in the same locality there are practices and beliefs which are not uniform; there are certain omissions, additions, or alterations, depending on the ability, beliefs, nationality, class and knowledge of the people.'[1] The very title *Life and Ritual in Old Siam* and its use of the word 'old' undoubtedly indicates that, at the moment of writing, he considered a great deal of it as belonging to a former time.

The dissertation does not deal solely with customs and traditions in a restricted sense. There is also abundant material about various types of rituals. He treats the ritual side of pregnancy, childbirth and childhood in several of his other works, and together they provide the best source for this aspect of the traditional culture in Thailand.

Dr Jane Richardson Hanks: *Maternity and its Rituals in Bang Chan* is another source of knowledge and understanding in this subject area. Her research was conducted in 1953-54 as a part of Cornell University's Thailand project. It was conducted just twenty miles Northeast of Bangkok in a typical Central Plain rice-growing village with 1,700 inhabitants, split into 336 families, of which around 10 per cent were Muslims.

She stated that the purpose of the study was 'to set down ethnographic data concerning childbirth, following out the economic, social, religious and cosmological aspects as needed to clarify the behaviour and the psychological attitudes noted'. Referring to Kaufman (1960) who undertook research in a village only eight kilometres from Bang Chan, she pointed out that there were 'striking differences', and used this observation to warn about just how careful one must be in making generalizations based on individual observations.

This social and cultural-anthropological work has, as far as I know, never been published in other than the original, mimeographed edition from 1963. This may seem strange, considering the knowledgeable solidity and thoroughness of the dissertation. The fact that there is a delightful, humane warmth shining throughout the book makes it even more valuable and worth of reading.

In her work, she occupied herself with the whole spectrum of events and functions during the period of pregnancy and in connection with the childbirth itself, but there is practically nothing about to what extent the patterns she described were observed by the women in the village. Nor is there anything about the many variations that undoubtedly also existed within the boundaries of this village.

Lise Rishøj Pedersen's *Aspects of Woman's Life in Rural Thailand*, published in 1968, is a third scholarly work in which pregnancy and childbirth are included. She worked on the subject in several villages, and also had the opportunity of a short stay in Laos. Her dissertation is, however, most essentially based on studies of a Lao Song Dam wet-rice village 24 kilometres West of Ratchaburi. The material was collected through interviews and conversations during a longish stay in the region in 1965–66. She concentrated mainly on major and general behaviour patterns and had no intention to identify which variations were found within the village itself, or the changes that occurred over the years.

Christine Mougne's *Changing Patterns of Fertility in a Northern Thai Village* (1978) is based on research done in the first half of the 1970s. There is a special section on 'Ethnography of Reproduction' in which there also are deliberations and information of importance to my work. Major and general behaviour patterns are described, with customs and traditions not given any profound or detailed treatment as such.

Valuable material is also found in two theses from 1962, written by students at the Bangkok Institute for Child Study (S. Cholvisuthi and C. Pitugsapol). They do not have extensive and representative data illustrating the topics of pregnancy and childbirth, but there are interesting accounts from the metropolitan area concerning 60 representatively selected mothers, in equal numbers from middle-class and lower-class families.

Also in Attagara's thorough and valuable book from 1967, about the *Folk Religion* in a village Southeast of Bangkok, there is a single section, 'Rites of Passage among the Laity' with the sub-section 'Childbirth', in which she described in general terms and without any great detail, rites during and after a childbirth.

The relatively few authors mentioned here are to my knowledge the only ones who have conducted research which has a direct connection with the subject of pregnancy and childbirth – and to several of them this theme is but a minor and less essential part of their research.

Perhaps H. Quaritch Wales ought to be included in this group. In 1933 he wrote an article, which he called 'Siamese Theory and Ritual Connected with Pregnancy, Birth and Infancy'. He stated that his sources had been 'a high nobleman and his wife', a pamphlet 'published some years ago' – the 'Code of Palace Law', and, finally, a medieval script 'Khun Jan Khun Phen'. It is interesting to note that in his opinion, most traditional customs and beliefs in connection with childbirth were rapidly about to vanish, so that one must presumably go to the 'more primitive Lao People' in Thailand's marginal regions to obtain further knowledge of customs and traditions of former times.

Many older authors have included remarks about childbirth customs. Many are romantic and adventurous descriptions, but some are solid reports written by

religious or foreign states' emissaries. One cannot, of course, attach much importance to these references, but they are not without interest in an overall assessment.

Several of the 'village studies' from the 1940s to the 1960s and some of the more popular books about Thailand from the same period mention aspects of traditional culture that may be of interest to this study. Some of these are also included in the references in the text though the 'information' in these books is more often misleading than guiding.

This section cannot, however, be concluded without giving special mention and emphasis to Professor S. J. Tambiah's highly-esteemed, scholarly works on social anthropology (1968, a, b, c; 1970, 1973) from his and my own simultaneous stays and work in Baan Phraan Muean. Whenever Tambiah has dealt with themes from this village it has been done so thoroughly that nothing has been omitted, overlooked, or ignored. Each individual work is an entirety, about which only the term 'eminent' can be used.

Apart from the fact that some of the existing pregnancy rites are included in his descriptions and assessments of the world of faith in the village, he does not occupy himself directly with pregnancy and childbirth. But indirectly, each work of his that relies on data from the village makes a considerable contribution to my own work.

From the last two or three decades of the 20th century almost nothing is to be found about this aspect of village culture, neither in relation to the development process and to changes in customs or traditions nor in relation to the consequences of these changes in society. Fortunately, Andrea Whittaker recently (1998, 1999, 2000, 2002 and 2004) contributed to our knowledge about the present day life of Isan rural women in her very careful, warm and valuable writings from a place not far from Khon Kaen.

Literature about childbirth and pregnancy from culturally related neighbouring countries is included in my search for studies and descriptions. It is astonishingly little that I have succeeded in bringing to light so far.

From Laos I only found the chapter 'Birth Rites' in Berval's beautiful and sympathetic book of 1959. This chapter, written by Charles Archaimbault, is very general. Nevertheless one gets a definite feeling that customs and traditions in this area agree to a wide extent with those found in Baan Phraan Muean in the early 1960s and my own not too systematic interviews in various places in Laos during the last few years leave the impression that this area of traditions has not changed nearly as much there, as it has on the Thai side of the Mekong River.

Just as general are C. V. Foll's descriptions in *An Account of some of the Beliefs and Superstitions about Pregnancy, Parturition and Infant Health in Burma* of 1959. Here also some relationship with Northeastern Thailand is reflected.

The regional similarities in these aspects of everyday life are corroborated also in Hart, Rajadhon and Coughlin: *Southeast Asian Birth Customs* from 1965. Rajadohn's part on Thailand is a reprint of the already-mentioned dissertation *'Life and Ritual in Old Siam'*. Hart writes from the Philippines and Coughlin from Vietnam. They are survey works based on sources from literature and conversations with individual people, presumably predominantly people with a higher education.

From Vietnam a little about the subject is found also from a Mekong Delta village in G. C. Hickey's *Village in Vietnam* (1964). This book is based on studies on the location from 1959 to 1964. Eveline Porée-Maspero (1951, 1954) has written about faith and cult at village level in Cambodia, and has given valuable material also about faith and superstition in connection with pregnancy and childbirth.

The above works are what I have found containing as a minimum one section of importance for my study of childbirth and its traditions. Several other works in the bibliography have also been referred to in the text. Others have just been consulted for possible inspiration and insight.

It should be noted that works on my subject, the traditional practice and beliefs connected with pregnancy and childbirth, especially as far as more recent research is concerned, are not only relatively few but – apart from Andrea Whittaker's – practically non-existent. This may partly be due to that the interests of international research have changed since I defined my research topic. However, research is scarce even into the highly interesting and topical issue of the impact of the development process on traditional belief and customs, and the results or consequences of such changes. This is not only surprising, but also disappointing. Surprising, because such changes and developments, the progress so to say, have long-term influence on the conditions of everyday life for the mother and the future of her child; disappointing, as my study has given evidence that the traditional Isan oral heritage relating to this subject is rich and much of it so undocumented that it should invite further serious research. My brief study visits to more than 30 villages besides my main target confirmed not only existing common traits but demonstrated as well a cultural diversity that ought to be studied and the knowledge of this cultural heritage preserved, before it is too late.

I can only hope there are studies written in Thai, which I have been unable to trace. If there are none, I cannot believe that it is because the area is evaluated as of no interest or importance. Perhaps the reason is rather to be found in a traditional reluctance and shyness preventing people from studying and dealing in the open with this subject which has been, and still is, a taboo in many cultures.

It may be almost too late to enter in studies of the old traditions and customs. However, I would not regard it as totally impossible in the Northeastern Thailand to find places where most of the traditions still exist and are followed by a rather large proportion of the families. As I have personally established there are still many places in Laos where this is the situation. Finally, considering that the subject area is so essential a part of the women studies domain, I would think that women researchers should be able to obtain more details than a male researcher.

Note

1. Phya Anuman Rajadhon (1961, p. 109)

Bibliography

Alabaster, H.	(1972) The Wheel of Law. Delhi: Varanasi.
Allport, G. W.	(1960) *The Individual and his Religion*. New York: Macmillan.
Ananthrawan, Chaakrit	(1995) (บทสูดขวัญ) [Sukhwan ritual texts in Loei. Changwat Loei]. Bangkok: Odeon Store Press.
Archaimbault, C.	(1964) 'Religious Structures in Laos'. *Journal of the Siam Society*, LII.
Attagara, Kingkeo	(1967) 'The Folk Religion of Ban Nai'. Ph.D. thesis, Indiana University.
Aung, M. H.	(1962) Folk *Elements in Burmese Buddhism*. London: Oxford University Press.
Bastian, A.	(1866) *Die Geschichte der Indochinesen* [History of the Indochinese], vols 1–4. Leipzig.
Benedict, R.	(1934) *Patterns of Culture*. Boston: Houghton Mifflin.
Bernot, L.	(1967a) *Les Caks* [The Caks]. Paris: Mouton.
——	(1967b) *Les Paysans Arakanais du Pakistan Oriental* [The Arakanai in East Pakistan (Bangladesh)], vols 1–2. Paris: Mouton.
Bertelsen, A.	(1907) 'Fødsel i Grønland' [Childbirth in Greenland]. *Bibliotek for Læger*. 99. 8. Gyldendal.
Berval, R. (ed.)	(1959) *Kingdom of Laos*. Saigon: France-Asie.
Beyer, C.	(1907) 'About Siamese Medicine'. *Journal of the Siam Society*, IV.
Birket-Smith, K.	(1929) *Report of the Fifth Thule Expedition 1921–24. The Caribou Eskimos*. Copenhagen: Gyldendal.
——	(1953) *The Chugach Eskimos*. Copenhagen: Gyldendal.
Blanchard, W.	(1958) *Thailand, Its People, Its Society, Its Culture*. New Haven: HRAF Press.
Bock, C.	(1884) *Templer og Elefanter eller Beretning om en Undersøgelsesreise gennem Siam og Lao* [Temples and elephants; the narrative of a journey of exploration through Siam and Lao]. Kristiania: Mallings Forlag.

Boonyakarnchan, Chaveelak, Srisa-ard, S. and Manochai, P. (1999) *Preservation of the Thai Oral Heritage* (available at www.tla.tiac.or.th/ifla99).

Bowring, Sir John   (1857) *The Kingdom and People of Siam with a Narrative of the Mission to that Country in 1855*. London: Parker.

Brandt, J. H.   (1961) 'The Negrito of Peninsular Thailand'. *Journal of the Siam Society*, XLIX.

Brinton, D. G.   (1897) *Religions of Primitive Peoples*. New York: Putnain's Sons.

Brohm, J.   (1963) 'Buddhism and Animism in a Burmese Village'. *Journal of Asian Studies*, 22.

Bronfenbrenner, U.   (1980) *Opvækst og Miljø* [The years of growth and the environment]. Copenhagen: Gyldendal.

Brun, V.   (1976a) 'Oral Tradition and Folk Religion in Northern Thailand'. In S. Egerod and P. Sørensen (eds), *Lampang Reports*. Copenhagen: Scandinavian Institute of Asian Studies.

——   (1976b) *Sug, the Trickster who Fooled the Monk*. SIAS Monographs, no. 22, Lund/London: Studentlitteratur/Curzon Press.

Brun, Viggo and Shumacher, Trond (1994) *Traditional Herbal Medicine in Northern Thailand*. Bangkok: White Lotus.

Bulletin of the UNESCO Regional Office for Education in Asia and the Pacific. (1982) no. 23.

Burges, A.   (1957) 'Traditional Systems of Child Care'. *Journal of Tropical Peadiatrics*, 3.

Burling, R.   (1965) *Hill Farms and Padi Fields. Life in Mainland Southeast Asia*. Englewood Cliffs: Prentice-Hall.

Cassell, E. J.   (1978) *The Healer's Art*. England: Penguin.

Chamarik, Sane   (2001) 'Oral Tradition in Thailand: a development perspective'. *IFLA Publications* 9,5, pp.49–68. Munich: Sauer.

Cholvisuthi, Sriswasai (1968) 'Patterns of Child-rearing Practices Among Thirty Mothers of Middle Socio-economic Status in Bangkok and Thonburi'. In T. Rasmussen (ed.), *Abstracts of Theses*. Bangkok Institute for Child Study.

Christmas, W.   (1894) *Et Aar i Siam* [A year in Siam]. Copenhagen: Gyldendal.

Cormack, J. G.   (1923) *Chinese Birthday, Wedding, Funeral, and other Customs*. Peking.

Coughlin, R. J.   (1965) 'Pregnancy and Birth in Vietnam'. In D. V. Hart, P. A. Rajadhon and R. J. Coughlin (eds), *Southeast Asian Birth Customs*. New Haven: Human Relations Area Files Press.

Crooke, W.   (1894) *Popular Religion and Folklore of Northern India*. Allahabad.

Curtis, L. J.   (1903) *The Laos of North Siam*. Philadelphia: Westminster Press.

Davis, R.   (1974) 'Tolerance and Intolerance of Ambiguity in Northern Thai Myth and Ritual'. *Ethnology*, XIII.

Davis, R.   (1984a) 'Muang Matrifocality'. *Mankind*, vol.14. No.4, 1984.

——   (1984b) *Muang Metaphysics. A Study of Northern Thai Myth and Ritual.* Bangkok: Pandora.

de Young, J. E.   (1958) *Village Life in Modern Thailand.* Los Angeles: University of California Press.

Dove, M. R. (ed.) (1988) *The Real and Imagined Role of Culture in Development.* Honolulu: University of Hawai'i Press.

Draper, John   (2004) *Isan: The Planning Context for Language Maintenance and Revitalization.* In SLLT, 4, (available at www.usq.edu.au/opacs/sslt/4).

Embree, J. F.   (1950) 'Thailand – A Loosely-Structured Social System'. *American Anthropologist.* 52.

Enfield, N. J.   (2002) 'How to Define "Lao", "Thai",and "Isan" Language? A View from Linguistic Science'. *Tai Culture*, VI, 1.

Egerod, S. and P. Sørensen (1976) *Lampang Reports.* Copenhagen: Scandinavian Institute of Asian Studies.

Erikson, E. H.   (1963) *Childhood and Society.* New York: W. W. Norton.

Faye, A. L.   (1885) 'Oplysninger om Forhold og Skikke vedrørende Svangerskab og Fødsel hos gamle Nordboere' [Information about customs related to pregnancy and birth among the ancient Nordic peoples]. *Norsk Magasin for Lægevidenskab.* 613–29, 673–707, 753–90.

Fei, Hsiao-Tung   (1939) *Peasant Life in China.* London: Routledge.

Firth, R.   (1967) *Tikopia Ritual and Belief.* Boston: Allen & Unvin.

Foll, C. V.   (1959) 'An Account of Some of the Beliefs and Superstitions about Pregnancy, Parturition and Infant Health in Burma'. *Journal of Tropical Paediatries*, 5.

Frazer, Sir J. G.   (1971) *The Golden Bough.* London: Macmillan.

Frick, J.   (1951) 'Magic Remedies Used on Sick Children in Western Valley of Sining'. *Anthropos,* XLVI.

Fukui, Hayao   (1993) *Food and Population in North East Thailand.* Honolulu: University of Hawai'i Press.

Gedney, W. J.   (1966) 'Some Questions on the Northeast'. *Asian Survey,* VI, 7.

Gideon, H.   (1962) 'A Baby is Born in Punjab'. *American Anthropologist,* 64.

Gohlert, E. W.   (1990) *Power and Culture: The Struggle Against Poverty in Thailand.* Bangkok: White Lotus.

Graham, W. A.   (1924) *Siam.* London: The de la More Press.

Granum-Jensen, F.   (2001) *Buddhisme og Åndemanere i Thailand.* Copenhagen: Systime.

Grimes, Ronald, L. (ed.) (1996) *Readings in Ritual Studies.* Englewood Cliffs: Prentice Hall.

Hale, A.   (1984) 'The Search for Jural Rule: Women in Southeast Asia – the Northern Thai Cults in Perspective'. *Man*, 14, 4.

Hall, H. F.   (1922) *The Soul of a People.* London: Macmillan.

Hanks, J. R.   (1963) *Maternity and its Rituals in Bang Chan.* Data Paper no. 51. New York: Ithaca, Cornell University.

Harper, E. B. (ed.)   (1964) *Religion in South Asia.* Seattle: University of Washington Press.

Hart, D. V., P. A. Rajadhon and R. J. Coughlin (1965) *Southeast Asian Birth Customs.* New Haven: Human Relations Area Files Press.

Hasegawa, Kiyoshi   (1993) 'Buddhism and spirit cults among the Thai-Lü in Yunnan'. *Tai Culture*, IV, pp. 32–52.

Havanon, N.   (1992) 'Rice, Labor, and Children: A Study of Peasants' Livelihood Strategies in Northeast Thailand'. In C. Goldschneider (ed.), *Fertility, Transitions, Family Structure, and Population Policy.* Boulder: Westview Press.

Heinze, Ruth Inge   (1977) 'Nature and Function of Some Therapeutic Techniques in Thailand'. *Asian Folklore Studies*, XXXVI: 2.

———   (1982) *Tham Khwan. How to Contain the Essence of Life.* Singapore University Press.

Henderson, J. W. (ed.) (1971) *Area Handbook for Thailand.* American University: Foreign Area Studies Division.

Hickey, G. C.   (1964) *Village in Vietnam.* New Haven: HRAF Press.

Hodgson, D.   (2001) *Gendered Modernities.* New York: Palgrave.

Hsu, F. L. K.   (1949) *Under the Ancestors' Shadow.* London: Routledge and Kegan.

——— (ed.)   (1972) *Psychological Anthropology.* Cambridge, Mass: General Learning Press.

Ingersoll, J.   (1966) 'Fatalism in Village Thailand'. *Anthropological Quarterly*, 39.

Irwin, A. J.   (1907) 'Some Siamese Ghost-lore and Demonology'. *Journal of the Siam Society*, IV, 2.

Izikowitz, K. G.   (1941) 'Fastening the Soul'. *Göteborg Högskolas Årsskrift*, XLVII.

Jackson, Peter   (1999) *Genders and Sexualities in Modern Thailand.* Bangkok: Silkworm Books.

Jahoda, G.   (1970) *The Psychology of Superstition.* Los Angeles: Pelican.

Jelliffe, D. B.	(1963) 'Custom and Child Health in Buganda'. *Tropical and Geographical Medicine*, 15.
Jung, G. C. G.	(1969) *Psychology and Religion*. Princeton: West and East.
Kabilsing, C.	(1991) *Thai Women and Buddhism*. Berkeley: Parallax Press.
Kampoon, Boontawe	(1988) *A Child of the Northeast*. Bangkok: DK books.
Kaufman, H. K.	(1960) *Bangkhuad, A Community Study in Thailand*. New York: J. J. Augustin.
Keyes, Charles F.	(1966) *Peasant and Nation: A Thai-Lao Village in a Thai State*. Cornell University.
——	(1975) 'The Northeastern Thai Village: Stable Order and Changing World'. *Journal of the Siam Society*, 63, 1.
——	(1984) 'Mother or Mistress but never a Monk: Buddhist Notion of Female Gender in Rural Thailand'. *American Ethnologist*, 11(2), pp. 223–241.
——	(1987) *Thailand: Buddhist Kingdom as Modern Nation-State*. Boulder: Westview Press.
Kiev, A.	(1960) 'Primitive Therapy'. In W. Muensterberger and S. Axelrad (eds), *The Psychoanalytic Study of Society*, vol. 1. New York: International Universities Press.
——	(1962) 'The Psychotherapeutic Aspects of Primitive Medicine'. *Human Organization*, XXI.
—— (ed.)	(1964) *Magic, Faith and Healing*. Glencoe: Free Press.
Kingshill, K.	(1960) *Kudaeng, The Red Tomb*. Bangkok: Siam Society.
——	(1991) *Ku Daeng Thirty Years Later: A Village Study in Northern Thailand 1954–1984*. DeKalb: Center for Southeast Asian Studies, Northern Illinois University.
Kislenko, A.	(2004) Culture *and Customs of Thailand*. Westport: Greenwood Press.
Klausner, W. J.	(1981) *Reflections on Thai Culture*. Bangkok: Suksit Siam.
Kluckhohn, C., H. A. Murray and D. M. Schneider (eds) (1961) *Personality in Nature, Society and Culture*. New York: Knopf.
Komonkitiskun, Jiranan (1992) 'Analysis of Women's Role and Status from Esarn Proverbs'. Research Report. Department of Foreign Languages, Khon Kaen: Khon Kaen University.
Kwon Ping, H.	(1978) 'Thailand's Broken Ricebowl'. *Far Eastern Economic Review*. December.
Lambert, W. W.	(1958) 'Some Correlates of Beliefs in the Malevolence and Benevolence of Supernatural Beings: A Cross-Societal Study'. *Journal of Abnormal and Social Psychology*.
Lehmann, A.	(1968) *Overtro og Trolddom* [Superstition and magic], 3rd edition. Copenhagen: Thaning og Appel.

Lewis, I. M.	(1966) '*Spirit Possession and Deprivation Cults*'. *Man*, 1, 3.
Lomas, P.	(1966) 'Ritualistic Elements in the Management of Child Birth'. *British Journal of Medical Psychology*, 39.
Le Bar, F. M. and A. Suddard (eds) (1960) *Laos, its People, its Society, its Culture*. New Haven: HRAF Press.	
Le Bar, F. M., G. C. Hickey and J. K. Musgrave (1964) *Ethnic Groups of Mainland Southeast Asia*. New Haven: HRAF Press.	
Le May, R.	(1926) *An Asian Arcady, The Land and Peoples of Northern Siam*. Cambridge: University Press.
Lück, Heike	(1996) *Khwan, Blutopfer und Besessenheit* [Khwan, blood-sacrifice and possession]. Berlin: SEACOM.
Luther, H. U.	(1978–79) 'Peasants and State in Contemporary Thailand'. *International Journal of Politics*, VIII, No. 4. Maclean, U. (1971) *Magical Medicine*. Middlesex: Penguin.
McIlwaine, J. and J. Whiffrin (eds) (2001) *Collecting and Safeguarding the Oral Traditions: an international conference*. IFLA Publications 95, München: Sauer.	
Malinowski, B.	(1948) *Magic, Science and Religion and other Essays*. Boston: Beacon Press.
Manderson, Leonore	(1981) 'Roasting, Smoking and Dieting in Response to Birth: Malay Confinement'. In *Cross-Cultural Perspective, Social Science and Medicine*,15B.
Mills, Mary. B.	(1995) 'Attack of the Widow Ghosts: Gender, Death and Modernity in Northeast Thailand'. In A. Ong and M. G. Peletz (eds), *Bewitching Women, Pious Men: Gender and Body Politics in Southeast Asia*, Berkeley: University of California Press, pp.244–273.
——	(1999) *Thai Women in the Global Labor Force: Consuming Desires, Contested Selves*. New Brunswick: Rutgers University.
Milne, L.	(1924) *The Home of an Eastern Clan, a Study of the Palaungs of the Shan States*. Oxford: University Press.
Mizuno. K.	(1971) *Social System of Dong Daeng Village. A Community Study in Northeast Thailand*. Discussion Paper No 17. Kyoto.
Møller, S. J.	(1940) *Moder og Barn i Dansk Folkeoverlevering* [Mother and child in Danish folklore] København: Munksgaard.
Morris, Rosalind	(2000) *In the Place of Origins. Modernity and its Mediums in Northern Thailand*. Durham, Duke University Press.
Mosel, J. N.	(1966) 'Fatalism in Thai Bureaucratic Decision-Making'. *Anthropological Quarterly*, 39.

Mougne, C.	(1978) 'Changing Patterns of Fertility in a Northern Thai Village'. *Nature and Man in South-East Asia*. London: SOAS.
Nash, M. (ed.)	(1966) *Anthropological Studies in Theravada Buddhism*. New Haven: Yale University Press.
Northrop, F. S. and H. H. Livingston (1964) *Cross-Cultural Understanding*. New York: Harper & Row.
Ong, A. and M. G. Peletz (1995) *Bewitching Women, Pious Men, Gender and Body Politics in Southeast Asia*. Berkeley: University of California Press.
Opler, M.	(1956) *Psychiatry and Human Values*. USA: Charles Thomas.
——	(1963) 'The Cultural Definition of Illness in Village India'. *Human Organization*, 22. 1.
——	(1967) *Culture and Social Psychiatry*. New York: Atherton Press.
Paul, B. D. (ed.)	(1955) *Health, Culture and Community*. New York: Russell Sage Foundation.
Pedersen, Lise Rishøj	(1967) *Thai kvinder - enlige og gifte* [Thai women, single and married]. Copenhagen: Nationalmuseet.
——	(1968) 'Aspects of Woman's Life in Rural Thailand'. *Folk*, 10.
Pendleton, R. L.	(1943) 'Land Use in NortheasternThailand'. *Geographical Review*, 33.
Phillips, H.	(1963) 'Relationships between Personality and Social Structure in a Siamese Peasant Community'. *Human Organization*, 22. 2.
——	(1965) *Thai Peasant Personality*. Berkley: University of California Press.
Phongphit, Seri (ed.)	(1986) *Back to the Roots: Village and Self-Reliance in a Thai Context*. Bangkok: Rural Development Documentation Centre (Rudoc).
——	(1988) *Religion in a Changing Society: Buddhism, Reform and the Role of Monks in Community Development in Thailand*. Hong Kong: Arena Press.
Phongphit, S. and K. Hewison (1990) *Thai Village Life, Culture and Transition in the Northeast*. Bangkok: Mooban Press.
Phongpaichit, Pasuk	(1998) *Women in Thailand*. Manila: Asian Development Bank.
Piker, S.	(1968a) 'The Relationship of Belief Systems to Behaviour in Rural Thai Society'. *Asian Survey*, VIII, 5.
——	(1968b) 'Sources of Stability and Instability in Rural Thai Society'. *Journal of Asian Studies*, XVII. 4.
Pitugsapol, Choochit	(1968) 'Pattern of Child-rearing Practice Among Thirty Lower Class Mothers in Bangkok and Thonburi'. *Abstracts of Theses*. Bangkok Institute for Child Study.

Ploss, H.   (1887) *Das Weib in der Natur- und Völkerkunde* [The folklore of women], vol. II. Leipzig.

——   (1911) *Das Kind in Brauch und Sitte der Völker* [Manners and customs in relation to children in various countries}, vol. I–II. Leipzig.

Porée-Maspero, E.   (1951) 'La Cérémonie de L'Appel des Esprits Vitaux Chez les Cambodgiens' [The ceremony for calling the 'Life Spirit' of the Cambodians]. *Bulletin de I'Ecole Francaise d'Extreme-Orient*, XLV, 1.

Potter, Sulamith. H.   (1977) *Family life in a Northern Thai Village*. Berkeley: University of California Press.

Poulsen, A.   (1979) 'Children in Ban Phran Muan, Fragments of a Picture'. Copenhagen: Ministry of Foreign Affairs, DANIDA (stenciled).

——   (1983) *Pregnancy and Childbirth – Its Customs and Rites in a NortheasternThai Village*. Copenhagen: Ministry of Foreign Affairs, DANIDA, (mimeograph copy).

——   (1984). 'Customs and Rites Connected with Pregnancy and Childbirth in a Northeastern Thai Village'. *Asian Folklore Studies*, XLIII, 1.

Premsilat, Suwilai et al (2004) (แผนที่ภาษาของกลุ่มชาติพันธุ์ต่างๆ ในประเทศไทย) [Ethnolinguistic Maps of Thailand]. Institute for Language and Culture for Rural Development (ILCRI), Mahidol University.

Raendchen, Oliver   (2002) Suu Khwan: Ritual Texts and Ceremony in Laos and North East Thailand. *Tai Culture*, VII,1.

Rajadhon, Phya Anuman (1952) 'The Ceremony of Tham Khwan of a Month Old Child'. *Journal of the Siam Society*, XL, 2.

——   (1953) 'Chao Thi and Some Traditions of Thai'. *Thailand Culture Series*, 6.

——   (1955) 'Me Posop, The Rice Mother'. *Journal of the Siam Society*, 43.

——   (1960) 'Fertility Rites in Thailand'. *Journal of the Siam Society*, 48.

——   (1961) *Life and Ritual in Old Siam*. New Haven: HRAF Press.

——   (1964) 'Thai Charms and Amulets'. *Journal of the Siam Society*, 52.

Rasmussen, K.   (1929) *Intellectual Culture of Iglulik Eskimos*. Fifth Thule Expedition 1921–24. Copenhagen: Gyldendal.

——   (1931) *The Netsilik Eskimos Social Life and Spiritual Culture*. Fifth Thule Expedition 1921–24. Copenhagen: Gyldendal.

Rasmussen, T. (ed.)   (1968) *Abstracts of Theses 1958–1967*. Bangkok Institute for Child Study.

Rhum, M. R.   (1994) *The Ancestral Lords, Gender, Descent and Spirits in a Northern Thai Village*. DeKalb: Northern Ill University.

Rosenberg, H.   (1900) *Siam*. Copenhagen: E. C. Gad.

Ruangsuwan, Jarubut   (1977) (ของดีอีสาน) [Treasures of Isan]. Bangkok: Department of Religion Press.

Russel, S. D. (Ed.)   (1989) *Ritual, Power, and Economy: Upland-Lowland Contrasts in Mainland Southeast Asia*. DeKalb: Northern Illinois University.

Saarathasananan, Saan (1986) (ฮีตสิบสอง) [Twelve Customs of Isan]. Udorn: Cultural Centre, Rajabhat Institute.

——   (1989) (พิธีสู่ขวัญและคำสู่ขวัญโบราณ) [Suukhwan Rites and Ritual Texts in Ancient Times (The Complete Version)]. Loei: 16, Sakon-Chiangkhaan Road, Soi 1.

Sarasittiyot, An-Julee (1997) (การอยู่กรรมของแม่ลูกอ่อน บ้านศรีบุญเรือง ตำบลนาภู่ อำเภอเพ็ญ จังหวัดอุดรธานี) [The Childbirth Fireside Ritual in Baan Siboonrueang, Tamboon Naaphuun, Amphoe Pen, Udornthani]. Mahasarakham: Srinakharinwirot University.

Schoenthal, R.   (1957) 'Herbal Medicines and Disease'. *Journal of Tropical Paediatrics*. March.

Sears, R. R., E. E. Maccoby and H. Levin (1957) *Patterns of Child Rearing*. New York: Row & Peterson.

Seidenfaden, E.   (1958) *The Thai Peoples, Book 1*. Bangkok: Siam Society.

Sittirak, Sinith   (1998) *The Daughters of Development. Women in Changing Environment*. London: Zed Books.

Smart, R. B.   (1931) 'Burmese Birth Customs'. *Journal of Burma Research Society*, XXI. II.

Smithies, Michael   (1995) *Descriptions of Old Siam*. Oxford: Oxford University Press.

Sparkes, Stephen   (1993) 'Gender and Cosmology in an Isan Village in Northeast Thailand'. Ph.D. thesis, University of Oslo.

——   (1995) 'Taming Nature-Controlling Fertility Concepts of Nature and Gender among the Isan of the Northeast Thailand'. In O. Bruun and A. Kalland (eds), *Asian Perceptions of Nature: A Critical Approach*. Richmond, Surrey: Curzon Press, pp. 63–87.

Spiro, M. E.   (1967) *Burmese Supernaturalism*. Englewood Cliffs: Prentice Hall.

Sudham, Pira   (1987) *People of Esarn*. Bangkok: Media.

Suvannathat, Chancha (1967) *A Study of Social Influences on the Development of Children in the Village of Napa*. Summaries, Bangkok Institute for Child Study.

——   (1979) 'The Inculcation of Values in Thai Children'. *International Social Science Journal*, 31. 3.

—— (ed.) (1971) *Summaries of the Study of Social Influences on the Development of Thai Children in the Villages of Ban Pranmuen and U-Meng.* Research Bulletin, no. 10. Bangkok Institute for Child Study.

Suwanlert, Sangun (1968, 1969) 'Psychiatric Study of Phii Pob', vols I and II, (mimeograph copy).

—— (1976) 'Neurotic and Psychotic States Attributed to Thai "Phii Pob" Spirit Possession'. *Australian and New Zealand Journal of Psychiatry*, 10, pp. 119.

Takagi, Ryo (1995) 'Interaction and power relations: A village headman (*kamnan*) election in Central Thailand'. *Tai Culture*, IV, 1, pp. 153–168.

Tambiah, S. J. (1968a) 'Literacy in a Buddhist Village in North-East Thailand'. In J. Goodny (ed.), *Literacy in Traditional Societies*. Cambridge: Cambridge University Press.

—— (1968b) 'The Ideology of Merit and Social Correlates of Buddhism in a Thai Village'. In E. R. Leach (ed.), *Dialectic and Practical Religion*. Cambridge: Cambridge University Press.

—— (1968c) 'The Magical Power of Words'. *Man,* 3, 2.

—— (1970) *Buddhism and the Spirit Cults in North-East Thailand*. Cambridge; Cambridge University Press.

—— (1973) 'Buddhism and This-worldly Activity'. *Modern Asian Studies*, 7, 1.

—— (1976) *World Conqueror and World Renouncer: A Study of Buddhism and Polity in Thailand against a Historical Background.* Cambridge: Cambridge University Press.

—— (1990) *Magic, Science, Religion and the Scope of Rationality.* Cambridge: Cambridge University Press.

Tandrup, A. (1980–81) 'Den voksende forarmelse af bønderne i Sydøstasien' [†the growing poverty among Southeast Asian peasants]. *Kontakt*, 2.

Tanabe, Shigeharu (1997) 'Suffering and Negotiation: Spirit-Mediumship and HIV/Aids Self-helps Groups in Northern Thailand'. *Tai Culture*, IV, 1, pp. 93–114.

Tannenbaum, N. and C. A. Kammerer (eds) (2003) *Founders' Cults in Southeast Asia: Ancestors, Polity, and Identity.* Monograph 52, Yale Southeast Asia Studies. New Haven: Yale University Press.

Taylor, K. W., H. S. Marcussen and J. Carlsen (1972) *Thailand – Udvikling for hvem?* [Thailand – Development for whom?]. Copenhagen: Institut for Udviklingsforskning.

Terweil, B. J.	(1975) *Monks and Magic: An Analysis of Religious Ceremonies in Central Thailand.* Lund/London: Studentlitteratur/Curzon Press.
Textor, R. B.	(1961) *From Peasant to Pedicab Driver.* Cultural Report Series. 9. New Haven: Yale University Press.
Torrey, E. Fuller	(1973) *The Mind Game. Witchdoctors and Psychiatrists.* USA: Bantam.
van Gennep, A.	(1961) 'On the Rites of Passage'. In T. Parson ed., *Theories of Society* vol. II. Free Press of Glencoe.
Trankell, Ing-Britt	(1996) 'Gender, Morality, and Commercial Spirits in Thailand'. Working Papers in Cultural Anthropology, No. 1. Uppsala University.
UNDP	(2003) Thailand *Human Development Report 2003*, Bangkok (available at http://hdr.undp.org/reports
Van Esterick, Penny	(1996) 'Women in Southeast Asia'. Monograph Series no.17, Occasional Papers. Northern Illinois University.
——	(2000) *Materializing Thailand.* Oxford: Berg.

Varaaswapti, Varakorn. (1977) 'Patterns of Child Rearing Practices in the North-East'. *Journal of Home Science*, 21, 1.

Wales, H. Q.	(1933) 'Siamese Theory and Ritual Connected with Pregnancy, Birth and Infancy'. *Journal of the Royal Anthropological Institute of Great Britain*, 63.
——	(1983) *Divination in Thailand.* Richmond: Curzon Press.
Walker, G. B.	(1968) *Hindu World*, Vol. I & II. St. Leonards: Allen & Unwin.
Wells, K. E.	(1960) *Thai Buddhism, its Rites and Activities.* Bangkok: Christian Bookstore.
Whiting, B. (ed.)	(1963) *Six Cultures: Studies of Child Rearing.* London: Wiley & Son.

Whiting, J. W. M., Child, J. L. (1953) *Child Training and Personality.* New Haven: Yale University Press.

Whittaker, Andrea	(1998) 'Woman's Desires and Burden: Family Planning in Northeast Thailand'. *Asian Studies Review*, 22(2), pp. 137–155.
——	(1999) 'Birth and the Postpartum in Northeast Thailand: Contesting Modernity and Tradition'. *Medical Anthropology*, 18, pp.1–29.
——	(2000) *Intimate Knowledge. Women and their health in North-East Thailand.* Sydney: Allen &Unwin.
——	(2002) 'Water Serpents and Staying by the Fire: Markers of Maturity in a Northeast Thai

	Village'. In L. Manderson and P. Liamputtong (eds), *Coming of Age in South and Southeast Asia*. Richmond, Surrey: Curzon Press.
——	(2004) *Abortion, Sin and the State in Thailand*. London: RoutledgeCurzon.
Wright, M. A.	(1968) 'Some Observations on Thai Animism'. *American Anthropologist*, 15. 1.
Young, E.	(1907) *The Kingdom of the Yellow Robe*. London: Constable and Co.
Young, G.	(1962) *The Hill Tribes of Northern Thailand*. Bangkok: Siam Society.

Index